LAW FOR
SOCIAL WORKERS

LAW FOR
SOCIAL
WORKERS

Seventh Edition

Hugh Brayne, BA, Solicitor
Gerry Martin, BA, Solicitor
Helen Carr, BA, Solicitor

OXFORD
UNIVERSITY PRESS

OXFORD

UNIVERSITY PRESS

Great Clarendon Street, Oxford OX2 6DP

Oxford University Press is a department of the University of Oxford.
It furthers the University's objective of excellence in research, scholarship,
and education by publishing worldwide in

Oxford NewYork

Athens Auckland Bangkok Bogotá Buenos Aires Cape Town
Chennai Dar es Salaam Delhi Florence Hong Kong Istanbul Karachi
Kolkata Kuala Lumpur Madrid Melbourne Mexico City Mumbai Nairobi
Paris São Paulo Shanghai Singapore Taipei Tokyo Toronto Warsaw

with associated companies in Berlin Ibadan

Oxford is a registered trade mark of Oxford University Press
in the UK and certain other countries

Published in the United States
by Oxford University Press Inc., New York

A Blackstone Press Book

First edition © H. Brayne and G. Martin 1990
Seventh edition © H. Brayne, G. Martin and H. Carr 2001

British Library Cataloguing in Publication Data

Data available

Library of Congress Cataloging in Publication Data

Data available

ISBN 1-84174-197-3

1 3 5 7 9 10 8 6 4 2

Typeset by Style Photosetting Limited, Mayfield, East Sussex
Printed in Great Britain
on acid-free paper by
Ashford Colour Press Limited, Gosport, Hampshire

CONTENTS

FOREWORD

The practice of social work operates within the framework of the law and the legal system. Some knowledge of the law, an awareness of its implications, expertise in applying it and, when necessary, the ability to communicate with lawyers (not always an easy task!) are, in my view, essential requirements for those working in local authority social services departments or other social work organisations. In addition, in the context of court cases specifically, the social worker needs to know or have access to advice about the precise kind of evidence a court or tribunal will require.

High profile inquiries and cases in the field of childcare, for example, Cleveland, Rochdale, Staffordshire, Leicestershire, Orkney, Ayrshire and North Wales, have exemplified and underlined, amongst other things, the importance of the role of the law and the need for an accurate knowledge of it. It seems to me that this message should pervade social work training, management and practice. It is now of even greater importance because of the implementation of the Human Rights Act 1998. Each local authority will have to ensure that its practices and procedures are compatible with the European Convention on Human Rights which became part of our domestic law in October 2000.

This book provides an excellent source of knowledge about legal matters for the social worker. It will also be very helpful to lawyers and others involved in the wide-ranging subjects covered which include child protection, housing, benefits, discrimination and legal procedure. The appearance of a seventh edition only eleven years after the original launch of the book reflects the extent of its success. The clarity of the contents and the fund of practical advice made available make it essential reading for all those concerned with social work.

Allan Levy QC
Bedford Row, London
September 2001

ACKNOWLEDGMENTS

Many people have been thanked for their help in earlier editions. We would once again like to add, in relation to the seventh edition, Di Cowgill, welfare rights adviser to Jockelson and Kibbler, Solicitors, who advised us in relation to recent benefit changes and Nony Ardill at Legal Action Group for her invaluable help with Chapter 15.

Thanks, as always, to the many students, solicitors, social workers and other professionals whose thoughts have clarified our thinking and concepts of this ever-stimulating area of law.

Helen would like to thank her family, especially Richard for helping her to create the time to work on this edition.

As Gerry Martin was not involved in the preparation of the seventh edition, we acknowledge the superb foundations he laid for the continuing success of this book in the first six editions. His unparallelled experience and knowledge of the law relating to children was matched only by his unique ability to explain the law simply and accurately.

We owe a very large thanks to the editorial team at Blackstone Press. We made a lot of amendments for this edition, not always legibly or consistently, and they have worked painstakingly and patiently to produce an excellent finished product. We hope their style and spirit lives on with OUP

We take responsibility for any mistakes in the seventh edition, but if we can find someone else to blame we will try.

PREFACE

There have been quite a few developments in law affecting social workers since the sixth edition. Many of the changes which we flagged up two years ago in 1999 — the complete rewriting of the legal aid scheme, the deluge of legislation affecting youth justice and children's evidence in criminal cases and, above all, the impact of the Human Rights Act on all areas — are now law.

Thus, as well as the need to update with minor changes (such as the change in name from 'guardian *ad litem*' to 'children's guardian', new case law, new government guidance, the abolition of the Central Council for Education and Training in Social Work, the arrival of the new Care Standards Commission and so on), we've also had to do quite a lot of actual rewriting of the original text.

We have added a new section explaining human rights in Chapter 1. You need this explanation early on because the way courts apply both new and existing laws has changed fundamentally: every provision of every statute and principle of law must now be interpreted by the courts in a way that is consistent with the basic rights set out by the Council of Europe after the Second World War, and consistent with the decisions of the European Court of Human Rights.

The law affecting the vulnerable — mental health and community care — has now been split into two chapters. Although there is some overlap, particularly in relation to the affairs of elderly people, we hope that the separate chapters will allow you to get a clearer understanding in each area. The reforms to the juvenile justice system — from quasi-criminal parenting orders and anti-social behaviour orders through to new ways of sentencing children — are now in place, though there is little case law to guide you as to how it is working. Meanwhile, the entire sentencing legislation for all criminal offences has been repealed and re-enacted in one statute. The actual law, however, is not affected. Perhaps one day the government will take community care law in hand in the same way — you will see that, despite our efforts to present the material in a clear and straightforward manner, it is nonetheless a morass of complex and sometimes contradictory statutes and cases which, from innocent-looking and benign seedlings, each planted with the best of intentions, have grown into a virtually impenetrable thicket.

Fortunately the landscape remains reasonably constant when we look at the law affecting children. The human rights of children and their families puts a fresh perspective on the Children Act 1989, but the basic framework of this Act remains robust, and the updates mainly involve informing you of new case law, changes to government guidance, and the impact of the Human Rights Act. This part of the book was originally written by Gerry Martin, and his excellent and informative framework for explaining in the clearest terms how the law relating to children actually works is a legacy and a style we will do our best to retain.

Hugh Brayne, Sunderland
Helen Carr, London
October 2001

ABBREVIATIONS

AA	Attendance allowance
ABWOR	Assistance by way of representation
ACPC	Area Child Protection Committee
ALAS	Accident Legal Advice Service
ASBO	Anti-social behaviour order
AST	Assured shorthold tenancy
ASW	Approved social worker
BA	Benefits Agency
BAAF	British Agencies for Adoption and Fostering
CAB	Citizens Advice Bureau
CAFCASS	Children and Family Court Advisory and Support Service
CB	Child benefit
CCETSW	Central Council for Education and Training in Social Work
CDCA	Carers and Disabled Children Act 2000
CDS	Criminal Defence Service
CLS	Community Legal Service
CPO	Child protection order
C(RS)A	Carers (Recognition and Services) Act 1995
CSA	Care Standards Act 2000
CSO	Child safety order
CSDPA	Chronically Sick and Disabled Persons Act 1970
CICB	Criminal Injuries Compensation Board
CRE	Commission for Racial Equality
DLA	Disability living allowance
DPEA	Disabled Persons (Employment) Act 1958
DP (SCR) A	Disabled Persons (Services, Consultation and Representation) Act 1986
DSS	Department of Social Security
DTQ	Detention, Treatment and Questioning
EOC	Equal Opportunities Commission
EPO	Emergency protection order

FC	Family credit
HA	Health Act 1999
HASSASSA	Health and Social Services and Social Security Adjudications Act 1983
HB	Housing benefit
HSPHA	Health Services and Public Health Act 1968
IP	Invalidity pension
IS	Income support
IT	Intermediate treatment
LASSA	Local Authority (Social Services) Act 1970
MHA	Mental Health Act 1983
MHA 1959	Mental Health Act 1959
MHRT	Mental Health Review Tribunal
MIB	Motor Insurers' Bureau
NAA	National Assistance Act 1948
NHSA	National Health Service Act 1977
NHSCCA	National Health Service and Community Care Act 1990
NSPCC	National Society for the Prevention of Cruelty to Children
PCCSA	Powers of Criminal Courts (Sentencing) Act 2000
RRA	Race Relations Act 1976
RHA	Registered Homes Act 1984
RO	Reporting officer
SB	Sickness benefit
SBA	Supplementary Benefit Act 1976
SDA	Sex Discrimination Act 1975
SSP	Statutory sick pay
TWOC	Taking without owner's consent
YOT	Youth Offending Teams

TABLE OF CASES

TABLE OF STATUTES

PART I   THE LEGAL CONTEXT OF SOCIAL WORK PRACTICE

ONE

Introduction

LAW IN SOCIAL WORK

In the beginning there were no social workers. But Parliament said 'let there be social workers', so they were created; Parliament also said 'this is what we want them to do'. (To be precise, it said 'let there be Committees and Directors of Social Services, let there be approved social workers, let there be probation officers, let there be minimum standards of qualifications'.) Whether the result was good is not our job to judge.

In your professional role you were created to perform — and only to perform — the jobs that Parliament has given you. Although there is plenty of room for good intentions, these do not define your job; the statutes do. The statutes tell you who you have responsibilities towards, and how they shall be exercised.

So our job in this book is to lay out who you have these responsibilities towards, what the law tells you you must do, or may do, and to try to explain what that means in practice. The result is a long book. We offer no apologies. The law is a big subject, and it affects you more than most people — even, perhaps, more than some lawyers. What we have aimed for is a book which covers the things you are likely, in practice, to need to know; not everything, and not every pernickety detail, because perhaps the most important point we remind you of (frequently, as you will see) is that you cannot and need not know it all. If you know enough, you will know when it is time to call in the lawyer. And if your knowledge of the law is good, you can work in partnership with the lawyer.

Why two parts to the book? Social workers have statutory responsibilities. They have them to children, in particular, but also to other vulnerable members of society, or people caught up in the criminal process. We have spelled out these statutory duties as clearly and fully as we think our publishers will let us get away with. We have summarised them at the end of this chapter.

So Part I is about the practice of social work. It covers not only the law which connects social workers to particular client groups, but also the parts of the legal system of England and Wales which you need to know about to understand how these laws are applied. We describe the court and tribunal system, and how courts operate in practice; we offer practical guidance on how the social worker should act in court; we describe the legal framework within which reports for court must be prepared, and give practical advice on writing them. These areas are all vital to your effective work: court appearances and reports are the points at which you make the most direct contact with the legal system. We have a separate chapter on how to plan your cases.

Another way of seeing Part I, therefore, is to call it the law of social work practice; that is, the law which dictates how you carry out your statutory duties as a social worker.

Part II by contrast deals with the law as it affects your clients. We had difficulty in selecting material for this part. Had we had sufficient time, and you sufficient money to buy it, we should have liked to write a section of the book called 'Everything you always wanted to know about the law but were too afraid to ask'. For your clients will, in one way or another, have experiences covering every aspect of every law. Fortunately, perhaps, this was impossible. We selected areas where we think that a social worker is in need of an understanding of the position of the client, and how the law affects that client, in order to be able to undertake the statutory duties to that client which are covered in Part I. That is why we concentrate on areas like housing and family relationships. Chapter 19, on anti-discrimination law, belongs in both Parts; but since most of this law is generic, rather than aimed specifically at social work practice, we place it in Part II.

But before we go into these areas, we have given a chapter of background (but essential) material on lawyers, legal help and advice services; for knowing the relevant law must go hand in hand with an understanding of how to apply it for the benefit of the individual concerned. So most of Chapter 15 concerns getting more specialist help than you yourself can provide.

You may find it odd that we consider it necessary to go into some detail in these areas; after all, do we not repeatedly stress that it is not necessarily your job to know this law, and that you must refer to lawyers for specialist advice? Could we not have omitted this section, as texts for social workers have traditionally done? The answer to the second question, we are sure, is no. In your work with clients to whom you owe statutory duties, you come up against people suffering a vast range of legal problems. These problems are part of your clients' world, and you will be drawn into discussing them, advising on them, maybe taking action about them, like it or not.

Although you should never be the principal source of legal advice for these clients, you cannot escape from the fact that you are often the first, and perhaps even the last. This places you very much in the front line. Moreover, unlike the situations where you can consult your agency lawyer, and perhaps discuss a course of action in a case conference, you are on your own talking to your client about their legal problems. For that reason, we cannot pare the material down too finely if you wish to be able to play a helpful role. We think you should have the outline of the most significant areas, partly in your head, and in any event on your bookshelf when you need it. We are aware of two regrettable trends affecting social work education:

(a)   many schools of social work have cut down on buying in law teachers for their students and are dumping the work on teachers who are not lawyers;

(b)   degree syllabuses are becoming so full of competing demands that hours devoted to learning law have been reduced.

There is also the general trend in higher education of making students do more of the work themselves. This is excellent when the students are properly prepared. We think that students need, in law, quite a lot of detail to work with on their own and enough explanation to guide them through it. Our book, and its forthcoming companion volume, *Legal Materials for Social Workers* (H. Brayne and G. Broadbent, to be published by Oxford University Press in 2002), is intended to give the student, and the practitioner, the material to take them through that minimum area of competence in law.

Before you get started, may we collect together some of the miscellaneous points that have occurred to us while writing the book, which did not fit into the text anywhere else?

(a)   As a social worker you have opted to work in a statutory framework. Criticism of the law is valid and useful; but any decision to ignore the law is unacceptable. Illegal imprisonment of children in care in Staffordshire — 'pin-down' — was the result of using the authority of the social services department to oppress individuals who should have been entitled to the protection of the law. We consider it an illusion to think you can protect your clients' interests better outside the legal framework than within it. At the very least it will destroy your credibility in court and your chance of obtaining appropriate court orders; at its worst, there may be a disaster, and you will be the first in line for any criticism. 'Professionals involved in child welfare and protection are not moral crusaders. They are empowered in law to act in certain prescribed situations in certain prescribed ways no more, no less' (*Making Enquiries into Alleged Child Abuse and Neglect: Partnership with Families*, Pennant, 1996).

(b)   We try not to presume to talk about what is good social work practice. We are lawyers, not social workers, and anyway there would not be space. Of course, we have our own thoughts, and some of these may creep in. Where possible, though, we have assumed that you bring your own professional knowledge to apply to the legal framework we provide. For example, we have assumed that you have some idea of the major child care inquiries that have recently taken place. We also assume that you will obtain equal opportunities training, so that we need only outline the legal framework.

(c)   Who have we aimed the book at? It is the local authority field social worker whom we have principally had in mind, but we expect much of the material to be of use to probation officers, social work managers, and solicitors in the child care area, as well as students of social work and their teachers.

(d)   The book describes the law of England and Wales. England and Wales is one of the jurisdictions of the United Kingdom. The others are Scotland and Northern Ireland.

(e)   A word about style. We try to avoid language that makes sexist assumptions. We therefore try not to write 'he' or 'she' unless we mean a person of that sex only. But statutes say 'he' as a shorthand for 'he or she' — in fact the 1978 Interpretation Act tells us that 'he' means 'she' as well. So when we quote a statute, we give you the actual wording, but do not intend ourselves to describe an all-male world. We try to avoid inappropriate labelling, but where words like 'the disabled' are statutory terms, we reproduce those terms for accuracy.

(f)   Again on the question of statutes, we would have liked to provide verbatim all of the statutory material referred to. That is the best way to see what it means. We could not do that without a fivefold increase in the size of the book. So instead you will find sections of legislation partially reproduced, where the actual words will be particularly helpful. Note that the square brackets [ ] and **bold** emphasis do not appear in the statute itself. We have added these, because emphasis helps us to explain what we think important. Further statutory material will be available in the companion volume of legal materials (see above).

(g)   We try to give a picture of forthcoming changes in the law, for example, in Chapter 14 where we anticipate the changes expected in mental health law. Sections of the text looking at planned changes in the law are written in italics.

We recommend getting into the habit of looking at — and acquiring — the texts of the major pieces of legislation relevant to your area. All legislation likely to affect social workers is collected together in the looseleaf *Encyclopedia of Social Services and Child Care Law* (published by Sweet & Maxwell and updated regularly), together with rules, regulations, circulars and text. We use it a lot and recommend it to you too.

This chapter finishes with a consideration of three separate and important topics. They form part of the framework for understanding the context in which you are working. Who is a social worker? What are your statutory duties? How do human rights laws affect your work?

WHO IS A SOCIAL WORKER?

At the beginning of this chapter we stated that Parliament created Committees and Directors of Social Services. This was done by an Act of Parliament in 1970. Surprisingly, given the good work that has been done by social workers since that Act of 1970, Parliament did not actually create social workers until 2000, when the Care Standards Act (CSA) was passed. Previous legislation, most recently the Health and Social Services and Social Security Adjudications Act (HASSASSA) 1983, did recognise the Central Council for Education and Training in Social Work (CCETSW) and give it statutory powers to regulate your training, but it did not as such recognise the role of the social worker. The CCETSW is to be abolished in 2002 when the main provisions of the CSA come into force and replaced under s. 54 with, in England, the General Social Care Council and, in Wales, the Care Council for Wales.

The CSA 2000, s. 55, defines a 'social care worker' as being synonymous with a 'social worker' (s. 55(2)(a)). A social care worker must be registered under s. 56 with the relevant Council (see above). It is a criminal offence for anyone else to use the title 'social worker' (s. 61). The Councils have powers to approve training courses, the recognition of foreign qualifications and post-qualification training, but the Government lays down the qualification requirements under s. 67 of the Act.

So who is required to register? Under s. 55, any of the following:

(a) anyone who engages in 'relevant social work' (meaning social work connected with any health, education or personal services — perhaps a little unhelpful as a definition, but it will have to cover anyone undertaking the duties set out in the Local Authority (Social Services) Act 1970, listed at pp. 6–10 below);

(b) a person employed in or managing a children's home, care home or residential family centre, or for the purposes of a domiciliary care agency, a fostering agency or a voluntary adoption agency;

(c) a person supplied by a domiciliary care agency to provide personal care in their own homes to persons who by reason of illness, infirmity or disability are unable to provide it for themselves without assistance.

The Government has the power to extend this definition.

AN OVERVIEW OF THE STATUTORY FRAMEWORK FOR LOCAL AUTHORITY SOCIAL WORKERS

We have heard it said (in relation to the authors of earlier editions) that there is a 'Brayne and Martin' view of social work, which emphasises the need to work within the statutory framework, in contrast to a view that what really matters is social workers using their expertise to help clients. Is this praise or criticism?

Rather than mend our ways, we decided instead to justify them here. For local authority social workers, the tasks you perform are set out within a legislative framework. These tasks are what you do. Unless you are employed by a different agency, you have no other functions than these. (The Crime and Disorder Act 1998 is an exception to this statement. This Act imposes statutory duties on the local authority as a corporate body, rather than on its social services function. That is why we have not included those functions in this section. You will see that we have made extensive reference to the Crime and Disorder Act 1998 where it is necessary, in particular in Chapter 12.)

Please be aware that, by and large, duties are placed by the legislation not on individual social workers but on the employing local authority of social workers. Children's guardians (formerly guardians *ad litem*) in child care work (p. 90) and approved social workers in mental health work, however, also have duties imposed on them as individuals.

Be warned (and, we hope, shocked when you learn) that the statutory powers and duties which follow are limited when applied to asylum seekers and their dependants (Immigration and Asylum Act 1999). In particular, s. 122 excludes children from the scope of local authorities' welfare services, s. 116 prevents asylum seekers being taken into community care accommodation and s. 117 excludes them from welfare services for the elderly and prevention and after-care for the sick.

Direct quotations in the following text are in **bold**. Where 'etc.' appears it is the wording from the statute, not a result of our laziness.

Local Authority (Social Services) Act 1970
Section 2 provides the framework:

> **Every local authority shall establish a social services committee, and . . . there shall stand referred to that committee all matters relating to the discharge by the authority of—**
>   **(a)   their functions under the enactments specified in the first column of Schedule 1 to this Act** [which are set out below].

> Section 7 provides: **Local authorities shall, in the exercise of their social services functions, . . . act under the general guidance of the Secretary of State.**

Section 7B requires a complaints procedure to be established for each social services authority.

Section 7C provides for the Secretary of State to set up inquiries into performance of functions.

Section 7D provides for the Secretary of State to take over the running of the authority's functions.

All statutory material which follows is based on what is listed in Schedule 1 (see s. 2 above). The duties described are those of the local authority, not the individual employee.

The order in the Schedule is according to the age of the Act concerned. We have re-grouped the duties according to subject matter. This Schedule to the 1970 Act is updated regularly by new legislation. (We have included the effects of legislative amendments (in particular the CSA 2000) not yet in force.)

Function assigned to social services committee	Page in this text

GENERAL

Local Authority (Social Services) Act 1970
ss. 6 and 7B Appointment of Director of Social Services, etc.; provision and conduct of complaints procedure.   pp. 82–83 and 318

CHILDREN

Children and Young Persons Act 1933
Part III Protection of the young in relation to criminal and summary proceedings; children appearing before the court as in need of care, protection or control; committal of children to approved school or care of fit person, etc.
pp. 255 and 285

Part IV Remand homes, approved schools and children in care of fit persons.
p. 279–80

Children and Young Persons Act 1963
Part III Powers relating to young persons in need of care, protection or control; further provisions for protection of the young in relation to criminal proceedings.
p. 255

Children and Young Persons Act 1969
Care and other treatment of children and young persons through court proceedings.
pp. 255 and 286

Family Law Reform Act 1969
s. 7(4) Supervision of ward of court.

Adoption Act 1976
Maintenance of adoption service; functions of local authority as adoption agency; application for orders freeing children for adoption; inquiries carried out by local authority in adoption cases; care, possession and supervision of children awaiting adoption.
p. 240

Children Act 1989
Welfare reports; consent to application for residence order in respect of child in care; family assistance orders; functions under Part III of the Act (local authority support for children and families); care and supervision; protection of children; functions in relation to community homes, voluntary homes and voluntary organisations, private children's homes, private arrangements for fostering children, child minding and day care for younger children; research and returns of information; functions in relation to children accommodated by health authorities and local education authorities or in care homes, independent hospitals or schools.
Chapters 5, 6, 7, 9 and 11

Education Act 1996
s. 322   Help for local education authority in exercising   Not covered
functions under Part IV of the Act (children with special   in this book.
needs).

Adoption (Intercountry Aspects) Act 1999
s. 2(4)   Functions under Article 9(a) to (c) of the   Not covered
Convention on Protection of Children and Cooper-   in this book.
ation in respect of Intercountry Adoption.

COMMUNITY CARE

National Assistance Act 1948
ss. 21 to 27   Provision of residential accommodation   p. 322
for aged, infirm, needy, etc.

ss. 29 and 30   Welfare of persons who are blind, deaf,   p. 315
dumb or otherwise handicapped or are suffering from
mental disorder; use of voluntary organisations for
administration of welfare schemes.

ss. 43 to 45   Recovery of costs of providing certain   p. 320
services.

s. 48   Temporary protection of property belonging to   p. 319
persons in hospital or accommodation provided under
Part III of the Act, etc.

s. 49   Defraying expenses of local authority officer   Not covered
applying for appointment as receiver of certain pa-   in this book.
tients.

s. 56(3)   Prosecution of offences (e.g., s. 51 failure to   p. 325
maintain spouse or children, s. 42 making a false statement
to get accommodation).

Disabled Persons (Employment) Act 1958
s. 3   Provision of facilities for enabling disabled per-   pp. 316
sons to be employed or work under special conditions.   and 320

Mental Health Act 1959
s. 8   Welfare and accommodation of mentally dis-   pp. 316
ordered persons.   and 320

(s. 131   Gives powers to local authorities to prosecute for
sexual offences involving mental patients, which are not
mentioned in Sch. 1 to the Local Authority (Social Services)
Act 1970.)

Health Services and Public Health Act 1968
s. 45   Promotion of welfare of old people.   pp. 316
                                                     and 320

These are not the only bits of legislation that will concern you. What they do is to tell you who you owe duties to. These are your clients. They are why you are a local authority social worker. In carrying out those duties you use your expertise to assist individuals where appropriate, or control them where required, and you need to know a lot of further law (and social work practice) to do this. What the law says and how it is put into day-to-day practice is not always the same. In 1998, the Social Service Inspectors at the Department of Health published a report called 'Someone Else's Children' (DoH, 1998). This sets out the results of a large-scale inspection of local authorities in England and Wales. It gives a dreadful picture of how the law is actually put into practice. It reveals 'a catalogue of concerns about how important decisions are made and the arrangements to ensure that children are safe' (1.3). Failure to understand and act within the legal framework is what let these children down.

HUMAN RIGHTS AND THE SOCIAL WORKER

The Human Rights Act 1998 came into force in October 2000, amidst a huge fanfare of publicity. Few readers will be unaware that the European Convention on Human Rights 1950 has become part of the law of England and Wales. Or has it? Few will be unaware that it brings about a significant shift in the way our courts will make decisions. Or does it? Most will know that all legislation now has to be compatible with the fundamental rights set out in the Convention. Or must it? In this final section of the chapter we will outline briefly how the new system will work, and attempt to indicate where it may impact on the work of a social worker.

New Rights?
The rights set out in the 1950 Convention are not in fact new rights for the UK. The UK was the prime force in drafting the Convention, believing that in fact it was essentially exporting fundamental rights and freedoms already existing under our own laws. The Government signed up to the treaty in 1951. But in international law, although signing a treaty commits the Government to obeying its terms, it does not change the law of the country. The only enforcement mechanism is the criticism which may come from any monitoring organisation set up by the treaty.

In 1965 the UK agreed to a right of direct petition to the European Court of Human Rights in Strasbourg. Since that date, anyone alleging a breach by the UK Government (which includes its public authorities) of their Convention rights has been able to have the dispute adjudicated by this international court. The UK has lost more cases than any other country. Why? Is it because our Government and laws fail to protect human rights? To some extent this is the answer. But the principal reason is that all allegations of breach had to go to the court in Strasbourg for adjudication, as the Convention rights were irrelevant in UK law.

A good example illustrating this is the 'gays in the forces' case, *R v Ministry of Defence, ex parte Smith* [1996] QB 517. (This is the first time we have cited a law report. The meaning of these letters and numbers is explained in the next chapter at p. 45.) Having been dismissed from the armed forces because of their homosexuality, and not for reasons of conduct, four officers tried to get the ban overturned by having the decision judicially reviewed in the High Court. The case went to the Court of Appeal, where it was thrown out. The judges agreed that under English law the only reason for overturning the Ministry's decision would be if it was made unlawfully, which would mean, in this case, a bizarre, irrational decision which no reasonable Government department could possibly come to. It would not be unlawful merely because it was wrong or a policy with which the judges disagreed. And most importantly, it could not be unlawful on the ground that the judges found it to be in breach of Convention rights. It would not even be unlawful if the judges acknowledged that the Court in Strasbourg would be bound to rule that the UK Government had breached the officers' rights by dismissing them. The Court of Appeal decided that this was not an irrational decision, and therefore it had been made lawfully. Predictably, the European Court of Human Rights upheld the complaint (*Smith* v *UK* [1999] IRLR 734), and only then was the Government forced to change its policy and admit homosexuals into the forces (or, more accurately, allow those already in the forces to 'come out of the closet').

New Ways of Enforcing the Rights
The principal effect of the 1998 Act is to allow allegations of a breach of Convention rights to be raised in front of English courts. It is achieved as follows:

(a)   When legislation is interpreted, if at all possible a meaning must be found which is compatible with Convention rights (s. 2).
(b)   If the legislation breaches Convention rights but is unambiguous, the courts must follow the legislation (s. 3(2)(b)) and not the Convention.
(c)   All public authorities (which will of course include a local authority) must not act in any way which is incompatible with a Convention right (s. 6) unless they are bound by clear legislation. A public authority can be taken directly to court for any alleged breach of a Convention right (s. 7).
(d)   Courts, as public authorities, must apply Convention law (s. 6(3)) and must take into account cases decided by the Strasbourg Court (s. 2).

How will this work in practice? First, be aware that where legislation clearly clashes with Convention rights, legislation wins. There is a new 'fast-track' procedure for amending legislation which is found by a court to be incompatible, but the unfortunate litigant may still have to tread the weary road to Strasbourg to find a remedy. There is a requirement for new legislation to be declared compatible with the Convention rights. (This does not guarantee that it is compatible, merely that its authors believe that it is. There is concern amongst some commentators, for example, that the Regulation of Investigatory Powers Act 2000, which sets out powers to intercept electronic communications, may be in breach of the Human Rights Act, even though the Act declares itself compliant.) There have already been examples of older statutes being found to have provisions that are incompatible with the Convention rights. For example, in *R (on the application of H)* v *Mental Health Review Tribunal* [2001] EWCA 415, (2001) *Times*, 2 April, s. 73 of the Mental Health Act was declared to be incompatible with the right to liberty (Article 5). (See further at p. 351, Chapter 14.) However, any law other than primary legislation (common law and secondary legislation, explained in Chapter 2) can be simply declared wrong if found incompatible with the Convention rights.

Will There be a Noticeable Change in the Law?
An expectation of radical changes in English law may lead to disappointment. By and large our laws comply with Convention rights, or our judges believe they do. It is important to be aware that for every individual right there is a corresponding provision balancing the right with the needs of the state or

society. Article 8 of the Convention (right to respect for private and family life) is an example. Paragraph 1 baldly describes the right:

> Everyone has the right to respect for his private and family life, his home and his correspondence.

But para. 2, after appearing to extend the right, quickly shows the limits to it:

> There shall be no interference by a public authority with the exercise of this right except such as is in accordance with the law and is necessary in a democratic society in the interests of national security, public safety or the economic well-being of the country, for the prevention of disorder or crime, for the protection of health or morals or for the protection of the rights and freedoms of others.

This leaves a great deal of discretion to the judges. They must exercise it by taking into account previous decisions of the Strasbourg Court, and, in due course, the body of case law built up in this country. We have chosen four cases to suggest that mounting a human rights challenge within our courts will not be easy. The first shows how the Strasbourg Court balances the individual right against the wider interests of society.

In *Scott* v *United Kingdom* [2000] 1 FLR 958, S's child (A) had been placed on the 'at risk' register because of S's alcohol problems. While subject to interim care orders A was placed with foster parents, and the local authority tried rehabilitation. The mother's alcoholism continued and the authority changed strategy, going instead for adoption. S missed the meeting where this was decided because she was being treated in a clinic. As you will see in Chapter 11, there is a procedure for a court to dispense with a parent's consent to adoption if this consent is being 'unreasonably withheld'. S's consent to adoption was dispensed with in 1994, when A was 'freed for adoption'. S complained to Strasbourg (where the decision was reached six years later). The European Court of Human Rights dismissed the complaint that her right to family life had been breached. It held that, while any restrictions of parents' rights must be carefully scrutinised, the evidence showed that A needed to be protected and that the authority's actions had been fair. S had had the chance to apply to dismiss the care orders or to appeal against the freeing order.

In the second, *R* v *Secretary of State for the Home Department, ex parte Mellor* [2000] 3 FCR 148, M was serving a life sentence for murder. He was refused permission to pass his wife a sperm sample so that she could have a child. Article 12 of the Convention provides:

> Men and women of marriageable age have the right to marry and to found a family, according to the national laws governing the exercise of this right.

M's argument was that as prisoners retain all their civil rights that are not expressly or necessarily taken away as a result of their sentence, this right remained. To grant his request did not affect prison security or discipline. The High Court, relying on a judgment of the Strasbourg Court in a previous case, held that the right to found a family did not mean a right at all times and in all circumstances and with all possible assistance to conceive children. Additionally, there was a need to uphold confidence in the judicial system.

In the third, another prison case, the Court of Appeal decided that it was not a breach of a mother's right to a family life to take her child away at 18 months old: *R (on the application of P)* v *Secretary of State for the Home Department* [2001] EWHC Admin 357, [2001] 2 FLR 383. As we said, do no not expect the Act to make society radically different.

Fourthly, in *R* v *Lambert* [2001] UKHL 37, [2000] 3 WLR 206, the Convention right at issue was the presumption of innocence in Article 6(2). Article 6 is important, so we quote it in full:

> 1. In the determination of his civil rights and obligations or of any criminal charge against him, everyone is entitled to a fair and public hearing within a reasonable time by an independent and impartial tribunal established by law. Judgment shall be pronounced publicly but the press and public may be excluded from all or part of the trial in the interests of morals, public order or national security in a democratic society, where the interests of juveniles or the protection of the private life of the parties so require, or to the extent strictly necessary in the opinion of the court in special circumstances where publicity would prejudice the interests of justice.
>
> 2. Everyone charged with a criminal offence shall be presumed innocent until proved guilty according to law.
>
> 3. Everyone charged with a criminal offence has the following minimum rights:
>
> (a) to be informed promptly, in a language which he understands and in detail, of the nature and cause of the accusation against him;
>
> (b) to have adequate time and facilities for the preparation of his defence;
>
> (c) to defend himself in person or through legal assistance of his own choosing or, if he has not sufficient means to pay for legal assistance, to be given it free when the interests of justice so require;
>
> (d) to examine or have examined witnesses against him and to obtain the attendance and examination of witnesses on his behalf under the same conditions as witnesses against him;
>
> (e) to have the free assistance of an interpreter if he cannot understand or speak the language used in court.

The defendant had been charged with possession of drugs with an intent to supply. Another defendant dealt with in the same judgment had been convicted of murder. The normal rule of criminal procedure is that the prosecution must prove the guilt of the defendant beyond reasonable doubt. However, there are some defences available where the *defendant* needs to prove, on the balance of probabilities (see Chapter 8), the truth of certain facts. In the case of murder, evidence of diminished responsibility can be put forward under the Homicide Act 1957, and the jury are then entitled to convict only for manslaughter. A defendant could also try to prove, for example, intolerable provocation. In the case of intent to supply, the defendant would need to show under the Misuse of Drugs Act 1971 that she or he did not know what was in the container. Both defendants appealed against conviction, using the Human Rights Act 1998 to claim that the statutes should now be interpreted in line with the Article 6(2) presumption of innocence, and arguing that it was therefore for the prosecution to prove that what the defendants were suggesting — provocation or lack of knowledge — was false.

The Court of Appeal and the House of Lords both dismissed the human rights claim. In the Court of Appeal Lord Woolf stated that the interpretation of Article 6(2) required a balancing act, so that the rights of the defendants to have the case proved against them are balanced with the rights of society in general. In this case, he said, the presumption of innocence was not in any way diminished: the prosecution must prove the case or fail. If a defendant wants to raise additional facts which statute requires her or him to prove, that does not remove the need for the prosecution to prove their case against her or him.

The Convention Rights

We have already cited three important rights — to a fair trial, to private and family life, and to marry and found a family. Space does not permit us to reproduce the remaining articles in full. Where helpful, in the chapters which follow the text will be set out. Please be content at this point with an overview only.

Article 2 establishes a right to life. This could be relevant to a social services department sued, for example, for failure to protect the right of a child not to be killed by an abusive parent.

Article 5 provides a right to liberty and security. This means that a person can be detained only following a proper, lawful procedure. Criminal procedure in this country probably already complies with this requirement. That means that anyone claiming illegal detention — such as, for example, a child locked up without following the procedures under the Children Act set out in Chapter 11 — already has a remedy under English law and does not need to invoke the Human Rights Act 1998. It may be arguable that the detention of immigrants pending the processing of their applications is in breach of Article 5.

Article 7 provides that there shall be no punishment without law.

Article 14 prohibits discrimination in the enjoyment of Convention rights.

The First Protocol to the Convention sets out a right of peaceful enjoyment of property, and a right to education.

Public Assistance in Enforcing Rights

You will discover in Chapter 19, which deals with laws to suppress discrimination on grounds of sex, race or disability, that in each of these areas there are publicly funded expert bodies whose task is to promote best practice and to assist individuals who allege they have been victims of discrimination. Is there any equivalent body with the twin tasks of (i) promoting best practice in the observation by the Government of human rights obligations, and (ii) assisting individuals to obtain redress if they allege that their rights have been breached? Such a body exists in Northern Ireland, but not in England and Wales. Redress of grievances connected to human rights abuses requires the use of the existing mechanisms for funding legal cases (see Chapter 15), or help from organisations such as the civil liberties watchdog Liberty.

Department of Health Guidance for Social Workers on Human Rights
Circular LAC 2000 (17) states:

> Social Service Departments should actively develop good practice in a manner suited to the new human rights culture, linking as appropriate the equality and race relations agenda.

This is, unfortunately but perhaps unavoidably, a rather bland statement. The Guidance will only work if human rights issues are taken into account in all aspects of social work. We have tried to raise issues of human rights as they occur throughout the text so that this culture can acquire some meaning for you. The DoH website is a very good source of further guidance: find it at www.doh.humanrights/index.htm. It includes discussion of the relationship between existing human rights cases, the articles referred to above, and social work situations.

A Postscript
As this edition goes to press in October 2001, the terrorist attacks on New York and Washington have led to the Home Secretary declaring that, if necessary, human rights legislation will have to be amended. Our optimistic belief that human rights provides a new foundation for all legal thinking may by snuffed out in new legislation or executive action, or by judges simply preferring to support state rights against individual liberty when using their wide discretion.

TWO

The Social Worker in the Legal System

Being a member of a skilled profession you need an understanding of the law. This is a book by lawyers for social workers. If it is to be useful to social workers we will need to clarify the differences that exist between the two professions, so that there can be a productive relationship.

LAWYERS

It may appear to be facile to state that lawyers, just like social workers, are ordinary people doing a particular job. Often we tend to reduce people to a 'group' and expect everybody within that group to act and react in a particular way. Just as your professional clients are individuals, so are lawyers. In your working life you can do no better than to cultivate a personal relationship with your agency lawyer so that all sides can work effectively together.

Having said that, perhaps initially it is still worth stating some often repeated, jaundiced and prejudiced views of lawyers by social workers. Such views may contain a grain of truth. (We will not repeat the jaundiced and prejudiced views held about social workers by lawyers!) We look at lawyers despite the fact that this chapter is about the social worker in the legal system. The aim is, in showing some of the fallacies that exist about lawyers, to begin to show you the workings of the legal system and to enable you to see your place within it.

'Lawyers do not enjoy life; they merely litigate their way through it'
Lawyers are often accused of seeing life through jaundiced eyes, as an endless journey from one pressing legal problem to another. A good lawyer, on being told of an acquaintance's engagement does not think 'congratulations!' but rather reflects on the fact that any property now acquired by the couple can, on the breakdown of the the relationship, be litigated about under the Married Women's Property Act 1882, s. 17 (as amended by the Law

Reform Miscellaneous Provisions Act 1970). Every good lawyer, as a paid-up member of the cynics' club, knows perfectly well that any relationship is guaranteed to break down, sooner or later. They know that it is guaranteed to break down because often their professional life is spent dealing with the consequences of such broken relationships.

It is also true to say that most lawyers are geared up to see life as a series of 'problems' to be solved for others. Lawyers should be trained to absorb the details of a particular situation, then to analyse that situation for the legal questions and to propose a course of action or more hopefully a series of courses of action. You should be extremely sceptical of a lawyer who says 'there is no alternative'. Most of life's problems have a number of possible legal solutions. The consequences of those different courses of action should be outlined but the actual choice of the course of action should be left to those instructing the lawyer. As the Kimberley Carlile report said: 'the lawyer should be ever present but should never dominate'.

Having arrived at that decision the lawyer can be expected to take such steps as are required to obtain the result that is desired, for example by going to court, and after that the lawyer will tend to withdraw from the scene.

Lawyers share with other professionals the problem of too much work required to be done in too little time. A social worker must appreciate that a lawyer will at any one time have a great number of cases with which they are dealing. The mere fact that you know everything about your case does not mean that your lawyer will be in the same helpful position. A social worker must never assume anything with a lawyer! The frequent comment from those who have been exposed to the legal process is 'those dealing with the case did not fully comprehend or appreciate the facts and I felt so frustrated. If only they had asked'. The social worker instructing the lawyer must, at an early stage, be certain that the lawyer does have a full picture of the social worker's stance and can see what the social worker can see.

'Lawyers are a bunch of cold fish'

One skill a good lawyer should have — and due to pressures of work, most lawyers do actually acquire this skill — is that of being detached from the client's situation. In other words they will not become 'involved'. Whilst this may be frustrating, it can also be a great help to the hard pressed social worker because the lawyer can be the person who points out the obvious, which the social worker, being close to the situation, may overlook. No committed social worker can do anything to prevent becoming involved with their clients; they will want their clients to 'succeed'. Running into the cold, detached approach of the lawyer can at the very least be described as stimulating!

Lawyers will expect to get results — to finish a case. The greatest failing that a lawyer can become prey to is that of seeing everything as 'just another case'. (Cases are the bread and butter of the lawyer's life. Lawyers greet each other saying 'any good cases?'.) In instructing lawyers, social workers will need to keep the 'human' element to the fore. A social worker needs to accept that whilst lawyers look to 'solve' legal problems, they often find it difficult to understand why social workers want to 'resolve' their clients' other problems. Of course, the lawyer is not going to have to see the social worker's clients after the case is over. They do not have to continue to work with the parents whose children have been taken away and therefore it is not surprising that sometimes they may appear to be harsh and uncaring.

What we have just said should not be seen as all gloomy. There is a positive virtue in the interaction between the differing approaches of the two professions. As long as social workers do not expect lawyers to be social workers and vice versa then a positive successful relationship will develop.

One of the advantages that has come from the reports into the deaths of children such as Kimberley Carlile and Jasmine Beckford, and 'The Cleveland Report', has been that the legal profession now recognises that there are particular skills required of a lawyer dealing with child care cases. Prior to these reports, in local authorities particularly, the child care cases were given to the most inexperienced lawyer and had to be fitted in amongst the stopping up of roads and the prosecutions of the 'fly in the pie' cases. This attitude is now dying and there is, increasingly, a new breed of lawyer which specialises in social services matters and child care cases.

Within your agency you should expect and demand the best possible professional legal support. If it is necessary to support you in this quest, one quote from the *Report of the Inquiry into Child Abuse in Cleveland 1987* ('The Cleveland Report') should suffice:

> The lack of appropriate legal advice at case conferences contributed to the failure of those most closely involved with the children to appreciate that the medical opinions they had acted upon might not provide a satisfactory basis for applications in care proceedings. This deprived them of a useful check in consideration of the advisability of the removal of the children from home. (Final Recommendations, para. 11.)

For lawyers in private practice the Law Society has created a Children Panel of solicitors. This covers lawyers who are involved in any cases where children are concerned. The aim has been that practitioners who wish to be included on that panel have to show that they have the relevant experience, knowledge and temperament to deal with such cases. After a short experience of courtroom practice you will be able to form your own judgments. A social worker should expect and indeed demand that they are able to get advice from a lawyer of at least the same or better standard.

'The lawyer's role is to get us out of the mire!'
The advice of lawyers is sought when there appear to be particular legal difficulties. The expectation is that the lawyer will be able to solve problems. But to be able to see that there are legal problems does suggest that the social worker will be able to know what the legal problems are in the first place. The aim of this book is not to replace the advice of a good lawyer. The book will not make it possible for the social worker to dispense with the lawyer. The knowledge of the essential legal foundation upon which all social work is

based will enable the social worker to be in a better position to benefit from the help of a lawyer.

'Lawyers are obsessed with procedure'

Lawyers are concerned not so much with the decisions and professional judgments made by you and your local authority, but with the way you make them. The Human Rights Act 1998 underscores the importance of procedure. Bear with the lawyer here, and accept the need for justice not only to be done but to seen to be done. The complexity of your role requires you to think especially clearly about your decision making.

This book can only hope to lighten the burden on social workers. It will never remove all the pressures that will, at times, exist. The professional social worker has the task of trying to resolve considerable, apparently conflicting, demands. Ultimately, the difficult decisions that any individual social worker may have to take will have to be justified by that social worker. The only correct answer that a social worker can give, when asked why they took a particular course of action, must include the statement 'that I took the step because that was what appropriate social work practice demanded within the framework of the law'. Without the ability to say that, the professional social worker will have failed themselves and, more important, their client.

THE DIFFERENT HATS YOU HAVE TO WEAR

Life would be much simpler if we all had one single job to do all the time. Nobody should become a social worker, however, if they want a simple life!

You will always have a variety of tasks and different roles to perform as a social worker. Balancing these is no easy task and needs to be worked at. Let us look at the variety of roles that a professional social worker can undertake within the legal sphere:

Local authority field worker As such you will have to carry a case load of individual clients to each of whom you will have a statutory duty. Where your client is a child you will have to ensure that the welfare of the children is promoted. This may mean that you have to seek statutory orders to protect them. In doing this you will become:

Applicant to the court This is when you, on behalf of your agency, apply to the court for an order. The matter is then passed out of your direct control and the future conduct of the matter has to be regulated to the demands of the court. Where requested or allowed by statute, the court will place the child's needs as paramount.

Witness In doing this you will need to be truthful to the court whilst still trying to ensure that your agency is satisfied by obtaining the order. If the court then decides that there are grounds on which an order may be made you will produce a report to assist the court and become a:

Reporter to the court   In this role your function will be to assist the court in deciding what is in the best interests of the child, which may mean, in a case, saying to the court that an order should not be made.

Children's guardian (formerly a guardian ad litem)   As an experienced and senior social worker you may find yourself being asked to fill this role. Your function will be to assess the child on whose behalf you have been appointed and then assess the actions and proposals of the local authority which has brought the case to court. In doing this you may be required to be critical of your professional colleagues in a neighbouring local authority. From April 1999 the procedural rules for the county court and the High Court were changed. Most of the changes have been made in an attempt to simplify and streamline the court procedures. One aspect has been to adopt, as far as is possible, plain English. This means that somebody bringing a civil (not a criminal) claim in court is no longer called the 'plaintiff' but is now the 'claimant'. Most of the changes do not directly affect the contents of this book. However, the court-appointed person who represents the child in civil proceedings is now called a 'litigation friend'. This change applies only to the county court and High Court. It does not apply in the Family Proceedings Court of the magistrates' court. The majority of social workers' experience will be within the Family Proceedings Court where children's interests are represented by children's guardians.

Throughout all these different roles you will remain employed by an agency and have to do the best you can for them. This may produce conflicts arising from the handling of individual cases. You may find that you are required by your team leader or area manager to take certain steps, such as seeking a court order, that you may not think is the 'best' course of action. As an employee you are legally required to follow the instructions of your employer. But as a professional, a social worker may find that their professional duty puts them in conflict with their role as employee. We hope this occurs rarely, but it remains a real possibility. For further exploration of these issues please see Chapter 8. (For the particular case of an approved social worker under the Mental Health Act — where the employer cannot give the social worker instructions, the responsibility is individual — please see Chapter 14.)

Underlying all these roles is the central dilemma for social workers in the legal system. This is the conflict that exists between the twin demands of being:

(a)   an adviser/friend to your client, or to those involved with your client such as their carers or parents. Such a role is often talked of as 'being an agent of social change'. That is to say that you will be seeking to make life better for your client; and

(b)   a statutory person in relation to your client. This is more commonly referred to as being 'an agent of statutory control'. This is where you are sometimes required to use statutory powers to protect your client.

We have already made it clear that your prime role has to be within the statutory framework that has created social workers. A social worker who fails to bear this in mind will ultimately fail themselves and their clients. This does not mean that your role as friend and adviser is or should be diminished. Nevertheless you need to build up your relationship with your client with your statutory role as your first consideration. This is to be honest with your client which is the best basis of the relationship.

WHO IS MY CLIENT?

We have already used the word 'client' and it is important that we clarify who the social worker's client is. Sometimes this is far from clear to the outsider. In any case involving children, each individual child on your case-load is your client. You need to build up an individual relationship with each child over and above that you may have with the child's parents. It only requires a reading of such reports as those into the deaths of Kimberley Carlile or Jasmine Beckford to see the dangers that exist where social workers lose sight of the child as their client, either through lack of insight or through being 'conned' by the child's parents. (While both of these reports were published some time ago, 1987 and 1985 respectively, they remain important teaching and learning documents. Although child-care tragedies continue to happen, there has been a trend for the reports not to be published. Most commentators continue to refer to the above reports. For a summary of these and other reports, see DoH, *Child Abuse: A Study of Inquiry Reports 1980–1989* (1991).)

This point about clients is not just applicable to children. For example, if you are dealing with an old person it is very easy to overlook that the old person is your client and that his or her needs should, as far as possible, prevail. The pressures of the family can lead you to concentrate on what the family may want, which often may not be what the old person wants.

A good social worker will, in any new case, ask 'who is my client?' and, having answered that question, constantly keep that client at the forefront of their mind. Failure to do this runs the risk of letting down the person on whose behalf you are supposed to be acting.

SOURCES OF LAW

We have already talked a great deal about the legal system and the law. Where do lawyers get their law from? In this section we shall study the following:

(a) the differences between common law and statute law;
(b) the 'rule of law' and natural justice;
(c) the distinction between private and public law;
(d) the differences between duties and powers; and
(e) regulations and guidance.

It will be necessary for you to be aware of the meaning of these terms since these are the common foundations of the law. As such, we will refer to them throughout the book without defining them again.

Common Law and Statute Law

We state that a social worker has 'statutory powers' — what does this mean? There is a distinct difference drawn by lawyers between statutory law and common law. Common law can be regarded for our purposes as established, traditional law as defined by the courts. Statute law is that law that has been passed by Parliament.

As society becomes more complicated the role of common law diminishes, since more and more statutes are passed dealing with more and more areas of behaviour within society. But common law is not wholly extinct: murder is not a statutory offence, it is a common law offence. This means that you cannot look in an Act of Parliament for a definition of murder, rather you have to look at decisions of courts in the past as to what defines murder. However, the penalty that must be imposed for murder is set out in a statute.

Statutes, delegated legislation and how to interpret them Parliament passes statutes by a process of debates and votes during which the original Bills are changed into their final form — the Act of Parliament. One of the growth areas of modern life is that of legislation. Parliament sits long into the night producing more and more Acts. It has been realised that no matter how long Parliament sits, it still will not be able to pass sufficient legislation in the detail that the running of a sophisticated democracy requires.

Therefore, in most Acts of Parliament there will be found a power for delegated legislation. Delegated legislation, as its name implies, gives the power to some person or body to pass legislation that has the same effect as if it had been passed by Parliament through its normal process of legislation. For the delegated legislation to come into force, normally it must be 'laid before Parliament'. This requires a copy of the proposed delegated legislation to be placed (or laid) on the table in the House of Commons and the House of Lords for a specified number of days. After that the legislation comes into force. It may require a vote without a debate, or the alternative form is where it comes into effect by 'negative resolution'. This means that it will come into force unless sufficient members of Parliament put their names down so as to require a vote to be taken.

We will come across a considerable amount of delegated legislation in the form of Regulations and Rules of Court. Later in the book we devote a great deal of space to considering the effect of the Children Act 1989. The Act sets out in detail how the courts, local authorities and others are to deal with the care and welfare of children. There are 108 sections in this particular Act and 15 Schedules, and the Bill which became the Act spent almost a year being debated in both the House of Lords and the House of Commons. Despite all this, the Act could not come into force as soon as it was passed, and it has had to be amended many times since it was first enacted. To ensure that the courts and local authorities could make the Act work in practice, there had to be a period of some two years to enable the necessary Rules of Court and Regulations to be issued, by means of delegated legislation.

For legislation introduced after the Human Rights Act 1998 came into force (October 2000), the Minister has to endorse the Bill with a statement of its compatibility with the rights laid down in the European Convention on

Human Rights, or make a statement that he is unable to so endorse the Bill but that he wishes the House to proceed with it.

Statutory interpretation   Having been through all these procedures, you would have thought that the law would be perfectly clear. However, it is not as straightforward as that. There will always be disputes as to what is the particular meaning of a statute, or indeed what is the meaning of a particular word within a statute. It is the function of courts to interpret statutes. This process is called statutory interpretation.

Statutory interpretation has evolved over centuries. When courts have had to decide what a statute says, there has developed a series of so-called 'rules' that guide the courts. Their effect is to set out the approach that should be adopted by the courts. There are three main 'rules': first, the 'literal rule' which says that the words in a statute are taken to have their literal meaning unless such an interpretation produces a nonsensical result. In that case the 'golden rule' applies which says if the literal meaning produces an absurd result then you look at it in the overall context of the statute. If these two 'rules' do not help then the 'mischief rule' is applied. This rule states that you interpret the meaning of the word in the light of what the problem or mischief was that the statute was passed to deal with.

An example of the application of statutory interpretation will be in relation to the meaning of the word 'significant' in the Children Act 1989, s. 31. As you will see in Chapter 7, the word occurs in the definition of the grounds on which a court may make a care order in respect of a child. No definition of the word is given in the Act and views differ on the word's meaning within the section. We said in earlier editions that soon after the section came into effect we had no doubt that there would be an appeal case that would seek a definition of the word. This proved to be true. If you look at Chapter 7, you will see there has been a number of cases on this very point. In trying to define 'significant' the courts have applied the rules of statutory interpretation. Having done that, the lower courts will now be bound to follow the High Court's and Appeal Court's interpretation in all future cases. The meaning of the statute is considered in the light of the unique facts of each case, and the court will always have the chance of saying 'but this case is different'.

The Human Rights Act 1998 has an impact on statutory interpretation, in that it provides that courts must strive to interpret legislation in a way which is compatible with Convention rights and the intention of Parliament (see Chapter 1). Where it is not possible to interpret the legislation in this way, the courts may strike down delegated legislation but not primary legislation (although they may make a declaration of incompatibility, which should prompt Government action).

The Distinction between Public Law and Private Law
A distinction that is made by lawyers, and the courts in particular, is that between public and private law.

Public law is that law which deals with those areas in which society, for good or ill, has decided to interfere in a direct manner with the behaviour of individuals. On the other hand, to regulate the behaviour of private individuals between themselves comes within the confines of private law.

For example, care proceedings are an area of public law. In that situation the state has decided that the task of bringing up children should be carried out within certain parameters, which are set out in the relevant legislation. If parents step outside those parameters then the state, in the form of the local authority, will step in and, in the extreme, take over the upbringing of the children by removing them from the parents. The local authority, in taking such actions, is acting on behalf of the public, and public law regulates the way in which that task is carried out.

In contrast, an example of private law would be a dispute between a car owner and a garage over the quality of a repair to the car. If the owner refuses to pay the bill because of dissatisfaction with the quality of the repair, the garage may sue the car owner in the county court. How the dispute is to be resolved by the court is set out in the law of contract and the rules of court. The outcome of the case, though, is not of interest to society as a whole, only to the parties to the dispute.

Sometimes, public law and private law will meet in the course of the same proceedings. An example would be during the course of divorce proceedings which are essentially private law. As you will find out in Chapter 5, under the provisions of the Children Act there are powers during divorce proceedings to require the local authority to carry out an investigation, if the court is concerned about the welfare of the children. One outcome of this investigation can be the local authority commencing care proceedings, which, as stated above, are public law.

Whilst the statutes and delegated legislation set out the powers and duties of public bodies, exactly how those duties and powers are carried out depends largely on two common law concepts, the rule of law and natural justice.

The Rule of Law and Natural Justice

If a director of social services (a post created by statute; see p. 33 below) wishes to provide particular services for children in need then they refer to the Children Act 1989 — a statute. In that Act they find the rules on which any recommendation can be made to the Social Services Committee (a creature of statute). Suppose that those in political control say that they are opposed to providing additional services for children in need — can the director ignore the criteria set out in the statute?

'Rule of law' Not according to the concept of the rule of law. This concept is that no matter how much any individual may dislike a particular law, whilst they remain a member of this particular society, they are required to obey the law. The rule of law in a democracy means that we are ruled by politicians in Parliament who can pass whatever laws they see fit, and the citizens have to obey those laws.

The rule of law also means that the courts' function is to interpret the will of Parliament expressed in statute and not to make it up for themselves, unless there is a 'gap' in the statute. This does not mean that the courts do not have a function in controlling the possible excesses of Parliament. They can rely on the idea of natural justice and (since 2 October 2000) the Human Rights Act 1998.

The Human Rights Act 1998 In passing the 1998 Act, Parliament has decided that in general it will be bound by the terms of the European Convention on Human Rights. However, it retains discretion as to whether or not each statute that it enacts will be compatible with the Convention. From 2 October 2000, each statute must contain a statement of compatibility or non-compatibility. Clearly, if the Government states that it does not intend a statute to be compatible, it must explain why and receive Parliament's consent. The 1998 Act also contains a new rule of statutory interpretation as we explained earlier.

'Natural justice' This is taken to mean that whatever the law is, citizens are entitled to have the law applied fairly, in accordance with common law, and the courts will uphold that right. Common law has laid down the ways in which the courts are to interpret statute. If the statute is not correctly applied then that will be a breach of natural justice.

Like all concepts in the legal field, it is not as simple as that. If a statute clearly says that the courts will have no power of review, then the courts will not have the power to intervene, although there have been a number of lengthy and complicated cases examining whether or not a statute can be made totally 'judge-proof'. This fascinating area is outside the scope of this book. If you wish to know more then you will need to read further on constitutional law.

Going back to our director of social services: if they were personally to take a dislike to the parents of the child who was seeking services, then they might decide merely to recommend to the Social Services Committee that the home should not receive services. They would have failed to have carried out the necessary procedures that are required by the statute.

In those circumstances the child could seek a judicial review of the 'decision' by stating that natural justice had been infringed since the law was not fairly applied. The court could make such a ruling, even though according to the Act the Social Services Committee may refuse to provide a particular service to a child in need. For the doctrine of natural law means that the decision must be arrived at through the correct procedures. The courts would then have the power to overturn the 'decision' of the Social Services Committee. This is applicable because the provision of services to children in need is within the area of public law.

Another relevant concept that is in many ways an extension of the natural law concept in the field of public law is the application of the *'Wednesbury* principles'.

The 'Wednesbury principles' They are called the *Wednesbury* principles since they were first stated by the judges sitting in a case called *Associated Provincial Picture Houses* v *Wednesbury Corporation* [1947] 2 All ER 680. By way of information, the actual case concerned the question of whether or not cinemas should be allowed to open on Sundays in the town of Wednesbury. The cinema lost.

The *Wednesbury* principles are applicable to the acts of local authorities and other public bodies which function within the field of public law. They state, broadly, that when coming to a decision the local authority must consider all relevant matters and exclude all irrelevant matters, and if it fails to do that the courts will have the power to overturn the decision. Even if the authority had excluded all irrelevant matters and considered all relevant matters, if the decision had been one that was so unreasonable that no reasonable authority could have come to that decision then, again, the courts will overturn the decision.

To apply this to services provided to children in need: if the councillors decided not to provide the services because they felt that there were too many services for children in need, they would not have considered relevant matters and they would have made their decision based on irrelevant matters. Therefore, they would have fallen foul of the *Wednesbury* principles.

Proportionality An additional requirement imposed by the Human Rights Act 1998, is the need for decisions to be proportionate to the outcome which is sought. So, for instance, in *Re C and B (Children) (Care Order: Future Harm)* [2000] 2 FCR 614, CA, the Court of Appeal allowed a mother's appeal against the making of a care order in respect of two of her three children with a view to placement for adoption. The Court accepted that there were reasons for concern, and that there was evidence on which the judge was entitled to conclude that there was a real possibility of future harm. However, there was no evidence of actual harm to the younger children, or that they were at immediate risk. Intervention had to be proportionate to the degree of risk, and a care order was not justified.

The Difference between Powers and Duties

The distinction and difference is relatively straightforward. It is sometimes forgotten in practice.

Where a statute imposes a duty on a person or a body then they have to carry out that duty. There is no choice, however hard the carrying out of the duty may be. Lack of finance, for instance, is not an acceptable reason for not carrying out the duty.

Where a statute gives a person or a body a power to do some act, the person or the body may exercise that power but they are not obliged to do so.

The distinction is important when a person is disgruntled by the behaviour of a statutory person or body. If there is a duty then the disgruntled person will be able to take court action to enforce that duty. If there is only a power, then it is unlikely that there will be any legal redress. Although if the person can show that the way in which the power was exercised was unreasonable, that could be challenged by a judicial review.

Whatever you are doing as a social worker, you should be clear in your own mind whether you are acting under a duty or a power, and regulate your actions accordingly.

Regulations and Guidance

No Act of Parliament will ever cover every situation. Most Acts give the power to make regulations. In the field of social services another important piece of government output is the guidance issued by the Secretary of State.

While regulations have the full force of a statute, the role of guidance is not so clear-cut. As will be seen on p. 32, the local authority social services functions are governed by the Local Authority Social Services Act 1970 (LASSA). Under s. 7 these functions must be exercised under the general guidance of the Secretary of State. Where guidance is issued to local authorities under this s. 7, it is not, in law, mandatory. Such guidance, nevertheless, must be followed unless there are justifiable reasons for not doing so. An explanation of the role of such guidance is to be found in the following quotation where Sedley J (the 'J' means a High Court judge: in this case Mr Justice Sedley) stated that local authorities have:

to follow the path charted by the Secretary of State's guidance, with liberty to deviate from it where the local authority judges on admissible grounds that there is good reason to do so, but without freedom to take a substantially different course. (*R* v *Islington LBC, ex parte Rixon* (1996) *The Times*, 17 April)

It is also worth noting that although local authorities have to follow guidance as set out above, if they do that, they cannot be guaranteed to get it right. Guidance issued by a government department will always only amount to a view of what the department think the law is. It is perhaps the clearest expression of their wish of what the law should mean. It remains the function of the court actually to decide what the legislation means. So we find the House of Lords making this point:

It is true that para. 4 of local Authority Circular LAC (93) 10 says

'It is the view of the department that the amendments introduced into the 1948 Act by section 1 of the Community Care (Residential Accommodation) Act 1992 will require authorities to make some direct provision for residential care under Part III of the 1948 Act'

The opinion of the department is entitled to respect, particularly since I assume the Act was drafted upon its instructions. But in my view this statement is simply wrong. (*R* v *Wandsworth London Borough, ex parte Beckworth* [1996] 1 All ER 129, HL, Lord Hoffman)

As the foreward to *An Introduction to the Children Act 1989* (Department of Health: HMSO 1989) says: 'The Government is not entitled to give an authoritative interpretation of the law and ultimately any interpretation is a matter for the courts'.

In the extreme, the Secretary of State has the powers to intervene to direct a local authority to take a particular course of action. For example, a juvenile is arrested for a murder which attracts a high media profile. The juvenile is remanded into the custody of the local authority. Under current guidance the local authority does not have to place the juvenile in secure accommodation. In this situation the Secretary of State may well be expected, in view of the attendant media hype, to direct the local authority to place the juvenile in secure accommodation.

Other guidance may be in the form of circulars and other documents that are not issued under s. 7 of LASSA. If a local authority does not follow this non-statutory guidance, it will be open to censure, either by the courts, parliament or the media, if things go wrong. The censure will not be by imposition of a legal penalty, but will be criticism of the course of action. However, if you look at the quotation on p. 66, you will see that the courts do not always agree with the interpretation of the law given in government guidance! This puts the local authority in a 'no win' situation, but that is often the nature of this area of work.

The social worker should always check whether the document they are using is or is not issued under s. 7 of the LASSA. If it is, this is indicated clearly in the preface to the document.

Lastly, you should not be confused by questions of good practice. Much is written about the best practice in social work. Such opinions set out the ideals of what is thought of the way in which social work principles should be put into day-to-day practice. It is not, however, statute law and much of what does amount to good practice is *not* issued in the form of either regulations or statutory guidance. Therefore, good practice must always give way to the requirements of statute, regulations and guidance, if these legal requirements conflict.

A great deal of this book concerns the Children Act. Despite there being over 100 sections in the Act, some 30 sets of regulations have been issued under it. Together with these go 10 books of guidance. So, merely looking at the Act will not give the full picture of what it is about. So detailed are the regulations and guidance that there is even a separate index published. We refer to these books of regulations and guidance throughout the relevant chapters. To help you understand these books the Government has issued a book of guidance on *The Care of Children: Principles and Practice in Regulations and Guidance*. This is worth reading and gives further explanation on the different concepts.

Although guidance can be linked to a particular Act (such as the Children Act 1989), sometimes it can stand alone. Three good examples are:

(a) *Working Together to Safeguard Children — Government Guidance on Inter-Agency Cooperation 1999* — this is guidance on inter-disciplinary working to protect children. We discuss this in fuller detail in Chapter 5. It is issued under s. 7 of LASSA.

(b) *Framework for the Assessment of Children in Need and their Families (2000)* — this again is 'stand alone' guidance on assessing children. In any application by a local authority to the court it is to be expected that the local authority will be asked whether or not any assessment that was carried out followed the guidance in this book.

(c)   *A Manual for Guardians ad Litem and Reporting Officers.*

The guidance referred to in (b) and (c) above is not issued under s. 7 of
LASSA. We recommend the study and use of all these books. They are
available on the DoH website at www.open.gov.uk/doh/quality.htm.

THE OMBUDSMAN

Mention of disgruntled persons brings us to the ombudsman. (It is a
Scandinavian term adapted to the English language. It should really be
'ombudsperson', especially as women serve in the role.)

The first ombudsman created was the Parliamentary ombudsman who
deals with the failings of government departments. There are now quite a
number of ombudsmen for different bodies; local authorities, the Health
Service and for 'private' organisations such as insurance companies and
banks. We shall look at the local authority ombudsman (technically called the
Parliamentary Commissioner for Local Government) as this is the person you
may have dealings with. Typically, in any year there are 15,000 complaints
to the local authority ombudsman, 6 per cent of which relate to social services
(37 per cent, in contrast, relate to housing departments).

The public ombudsman schemes are a creation of statute designed to
provide a possible source of redress where private individuals have suffered
through the poor administration of a public body, such as a local authority.

We say 'poor administration'. which is also termed 'maladministration',
because the ombudsman is only concerned with this area. That means that
the person seeking to use the ombudsman must not have any way of seeking
a legal redress through the courts. What the ombudsman looks at is not the
failure of the local authority to obey the law but its failure to implement the
law in a competent way.

To take the situation, referred to earlier, of the attempts to provide services
to children in need, the ombudsman may be turned to in a situation where
the system fails, rather than when the law is broken. So if the application form
was lost in the civic centre, the report to the Social Services Committee
(although on its agenda) was not presented etc, and if as a result of these
failings the applicants suffered, then they would have the chance to apply to
the ombudsman. Children and young persons have as much right to go to
the ombudsman as do adults.

To apply, it is necessary to have satisfied the ombudsman that all other
procedures of internal complaint to the local authority have been tried and
exhausted, without giving the complainant redress. (While many complaints
will be covered by the local authority complaints procedures, the ombudsman
can investigate delays in making complaints or allegations that councils are
trying to exclude people from using the complaints process.) Then the
complainant has to approach the ombudsman through a local councillor.
This is designed to act as a filter, since the requirement to use a councillor
should mean that the councillor will have considered all other forms of
redress and will have used their influence to solve the difficulty. If the

complainant can find no councillor willing to make the application, the complainant can approach the ombudsman direct. This having been done, the ombudsman then has wide powers of investigation and the ability to look at files and compel people to give information.

An officer of the ombudsman sends a copy of the complaint to the chief executive of the local authority asking for comments.

When the investigations are complete the ombudsman prepares a report. This report is made publicly available, with the expectation that if there is a finding of maladministration then the local authority will remedy the fault and, in the appropriate case, pay compensation. The local authority must respond to the report. If the local authority fails to carry out the recommendations of the ombudsman then a further report will be published. This, however, is the only sanction that the ombudsman has. There are no powers of compulsion available to the ombudsman to require the local authority to carry out any of the recommendations contained in the report.

On the matter of complaints, the ombudsman is not the only recourse that may be available. Many local authorities have systems of complaints procedures. Very important, in respect of the Children Act, there is the requirement for a complaints procedure (s. 26; see Chapter 4: The Law and Children).

STATUTORY CONTEXT OF LOCAL AUTHORITY SOCIAL SERVICES

The introduction to this book begins with the statement that the social worker is a creation of statute, and we will repeat that point on a number of occasions throughout. Before that, we will look at the developments that led to the passing of the statute.

Brief Historical Background

The Social Services function derives from the original role of the local parish council that was responsible for the administration of the 'poor law'. That law was the beginning of the concept of the basic safety net that would, when a person was at the end of the line, keep them from falling into the gutter. The original philosophy was that the responsibility for the person's misfortune was their own, and they were given basic relief, at the merest subsistence level, for which they had to work.

There is a perceptible difference between the 'safety net' idea and the 'prevention' idea that is reflected in the various statutory solutions. The legislative history shows the divergence that has occurred. The administration of the old 'poor law' was taken over by national government, since it was seen to be important to provide a uniform national level of subsistence benefit. While that was done, other areas that had grown up from the poor law, such as the 'work house', stayed with the local authorities in the form of their responsibilities for old people and the provision of homes for them. This explains why the statutory basis for providing accommodation for old people is to be found in the National Assistance Act 1948. (For further details, see

Chapter 13.) It is worth remembering that it was not until the reforms made in the post-war period that the residues of the old 'poor law' structures were removed.

Children, at the time of the poor law, were seen, at best, as chattels of their parents, and, at worst, as a heavy charge on the parish to be discharged at the earliest possible date. Services for children, on the other hand, developed as an adjunct to the health services. It was the drive for public health, through the supply of adequate water supplies and drainage, that led to the appointment of Medical Officers of Health, who dealt with the mass outbreaks of diseases. This in turn led to the development of a Public Health Service. Part of that work dealt separately with children, originally with children's health. The National Health Act 1946 set up a national system for health care, in its widest sense. At that stage the function of protecting children was exercised by the 'Children's Officer' who was employed by the Health Authority. That person carried out the functions that are today exercised by the social worker. Within the hospital service there was the evolution of the 'almoner' who dealt with the non-medical problems of the patients, and who developed into the hospital social worker.

It was only following the Seebohm report and the subsequent Local Authority Social Services Act 1970 that the profession of the social worker that we know today began to be established, with the transfer of the modern social services function to the local authorities. In the particular field of child protection, for instance, this move had followed the passing of the Children and Young Persons Act 1969. This Act was the main basis of work involving children until the passing of the Children Act 1989, which now provides a comprehensive legal framework for the protection of children.

Present Structure

The prime Act imposing the social services function on local authorities (metropolitan boroughs and county authorities) is the Local Authority (Social Services) Act (LASSA) 1970. This requires local authorities to establish a Social Services Committee which shall administer the social services functions of the local authority. The Act specifies what those functions are. (Please see the overview of the statutory framework in Chapter 1 for a list of the functions under this Act.) These functions are exercised under the general supervision of the Secretary of State — the Secretary of State now being that of the Department of Health. Some of the specific provisions include the power for the Secretary of State to direct the local authority to take certain steps in relation to its social services function.

For example, under the Children Act 1989 there is a provision in s. 44(5) which deals with the exercising of parental responsibility once an emergency protection order has been granted. Paragraph (c) requires that the exercise of these powers 'shall comply with the requirements of any regulations made by tary of State for the purposes of this subsection'. This subsection requires the Secretary of State to act by way of regulations, but in some cases the Secretary of State can act directly. For example, under s. 22, the general duty of the local authority to children can be overriden for the purposes of protecting members of the public from serious injury. By virtue of 22(7), in that situation the Secretary of State can tell the local authority what to do. This may be applicable in the case of a child suspected of murder where the matter might become a case for public concern. There the Secretary of State would have the politically useful powers of being able to say 'I have directed the local authority to do . . .'.

While LASSA sets out the framework for the provision by the local authority of social services, it is not very specific about the particular way this is to be organised. It may or may not be of comfort to you to know that the only person within the social services department who actually warrants a specific mention in the Act is the director of social services, a person whom the Social Service Committee must appoint! This person does not have to be qualified or even knowledgeable in social work.

Having established the overall framework in LASSA, other specific duties, responsibilities and powers are to be found in other relevant Acts such as the Children Act 1989 or the Registered Homes Act 1984 to which we have referred above.

CONFIDENTIALITY

The Basic Duty

You as a professional have a duty to maintain the confidentiality of information you have obtained from and about your client. Because you will work largely in the community, you are likely to gather a great deal of knowledge simply from visiting your client's home and sharing problems with him or her. People who are not your clients will give important information about their lives and other people's lives. It is important not to abuse that privilege. The basic rule of thumb, then, is that you must not give information you have received to anyone else unless you have the permission of the source. However, in the course of your career you will face dilemmas as to whether and when to break the duty of confidentiality. What we will examine here is, first, the basis of your duty and, secondly, the occasions on which you are able to break the duty because of other, greater duties which justify disclosure of information. It is important to realise that this is an area in which the law is continually developing and gives no clear answers. Different weight is given in different cases and at different times to the critical importance of confidentiality as a human right and as the core of the professional/client relationship and the need to disclose information to ensure effective multi-agency care, public protection and risk reduction. Do not forget, even if you decide to disclose information, what you disclose and who you disclose it to should be as restrictive as possible.

Explaining the basis of confidentiality is difficult, as neither its legal nor its ethical foundations are clear. The duty of confidentiality arises partly from your duty of care as a professional to your client, and is part of your duty as an employee of social services and a member of a professional body. There is a DHSS circular for social services departments which provides invaluable guidance on confidentiality (LAC (88)17), which appears to be little known.

If you are in doubt about a decision to disclose, you should refer to that circular, as well as consulting with your professional colleagues, your department's lawyers and your professional body. Whatever decision you take, you should make full notes justifying that decision in your client's file.

Other approaches would emphasise both the moral duty to keep confidences and clients' rights to autonomy. One basic, but important, reason for the general duty of confidentiality is that it is in the best interests of society and of your client that people are prepared to give information to social workers to protect the vulnerable. To reveal sources of information could lead to a reluctance to provide such vital information. The leading case on this is *D v NSPCC* [1978] AC 171. Here, a parent wanted to know who had made an unfounded complaint of child abuse against them. The House of Lords said that the identity of an informer must be protected. This is described as 'public interest immunity'. Therefore local authority and NSPCC records, including the records of individual social workers or of case conferences, generally have enjoyed immunity from disclosure.

The Human Rights Act 1998 has given rise to a new emphasis on the right to privacy. Article 8 of the European Convention on Human Rights provides that:

1. Everyone has the right to respect for his private and family life, his home and his correspondence.
2. There shall be no interference by a public authority with the exercise of this right except such as in accordance with the law and is necessary in a democratic society in the interests of national security, public safety or the economic well-being of the country, for the prevention of disorder or crime, for the protection of health or morals, or for the protection of the rights and freedoms of others.

Disclosure of information without consent may, therefore, give rise to a legal claim. However, the exceptions listed in Article 8(2) indicate the necessary balancing exercise between individual rights and the broader interests of society. Do not forget, though, that disclosure should be appropriate for the purpose you wish to achieve, and should be made only to the extent necessary to achieve that purpose.

The Balancing Act — When are you Justified in Disclosing Confidential Information?

Even in discussing the nature of confidentiality, it is apparent that the duty on you must be limited. If someone discloses to you that they have been abused, or that they have abused a child, you are not necessarily bound by confidentiality. What is necessary is that you balance the duty of confidentiality with the duty to disclose.

The main exceptions to the duty of confidentiality are as follows:

(a)   with the consent of your client or your informant;
(b)   where disclosure is in the interests of your client;

(c)   the public interest;
(d)   where the court orders disclosure; and
(e)   statutory duty.

The consent of your client or informant   The duty is owed to your client or to the person who gave you the information. If they agree that information can be passed on to other people, this consent would be a complete defence against any claim for breach of confidentiality. You must always be clear as to your client's or informant's capacity to give consent. In the case of a child, or in the case of someone who is mentally disordered, it is important to be sure that they have the ability to understand the choices you are asking them to make.

Disclosure in the interests of your client — the 'need to know' exception   It is very important that professionals do not work in isolation. They need to relate to each other on a multi-disciplinary basis and ensure that relevant information is given to each other so that they can act in the best interests of the client. Disclosure to other professionals working on a particular case with you is therefore legitimate. *Working Together* (DoH 1999) comments (at para. 7.27):

> Research and experience have shown repeatedly that keeping children safe from harm requires professionals and others to share information: about a child's health and development and exposure to possible harm; about a parent who may need help to, or may not be able to, care for a child adequately and safely; and about those who may pose a risk of harm to a child. Often, it is only when information from a number of sources has been shared and is then put together that it becomes clear that a child is at risk of or suffering harm.

and further (at para. 7.29):

> Professionals can only work together to safeguard children if there is an exchange of relevant information between them.

This legitimises, for instance, disclosure of information to a school, but limited to the extent that it is necessary to share knowledge (see further discussion at Chapter 5). Beyond this, the degree of confidentiality in child protection work will be governed by the need to protect the child. Social workers must make it clear to the child and the family that, with regard to any information they may disclose, confidentiality may not be maintained if the withholding of the information will prejudice the welfare of the child.

Public interest — where there is a threat of serious harm to others   Professional codes of conduct recognise that there are extreme cases when the public interest outweighs the rights of the client or an informant in keeping information confidential. Social work records, such as the records of individual social workers or of case conferences, generally have had immunity from disclosure. As we have said before, the rationale for this is the need to look after the welfare of the children. It is important not to damage what is likely to be a long term relationship between social workers and families. Your department will generally have to make the decision, but those who feel aggrieved will be able to challenge your decision in court. The courts will order disclosure where there is a public interest in so doing. In *Re M (A Minor) (Disclosure of Material)* [1990] 2 FLR 36, the Court of Appeal considered the situation where it might be necessary for local authorities in child care cases, for the benefit of the child, to volunteer disclosure of certain records, such as contemporary notes in a neglect case. The test that the court held to be correct was whether real harm would result from failure to disclose. The courts will go through a balancing exercise to decide whether information should be disclosed or not.

The key here to the decision to disclose is the risk of serious harm to others. *W* v *Edgell* [1989] 1 All ER 1089, is a helpful illustration of the protection given to professionals when they make the decision to disclose information which is normally confidential. W had been convicted of manslaughter after multiple killings in circumstances of extreme violence. He was detained under the Mental Health Act 1983 as a patient in a secure hospital. Dr Edgell was instructed by solicitors acting on behalf of W to prepare a psychiatric report for use before a Mental Health Review Tribunal (MHRT). Dr Edgell's opinion was that W remained very dangerous. W dropped his application to the MHRT when his solicitors received the report. However, Dr Edgell believed that the hospital and the Home Office ought to know the contents of the report. W applied to the court for an injunction preventing its disclosure. The House of Lords found that the public interest justified disclosure to the medical director of the hospital and to the Home Office, as the report contained information about W's dangerousness which was not know to these parties. In these circumstances, the public interest in protecting the public from violence took precedence over the general public interest in ensuring the confidentiality of medical consultations. This was an extreme case and it is clear that the public interest exception requires, first, that there is a real and serious risk of danger to the public, and that it is a continuing risk; secondly, that disclosure must be to a person with a legitimate interest in receiving the information; and, thirdly, that even where disclosure is justified, it should be limited to the most necessary information.

Public interest — the fair administration of justice It is a clear principle of law that local authorities are under a duty to disclose information to a child's parents and/or the child's legal advisers. This is a matter of fairness and it is in the best interests of the child. In *R* v *Hampshire County Council, ex parte K* [1990] 2 QB 71, a child who had allegedly been sexually abused was examined by a police surgeon. He found no physical evidence of abuse but, because of what the child had said, sexual abuse was suspected. After a further examination two months later, another paediatrician concluded that there had been sexual abuse. The parents obtained judicial review to quash the council's decision to withhold medical reports and its refusal to allow a further medical examination of the child by a paediatrician instructed on the parents' behalf. The court held that every child had an interest, as part and parcel of their general welfare, not only in having their own voice sympathetically heard and their own needs sensitively considered, but also in ensuring that their parents were given every proper opportunity of having the evidence fairly tested and preparing themselves in advance to meet the grave charges against them. Note, however, that the duty to disclose here is limited by public interest immunity, so information which does not have to be disclosed because keeping it confidential is in the public interest, will not have to be disclosed because of the requirement that justice should be done and seen to be done.

Court order for disclosure If matters go to court then the public interest in the efficient conduct of justice overrides the obligation of confidentiality. In particular, in children's cases all information must be put before the court and you are obliged to answer questions put to you by the judge. You cannot hide behind confidentiality. However, once information becomes part of the court proceedings, it can be disclosed only with the leave of the court. This rule applies whether proceedings are pending or concluded. The purpose of the rule is to impose confidentiality on the parties so that no improper disclosure of documents is made to a third party. Having said that, it is a common practice for a court in children's proceedings to give leave for disclosure of evidence for use in criminal and other legal proceedings. The court will give leave if it determines that confidential information about someone is relevant in any action and should be disclosed. In such a case there can be no defence against the production of that information on the grounds that the information is confidential or that there has been no consent.

There are two exceptions to the right of the court to order the disclosure of relevant information. One is the right of legal professional privilege, where information passing between client and lawyer in connection with litigation is privileged from disclosure. The other is the right to keep information privileged from disclosure on the grounds of public interest immunity. So how does the court decide whether to allow disclosure on the grounds of public interest? The cases indicate that the justification for doing so must be 'pressing', and the court must address 'all questions of confidentiality, weighing in particular the interests of the particular child against other public interest considerations'. So, for instance, in *Re A (A Minor) (Disclosure of Medical Records to the GMC)* [1999] 1 FCR 30, where there was an application by the General Medical Council for leave for disclosure of court documents and evidence in a case where allegations of child abuse had been made against the father of a child who was a doctor, leave was given on the grounds that the documents sought should be disclosed in order to enable the council to carry out its statutory duties to protect the public against possible medical misconduct. Similarly, in *Re L (Care Proceedings: Disclosure to Third Party)* [2000] 1 FLR 913, leave was given for the judgment in care proceedings to be disclosed to the United Kingdom Central Council for Nursing,

Midwifery and Health Visiting (UKCC). Here, the mother was a registered nurse who during the course of proceedings was found to be suffering from a severe personality disorder. Following the inquiry into the deaths of children at the hands of Beverley Allitt, NHS guidance is that no one with a severe personality disorder should be employed as a nurse. The judge in *Re L* found that she had to consider the effect of disclosure on the child who was the subject of proceedings. It was found that the child's welfare would not be compromised in any way. The public interest in the UKCC being able to carry out is statutory function of protecting the public against unsafe nurses justified disclosure.

Clearly, then, there is strong public interest in the disclosure of evidence against health professionals. What about in other circumstances? In *Re V (Sexual Abuse: Disclosure)*; *Re L (Sexual Abuse: Disclosure)* [1999] 1 FLR 267, the Court of Appeal reversed a decision of the Family Division which had enabled its finding that Mr L had sexually abused his two daughters and a stepdaughter to be passed to the local authority for the area to which Mr L had moved. Butler-Sloss LJ determined that in the case of Mr L, there was no pressing need for disclosure. The Court was concerned at the potential lack of control of information. Further, the statutory provisions on disclosure of information on sex offenders were thought by the Court to exclude the general principle of disclosure on the basis that there was a prescribed manner for providing the public with protection. Commentators have expressed concern at the implications of this decision, particularly when it comes to passing on to other local authorities allegations of child abuse rather than information about proven abuse. Human rights considerations may also impact upon courts' decisions to disclose information. As we have already pointed out, Article 8 of the Convention requires that there should be no unlawful interference with a person's private and family life. However, in *R v Secretary of State for Health, ex parte C* [2000] 1 FLR 627, Lord Woolf MR held that including someone's name in an index of unsuitable people who were not to be appointed to a position involving contact with children was lawful and did not fall foul of the Convention.

Statutory duty   Certain Acts of Parliament require the production of confidential information. These include the Prevention of Terrorism Acts, Road Traffic Acts, Public Health Acts, the Police and Criminal Evidence Act 1984 and the Misuse of Drugs Act 1971. We look in more detail at your duty to disclose to the police when we consider what the duty of confidentiality means in practice.

Confidentiality in Practice

Information in files   You must record everything carefully in your files. Is it then safe from being revealed? The answer is 'No'.

The persons who may gain access to the information in your files are as follows:

(a)   If you take your file to court and refer to it from the witness-box, the other lawyers can demand to see it. What a lawyer sees is generally going to be available to be seen by their client. In some cases the court may order that only the lawyer is allowed to see certain information.

(b)   If a children's guardian is appointed then they can see it under the provisions of s. 42 of the Children Act.

(c)   People about whom information is recorded can usually see that part of the files under the Access to Personal Files Act 1987.

(d)   Normally, if the police want to obtain information they must approach social services with a request, although exceptionally you can make the approach to them yourself for the purpose of protecting a person from a serious crime — for example, a victim of abuse. You will always need legal advice on this point, but should not automatically assume you have a duty to report admitted criminal activities to the police. Police can see your files against your wishes only by getting an order from a circuit judge. The Circular LAC(88)17 provides:

28.   Disclosure to police. The disclosure of personal information may exceptionally be justified if it can help to prevent, detect or prosecute a serious crime. . . . Before such a disclosure is made at least the following conditions must be satisfied:

- the crime must be sufficiently serious for the public interest to prevail. A record should be kept of when information is disclosed for this purpose;
- it must be established that, without the disclosure, the task of preventing or detecting the crime would be seriously prejudiced or delayed;
- satisfactory undertakings must be obtained that the personal information disclosed will not be used for any other purpose and will be destroyed if the person is not prosecuted, or is discharged or acquitted;
- request from a police officer of suitably senior rank e.g., superintendent or above.

29.   It is impossible to be precise about what constitutes a 'serious crime'. This is something for individual authorities in consultation with their legal advisers. The Police and Criminal Evidence Act 1984 provides a guide to what may be regarded as sufficiently serious to justify disclosure in the public interest, but it should not be treated as either conclusive or exhaustive. Section 116 contains definitions of what it calls 'serious arrestable crime', i.e., one which has caused or may cause:

- serious harm to the security of the state or to public order;
- serious interference with the administration of justice or with the investigation of an offence;
- death
- serious injury
- substantial financial gain or financial loss.

30.   In addition, evidence may come to the attention of staff which may justify disclosure on their own initiative to the police so as to protect another individual. The most common example of this is in cases of child abuse.

Confidentiality and the Police: the Crime and Disorder Act 1998   The Crime and Disorder Act 1998 has an important impact on the principle of confidentiality. The Act blurs the distinction between criminal activity and welfare provision that the Children Act established.

We discuss the effect of the 1998 Act at various points in the rest of the book, particularly in Chapter 12. In that chapter we look at the sex offenders order. That order is applied for by the police where they believe that a person is a danger to children or elderly people. In assessing whether or not to apply for such an order the police may seek information from a local authority. According to the principles of confidentiality we have studied so far, it may not be possible for the local authority to release the information that it has. However, s. 115 of the Crime and Disorder Act 1998 gets around this difficulty as follows:

115.—(1)   Any person who, apart from this subsection, would not have power to disclose information—
    (a)   to a relevant authority; or
    (b)   to a person acting on behalf of such an authority,
shall have power to do so in any case where the disclosure is necessary or expedient for the purposes of any provision of this Act.

The relevant authorities are the police, other local authorities, probation and health authorities.

It needs to be understood that this section does not impose a duty to disclose. It merely gives a power to disclose. Therefore, before such disclosure occurs the local authority would need to consider whether the disclosure should take place in the light of the principles discussed above.

Confidentiality and child protection conferences and reviews   For full discussion of the workings of these conferences and reviews see Chapter 5. In that chapter we look at the particular questions of confidentiality relating to conference minutes. At this point in the book we are looking only at the wider implications of confidentiality in the child protection system.

We saw above the difficulties of promising confidentiality when being told of abuse. If you are told of abuse you will be under a statutory duty to safeguard and promote the welfare of the child or young person concerned. This may mean that you have to apply for a court order. What if you also feel that the alleged abuser ought to be prosecuted? Clearly the process of prosecution may be one way of safeguarding and promoting the child or young person's welfare: it would cause the abuse to stop.

In that situation can you tell the police? There are a number of issues involved. If care proceedings have begun, the court is involved. This means that the court rules apply. Rule 23 of the court rules made under the Children Act states that any documents used in the case are court documents. As we have already pointed out, to show them to any person who is not party to the court proceedings requires the permission of the court.

In *Re G (Social Worker: Disclosure)* [1996] 1 FLR 276, one child of the parents had previously been made subject to a care order and was living with the child's grandparents. The parents had been charged with criminal offences relating to injuries caused to the first child. The case had not proceeded to a full hearing for lack of evidence. Another child was born, and because of the concerns relating to the first child it was made subject to an interim care order. During these proceedings the local authority, supported by the police, sought a ruling that they were entitled to disclose to the police any information obtained from the parents about the injuries to the first child. The parents and the guardian *ad litem* argued that the local authority were only able to give any information with leave of the court in accordance with rule 23.

The Court of Appeal drew a distinction between actual documents that have been filed with the court and those which have not yet been filed, even though they may at some stage be filed. The former clearly are court documents and do need the permission of the court to disclose them or their contents. Information that was recorded as part of the investigation and had not been filed did not form court documents. Therefore leave of the court was not required. To require social workers to seek leave would be to drive a coach and horses through interdisciplinary arrangements for investigation into child abuse, and might even put the child's welfare at risk. The court did draw a distinction between the duty of the local authority social worker and that of the guardian *ad litem*. As the guardian was appointed by the court, it would appear that if the guardian wanted to disclose any information to anyone who was a party, leave would have to be obtained.

Developments since the Children Act came into force have shown that the courts are more often requiring disclosure of such information in the interests of the child concerned. The view of the courts is that proceedings under the Children Act are to be seen as inquisitorial, with the court taking the initiative, rather than adversarial, with the parties revealing what they see fit. In practice this attitude will present real difficulties for the social worker in dealing with clients' families. This particularly applies in cases where there is the possibility of the parents of the child becoming subject to criminal proceedings.

Current Developments on Confidentiality
The current leading case on this is the decision of the House of Lords in *Re L (Police Investigation: Privilege)* [1996] 2 WLR 395, [1996] 1 FLR 731, which has greatly extended the willingness of the courts to disclose confidential information collected under the child protection procedures.

The parents were heroin addicts. They had two children. One was admitted to hospital having consumed (according to the mother, accidentally) a quantity of methadone. The children were subsequently made the subjects of interim care orders. In the course of those proceedings, the parents sought leave from the court to disclose the court papers to a consultant chemical pathologist. This was to obtain a report which they hoped would be favourable to them. The court gave them leave and also directed that the report be filed in the court and made available to all the other parties.

The pathologist reported to the mother's solicitor that the mother's version of events was not at all probable. During a child protection conference the police became aware of the contents of this report. They felt they ought to see the report, so as to consider whether or not to bring criminal proceedings against the parents. The police applied on notice to be joined as a party to the care proceedings in order to seek disclosure of the pathologist's report for the criminal investigation. The guardian supported the police authority's application. The House of the Lords held that the report should be disclosed.

In other proceedings the parents might have been able to claim privilege for documents obtained by their solicitor. This is known as litigation privilege. For example, you are injured in a car accident; your solicitor gets a medical report during proceedings against the other driver. If that report said that your injuries were not as bad as you claimed, your solicitor could not be forced to show that report to the other side or to the court.

The House of Lords said that this litigation privilege did not apply to proceedings under the Children Act as these were non-adversarial. So any party has to think carefully about any information they seek to obtain as it will have to be disclosed.

While the decision in *Re L* was the result of public law proceedings, the decision in *Vernon* v *Bosley (No. 2)* [1997] 1 All ER 614 means that such disclosure will also be made in any private law proceedings.

The continuing trend towards disclosure in what the court views as the interests of the child is shown in *Re EC (A Minor) (Care proceedings: Disclosure)* [1996] 2 FLR 725. Here a four-month-old baby died from head injuries. The local authority started care proceedings relating to the other child in the family. The police interviewed all the people who may have been responsible for the injuries to the baby. However, the father, during the hearing of the care proceedings, admitted throwing his infant daughter against a settee, resulting in injuries which caused her death. At the end of the case the judge allowed disclosure to the police of that information and of the medical evidence.

The police also wanted to see the transcript of the evidence so as to enable them to decide how to investigate the possible prosecution of the father. (The statement by the father in his evidence during the proceedings, that he had injured the baby, could not be used against him in any criminal proceedings because of the provisions of s. 98 of the Children Act: see Chapter 8.) The Court of Appeal allowed the transcripts of the evidence to be disclosed to the police. The justification for this was that if the father was guilty of the unlawful killing of the baby, then the child's best interests (that is the child who was the subject of the care proceedings) and the best interests of other children were served by his being prosecuted and convicted and punished. No benefit would accrue to the child and other children as a result of the evidence not being disclosed, and she would be caused no harm by disclosure.

The court felt that if the admission was true, this was a grave crime involving the killing of a young child. In those circumstances, the public interest in the administration of justice — by proper investigation and the prosecution of a crime of such gravity — was a weighty factor indeed favouring disclosure.

A further extension of the principle of allowing the wider public interest to outweigh confidentiality can be seen in *A County Council* v *W (Disclosure)* [1997] 1 FLR 574. Here the General Medical Council were allowed access to documents from care proceedings. The father involved in the care proceedings was a doctor, and both the police and the local authority felt that the General Medical Council ought to be notified of the fact of the care proceedings. This was with a view to bringing disciplinary proceedings against the father. Disclosure was allowed on the basis that the disciplinary proceedings would possibly protect other children.

The implication of these cases is that during a child protection investigation you must make it clear to all those involved that if they give you any information that may indicate that they have committed criminal offences, you may be compelled to reveal that information to the police. Certainly you can give no guarantee that information may not be given to the police or other authorities at some stage.

It remains to be seen what further developments may occur in this area. For the practising social worker the advice must remain that no assurance of complete confidentiality should ever be given.

Sex Offenders' Register

A national sex offenders' register compiled under the Sex Offenders Act 1996 was launched on 1 September 1997. Under the provisions, anyone jailed for more than 30 months for a sex offence will be on the register for life; jailed for six to 30 months, on for 10 years; jailed for less than six months, for seven years; for a non-custodial sentence, for five years. Offences which are covered by the new law include rape, intercourse with a girl under 13 and indecent assault.

The register affects only those currently jailed or convicted in future. It does not apply to previous offences.

Protection of Children Act 1999

The purpose of the Protection of Children Act 1999 is to create an efficient system for identifying those persons considered to be unsuitable to work with children. It creates several new duties for both the Department of Education and Employment and child care organisations. The Department of Health must keep a list of persons who are considered unsuitable to work with children. This is in addition to the existing powers of the Department of Education and Employment to maintain a list of people who are unsuitable to be employed. The list is compiled from information supplied by child care or other organisations. Child care organisations are required to report to the

Department of Health any person they consider has harmed a child or placed a child at risk of harm. Other organisations can report a person in a similar situation. Before employing anybody who has dealings with children, a child care organisation must refer to the list. If the person is included on the list, the child care organisation must not employ that person. Where it is proposed to place a person's name on the list, that person may register objections against it. Ultimately he or she will be able to appeal to an independent tribunal against the inclusion.

WHAT IF THINGS GO WRONG?

Local authorities have responsibilities and duties towards you as their employee. The nature and volume of your work, with its associated risks of violence and abuse, place you under a great deal of stress. You have to balance individuals' needs with limited resources, and you are responsible for decisions which have significant implications for people's lives. In *Walker* v *Northumberland County Council* [1995] IRLR 35, where a social worker suffered a nervous breakdown as a result of stress, the court made it clear that all employers have a duty of care and a duty in contract to ensure that the employee is kept safe from psychiatric as well as physical harm. Local authorities who breach this duty may be liable to pay substantial compensation to social workers. In September 2001 headline news was made by a former social worker who received £140,000 damages in settlement of her claim against Worcestershire County Council for a stress-related illness developed through work. In *Gogey* v *Hertfordshire CC* [2001] 1 FLR 280, CA, a worker in a care home was suspended when concerns were raised about allegations of abuse made by a vulnerable child. The facts on which those concerns were raised were not clear. The Court found that the local authority could suspend the worker only if it was 'reasonable and proper' to do so. So the law should protect you from excessive work pressure and being treated in an arbitrary manner.

Many social workers are concerned that they may be personally liable if they make mistakes. There is no doubt that if things go wrong you will have to explain your decisions. If you have taken reasonable care and acted within an acceptable level of professional competence then you will be able to do this. If you do make a professional misjudgment there may be several consequences. First, the case may become the subject of an inquiry and you may be blamed in the report. Many feel that such an emphasis on individual social workers is unfair. Secondly, you are subject to the risk that you will be disciplined, and even dismissed, as a result of your mistake. The incompetent social worker will always take this risk. Lastly, the person who suffers may be able to sue for compensation for the effects of your mistake. He or she is far more likely to sue the local authority than you, and even if you are sued you will be indemnified by the local authority. It is worth noting that the courts are increasingly holding local authorities to account for the mistakes of their employees. Traditionally, local authorities have been protected by the courts from such action for policy reasons — local authorities should be able to carry out the difficult task of child protection without the risk of being sued. For these reasons the House of Lords, in *X (Minors)* v *Bedfordshire County Council* [1995] 3 All ER 353, dismissed claims by children trying to sue for failures by local authorities. Recently, however, there has been a shift away from this legal immunity. Local authorities can be sued for negligence, and there has been a range of cases demonstrating this. Among these are *S* v *Gloucestershire County Council* [2000] 1 FLR 825, where the child was sexually abused by foster parents; *W and Others* v *Essex County Council* [2000] 2 All ER 237, where the foster parents had not been told by the social worker that the foster child had come into care for abusing his sister; and *Barret* v *Enfield London Borough Council* [1999] 3 All ER 193, where a social worker was careless in implementing decisions made about a child in care.

The House of Lords has recently considered the extent of the duty of care of local authorities and the professionals it employs to carry out its statutory responsibilities, in *Phelps* v *London Borough of Hillingdon* [2000] 4 All ER 504. Their Lordships make it clear that local authorities are vicariously liable for professional misjudgments; and where a duty of care arises between a professional and a particular child, the professional can be sued if there is a breach of that duty. The judgment of the European Court of Human Rights in *Z and others* v *The United Kingdom* [2001] 2 FLR 612 (the name by which the *X* v *Bedfordshire County Council* case was taken to Europe) decided that the traditional approach was inconsistent with the Convention. The Court awarded the children substantial damages against the local authority for years of emotional and physical abuse by the birth parents which resulted in long-term psychiatric damage. The authority's failure to remove the children from the home over a period of four and a half years meant that the authority had breached Article 3 of the Convention — 'No one shall be subjected to torture or to inhuman or degrading treatment or punishment' — and the failure of English law to allow the children to sue was a breach of Article 13 — 'Everyone whose rights and freedoms as set forth in this Convention are violated shall have an effective remedy before a national authority notwith-standing that the violation has been committed by persons acting in an official capacity'.

CASE REFERENCES

When we want to know what the law is, we first read the statute. As we explained above, though, this is not always the whole solution. Often it is necessary for the courts to interpret what the words of the statute mean. If there is no statute we fall back on the common law. For both of these approaches by the courts we need to look at the law reports. As a good social worker you should spend some time reading law reports, even if only the summaries that accompany decisions. To help you find the full reports we set out the information below.

How to Find a Law Report in the Library

(a) Find the meaning of the abbreviation for the law report.

(b)   Find the series of law reports on the library shelves.
(c)   Find the year, and the volume number within that year.
(d)   Find the page number on which the case begins.

[1999]	3	All ER	486
year	volume number	abbreviation	page number

The Law Reports
Frequently used series of general law reports are:

The All England Law Reports (abbreviated to All ER)
The Law Reports, currently issued in four series:
   Appeal Cases (AC)
   Chancery Division (Ch)
   Queen's Bench (QB)
   Family Division (Fam)
The Weekly Law Reports (WLR)
Family Law Reports (FLR)

Summaries of recent cases can be found in *The Times* and the *Financial Times*, and in professional journals such as the *Solicitors Journal,* the *New Law Journal, Family Law* and the *Law Society's Gazette.*
Note that some citations use round brackets instead of square brackets around the date of the report. Round brackets indicate that it is the volume number, and not the date of the report, which is essential if you are to locate it on the shelves. The use of round and square brackets can be summarised as:

[ ]   Date is essential. The volumes are arranged on the shelves by year, and the volume number is used only to distinguish between different volumes published in the same year, e.g., [1999] 1 FLR 40.
( )   Date is not essential, but volume number is essential, i.e., the arrangement on the shelves is by volume number, not by date, e.g., (1980) 70 Cr App R 193.

More and more cases are now being published on the World Wide Web. A new citation system has been introduced for all Court of Appeal and High Court (Administrative Division) judgments decided since 11 January 2001, to facilitate this. The new citation should appear in front of the familiar citations set out above. The new citation is media neutral, as page numbers are irrelevant on the Web.
The three new forms of citation are as follows:

Court of Appeal (Civil Division)	[2001] EWCA Civ 1, 2, 3 etc.
Court of Appeal (Criminal Division)	[2001] EWCA Crim 1, 2, 3 etc.
Administrative Court	[2001] EWHC Admin 1, 2, 3 etc.

Eventually, all High Court judgments will be cited in this way, which fits in with international practice and makes it easier to find cases electronically. Here is an example: *Re O (Supervision Order)* [2001] 1 FLR 923 is a Court of Appeal decision published in the Family Law Reports. It should now be cited as : *Re O (Supervision Order)* [2001] EWCA Civ 16; [2001] 1 FLR 923. The '16' means that it was the sixteenth case heard in the Court of Appeal Civil Division in 2001. 'EW' stands for England and Wales.

THREE

How the Courts Work

As a practising social worker you are working within the legal framework. To work successfully within that framework you will need to know the rules that govern it. When a dispute cannot be resolved by the people involved, the solution of our legal system is usually for the dispute to be decided by a judicial hearing. Sometimes there is a need to attend a judicial hearing even if there is total agreement between the persons involved; for example, if a couple agree to get divorced, then no matter how much they settle things by agreement they will never get a decree of divorce without a judicial hearing. At some time, every social worker is going to have to attend some form of judicial hearing.

We use the term 'judicial hearing' since it is somewhat wider than just 'court'. For example, apart from courts there are Mental Health Review Tribunals, Registered Home Tribunals and others which a social worker may be required to attend. From now on, where we use the term 'court', it is intended to include these other forms of judicial hearings. This chapter considers only the particular structure of courts in England and Wales. (Those in Scotland and Northern Ireland have a different legal system.) So what we mean by the term 'court' in this particular chapter is 'courts and other judicial hearings in England and Wales'.

(You will, by now, be coming to understand the complicated way that we lawyers approach language!)

GENERAL STRUCTURE

Criminal and Civil Courts

There are two main divisions of the courts:

(a) criminal; and
(b) civil.

Surprisingly the criminal courts deal with criminal cases and the civil courts with civil matters! (Which to all intents and purposes you can regard as 'everything else'.) Most people think that they have a reasonable idea of what a crime is, but in practice they find out that it is not as clear as they thought. The main distinction that could be made is that the outcome, known to lawyers as the 'remedy', that each gives is different. A criminal court will impose a punishment (which does not just include a term of imprisonment), whereas a civil court will normally make a judgment of a financial kind, although it can make an order that someone should do or not do a particular act, or it can define a person's rights.

To draw the clear and simple division of cases into civil and criminal is often an over-simplification. Frequently the same facts can give rise to both a criminal and a civil 'offence'. We take a common case — the 'simple' road accident. If a person driving hits another car then the person may have committed a criminal offence and also be liable to be sued in civil law for damages. The civil case (known as the 'claim') for damages would be totally separate, unconnected with the careless driving charge. A person may be successfully sued for damages arising out of a road accident, without there being any proceedings for driving offences, or vice versa.

Let us look at another example from a field in which you may become involved. You will deal with old people; private homes for old people need to be registered with the local authority under the Registered Homes Act 1984. One part of the Act requires the owner of the home to keep accurate records of drugs kept in the home. Failure to keep such records can give rise to the possibility of a criminal prosecution in the magistrates' court or to civil proceedings in the magistrates' court to have the home closed as an emergency measure; or to civil proceedings before the Registered Homes Tribunal to have the home closed as a non-emergency measure.

We now turn, in more detail, to the actual court structure. The diagram on p. 51 gives an overall picture.

All courts are arranged in a hierarchical structure. This means that a lower court must follow decisions of any court higher than itself in the judicial 'ladder' and that there is also a system of appeals against the decision of one court from one level to another. Cases begun in the lower courts can, normally, work their way up to the highest court, by way of appeal. If you spend any point actually in court, then at some point you are going to hear some disgruntled person saying 'I'll take it to the highest court in the land . . . I'll take it to the House of Lords'. We will return to the question of appeals at a later stage.

Modernising the Court System

We need to sound a note of caution here. The court system — both civil and criminal — is undergoing careful scrutiny, with the aim of making it more effective and more efficient. Lord Woolf carried out a major review of civil justice in his enquiry *Access to Civil Justice* in 1994. New Civil Procedure Rules came into force in April 1999, the impact of which is still being assessed. The latest Consultation Paper, 'Modernising the Civil Courts', has just been published with a view to rationalising the county court system and maximising the use of information technology. Lord Justice Auld's report on criminal justice, which will have a major impact on magistrates' courts and jury trials, was published in October 2001.

THE CRIMINAL COURTS

This section looks at the two main criminal courts, namely:

(a)   the magistrates' court; and
(b)   the Crown Court.

(The youth court is dealt with in Chapter 12.)

The Queen's speech on 20 June 2001 included proposals to reform sentencing law; reform of the double jeopardy rule to allow retrial of a defendant previously acquitted of murder where there is compelling new evidence; new measures to govern the registration of sex offenders; and a new complaints scheme. In addition the government will introduce legislation to reform the structure of the criminal courts in the light of the Auld report's 300 plus recommendations. So what you read here is all about to change in the very near future.

The social worker, in their official capacity, will appear in these courts only when presenting pre-sentence reports to assist the court in deciding what type of punishment should be passed (unless the social worker is called as a witness to an alleged crime arising from their work, for example if they have been assaulted by a client or the client's carer, or are able to give evidence in prosecution for abuse of a child).

Criminal Proceedings in the Magistrates' Court

All criminal cases begin in the magistrates' court. The vast majority (95 per cent) start there and stay there. They stay there because either there are no powers for the cases to be transferred anywhere else or the person involved (the defendant) agrees to the case being dealt with by the magistrates. You will appreciate because of the volume of cases dealt with by magistrates that they are the backbone of the criminal system. Specially selected magistrates deal with juvenile crime in the youth courts.

For all this, magistrates are not professionals; they rejoice in the fact that they are amateur, albeit with some training. Their function is to decide what are the facts of the cases on the evidence that is put before them. (You should see Chapter 8 for fuller details on evidence.) Magistrates also apply the relevant law in the case. They are not expected to know all the law. The person on whom this burden falls is the only professional lawyer employed by the magistrates' court, namely the court clerk. (Regrettably a majority of courts are actually clerked by unqualified clerks under the overall supervision of a qualified court clerk.) The clerk will advise the magistrates (collectively known as the 'bench') on points of law that arise during the course of any trial and again when the magistrates consider the appropriate form of sentence or penalty. We say 'any trial', since the vast majority of criminal

Diagram 3.1

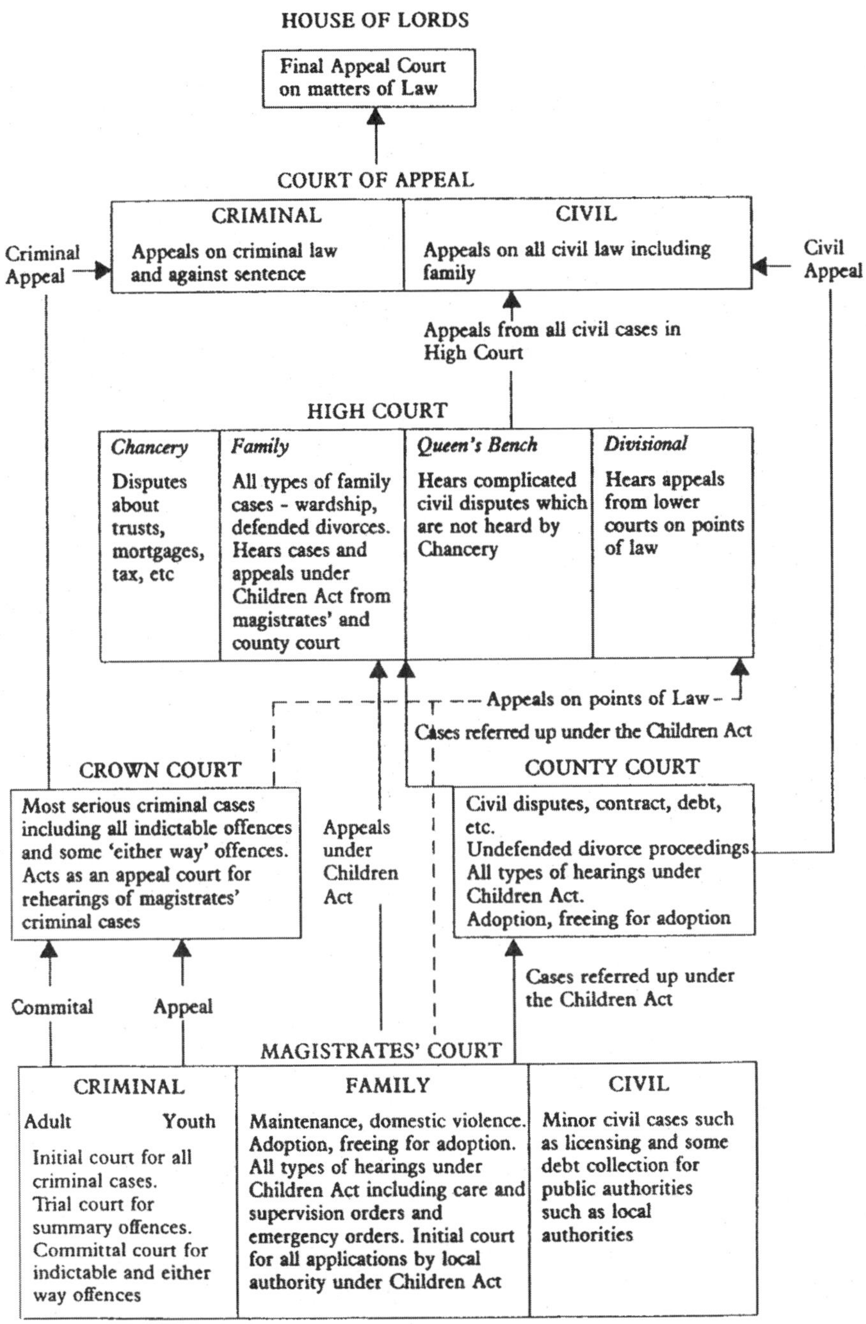

HOUSE OF LORDS

Final Appeal Court
on matters of Law

COURT OF APPEAL

CRIMINAL	CIVIL
Appeals on criminal law and against sentence	Appeals on all civil law including family

Criminal Appeal →

Civil Appeal ←

Appeals from all civil cases in
High Court

HIGH COURT

Chancery	*Family*	*Queen's Bench*	*Divisional*
Disputes about trusts, mortgages, tax, etc	All types of family cases - wardship, defended divorces. Hears cases and appeals under Children Act from magistrates' and county court	Hears complicated civil disputes which are not heard by Chancery	Hears appeals from lower courts on points of law

- - - - Appeals on points of Law - - -
Cases referred up under the Children Act

CROWN COURT   COUNTY COURT

	Appeals under Children Act	
Most serious criminal cases including all indictable offences and some 'either way' offences. Acts as an appeal court for rehearings of magistrates' criminal cases		Civil disputes, contract, debt, etc. Undefended divorce proceedings. All types of hearings under Children Act. Adoption, freeing for adoption

Commital   Appeal

Cases referred up under
the Children Act

MAGISTRATES' COURT

CRIMINAL	FAMILY	CIVIL
Adult Youth Initial court for all criminal cases. Trial court for summary offences. Committal court for indictable and either way offences	Maintenance, domestic violence. Adoption, freeing for adoption. All types of hearings under Children Act including care and supervision orders and emergency orders. Initial court for all applications by local authority under Children Act	Minor civil cases such as licensing and some debt collection for public authorities such as local authorities

cases in the magistrates' court — and, indeed, in the Crown Court — proceed on a guilty plea.

All criminal cases start in the magistrates' court. There are three types:

(a)   summary offences;
(b)   indictable offences; and
(c)   either way offences.

Summary offences   These are the most common offence. Examples would be: common assault, less serious criminal damage, taking a motor vehicle without consent (this offence is known by the acronym 'TWOC'). They can normally be dealt with only in the magistrates' court. Therefore, the court has the limited powers of sentence described below.

As you would expect, summary offences constitute the vast majority of criminal offences dealt with in our courts. They are generally regarded as commonplace and mundane. The social worker should always bear in mind that for the particular individual involved in 'their' case, this is the total of their experience of the court system. Whether it be the first and only time that person goes to court, or whether it is the latest in a long line of appearances, it is of great importance to them. It is too easy for all of us involved in the court system to become blasé about the process.

Indictable only offences   These are cases that are 'just passing through' the magistrates' court. They are the serious offences, such as murder, rape and arson that, for an adult (over 18), can be dealt with only by the Crown Court. A person accused of murder cannot decide to go to the local magistrates' court and get the case dealt with there.

Why then do the cases not just go straight to the Crown Court? The reasons for this are historical and practical. The practical reason is that where, for instance, a person is accused of murder, it requires a great deal of time for both the prosecution and the defence lawyers to prepare their cases before the trial can take place in the Crown Court. Meantime, the question of what is going to happen to the accused person has to be dealt with. The magistrates will decide whether the accused person should be remanded into custody or be granted bail (which would be rare in cases such as murder).

The magistrates can also be asked by the defence to act as a filter, throwing out cases that have no prospect of conviction in the Crown Court. Before a person accused of an offence can be sent from the magistrates' court to the Crown Court, the magistrates must, if called on to do so, be satisfied by evidence produced by the prosecution that there is a 'case to answer'. The procedure on this has recently changed. A defendant could previously insist on hearing, and challenging, the prosecution witnesses before the magistrates decided whether there was a case to answer at Crown Court. Under the Criminal Procedure and Investigations Act 1996, the magistrates can only consider written prosecution evidence in deciding whether to send the case for trial, and will usually do so without having a hearing at all. If the defence wish to argue that there is no case to be committed to Crown Court, they will usually be limited to a written submission.

Usually, an indictable only offence is dealt with in the youth court if the accused is under 18 — see Chapter 12.

Either way offences These are hybrid offences which, as the name implies, can be dealt with either by the magistrates' court or by the Crown Court before a judge and jury. An example of such an offence is theft. What may appear to be the theft of a small amount may be regarded by many as trivial, but for the defendant the consequences of being convicted of such an offence may be extremely serious. Therefore Parliament has decided, for the present, that the person accused of such an offence can insist on the case being tried before a judge and jury in the Crown Court. (The Government is proposing to abolish a defendant's ability to elect for jury trial in either way offences instead of offering the option of a judge and two lay magistrates.).

However, if the magistrates consider the case to be not too serious, they can offer the defendant a 'summary' trial. This has the advantage of being dealt with more quickly and sometimes, if the person pleads guilty, on the spot.

If the magistrates or the defendant insist on Crown Court trial, the defence can require the magistrates consider the prosecution evidence to see if there is a case to answer, before committing the case for trial at Crown Court. Magistrates alone would then have the power to decide where the case is tried. A right to appeal to the Crown Court would be made available to the defendant.

The magistrates' court is divided into different parts. There is the division into the criminal and civil, but there is also the distinction in criminal proceedings between the adult and youth courts, which deal with juveniles under the age of 18. The criminal functions of the magistrates' court are exercised by both the adult and the youth court benches. For fuller details see Chapter 12. The magistrates also have important family (civil) functions, which we will consider after looking at the Crown Court.

Magistrates' Courts' Powers of Sentence
Magistrates have restricted powers in relation to the sentences that they can impose. We tend to associate the word 'sentence' with the idea of 'locking someone up'. Many of the offences dealt with by the magistrates' court carry no power of imprisonment, and the heaviest penalty then can only be a fine or probation. Where the magistrates have the power to imprison a person the maximum length of the sentence will be governed by the statute. Even where an offence may carry a maximum penalty of several years' imprisonment if it were dealt with by the Crown Court, the magistrates are limited in the length of sentence they can impose. For any one offence committed by an adult they can impose a maximum of only six months' imprisonment, assuming the offence merits such a sentence. In addition, if a person has committed more than one offence, each of which is an either way offence and each of which could have a six-month sentence imposed for it, then the total maximum sentence the magistrates could impose would be 12 months' imprisonment

(i.e., two six-month sentences to run consecutively). If the magistrates think that their powers, in relation to either way offences only, are inadequate, then after conviction they could commit the person to the Crown Court for sentence. (The youth court does not have this power, although its maximum sentencing powers can be two years. If it thinks an offence particularly serious, i.e., homicide or one that can carry a 14-year prison sentence for an adult, such as causing death by dangerous driving, or an indecent assault on a woman, the youth court may send the case to the Crown Court for trial and sentencing — see Chapter 12.)

Crown Court
The Crown Court is the archetypal court, in that it has the judge in gown and wig, being addressed by lawyers, normally in gowns and wigs, and the jury sitting in judgment on the defendant. Whereas the magistrates, in their court, are the deciders of both fact and law (after being advised on the law by their clerk), in the Crown Court there is a separation of these functions. The judge, being a professional lawyer (usually a barrister, but occasionally a solicitor), is the authority on the law. The jury, composed of randomly selected lay people, is the body which decides what the facts are, based on the evidence which they hear.

If you go to watch proceedings in a Crown Court, and every social worker should ensure that they attend the courts with which they are going to deal before they actually have to appear there, you will observe that sitting in front of the judge there is a court clerk. The role of the clerk in the actual trial is much less active than that of the clerk in the magistrates' court, although the judge may seek advice on complicated points of law, which can amount to asking the clerk to find a particular place in a law book!

When sentencing an adult, the powers of sentence of the Crown Court are limited only by the lengths of sentence that are set out either in the statute governing the crime or by common law. The Court's powers on sentencing a person under 18 are more limited — see Chapter 12. The Crown Court can impose a maximum penalty of life imprisonment and almost unlimited financial penalties for some offences.

The Crown Court hears some criminal appeals from the magistrates' court.

The Auld Review and Other Proposals
The Government appears to be determined to overhaul the criminal justice system. It set up the Auld review (named after Lord Justice Auld who is conducting it), with broad terms of reference. The report (available at www.criminal-courts-review.org.uk) was published on 8 October 2001 and contains more than 300 recommendations which will transform the administration of criminal justice.

The Government has also indicated that it wishes to limit the right to jury trial. Bills to this effect have twice been defeated in the House of Lords, but the Government has made it clear that it intends to push through changes. The Auld review is reportedly considering an intermediate tier of jurisdiction which would deal with some offences by way of a District Judge sitting with two lay magistrates, leaving only the most serious offences to be tried by jury.

THE CIVIL COURTS

This section will look at the following courts:

(a)   magistrates' court;
(b)   county court;
(c)   High Court; and
(d)   tribunals.

Civil functions cover such areas as:

(a)   matrimonial cases;
(b)   contact with children cases;
(c)   child care cases;
(d)   contract cases;
(e)   personal injuries cases;
(f)   licensing cases;
(g)   employment cases; and
(h)   social security cases.

The social worker will have to appear in these courts in the following circumstances:

(a)   *In family matters*
   (i)   As an applicant and/or witness in applications for an order under the Children Act. (Details of the relevant law are dealt with in Chapters 6 and 7.)
   (ii)   As a 'welfare officer' presenting a report to the court to assist it in deciding what, if any, type of order should be made. (Reports are dealt with in Chapter 9.)
   (N.B. These two functions may be carried out by the same person in the same hearing, though at different times.)
(b)   *In civil matters other than family matters*
   (i)   In the magistrates' court: As an applicant or witness in applications for some statutory order connected with their employment, for example an application under the Registered Homes Act or National Assistance Act (see Chapter 13).
   (ii)   In other civil courts: In applications for orders before tribunals such as the Mental Health Review Tribunal; as a witness on behalf of clients (possibly an advocate) before other tribunals such as a Social Security Appeal Tribunal.

We shall look in detail at a hearing of an application by a local authority for a statutory order under the Children Act in the magistrates' court. This is to enable you to get an overall picture of the format of a hearing of a case which is probably the one hearing that the social worker will most frequently attend. In most courts there is a similar approach to hearings. Details of the applicable law should be obtained from Chapter 7.

It is worth making clear, however, that much of the local authority social worker's time will not be spent with dealing with applications for care orders, since work with children does not inevitably end in an application to the court. It is the very philosophy of the Children Act 1989 to try to avoid the need for formal court orders.

The Hearing in the Family Proceedings Court

It will be before a family panel of magistrates that an application for a child protection order, a care order or a supervision order will be made. Most applications have to be made either by a local authority or the NSPCC.

For the purposes of the social worker the important civil function of the magistrates' court is exercised in family cases (the family function) by the family panel (drawn from both the adult and youth court bench of the magistrates' court).

Rules of court   The rules of court govern the procedure of the court. Those issued under the Children Act 1989 will be the ones the social worker will come across most often. Throughout this book, when we refer simply to the 'rules', we mean the rules of court under that Act. There are two sets of rules: one for the magistrates' court and one for the county court and High Court. In most cases they have identical numbering, except that the county court/ High Court rules are prefixed with '4'. For example, rule 18 of the magistrates' court rules deals with the admission of expert evidence: the admission of expert evidence in the county court/High Court is dealt with under rule 4.18. In this book we have omitted the '4', and treat the rules as identical. Where there is a difference in numbering we state it.

Rule 25 sets out the procedure in a case where the local authority applies for an order. (More information on evidence and courtroom procedure can be found in Chapter 8.)

(a)   The applicant (i.e., local authority or NSPCC) will make an opening statement, through their lawyer, outlining the basis of the case.

(b)   The applicant will call witnesses (who will certainly include social workers) to support their case. It is necessary to submit a written statement of evidence in the magistrates' court before the hearing. This may either shorten or lengthen the hearings. This is because a written statement can allow agreed evidence to be quickly introduced but also allows more detailed evidence to be produced which gives the 'other side' plenty of scope for cross-examination. Following *Practice Direction* [1995] 1 All ER 586, in the county court and High Court the written statement is the evidence. The trend in the Family Proceedings Court is to place greater reliance on the written statement. Opening evidence will tend to be confined to confirming the written statement. Witnesses are immediately cross-examined as in (c).

(c)   The other parties (or more usually their lawyers) to the proceedings (which includes the child through their guardian *ad litem*, the parents and grandparents) can cross-examine the applicant's witnesses (see Chapter 4: The Law and Children).

(d) The applicant can re-examine their witnesses.

(e) The other parties may make an opening statement.

(f) The other parties may call witnesses to rebut the applicant's case.

(g) The applicant may cross-examine the other parties' witnesses.

(h) The applicant, through their lawyer, can make a closing statement.

(i) The other parties to the proceedings, normally through their lawyer, can make a closing statement.

(j) The magistrates decide whether the grounds for the order are satisfied.

(k) If there are grounds for making an order, then the applicant and the other parties, in that order, make representations as to the kind of order that should be made. These representations can be supported by evidence given under oath.

(l) The children's guardian if appointed (see Chapter 4, p. 90), will present their report and can give evidence if required. (See also Chapter 8 on evidence and Chapter 9 on reports.)

(m) The magistrates decide what order they are going to make. The court may decide not to make any order at all (s. 1(5)). (All references in this part are to the Children Act 1989.)

The making or refusing of the order ends the proceedings, unless there is an appeal.

In other family proceedings, such as matrimonial proceedings, which are not begun by the local authority or the NSPCC, the order of proceedings will be recognisably similar. That is to say, the person making the application to the court will open the proceedings with the other parties giving evidence in turn. If the social worker is involved at all it will normally only be at the report stage.

Interim Hearings

The proceedings that have been described above are called full hearings since, subject to any appeal, once the order is made the case is closed. (But social workers will know that getting a court order does not mean that they can close their case files!)

Often when a case comes before a court, for a variety of reasons, the court cannot make a final order. There will therefore be a need to adjourn the hearing to another date and, in the meantime, sometimes to make an interim order. This will state what the parties should do during the time the case is adjourned. For instance, if the local authority were making an application for a care order, and an adjournment was needed to enable a report to be obtained from a child psychiatrist, then it would need to be decided where the child is to stay in the meantime. Such directions will be contained in an interim order.

(The more cynical of social workers sometimes hint that it is the very function of lawyers to ensure that a final order is never made and that life consists solely of interim orders!)

Interim orders can be made in any court proceedings. What the social worker has to appreciate is that they are very common and that you should not be misled by the term. It is easy to fall into the belief that because the applicant is only asking for an interim order it will automatically be a short hearing. Evidence or representations are required, unless the interim arrangements are agreed.

Direction Hearings

An important part of preparing a case for hearing is the Direction Hearing. This is designed to enable the court and the lawyers to decide what procedural matters need to be dealt with. It is very important in the process of managing the case, to ensure that the final hearing takes place as quickly as possible, is as short as possible and deals with those points that are actually in dispute. See p. 222 for a full discussion.

Hearings in County Court and High Court

The majority of the social worker's dealings with the county court and the High Court will be in connection with children. We shall look mainly at such cases in this section. However, we will briefly mention the other cases that are heard by these courts to complete the picture.

The frequency of such appearances will depend on the nature of your actual placement. Such appearances will be:

(a)   the result of your authority applying for a care or supervision order;

(b)   at the request of the court, where it appears during family proceedings that it may be appropriate for a care or supervision application to be made by the local authority (Children Act 1989, s. 37); or

(c)   the most frequent, where the court requires a welfare report to assist it to decide what order should be made in family proceedings (Children Act 1989, s. 7).

Transfer of Cases

Under the Children Act there is the generic concept of family hearings. Under the public law all cases have to be started in the magistrates' court. For the more complex cases there are procedures whereby the cases can be transferred to the county court and then to the High Court. These are dealt with in the Children (Allocation of Proceedings) Order 1991. Essentially, the grounds for transfer are whether the proceedings are exceptionally grave, important or complex, or because there are already proceedings in the other court or the case can be dealt with more quickly by the other court.

Before the Act came into force, the Government indicated that it both expected and wanted the majority of cases to stay in the magistrates' court. The reasons for this seem to be largely questions of costs, since, as the magistrates are unpaid lay people, costs per hour in the magistrates' court are far less than in the higher courts with professional judges. (This argument ignores the cost, including financial costs, of bad decisions.)

When the Act first came into force there appeared to be a number of magistrates' courts which were reluctant to transfer cases up. The High Court has made a number of comments in different cases about the need to transfer cases up to the higher courts. See, for instance, *C* v *Solihull Metropolitan Borough Council* [1993] 1 FLR 290 or *Re H (A Minor)* [1993] 1 FLR 440 (the details of the cases are given later in the book). In the latter case the court said that magistrates should not hear a case expected to last in excess of two, or at the most three, days. Cases involving serious disputed sexual or other abuse, or cases where children or young people are seeking to make representations which are different from those of the guardian *ad litem*, should not be heard in the magistrates' court.

If the magistrates refuse to transfer a case to the county court, this decision can be appealed. It is a matter for your legal advisers to deal with. It is important that you try to ensure that the case is heard in the right court. (See Case Planning in Chapter 10 for more discussion of this.) Most people within the child care system still feel that the full-time professional judges in the county court or the High Court will ensure a more satisfactory hearing. That is not to criticise the magistrates but to accept that there is more expertise in the higher courts.

County Court

The county court is the court where most divorces are processed, and it follows that it is the court in which s. 8 Orders (see Chapter 16) will be made ancillary to those divorce proceedings. Under the Children Act 1989, s. 7, in the course of the divorce proceedings the court has the power to ask either the local authority or the probation service to prepare a report. For the requirements of such a welfare report see Chapter 9.

When presenting your report you will find that the hearing in the county court follows a similar outline to that described for the magistrates' court. The report will be presented at what is stage (k).

The county court family hearing takes place in 'chambers', which means that the hearing will be in private. (But rarely in the judge's private chambers from which the term derives; most chambers do not have the room to take all the people who will be involved in the hearing.)

There is, no longer, a hearing of initial oral evidence by the applicant. The county court is familiar with the idea of using written statements as the means of setting out both the competing claims of the opposing parties and the evidence that goes to support those claims. The judge, having had the opportunity to read those before the hearing date, will already be in a position to see the areas of dispute. This does not mean that the side opposing the application will not spend a great deal of time cross-examining the applicant's witnesses, and in turn the applicant may spend an even greater length of time re-examining their witnesses!

As the judges are professional lawyers, you will hear them assist the lawyers who are appearing before them, by indicating when the lawyer has to pursue a particular point and when this is not needed. You will hear such statements as: 'I am with you on that point; you have no need to pursue that point; what is your submission on this point?' This may appear confusing to the outsider but is designed both to speed the hearing and to ensure that the lawyers and the judge address the correct questions.

How individual judges approach and 'run' hearings varies with the individual. That is to say that judges are just ordinary people, with certain qualifications, who have their own ways of doing things. Some you will like and some you will not. You will soon learn which judge you prefer to be in front of and which you would prefer to avoid.

If you are not presenting a report and are involved in the full hearing merely as a witness (say in a claim for damages arising out of a road accident) the hearing will be in a similar format to that of the magistrates' court, but without the need for reports.

High Court

The historical role of the High Court in children's cases was that of wardship where the High Court steps in and takes over as the child's parent. (The child then becomes referred to as a ward.)

Prior to the passing of the Children Act, most of the local authority social worker's experience of the High Court would have been in wardship proceedings. Under s. 100, local authorities no longer have the right to apply in wardship proceedings for a statutory order (that is, they cannot get a care or supervision order this way). It was thought by many that this would mean a total end to such wardship hearings.

As stated previously, under the Children Act the High Court is expected to hear the more complex cases involving children under the Act.

In addition, it has a very important function of supervising the workings of the Act, being the court which hears appeals against the decisions of magistrates and the county courts. In this way, gradually, a uniformity of practice in these courts should be brought about.

Is wardship dead?   The practice under the Act has revealed that wardship is still being used by local authorities in particular to get the High Court to make specific orders in difficult cases. In *Re S (A Minor) (Medical Treatment)* [1993] 1 FLR 376, the authority sought an order in wardship to allow a blood transfusion to be given to a child of Jehovah's Witnesses whose parents were refusing to allow this. The court readily granted the order. The interesting aspect of the case was the lack of comment by the court as to why wardship was being used rather than any other order under the Act. (The authority could have applied for an emergency protection order, which we discuss in Chapter 6.) Such wardship applications are using known as the inherent jurisdiction of the court rather than the statutory powers of the Childrens Act. There seems to be a continuing role that will be used for wardship in such cases, and the High Court does not appear to be raising difficulties.

Additionally, people other than local authorities can, in certain limited situations, apply to the High Court, and in those circumstances the local authority may well be joined as a party in the proceedings because of immediate interest in the welfare of the child. Social workers still have to be involved in such cases.

The hearing in the High Court   The hearing in the High Court is very much a copy of the county court hearing. In principle you should expect a 'better class' of hearing in the High Court, since the judges are expected to be of the highest calibre. Practical experience will allow you to draw your own conclusions as to whether or not this is so.

The hearings are again in chambers. The courtrooms used may well be the same rooms as are used for the county court. Indeed you may find yourself appearing before a judge who also conducts hearings as a county court judge. This is because there are provisions for county court judges to be appointed as 'deputy' High Court judges, because of the continuing lack of available High Court judges to meet all the demands for hearings before them.

Procedural Changes
From April 1999 there have been a considerable number of procedural changes. These affect the county court and High Court.

Civil Hearings other than Family Hearings
All the courts discussed above exercise a civil jurisdiction other than in family matters. These cover such matters as contract disputes, licensing, claims for compensation arising from accidents, etc. Normally a social worker will not deal with these courts in the course of their work. Perhaps the main distinction between these hearings and family hearings is that 'normal' civil hearings will take place in open court and will be public. The form of the hearing will be similar to that of a family hearing, although obviously in a contract dispute there will be no place for a welfare officer!

Appeal Hearings
The courts of England and Wales are part of an appellate structure. Accordingly, there are normally provisions for a party unhappy with a decision of a lower court to appeal to a higher court.

This section looks at the question of appeals in family matters, since that is the main concern of social workers. The general principles are applicable to other cases.

A dissatisfied party may want to appeal for the following reasons (it is rare to find anybody who is satisfied with a hearing appealing!):

(a)   They think the court got the facts of the case wrong.
(b)   They think that the court got the law applying to the case wrong.
(c)   They think that the court in exercising its discretion in the case came to the wrong decision.

Most appeal hearings do not involve hearing the case all over again with the same witnesses. The appeal court will look at what reasons the lower court gave for arriving at its decision. In some courts the reasons (the judgment) are available in writing. Having heard representations from the parties and having looked at the judgment, the appeal court will give *its* judgment.

Accordingly it will be difficult to succeed in an appeal on ground (a) — it would only be in exceptional circumstances that a lower court will be held to have got the facts wrong, since that court at least has heard the evidence directly.

Most decisions are on ground (b) — that the lower court misstated or misunderstood the law. The clarification of the law is a prime function of the appeal system.

In the field of family matters it is ground (c) that presents the greatest difficulty. It will be appreciated when dealing with such family proceedings that there can rarely be only one correct decision. The question whether or not to grant a contact order or a residence order will always be a question of balancing a variety of possibly conflicting demands. In any of these types of cases there will always be a certain amount of discretion as to whether or not an order should be made. The appeal courts, generally, will not interfere in such a case provided that the exercise of that discretion was not unreasonable. Thus an appeal court may say that it would have arrived at a different decision, but if the original decision was within the area of the lower court's discretion then it will not interfere.

So although there is a system of appeals it does not mean that any decision can be overturned. Just because a decision goes against you, do not think that you will have grounds for an appeal.

If you look at the diagram of the court structure (p. 51) you will see that the two highest courts of appeal are the Court of Appeal (which has separate branches — criminal and civil) and the House of Lords. Beyond the House of Lords there may be a final appeal to the European Court of Human Rights in some cases. To give some understanding of the actual workings of the appeal system: the Court of Appeal will hear about 1,000 cases a year and the House of Lords hears about 50 cases a year. So it will be a rare occasion when you have a case going to either of these courts.

The actual practicalities of appeals are beyond the scope of this book. If you do find yourself in a situation which you think should be the subject of an appeal, you should consult immediately with your lawyer.

Tribunals

A great deal of dispute resolution within the English legal system is carried out by tribunals. They hear a large number and a great variety of cases, generally between the citizen and the state, such as in Social Security Appeal Tribunals; but they also hear citizen against citizen disputes, as in Employment Tribunals. Tribunals are created by statute and are administered by the relevant government department. Tribunals generally consist of three people, with only the chair being legally qualified. Their numbers have dramatically increased over the last 50 years. Their purpose is to provide a quicker and less formal forum than the courts and to allow cases to be adjudicated by people with an expertise in the particular jurisdiction, so for instance psychiatrists sit on Mental Health Review Tribunals and surveyors on Lands Tribunals. Tribunals tend to be of particular importance to social work clients as their lives are likely to be more dependent on decisions made by state bodies.

New tribunals are created relatively frequently, partly in response to the increasing complexity of society and also stimulated by Article 6 of the European Convention on Human Rights (the right to a fair trial). A recent example relevant to social work practice is the Protection of Children Act Tribunal, set up by s. 9 of the Protection of Children Act 1999. The 1999 Act provides for the Secretary of State for Health to maintain a list of people considered unsuitable to work with children. This is to prevent those listed from being employed in positions which allow them regular contact with children. The particular types of employment are those concerned with providing accommodation, social services, health care or supervision to children. The process starts with a referral from the child care organisation which dismissed the person because of misconduct which harmed a child or placed one at risk. The individual is automatically provisionally placed on the list. The entry on the list is made permanent if the Secretary of State is satisfied that the organisation reasonably considered the individual guilty of misconduct and that the individual is unsuitable to work with children. Individuals who are named have a right of appeal against inclusion on the list to the new tribunal.

The tribunal system is criticised on a range of issues. Tribunals are not clearly independent of the government body whose decision is being challenged. Procedures and the quality of decision-making vary enormously. Informality and simplicity of procedure is difficult to achieve in many of the complex social welfare fields in which tribunals operate, so that unrepresented parties feel themselves to be at a disadvantage, yet in the vast majority of tribunals there is no publicly funded legal help available (exceptions being the Mental Health Review Tribunal and the Immigration Appeal Tribunal) to pay for lawyers. As the Legal Action Group points out, those who are unrepresented encounter pitfalls, such as being unaware that an application is without merit, misunderstanding tribunal procedures, preparing inadequately for the hearing or putting forward irrelevant facts and arguments. The best advice you can give to a client taking a case to a tribunal is to go to their local advice centre as soon as possible for specialist assistance.

The Government set up a comprehensive review of the tribunal system in June 2000 (the Leggatt Review). The report was published in August 2001, entitled 'Tribunals for Users: One System, One Service', together with a consultation paper seeking views on its main recommendations. It addresses many concerns about the tribunal service — the need for an enhanced role for the Council on Tribunals, a greater standardisation of tribunal procedures, better judicial training and clearer separation from government departments. The proposal for a unified tribunal service is particularly welcome. The report does not support increasing funded legal representation, preferring to focus on prior advice and supplied procedures. The report can be found on the Lord Chancellor's Department website: www.lcd.gov.uk.

FOUR

The Law and Children

In the next four chapters we look at how the law relates to and affects children in particular. The following two chapters then look at how to behave in court, giving evidence and writing reports. Chapters 4 to 9 contain pieces of a complicated jigsaw. In Chapter 10, which discusses investigation and case planning, we will give you some guidance on putting the pieces into place. You may wish to read it first to get an overview of the system, a feel for the process. If you do that, do not forget to come back here for all the pieces of the jigsaw.

The stated aim of the Children Act 1989 was to clarify and codify the law relating to children. In doing this it repealed a considerable amount of existing legislation that had developed piecemeal over the years. You are lucky in that, now, you can look to one piece of legislation to provide most of the answers to the questions that you may have relating to children and the law. (You will note that, as lawyers, we do not give a totally unequivocal answer!)

The aim of this chapter is to look at the overall structure and philosophy of the Act and at some common definitions in relation to children and the law. This is to give you a basic understanding of the law in this area, before we look at the different provisions of public law (the child client in relation to the local authority and other statutory bodies) and the private law (the law relating to relationships between individuals such as divorce and separation). You should read and digest this chapter before diving into the other chapters on children, where we will be using the definitions and concepts discussed in this chapter. However, this book is not a book on the Children Act. You must have your own full copy of the Act to function adequately in this area.

In this chapter we shall look at:

(a) the overall structure of the Children Act;
(b) the philosophy behind the Children Act;
(c) some relevant concepts;
(d) local authority support for children and families: Children Act, Part III:
    (i) being 'looked after';

(ii)   'accommodation';
(iii)   the complaints procedure relating to a local authority's service for children;
(e)   principles applicable to court proceedings under the Children Act;
(f)   the role of children's guardians; and
(g)   process under the Children Act.

THE OVERALL STRUCTURE OF THE CHILDREN ACT

The Act has over 100 sections and 15 schedules. It is a very large piece of legislation. It is divided into 'Parts'. These 'Parts' group together different sections under headings to assist with understanding.

We reproduce, below, an outline of the Parts in the Children Act. Shown alongside, in parentheses, are the chapters in the book where we look at those Parts. We do not have the space to examine every Part in great depth. We concentrate on those Parts the 'field' social worker will have to be familiar with. It will help to keep in mind this overall structure as it reflects the philosophy behind the Act and assists in comprehension of the particular sections:

Part I: Introductory (Chapter 4).
Part II: Orders with respect to Children in Family Proceedings (Chapters 4 and 15).
Part III: Local Authority Support for Children and Families (Chapters 4, 5 and 11).
Part IV: Care and Supervision (Chapter 7).
Part V: Protection of Children (Chapter 6).
Part VI: Community Homes.
Part VII: Voluntary Homes and Voluntary Organisations.
Part VIII: Registered Children's Homes.
Part IX: Private Arrangements for Fostering Children.
Part X: Child Minding and Day Care for Young Children.
Part XA: Child Minding and Day Care for Children in England and Wales (inserted by the Care Standards Act 2000).
Part XI: Secretary of State's Supervisory Functions and Responsibilities.
Part XII: Miscellaneous and General.

Because we do not have enough space for everything, parts VI to XII are not specifically referred to in this book, as these Parts tend to be concerned with the regulatory function of local authorities and are therefore not a daily concern for field social workers. These are important Parts of the Act that may, on specific occasions, need to be referred to in your work.

You will see that Part III Local Authority Support for Children and Families is comprehensively referred to in three chapters in the book.

The Children Act Bus
To give an idea of how the Children Act 1989 is constructed, imagine a bus. Part III will be the chassis. It is the essential underpinning of the vehicle. We

will look at this in detail shortly. Before we do that we need to look at the philosophy of the Act, which can be regarded as seeing into the minds and the plans of the designers of the bus (bearing in mind that the finished article does not always look the same as it did on the drawing board). After that we will describe some principles which may be seen as the framework which holds the body of the bus onto the chassis. To continue (along the same road with!) the metaphor, the court orders available under the Act are the horn, to be used only when absolutely necessary. We leave it to you to extend this metaphor further — mentioning the comment of one social worker, 'and we are the ones outside pushing it along the road!'

We will look at the Children Act 1989 in this order. In particular, we will look at the local authority support in Part III before we consider court orders.

THE PHILOSOPHY OF THE ACT

To a traditional lawyer, talk of the philosophy of a piece of legislation is incorrect. The words of the statute are all that there are, and the meaning is to be found in those words. That said, much has been made of the Children Act's philosophy. What this really means is the philosophy of those who framed the Act. Knowing the basis on which they worked helps a proper comprehension of the Act.

A comprehensive exposition of much of the philosophy can be found in *The Introduction to the Children Act 1989, The Care of Children, The Principles and Practice in Regulations and Guidance* and the 10 volumes of *Guidance and Regulations on the 1989 Children Act* published by the Department of Health. Social workers need to be familiar with all these. A word of clarification and warning; these excellent books contain guidance which has to be considered by all local authorities, as they are issued under s. 7 of LASSA 1970 (see p. 28). They are not the final statement of the law. They reflect the government view of what it *hopes* the words of the Act say. Therefore, while you should read them, do not take them to be the final, definitive statement of the law. So, in *Re M (A Minor) (Secure Accommodation Order)* [1995] 2 WLR 302 (for more about this case see p. 239) we find a Court of Appeal judge saying: 'In my judgment section 1 was not designed to be applied to Part III of the Act of 1989. To that extent I would disagree with volumes 1 and 4 of the Department of Health's Children Act Guidance and Regulations, although I do agree that the welfare of the child is an important consideration.' It is the courts that finally decide what the law means and, whilst helped by guidance, the social worker has to consult with their own lawyers for the best interpretation.

So what is the underlying philosophy of the Act?

[T]he Act's philosophy [is] that the best place for the [child] to be brought up is usually in the [child's] own family and the [child] in need can be helped most effectively if the local authority, working in partnership with the parents, provides a range and level of services appropriate to the [child's] needs. To this end the parents and [the child] (. . . where [the child] is of sufficient understanding) need to be given the opportunity to make their wishes and feelings known and to participate in decision-making. (*Guidance and Regulations on the 1989 Children Act*, vol. 2.)

Thus the philosophy is that the child should be brought up with the child's family, and the local authority should be providing support to that end. This needs to be both understood and, more importantly, accepted by all those who carry out statutory work under the Children Act. There may be those who disagree with this particular child care philosophy. That is irrelevant to the fact that the law is framed on this basis and therefore is to be adhered to. To do otherwise is rather like saying, when asked for directions to get somewhere, 'well, I wouldn't start from here'.

In addition to this concept is the belief that the state, in the shape of the local authority, should not, normally, take control of a child's life unless some strict statutory criteria are met. These criteria are the grounds for care and supervision orders contained in s. 31 (we deal with this in Chapter 7).

SOME RELEVANT CONCEPTS

The Welfare of the Child

This is one concept that causes a great deal of confusion. We return to it at a number of points throughout the book. Many commentators and practitioners state blandly that the Children Act puts the welfare of the child as the paramount consideration. This is not true. The Children Act requires the welfare of the child to be the paramount consideration only when the court is making a decision under its powers under the Act. Even then, if the Act lays down other statutory considerations, the welfare of the child is not paramount.

There are three different welfare tests to be applied. These are as follows:

(a)   A person who has the care of a child but not parental responsibility can do what is reasonable in all the circumstances for the purpose of safeguarding or promoting the child's welfare (s. 3(5)).

(b)   A local authority must safeguard and promote the welfare of a child, in its area, who is in need (s. 17). See p. 74.

(c)   A court making a decision as to the upbringing of a child must have the welfare of the child as the paramount consideration (s. 1(1)). See p. 84. This is unless there are statutory requirements that apply different criteria. (For example the court can never make a care order if the significant harm test is not satisfied. This is true even if the welfare of the child would be best served by the care order.)

It is only when a court is dealing with a case that affects a child directly that that child's welfare is paramount. So, when the House of Lords was considering what should happen to a young baby born to a 16-year-old mother in care, it had to put the welfare of the baby as being paramount above that of the baby's mother (even though the mother was under 16 and, as such, a child). This was because the court was dealing with an application concerning the baby not the mother (*Birmingham City Council* v *H (No. 3)* [1994] 2 WLR 31.

The welfare concept would be better expressed if it were stated that the Children Act requires everybody to safeguard and promote the welfare of children as far as is possible, because that is the primary and universal duty.

Human Rights and the Welfare of the Child

It will be important to notice how the courts respond to the potential conflict between the welfare principle and human rights provisions. Article 8 of the Human Rights Convention specifically relates to respect for family life, which may cause difficulties unless the court is satisfied that interference by a public authority is warranted. The Human Rights Act 1998 will certainly encourage greater clarity in local authority and social work decision making. The need for proportionality will be important too (see *Re C and B (Children) (Care Order: Future Harm)* [2000] 2 FCR 614, CA, referred to at p. 27). Overall, however, lawyers' views are that the requirement that the welfare of the child be the court's paramount consideration is consistent with Convention case law and within the margin of appreciation (allowance for local circumstances) permitted to national authorities under Article 8, and is therefore compatible with that Article.

Respect for the Child

This is a concept that is difficult to define but which pervades all the questions of how the law looks at the child. In dealing with children you need to recognise that the law regards the child as your client. You cannot escape the comment made on behalf of the British Association of Social Workers to the Jasmine Beckford inquiry, which fully endorsed it: '[the] clear and unequivocal view that in any child abuse case the primary client for the social worker is the child. The many conflicts are easier to resolve if social workers always bear in mind who is the primary client.' There will always be a conflict between parent and child at some stage of the child's development. Part of the growing process is the assertion of the child's independence. When the state becomes involved in the essentially private area of family life, the real difficulty is for the state to ascertain when that independence should be allowed to become a reality. Clearly a six-month-old baby cannot be independent, and if the parents fail the child then the state must step in and assume parental responsibility. But what is to be said for a 12-year-old child or a 16-year-old young person? If their parents fail, what consideration has to be given to the wishes of the child or young person?

For a statutory recognition of this concept we need to look at s. 22 of the Children Act 1989:

> (4) Before making any decisions with respect to the child whom they are looking after, or proposing to look after, a local authority shall, so far as is reasonably practicable, ascertain the wishes and feelings of—
>   (a)   the child;

(b)   his parents;

(c)   any person who is not a parent of his but who has parental responsibility for him; and

(d)   any other person whose feelings the authority consider to be relevant, regarding the matter to be decided.

(5)   In making any such decision a local authority shall give due consideration—

(a)   having regard to his age and understanding, to such wishes and feelings of the child as they have been able to ascertain;

(b)   to such wishes and feelings of any person mentioned in subsection (4)(b) to (d) as they have been able to ascertain; and

(c)   to the child's religious persuasion, racial origin and cultural and linguistic background.

The fact that the child is mentioned before the parents, or any other person in this section, suggests that the child's wishes are to be the first consideration. This applies whether or not the child is subject to a court order. It should also be borne in mind that if any matter concerning the child is taken to court, then the court will apply the welfare principle, placing the child's welfare as paramount, i.e., coming before and overriding anyone else's welfare or convenience.

The statutory responsibilities are expanded by the decisions of the courts, notably the *Gillick* case described below. In dealing with any children, you have to ensure that an appropriate level of respect is given to the child as an individual who is entitled to separate consideration in his or her own right. As the Cleveland Report put it, 'the child is a person not an object of concern'. As a result of the respect principle, you will find courts and local authorities are required, throughout the Act, to take into account the wishes and feelings of the child. (This does not necessarily mean carrying out those wishes.)

Respect for the child does not mean the child has absolute rights above all others. This point is well made in the following extract:

10.1   Mention of children's rights provokes a sour response in some quarters, along the lines that the Children Act destroyed parental authority to control and discipline children. There is indeed a set of difficult issues about control and discipline, but they are of long standing and have little to do with the Children Act. Underlying the Act is a strong sense of the value of children, and one of its main purposes is to safeguard and promote their welfare. In the narrower area of rights, however, it specified circumstances in which they were to be consulted about what was provided for them, and their views were to be taken into account. It is also clear that they have a right not to be physically or sexually abused, and to have factors such as race, culture and religion considered when decisions are made about them.

10.2   These are and remain important. Around them, however, have grown myths of child dominance and omnipotence. A proportion of staff polled for their views by one voluntary body believed that the Children Act 'enabled young people to make decisions that they are ill-equipped to make'. A similar proportion percipiently observed that staff used the Children Act as an excuse for inaction in protecting young people. This view was echoed in a personal submission which deplored 'the growing tendency for the SSD spokesperson to say that the Children Act prevented them from doing their job properly'. The Children Act does not say that children must always have their own way, or that they must always be believed. Such loose attributes are made by adults grasping for excuses for welshing on their responsibilities to children (Sir William Utting: *People Like Us*, Department of Health, 1997)

Partnership under the Children Act

One word that you will constantly come across when reading about the Children Act is 'partnership'. If you read the Children Act carefully, though, you will not find the word 'partnership' anywhere. Therefore it is not a legal requirement under the Children Act. On the other hand, if you read the volumes of guidance and many of the training materials available you will find that reference to 'partnership' occurs frequently:

> . . . the Act's philosophy that the best place for the child to be brought up is usually in his own family *[The wording chosen here can be criticised. Section 17 makes clear that the first duty is to promote and safeguard the child's welfare and only then to try and keep the child with the family. See page 75.]* and the child in need (who includes the child with disabilities) can be helped most effectively if the local authority, working in partnership with the parents, provides a range and level of services appropriate to the child's needs. To this end the parents and the child (where he is of sufficient understanding) need to be given the opportunity to make their wishes and feelings known and to participate in decision-making. (DoH, *Guidance and Regulations*, vol. 2)

Indeed the Department of Health has issued a volume of guidance actually called *The Challenge of Partnership in Child Protection: Practice Guide* (Department of Health, 1995).

It is clear from the comments we have already made about the need to follow guidance that a local authority is required to work, as far as possible, in partnership with children and their families. The principle can be seen to be reflected in the statute as follows:

(a)   accommodation of children looked after should be provided as a consumer-led service (s. 22);

(b)   that accommodation should be near the children's parents;

(c)   contact with parents is presumed if a child is in care (s. 34), and during emergency protection (s. 44) or police protection (s. 46);

(d)   care orders do not remove parental responsibilities (s. 2(6));

(e)   abolition of care by stealth, i.e. that the placing of a child or young person into local authority accommodation can no longer lead, of itself, to that child or young person becoming subject to any form of statutory control; and

(f) the duty of the local authority to consult parents when they accommodate a child (s. 20) or provide services (s. 17).

However, it is important to note that the concept of partnership does not remove the overriding duty of the local authority to safeguard and promote the welfare of the child. Allowing partnership to become paramount is both misapplying the law and bad practice. As 'Someone Else's Children' (DoH, 1998) stated:

> [Social Service Department's] were overwhelmingly committed to the concept of partnership with children's families. This was sometimes detrimental to the best interests of the child, as successive attempts were made to assess and rehabilitate. This practice was driven by a view often reinforced by local authority legal advisers that it was essential to demonstrate to GALs and the courts that no stone had been left unturned before resorting to the judicial system. Such defensive practices contributed to case drift. (1.34)

Informed Consent

Doctors cannot treat a person without consent. How do they obtain consent to treat a child? The starting point is that as a general rule anyone (including a local authority) with parental responsibility can give a valid consent (but note the limitations on the local authority's power when it has parental responsibility by virtue of an emergency protection order — see p. 123). However, there are limits on the powers of those with parental responsibility. First, irreversible medical treatment for non-therapeutic purposes (such as sterilisation) should take place only with the leave of the court. Secondly, the age of the child has significance.

The child's consent and Gillick competence There is in the Act a statutory recognition of the decision in *Gillick* v *West Norfolk and Wisbech Area Health Authority* [1986] AC 112 (the *Gillick* case) in which the House of Lords discussed the relationship between parent and child and the responsibilities that arise from that relationship. (The case concerned the question whether or not a parent was entitled to be informed that a child under the age of 16 was going to be given contraception.) What the House of Lords indicated was that there is a tapering relationship between parent and child. The older and more mature a child becomes the less the parent is entitled, as a matter of right, to know about the child's affairs. The child does not have to wait for the age of majority (18) to be able to decide matters in his or her own right; that informed choice can be made at an earlier age.

Prior to the *Gillick* case a child could consent to medical treatment at the age of 16. The decision in the *Gillick* case indicates that the consent to such treatment can be given at an earlier age. There is no fixed age, it will depend on the particular child concerned. So when the Act talks of medical or similar examinations of children, we find the following type of statement: 'but if the child is of sufficient understanding to make an informed decision he may refuse to submit to the examination'.

One difficulty that is raised by the idea of informed consent is 'what happens if the child refuses to consent?'. Volume 3 (2.32) of the *Guidance and Regulations* makes it clear that in that situation it is a matter for the doctor to decide. This is in accordance with official guidance given on patient consent to treatment or examination.

A number of cases (some decided under the Children Act) have complicated the concept of informed consent. The first of these is *Re R* [1991] 3 WLR 592. In this case (decided before the Children Act came into force) the Court of Appeal held that although a 16-year-old girl could be said to be '*Gillick* competent', that fact did not prevent the court ordering that she be given drugs against her will. The Court, in a much criticised decision, drew the distinction between the ability of the girl to give consent and her right to refuse consent. It said that while she could give valid consent, if she refused this did not mean that others such as parents or the court could not still impose consent on her behalf.

As the Court said:

> The failure or refusal of the 'Gillick competent' child is a very important factor in the doctor's decision whether or not to treat, but it does not prevent the necessary consent being obtained from another competent source.

Similarly, in *Re W (A Minor) (Consent to Medical Treatment)* [1993] 1 FLR 1, the Court of Appeal again overrode the refusal of an anorexic to accept treatment. What the Court is saying is that the welfare of the child is not something to be decided solely by the child. The welfare of the child can be decided by others, particularly the court.

This approach can best be seen in *South Glamorgan County Council* v *W and B* [1993] 1 FLR 574. Here Douglas Browne J was faced with the problem of a young person who clearly was beyond parental control. She was aged 15. She had refused to do anything she was told. She had, in fact, barricaded herself in the front room of her father's house for 11 months. The local authority wanted an interim care order to have the child assessed. The difficulty was the provisions in s. 38(6) which deal with the court's powers to make orders for assessments to be carried out when making interim care orders (we look at these in Chapter 7). This particular subsection has provision for informed consent by the young person, stating '. . . but if the child is of sufficient understanding to make an informed decision he may refuse to submit to the examination or other assessment'. The local authority and those acting for the girl put the view to the court that if she refused to submit to the assessment then there was little that anyone could do. The judge would not accept this and gave directions under the inherent power of the court (s. 100) for the authority to remove the child. In effect, he bypassed the provisions of the Act relating to informed consent. He did this without making the girl a ward of court. He said:

In my judgment the court can in an appropriate case — and they will be rare cases — but in an appropriate case, when other remedies within the Children Act have been used and exhausted and found not to bring about the desired result, can resort to other remedies, and the particular remedy here is the remedy of providing authority, if it is needed, for the local authority to take all necessary steps to bring the child to the doctors so that she can be assessed and treated.

In *Re C (A Minor) (Medical Treatment: Courts' Jurisdiction)* (1997) *The Times*, 21 March, the court extended the concept of its inherent power to allow a young person to be detained in a clinic. This bypassed the question of the need for a secure accommodation order under s. 25 (see p. 238).

There have been a number of cases concerning the ability of children or young people to appoint guardians or solicitors to act on their behalf. In *Re S (A Minor)* [1993] 2 FLR 437, the Court of Appeal held that a child of 11 could not remove the Official Solicitor as guardian. The court said:

The 1989 Act enabled and required a judicious balance to be struck between two considerations. First was the principle, to be honoured and respected, that children were human beings in their own right with individual minds and wills, views and emotions, which should command attention. Second was the fact that a child was, after all, a child.

In *Re H (A Minor) (Care Proceedings: Child's Wishes)* [1993] 1 FLR 440, the court said a 15-year-old did not have the right to address the court on his own behalf.

These cases point to a view of the courts that, despite the apparent philosophy of legislation, the court retains the right to make such difficult decisions for itself, and, if it feels able, to substitute its view for that of the child or young person.

This may cause some confusion for social workers. These decisions may not do a great deal to advance the case for children and young persons to be autonomous. The Children Act does give clear statements that the wishes of the child have to be taken into account, and from that flows the idea of informed consent. The social worker has the requirement to follow the Children Act. However, in some extreme circumstances (such as in the *Glamorgan* case) there may be the need to seek court approval to override the wishes of children if you consider that their decision is not in their best interests. In doing that you will be asking the court to override the refusal or consent of the child or young person because, in essence, the court will be finding that it is not informed consent.

The concept of an informed consent is not just applicable to the question of medical examinations; there are other areas where the child may give or refuse an informed consent, such as whether or not a visitor should be appointed under the provisions of the Children Act, Sch. 2, para. 17. (For a similar approach, see the Code of Practice under the Mental Health Act 1983, para. 29.)

The position of parents   The court also has powers to override the decisions of parents to consent to medical treatment. In *Re A (Children) (Conjoined Twins: Surgical Separation)* [2000] 4 All ER 961, the Court of Appeal sanctioned, against the wishes of the parents, the separation of conjoined twins, despite the fact that the result would be the death of the weaker twin. The court in these circumstances makes it decision based on the best interests of the child and not on the reasonableness of the parents' refusal of consent.

Diminishment of Court Proceedings

This is applicable only in the public law area of the Act. Its provisions are to be found tucked away in Sch. 2, Pt. I, para. 7, which states:

> Every local authority shall take reasonable steps designed—
>   (a)   to reduce the need to bring—
>   (i)   proceedings for care or supervision orders with respect to the children within their area;
>   (ii)   criminal proceedings against such children;
>   (iii)   any family or other proceedings with respect to such children which might lead to them being placed in the authority's care; or
>   (iv)   proceedings under the inherent jurisdiction of the High Court with respect to children;
>   (b)   to encourage children within their area not to commit criminal offences;
>   (c)   to avoid the need for children within their area to be placed in secure accommodation.

This provision imposes a duty on local authorities, and in carrying out your duties you should be looking for ways in which to give effect to it.

LOCAL AUTHORITY SUPPORT FOR CHILDREN AND FAMILIES: CHILDREN ACT 1989, PART III

Why is support supplied by the local authority? To safeguard and promote the welfare of children who are in need, and to enable the child to be brought up with his or her family. In doing that the local authority works in partnership with the child and the child's parents. The aim is to provide positive support to avoid the need, as far as possible, for the local authority to have to seek statutory control. It is to be viewed as a supportive partnership.

Section 17 states this approach as follows:

> (1)   It shall be the general duty of every local authority (in addition to the other duties imposed on them by this Part)—
>   (a)   to safeguard and promote the welfare of children within their area who are in need, and
>   (b)   so far as is consistent with that duty, to promote the upbringing of such children by their families, by providing a range and level of services appropriate to those children's needs.

Again, whereas the welfare principle (below, p. 84) for courts requires them to treat the child's welfare as the paramount consideration, for local authorities the requirement is that they *safeguard and promote the welfare* of children within their areas who are in need. To discharge this duty the local authority has to carry out a balancing act. There will always be a conflict between what it may want to do for an individual child and what it can do, given its resources and the demands of other children whose welfare it has to safeguard and promote. 'The outcome of any service provision under this power should be evaluated to see whether it has met the primary objective, namely to safeguard and promote the child's welfare' (*Guidance and Regulations,* vol. 2, p. 6).

Who is a Child in Need?
The local authority's duty to safeguard and promote the welfare of a child extends only to those children who are 'in need'. For a definition of this we have to look at s. 17(10):

(10)   For the purposes of this Part a child shall be taken to be in need if—

(a)   he is unlikely to achieve or maintain, or to have the opportunity of achieving or maintaining, **a reasonable standard of health or development** without the provision for him of services by a local authority under this Part;

(b)   his **health or development** is likely to **be significantly impaired**, or further impaired, without the provision for him of such services; or

(c)   he is **disabled**, and 'family', in relation to such a child, includes any person who has parental responsibility for the child and any other person with whom he has been living;

(11)   For the purposes of this Part, a child is disabled if he is blind, deaf or dumb or suffers from mental disorder of any kind or is substantially and permanently handicapped by illness, injury or congenital deformity or such other disability as may be prescribed; and in this Part—

'**development**' means physical, intellectual, emotional, social or behavioural development; and

'**health**' means physical or mental health.

It is clear from this definition that the majority of children and young people with whom the local authority is going to come into contact will fall within the definition of being 'children in need'. The definition has been made this broad to emphasise the preventative element of the local authority's role. There are three different elements of the definition:

(a)   reasonable standard of health or development;
(b)   significant impairment of health or development;
(c)   disability.

These are separate and distinct bases on which 'need' should be considered. *As Guidance and Regulations,* vol. 2 says: 'It would not be acceptable for an authority to exclude any of these three — for example, by confining services to children at risk of significant harm' (we look at significant harm at p. 136). The local authority must consider the provision of services for those who fall within any of the headings. It is the local authority that makes the decision as to whether or not a particular child is or is not in need (*Re J (Specific Issue Order: Leave to Apply)* [1995] 1 FLR 669). The need for a holistic model for assessing children's needs is emphasised in *A Framework for the Assessment of Children in Need and Their Families* (The Stationery Office, 2000), jointly published by the Department of Health, the Department of Education and Employment and the Home Office.

Services for a Child in Need

Having established that the child is in need, the local authority has the power to provide the appropriate services.

These services may be supplied direct to the child or to other members of the child's family (s. 17(3)). A wide definition of 'family' is given so that it encompasses any family grouping you are likely to encounter. It is acceptable to target the services on someone other than the child, provided that this is done with the aim of promoting and safeguarding the welfare of a particular child in need, who is your client.

So if a mother was finding it difficult to cope with a child because she also had the responsibility of looking after an elderly parent, it would be possible to use the budget for the provision of services to children under s. 17 to provide the elderly parent with day care facilities, so as to enable the child's mother better to look after the child.

Cash help The services can, if necessary, be provided by means of cash assistance, as the Children Act 1989, s. 17(6)–(9) show:

(6) The services provided by a local authority in the exercise of functions conferred on them by this section may include giving assistance in kind or, in exceptional circumstances, in cash.

(7) Assistance may be unconditional or subject to conditions as to the repayment of the assistance or of its value (in whole or in part).

(8) Before giving any assistance or imposing any conditions, a local authority shall have regard to the means of the child concerned and of each of his parents.

(9) No person shall be liable to make any repayment of assistance or of its value at any time when he is in receipt of income support or family credit under the Social Security Act 1986.

These important powers mean that if the need can be met by cash then there is nothing to stop the local authority giving cash. For the majority of people who receive that cash, as they are likely to be in receipt of family credit or income support, they will not have to repay the money received.

Note that the Carers and Disabled Children Act 2000 inserts a new s. 17A into the Children Act 1989, which allows local authorities to make direct payments to persons with parental responsibility for a disabled child instead of services which would otherwise have been provided for them by the local authorities.

Specific Duties

In addition to the general duty in the Children Act 1989, s. 17, there are contained in Sch. 2 to the Act a number of specific duties dealing with all children and children who are looked after.

As explained earlier, a duty is something that *must* be carried out. Against this, those drafting the legislation often slip in words that dilute the force of a duty. You will see such phrases as 'shall take reasonable steps, such steps as are reasonably practicable, shall provide services designed to' etc. The addition of qualifications to the imperative 'shall' has the effect of diminishing the force of the duty. Unfortunately, it is then open to a particular local authority to say that the provision of a service is not a reasonable step because there is not sufficient money available. So, while there is the distinction between duties and powers, a qualified duty is little more than a mere power.

The Children Act 1989, Sch. 2, imposes *specific* duties on the local authority when dealing with all children as follows:

1. *Identification of children in need and provision of information*
   (1) Every local authority shall take reasonable steps to identify the extent to which there are children in need within their area.
   (2) Every local authority shall—
      (a) publish information—
         (i) about services provided by them under sections 17, 18, 20 and 24 [s. 17 is the general provision of services to children in need, s. 18 is about day care provision for children, s. 20 is about the provision of accommodation and s. 24 is about the provision of advice and assistance]; and
         (ii) where they consider it appropriate, about the provision by others (including, in particular, voluntary organisations) of services which the authority has power to provide under those sections; and
      (b) take such steps as are reasonably practicable to ensure that those who might benefit from the services receive the information relevant to them.

One of the great improvements made by the Children Act is that where a local authority is required to provide a service, it is required to give publicity to that service and also to services provided by voluntary groups. That information has to be published and steps have to be taken to ensure that it reaches the people who need it.

2. *Maintenance of a register of disabled children*
   (1) Every local authority shall open and maintain a register of disabled children within their area.

(2)   The register may be kept by means of a computer.

This, it will be noted, is one of the few examples of a clear statutory duty with a little tilt towards our modern age permitting the use of computers! Despite this modern approach to equipment, the labelling of children with disabilities as 'disabled' is regrettable and avoidable in modern legislation.

3.   *Assessment of children's needs*
   Where it appears to a local authority that a child within their area is in need, the authority may assess his needs for the purposes of this Act at the same time as any assessment of his needs is made under—
      (a)   the Chronically Sick and Disabled Persons Act 1970;
      (b)   the Education Act 1981;
      (c)   the Disabled Persons (Services, Consultation and Representation) Act 1986; or
      (d)   any other enactment.

4.   *Prevention of neglect and abuse*
   (1)   Every local authority shall take reasonable steps, through the provision of services under Part III of this Act, to prevent children within their area suffering ill-treatment or neglect.
   (2)   Where a local authority believes that a child who is at any time within their area—
      (a)   is likely to suffer harm; but
      (b)   lives or proposes to live in the area of another local authority they shall inform that other local authority.
   (3)   When informing that other local authority they shall specify—
      (a)   the harm that they believe he is likely to suffer; and
      (b)   (if they can) where the child lives or proposes to live.

The appearance of the words 'reasonable steps' diminishes somewhat the duty of this paragraph. The steps may be taken to prevent 'ill treatment or neglect'. This is not the same as the 'significant harm' test in s. 31 of the Act (see p. 136). It is a lower standard and enables help to be given at an earlier stage. Neglect is not defined in the Act and therefore has to be given its normal meaning. We find that ill-treatment includes sexual abuse and forms of ill-treatment which are not physical: s. 31(9).

5.   *Provision of accommodation [to the suspected abuser] in order to protect child*
   (1)   Where—
      (a)   it appears to a local authority that a child who is living on particular premises is suffering, or is likely to suffer, ill treatment at the hands of another person who is living on those premises; and
      (b)   that other person proposes to move from the premises; the authority may assist that other person to obtain alternative accommodation.
   (2)   Assistance given under this paragraph may be in cash.
   (3)   . . .

This is one of the most potentially useful provisions of the whole schedule. It is one of the few provisions that relate directly to the Cleveland experience, such a course of action being recommended in the Report.

To give an example of it in action: there is a report of a girl possibly being abused by her mother's cohabitee. A joint investigation with the police should be undertaken by the Social Services Department. We look later at the types of order the local authority could apply for. If an emergency protection order or an interim care order is applied for, the court has the power to exclude the suspected abuser from the home. What Sch. 2, para. 5 does is give the power to the Social Services Department to suggest to the suspected abuser that he leaves the house while investigations and inquiries are carried out. If he is prepared to do this then the Social Services Department can not only help him find accommodation, but also pay for that accommodation. The limit in the power is that there can be no compulsion applied to the man. All that is left is the use of exhortations and cajoling.

This may be less traumatic for all concerned. The use of this power should not be seen as a replacement for any statutory order, however. If you feel that a statutory order is required then the order should be applied for.

This power is in addition to the power of a court to exclude a suspected abuser when making either an emergency protection order or an interim care order (see p. 123).

6. *Provision for 'disabled' children*
    Every local authority shall provide services designed—
    (a) to minimise the effect on disabled children within their area of their disabilities; and
    (b) to give such children the opportunity to lead lives which are as normal as possible.

The wish to see children leading more normal lives should not obscure the need for local authorities to ensure that adequate provision is made to cater for children's disabilities. A first step could be to ensure that they are referred to as children with disabilities and not labelled, as in the statute, as disabled children.

7. *Provision to reduce need for care proceedings etc.* [This has already been described as the diminishment of court proceedings principle.]

Local authorities should take steps to avoid any child being involved in any court proceedings, whether civil or criminal.

8. *Provision for children living with their families*
    Every local authority shall make such provision as they consider appropriate for the following services to be available with respect to children in need within their area while they are living with their families—
    (a) advice, guidance and counselling;

(b)   occupational, social, cultural or recreational activities;

(c)   home help (which may include laundry facilities);

(d)   facilities for, or assistance with, travelling to and from home for the purpose of taking advantage of any other service provided under this Act or of any similar service;

(e)   assistance to enable the child concerned and his family to have a holiday.

This paragraph requires the local authority, in accordance with the philosophy of the Children Act 1989, to support the child who is living with his or her family. As can be seen, there is a wide range of provisions that the local authority should consider making.

9.   *Family centres*

(1)   Every local authority shall provide such family centres as they consider appropriate in relation to children within their area.

(2)   'Family centre' means a centre at which any of the persons mentioned in subparagraph (3) may—

(a)   attend for occupational, social, cultural or recreational activities;

(b)   attend for advice, guidance or counselling; or

(c)   be provided with accommodation while he is receiving advice, guidance or counselling.

(3)   The persons are:

(a)   a child;

(b)   his parents;

(c)   any person who is not a parent of his but who has parental responsibility for him;

(d)   any other person who is looking after him.

The fact that this is the first statutory mention of 'family centre' may be surprising, in view of their long history in the overall picture of child protection. You will notice that this paragraph clearly states that the assistance of a family centre can be given to someone other than a particular child. This, again, is on the basis that the overall aim must be to safeguard and promote the welfare of a particular child.

10.   *Maintenance of the family home*

Every local authority shall take such steps as are reasonably practicable, where any child within their area who is in need and whom they are not looking after is living apart from his family—

(a)   to enable him to live with his family; or

(b)   to promote contact between him and his family,

if, in their opinion, it is necessary to do so in order to safeguard or promote his welfare.

Again we see the philosophy spelt out, requiring the local authority to take steps to enable children *who they are not looking after* to live with or to have contact with their family.

There may be a conflict between the responsibilities of the Social Services Department and the Housing Department. This is especially true in those non-county authorities where these twin responsibilities are shared by the same authority. Suppose the Housing Department evicts a family for non-payment of rent. (You will see in Chapter 17 further details of the relevant housing law.) Should the Social Services Department then take over the responsibility for keeping the family home together? The law appears to be in conflict at this stage. The House of Lords has said that the child cannot make an application for housing in his or her own right. (*R v Oldham Metropolitan Borough Council ex parte G (A Minor)* [1993] 2 FLR 194).

In the case of *R v Northavon District Council ex parte Smith* [1994] 2 FLR 671, the House of Lords said that when a family has been refused accommodation under the Housing Act 1985, on the grounds that they were intentionally homeless, the housing authority was not obliged to reconsider providing a home under the Children Act 1989. Children in need, however, should not remain unassisted because of the overlap between the two codes. This should not amount to the housing authority giving them a house.

The Social Services Department's responsibility implies the need to ensure that the family is kept together, although clearly it cannot take on an open-ended commitment to pay the rent and arrears. Ultimately, it may be that the Social Services Department would have to seek care orders to house the children. This is because the statutory duty is to the individual children rather than to the family as a whole.

11. *Duty to consider racial groups to which children in need belong*
     Every local authority shall, in making any arrangements—
       (a) for the provision of day care within their area; or
       (b) designed to encourage persons to act as local authority foster parents, have regard to the different racial groups to which children within their area who are in need belong.

This is a requirement for the local authority to take account of our multicultural society in the provision of day care and recruiting foster parents. Where a local authority is 'looking after' a child, there is a requirement before making any decisions in respect of that child to give due consideration to the child's religious persuasion, racial origin and cultural and linguistic background (Children Act 1989, s. 22(5)(c)) (see 'Respect for the Child' (above)).

The Meaning of 'Looked After' and 'Accommodation'
Before concluding our study of Part III of the Children Act 1989, we need to examine the meanings of the terms 'being looked after' and 'accommodation', which have already come up in our description of Part III services to children in need.

Looked after This term is not actually defined specifically in the Children Act 1989. It is an important concept because, once a child has been looked after, the child is entitled to a range of services. The local authority has certain duties towards the 'looked after' child. To become 'looked after', the child, first, has to be in need. Being in need is the ticket that gets the child onto the Children Act bus. Being 'looked after' is first referred to in s. 22. To be looked after the child either has to be the subject of a care order, or be supplied with accommodation by the local authority. By being looked after the child has access to a range of services. The local authority will have control over the 'looked after' child only if the child is the subject of a care order. It is important to note that once a child is looked after the child becomes subject to the Placement of Children Regulations. We discuss this more fully in Chapter 11.

Accommodation This term could be somewhat confusing, as the supplying of accommodation by a local authority is not, of itself, indicative of any particular legal situation.

A child may be supplied with accommodation by a local authority without being the subject of any statutory control by that local authority.

No matter how long a child is looked after by a local authority and supplied with accommodation, the child never becomes the subject of statutory controls until an application is made for a care order or supervision order and that order or an interim order is granted. This means that a parent of such a child may at any time remove that child from the local authority accommodation. This is in contrast to the previous law where, after a six-month period in local authority accommodation, notice had to be given before removal of the child.

Accommodation is defined in s. 22(2) of the 1989 Act as meaning accommodation which is provided for a continuous period of more than 24 hours. There are provisions in s. 23 which allow the local authority to discharge its duty to supply accommodation by placing the child with its close family, or a relative or other suitable person, or placing the child in a suitable home. These provisions are subject to the various regulations which come under the heading of the placement of children. These are dealt with in vol. 3 of the *Guidance and Regulations on the 1989 Children Act*. We look more closely at those regulations and their implications in Chapter 11.

The Complaints Procedure Relating to a Local Authority's Services for Children

For whatever reason, the parents may feel aggrieved with the actions of the authority. Under the Children Act 1989, s. 26(3) to (8), there are important provisions requiring local authorities to establish a representations procedure in relation to the discharge of any of their functions of providing support for children and their families under Part III of the Act.

The provision requires the authority to consider representations (including complaints) from:

(a) any child or parent of such a child in need or being looked after by the authority;

(b)   a person with parental responsibility for such a child;

(c)   any local authority foster parent; and

(d)   any other person the authority consider has sufficient interest in the child's welfare.

You will note that the procedure is based on a particular child's experience, which will exclude representations being made about the authority's general policies. Those representations should be properly made through the elected councillor members of the Social Services Committee. The expression 'representations' is wider than 'complaint' and will allow for comments about the way in which a particular case is being handled.

The regulations (the Representation Procedure (Children) Regulations 1991) require the local authority to appoint an officer to be responsible for the coordination of complaints. Any representations are to be put in writing by the officer, even if given verbally.

There must be at least one person independent of the authority who takes part in the procedure. The consideration of the complaint must take place within 28 days of the complaint being received.

After consideration, all people who may be interested must be notified within 28 days of the result. If the complainant is not satisfied, then the local authority must, again within 28 days, appoint a panel to consider the representations. The panel also has to contain at least one independent person. It is possible for the independent person to be the same person who considered the written representations. Alternatively, a separate independent person may be appointed.

This panel can consider both written and oral representations. If the independent person on the panel is different from the one who considered the written representations, then that independent person may make oral representations before the panel.

Importantly, the person making the representations has the right to be accompanied by someone who may speak on that person's behalf. This clearly would include a solicitor.

Where representations are made and have been considered, the authority shall:

(a)   have due regard to the findings of those who considered them (i.e., so that the representation procedure is not a toothless public relations exercise);

(b)   take steps to notify in writing those who have made the representations of the decisions reached and of action to be taken;

(c)   give appropriate publicity to this procedure.

The regulations require the local authority to prepare regular reports of the complaints and their outcomes. These should be supplied to the Social Services Committee and be published in an annual report.

Failure to comply with the representations procedure will mean the local authority may be subject to judicial review and the ire of the Secretary of State. However, before an application may be made for judicial review, the representations procedure must be exhausted (*R* v *Royal Borough of Kingston-upon-Thames* [1994] 1 FLR 798).

A social worker in any dealings with their client will need to inform them of the availability of this procedure, and if necessary assist the clients in making representations.

It is worth noting that 'Someone Else's Children' stated:

> . . . young people we met had little confidence in the complaints process and felt that their concerns were not heard:

> > 'You never get believed but have to believe everything told to you. They never tell you what people say about you, but what I say has to be written down.'

> Young people told us that, when they were better informed about the process, their confidence in it increased. (4.30)

The Department of Health has responded to concerns about complaints procedures and published a Consultation Document, 'Listening to People — a Consultation on Improving Social Services Complaints Procedures'. This raises key issues about advocacy for children, the necessity of rapid responses to complaints by children, and the need for local authorities to freeze decisions which have a significant impact on the life of an individual pending the outcome of the complaint, unless good reason can be found otherwise. Any new procedures would, of course, have to be based on a Human Rights Act compliant 'fair trial' procedure. The draft regulations drawn up under the Children (Leaving Care) Act 2000 (due to be implemented from 1 October 2001) indicate that the current complaints procedure under the Children Act will be extended to cover care leavers, and propose a new local resolution stage and access to an advocate as new features of complaints procedures.

PRINCIPLES APPLICABLE TO COURT PROCEEDINGS UNDER THE CHILDREN ACT

In order to avoid continual repetition of basic points and the repeated statement of section numbers, we have defined below what we call 'principles'. You should keep in mind that this terminology is not always found in the Act, but is designed for ease of reference.

The Main Principles

There are three main principles that guide courts under this Act, all of which are to be found in s. 1. They are:

(a)   the welfare principle (s. 1(1));
(b)   the non-delay principle (s. 1(2)); and
(c)   the no order principle (s. 1(5)).

The welfare principle   When a court (*but only a court*) considers any matter concerning the welfare of the child, the court shall treat the child's welfare as its paramount consideration. This means that although the Act tries to balance the rights of the child and the rights of the parents, finally the court must do what the court sees as being best for the child. (That is the function of the court, to arrive at a hard decision, which not all the parties may agree with.) The welfare principle in s. 1 does not apply to all decisions by the court. Within the Act there are sections that have specific statutory requirements for the court to consider. If the Act gives such requirements the court must follow these. It cannot apply only the s. 1 paramount welfare principle. For example, s. 10(9) deals with applying for leave to make an application for an order by a private individual. There are specific grounds for the court to consider (*Re A & W* [1992] 3 All ER 872). Where an application is made to place a child in secure accommodation under s. 25, again, specific statutory criteria apply (*Re M (A Minor) (Secure Accommodation Order)* [1995] 2 WLR 302). The court said in that case:

> This duty cast upon the local authority to safeguard and promote the welfare of the child is not the same duty cast upon the court by section 1 to place welfare as the paramount consideration. Other considerations can and frequently do affect the local authority's approach [*per* Butler Sloss LJ].

So, even if a court is dealing with a specific case involving children under the Children Act, the welfare principle may not be paramount. It cannot override statutory time limits, such as the length of time an emergency protection order may last. It will not allow the court to go behind established principles of law. In *Re M (A Minor) (Appeal) (No. 2)* [1994] 1 FLR 59 the guardian *ad litem* sought to introduce evidence before the Court of Appeal of the effect on the child on being told that the child would have to return home to the mother. The child became hysterical and distressed. The court would not allow this. Yet another example is the case of *Nottinghamshire CC v P* [1993] 3 WLR 637 discussed on p. 87 below.

The non-delay principle The court 'shall have regard to the general principle that any delay in determining the question is likely to prejudice the welfare of the child'. The 'question' here means the question on upbringing the court is deciding. One of the most depressing features of the legal system's response to children is that of delay. There are myriad reasons for this. All those concerned with children are anxious to avoid delay. The introduction of this particular section does nothing of itself to reduce the causes for those delays. In any proceedings involving children, both in private law and public law, there are sections which provide that the court shall:

(a)   draw up a timetable with a view to determining the question without delay; and
(b)   give such directions as it considers appropriate for the purpose of ensuring, so far as is reasonably practicable, that that timetable is adhered to.

These provisions are to be found for private law in s. 11 and for public law in s. 32.

The rules, under the Children Act, require the holding of a directions hearing (rule 14) for the Court to make arrangements for preparing the case and hearing it. The first item to be addressed is the timetable for the proceedings. The non-delay principle will be applied.

The no order principle   The court should *not* make an order unless it considers 'that doing so would be better for the child than making no order at all' (s. 1(5)). This small section has the potential for being the most dangerous part of the Act. The first Annual Report on the Children Act (CM 2144) showed a considerable drop in the number of court proceedings taken under the Children Act compared with similar provisions under the former law. Whilst the cutting of the number of orders may not, of itself, be a bad thing, it does not appear to be that simple. For instance, the figures show that only 2,300 emergency protection orders were made compared with 5,000 place of safety orders in the previous year. Only 1,600 care orders were made compared with 6,200 care orders under the old law. There is anecdotal evidence that many social workers and local authority legal departments are taking the view that the 'no order principle' means that cases should not be taken to court. This view is, to some extent, supported by the report itself:

> 2.20   A recent [Social Services Inspectorate] study examined these decision-making processes in four local authority areas in an attempt to address this issue. Arising from the study and Departmental discussions with a number of local authorities was a belief that the 'no order' principle requires authorities to demonstrate that working in partnership has broken down or been exhausted before an order will be made.
>
> 2.21   This was not the intention of the legislation. Where a local authority determines that control of the child's circumstances is necessary to promote his welfare then compulsory intervention, as part of a carefully planned process, will always be the appropriate remedy. Local authorities should not feel inhibited by the working in partnership provisions of the Children Act from seeking appropriate court orders. Equally, the existence of a court order should not of itself impede a local authority from continuing its efforts at working in partnership with families of children in need. The two processes are not mutually exclusive. Each has a role to play, often simultaneously, in the management of a child at risk.

Since that first report was published, there has been an increase in the number of applications for orders to the courts. However, the general point about the misunderstanding of the no order principle remains true. To put it simply, the 'no order principle' is a principle for the court, not for social workers. The duty of the social worker is to promote and safeguard the welfare of children who are in need. Therefore, the 'no order principle' should not in any way inhibit the social worker from taking statutory steps, including going to court, to carry out this duty. It is not the function of the social worker to second guess the court and say that, 'well the court may apply the no order principle and therefore I will not take any action'. Only when it is clear that it is a hopeless case should you consider not going to court because of the no order principle.

Sadly, it remains our view that because of a misunderstanding of the no order principle there may be many timebombs of cases where statutory steps have not been taken to protect children. These cases may explode with the death of a child with all the attendant adverse publicity and trauma.

How Are These Put Into Effect?
In addition to these three main principles we find others:

No compulsory intervention by the state without an application This is a reflection of the philosophy of the Act and is applicable to both private and public law elements of the statute. Where a court is faced with a child that it perceives to be at risk then the court has no power permanently to commit the child into the hands of the state without there being before it an application by the local authority or authorised person. You will not be able to obtain any court order without having made an application to the court. This remains the same despite the provisions of the Crime and Disorder Act 1998 (see p. 119). That Act does allow the court to make a care order without satisfying the full provisons of s. 31 (see p. 135). However, the court will not have this power unless and until the local authority with responsibility for social services provision decides to make the application.

A salutary case to read is *Nottinghamshire CC v P* [1993] 3 WLR 637. In this case the local authority applied for an order under s. 8 of the Children Act that a self-confessed child abuser stepfather vacate the household and that the children should have no contact except under supervision. The court held that, since the effect of the order was in fact to make a residence and contact order, it could not make that order. Local authorities are specifically excluded from applying for such orders (s. 9(2)). As the authority wished to ensure that the children were not put at risk by seeing their father unsupervised, it would appear that they would have been better to apply for a care order. This is the view that the High Court judge and the Court of Appeal took.

As the report of the judgment states:

> . . . the route chosen by the council was wholly inappropriate. In cases where children were found to be at risk of suffering significant harm within s. 47 a clear duty arose on the part of the local authorities to protect them. . . . The council persistently and obstinately refused to undertake what was the appropriate course of action and thereby deprived the judge of the ability to make a constructive order. . . . The position was one which it was hoped would not recur.

Here the Court of Appeal found itself totally frustrated by being unable to make the order asked for. The local authority was seeking to obtain the effect of a care order by the back door. This is clearly contrary to the concept that the only basis on which statutory control can be obtained is by an application which satisfies the significant harm test. This is another example of where the actual goal of social work intervention appears to have been lost sight of. The only duty for the social worker is to promote and safeguard the welfare of children who are either in need or being investigated under s. 47. When carrying out this duty it will often be necessary to take court proceedings. The prime way of protecting children will be by applying for care or supervision orders under Part IV. Applications for other orders under the Children Act should only be made if it is clear that such applications will actually protect the children. Importantly, the application for a care or supervision order will enable the court to make any other orders under the Act (see p. 95). The converse is not true. An application for a s. 8 order does not give the court the power to make a care or supervision order.

The welfare checklist   This is to be found in the Children Act 1989, s. 1(3) and is applicable to all court proceedings in both private and public law, except *it does not apply to court proceedings under Part V* (the emergency protection of children). It consists of a uniform checklist to which the courts need to have regard when they are faced with a dispute concerning any child. t is applicable whether the dispute is between individuals, or a local authority is applying for an order. It states that the court, in deciding any question with respect to the upbringing of a child, must have regard to the following:

(a)   the ascertainable wishes and feelings of the child concerned (considered in the light of his age and understanding);
(b)   his physical, emotional and educational needs;
(c)   the likely effect on him of any change in his circumstances;
(d)   his age, sex, background and any characteristics of his which the court considers relevant;
(e)   any harm which he has suffered or is at risk of suffering;
(f)   how capable each of his parents, and any other person in relation to whom the court considers the question to be relevant, is of meeting his needs;
(g)   the range of powers available to the court under the Children Act in the proceedings in question.

If you are seeking an order from the court, appropriate attention must be given to the checklist in your presentation of evidence and within your report. Also, expect in any disputed case to be cross-examined under each heading.

It should be understood that each point in the checklist is considered separately. There is no priority in the order in which the points appear.

'Mix and match'   This is a useful expression derived from the Department of Health publication, *An Introduction to the Children Act*, where it states:

[a] full menu of orders is also available to a court hearing a local authority application for a care or other order in respect of a child. Thus a court might, for example, order that a child live with a suitable relative or friend rather than make a care order in favour of the local authority. Or it may

mix and match by, for example, ordering that a child live with a non-abusing parent and making a supervision order at the same time.

What it means is that the court should always seek to choose the best order for the child, and that choice is not limited to the orders that the parties have applied for. But the court cannot make a care or supervision order unless it has been applied for.

How this works in practice can be seen in the case of *C v Solihull Metropolitan Borough Council* [1993] 1 FLR 290. A 12-month-old child had suffered a non-accidental injury. The magistrates' court refused to grant a local authority application for a care order but returned the child subject to a supervision order with no conditions attached. On appeal, the High Court made a residence order which no one had applied for, with conditions attached, and an interim supervision order.

Family proceedings   Most proceedings in any area of family law are defined as 'family proceedings'. Inclusion in this category means that, if they have any family proceedings before them, the courts are free — in fact obliged — to apply the mix and match principle, and make the best order for the child, not necessarily the one applied for, and quite possibly where no one has applied for an order under the Act.

The list of family proceedings is given in the Children Act 1989, s. 8(3) and (4):

(a)   High Court proceedings relating to children under the residual powers of wardship (see Chapter 3);

(b)   Matrimonial Causes Act 1973 — proceedings for divorce and other related matters (see Chapter 16);

(c)   Domestic Violence and Matrimonial Proceedings Act 1976 — cases relating to violence between couples (see Chapter 16);

(d)   Adoption Act 1976 (see Chapter 11);

(e)   Domestic Proceedings and Magistrates' Court Act 1978 — disputes between married parties in the magistrates' court (see Chapter 16);

(f)   Matrimonial Homes Act 1983 — concerning disputes over property between married couples (see Chapter 16);

(g)   Matrimonial and Family Proceedings Act 1984 — involving divorce proceedings (see Chapter 16);

(h)   Children Act 1989, Pts I, II and IV (see the other various chapters relating to children); and

(i)   Sections 11 and 12 of the Crime and Disorder Act 1998.

It is important to remember that proceedings under Part V of the Act (protection of children) are *not* family proceedings. So there can be no 'mix and match', only an EPO, or a CAO or no order at all.

Family assistance order   In any family proceedings the court can, under the Children Act 1989, s. 16, make a family assistance order, where the court is satisfied that there are exceptional circumstances and the people named in the order agree. Only the court can make the order; it cannot be applied for by a party. When a family assistance order is made the officer named in the order is to advise, assist and (where appropriate) befriend the person named in the order.

This order is intended to be a short-term order; it can last only for a maximum of six months. It is to help the family over the difficulties that have led to the court appearance.

In *Re C (Family Assistance Order)* [1996] 1 FLR 424, when the local authority said that it did not have the resources to implement the order, the court held that it had no power to force the authority to do so. Nor would the court compel a local authority under a family assistance order to accompany a child to visit that child's father in prison (*S v P (Contact Application: Family Assistance Order)* [1997] 2 FCR 185).

THE ROLE OF CHILDREN'S GUARDIANS

Following the creation of CAFCASS (see p. 91 below), the term 'children's guardian' is to be used instead of 'guardian *ad litem*' (Family Proceedings (Amendment) Rules 2001 (SI 2001 No. 821)).

The role of the guardian is one, historically, that has been long known to the court. Out of the context of child care, the guardian — also known as the child's 'next friend' — acted on behalf of children in court actions such as a claim for damages arising from an accident.

Guardians were introduced into children's cases because the court needed to have a person to give the child's point of view when it was perceived that there was or might be a conflict of interest between parent and child. Guardians have been a common feature of wardship proceedings. They were introduced into the statutory framework of child care law following the Maria Colwell inquiry. In that case Maria was killed by her stepfather, having been returned from the care of the local authority following the revocation of the care order with the consent of the local authority. It was felt that the tragedy could have been avoided if Maria had been separately represented in the proceedings. A person acting solely on behalf of Maria could have argued that it was not in Maria's best interest for the care order to be revoked.

The Children Act 1989 contained the power for courts to appoint guardians *ad litem*. In tandem with the lawyer acting for the child, the system ensures that the child's interests are protected and his or her rights respected and upheld by the court.

Since the commencement of the Children Act 1989, you can expect guardians to be involved in proceedings concerning children, even at the stage of the application for an EPO (details of this order are in Chapter 6). The practical difficulty is one of resources, there not being sufficient suitably qualified people to act as guardians. In some parts of the country, this shortage is delaying proceedings.

Rules of court set out the functions of the guardian. The way in which the guardian works is by a process of investigation involving interviewing the local authority personnel, the child, the parents, relatives and any other persons the guardian considers relevant. The guardian then prepares a report stating what the guardian considers to be in the best interest of the child's welfare. This report must be made available to all parties to the proceedings in advance of the final hearing. The status of the guardian's recommendations we consider in Chapter 8: Reports.

The guardians have the advantage of s. 42, which provides that a guardian has the power to inspect any local authority or NSPCC records relating to the child who is the subject of the court proceedings. In addition, in *Re R (Care Proceedings: Disclosure)* [2000] 2 FLR 751, CA, the Court held that the guardian had a right to see a report compiled by the Area Child Protection Committee on the child's half sibling who had been killed by the child's father. Having inspected those records the guardian may take copies, and those copies shall be admissible as evidence both in the guardian's report and, if the guardian gives oral evidence, during the proceedings.

Your approach to the handling of any case must be carried out in the full knowledge that an officer of the court, the children's guardian, is possibly going to have the chance both to look at and produce in court all the records that you have made. More important, that person may be able to draw the court's attention to the fact that although you claim to have done a particular thing, there exists no record of this fact in your case notes. The moral of this is: accurately and comprehensively record all your actions and decisions as soon as possible after the events.

The children's guardian is clearly becoming a much more common feature of social work practice, within court proceedings, than has been the case in the past. (This does suppose that there will be sufficient resources in terms of personnel — a problem that is not adequately addressed by the Act.) A useful resource book on being a guardian is *Manual of Practice Guidance for Guardians ad Litem and Reporting Officers* (HMSO, 1995). We noted on p. 21 that in some proceedings the children's guardian will be called a 'litigation friend'.

CHILDREN AND FAMILY COURT ADVISORY AND SUPPORT SERVICE

The Children and Family Court Advisory and Support Service (CAFCASS) has been created by the Criminal Justice and Court Services Act 2000, ss. 11 to 17 and Sch. 2. It is designed to carry out the functions set out in s. 12 of that Act, i.e. to:

(a) safeguard and promote the welfare of children;
(b) give advice to any court about any application made to it in any family proceedings;
(c) make provision for the children to be represented in such proceedings; and
(d) provide information, advice and other support for children and their families.

CAFCASS — a non-departmental public body accountable to the Lord Chancellor — came into operation on 2 April 2001. It unites the Family Court Welfare Service (FCWO) (which advises the courts in private law cases), the Guardian *Ad Litem* (now to be known as children's guardian) and Reporting Officers Service and the Children's Division of the Official Solicitor's Department. This integration should allow guardians to be freed from the previous potential conflict of interest as they were funded and administered by local authorities. It also releases the FCWO from the control of the Home Office. In addition there is the potential for a national and child-focused service to assist the courts in making critical decisions about children which allows for a beneficial sharing of expertise. The new service will be responsible for the annual production of 45,000 reports impacting upon the lives of 65,000 children.

Generally the establishment of CAFCASS is welcomed by the relevant professional organisations, but there are some significant concerns. First, there are proposals to provide fixed fees for children's guardians which would in effect limit the amount of time that such guardians (who are self-employed) can spend on a case, with serious implications for the effectiveness of the service. Secondly, it is not clear what the relationship will be between the Community Legal Service and CAFCASS, and whether it will lead to the refusals of legal aid for solicitors to act for children as CAFCASS can be argued to provide a sufficient system of representation. It is also critical that the development of the organisation is compatible with the Human Rights Act 1998. It is not possible to give more information about the operation of CAFCASS until the detailed regulations and guidance appear. However, the website at www.open.gov.uk/lcd/cafcasfr.htm will provide these as they are published.

PROCESS AND PROCEDURES UNDER THE CHILDREN ACT

The Children Act 1989 is, as we have already seen, a very large and complicated document, and there are vast numbers of regulations and court rules that have been made under it. The philosophy of the Act aims to avoid court hearings by evolving a complex series of support mechanisms.

The social worker will find within their agency a whole series of procedures that are applicable to their own agency. These are based on the various regulations and guidance issued under the Act, together with local agreed practice. There are procedures to be undertaken before considering proceedings and at the stage when proceedings are to be begun.

In addition the local court also has its own ways of working. It expects not only the statutory forms to be completed and the time limits observed, but the local practices to be conformed with.

What you need to keep clear in your own mind is that the law can easily become clouded by practice and process. This should not be allowed to happen. For instance, it might be good practice when applying for an EPO (see Chapter 6) to supply the court with a written statement of the circumstances surrounding the case. This may develop in your local court to be routine. But neither the Act nor the rules *require* such a statement. It would be easy in these circumstances to come to believe that without such a statement you cannot apply for an EPO. If that were the case then practice and process would have obstructed the law.

A further example would be where the local court states that all EPOs are to be applied for on notice to all parties. Again this may be a good idea and good practice. But the Act and rules do allow for applications to be made without all the parties being notified. Again, what is good practice has obscured the law and should not be a straitjacket.

The Department of Health has produced a comprehensive pack of planning materials for 'Looked After Children and Young People'. It is an invaluable resource to ensure appropriate planning with participation, by input from the clients who are looked after. It encourages excellence in practice. However, it should be understood that these procedures do not change the law relating to children and young people. While the use of these procedures and resources should be standard good practice, they are not legal requirements. Under the Children Act a child or young person can be looked after whether or not the Department of Health guidelines are followed.

As a practising social worker you should constantly be asking yourself whether a particular step is required by the law, or whether it is just a matter of practice and process. Not that you should have bad practice; rather, be able to distinguish when that practice should be overridden to protect a child.

FIVE
The Protection of Children

At this stage of the book you may feel that the repetition of the statement that a social worker functions within a statutory framework is unnecessary. We do not think that a social worker can have that basic point reiterated too often.

We have already looked at the provisions of Part III of the Children Act 1989 (see Chapter 4). We have seen that these reflect the underlying philosophy of the Act: that children should be at home with their families and that the local authority, in partnership with the parents, provides a range of services to children in need to enable this to happen. This is the essence of protecting children according to the Act. In this chapter we are going to look at those cases where the local authority is required to go beyond that stage and to act in a more interventionist manner.

The majority of children will be safe and protected without anything but the smallest help from the local authority. Some children in need will require s. 17 support services. For a small number, who may make up a large part of a field social worker's workload, there is a requirement for the local authority to intervene more positively by seeking a court order. In saying that, it should not be forgotten that the supply of services to children in need is done with the overall aim of protecting children, both from actual harm and the over-anxious interference of the state, in the shape of the local authority.

This chapter will look at the steps that are required to protect children before and leading up to the beginning of court proceedings by a local authority. We shall consider:

(a) finding out whether a child may be at risk: investigations under s. 37 and s. 47;
(b) the process of investigation;
(c) the structures designed to protect children: *Working Together;* the child protection register; the child protection case conference; and
(d) protecting the child without a court order.

In the next chapter we shall look at how to protect a child with a court order.

FINDING OUT WHETHER A CHILD MAY BE AT RISK

The Powers of the Court under s. 37

In the course of any family proceedings not involving a local authority, a court may have legitimate reasons to be concerned about the care of children. If that is the case then the court can use the Children Act 1989, s. 37. This gives the court power to give directions to a local authority to investigate and consider whether care proceedings should be brought:

(1)   Where, in any family proceedings [i.e., other than care proceedings] in which a question arises with respect to the welfare of any child, it appears to the court that it may be appropriate for a care or supervision order to be made with respect to him, the court may direct the appropriate authority to undertake an investigation of the child's circumstances.

(2)   Where the court gives a direction under this section the local authority concerned shall, when undertaking the investigation, consider whether they should—

(a)   apply for a care order or for a supervision order with respect to the child;

(b)   provide services or assistance for the child or his family; or

(c)   take any other action with respect to the child.

(3)   Where a local authority undertake an investigation under this section, and decide not to apply for a care order or supervision order with respect to the child concerned, they shall inform the court of—

(a)   their reasons for so deciding;

(b)   any service or assistance which they have provided, or intend to provide, for the child and his family; and

(c)   any other action which they have taken or propose to take, with respect to the child.

(4)   The information shall be given to the court before the end of the period of eight weeks beginning with the date of the direction, unless the court otherwise directs.

(5)   The local authority named in a direction under subsection (1) must be—

(a)   the authority in whose area the child is ordinarily resident; or

(b)   where the child does not reside in the area of a local authority, the authority within whose area any circumstances arose in consequence of which the direction is being given.

(6)   If, on the conclusion of any investigation or review under this section, the authority decide not to apply for a care order or supervision order with respect to the child—

(a)   they shall consider whether it would be appropriate to review the case at a later date; and

(b)   if they decide that it would be, they shall determine the date on which the review is to begin.

This is a comprehensive section that has wide implications for the local authority. It gives the residual power to the court to require the state, via the local authority, to consider intervention in the affairs of a family. The court can exercise the power in any family proceedings and the use of these powers can lead to a supervision order, or indeed a care order, being made. For instance, if a court was considering an application for a divorce and became concerned about the welfare of the children, it could ask the local authority to undertake a s. 37 investigation.

The procedure is dealt with under r. 27 of the Magistrates' Court Rules and r. 26 of the County Court and High Court Rules. Before making a direction under s. 37, the court would deal with the main application before it. This would normally be by way of making an interim order pending the s. 37 investigation. It would then adjourn the hearing. A written direction is to be served on the local authority. If, after investigating, the local authority decides not to apply for an order (i.e. in accordance with s. 37(3) above) then it needs to inform the court in writing.

Even if a care or supervision application is not made, the local authority is still required to explain its actions, the reasons for non action, and its plans for the future. If the court makes a direction under s. 37, the court can appoint a guardian to act on behalf of the child.

Although it is possible to envisage circumstances in which the local authority and guardian may disagree over the course of action, it remains solely the choice of the local authority as to whether or not to apply for an order. If in those circumstances the court prefers to pay greater attention to the views of the guardian, which is to be expected, then the court cannot compel the local authority to make an application for a care order.

Interim Care or Supervision Orders Pending s. 37 Investigations
There are provisions in the Children Act 1989, s. 38, for making interim orders during the s. 37 investigations:

(1)   Where—
(a)   in any proceedings on an application for a care order or supervision order, the proceedings are adjourned; or
(b)   the court gives a direction under section 37(1),
the court may make an interim care order or an interim supervision order with respect to the child concerned.

This section, strictly speaking, is an exception to the principle that we have stated that no care or supervision order may be made without an application being made to the court. Under s. 37 of the 1989 Act, no application need be before the court for it to have the power to make an interim care or supervision order. Before you rush to consign the book to the dustbin, though, we can say that before a *full* care or supervision order can be made it is necessary for a local authority actually to make an application, so we can claim that our principle is intact!

If the court has ordered a s. 37 investigation and is thinking of making an interim care or supervision order, it must be certain, first, that the normal test for an interim order is satisfied. Section 38(2) states:

> (2)   A court shall not make an interim care order or interim supervision order under this section unless it is satisfied that there are reasonable grounds for believing that the circumstances with respect to the child are as mentioned in section 31(2) [i.e., the grounds for a care order — the likelihood of significant harm, the child beyond parental control].

The words 'reasonable grounds for believing' mean that the grounds do not have to be 'proved' before an interim order can be made, but merely that there have to be some grounds for believing that a full order may be made. The making of an interim order *does not* presuppose that a full order will be made.

We discuss this section further in Chapter 7.

Section 8 Residence Orders During or After s. 37 Investigation

An alternative course open to the court would be to make a s. 8 residence order. (For further discussion of these, see Chapter 16.) It has the power in any family proceedings to make a s. 8 order, even though it has not disposed of the main proceedings (s. 11(3)).

Time Limits

One of the practical difficulties is the requirement that the investigation under the Children Act 1989, s. 37, be completed within a period of eight weeks, unless 'the court otherwise directs'. The resource implications for s. 37 are immense, and in the absence of greatly increased resources the court may need to 'otherwise direct' in many cases!

The Local Authority's Duty to make Enquiries Where a Child may be 'At Risk' (s. 47)

Section 47 makes it clear that the main responsibility for the protection under the Act falls on local authorities. Section 47 provides as follows:

> 47.—(1)   Where a local authority—
>   (a)   are informed that a child who lives, or is found, in their area—
>   (i)   is the subject of an emergency protection order; or
>   (ii)   is in police protection, or
>   (iii)   has contravened a ban imposed by a curfew notice within the meaning of Chapter I of Part I of the Crime and Disorder Act 1998; or
>   (b)   have reasonable cause to suspect that a child who lives, or is found, in their area is suffering or is likely to suffer **significant harm**,
> the authority shall make, or cause to be made, such enquiries as they consider to be necessary to enable them to decide whether they should take any action to safeguard or protect the child's welfare.
>   (d2) [a requirement added by the 1998 Crime and Disorder Act.] In the case of a child falling within paragraph (a)(iii) above, the enquiries shall be commenced as soon as practicable and, in any event, within 48 hours of the authority receiving the information.

Working Together, para. 5.33 makes it clear that the objective of local authority enquiries conducted under s. 47 is to determine whether action is needed to promote and safeguard the welfare of the child or children who are the subject of the enquiries. The 'Framework for the Assessment of Children in Need and Their Families' provides a structure for helping to collect and analyse information obtained in the course of the s. 47 enquiry. *Working Together* stresses that this 'core assessment' is critical to the s. 47 enquiry process, and that it should be completed by the time of the child protection conference or within 42 days of the commencement of the assessment.

What this means is:

(a)   that the local authority has a duty to make enquiries which can be triggered by others taking action. (Being a duty means that the local authority has no option.) This can be by someone obtaining an emergency protection order (see p. 120), or the child being taken into police protection (see p. 132) or the child breaching a curfew order (see p. 117); and

(b)   that the local authority has an overall duty to make enquiries as soon as it has 'reasonable cause to suspect' the possibility of significant harm. This is relatively low-level threshold for triggering action, and clearly is lower than those in s. 38 (interim orders), or in ss. 44 and 46 (EPOs), which involve a compulsory intervention in the lives of both child and family (see Chapter 7). There has been inserted in the case of a breach of a child curfew order only, a requirement for the enquiries to be commenced as soon as practicable and, in any event, within 48 hours of the authority receiving the information. (It is difficult to see why this particular provision was inserted. Failure to start the enquiries within this timescale will presumably incur the wrath of the Secretary of State.)

The 'any action' referred to in this section may constitute applying for a court order or providing any form of support under Part III. *Working Together* emphasises that placing a child's name on the child protection register, or initiating care proceedings are not the only ways of protecting children. Providing access to a wide range of support services to help children in need is likely to be equally important.

Despite this emphasis, importantly s. 47(3) goes on to state that the enquiries should in particular be directed towards establishing whether the local authority should make any application to court. This reinforces the point that s. 47 actually requires the making of applications to court, if the conditions are satisfied.

In making its enquiries, the statute requires the local authority actually to see the child unless it is satisfied that it has sufficient information (s. 47(4)).

If in making the enquiries the local authority finds matters concerned with the child's education it is required to consult the relevant education authority (s. 47(5)).

Where the local authority does try to carry out this statutory duty and is refused access to the child, or is denied information as to the child's whereabouts, the authority is required to apply for an emergency protection order, a child assessment order, a care order or a supervision order unless satisfied that the child's welfare can be satisfactorily safeguarded without doing so (s. 47(6)). This requirement to make an application if access is refused, again, is a statutory duty, albeit that there is a narrow area of discretion.

Once the local authority has concluded its enquiries under s. 47 it has to consider what is to be done:

47.—(7)   If, on the conclusion of any enquiries or review made under this section, the authority decide not to apply for an emergency protection order, a child assessment order, a care order or a supervision order they shall—
(a)   consider whether it would be appropriate to review the case at a later date; and
(b)   if they decide that it would be, determine the date on which that review is to begin.

The section requires the local authority to be positive, even if not applying for an order.

Section 47(8) lays down the overriding statutory requirement for the local authority:

(8)   Where, as a result of complying with this section, a local authority conclude that they should take action to safeguard or promote the child's welfare they shall take that action (so far as it is both within their power and reasonably practicable for them to do so).

If it believes that proceedings are required, the local authority shall take proceedings. There is the slight qualification of 'so far as it is both within their power and reasonably practicable for them to do so'. This section does not only cover proceedings. If the local authority concludes as a result of its enquiries that the child needs some form of support, it must supply that support. If it fails to do so then its decision may be liable to judicial review.

The types of order that the authority could apply for are discussed in the next two chapters.

To assist with this investigation the local authority may have assistance from other bodies and authorities:

47.—(9)   Where a local authority are conducting enquiries under this section, it shall be the duty of any person mentioned in subsection (11) to assist them with those enquiries (in particular by providing relevant information and advice) if called upon by the authority to do so.
(10)   Subsection (9) does not oblige any person to assist a local authority where doing so would be unreasonable in all the circumstances of the case.
(11)   The persons are—
(a)   any local authority;

(b) any local education authority;
(c) any local housing authority;
(d) any health authority; and
(e) any person authorised by the Secretary of State for the purposes
of this section.

This responsibility is *additional* to the duty to take court proceedings and covers any form of action. We therefore have an overall picture of the requirement for the local authority to do all within its power to safeguard or promote the welfare of a child brought to its attention as being at possible risk. The aim of the legislation has been to avoid the local authority being put in a situation of saying 'we would like to do this but we do not have the legal power'.

This is merely emphasising the concept of 'diminishment of court proceedings' discussed in Chapter 4, which, in turn, is a reflection of the overall philosophy of the current law relating to children. This is that the local authority shall do all that is within its power to safeguard children and should apply for court orders only as a final and last resort, but always bearing in mind that it should apply for a court order if that is necessary.

THE STRUCTURES DESIGNED TO PROTECT CHILDREN

We now look at the framework (statutory and otherwise) that has been built up with the aim of protecting children. This framework has been assembled, piecemeal, as society's response to particular problems at particular times. The chapter does not set out to be a critique of that system; rather it is a straightforward exposition. This point is made because the system is not perfect and any practitioner will be able to locate faults and failings.

The main burden of protecting the child falls on the local authorities which exercise the social services function, as defined in the LASSA 1970. These are county councils, metropolitan councils and London borough councils.

Many professionals who you will encounter at child protection conferences will be unclear as to the statutory basis on which they are there, or the basis on which the conference was convened. They will also have different priorities regarding what they perceive as being the outcome of the process. Part of this is due to the historical development of such procedures, which we examined in Chapter 2, coupled with the lack of a single statutory source which can be consulted by all professionals to understand the structures and obligations.

The Present Structure
The child protection structure is not laid down in any one piece of legislation, nor by the decisions of the courts in common law; rather it has evolved through a series of reports, government circulars and individual decisions by local authorities. It needs to be understood that the legal power of a circular is less than that of a piece of legislation. To disregard a circular will not mean that the 'offender' has disobeyed the law but nevertheless circulars are powerfully persuasive. Failure to follow the circulars will provoke the ire of

the Department of Health and would no doubt bring financial penalties and the threat of the local councillors being removed from their elected offices, but there are no statutory penalties. This is in contrast to the default power of the Secretary of State under the Children Act 1989, s. 84, which clearly states the powers of the Secretary of State where a local authority fails to carry out its duties under the Act (i.e., its statutory duties).

Thus there is no mention in the Children Act of the child protection system as is set out below. Schedule 2, para. 4(1) merely says:

> Every local authority shall take reasonable steps, through the provisions of services under Part III of this Act, to prevent children within their area suffering ill-treatment or neglect.

We saw, above, the specific duty to make enquiries in s. 47. But nowhere in the Act will we find a detailed description of the child protection framework in which the local authority will carry out its duties. The one document that gives guidance is *Working Together*. This looks at the entire area of cooperation between agencies seeking to protect children. The original circular was issued at the same time as the Cleveland Report was released. It was the breakdown of cooperation between agencies that was at the heart of the Cleveland issue. *Working Together* seeks to overcome such difficulties. *Working Together* is issued under s. 7 of LASSA 1970 and should be treated as such (see p. 28). As previously mentioned, there is a helpful practice guide published in 1995 by the Social Services Inspectorate, *The Challenge of Partnership in Child Protection*, HMSO. As a practice guide it goes beyond setting out the strict requirements and shows how these may be implemented. It should be read along with *Working Together*, but it is not equally authoritative in law. The remainder of the chapter describes the system as set out in *Working Together* published in 1999.

A social worker dealing with children will spend a great deal of their time dealing with the child protection system, probably more than the time that they will spend in court. So what is the structure?

The Area Child Protection Committee This is more commonly referred to by its initials, ACPC. It is the framework underpinning the child protection system.

The ACPC will be established in each local authority area. The ACPC is an inter-agency forum for agreeing how the different services and professional groups should cooperate to safeguard children in their area, and for making sure that arrangements work effectively. The functions of the ACPC, as set out in *Working Together*, are as follows:

(a) to develop and agree local policies and procedures for inter-agency work to protect children, within the national framework provided by *Working Together* (this is done by the issuing of Local Procedural Handbooks, which are issued to hospitals, schools and other bodies who deal with children, setting out what is to be done in cases of suspected child abuse);

(b)   to audit and evaluate how well local services work together to protect children, for example through wider case audits;

(c)   to put in place objectives and performance indicators for child protection, within the frameworks and objectives set out in Children's Services Plans;

(d)   to encourage and help develop effective working relationships between different services and professional groups, based on trust and mutual under-standing;

(e)   to ensure that there is a level of agreement and understanding across agencies about operational definitions and thresholds for intervention;

(f)   to improve local ways of working in the light of knowledge gained through national and local experience and research, and to make sure that any lessons learned are shared, understood, and acted upon (these issues can arise from local inquiries or national inquiries, for instance the Laming Inquiry into the death of Anna Climbie);

(g)   to undertake case reviews where a child has died or, in certain circumstances, been seriously harmed, and abuse or neglect are confirmed or suspected; to make sure that any lessons from the case are understood and acted upon; to communicate clearly to individual services and professional groups their shared responsibility for protecting children, and to explain how each can contribute (details on the operation of case reviews are set out in Part 8 of *Working Together*);

(h)   to help improve the quality of child protection work and of inter-agency working through specifying needs for inter-agency training and development, and ensuring that training is delivered (this emphasises the key importance of training in tackling child abuse); and

(i)   to raise awareness within the wider community of the need to safeguard children and promote their welfare, and to explain how the wider community can contribute to these objectives.

ACPCs and Children's Services Planning   The responsibility of social services departments to produce a children's services plan is explicit in *Working Together*. The plans should 'look widely at the needs of local children, and the ways in which local services (including statutory and voluntary services) should work together to meet those needs' (*Working Together*, para. 4.7). The local authority should take a holistic view of how it can better promote the welfare of children; it should consider the roles played by education, housing, youth services, culture, leisure and other departments as well as social services, and produce a plan to which all local services are committed. ACPCs must contribute to the plan and work within its framework. ACPCs should have 'a clear role in identifying those children in need who are at risk of significant harm, or who have suffered significant harm, and in identifying resource gaps (in terms of funding and/or the contribution of different agencies) and better ways of working' (*Working Together*, para. 4.9).

ACPC Protocols   *Working Together* (para. 4.18) makes it clear that it is a major responsibility of the ACPC to put in place local protocols covering:

(a) how s. 47 enquiries and associated police investigations should be conducted, and in particular, in what circumstances joint enquiries are necessary and/or appropriate;

(b) quick and straightforward means of resolving professional differences of view in a specific case, e.g. on whether a child protection conference should be convened;

(c) attendance at child protection conferences, including quora;

(d) involving children and family members in child protection conferences, the role of advocates as well as including criteria for excluding parents in exceptional circumstances;

(e) a decision-making process for registration based upon the views of the agencies present at the child protection conference;

(f) handling complaints from families about the functioning of child protection conferences; and

(g) responding to children involved in prostitution.

As a field social worker you will not normally be involved with the ACPC, unless you have the misfortune to be caught up in a case review arising out of the serious injury or death of a child where child abuse has been suspected, as the ACPC has the responsibility, according to *Working Together*, for carrying out such reviews.

Statutory responsibility   There is a clear distinction between the local authority's statutory duty for the protection of children and that of the other agencies, which do *not* have statutory responsibilities. The local authority's duties are set out in the Children Act 1989, s. 47, which we discussed above.

The other agencies, such as health visitors, doctors or teachers, are, naturally, professionally concerned and involved but are not given any direct responsibility by statute.

It is within this context that the child protection conference functions. Just because the other agencies do not have statutory responsibilities does not mean that they should not cooperate with the local authority. The agencies other than the social services department, in circulars issued by their respective departments, are exhorted to provide cooperation with the local authority in respect of child protection.

Child protection register   The ACPC will monitor the information that comes from the child protection register (known variously as the 'at risk register' or often 'the abuse register'). The function of this register is often misunderstood. It is essentially a management tool that records the fact that a child has been or is suspected of being abused or is believed to be at risk of being abused. It should serve to 'ring alarm bells' when a professional faced with a new situation of proved or suspected child abuse consults the register on a later occasion. It will give them the details of previous incidents and inform them who are the professionals currently involved so that a full and adequate investigation can be carried out.

It is not a 'legal' document, it has no statutory force and of itself offers no 'real' protection, in that the mere act of placing a child's name on the protection register does not give any agency the legal grounds to take any action in relation to that child.

The maintaining of the register is normally carried out by a designated officer within the social services department, although in some parts of the country this function is carried out by the NSPCC. Access to the register is restricted to those professionals who are offering services direct to the child. There must be careful control over access to the information since there will normally be little or no judicial check on what the register contains. In the year ending 31 March 2000 about 30,300 children were on child protection registers, which represents 27 children per 1,000 of the population under 18 years of age. There were 29,300 registrations during that year, and 30,500 children were deregistered. Of the registrations, 44 per cent were as a result of neglect, which represents an increase on previous years. The proportion of children registered as a result of physical or sexual abuse has fallen. The proportion of child protection conferences not leading to registration has fallen to 25 per cent.

Entries on the child protection register   This does not mean that the register can be filled with unchecked gossip. Although the register is not a statutory device, the placing of a person's name on the register is capable of being reviewed, in exceptional circumstances, by the courts. In *R v Norfolk County Council ex parte M* [1989] 2 All ER 359 it was suspected that a plumber who had visited a child's house had indecently assaulted her and exposed himself to her. The case conference decided that his name should go on the register and that his employers should be told. He successfully claimed that there had been no adequate investigation and that it was an abuse of process, in those particular circumstances, to place his name as the abuser on the register.

Against this should be placed the decision in *R v Harrow London Borough Council ex parte D* [1990] 3 All ER 12, where the mother of children who were placed on the register sought judicial review of that decision. She complained that she had not had the chance to know the allegation against her even though she had made a written submission to the conference. The Court of Appeal refused to grant a judicial review. It held that in the circumstances of the case the council had to act fairly: 'In balancing the adequate protection for the child and fairness for the adult, the interest of the adult may have to be placed second to the needs of the child.' Whilst approving the decision in the *Norfolk* case, the court pointed out that the main failing there had been the informing of the employer, rather than, necessarily, placing the names on a register. Accordingly, every time, a decision to place a person's name on the register should be taken only after careful consideration.

Similarly, in *R v Lewisham London Borough* [1991] 2 FLR 185, the court held that where unproved allegations of sexual abuse were made against a foster parent, the authority must not adopt a policy of telling all future foster parents of the children who had been fostered that he was a sexual abuser. The council had to weigh in each case the interests of the children against the harm done to the foster parent. This again points to an approach of carefully checking all facts and making careful decisions about their disclosure. The results would have been different if the allegations were well founded and the social workers acted in good faith (*R v Devon County Council ex parte L* [1991] 2 FLR 541).

In *R v Hampshire CC ex parte H* [1999] 2 FLR 359, the Court of Appeal pointed out that while judicial review could be available in respect of decisions of child protection conferences, it would be rare for it to be the appropriate procedure, complaints procedures being more apt. However, the Court stressed the need for evidence to justify entering a name on the child protection register.

Child Protection Conference   This is the basic instrument of the case by case child protection system. It has a double purpose: (i) to make judgments about the likelihood of a child suffering significant harm in the future; and (ii) to decide whether future action is needed to safeguard the child and promote his or her welfare, how that action will be taken forward and with what intended consequences. It is the format in which the multi-disciplinary consideration of a child seen to be 'at risk' takes place. It is multi-disciplinary since at the conference there will (or should) be representatives from all the agencies who have dealings with the child, or the child's family. Its central role and its relationship with the other structures and legal obligations of the local authority in the protection of children are made clear in diagrammatic form in Appendix 5 of *Working Together*, reproduced at the end of this chapter. Amongst those represented at the conference may be:

(a)   *The social services department*:   The individual social worker, that social worker's team leader, other social workers who have had dealings with the case, those within the department who have special responsibilities for children.

(b)   *The local authority solicitor*:   The solicitor will not normally be a member of the social services department, and therefore may have a different perception to that of the social services department.

(c)   *The education department*:   The child's teacher, the child's head teacher (often it is only the headteacher who attends), the education welfare officer.

(d)   *The health authority*:   There will be people drawn from both the community-based health services (the general practitioner side) and, if relevant, the hospital-based services. From the community side there may be: the district nurse; the health visitor (in most cases the managers for these will also attend); the general practitioner. Then from the hospital side: the accident and emergency consultant; the paediatric consultant; the child psychiatrist, a particular consultant for a relevant specialism.

(e)   *The police authority*:   Members of the local child protection team (if such is established) or the investigating officer.

(f)   *The probation service*:   If the parent or other relevant member of the family has or has had dealings with the service.

(g)   *The family or carers of the child/young person and the child/young persons themselves*:   *Working Together* stresses the need for the involvement of the family concerned with the whole of the child protection procedures.

(h)   *Others*:   There may be a number of other persons who are present as they have an interest in the child being discussed. The NSPCC is an obvious example.

The relevant ACPC protocol should specify a required quorum for attendance and list who should be invited to attend. Accordingly, the child protection conference may well have an average attendance of 10, and on some occasions can have over 20 people present. Those attending should be there because they have a significant contribution to make, either because of professional expertise or from knowledge of the family, or both.

Terminology
One problem that you should be aware of in this area is that of terminology. In describing meetings to discuss the future of children there is no agreed vocabulary, there are no statutory definitions. So the same term is used by different people to mean different events.

Often you will find that an internal agency meeting about a particular case is referred to by some participants as a 'case conference'. An example of this occurs in the Jasmine Beckford Report where both an internal meeting and those involving all agencies are shown, in the appendix, as 'case conferences'.

Similarly, *Working Together* uses the term 'case review' to describe an investigation by the ACPC arising out of a child's death or serious injury. In practice, within agencies the term 'case review' tends to be used for internal reviews of particular cases. So the meetings that have to be held regularly by the regulations governing the handling of children in care tend to be called 'statutory reviews'.

Sometimes these internal discussions are called 'case discussions' or just 'reviews'. We cannot give any positive guidance, other than to encourage the use of a consistent terminology, preferably based on the national guidance contained in *Working Together*. Therefore we will use the expressions 'child protection conference' and 'the child protection review' as adopted by *Working Together* from here on.

The 'child protection conference' is used to describe the first inter-agency conference convened under the child protection procedures to share information about a particular child.

The 'child protection review' describes a subsequent meeting to review the particular child's case.

From your practical point of view, you need to be clear when attending a 'meeting' about a child what the meeting is and what its purpose is. When talking with others about such meetings do not assume that there is a common vocabulary — clarify everbody's understanding of particular words.

Form of Child Protection Conference
As we have shown, the child protection conference is multi-disciplinary. But the calling of the conference will be the direct responsibility of the social services department or the NSPCC, both of which have statutory powers.

The initial conference should be called only after an investigation under s. 47 of the Children Act 1989. In some local authority areas the maintenance of the child protection register is delegated to the NSPCC. Any other agency involved with the child should have their request for a conference dealt with as soon as possible.

The child protection conference will look at the child in question and recommend at the initial conference whether the child's name should be placed on the child protection register. The entry of a name can be in various categories, depending on whether or not abuse is known or suspected and whether the abuse is physical, sexual, emotional or neglect. The classifications are made for management purposes to give an overview of trends, if any.

The form and style of the conference will depend greatly on the person chairing the conference. *Working Together* states:

5.53   The initial child protection conference brings together family members, the child where appropriate, and those professionals involved with the child and family, following section 47 enquiries. Its purpose is:

- to bring together and analyse in an inter-agency setting the information which has been obtained about the child's health, development and functioning, and the parents' or carers' capacity to ensure the child's safety and promote the child's health and development;
- to make judgments about the likelihood of a child suffering significant harm in future; and
- to decide what future action is need to safeguard the child and promote his or her welfare, how that action will be taken forward, and with what intended outcomes.

This sets out the importance of planning for a child who is the subject of a s. 47 enquiry. The child protection conference agrees the child protection plan in outline. It is for the key worker and the core group (see p. 217) to develop the details.

Involving the child, the parents and other family members   Parents used to be systematically barred from child protection conferences and review meetings. The reason often given was that the people present would be inhibited from talking frankly. This was challenged, and the decisions of the European Court of Human Rights over the failure of local authorities to involve parents in the decision-making process were partly responsible for the changes in practice and procedure.

The current version of *Working Together* states:

5.57   Before a conference is held, the purpose of a conference, who will attend, and the way in which it will operate, should always be explained to a child of sufficient age and understanding, and to the parents and involved family members. The parents should normally be invited to attend the conference and helped fully to participate. Social services should give

parents information about local advice and advocacy agencies, and explain
that they may bring an advocate, friend or supporter. The child, subject to
consideration about age and understanding should be given the opportunity to attend if s/he wishes, and to bring an advocate, friend or supporter.
Where the child's attendance is neither desired by him/her nor appropriate,
the social services professional who is working most closely with the child
should ascertain what his/her wishes and feelings are, and make these know
to the conference.

5.58   The involvement of family members should be planned carefully. It
may not always be possible to involve all family members at all times in the
conference, for example, if one parent is the alleged abuser or if there is a
high level of conflict between family members. Adults and any children
who wish to make representations to the conference may not wish to speak
in front of one another. Exceptionally, it may be necessary to exclude one
or more family members from a conference, in whole or in part. The
conference is primarily about the child, and while the presence of the family
is normally welcome, those professionals attending must be able to share
information in a safe and non-threatening environment. Professionals may
themselves have concerns about violence or intimidation, which should be
communicated in advance to the conference chair. ACPC procedures
should set out criteria for excluding a parent or carer, including the
evidence required. A strong risk of violence or intimidation by a family
member at or subsequent to the conference towards a child or anybody else
might be one reason for exclusion. The possibility that a parent/carer may
be prosecuted for an offence against a child is not in itself a reason for
exclusion although in these circumstances the chair should take advice
from the police about any implications arising from an alleged perpetrator's
attendance. If criminal proceedings have been instigated the view of the
Crown Prosecution Service should be taken into account. The decision to
exclude a parent or carer from the child protection conference rests with
the chair of the conference, acting within ACPC procedures. If the parents
are excluded or are unable or unwilling to attend a child protection
conference, they should be enabled to communicate their views to the
conference by another means.

Note that parents and others can use the complaints procedure if they feel
they have not been treated properly by the conference; and they may also, in
more limited circumstances, use judicial review procedures or challenges
under the Human Rights Act 1998. Clear, fair and transparent procedures
are obviously vital.

In *Scott v UK* [2000] 1 FLR 958, the European Court of Human Rights
held that there had been no breach of the mother's rights under Article 8 of
the Convention when a local authority decided that as a result of her
continued alcohol problems, it would no longer plan to rehabilitate her with
her child. What is important here is that a broad view was taken of the
decision-making process. While the mother had not been present at the actual

meeting when the decision against rehabilitation was made, she had been involved in the overall planning process. The more you can involve the parents, the better the general process of decision-making is seen to be. In this way an individual procedural error can be remedied and human rights litigation avoided. Of course, parental involvement is important not just for human rights reasons, but also because participation increases the prospects of a successful intervention.

Confidentiality of child protection conference/reviews All discussions that take place within the child protection conference or review are intended to be confidential. Without total confidentiality the professionals attending will be unable to share frankly all their information and concerns. All professionals involved in child protection, including medical practitioners, have been informed by their appropriate professional bodies that their duty of confidentiality to their client/patient is overridden by their duty to contribute to the protection of a child at risk. Thus at a child protection conference or review there should be no difficulties about a frank exchange. *Working Together* states:

> 7.27 Research and experience have shown repeatedly that keeping children safe from harm requires professionals and others to share information; about a child's health and development and exposure to possible harm; about a parent who may need help to, or may not be able to, care for a child adequately and safely; and about those who may pose a risk of harm to a child. Often, it is only when information from a number of sources has been shared and is then put together that it becomes clear that a child is at risk of or is suffering harm.

> 7.28 Those providing services to adults and children will be concerned about the need to balance their duties to protect children from harm and their general duty towards their patient or service user. Some professionals and staff face the added dimension of being involved in caring for, or supporting, more than one family member — the abused child, siblings, an alleged abuser. *Where there are concerns that a child is, or may be at risk of significant harm, however, the needs of that child must come first. In these circumstances the overriding objective must be to safeguard the child* [emphasis added].

We have discussed above the duty under the Children Act to share information, whilst noting the limitations on that duty. It is clear that the courts could compel the details of the discussions at child protection conferences or child protection reviews to be revealed. You will recall from the discussion of confidentiality in Chapter 2 that in *Re M (A Minor) (Disclosure of Material)* [1990] 2 FLR 36, the court specifically excluded the records of the child protection conference. The court said:

> case conferences bring together people of different disciplines from the local community to discuss the protection and welfare of a child . . . For

them also the disclosure of the contributions made at a case conference and recorded may have adverse results and the possibility of such disclosure may even inhibit some from attending, an effect which could only be to the detriment of children in the community. Such records ought not to be lightly exposed to general scrutiny and the work for children jeopardised without careful and cogent reasons for their disclosure.

It is not clear whether those records of the conference or review are local authority records. If they are local authority records, then the children's guardian will be able to see them under s. 42. They will also be open to inspection by individuals under the Access to Personal Files Act 1987 (although that access may be refused on the grounds of the risk of serious harm being caused if they were revealed — see Chapter 9: Reports, for further discussion of this Act).

The questions of confidentiality and parental involvement within conferences are ever-changing. Many professionals feel acute personal dilemmas as they are unhappy about and unsure how to cope within a regime of more open decision-making. Most of the questions that are raised are ones of professional ethics and, as such, beyond the scope of this book. The law suffers from a lack of clarity but is increasingly pointing towards the concept of openness and participation, balanced by an appreciation of the Human Rights Act 1998.

Decisions at child protection conference   What must be appreciated, and often is not, is the fact that the child protection conference does not decide whether any statutory proceedings should commence in relation to a particular child. The conference can make a recommendation that proceedings are commenced but the responsibility for the actual decision and the commencing of the proceedings lies squarely with the local authority. It is conceivably possible for a local authority, having considered the recommendation of the child protection conference, to decide to reject the recommendations and not to commence proceedings. This would have to be when the local authority is satisfied that the child's welfare can be satisfactorily safeguarded without proceedings being commenced, in accordance with the Children Act 1989, s. 47(6). The same is true in relation to the placing of the child's name on the register. It must be stressed that not to follow the recommendation of the case conference would be a wholly exceptional circumstance.

A similar situation exists in relation to a decision to prosecute for a criminal offence arising out of the abuse of a child. The Home Office circular on this area, similarly called *Working Together,* stresses the fact that while the decision to prosecute or not should be taken in consultation with the child protection conference, nevertheless the responsibility will still rest with the police and then with the Crown Prosecution Service.

Key worker   The child protection conference, once it has decided that a child's name is placed on the register, will require that a *key worker* be appointed. The key worker is then required to draw up a plan that will address the concerns that have led to the child's name being placed on the register. The key worker will be either a local authority social worker or an NSPCC social worker.

5.75   When a conference decides that a child's name should be placed on the child protection register, one of the child care agencies with statutory powers (the social services department or the NSPCC) should carry future child care responsibility for the case and designate a member of its social work staff to be the key worker. Each child placed on the child protection register should have a named key worker.

5.76   The key worker is responsible for making sure that the outline child protection plan is developed into a more detailed inter-agency plan. S/he should complete the core assessment of the child and family, securing contributions from Core Group members and others as necessary. The key worker is also responsible for acting as lead worker for the inter-agency work with the child and family. S/he should co-ordinate the contribution of family members and other agencies to planning the actions which need to be taken, putting the child protection plan into effect, and reviewing progress against the objectives set out in the plan. It is important that the role of the key worker is fully explained at the initial child protection conference and at the core group.

Core group   Whilst at the early stages the child protection conference may need to be quite large, *Working Together* advises the appointment of a 'core group' once long-term planning has been formulated. This group would include the key worker and should work to implement and review the plan. Any major changes such as deregistration of the child should be taken back to the child protection conference. The core group can provide a much less intimidating forum for children and parents to work with the authority.

Other Child Protection Structures
It should not be assumed that the system outlined above is the only form of child protection. As has been made clear, the statutory duty on the local authority is the prime basis for protection. The obtaining of an emergency protection order under the Children Act 1989, s. 44, or the obtaining of a child assessment order under s. 43, can, and on many occasions does, take place without a child protection conference being convened. Indeed it would not be acceptable for a local authority to say that no action was taken because a conference could not be convened to 'approve' its actions. If you are a social worker faced with a situation of risk involving a child then you may well be required to take action on your own initiative without the opportunity to consult with senior management within your own department, let alone a child protection conference.

Similarly, there are also provisions for police officers to remove children to accommodation in an emergency, such action again to be taken without the elaborate consultation with a child protection conference. (Fuller details of these points of law are dealt with in Chapter 6.)

There are other ways of protecting the child, both by leaving the child at home or by providing other accommodation.

Protecting the Child without a Court Order

Leaving the child at home and providing support   This is perhaps the most difficult course of action to adopt as it is very risky. Something may go wrong and somebody is going to get the blame. Past experience shows who that person will be, namely, the social worker. There will always be a tendency, especially on the part of senior management, to 'play safe' by seeking some form of court order. Part of this pressure will come, inevitably, from lawyers, who will feel reassured by there being some form of court order.

Because a child has become the subject of the child protection procedures, this should not inevitably end in an application to the courts. What the social worker needs to bear in mind is the fact that any court order is not an end in itself, merely one of the possible options when looking at the overall welfare of the child. Lawyers, as explained in Chapter 2, will largely mark progress by moving from one court hearing to another, and may be concerned if there are no hearings. It is at this stage that the social worker has to ensure that the social work priorities do not become overwhelmed by the legal machine — the lawyers are there to help the social workers, not to tell the social workers what is to be done.

Under the Act there is the positive duty to consider leaving the child in the home situation, and providing assistance for that purpose should not be overlooked. It is part of the 'diminishment of court proceedings principle' that gives rise to this duty. Under the Children Act the provisions are carefully drawn to ensure that there should be few or no barriers to providing support to the child and his or her family within the home setting wherever possible. We must make it clear that even if a care order is made, this does not mean that the child has to be removed from the home (see Chapter 7).

We would again draw your attention to our comments from Chapter 4 when we were looking at the no order principle. Not going to court may be a good, positive step that safeguards and promotes the welfare of the child concerned. The decision not to go to court is one that should be taken only in an established definite manner, not as a drifting lack of response. There is an ever-present danger of thinking that 'the Children Act is about partnership and the no order principle and therefore we will not or cannot take any action'. This is the road that leads to ACPC case reviews!

Local authority accommodation   A further way of protecting children may be by providing accommodation through the local authority. This area is discussed fully in Chapter 11. At this stage we look at it only in outline as a way of protecting children.

Where a local authority provides accommodation without a court order, this *does not* mean that the child is in 'care'. The provision of accommodation does not affect the parental responsibilities of any person.

If a local authority is providing accommodation for a child the local authority is 'looking after' the child. The expression 'looking after' is not completely defined within the Act, but can cover both children subject to court orders and those who are not.

Section 20 places a duty on an authority to provide accommodation for a child for whom there is no one with parental responsibility or who has been abandoned, or where the person who has been caring for the child is unable to provide suitable accommodation or care.

The local authority also has power to provide accommodation for a child even though there is someone who is willing and able to provide accommodation, if the local authority considers that the provision of accommodation would promote the child's welfare. This is the power that may well be used to protect a child by removing the child from the unsatisfactory home setting.

The difficulty with this approach is that the provision of accommodation for a child under the age of 16 under this section is subject to parental consent. Without that consent no accommodation can be provided. If a child has been provided with accommodation and parental cooperation is withdrawn then, if you are seeking to protect the child, you should consider applying for an emergency protection order (see Chapters 6 and 11).

Refuges A final consideration is the use of refuges. As a child grows and develops it is almost inevitable that there will be some conflict between parent and child. It is part of the child's learning to become independent. In most cases that conflict can be dealt with in the family setting. Sometimes it leads to open hostility and dispute, with the child eventually leaving home.

Such decisions are often taken with no thought by the young person. In some circumstances such a course of action may well be the quickest way of avoiding continuing abuse. Whatever the circumstances, it is clearly a situation in which the young person can be at considerable risk, both physically and emotionally. In this situation you may wish to use a refuge for the young person.

In the absence of a court order parental responsibility will remain with at least the mother, if the parents are unmarried, or both parents, if they are married (s. 2). In normal circumstances, to assist a child to stay away from a person who has parental reponsibility would be an offence under the Child Abduction Act 1984, s. 2, or there may be an offence of abduction under the Children Act 1989, s. 49.

It will be understood that in the absence of a specific statutory exemption, anybody operating a refuge for such young people will be committing an offence. This is the purpose of s. 51 which provides that where the Secretary of State has issued a certificate in respect of a specific home designating it as a refuge then any person providing a refuge at that home will not commit an offence in relation to the abduction of children (s. 51(5) and (7)). It is possible for a local authority to arrange for a foster parent to provide a refuge, and to have that foster parent so designated by the Secretary of State (s. 51(2)).

The use of a refuge, as such, is not a regular method of dealing with young people by a local authority, but nevertheless it is a method of temporarily assisting the young person who wishes to leave home.

Table 5.1   Individual cases flow chart

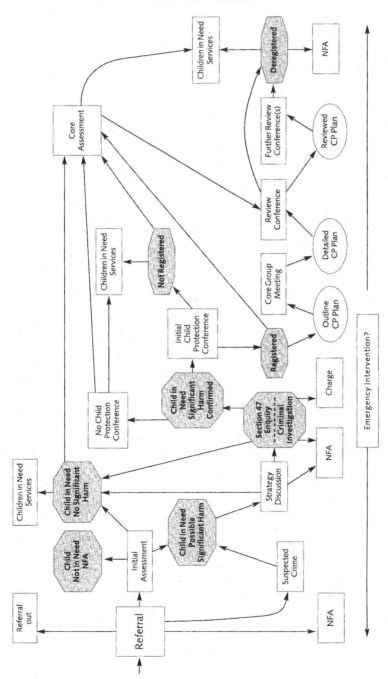

SIX

The Emergency Protection of Children

(Please note that all statutory references in this and the following chapter are to the Children Act 1989, unless otherwise stated. The acronyms 'EPO', 'CSO' and 'CAO' stand for emergency protection order, child safety order and child assessment order, respectively. The rules referred to are the Court Rules applicable to either the magistrates' court, or county court or High Court as explained on p. 56.)

By using emergency powers in the Children Act 1989, society is intruding into the essentially private world of the family. The only justification for such an interference is to protect vulnerable children. As a social worker you are required to use these powers in certain circumstances. That use will have a profound effect on the child involved, the child's family and on you. It is not the function of this chapter to examine those consequences. This does not mean that we are unaware of these consequences. We have borne in mind the following paragraph taken from 'The Cleveland Report':

> Those who work in this field must have an empathy with children and 'their feet on the ground'. They must be able to cope with the stress that is experienced by all who deal with these children. It should not be seen as a failure for some to take the sensible course of saying that he/she is not suited to do that sort of work.

We hope that the knowledge of the powers that you have will reduce the stress caused by uncertainty.

OVERALL STRUCTURE

We have discussed in Chapter 4 the powers to take steps to promote or protect the welfare of a child without taking proceedings, in accordance with the general 'diminishment of court proceedings principle'. In Chapter 5 we looked at the different areas of:

(a) finding out whether a child may be at risk: investigations under s. 37 and enquiries under s. 47;

(b) the process of investigation;

(c) the structures designed to protect children: *Working Together;* the child protection register; and the child protection conference; and

(d) protecting the child without a court order.

This chapter will look at what needs to be done when these procedures do not adequately safeguard and promote the welfare of the child and it is necessary to resort to an application for a court order.

TAKING ACTION

The legal framework provides three possibilities open to you when there is a child at risk:

(a) leaving the child at home and providing support;

(b) removing the child from the home on a temporary basis; and

(c) removing the child on a permanent basis.

All these approaches must be carried out in the overall context of the child protection system that is described in the previous chapter. Social workers do not function on an individual basis. You are always a member of a team, which includes not only the members of your area team, but higher management, and your agency lawyers. They are there to ensure that you can deliver the best possible service and protection to the child concerned. You will also have to work with other agencies.

Having stated that, it is absolutely essential that a social worker working within this area is completely familiar with the law that is applicable. A lack of knowledge of the legal basis on which you can operate will lead to a lack of confidence on your part and the inappropriate choice of course of action. Law should be used, in a positive, creative way, to ensure that the right decision is made, and not as a justification for avoiding making 'mistakes'.

LEAVING THE CHILD AT HOME AND PROVIDING SUPPORT

We have already discussed this course of action in the previous chapters. We repeat it in this chapter as a reminder, to ensure that the first reaction to a perceived risk is not an instant application for a court order since that would be inconsistent with the 'diminishment of court proceedings principle'.

That is not to say that court orders should never be sought. Section 47(8) states that if the authority concludes that a course of action would promote or safeguard a child's welfare then it *shall* take that action.

What the social worker has to bear in mind is the fact that any court order is not an end in itself, merely one of the possible options that should be used in the correct circumstances. It is the task of the social worker, with their colleagues and management, to ascertain what that correct moment is. Do not allow the social work priorities to be overcome by the legal machine nor allow the social work priorities to obscure what are the legal duties.

If the option of leaving the child at home without a court order is not going to provide adequate protection then you *must* look for alternatives. As will be seen, a child may be left at home even if the local authority has a care order (see Chapter 7).

There are two orders under the Crime and Disorder Act 1998 that may ensure that the child remains at home:

(a)   the sex offenders order (see page 303). This order is aimed more at the perpetrator than at the child. It nevertheless may offer some protection; and

(b)   the child safety order.

Child safety orders: Crime and Disorder Act 1998, s. 11

These are orders brought in by the Crime and Disorder Act 1998. Following pilots of the orders they became available nationally in June 2000. It has to be said that they can be viewed as being skewed more towards the punitive than to the welfare principle. They only apply to children under the age of ten. As a child under the age of ten cannot, in law, commit a criminal offence (see Chapter 12), the child safety order is now available. The grounds for imposing such an order are behaviour that would be criminal but for the child's age. It is the local authority with social services responsibility who has to apply for the order.

The grounds   Under s. 11(3) of the 1998 Act, the conditions for imposing a CSO are:

(a)   that the child has committed an act which, if he had been aged 10 or over, would have constituted an offence;

(b)   that a child safety order is necessary for the purpose of preventing the commission by the child of such an act as is mentioned in paragraph (a) above;

(c)   that the child has contravened a ban imposed by a curfew notice; and

(d)   that the child has acted in a manner that caused or was likely to cause harassment, alarm or distress to one or more persons not of the same household as himself.

'Offence' in s. 11(3)(a) means any criminal offence ranging from murder to dropping litter.

In our view s. 11(3)(b) may be subject to much legal argument. Imagine a committed litter dropper. There is no power within the CSO that would actually stop the child dropping litter. It follows that it can be argued that the CSO should not be made. More significantly it is difficult to imagine a scenario where a CSO is being genuinely considered where it would not be more appropriate to take proceedings under the Children Act. No doubt this is why only seven CSOs have been made between April 2000 and September 2001.

Section 11(3)(c) refers to a breach of a curfew notice imposed by s. 14 of the Crime and Disorder Act 1998.

Section 11(3)(d) is largely self-explanatory. It should be noted that the provision that specifies the person to whom harm, alarm or distress is caused or likely to be caused should not be of the same household. (Harassed parents cannot apply!)

The application for a CSO is to the Family Proceedings Court. These are not specified proceedings under s. 41 of the Children Act 1989 (see p. 89). This means that there will be no children's guardian appointed. They are, however, family proceedings under the Act (see p. 89). This means the court must apply the s. 1 principles set out in Chapter 4, such as the welfare principle, the no order principle and so forth. Before making an application the local authority must consider its duty under s. 17 of the 1989 Act as to whether the application will safeguard and promote the welfare of the child. In deciding to apply for a CSO, the local authority is not bound by the provisions of s. 37 of the Crime and Disorder Act 1998 (see Chapter 12). As will be seen, this is the provision that states that it is the principal aim of the youth justice system to prevent offending by children and young persons. A child under the age of ten is not within the youth justice system and cannot commit an offence.

What may be in the order?   Section 11(1) of the 1998 Act places the child under the supervision of a responsible officer (who will either be a social worker or a probation officer) for a minimum period of three months, or exceptionally up to 12 months. The court may specify any requirements which the court considers desirable in the interests of:

(a)   securing that the child receives appropriate care, protection and support and is subject to proper control; or
(b)   preventing any repetition of the kind of behaviour which led to the CSO being made.

The Act is silent on the actual requirements. The guidance issued by the Home Office (see H. Brayne and G. Broadbent, *Social Work and the Law: Cases and Materials*, OUP, to be published 2002, Chapter 8) gives examples, such as:

- attendance at school or extra curricula activities such as sporting activities or homework clubs;
- avoiding contact with disruptive and possibly older children;
- not visiting areas, such as shopping centres, unsupervised;
- being home during certain hours, probably the evenings; or
- attending particular courses/sessions to address specific problems (for example educational support, behavioural management).

The procedure for making a CSO   Section 12 of the Crime and Disorder Act 1998 imposes specific requirements on the court before it can make an order. The court must:

(a)   obtain and consider information about the child's family circumstances and the likely effect of the order on those circumstances (this
information can be either in oral or written form);

(b)   explain to the parent or guardian of the child in ordinary language—

(i)   the effect of the order and of the requirements proposed to be
included in it,

(ii)   the consequences which may follow if the child fails to comply with
any of those requirements, and

(iii)   that the court has power to review the order on the application
either of the parent or guardian or of the responsible officer (this normally
would be done at court, although the draft guidance does suggest that it could
be done in the form of a letter sent by the court); and

(c)   avoid, as far as practicable, imposing requirements which would either
conflict with the parent's religious beliefs, or interfere with the times at which
the child normally attends school.

When making a CSO the court could make a parenting order under s. 9 of
the Crime and Disorder Act 1998 (see p. 258).

Variation, discharge and breach of the CSO   While the order is in force, the
responsible officer or the parent may apply to discharge or vary the order. Any
provisions can be taken out or be added. The guidance states that it is not
possible to extend the length of time of an existing order. It is not clear how
the guidance comes to this conclusion.

There is a startling power following a breach of a CSO contained in
s. 12(6) and (7) of the Crime and Disorder Act 1998. If the responsible
officer applies to the court and satisfies the court that any requirement in the
CSO has been breached, the court may discharge the order and substitute a
care order under s. 31 of the Children Act 1989. In making a care order in
these circumstances, s. 12(7) of the 1998 Act specifically states that the
threshold criteria in s. 31 *do not* have to be satisfied.

The point at which the court decides that the care order route is appropriate is the point at which the proceedings become specified proceedings. As
soon as practicable after that point the court should consider the appointment
of a children's guardian and the need to draw up a care plan.

REMOVING THE CHILD FROM THE HOME ON
A TEMPORARY BASIS

There are six possible ways in which this can be brought about:

(a)   with consent of the parent;

(b)   by obtaining an emergency protection order (EPO) (s. 44);

(c)   by obtaining a child assessment order (s. 43);

(d)   by the police removing the child to suitable accommodation (s. 46) or
under a child recovery order (s. 49);

(e)   by obtaining an interim care order (s. 38); and

(f)   by obtaining a care order (s. 33).

This chapter will concentrate on the first four options. For full consideration of the interim care order and care order please see Chapter 7.

Emergency Protection Order (s. 44)
An EPO is a short-term order that either:

(a)   removes the child on a short-term basis; or
(b)   allows the child to be kept in a place of safety (for instance, a hospital); or
(c)   requires the alleged abuser to leave the family home (see p. 123).

Table 7.1   Key features of the Emergency Protection Order

Feature	Provision	Section	Note
Grounds	Child likely to suffer significant harm or cannot be seen where child is at risk of suffering significant harm.	s. 44(1)	See full discussion of signficant harm in Chapter 7, p. 136.
	Must apply the welfare principle and the non-intervention principle but not the welfare checklist.		
Duration	8 days possible extension for additional 7 days.	s. 45(3), (5)	Could be for a shorter period.
Discharge	Certain persons may be able to apply for discharge between 72 hours after commence-ment of order and 8 days.	s. 45(8), (9)	Cannot apply during extension of EPO.
Parental responsibility	Grants a very limited parental responsibility to the local authority.	s. 44(4)	
	The parent of the child does not lose parental responsibility.		

Feature	Provision	Section	Note
Directions	Court has the power to order contact, medical and/or psychiatric reports assessment etc.	s. 44(6)	
Emergency	The EPO may be made by a single justice with the leave of the clerk if the parents are not alerted to the proceedings.	Family Proceedings Court (Children Act 1989) Rules rr. 2(5), 4(6)	The order should be made by a full court if possible. Decisions about whether to inform parents about the application must bear in mind any danger to the child(ren) involved.
Child	Must be named or described as clearly as possible.		

The EPO may be granted for a period of up to an initial eight days, extendable, once only, for a period of up to a further seven days. These are the maximum periods allowed. It may well be that the court will decide that the order should last for a shorter period.

Such an order is not an end in itself. It is to be seen as a step in the local authority's investigation under s. 47 which will lead to the local authority being satisfied about the child's welfare or will lead it to begin care proceedings.

The different forms of EPO   The EPO is not designed to be granted without careful consideration of the grounds by the court. There are two forms the applications can take:

(a) *The any person basis under s. 44(1)(a).*   Here, the court, on the application of any person, may grant an order if a version of the significant harm test is satisfied. (This is the first time we have come across the 'significant harm' test. It is the basis for all orders that give control over a child to an agency. For a full discussion of the meaning of significant harm, please see Chapter 7: Care and Supervision Orders.) Where any person applies to it, the court may grant an EPO only if the court is satisfied that there is reasonable cause to believe that the child is likely to suffer significant harm unless removed to accommodation provided by the applicant or unless allowed to remain in present accommodation.

The 'any person' may include a social worker. This type of application is designed to cover situations where perhaps a social worker is notified of a child with severe injuries and feels that the child should be removed from home for the protection of the child. The ground is that the child is *likely* to suffer significant harm. That means that there appears to be a possibility that the harm will be repeated — so a 'one-off' incident cannot be a ground for granting an EPO under this subsection. The applicant has to satisfy the court that there are reasonable grounds for believing that the child is likely to suffer significant harm. The social worker or other applicant has to be able to put evidence before the court that will satisfy the court as to this likelihood.

Alternatively, the 'any person' EPO envisages the situation where a child has been admitted to hospital and the parents are threatening to remove the child, and the court believes the removal would be likely to cause the child significant harm. It would be possible to make an application where a child is being looked after by a local authority in accommodation and the parents are again threatening to remove the child.

(b)   *The investigation basis under s. 44(1)(b).*   Here, if the investigations of a local authority or the NSPCC are obstructed then the court may grant an EPO without being satisfied on the significant harm test — but, like the CAO (discussed below), *the applicant* has to be satisfied there is a risk of significant harm. Under this subsection an EPO will be granted only where access, for the purposes of investigation, is being unreasonably refused.

An application under s. 44(1)(b) is to be made by the local authority only as part of a continuing investigation under s. 47. That is the investigation the authority or NSPCC has to carry out when it has reasonable cause to suspect that a child is suffering or is likely to suffer significant harm. (This again reminds of the need for the social worker to keep careful case notes of their actions, since it would seem perfectly reasonable for the court to ask what steps had been taken under s. 47, and in the absence of being satisfied, it will be reluctant to grant an EPO.)

An order may be granted in the absence of the parents (i.e. without notice of the hearing), but as with the child assessment order there are provisions for the parents to seek to have the order discharged under s. 45(8). At that stage it would be possible for the parents to state that access will be granted and, if the statement is believed by the court, for the basis of the local authority application to be totally undermined. The court would need to be satisfied that the access was being unreasonably refused by the parent. The court would have to ask whether this parent was, in all the circumstances, being unreasonable. The local authority would have to show that access was required as a matter of urgency. An application on these grounds may be simpler to obtain than one where you have to satisfy the court that the child is actually suffering significant harm.

Common elements between these different forms of EPO   Even though the court may be satisfied that the grounds for an EPO exist, it still need not grant one, for it has to apply the 'welfare' principle and the 'non-intervention' principle which are contained in s. 1. This means that it has to be satisfied that the order is in the best interests of the child and necessary for its protection. It does not have to consider the welfare checklist in s. 1. Presumably, the justification for the exclusion of the welfare checklist is that there is not the time to collect the necessary evidence.

The various safeguards in this section all point to the need for the social worker to be adequately prepared before rushing off to seek an EPO. Adequate preparation means that you will need to have answers ready for all the points that the court requires: the grounds (harm or obstruction of your investigation), the welfare of the child and the need to intervene.

What may be contained in an EPO   An order does not give the applicant an unfettered licence in respect of the child. Looking at the relevant subsections, in turn, s. 44 states:

(4)   While an order under this section ('an emergency protection order') is in force it—
     (a)   operates as a direction to any person who is in a position to do so to comply with any request to produce the child to the applicant;
     (b)   authorises—
          (i)   the removal of the child at any time to accommodation provided by or on behalf of the applicant and his being kept there; or
          (ii)   the prevention of the child's removal from any hospital or other place in which he was being accommodated immediately before the making of this order; and
     (c)   gives the applicant parental responsibility for the child.
(5)   Where an emergency protection order is in force with respect to a child the applicant:
     (a)   shall only exercise the power given by virtue of subsection (4)(b) in order to safeguard the welfare of the child;
     (b)   shall take, and shall only take, such action in meeting his parental responsibility for the child as is reasonably required to safeguard or promise the welfare of the child (having regard in particular to the duration of the order); and
     (c)   shall comply with the requirements of any regulation made by the Secretary of State for the purpose of this subsection.

Not to produce the child is a criminal offence (s. 44(15)). If you have such an order and ask for the child to be produced and he or she is not produced, you must draw the person's attention to the explanatory notes attached to the order and warn them that failure so to do will render them liable to criminal proceedings.

If the child is produced then you may take him or her to, and/or keep him or her in, accommodation.

Power to exclude alleged abuser   The Family Law Act 1996 amended the Children Act to include s. 44A — a power in EPOs to require an alleged abuser to leave the house in which the child is living. The court would have to be satisfied of the following:

(a)   that there is reasonable cause to believe that if a person is excluded from a dwelling house in which the child lives, the child will cease to suffer or cease to be likely to suffer significant harm; and

(b)   another person living in the same house, whether or not a parent, is able and willing to give to the child the care which it would be reasonable to expect a parent to give; and

(c)   that person consents to the inclusion of the exclusion requirement.

There are also powers of arrest available, subject to certain requirements. The difficulty with this power is that it does require the consent of the person who is to care for the child. This would normally be the mother. In the absence of her consent it is not possible to compel the alleged abuser to leave. While this power is a welcome addition to an EPO, the requirement of consent means it is not the answer in all circumstances. Note that an identical power to exclude an alleged abuser exists in relation to interim care orders (see p. 146).

In *Re W (Exclusion: Statement of Evidence)* [2000] 2 FLR 666, FD, the judge set out guidance on the relevant procedure. While it is not necessary for the local authority to make a specific application, there does need to be a separate statement of evidence supporting the case for an exclusion require-ment. The consent can be given orally in court, or in writing. If it is in writing, it should clearly state that the person giving consent understands the provision.

(See Chapter 16 for discussion of how the law deals with domestic violence.)

Limited power of removal under EPO   The power to remove the child is to be used only where it is necessary to safeguard the welfare of the child. This means that if you have obtained an order and then go to the house and find the child is safe, you are not permitted to remove the child.

It is easy to imagine an extreme case where this might be applied: you receive an anonymous telephone call stating that it sounds as if a child is being beaten to death in a certain house. You go to the house, knock on the door, get no answer but hear the sounds of a child sobbing and screaming. You knock next door and are told that there is a child in the house and that 'they are an odd lot'. You go to court and are granted an EPO under s. 44(1)(b) (on the grounds that you are investigating and your investigation is being obstructed). You go to the house with the EPO, a surprised parent opens the door holding a cheerful, smiling toddler with no visible signs of injury. The parent readily agrees to you examining the child undressed and there are no signs of injury. When asked about the noise of crying, the parent says that they were listening to a play on the radio, about a child-beating case, which may explain the sounds, and they had the radio up very loud and therefore your knocks were not heard. End of case and clearly s. 44(5)(a) applies and you would have no grounds for the removal of the child, despite holding the EPO.

Most cases are not as clear-cut as that and it is to be expected that the workings out of this particular subsection in practice may be difficult. The only sensible advice is to err on the side of caution and not be afraid to remove the child if in doubt. To assist you in making the decision, as to whether removal is necessary, you may want to have the assistance of some other professional person when you go to the house. In these circumstances you may ask the court to make a direction under s. 45(12), which states that the court may direct that the applicant may be accompanied by a doctor, nurse or health visitor, if the applicant so chooses.

Parental responsibility under an EPO   The local authority, or whoever was the applicant, will also have parental responsibility, but this does not mean that the parent of the child loses parental responsibility. The exercise of parental responsibility under an EPO in accordance with s. 44(5) means that only steps that are reasonably required during the order (which will be eight, or at the very most 15, days) may be taken by the person with temporary parental responsibility. This does not mean that a child may have their school permanently changed, only temporary educational provision made. It does not mean that a child may be allowed to undergo a cosmetic surgery operation, but would allow for an emergency operation.

'*Religious objections to treatment*'   The position of children of Jehovah's Witnesses and parents with similar religious objections to treatment needs particular mention. In the first case reported under the Children Act of a child needing a blood transfusion (*Re S (A Minor) (Medical Treatment)* [1993] 1 FLR 376), the local authority did not apply for an EPO but made the child a ward of court. Although commentators agreed that there was no need to do this, the court agreed to the order in wardship and made no reference to the powers under an EPO. In *Re R (A Minor) (Blood Transfusion)* [1993] 2 FLR 757, Booth J stated that the use of an EPO in such cases was not appropriate. Either the inherent jurisdiction of the High Court should be used, or the local authority should apply under s. 8 to a High Court judge.

Contact and medical examinations during an EPO (s. 44(6))   There is a general presumption that the parent will have reasonable contact with the child whilst an EPO is in force, unless a direction under s. 44(6) is made.

Medical examinations are allowed only for purposes that promote or safeguard the welfare of the child. This means that any examinations required for the purpose of preparing your case prior to applying for a care order would not be permitted unless you have the additional power contained in s. 44(6).

This subsection sets out the directions that the court can make at the time of granting the order. The court may decline to make any directions under this subsection. The directions which can be given cover:

(a)   the contact which is, or is not, to be allowed between the child and any named person;
(b)   the medical or psychiatric examination or other assessment of the child.

The question of medical examinations is further dealt with in s. 44(7) and (8), which provide:

(a)   that a child may give informed consent to any medical examination;
(b)   that the court may order that there should be no medical or psychiatric examination, or that such an examination *shall take place only if further permission* is obtained from the court.

It needs to be noted that if you are seeking an EPO and you or your agency feels that there may be the need for some form of medical examination, then you should, at the time of the application, seek a direction from the court.

There may be some lawyers who would argue that in the absence of any directions it would be possible under the powers of parental responsibility to have an examination carried out. Our advice, nevertheless, is to seek a direction from the court. If it is not sought at the time of the initial application and it is decided that such an examination ought to be carried out then a direction should be sought under the provisions of s. 44(9). This point of view is reinforced by rule 18(1)of the relevant court rules, which states:

No person may, without leave of the court, cause the child to be medically examined or psychiatrically examined or otherwise assessed, for the purposes of the preparation of expert evidence for use in the proceedings.

Section 44(9) deals with applications to vary the order whilst it is still in force. If directions have been made about either contact with parents or other people, or medical examinations, then an application can be made to vary these.

Returning the child before the EPO expires   Given the drastic effect of an EPO, the Act contains various provisions to mitigate the disruption caused to the child and family.

The first requires that although an EPO may have been granted, the child should be kept away from 'home' only as long as is required, and if it is safe the child should be returned 'home'. Section 44(10) states that:

(10)   Where an emergency protection order is in force with respect to a child and—
(a)   the applicant has exercised the power given by subsection (4)(b)(i) [removed a child] but it appears to him that it is safe for the child to returned; or
(b)   the applicant has exercised the power given by subsection (4)(b)(ii) [prevented the child from being removed from accommodation] but it appears to him safe for the child to be allowed to be removed from the place in question,
he **shall** return the child or (as the case may be) allow him to be removed.

This means that if the danger is over the child is returned. In the case of a child needing the emergency operation, once the operation takes place then the child should be 'returned' (albeit that the child may stay in hospital).

In the sphere of inter-disciplinary working this subsection can cause a few problems. Suppose a girl was removed by an EPO because she was allegedly being sexually abused by her father. If the father was then arrested and remanded in custody, this subsection states that she should be returned to her home — assuming that the father's alleged sexual abuse was the only basis of the application.

Once it is safe to return the child, then, you *must* do so. You can return the child to a different person — not the parent, not the person caring for the child at the time of the EPO — only with the court's permission (s. 48(11)).

We hope that good use is being made of this duty to return in s. 44(11). Although there is a need for the normal caution required when dealing with children's lives, it must not be excessive. If there is no need to keep the child, the Act says the child should be returned.

It should be of some reassurance to know that the returning of a child under this subsection does *not* bring the EPO to an end. This is provided for in s. 44(12) which states that if, having returned the child, at any time whilst the order is still in force, it appears to the applicant that the child should again be removed, then that can be done. This is without the need for a fresh application. So suppose the parent of the child who had the emergency operation did try to remove the child from the hospital against medical advice, the current EPO would give the power to stop this. If the father charged with sexual abuse, having been remanded in custody by the magistrates, was granted bail by a Crown Court judge, and was returning to the family home, the girl could be removed under the current EPO. In the situation outlined, it may be worth considering having a power of exclusion attached to the EPO.

Applications to discharge an EPO   The next 'check' on the EPO is the right of the parent to challenge the order. This right of challenge is not total. The relevant section is s. 45.

The right to apply for a discharge is not available for the first 72 hours of an EPO. Neither does it apply for a parent who was present at the hearing of the application for the EPO (i.e., was given the chance to put their side of the case to the court). Such a parent has no right to seek to have the order discharged at any time.

Similarly there is no right to have an order discharged after that order has been extended. This is because rule 4 of the relevant court rules requires that an extension application take place only after notice has been given to all parties. So again, the parents will have had their chance to put their side of the case.

The application to discharge the order can be made by the child (through his or her guardian, see Chapter 4) or the child's parents.

We have almost completed looking at the EPO and its workings but before making some practical points we need to look at s. 45(10) which provides:

(10)   No appeal may be made against the making of, or refusal to make, an emergency protection order or against any direction given by the court in connection with such an order.

This point was clearly made in *Hounslow London Borough Council* v *A* [1993] 1 FLR 702 and *Re P (Emergency Protection Order)* [1996] 1 FLR 482.

The Act therefore only allows for any particular EPO to be discharged, not to be appealed against. This would not exclude an application for judicial review if the circumstances were appropriate. A suitable example of this would be where the notice of an extension hearing was not given in accordance with the rules of court but the court nevertheless went ahead and granted the extension. In these circumstances an affected party can seek judicial review of the action of the court. If the EPO was made by the High Court, there can be no judicial review of that decision.

Additional powers to protect children   Section 48 of the Children Act gives additional powers which you should consider. For instance, you may not know exactly where the child is who may be in need of emergency protection. The court may include a provision in the EPO requiring a person who may have information about the child's whereabouts to disclose that information (s. 48(1)). The order may also authorise an applicant to enter premises and search for the child, although this section in any event requires that the parents or whoever is in control of the premises cooperates. If you are prevented from entering premises or gaining access to the child, or it appears to the court that you may be, the court can issue a warrant authorising the police to assist the entry and search.

You may believe that there are other children on the premises who also ought to be the subject of an EPO. If so, you may seek an order authorising a search for them. If the child is found and you are satisfied that the grounds for an EPO exist, the order authorising the search has effect as if it were an EPO. This is useful when you are not able to identify all the children in the family, or, for instance, where there is evidence of the existence of a paedophile ring but the number and identities of the children involved are unknown.

Lastly the Act gives you powers through the mechanism of recovery orders (s. 50) in respect of a child in care, or the subject of an EPO or in police protection, where the child has unlawfully been taken away, has run away or is staying away from the 'responsible person'. A responsible person is anyone who has the care of the child by virtue of a care order or an EPO. The order operates as a direction to produce the child, or to disclose his or her whereabouts, and authorises a constable to enter named premises and search for the child, using reasonable force if necessary.

Practical considerations for EPOs

(a)   *Record-keeping*:   There is a clear need for meticulous record-keeping on the part of the social worker involved so that the evidence of the investigation, which is one branch of the grounds for an EPO, can be shown, together with the details of obstruction by the parents that would be required.

(b)   *Before taking action*:   Whatever the situation is in which you intend seeking an EPO, always stop to think clearly about why you want an EPO and what you are going to do with it. Always try and consult with a colleague, even if your particular management guidelines allow you to take such steps without consultation.

(c) *Refusal of an EPO*: If an EPO is refused then, in principle, there does not appear to be any bar to making another application. This is particularly true if further information becomes available concerning the likelihood of potential harm to the child.

(d) *Identification*: A small practical point is that under s. 44(3) a person seeking access to a child for an investigation shall produce some duly authenticated document stating that they are authorised to seek access. All local authority social workers are such authorised persons. Failure by you to produce such proof, if asked for, is just the sort of point that a lawyer acting for a parent would love to have as an opening question in cross-examination. The mere failure to have identification does not on its own prevent you obtaining the order, but it makes you look less professional to the court.

Also, the explanatory notes that are part of the statutory form of the EPO have a box telling the parent to ask anyone who tries to carry out the order for evidence of their identity.

(e) *Out of hours applications*: The expression 'court' would normally mean just that, a court sitting in a courtroom of some description. The magistrates' courts' rules allow a single justice (magistrate) to hear an application (rule 2(5)). If the hearing is to be made without notice, leave of the clerk to the justices has to be obtained (rule 4(4)). Therefore, in applying out of the normal court time for an order, the applicant needs to contact the justices' clerk first, if the hearing is to take place without the parents.

Time limits Before leaving this section, some comment has to be made about the difficulties of the time constraints imposed by the provisions relating to the EPO. Fifteen, let alone eight, days is a very short period of time, particularly for lawyers and courts. Given the chance for parties to seek a discharge of the order and to seek contact with the child, the entire time between the granting and expiration of the order could be occupied with court hearings instead of carrying out the intended assessment.

To set this in some context, we reproduce below a list of possible tasks following an EPO (this, slightly modified, is taken from *Blackstone's Guide to the Children Act 1989*):

(a) Arrange for accommodation for the child.

(b) Place the child with foster parents or in an institution, and explain to the child what is happening and give sufficient information to those who will be caring for the child to do so appropriately.

(c) Explain to the parents why their child has been removed from them, and discuss concerns and allegations with them.

(d) Spend further time with the child, to be satisfied that the child's welfare is being met, and also ask the child about any concerns or allegations.

(e) Take the child for medical examination and/or treatment, and obtain the doctor's diagnosis, having obtained leave of the court, if required.

(f)   Make decisions about who the child should be allowed to have contact with (from those listed in s. 47(11)).

(g)   Arrange for such contact to take place.

(h)   Instruct the authority's solicitor in time for extension hearings. Consider making application for directions governing contact or medical examination. Instruct the local authority solicitor to commence appropriate proceedings, and provide sufficient information for the solicitor to do so.

(i)   Discuss the case with a children's guardian if one has been appointed.

(j)   Convene a child protection conference, trying to get a sufficient number of those involved with the family to attend.

(k)   Keep under review whether it is safe to return the child home.

(l)   Decide, with senior social work staff, whether action needs to be taken to promote or safeguard the child's welfare.

(m)   Attend court in respect of an application for an interim care order.

Child Assessment Order (s. 43)

This provision allows the local authority to obtain an order for compulsory assessment of the child's state of health and development, if need be by removing the child from the home. It was introduced at a very late stage in the Bill's passage through Parliament. Prior to its introduction the Government had stated that it was against the idea of such orders. It would probably be better called a child investigation order, since it allows only a limited amount of assessment. The figures from the Annual Reports on the Children Act show that the order has not proved very popular.

The CAO can trace its history back to the Kimberley Carlile report. In that case the social worker was prevented by the stepfather from seeing Kimberley. There were doubts as to whether or not the legal powers then available were sufficient. The report recommended the institution of an order such as the CAO.

We have placed it in this chapter even though, strictly speaking, it is not an emergency order. It is intended that the order be applied for in an ordinary court and with the parents being represented. It is not available on a 'without notice' basis (that is without giving seven days' notice of the application in advance). What then does it provide?:

(1)   on the application of a local authority . . . for an order under this section, the court may make the order if, but only if, it is satisfied that—

   (a)   the applicant has reasonable cause to suspect that the child is suffering, or is likely to suffer, significant harm;

   (b)   an assessment of the state of the child's health or development or of the way in which he has been treated, is required to enable the applicant to determine whether or not the child is suffering, or is likely to suffer, significant harm; and

   (c)   it is unlikely that such an assessment will be made, or be satisfactory, in the absence of an order under this section.

(2)   . . .

(3)   A court may treat an application under this section as an application for an emergency protection order.

(4)   No court shall make a child assessment order if it is satisfied—
    (a)   that there are grounds for making an emergency protection order with respect to the child; and
    (b)   that it ought to make such an order rather than a child assessment order.

To obtain an order you need to show to the court not that, objectively speaking, the child *is* at risk, but that you have reasonable cause to believe the child is at risk. Then you must show that an assessment of health and development is required to actually find out whether the child is suffering or is likely to suffer significant harm. Having satisfied the court of this you then have to show that you could not make a satisfactory assessment without the order.

Whenever there is a child at risk the question of whether or not the child would be safe if left in his or her home will be uppermost in most people's minds. The Act deals with this in this particular section by stating that the court shall not make a child assessment order if it thinks that the child *should be* removed from the home. This would be done by means of an emergency protection order (EPO) which we discuss above.

If there are no grounds for making an EPO then the court may grant the application for the CAO. This 'fail safe' measure may explain why the courts are reluctant to grant a CAO, preferring to grant an EPO. We suspect that such an attitude prevails with senior management within local authorities.

In some circumstances, though, it may well be that there are just no grounds for an EPO until after an assessment order is granted.

Just as the CAO is not intended to be dealt with on a 'without notice' basis, neither does the assessment have to begin on the day the order is made. Section 43(5) specifies that the date on which the order may begin can be set by the court. This would enable a plan for an assessment to be made, in advance, to begin at some future date.

The order may last for only *seven days*. It is difficult to make an adequate form of assessment within that time-scale. This is particularly true when you consider that the *Framework for the Assessment of Children in Need and their Families* (see p. 29) talks of the first week being the investigation period and of assessment taking up to 12 weeks. Clearly, all that the assessment in a CAO is capable of achieving is to show whether other court orders should or should not be applied for. From a social work practice point of view, it cannot be an adequate form of assessment.

If an order is granted then its purpose will be to allow this limited type of assessment to be carried out. To this end the order may include directions for the child to be produced for medical or psychiatric examination. Such examinations are subject to the informed consent of the child (discussed on p. 71).

The order does allow the child to be compulsorily removed from the home, but only for the purposes of the assessment, and, if that occurs, there is provision for reasonable contact by the child with parents or other persons. These are contained in s. 43(9) and (10):

(9)   The child may only be kept away from home—

(a)   in accordance with directions specified in the order;
(b)   if it is necessary for the purposes of assessment; and
(c)   for such period as may be specified in the order.

(10)   Where the child is to be kept away from home, the order shall contain such directions as the court thinks fit with regard to the contact that he must be allowed to have with other persons while away from home.

Therefore, the child may be removed only if the court order says so. This would be where it was necessary for the child to attend for a short residential assessment. It is not designed to *protect* the child by removal from the home — that is the function of the EPO.

An application for a CAO cannot be made on a 'without notice' basis. It must be made when the parents have been told of the hearing and have the chance to be represented there (rule 4(4)).

Variation and discharge of a CAO   It may be that the order having been made, the arrangements for the assessment cannot be carried out on the set date. If a variation becomes necessary, or even if a discharge of the order is required, the court can do this under rule 2(3).

Removal by the Police to Accommodation (s. 46)

This is the last point to be considered in the area of the emergency protection of children. The police are very much in the 'front line' when it comes to dealing with social problems. It is therefore to be expected that they will, in the course of their duties, come across children at risk who need protection. As there may be the need to take instant action, the police are given powers under the Children Act to take the children into police protection. These powers apply to children whom the police find and contain no provisions enabling the police to search for a child. They can be used for runaways or for abandoned children, or where the police come across children with drunk parents or living in unhygienic conditions.

The police are not equipped to deal with children at risk, and therefore the police are required to arrange to place the children in suitable accommodation. They also have the power to ensure that a child remains in suitable accommodation such as a hospital (s. 46(1)(a) and (b)). Neither of these powers (to remove a child or to keep a child in a safe place) requires a court order. The police therefore have powers which a social worker does not.

As soon as the police have taken a child into their protection they have to notify the relevant local authority, notify the child, if appropriate, of what steps are to be taken, take steps to discover the wishes of the child concerned, move the child to suitable accommodation and inform the designated officer of the fact that a child has been taken into police protection (s. 46(3)).

The 'designated officer' within the police is clearly the liaison point between the local authority and the police in these cases, and every social worker should be aware of who this person is — every police force is required to appoint one.

The police also have to inform the child's parent of the fact that the child has been taken into police custody. The police do *not* obtain parental responsibility for the child by taking the child into police custody but must do what is reasonable to safeguard or promote the child's welfare (s. 46(9)).

If the police think that an EPO should be sought then they have to apply for it. They can do this whether or not the local authority is aware of the application or, more importantly, whether or not the local authority agrees with the making of such an application (s. 46(7) and (8)). If a child is in police protection that triggers the duty for a local authority to carry out an investigation under s. 47.

No child may be kept in police protection for more than 72 hours, and during that time the police shall allow both the child's parent and anybody having a contact order under s. 8 to have reasonable contact with the child (s. 46(10)).

However, if the child in police protection has been placed in local authority accommodation then it is for the local authority to arrange contact (s. 46(11)). Therefore, for the best of reasons, whenever the police take a child into their protection, they will wish to accommodate the child with the local authority as soon as possible. Either the police or, more probably, the local authority can apply for an EPO if appropriate.

The question of whether the social worker should use their own powers under the Act or turn to the police will be a decision that will greatly depend on the circumstances of the particular case and the extent and nature of the cooperation and liaison between the local police and the social services department.

In an extreme case, if you believe that a child is in serious physical danger, you can ask a police officer to exercise their powers under the Police and Criminal Evidence Act 1984, s. 17, to enter any premises and to search for and remove the child. No court order is required. The police may also arrest without warrant any person who has committed any offence where the arrest is necessary to protect a child from that person (Police and Criminal Evidence Act 1984, s. 25). The police also have powers under the Crime and Disorder Act 1998 to remove truants either to home, or to a place of safety (see p. 256).

REMOVING THE CHILD ON A PERMANENT BASIS

This is the final step that can be taken, and the Act envisages that it should be taken only as a last resort. The steps relating to this are discussed in the next chapter.

SEVEN
Care and Supervision Orders

Care and supervision orders require exactly the same grounds to have been proved to the court. What, then, is the difference between the two orders?

Essentially, the decision over the choice of orders is one concerning control over the child involved. The court decides, in the case of a care order, that the local authority needs to have effective parental control over the child. This need not involve the removal of the child from home. It needs to be understood that a care order gives the local authority the power to protect a child through acquisition of parental responsibility. That may involve removing the child, but equally it can and does permit the child to be left at home. If the court makes a supervision order the child will not normally be removed from home, although there are powers to direct the child to live at a specified address for a limited period. Supervision orders are less intrusive, and if the balance between a care order and a supervision order is equal, the court should adopt the least interventionist approach.

In *Re O (Supervision Order)* [2001] EWCA Civ 16, [2001] 1 FLR 923, the Court of Appeal considered the relationship between a care order and a supervision order in the light of the need for intervention to be proportionate to the risk to the child, as required by the Human Rights Act 1998. In the particular case the risk was felt by the Court to be at the low end of the scale, and that provided the parents cooperated and the local authority delivered the necessary range of services to protect the child, a supervision order (rather than the care order requested by the local authority) was appropriate. The Court indicated that previous case law was not necessarily helpful on this distinction, as each case has to be decided on its own facts and the requirements of the Human Rights Act 1998 must be considered.

Therefore, the actual decision as to which type of order the court will make will depend on how serious the court considers the case to be. To this end the social worker can make recommendations to assist the court.

CARE ORDERS

To restate a principle from Chapter 4: the only way in which a child may be 'in care' under the Children Act 1989 is by an application for a care order being made to the court and the court granting the care order. Without a care order the child is not 'in care'.

Obtaining a Care Order

Why should a care order be applied for? This question is posed before the more obvious question of 'What are the grounds for a care order?'. This is because the social worker needs to be asking the first question at all times when considering the handling of any individual case. A care order should be applied for only when the principle of the diminishment of the need for court proceedings has been tried or considered and been found to be unsuccessful or inapplicable. This means that what we have set out in Chapters 4 and 5 — the support for the family in cash or otherwise or alternative forms of accommodation — has been considered. Having done this and having found that none of these courses of action is suitable, there remains the duty to commence care proceedings if this is the appropriate way to promote and safeguard the welfare of the child. This is in accordance with s. 47. In particular, do not allow confusion over the 'no order principle', which we discussed in Chapter 4, to obscure the need to seek care or supervision orders.

Section 31(1) of the 1989 Act determines who may apply for a care order:

(1)   On the application of any local authority or authorised person [only the NSPCC is authorised], the court **may** make an order—
    (a)   placing the child with respect to whom the application is made in the care of a designated local authority; or
    (b)   putting the child under the supervision of a designated local authority or a probation officer.

You will see that a distinction is made between the application, which can be made by *any* local authority or the NSPCC, and the actual care order which is made to a designated authority. If a local authority finds a child within its area who should be the subject of a care order application but the child lives in a different area, then there is nothing to stop that local authority applying for a care order which will be made in the name of the child's 'home' authority. Alternatively, under s. 31(8), the care order could be made to the local authority in whose area the circumstances which caused the application to be made arose.

The Grounds for a Care Order

What, then, are the grounds for a care order? These are contained in s. 31(2):

(2)   A court may only make a care order or supervision order if it is satisfied—

(a)   that the child concerned is suffering, or is likely to suffer, significant harm; and
   (b)   that the harm, or likelihood of harm, is attributable to—
      (i)   the care given to the child, or likely to be given to him if the order were not made, not being what it would be reasonable to expect a parent to give to him; or
      (ii)   the child's being beyond parental control.

These grounds are known as the 'threshold criteria' since they set out the minimum criteria which should exist before there is justification for the court even to contemplate compulsory intervention in family life. The court need go on to apply the welfare principles contained in s. 1 only if it is satisfied that the threshold criteria apply.

Significant harm   What does this mean? The obvious first question is what is 'significant' in relation to 'significant harm'. On this the Act is silent. We said in earlier editions that trying to define 'significant' would be one of the first subjects of litigation in the higher courts. This proved to be the case. The attitude of the High Court and Court of Appeal appears to be that the question of significance is not so much a question of law, but rather one of fact for the lower courts. What is significant can only depend on the facts that the lower courts have considered. You will recall when we discussed the general principles of appeals in Chapter 3 that questions of fact and questions of discretion are the most difficult questions to get an appeal court to review. It appears that after the first flurry of cases the approach is now accepted that what is significant is a matter for the court to decide as a question of fact.
   An examination of some cases shows this approach. In *Humberside County Council* v *B* [1993] 1 FLR 257, Booth J heard a case in which the mother and father were both diagnosed as suffering from schizophrenia. The child involved was six months old at the time of the High Court hearing. Whilst the baby was developing well, there were occasions when she was left unattended. When an aunt was looking after the baby she found her to have bruising on her arms and thighs. A paediatrician had concluded that these were consistent with non-accidental injury. The local authority was granted an interim care order, and thus the magistrates were satisfied that there was a likelihood of significant harm. On appeal the High Court was asked to rule that the harm suffered by the baby was not significant. The judge formulated a two-stage process that the courts have to go through:

So it can be seen that the definition of harm is a very wide one. [T]he local authority has submitted that the question whether or not a child is suffering or likely to suffer significant harm is a question of factual proof as to which the welfare of the child is not relevant: that submission I accept. . . .
   The court, on being satisfied as to the criteria, is then required to have regard to the welfare of the child, and to the matters set out in s. 1 of the Act. In my judgment it is at that stage that the court is determining a question with respect to the upbringing of the child so that the welfare of

the child must be the court's paramount consideration. . . . It follows therefore in my judgment that the court has to follow a *two stage process* in determining whether or not to make a care or supervision order. *The first stage* is to determine whether or not the significant harm test in s. 31(2) is satisfied. If it accepts that as a matter of factual proof, and the criteria is satisfied, then the court must go on to *the second stage* where it must consider whether or not to make an order, and at that stage it must apply the provisions of s. 1 of the 1989 Act. The court is not confined in those circumstances to making a care or supervision order. . . . [s.] 1(3)(g) requires the court to consider the range of its powers under the Act. . . .

Where the justices fell into error [which was the granting of the interim order] . . . was to confuse the welfare considerations under s. 1 with their findings as to the likelihood of significant harm which . . . is a matter of factual proof. Having been satisfied as to that criterion on the evidence before them, it was then for the justices to consider whether or not to make an order. In relation to that, it was incumbent upon them . . . to consider all the circumstances of the case including the nature of significant harm which they considered would be likely that [the baby] would suffer, in relation to all matters under s. 1 of the Act including the harm which she would be likely to suffer by the continuing separation from the parents. (emphasis added)

In *Re O* [1991] 2 FLR 7, the court examined 'significant harm' and said that the s. 31 criteria were made out when the local authority had done all that they could in relation to truancy. Non school attendance itself was liable to cause harm, and in the long run this could be significant.

This perhaps was an unexpected result, particularly when the Children Act introduced the Education Supervision Order (s. 37 which we discuss on p. 152). It abolished the previous power to take a child into care for non school attendance. The decision in this case may have the effect of reintroducing this power.

The court made these comments:

In relation to whether the harm is significant, on behalf of the [child] it is said that the comparison which has to be made is with a similar child under s. 31(10) and that there is no evidence that she has suffered significant harm compared with a similar child.

In my judgment, in the context of this type of case, 'similar child' means a child of equivalent intellectual and social development, who has gone to school, and not merely an average child who may or may not be at school. In fact, what one has to ask oneself is whether this child suffered significant harm by not going to school. The answer in my judgment, as in the magistrates' judgment, is obvious.

To clarify, in considering an application for a care or supervision order, a court must:

(a)   be satisfied that the grounds in s. 31 (the threshold criteria) are met; and

(b)   decide whether, by applying the grounds in s. 1, to make an order and what order to make (see the diagram on p. 156).

At What Stage is Significant Harm to be Assessed by the Court?

In *Northampton County Council* v S [1992] 3 WLR 1010, the court considered at what time the significance of the harm should be considered. In this case the mother had two children, a girl born in 1986 and a boy born in 1989. The children had different fathers. Following a non-accidental injury the children were taken into voluntary care under the old law. The Children Act then came into force. The local authority applied for a care order. The father of the boy sought a residence order that the boy only was to live with the boy's grandmother. The magistrates granted the care order. The father appealed to the High Court. The High Court had to consider the meaning of 'suffering significant harm'. What is the effect of the present tense? It held that the phrase referred to the period immediately before the action commenced. Ewbank J said:

> That means the court has to consider the position immediately before the emergency protection order, if there was one or an interim care order, if that was the initiation of protection, or, as in this case, when the child went into voluntary care. In my judgment, the family proceedings court was quite entitled to consider the position when the children were with the mother prior to going into care and was correct in doing so.

The case of *Newham London Borough Council* v *AG* [1993] 1 FLR 281 saw some important points made by the Court of Appeal. The case concerned a girl who was aged 2 years 3 months. Her mother was aged 20 and was a schizophrenic. The local authority had concerns about both the mother and the grandmother. The grandmother appeared to be unable to accept that her daughter was ill. In September 1989, the mother was admitted to hospital after swallowing bleach. She discharged herself. Again she was admitted to another hospital. The mother had told a health visitor that she had hit and pinched the baby three or four times when in the previous hospital. She had threatened to give bleach to the baby. To protect the girl the local authority made an application in wardship in February 1990 (that is before the Children Act came into force). Importantly, however, the judge did apply the significant harm threshold test under s. 31 of the Children Act, and this approach was supported by the Court of Appeal. It enabled the Court of Appeal to consider the application of the significant harm test. Stephen Brown, President of the Family Division, gave the leading judgment and said:

> [1] . . . we should not approach the interpretation of s. 31(2) of the Children Act on the basis that the phrase 'likely to suffer' should be equated with 'on the balance of probabilities'. . . [However, this comment should be read in the light of the decision of the House of Lords in *Re H*

and R (Child Sexual Abuse: Standard of Proof) [1996] AC 583, see p. 141 below.]

[2] . . . It is true that first of all the court has to be satisfied that the child concerned is suffering or is likely to suffer significant harm, but in looking to the future the court has to assess the risk. Is this child likely to suffer significant harm? . . . It is important to bear in mind that the judge had to make an assessment of the future risk in the light of the evidence before him. That is entirely a matter for the judge. It is the duty he has to discharge in the exercise of his discretion . . .

(We have numbered the paragraphs for clarity.)

As can be seen, the higher courts seem to be saying that the question of significance is one of fact.

This does not mean that there are no aids to understanding the meaning of 'significant'. To help us understand s. 31(2) we have s. 31(9):

(9)   In this section—

. . .

'harm' means ill-treatment or the impairment of health or development;
'development' means physical, intellectual, emotional, social or be-haviourial development;
'health' means physical or mental health; and
'ill-treatment' includes sexual abuse and forms of treatment that are not physical.

Section 31(10) continues the clarification of terms:

(10)   Where the question of whether harm suffered by a child is significant turns on the child's health or development, his health shall be compared with that which could reasonably be expected of a similar child.

When lawyers are looking for a meaning of a word that is not statutorily defined they turn to dictionaries. This is in accordance with the rule of statutory interpretation described on p. 24. In this case dictionaries do not appear to help: 'significant: having, conveying a meaning; full of meaning, highly expressive or suggestive, important, notable' (*Oxford Dictionary*). Fowler's *Modern English Usage* says 'the primary sense of significant is conveying a meaning or suggesting an inference'.

This guidance appears to indicate that 'significant' encompasses more than just the question of magnitude of harm. For example, what is the effect of bruising caused by a child being pushed over; is this likely to be seen as insignificant as against a fractured arm caused by a parent hitting the child? The latter must amount to significant harm. Added to this is the question as to what an accidental broken arm amounts to. It may not be 'significant' or lead to any conclusion. If we are told the story behind the accident, a child left alone in a house perhaps, then it may be 'significant'. This use of the dictionary definition was indeed endorsed in *Humberside County Council* v *B* [1993] 1 FLR 257.

A court's view may be 'Well, we don't think that such a point is significant'. From the social worker's point of view, if you believe that the harm is significant then you should take the appropriate steps. The court will decide whether it shares the social worker's view as to what is significant.

Looking further at the subsection we see that it is possible to obtain a care order on the basis of present significant harm or the likelihood of future harm, in contrast to an EPO which can *only* be granted on the likelihood of future harm.

Nevertheless, a care order cannot be based purely on past harm. A decision under the Children and Young Persons Act 1969 continues to be relevant. In *Re D (A Minor)* [1987] AC 317, the House of Lords decided that a court could infer future harm from past events. In this case the mother's drug addiction during pregnancy provided the grounds for a care order afterwards because the resulting harm continued. This view prevailed in *Northampton County Council* v *S* [1992] 3 WLR 1010, referred to above.

Next the harm or likelihood of harm has to be attributable to the fact that the care given or likely to be given to the child (as appropriate) is not what a parent would reasonably be expected to give to the child.

This means the care that should be given to this particular child whose case is before the court by a '*reasonable*' parent. Therefore you have to look at the child in his or her context (home, surroundings, locale etc.) and ask what a reasonable parent in that situation would be expected to do. This was the point made in *Re O* [1992] 2 FLR 7, mentioned above.

This gets around the difficulty that if you were to look at most of your clients' situations then often you might be able to say that it would be possible to offer the children a 'better' home. The failing of the parent should be such that it is incapable of being overcome by the range of support services that the local authority is allowed to deploy as we have described in previous chapters.

In *Northampton County Council* v *S* [1992] 3 WLR 1010 (the facts are given above), the point was made that the carer to be considered was the one responsible for the child prior to action being taken. In this case it was suggested that the grandmother could care for the child now, and that with the grandmother the child would not be likely to suffer significant harm. The court ruled that this was not relevant and that it should not look at the hypothetical care that might be given by others who could now be considered as possible carers. The judge said:

> . . . the question arises whether the justices ought to consider the care being offered by the grandmother in assessing the threshold condition rather than the care which is actually being provided by the mother. The answer in my judgment is clearly 'No'. The threshold test relates to the parent or other carer *whose lack of care has caused the harm* referred to in section 31(2)(a). The care which other carers might give to the child only becomes relevant if the threshold test is met. The fact that the threshold test is met does not

mean that the family proceedings court does have to make a care order. They have the choice once the threshold conditions are met of making a care order, of making a supervision order, or of making any other order under the Children Act [or, we would add, making no order] [emphasis added].

The decision in this case was endorsed and specifically approved in the case of *Re M (Minor) (Care Order: Significant Harm)* [1994] 2 FLR 577. The House of Lords stated that it would be contrary to the intention of the Act to use any other approach.

So, the point at which the court is to consider whether or not the threshold criteria are met is at the point immediately before either the care/supervision court proceedings were started, or emergency protection proceedings were begun.

Some may think that this approach is unfair to parents. A considerable delay may occur between the beginning of the proceedings and the final hearing. During that time things could have changed considerably. Should any changes not be taken in account by the court?

The answer is that such changes will be considered by the court, at the second of the stages, set out by the decision in *Humberside County Council* v *B* (above). That will be when the court considers, with the application of the welfare criteria in s. 1, whether or not to make an order.

The Meaning of 'Likely': The Standard of Proof in Allegations of Abuse

One of the vexed questions of interpretation of s. 31 is the meaning of 'likely' in s. 31(2). This was considered by the House of Lords in *Re H and R (Child Sexual Abuse: Standard of Proof)* [1996] AC 583, [1996] 1 WLR 8, [1996] 1 All ER 1, [1996] 1 FLR 80. In this case the House also considered the standard of proof that is required in cases where allegations of abuse are made.

The facts of the case were as follows: The mother had four children. Two, C and D, aged 16 and 13, were the children of her husband, from whom she was separated. Two, T and M, aged 9 and 2, were the children of the mother's cohabitee. In 1990, C alleged that the cohabitee had sexually abused her. He was charged with rape but was acquitted. The local authority then proceeded with applications for care orders in respect of the three younger children under s. 31 of the Children Act 1989, based only on the alleged sexual abuse of C. The judge found that the mother and her cohabitee were lying and expressed considerable suspicion that the alleged abuse *had* taken place. But he held that, as the case depended solely on C's allegations, he was *not* satisfied on the balance of probabilities proportionate to the gravity of the offence that the allegations were true. Therefore he could not proceed to consider whether the children were likely to suffer significant harm in the terms of s. 31(2)(a). He dismissed the applications.

The local authority, supported by the guardian *ad litem*, appealed on the ground that even if the judge was not satisfied that abuse had in fact occurred, nevertheless the allegation itself and the judge's suspicion ought to be taken into account so as to fulfil the requirements of s. 31 relating to the interpretation of 'likely to suffer'. The House of Lords, in dismissing the appeal, held that the judge had been right to adopt a two-stage approach, and had fairly weighed up the matter relating to the allegations of sexual abuse. They concluded that the allegations had not been established to the requisite standard of proof, which is the balance of probabilities. The judge had rightly dismissed the applications. It was not open to him on the evidence, since he had rejected the only allegation which gave rise to the applications, to go on to a second stage and consider the likelihood of future harm to the children. The majority of the House adopted what was claimed to be the traditional test:

> The balance of probability standard means that a court is satisfied an event occurred if the court considers that, on the evidence, the occurrence of the event was more likely than not. When assessing the probabilities the court will have in mind as a factor, to whatever extent is appropriate in the particular case, that the more serious the allegation the less likely it is that the event occurred and, hence, the stronger should be the evidence before the court concludes that the allegation is established on the balance of probability. Fraud is usually less likely than negligence. Deliberate physical injury is usually less likely than accidental physical injury. A stepfather is usually less likely to have repeatedly raped and had non-consensual oral sex with his under age stepdaughter than on some occasion to have lost his temper and slapped her. Built into the preponderance of probability standard is a generous degree of flexibility in respect of the seriousness of the allegation.
>
> Although the result is much the same, this does not mean that where a serious allegation is in issue the standard of proof required is higher. It means only that the inherent probability or improbability of an event is itself a matter to be taken into account when weighing the probabilities and deciding whether, on balance, the event occurred. The more improbable the event, the stronger must be the evidence that it did occur before, on the balance of probability, its occurrence will be established. (*per* Lord Nichols in majority judgment)

Many commentators have found it difficult to understand this test as being different to the test the House purported to reject. However, the concluding remarks of Lord Nichols seek to justify the position:

> These are among the difficulties and considerations Parliament addressed in the Children Act when deciding how, to use the fashionable terminology, the balance should be struck between the various interests. As I read the Act, Parliament decided that the threshold for a care order should be that the child is suffering significant harm, or there is a real possibility that he will do so. In the latter regard the threshold is comparatively low. Therein lies the protection for children. But, as I read the Act, Parliament

also decided that proof of the relevant facts is needed if this threshold is to be surmounted. Before the section 1 welfare test and the welfare 'checklist' can be applied, the threshold has to be crossed. Therein lies the protection for parents. They are not to be at risk of having their child taken from them and removed into the care of the local authority on the basis only of suspicions whether of the judge or of the local authority or anyone else. A conclusion that the child is suffering or it likely to suffer harm must be based on facts not just suspicion.

The effect of this important judgment is to make it harder for the local authority to satisfy the standard of proof required by the courts. Since the decision by the House of Lords there have been a considerable number of decisions by the Court of Appeal which have followed this line of legal authority.

The courts have said that the test applies not just in public law applications by local authorities, but also in private law applications by individuals for s. 8 orders. So in *Re N (Residence: Hopeless Appeals)* [1995] 2 FLR 230:

One question touched upon in the course of this appeal was this: when deciding a child's future, must the court totally ignore the real possibility that a prospective carer has committed past sexual abuse when that abuse is not proved to the requisite standard of proof? By the majority decision of this court in *Re H and R (Minors)* that question was answered 'Yes' in the context of care orders. Unless the judge finds the alleged past sexual abuse proved on the balance of probabilities the threshold test set down by section 31(2) of the 1989 Act is not met. The court cannot find itself satisfied that the child 'is likely to suffer significant harm' in the future and accordingly the state cannot be allowed to intervene in the affairs of the family to protect that child. Does that same approach necessarily apply in the present context, one of competing applications for residence orders?

Being beyond parental control 'Being beyond parental control' in s. 31(1)(b)(ii) should present few difficulties as this definition is imported from previous legislation and is largely a self-explanatory matter of fact for the court to decide. An example of the use of this concept can be found in *South Glamorgan County Council* v *W and B* [1993] 1 FLR 574, which we discussed in Chapter 4 and also in *M* v *Birmingham City Council* [1994] 2 FLR 141. At the end of that chapter there is a flow diagram that shows a summary of the evidential steps to obtaining a care or supervision order. If you are the applicant you should ensure that you have evidence and argument on each point.

Interim Care Orders

Most interim care orders are going to be made in the situation where for one reason or the other the full hearing cannot yet take place. Section 38(1) provides:

(1)   Where—
    (a)   in any proceedings on an application for a care order or supervision order, the proceedings are adjourned; or
    (b)   the court gives a direction under section 37(1),
the court may make an interim care order or an interim supervision order with respect to the child concerned.

We have already discussed (on pp. 96–97) the provisions relating to interim orders made following the court's direction to a local authority to make an investigation under s. 37. To recap:

(a)   the court must have reasonable grounds for believing there are grounds for the full care order;
(b)   the making of the interim order does not mean that there will be a full order; and
(c)   the court must act judicially in making an order.

This does not mean that there will always have to be a hearing with evidence being given. Inevitably after the first interim order is made, within the constraints of the timetable provisions below, there are occasions on which everybody is agreed that for one reason or another a further interim order will need to be made — the medical report is not available, there is no available court time etc. In this case the court could make an interim order without hearing evidence but merely hearing representations from the applicant, as happened in *Devon County Council* v *S* [1992] 3 All ER 793.
    Section 38(4) sets out a timetable for the granting of interim care orders. It is not reproduced verbatim here since it is unnecessarily complex and unclear. What it appears to say is as follows:

(a)   an initial interim order may not last more than eight weeks;
(b)   if the initial interim order has been made for a period of less than eight weeks then any subsequent orders may be made for a period or periods that will not exceed that eight-week period starting on the date on which the initial order was made;
(c)   if any interim orders are made after that initial eight-week period then those further interim orders may not exceed a four-week period, although they may be made for periods less than four weeks; and
(d)   any number of interim orders could be made subject to the non-delay principle.

This approach was approved in *Gateshead MBC* v *N* [1993] 1 FLR 811. Importantly, when making an interim order, the court may give directions as follows:

(6)   Where the court makes an interim care order, or interim supervision order, it may give such directions (if any) as it considers appropriate with regard to the medical or psychiatric examination or other assessment

of the child; but if the child is of sufficient understanding to make an informed decision he may refuse to submit to the examination or other assessment. [This is another example of *informed consent.*]

Assessments during Interim Care Orders

In *Re C (A Minor) (Interim Care Order: Residential Assessment)* [1996] 4 All ER 871, [1997] 1 FLR 1, a four-month-old child was admitted to hospital suffering from non-accidental injuries. The child's parents, aged 16 and 17, were not able to give a satisfactory explanation of the injuries. An EPO was made, and then an interim care order under s. 38 of the Children Act 1989. The field social workers decided that in-depth assessment of the child and the parents together needed to be undertaken as soon as possible at a residential unit. However, their managers refused to agree to, or pay for, the residential assessment and decided to apply for a care order so that the child could be placed in a permanent alternative placement with a view to adoption.

At first instance, the judge held that she had jurisdiction under s. 38(6) to order a residential assessment. Having weighed the cost (estimated at £18,000 to £24,000) against the recommendations from the professionals involved, she decided to exercise her discretion by ordering the local authority to carry out the residential assessment.

The House of Lords held that s. 38(6) was to enable the court to obtain the information for its decision. In all other respects, under an interim care order, control over the child rested with the local authority. The court did have power to override the views of the local authority on whether to carry out a full assessment, so as to enable the court to decide whether or not to grant the local authority's application for a care order. The care plan here indicated that the local authority was going to place the child for adoption. To allow the local authority to decide what evidence was to go before the court at the final hearing would allow the local authority by administrative decision to pre-empt the court's judicial decision.

Section 38(6) and (7) did confer jurisdiction on the court to order or prohibit any assessment which involved the participation of the child, and was to provide the court with the material which was required to enable it to reach a proper decision at the final hearing. In exercising its discretion the court would have to take into account the cost of the proposed assessment and the fact of local authorities' lack of resources. In this case their Lordships ordered the assessment.

Directions in Interim Care Orders

The Act specifies in s. 38(7) what directions may be given. This subsection is an exact reproduction of s. 44(8) and (9) relating to EPOs which are discussed in Chapter 6: The Emergency Protection of Children. For comments relating to this similar subsection, see p. 97.

The important provisions of rule 18 must be noted:

(1)   No person may, without the leave of the justices' clerk or the court, cause the child to be medically or psychiatrically examined, or otherwise

assessed, for the purpose of the preparation of expert evidence for use in the proceedings.

. . .

(3)   Where the leave of the justices' clerk or the court has not been given under (1) no evidence arising out of an examination or assessment to which that paragraph applies may be adduced without the leave of the court.

The message here is quite clear. If you are going to have any medical examination, investigation, or any other type of assessment carried out, then obtain the leave of the court.

The final provision relating to interim care orders is s. 38(10):

(10)   Where a court makes an order under or by virtue of this section [an interim order] it shall, in determining the period for which the order is to be in force, consider whether any party who was, or might have been, opposed to the making of an order was in a position to argue his case against the order in full.

This is designed to cope with a situation where a parent has not had the opportunity to instruct lawyers to act on their behalf at the time of the interim hearing. The court should then consider making an interim order for just sufficient time to enable a lawyer to be properly instructed. This is another reflection of the Act's aim to try and reduce the delays that can be present in such cases.

Power to Exclude Alleged Abuser during Interim Order

The Family Law Act 1996 amended the Children Act to include a new s. 38A — a power in interim care orders to require an alleged abuser to leave the house in which the child is living. The court would have to be satisfied of the following:

(a)   that there is reasonable cause to believe that if a person is excluded from a dwelling house in which the child lives, the child will cease to suffer or cease to be likely to suffer significant harm; and

(b)   another person living in the same house, whether or not a parent, is able and willing to give to the child the care which it would be reasonable to expect a parent to give; and

(c)   that person consents to the inclusion of the exclusion requirement.

There are also powers of arrest available, subject to certain requirements. The difficulty with this power is that it does require the consent of the person who is to care for the child. This would normally be the mother. In the absence of her consent it is not possible to compel the alleged abuser to leave. While this power is a welcome addition to the interim care order, the requirement of consent may mean that it is not used as much as could be expected.

What is the Effect of a Care Order?

This is set out in s. 33:

(1)   Where a care order is made with respect to a child it shall be the duty of a local authority designated by the order to receive the child into their care and to keep him in their care while the order remains in force.

This subsection is relatively straightforward and requires little explanation, except for one point. We have previously mentioned that the definition of the concept 'care' is not always clear. Where the Act talks of a child being in care, this means subject to a care order (s. 105). Sometimes, however, the Act uses the word 'care' without any definition. This is potentially problematic, since some crucial issues may turn on this word. Section 33 continues:

(2)   Where—
      (a)   a care order has been made with respect to a child on the application of an authorised person [i.e., NSPCC, see Chapter 6]; but
      (b)   the local authority designated by the order was not informed that the person proposed to make the application [there is a requirement for the local authority to be informed of applications],
the child may be kept in the care of that person until received into the care of the local authority.
      (3)   While a care order is in force with respect to a child, the local authority designated by the order shall—
      (a)   have parental responsibility for the child; and
      (b)   have the power (subject to the following provisions of this section) to determine the extent to which a parent or guardian of the child may meet his parental responsibility for him.
      (4)   The authority may not exercise the power in subsection (3)(b) unless they are satisfied that it is necessary to do so in order to safeguard or promote the child's welfare.
      (5)   Nothing in subsection (3)(b) shall prevent a parent or guardian of the child who has care of him from doing what is reasonable in all the circumstances of the case for the purpose of safeguarding or promoting his welfare.

These subsections are the core of the effect of a care order. The main function of a care order is that it gives the local authority parental responsibility; it makes the local authority the child's parent — with all the implications that are contained in that phrase. You will notice that there is an immediate qualification to this in s. 33(3)(b), which states that the local authority has the power to determine the extent to which a parent may meet their parental responsibility to the child.

Parental Responsibility under Care Order
This is a reminder that the mere fact of making a care order and giving parental responsibility to the local authority does not remove parental responsibility from the parents (s. 2(5) and (6)). What happens is that the principal responsibility rests with the local authority, with the parents' responsibility remaining an ever-present feature. Indeed, s. 33(3)(b) echoes

the philosophy of the Act in that it seeks to encourage the local authority to look at ways in which it can share the care of the child with the child's parent, albeit that this is by way of a power not a duty on the local authority.

Section 33(4) then goes on to indicate that although the local authority may share the care of the child with his or her parent, it may not exercise this power unless it is necessary to do so in order to safeguard or promote the child's welfare. This means that a local authority should not adopt the attitude that, in every case where a child has parents, there should be steps to rehabilitate the child with those parents. It is more subtle than that. Local authorities are encouraged to look towards rehabilitating a child, but only in those cases where this will safeguard or promote the child's welfare.

What s. 33(5) is saying is that, although the granting of a care order does give the local authority parental responsibility, it does not mean that the parents can wash their hands of their responsibility for the child, especially where the local authority is seeking to share the care of the child with the parents. If, for example, a child subject to a care order was placed back with a parent (which would need to be done in accordance with the Placement of Children Regulations) and the child was neglected by the parent, then it would not be open to the parent to say 'it was the local authority's fault — we were not responsible because the local authority had a care order'.

Section 33(6), (7), (8) and (9) impose limitations on the power of the local authority in possession of a care order in respect of the child. They state, in summary, that whilst a care order is in force the local authority may not:

(a)   cause the child to be brought up in a different religious persuasion (this can present problems in the choice of foster parents);

(b)   cause the child to be adopted without a court order;

(c)   appoint a guardian for the child (that is a testamentary guardian for when the parents die); or

(d)   cause the child to be known by a different surname (again this needs to be watched with foster parents) or allow the child to be removed from the United Kingdom without the leave of the court (except for periods of less than four weeks).

In making applications to court it is always necessary for the local authority to present its plans for contact (s. 34(11)) and its proposals for the future care of the child if a care order is made (*Manchester City Council* v *F* [1993] 1 FLR 419). We discuss this in the section 'Preparing for Court' in Chapter 10. Once a care order is made the local authority has the task of deciding how to look after the child.

The decision in *Kent County Council* v *C* [1992] 3 WLR 808 is worthy of note in relation to the local authority's discretion after a care order. The local authority had indicated that it proposed to try to rehabilitate the child with the family. On hearing of this the magistrates added a direction to the care order that the guardian should continue to be involved with the child. This was to assess the success of the rehabilitation programme. The High Court said that this was not allowed by the legislation. The local authority's discretion, granted by the Act, should not be fettered in this way. To challenge the local authority, use has to be made of the provisions of s. 34 for contact. This we discuss in Chapter 11 'The Child Looked after by the Local Authority', and particularly the decision in *Re B (Minors) (Care: Local Authority's Plans)* [1993] 1 FLR 543. We also look further at the child in care in Chapter 11.

It is necessary to re-state that the making of a care order does not automatically mean that the child must be removed from the home. The local authority's duty once a care order is made is still that contained in s. 17, i.e., to safeguard and promote the child's welfare and, as far as is consistent with that duty, to encourage the child to be with his or her family. A care order adds to this a *power*, if necessary, to remove the child.

Discharge of Care Orders
The procedure for the discharge of care orders is identical to that for supervision orders. See Chapter 11.

SUPERVISION ORDERS

The grounds for making a supervision order are exactly the same as those for a care order. They are set out in s. 31(2) (i.e., the likelihood of significant harm or the child being beyond parental control). Indeed the whole of the provisions of s. 31 are applicable to the making of a supervision order. Therefore the questions of the meaning of 'significant harm', etc. which we discussed when looking at care orders are just as applicable. For the few who have forgotten what these questions were please see pp. 135–42 above!

What is the Effect of a Supervision Order?
A supervision order is an alternative to a care order. In the Act there is no guidance as to when a supervision order should be made rather than a care order. The decision is going to be the decision of the court, although the court will listen to the representations of all the parties, which can include a children's guardian, before coming to that decision. The order is made either to a local authority or a probation officer.

An interesting case which considered the need for a supervision order is *Re K (Supervision Orders)* [1999] 2 FLR 303. Here the local authority and the mother agreed that the threshold criteria in s. 31 were satisfied. They also agreed that a supervision order would be the appropriate way to safeguard the interests of the children. However, the children's guardian thought that the obligations of the local authority to safeguard the interests of the children under s. 17, as children 'in need', were sufficient to deal with their welfare. The judge found that as a concession had been made by the mother which appropriately reflected the gravity of the case, there was no need for a full investigation by the courts. He made it clear that a guardian should not lightly propose a contentious hearing. While accepting that the least intrusive order possible should be made, the supervision order imposed duties on the mother as well as on the local authority, which would be useful if the mother did not continue to cooperate, and that in practice the result of the supervision order would be to secure the allocation of a social worker and therefore greater protection for the children.

The effect of a supervision order is contained in s. 35:

(1) While a supervision order is in force it shall be the duty of the supervisor—
    (a) to advise, assist and befriend the supervised child;
    (b) to take such steps as are reasonably necessary to give effect to the order; and
    (c) where—
        (i) the order is not wholly complied with; or
        (ii) the supervisor considers that the order may no longer be necessary, to consider whether or not to apply to the court for its variation or discharge.

There are no definitions of the terms 'advise', 'assist' or 'befriend' to give any guidance. The order need not specify a particular person in respect of a local authority. A probation officer can be a supervisor with the agreement of the probation authority and where the probation officer is already dealing or has dealt with another member of the child's household (Sch. 3, para. 9 — this means that the majority of supervision orders will be made in favour of the local authority). Schedule 3 gives more detailed guidance on what a supervision order means.

The first paragraph of the Schedule introduces the new idea of the 'responsible person' who is either a parent or someone with whom the child is living. This 'responsible person' can have duties imposed upon them in addition to any requirements that are imposed on the supervised child. But the responsible person has to consent to playing this role.

The court, under a supervision order, can require the supervised person to obey certain directions given by the supervisor. Amongst these are that the supervised child:

(a) be required to live at a specified address for a specified period;
(b) present themself to a specified person at a specified time and place; and
(c) participate in specified activities.

In addition, the responsible person can be required to:

(a) take all reasonable steps to ensure that the supervised child complies with directions given by the supervisor or contained in the order;
(b) keep the supervisor informed of the supervised child's address; and
(c) attend at a specified place to take part in any specified activities.

The attendance requirement and specified activities requirement are the extension of the former 'intermediate treatment' requirements. These were originally devised in criminal proceedings as an alternative to a custodial sentence. The Act now creates three distinct supervision orders — the one made in the course of civil proceedings which we are considering here, the education supervision order which we look at below, and one made in criminal proceedings which we consider in Chapter 12.

The supervision order can require the supervised child to submit to a medical or psychiatric examination, or to submit to such examinations as are required by the supervisor. This requirement is subject to the informed consent of the child, if the child has sufficient understanding. It is also possible for the court to require specified medical or psychiatric treatment, but if psychiatric the court must have first heard the evidence of a Mental Health Act approved doctor. The order can also require the child to keep the supervisor informed of his or her address.

There are time limits on the supervision order. Any particular supervision order may not last, initially, for more than a period of one year, but the supervisor can apply to the court to have it extended for up to three years from the date on which the order was first made. The significant harm test need not be satisfied.

Interim Supervision Orders
Just as there are specific provisions for interim care orders, so there are provisions for interim supervision orders. These are also contained in s. 38 as set out on pp. 143–44 above. So it is not necessary to prove the grounds for making a supervision order, only to show that there are reasonable grounds for believing an order may be made. There are also the complicated timetable provisions etc (see above).

Interim Supervision Order when making a s. 8 Order

The effect of s. 38(3)

(3) Where, in any proceedings on an application for a care order or supervision order, a court makes a residence order with respect to the child concerned, it **shall also make an interim supervision order** with respect to him unless satisfied that his welfare will be satisfactorily safeguarded without an interim order being made.

This section covers the situation where the court, instead of making an interim care order, decides to make a s. 8 residence order, say to a grandparent. As a 'fail safe', the court is required to make an interim supervision order. An example of this in practice is *C* v *Solihull Metropolitan Borough Council* [1993] 1 FLR 290, which we discussed at p. 89.

It needs to be stressed again that the making of any particular interim order does not mean that type of order will be made as a final order.

Can you Replace a Supervision Order with a Care Order?
The answer is clearly 'No'. The 'no order without an application' principle means there has to be a fresh application by the local authority. In making

any new application the threshold criteria must be satisfied afresh. So in *Re A (Supervision Order: Extension)* [1995] 3 All ER 401, [1995] 1 FLR 335, [1995] 1 WLR 482, [1995] 2 FCR 114, 93 LGR 119, the local authority obtained a 12-month supervision order in respect of an 11-year-old child. Before the expiry of the 12-month period the local authority applied for an extension of the order. The guardian *ad litem* recommended that a care order be made in place of a supervision order. The Court of Appeal held that on an application for an extension of a supervision order, the court could make only a further supervision order and could not make a care order.

Discharge of a Supervision Order
This is dealt with in s. 39. We discuss the procedure, which is identical to that of the discharge of a care order, in Chapter 11.

Education Supervision Orders (s. 36)
If a local education authority (which in most areas is the same authority as the social services department) can satisfy the magistrates' court that a particular child is both of compulsory school age and not being properly educated (s. 36(3)), the court may make an education supervision order. Section 36(4) defines a child as being properly educated only if the child is receiving efficient full-time education suitable to age, ability and aptitude and any special educational needs that the child may have. An application for an order cannot be made if the child is in the care of the local authority, and the education department must consult with the social services department before the application is made.

Under Sch. 3, Part III, there are detailed provisions as to the effect of the order. In essence the supervisor has to advise, assist and befriend the child and give directions to the child to ensure that the child is properly educated. Chapter 3 of Vol. 7 of *Guidance and Regulations* considers the order in detail.

The directions might include directions for the child and parents to attend meetings to discuss the child's education, or for the child to see an educational psychologist. Under the provisions there is the need to consult with the parents and child before the directions are made. For the parents persistently not to comply with directions that are reasonably given will leave them open to be fined, on conviction, in the magistrates' court. There is no penalty for the child.

The education supervision order lasts for 12 months or until the child is no longer of compulsory school age (whichever is the shorter). It can be extended for up to three years.

The order was designed to ensure that children did not go into care merely for non school attendance. It is possible that the decision in *Re O* [1991] 2 FLR 7, discussed at p. 137, has somewhat undermined this.

PRACTICAL POINTS

(These should be read in conjunction with our comments on case planning in Chapter 10.)

Having reached the stage where you are to make an application to court for an order, you first have to decide whether you are going to apply for a care or supervision order and to prepare your application on this basis. Bear in mind, however, that the decision about the type of final order is going to be made by the court, assuming that the court does not decide that it would be in the best interests of the child not to make any order, or a s. 8 order instead (see Chapter 4; and Chapter 16, p. 389).

Applications for all orders under the Act have to be commenced by lengthy application forms that are prescribed in the rules. These are extremely useful as they ensure that the court has background detail concerning the child and the child's family and the nature of the order sought. This will enable the court and the other parties to have as full a picture as possible concerning the child, even before any hearing takes place.

The adequate completion of the forms is essential since, once you have stated the basis of the application and what you are going to rely on for the application, to amend it you have to seek the leave of the court. Therefore, you need to get it right first time if possible. Your agency lawyer will want to be consulted in most cases. The decision as to whether the lawyer or the social worker fills in the form should be a matter of good practice between the persons concerned.

These statutory forms have to be filed in all applications. There are provisions under rule 4(4) for the proceedings to be held without notice (i.e., when in an emergency it is necessary for the application to be made by one party in the absence of the other parties), and in those circumstances for the application to be filed with the court at a later date.

Directions Hearings

The application forms enable the magistrates' court (since all new public law applications have to begin in the magistrates' court) to decide whether the case will be dealt with in that court or in another court, that is to say in a higher court or in a different geographical location. At the same time the court will be able to consider whether at this stage a children's guardian should be appointed. These decisions will be made at a directions hearing. The procedure for these hearings is set out in rule 14. This states that the clerk of the court may make directions concerning the conduct of the proceedings, including:

(a) the timetable for the proceedings;
(b) varying the timetable (including the time limits set out in the rules);
(c) whether the attendance of the child is required;
(d) the appointment of a children's guardian;
(e) the timetable and arrangements for the service of documents;
(f) what evidence (including experts' reports) will be submitted;
(g) what welfare reports will be required under s. 7 (see Chapter 9);
(h) whether the case should be transferred to another court because of the need for speed, or the complexity and seriousness of the case; and
(i) whether to consolidate the case with other proceedings (such as divorce proceedings).

After the application has been lodged it will need to be supported by evidence which in all courts will be by means of written statements (see Chapters 8 and 9).

These provisions mean that the social worker is going to have done a considerable amount of background work prior to seeing the agency's lawyer and supplying the lawyer with a report from which a detailed proof of evidence can be prepared and draft witness statement (see Chapter 9) Guidance on the directions hearing and planning is to be found in *Re D (Minors) (Time Estimates)* [1994] 2 FLR 336 and in the suggested form of directions in the *1993/94 Annual Report* of the Children Act Advisory Committee. Involvement of the lawyer in drafting the application and dealing with the directions is preferable.

Once the proceedings have begun it must be remembered that the court will be looking to have the final hearing at the earliest possible stage. Under s. 32 the court is under a duty to draw up a timetable for a hearing for care proceedings.

There have been a number of cases in which the High Court has given directions as to how the magistrates' court should deal with hearings under the Children Act. The requirement under rule 21 for the magistrates' court to give written reasons for their decisions appears to have caused some difficulties for the magistrates.

In *Hertfordshire County Council* v *W* [1993] 1 FLR 118, the magistrates thought that when dismissing an application for an interim care order they were not required to give written reasons. The High Court held that they must do so.

In *Hillingdon London Borough Council* v *H* [1992] 2 FLR 372, the High Court said that the magistrates had to give written reasons at the time of the announcement of their decision. They could not meet later to give full written reasons. This point was emphasised in *Hertfordshire County Council* v *W* [1993] 1 FLR 118. Here the magistrates failed to give reasons for their decision at the time of announcing the decision. As a result their decision was held to be void.

In *Oxfordshire County Council* v *R* [1992] 1 FLR 648, important guidance was given to magistrates about how to approach the setting out of their reasons for their decisions. This guidance states that:

(a)   There are certain minimum findings and reasons which must be stated, so that the parties and the appellate court can see how the magistrates have approached their task.

(b)   A good starting point is the statutory framework within which the magistrates are working (under s. 1; see p. 94). Using the statutory criteria as a checklist, the findings of fact and reasons can be built around them without undue length.

(c)   A useful pro forma which provides a logical pattern for the statement of findings and reasons can be found at p. 157 of *Family Proceedings* by P. Dawson and R. Stevens. (This sets out that the magistrates should record details of the applicant, the respondent, the nature of the proceedings, the facts not in dispute, the facts in dispute, the findings of the court, the extent to which witnesses were believed or not believed, the information upon which the court relied in reaching its decision, the legal cases considered, whether a welfare report was considered and how they applied the welfare checklist.)

(d)   Magistrates should not delay their decision.

Another new experience for magistrates is that of the submission of draft orders agreed by all parties. In *Devon County Council* v *S* [1992] 2 FLR 244, the court was given an agreed order. Nevertheless, the magistrates insisted on hearing evidence before interim and final order. The High Court said that whilst the court should not merely rubber-stamp such an order, it was not necessary to have a full hearing of evidence. What was needed was sufficient evidence to enable them to make the judicial act of making the order.

Appeals

Lastly, we will look, briefly, at the particular methods of appealing decisions in relation to care and supervision orders. There is a particular provision for appeals in s. 40.

The aim is to allow the court to decide what will happen to a child where an application for an order is dismissed and there is to be an appeal. This is another safety net provision, in that no application will be made without an investigation by the local authority or authorised person, and it therefore follows that there should have been reasonable grounds for concern. The safety net that is provided gives the court the power to make an order of the type originally sought, pending the hearing of the appeal.

The requirement that needs to be satisfied is that there must have been an interim order made at an earlier stage in the proceedings. This means that at an earlier stage a court believed that there were reasonable grounds for believing that a final order might be made.

The order made pending appeal is not an interim order since the dismissal of the application is an end to the proceedings as far as the lower court is concerned. The length of time that the order will last is strictly limited to the 'appeal period', which means that the order will only last until the hearing of the appeal. There are provisions for the appeal court to extend the period until it is practicable for it to hear the appeal. In *Re O* [1992] 2 FLR 7, the court held that the magistrates had no power to stay (suspend) such an order pending an appeal.

As we have indicated earlier, if you are involved in a case where your application is dismissed you should immediately seek the advice of your agency lawyer.

Figure 7.1   Getting Care Order/Supervision Order

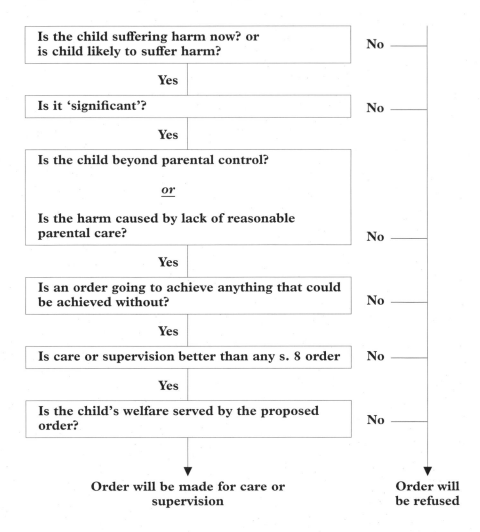

EIGHT

Evidence: How to Behave in Court and Evidence from Children

Law is about resolving conflicts. The courtroom is the place where the parties to unresolved conflicts end up, so it is vital to know how to use the court to obtain the outcome that you seek. You will have lawyers to prepare the ground and to argue the case for you, but they will not go into the witness-box for you, nor put their names to the reports or written statements you have to submit to the court. It is those who have first-hand knowledge of the relevant facts — social workers amongst others — who have to do that.

You need to know what is happening in court, particularly the rules which govern what can be said and what is excluded. This chapter sets out the rules of evidence that you will encounter; we follow it with a chapter on a particular type of evidence which you have to give, the report to the court.

What you will probably be most anxious about is appearing in court. First, therefore, we need to set the context with a look at the way in which courts approach evidence. We will be particularly concerned, later on, with how they approach evidence from children.

HOW TO APPROACH EVIDENCE

Rules of evidence are quite technical. They are the subject of weighty tomes. But do not allow fear to overwhelm you; the reason why the rules are so complex and abstruse is that the theory is distilled from the practice; what actually goes on in court is what counts, and theories have been built up over centuries to try and explain it. At a time when almost all cases went to juries, the judges wanted strictly to control what juries were allowed to hear. So the rules of evidence started as a set of rules to keep the jury from hearing evidence that they were once thought ill-equipped to weigh up. Sometimes, as a result, a rule is followed which has no rational basis in today's cases; sometimes what is thought to be a rule, such as the rule against hearsay, is not even fully understood by the courts and lawyers themselves. And as we shall see, increasingly in cases involving families and children, the courts are relaxing the grip of the evidential rules.

Our suggestion is to approach evidence from a commonsense point of view; know what it is you, as a witness, have to say that is relevant to this case, get on with it, but give way when your idea of what is common sense does not correspond with that of the court, or of the lawyer cross-examining you.

Why Evidence is Important

There are various models on which justice can be based. We shall caricature two of them, before going on to look at the model we think applies in the courts of England and Wales.

The arbitrary model: a senior and respected judge had spoiled a fine career with a bad decision. He was summoned before the Lord Chancellor to explain how he went about trying cases. He described how he would roll dice for each of the litigants, and decide in favour of the party with the best score. When asked to explain why the present decision was so bad, he said that as he was getting old, he must have misread the dice! So this model (taken from fiction, not the Law Reports!) gives a random outcome, unless you believe in divine intervention. There can be no room for witnesses and evidence. If you think this model has, in fact, been applied in a case you have been involved in, consider an appeal.

The compassionate model: here the court sets some kind of test/ordeal in order to form a judgment over which party merits its compassion. Solomon, for example, in his famous judgment, said that since the two parties were unable to agree which one should have the custody of a child, he would split the child down the middle and give them half each. When one of them, in horror, said she would give up her claim in order to save the child, Solomon recognised that she was the one with the true interests of the child at heart, and he awarded her custody. The role for a compassionate assessment of the competing interests of the parties is not excluded from our system; however, the difference between our system and Solomon's is that the court cannot invent tests; it must exercise compassion along criteria recognised by law, and on the basis of the admissible and relevant evidence before it.

The evidence model is a more complex model. It has to be, because it is based on a system of justice which aims to be predictable not arbitrary. A court cannot make decisions on the basis of whim, or pure compassion; it must remain aloof from the contest, and hear what all parties have to say. It must not take into account anything that they say, however, apart from what the law deems to be relevant to this particular type of dispute. Unlike the compassionate model, it cannot set tests (or traps) for the parties.

Lord Diplock, giving a judgment in the House of Lords, explained it in this way:

> The requirement that a person exercising . . . judicial functions must base his decisions on evidence means no more than it must be based upon material which tends logically to show the existence or non-existence of facts relevant to the issue to be determined, or to show the likelihood or unlikelihood or the occurrence of some future event the occurrence of which would be relevant. It means that he must not spin a coin or consult

an astrologer, but may take into account any material which as a matter of reason has some probative value . . . [R v *Deputy Industrial Commissioner, ex parte Moore* [1965] 1 QB 456].

Perhaps of the three models, the evidential model is the best. But it has its shortcomings, as is reflected by the following anecdotal story:

> It was a hot summer's day in the county court. Everbody was feeling testy. The old judge was listening to a particular witness, who was talking about the contents of a document that the witness had written and had sent to a person involved in the case. Mr Darby, the barrister, had a copy of the document in his hands and was slowly drawing out its contents from the witness. 'Mr Darby,' said the judge 'do you have a copy of this document?' 'Yes your Honour I do.' 'Am I to see it then?' 'No your Honour.' 'Am I not to know the truth of this wretched document. Am I not to hear the truth then, Mr Darby?' 'No, your Honour, that is not your function.' 'What, then, pray, Mr Darby, is my function?' 'Why, your Honour, your function is to hear the evidence, not the truth. And as your Honour will be aware those are not the same thing!'

A Deputy Director of Social Services, echoing this judge, said on radio in 1995 that courts should concern themselves with the truth not the evidence. He was clearly frustrated by the severe difficulties in getting the evidence of young children against their alleged abusers into court (see below). But there clearly are limits to how much evidence can be put before the court. Some limits are defined by the concept of privilege, e.g., to protect the identity of a police informant, or to preserve the confidentiality of discussions between client and lawyer (see p. 33). Other limits may be dictated by policy considerations. Consider the dilemma, for example, in ordering a blood test that might reveal that the man whom a child has called 'Daddy' for many years is not in fact his or her biological father. (See *Re H* [1996] 2 FLR 65, where the Court of Appeal held that this sort of evidence should be obtained, thereby overturning earlier decisions that the whole truth might be too damaging to a child.)

The case of *R v Smith and others* [2000] 1 All ER 263, is a fine example of the distinction between evidence and truth. J and others were on trial for conspiracy to rob and possession of a weapon. Halfway through the evidence the defence made a submission to the court that the prosecution evidence was so insubstantial that the case should be dismissed. The Court of Appeal agreed that, although the police had observed some suspicious comings and goings, and had found some equipment for robbery in a flat, nothing of any cogency connected J with the alleged offence. The defence submission should, as a matter of law, have been accepted, but the trial judge had wrongly rejected it and the case had continued. On cross-examination J had admitted his guilt. Was the conviction unsafe? Yes: it was overturned, because on the admissible evidence the case should have been thrown out before the truth was revealed.

Relevance of Evidence

The evidential model requires decisions to be based on the evidence. The law requires that evidence must be relevant. This concept of relevance is vital to your understanding of what goes on in court. Relevance has a commonsense meaning. If you are dealing with care proceedings, for example, your professional judgment and experience will lead you to a decision, which you have defended admirably through discussions and child protection conferences, that this child would be better off not living at home. But since not you but the court has to make the final decision, will it agree with you on which points are relevant?

The answer is that a court can treat as relevant only those matters which statute, or case law, has said are relevant. In the present example of care proceedings, therefore, you will not know which of your available facts and opinions to put before the court without looking at the Children Act 1989, s. 31, which tells you that the court can make a care order if — and only if — satisfied that the child has suffered significant harm, or is likely to suffer such harm, and that this is attributable to the standard of care of the parents or to the child's being beyond parental control. (For more detail on this see Chapter 7.) The court will also want to be satisfied that the proposed order is in the best interests of the child (s. 1).

This means that only those facts that are relevant to these matters are to be given in evidence; if you start to talk about something else, the court will ignore you, or tell you to stick to the point. A professional witness should not be thrown by this; you should know what is the point because you know what the law says is relevant. To the lay witness, who does not know the law which underlies the dispute, to be told to stick to the point is of course a waste of time; they will tend to think that is precisely what they are doing.

Facts in Issue

We are now able to state our most important evidential rule; all evidence must be relevant. Here is a definition of relevance: evidence of a fact is relevant if it logically helps to prove or disprove a *fact in issue*.

This definition is not connected in any way to whether the evidence is believable or not. That is a matter for assessment by the judge, magistrate, jury or tribunal after the evidence has been received; but for defining whether the evidence is relevant to the case, you have to assume that the evidence *could* be believed.

A fact in issue, of course, has to be explained. A fact is in issue — and therefore relevant — where the court cannot decide the case according to the law without first deciding whether that fact is true or false. Take 'significant harm' under the Children Act 1989, s. 31: the issue that the court has to determine is whether such harm has occurred, or is likely to occur. This is a fact in issue. The facts in issue in any particular case will be limited to those which the parties involved disagree on. In proceedings under s. 31, for example, the fact in issue might be how a bruise was caused. Relevant evidence on this particular fact will be that tending to prove or disprove that it was caused non-accidentally. Medical evidence, facts observed by neighbours, your own observations and opinions on the family's behaviour — these will be relevant. So will the evidence of the parent, which would also tend to show how the bruise was caused — it would help to disprove, if believed, the allegations that the bruise was attributable to a poor standard of care.

Several facts are always in issue at any one time. To seek to prove significant harm to a court, several incidents may be alleged; the harm alleged to be due to lack of parental care may show up as criminal behaviour by the child, poor school attendance, disturbed behaviour and so on. Evidence on all these facts will then be admissible as relevant, because they all come within the ambit of the criterion set out in the law — that significant harm has occurred or is likely to occur.

Rules under the Children Act 1989 help the courts and the parties to identify what are the facts in issue in a children case. Applications for any order must be accompanied by a form setting out, in particular, what the grounds for the desired order are and the applicant's future plans for the child. Other parties have to reply by stating what aspects of the applicant's case they agree or disagree with and what allegations of fact they wish to put forward.

Previous decisions of the courts also help to determine what factual evidence will be relevant. Again, taking 'significant harm' as an example, the courts have given some guidance on what might amount to significant harm. Truancy from school has been recognised as constituting 'significant harm' (*Re O* [1992] 2 FLR 7: see p. 137), and so evidence of truancy becomes relevant. Disagreements about whether, when or how the truancy took place become facts in issue. Another example of case law clarifying what has to be proved, comes again from the 'significant harm' test. Section 31 provides that it must be proved (among other things, as a ground for a care order) that the child '*is* suffering'. Does 'is' mean *now* — in court, today? In *Re M (Minor) (Care Order: Significant Harm)* [1994] 2 FLR 577 (see p. 141), it was held that the time to look at harm is the date that the court proceedings commenced.

Evidence or Representations

By and large, when making a finding on the relevant facts, the courts can only take into account 'evidence'. Evidence, as we see later in this chapter, means the testimony of witnesses, the contents of documents and the production of objects in court.

But there is another category of information which the court can take into account in making certain decisions; this information is not treated as 'evidence' and is not subject to the same rules.

Let us consider an example. Having ascertained the necessary facts in a care case, that a child has suffered harm due to lack of parental care, or in a criminal case that a person has committed an offence, the court can now hear 'representations' from people who are not testifying as witnesses of fact, in particular the lawyers. These representations are not subject to rules as to what is allowed to be said, and are, of necessity, based on much second-hand information and are full of opinion. For example, in a mitigation speech after a conviction, the lawyer may say 'I have heard from the defendant's employer that a job awaits him if he is not sent to prison, and in my opinion this would be a much better outcome'.

It will also be the role of the social worker to make representations. For example, assume that the court is satisfied that significant harm has occurred under s. 31, and that this relates to the standard of parenting. You may be asked to give a welfare report to the court and be available for questioning on it, for the purpose of representing to the court what particular order should be made and why.

You will normally provide your written evidence (on the facts in issue) and your representations (on your opinion as to how the court should decide in the light of the evidence) in one statement. When you are cross-examined it will be on both aspects — evidence and representations. On other occasions you will be delivering a report not on behalf of your agency, but as a servant of the court (see next chapter for when you take on these different roles); the same principles apply, your report and any questioning you may undergo in court do not consist, technically, of evidence but of representations, and the rules of evidence are relaxed.

Whether you are giving evidence or making representations, what you say must be justifiable and can be challenged.

Lastly, if what you say in the course of a representation is challenged as factually inaccurate, the court must either ignore it or require you to prove the point on evidence. For example, in a welfare report in care proceedings, you say that the family live in great squalor; the parents may challenge you, and you will either concede the point as unimportant or call evidence to support the point. If, in a pre-sentence report on a juvenile, you say that he has an alcohol problem, for example, or missed several appointments with you without excuse, and the juvenile challenges these allegations, the court will ignore them unless you can prove them by producing evidence.

The Standard of Proof

Let us again assume that the issue is whether there has been significant harm caused to the child because of a lack of parental care. The court has heard medical evidence on one side showing that the bruise is not consistent with an accident; evidence that the father has been heard to beat another child in the family; that there was a three-day delay before bringing the child to the doctor: yet on the other side there is medical evidence that suggests a plausible accident consistent with what the parents are saying; there is evidence from a relative of domestic harmony.

How does the court decide what actually happened and why? It must do so, in a civil case, on the balance of probabilities. This means it metaphorically puts all the admissible evidence for each side into a pair of imaginary scales; the more convinced the judge or magistrates are by a particular bit of evidence, the more it weighs; it then looks to see which way the scales tip. If they tip at all, the facts on that side of the balance are accepted for the purpose of this case. That may not be the end of the case, as there has to be a further balancing exercise for each set of relevant facts; for example, after finding, on the balance of probabilities, that the child has suffered significant harm, the evidence on the question 'Was it caused by a lack of parental care?' must be weighed in the same way.

What happens, however, if the scales do not move at all and there is perfect balance? In other words, the court is unable to decide whom to believe and whose evidence is more convincing. The answer is that whoever is alleging a fact has the burden of proving that fact. In care proceedings, it will be the social service agency that alleges the harm, and that it is due to lack of parental care. It therefore has the burden of proof on each of these allegations, and must discharge that burden by producing relevant evidence on each which the court accepts as more cogent than the evidence put to rebut these allegations. If they are not proved on the balance of probabilities and the scales refuse to tip, the care order cannot be made. If the scales do tip, the agency must still convince the court on the balance of probabilities that the order it seeks is the best outcome for the child.

The burden of proof in a criminal case is more onerous. Here, the party making the allegations — the prosecution — has to prove each and every element of the alleged crime beyond reasonable doubt. The benefit of any doubt, in theory if not always in practice, must go to the defendant, who is thus not obliged to prove his or her innocence.

The same set of facts may be in issue when a child has allegedly been sexually abused. The alleged perpetrator may be acquitted in the criminal proceedings because there is some reasonable doubt about his or her guilt. But nevertheless in the civil court, a care order is made because the court is satisfied that, among other things, a person committed those acts — the court is satisfied on the balance of probabilities.

Does the civil standard apply in all civil cases? Surprisingly, not always. Sometimes the court will wish to be convinced beyond the mere balance of probabilities before deciding a fact in issue. An example of this occurs where, in care proceedings, it is alleged that an identifiable person has abused a child. The allegation must concern behaviour that is also criminal, so that if it were made in the course of a criminal trial, it would have to be proved beyond reasonable doubt. The matters are not tried together, since in one instance the court is concerned with the future of a child, and in the other, the potential guilt and punishment of an offender. But the principles do overlap, and the case of *In re G (a minor)* [1987] 1 WLR 1461, suggests that where allegations of criminal conduct are made in care proceedings against a named individual, before accepting those allegations as true, a higher standard of proof is required than merely the balance of probabilities, but still not proof beyond reasonable doubt. And in *Re W (Minors)* [1990] 1 FLR 203, Butler-Sloss LJ said:

> Grave allegations of sexual abuse made in a statement by a child . . . would, unsupported, rarely be sufficiently cogent and reliable for a court to be satisfied on the balance of probabilities that the person named was indeed the perpetrator.

Contrast this cautious approach to the child's evidence with the decision of the Court of Appeal to convict a man for rape on the evidence of a six-year-old (*R* v *Norbury* (1992) 95 Cr App R 256).

Even without naming the abuser, the court could — and in *Re W* did — still make an order to protect the child, deciding that on the balance of probability significant harm has occurred or is likely, without deciding who caused it. Therefore, in *Lancashire County Council* v *B (A Child) (Care Orders: Significant Harm)* [2000] 2 WLR 346, where the court could not decide if it was the childminder or the parents who had injured the child, the significant harm was still made out.

What is the position where — in a civil case — allegations supporting, say, an application for a care order are made against someone not a party to the case? This happened in *Re S (Minors)* [1997] 1 FLR 497. The local authority wished to bolster its case by referring to allegations that the step-father had assaulted his niece (now an adult). The step-father did not want this issue decided in his absence, and he was allowed to intervene in the case to defend himself against these specific allegations.

Sometimes the burden of proof is laid down by statute or regulation. An example of this is the Sex Discrimination (Indirect Discrimination and Burden of Proof) Regulations 2001, SI 2660, which were brought in to comply with a European Union directive. Someone alleging sex discrimination must establish sufficient facts for the tribunal to presume that direct or indirect discrimination could have occurred. The respondant then has the burden of proof to show that it did not.

Confusion on Burden of Proof in Abuse Cases

The courts at times seem determined to avoid clear thinking in this difficult area of what is the burden of proof in abuse proceedings. They sometimes lose sight of the objective, which is to protect children, and stray into the arena of armchair philosophy and probability theory. Take a look at *Re H and R (Child Sexual Abuse: Standard of Proof)* [1996] AC 583, [1996] 1 FLR 80, a decision by the House of Lords by a majority of 3:2. Their Lordships decided that, as a matter of principle, serious abuse is less likely to occur than minor abuse, and therefore requires more cogent evidence. They cited no evidence and offered no justification for this pronouncement. This means, when you stop and think about it, that the greater the risk to the child in terms of seriousness, the harder it is to obtain a court order based on likelihood of significant harm. What makes this decision — to refuse a care order under the Children Act 1989, s. 31 — even more bizarre is that every time any judge looked at the actual evidence the judge found the child's allegations more credible than the man's denials. Nevertheless, the child's siblings were denied the protection of the 1989 Act because the allegations against the man were so serious! The case was followed by the Court of Appeal in *Re G (A Child) (Non Accidental Injury: Standard of Proof)* [2001] 1 FCR 97.

This case, and the problems the courts have created in protecting children from future harm, have been considered further at pp. 136–43 when we looked at child protection.

We have also considered in Chapters 7 and 17 the power of the court in family proceedings to have the abuser evicted. Will these questionable presumptions about probability make the power useless if the court refuses to name the abuser except in clear-cut cases?

Inferences and Presumptions

Having said that the party raising allegations must prove each and every one of them, we find that this principle is breached by the application of inferences and presumptions. Some of these are common sense, since if inferences could not be drawn from facts, little could ever be proved. Another way of understanding inferences is that they are the product of circumstantial evidence. If a person is identified running away from a jeweller's shop carrying a bag marked 'swag', and evidence shows that items found in the bag are identical to items missing from the shop, a good inference is that this person took them, dishonestly intending to keep them. The court has to make the inference in order to convict, for there is no direct evidence, particularly of the defendant's dishonest intentions.

Let us give an example from an actual case, *Whelehan* v *DPP* [1995] RTR 177. It is 1.20 a.m. The accused is sitting in his stationary car on a road; the keys are in the ignition. Has he been driving? If he has, he will be guilty of driving with excess alcohol in his blood. The accused will not admit to driving, so he can be convicted of the offence only if the inference is a strong one. Do the circumstances suggest that he was driving? Yes.

Inferences in most cases are less clear-cut than this example. Can the court infer, for example, from the fact that a parent delayed seeking medical help for a child's injury, that the parent inflicted the injury? On its own the inference is unsafe, but combined with other evidence, such as the nature of the injury, or the doubtful explanation given for it, the inference becomes reasonable — but it is not conclusive. The court may or may not draw the inference depending on the other evidence presented, the credibility of all the evidence, and of course the judge's or the magistrates' own experience (or prejudice).

Some inferences may be drawn because legislation provides for them. For example, under the Criminal Procedure and Investigations Act 1996, a defendant on a criminal charge must supply details of the nature of his or her defence before trial. If he or she does not, the court may draw adverse inferences from this (though it cannot convict on inference alone — there must be some additional evidence which together with the inference proves the case beyond reasonable doubt).

Often a court should be warned against a 'commonsense' inference. In child abuse cases it takes experience to realise that a child may conceal the abuse because of threats made and/or misplaced guilt. A jury might infer that the alleged abuse did not take place, and it might require expert evidence to explain the psychological processes which can lead a child to denial and delay.

Inferences can therefore be described as commonsense conclusions, applied with caution. What of presumptions? Here, the law is more rigid. The law will make certain presumptions in the absence of evidence to the contrary. The Court of Appeal has stated that it can be presumed that a one-month-old baby should be with the mother. The existence of this presumption means that the father needs positive evidence to rebut it (*Re W* [1992] 2 FLR 332, *Re D* [1999] FLR 134). Another example in family law is that a child benefits from contact with the father, unless the contrary is proved (*Re R* [1993] 2 FLR 762).

Judicial Notice

Certain facts are so well known that they do not have to be proved, for example that Monday follows Sunday, or that we should drive on the left. The judge takes 'judicial notice' of the fact. But courts are most reluctant to put themselves in the position of witnesses of fact; if in any doubt, they will require evidence on a point which you might well feel is self-evident. For example, in *Preston-Jones* v *Preston-Jones* [1951] AC 391, the court refused to take judicial notice of the normal period of gestation, and refused to declare that a man was not the father of a child, merely because he had last had intercourse with the mother 12 months before the birth. The court insisted on hearing expert evidence on the normal and maximum lengths of gestation.

This decision, and others like it, might prompt a robust commentator to agree with Dickens' Mr Bumble, that 'the law is an ass'; whatever your own view, be prepared to prove it with evidence on all points that form part of your case. But don't be surprised if, having gone to the length of getting a witness available on a point, the court criticises you for wasting its time by trying to prove the obvious. Getting to know your bench is at least as important as reading the evidence textbooks.

Who will the Court Believe?

In a criminal case, the magistrates or the jury decide whether they believe one story or another. (However, please recall the discussion above on burden of proof: they should apply a different standard when weighing the credibility of the prosecution's story against the credibility of the defence story. The defence do not have to prove their story, and the prosecution must prove theirs beyond reasonable doubt. This was reaffirmed by the High Court in *Evans* v *DPP* [2001] EWHC Admin 369, *The Times*, 9 July, which affirmed that the right to have the prosecution prove the case is a human right under Article 6 of the European Convention.) In a civil case, it is the magistrates or the judge. It is very much up to these fact finders to decide what is credible and what is not, and an appeal on the basis of 'well I wouldn't have believed that evidence' will fail, unless no reasonable court hearing that evidence could possibly have believed it. Calling a psychologist to bolster the credibility of a witness is frowned upon (*R* v *Robinson* [1994] Crim LR 356) in criminal cases, but is allowed in civil cases (though dislike of being told who to believe may perhaps make the judge sceptical of such expert evidence).

The decision on the evidence will always be that of the judge, magistrates or jury. The following is an example of that principle. A judge was entitled to reject the unanimous evidence of social workers, guardian *ad litem* and consultant paediatrician, who all advised in favour of adoption rather than the child remaining with the mother. The judge felt the non-accidental injuries were not the mother's fault and, so long as the decision was explained by the judge and not perverse, the Court of Appeal would not overturn it: *Re B (Care: Expert Witnesses)* [1996] 1 FLR 667.

Is Evidence always Required?

There is no simple answer to this point. In most civil proceedings, the parties can agree to a particular outcome, or part of the case, thus avoiding the need for the facts to be proved, since none is in issue. However, in cases where social workers are concerned, this is rare. In care proceedings, even if the parent does not oppose the proceedings, the court should make the order only if the grounds are made out to its satisfaction — because that is what the statute requires. And there may be other reasons for wanting a full hearing of the evidence. *Re M (Threshold Criteria: Parental Concessions)* [1999] 2 FLR 728 is an interesting example. Three adopted children each alleged sexual abuse against the adoptive father. In criminal proceedings he was acquitted, but (as we saw above) this means only that the evidence did not satisfy the jury beyond reasonable doubt, not that he did not do the deed. But the adoptive father did not want to continue as an adoptive parent. He conceded that the criteria for a care order were made out by his bad parenting and subsequent rejection of the children. However, the Court of Appeal decided that the children needed to be listened to, and the issue of abuse also needed to be decided in case the adoptive father ever applied for contact. Therefore the Court would hear and make a finding of fact on the abuse allegation in the civil case (see Chapter 7.)

Sometimes, of course, the evidence can be dispensed with, or perhaps no proceedings at all are needed. For example, a defendant in a criminal case pleads guilty; or a court makes an interim care order without hearing the full argument or evidence, because the parties agree (see further Chapter 7).

Types of Evidence

Our courts are the product of history. The rules evolved when few people could read or write, and it was necessary to have oral evidence or do without. Nowadays, there could be a choice, but despite some erosions of the rule, the norm is still for evidence to be presented orally. There are obvious criticisms of this rule — the expense and delay, and, as we shall see in criminal cases, the loss of potentially useful evidence — but it has the attraction of giving parties their day in court, the chance to see clearly what the case for or against them is, and to challenge the evidence of the other parties directly. This is the process of 'justice not only being done, but being seen to be done'.

Most of the discussion below will be concerned with oral evidence. But you have to be aware that there are two other categories of evidence, documentary (which includes audio and video tapes, and photographs) and real. The court allows documents as evidence. But there are problems in the form of the hearsay rule if you actually want to get the court to read what the documents say and to take account of the contents. Reports (see next chapter) and written statements (see below) are, by definition, documentary evidence.

Real evidence means things which relate to the facts in issue — for players of Cluedo, the piece of lead piping or the revolver which were the murder weapons; on a more mundane level, the brake cylinder which was allegedly defective and led to the crash. Surprisingly, people are real evidence, including their demeanour in court, which is relevant to whether they are to be believed.

The same fact can be proved by all three types of evidence: for example, the particular fact in issue is an alleged injury to a child. Oral evidence can be given by a witness, who states that she saw the injury being inflicted, or the resulting injury; X-ray evidence (i.e., documentary) can show a fracture (but oral evidence from a doctor is needed to interpret this evidence); a scar on the child's body could be looked at by the court as real evidence (although there would have to be compelling reasons to put a child through that when other satisfactory documentary or oral evidence is available, such as a photograph, a medical report or medical testimony).

BEING A WITNESS

Traditionally, the Law of England and Wales has favoured oral evidence. Witness evidence can be tested by cross-examination, and the credibility of the evidence can be judged from the demeanour of the witness. Courts have only recently moved towards allowing more written evidence in trials. In all civil proceedings which you encounter as a social worker (Children Act cases being the most important) any evidence from a witness must first be put before the court as a written statement. You will only go into the witness-box after the judge (or magistrates) and the other party have read your statement.

In criminal cases, however, the oral tradition remains paramount. In child protection work you are working with the police, whose duties include charging suspects; the best way to protect a child's interests may be for an abuser to be prosecuted. Therefore, you also need to understand matters of criminal evidence and procedure.

In what follows, we are assuming that you are preparing to appear as a witness in a civil case brought by social services. Where the procedure differs in criminal cases, we point this out.

Your agency lawyer should prepare, or assist you in the preparation of, documentary and real evidence. But no one can be a witness for you. In this part of the chapter, we will describe the procedures for oral testimony, and as we go along try to answer some common questions which cause anxiety.

Must I give Evidence?

Usually, as an agency social worker, this question will not arise; you have the relevant personal knowledge of the facts, and you will have to give evidence. Alternatively you could drop the case! Reluctant witnesses can be compelled by all courts and tribunals to attend to give evidence; but since you will probably have initiated the case, there is no point having an order taken out against yourself. It is possible, however, that another party will want to force you to attend, for example to testify in a case where you are no longer the key worker, perhaps on behalf of a parent.

If you are likely to require a witness from outside your agency, for example a health visitor, then frequently you will find that a witness order is required, as they are instructed by their employer not to attend court unless one has been served. You, and your lawyer, must be aware of which agencies have adopted this policy.

In what Order do Things Proceed?

Whoever has to prove the case will usually be required to call their witnesses first. In a criminal case, therefore, prosecution witnesses testify before defence witnesses. In care proceedings, the applicant (your department or the NSPCC) goes first. When it is your turn the usher leads you to the witness-box and gives you a choice of card. One contains the oath, the other the non-religious affirmation. Which you take is a matter of choice, although because most people take the oath, you may make yourself more conspicuous if you make the affirmation. The wording of the oath differs for different religions, and the book you hold in your hand should be appropriate to your religion.

There are three stages in giving evidence as a witness: examination, cross-examination and re-examination. In the examination and re-examination you are being questioned on behalf of your own 'side' — usually, of course, the lawyer for your employing authority. On cross-examination you are being questioned on behalf of all the other parties in turn.

Examination   This stage is bypassed in almost all civil proceedings, including Children Act cases, because any person, on behalf of any party, who has something to say in a civil case must submit to the court and the other parties a statement of what it is they will be saying as a witness. That statement is read in advance of the hearing, and witnesses go straight into the ordeal of being cross-examined. In the family proceedings court, some magistrates will ask the witness to go over the evidence before there is a cross-examination, even though there is a witness statement. In that case what we say below about examination in criminal proceedings will apply.

Examination in criminal proceedings   In a criminal case, 'special measures' are applied to permit a vulnerable witness to pre-record his or her evidence on video tape. The examination stage is also bypassed. This is discussed at the end of this chapter. What follows is directed at the non-vulnerable witness, such as the social worker.

If you are involved in a criminal case, your evidence will first be taken orally. (The statement you will have made to the police does not go before the court unless you are to be cross-examined about it.) The process is called examination in chief.

On examination, you will be asked questions by the prosecution lawyer. The questions must not be put in such a way as to suggest the answer — that would be a leading question. For example, you cannot be asked 'Did you see him hit the child?' but instead 'Did you see anything?'; 'Yes'; 'What did you see?'. Leading questions are permitted where the answer is not in dispute, such as when you are asked at the beginning of your examination 'Are you Joan Wilson, of 10 Burdon Terrace, Cliffside, and are you employed by Northshire Social Services Department in Area 3?'.

So under examination, you cannot be told what to say. You have to produce the 'right' answers of your own accord. One of the worst fears of a lawyer is of the witness who does not come 'up to proof', because the lawyer is prevented from saying 'Wait a minute, that's not what you told me before'. A lawyer cannot cross-examine his or her own witness, and is stuck with the answers he or she receives.

Therefore you need to know exactly what it is that you are going to say in evidence. Preparation comes in here. The term 'up to proof' in fact derives from a document called a proof of evidence. When legal proceedings are likely, the lawyer who plans to call you will take a statement (or proof of evidence) from you, have it typed up and have it signed by you. In a criminal case, the statement is usually taken by a police officer, and the statement will usually be disclosed to the defence before trial.

In civil cases the witness statements are filed at court and revealed to all the parties in advance. If any statement needs amending, the court's permission is needed. So a statement has to be drafted with the greatest care and attention to accuracy.

The prosecution lawyer will now assume that when you go into the witness-box your evidence will follow the witness statement. Questions will be asked to bring out that material. You will not have the proof in front of you. It is permissible and sensible to re-read your statement shortly before going into the witness-box, and even at this late stage it is better to tell the prosecution lawyer that parts are inaccurate than to have inconsistencies exposed in the witness-box.

Cross-examination   This stage applies in both civil and criminal cases.

You gave your evidence by written statement. Alternatively, the examination finishes, and you are asked to 'wait there'. All other parties' lawyers now have the opportunity to cross-examine you in turn. The most important part of the English trial is the cross-examination. The emphasis in English/Welsh law on the oral presentation of evidence is so that it can be tested. This is where the testing takes place. Cross-examination allows the advocate to put to you leading questions, i.e., questions which do suggest the answer. 'I think you've got it wrong; it wasn't half-past five when you called, it was well after six, wasn't it?' 'How can you be so sure?' 'So you were wearing a watch; how is it that you do not have one on today? Do you usually take your watch off before coming to court?' and so on. Something we, and the courts, would wish you to avoid is finding yourself being cross-examined on aspects of the statement that are put in the lawyer's words, not your own. Courts will rightly be angry if you express doubts about what is in your statement (*Alex Lawrie Factors Ltd* v *Morgan* (2000) *The Times*, 18 August). Before you sign it, read your statement and ask yourself if you are ready to be cross-examined on it.

Cross-examination can be an unpleasant experience. You will perhaps take a dislike to the person subjecting you to this. But understanding the purpose of cross-examination may assist in remaining objective about it.

If a witness makes any factual allegation, the other parties are assumed to accept it as correct unless they challenge it in cross-examination. So even when it is quite obvious that you are not going to change your story, you will have to answer questions such as 'That's not what happened, is it?' or even 'I suggest to you that what you have said is pure fabrication'. The lawyer does not expect, or even hope, that you will buckle under the weight of this skilful cross-examination and suddenly admit that you have made it all up. But he or she has a duty to put the question to you, and the benefit for that lawyer may be that it flusters and confuses you. To avoid this result, it helps to realise that this kind of question is often just a ritual. Do not take it personally just because someone is insinuating that you are wrong in your recollection or judgment.

More worrying is the apparently friendly question which softens you up for the sharp follow-up question. You may wonder what the questioner is getting at. If you are unsure, then the best advice is to answer the question in as matter of fact a way as you can, and let him or her reveal the strategy. Long, complex answers, given under pressure, may well contain things that you are not confident about, or even that contradict your earlier evidence. Short replies — but not monosyllabic — create fewer hostages to fortune. (If in doubt, remember KISS — Keep It Simple, Stupid!)

But giving evidence is an art, and giving short answers may itself allow a false picture of your position to emerge. Consider the following exchange:

Q: You were concerned about June?
A: Yes.
Q: Very concerned?
A: Yes.
Q: Did you discuss this with your management?
A: Oh yes, we had many meetings and case conferences.
Q: There was considerable concern throughout the department?
A: Yes.
Q: June was a constant preoccupation?
A: Yes.
Q: Then why did you visit only twice before you applied for a protection order?

How should the witness have answered these questions? Perhaps he or she was too eager to give the apparently 'correct' answer. There is no correct answer except what you consider to be the truth. The witness has acquiesced with an exaggeration of the truth, falling into the same trap as the witness who does not know when to stop.

Occasionally a skilled cross-examiner will trip you up. You will say something which you think on reflection is wrong. The immediate temptation is to cover your tracks, to pretend it is consistent with the other evidence you have given. But you risk digging yourself into a deeper hole, and a good cross-examining lawyer will allow you to dig deep before pointing out the inconsistencies in what you have just said. We suggest: 'I think I have just said something which gives the wrong impression', or even 'I made a mistake when I said that; what I meant to say was. . .'.

Tips for answering questions   There is a convention which you can use to your advantage. It can be used in examination and cross-examination. Although the lawyer asks you the questions, your answers must be addressed to the bench. This means, to do it properly, turning your head to face the bench after the lawyer has finished framing the question. Doing this slowly, particularly after a difficult question in cross-examination, gives you thinking time, and shows you to be in control of the situation.

Sometimes you will be told to 'Watch the pen!' To the uninitiated this makes no sense at all. Apart from the High Court, where there will be a stenographer or a tape recorder, you will find that the clerk of the court or the judge is taking a longhand note of everything that is said. Watching the pen means pausing frequently as you speak, resuming only when the pen is still. If you comply with this requirement, not only will the court be impressed by your obvious control of the situation and your court experience, but you will also gain valuable time to think about what it is you wish to say next. If you feel nervous, this is natural. So, in fact, do the lawyers and the other witnesses. Perhaps the judge is nervous. Speak slowly and deliberately, pause for breath, and remember that how you feel is probably worse than how you look.

Re-examination   This is the mopping-up operation. It is too late to introduce new evidence, but your own lawyer will get you to clarify points that have been raised in cross-examination, to explain inconsistencies. If you have taken a straightforward approach to the cross-examination, this will be mercifully brief. It may not even happen at all.

We will now consider some more questions which commonly concern witnesses.

Can Anyone Help me with my Evidence?
The simple answer is 'No'. Once in the witness-box, you are on your own. Preparation of your evidence gives some assistance, as long as it is still your own evidence and truthful.

Can I Refuse to Answer Questions?
No, unless the answer would incriminate you — i.e., leave you vulnerable to criminal charges. This is an unlikely risk to you personally. In fact, since the Children Act, s. 98, you are unlikely to see a witness be allowed to refuse to answer a question on this ground, for it no longer applies in a case involving children. The result is that in care proceedings a person alleged to have abused a child must answer questions about the allegations, even if the answers could lead to a criminal prosecution. The Act puts the need to protect children above other civil liberties.

Transcripts of civil proceedings can be disclosed to the police for use in criminal cases, if the judge gives permission. This makes the right not to answer questions a little meaningless, since the witness can then be cross-examined in a criminal trial as to why he or she refused to answer questions (*Re L* [1999] 1 FLR 165).

Can I Refer to Notes?

You can refer to your written statements in a civil case.

The court will also allow a witness to refer to notes that were made by that witness, or verified by that witness, 'substantially contemporaneously' with the events that are recorded in them. This means as soon as possible in the circumstances. You may therefore refresh your memory from the case notes, if, in accordance with good practice, you made these notes when the incidents were fresh in your mind, and not days or weeks or months later. You would not be able to refer to anyone else's notes to help you remember the facts — the maker of the notes would have to be called personally or, in a children's case, those notes could themselves be evidence. Before being allowed to refresh your memory, you will be asked a few questions about when you made the note.

You may be asked to explain why you took, or failed to take, a particular course of action, and in that case you may refer to case notes made by yourself, or anyone else. This is, technically, different from refreshing your own memory.

Your notes will be kept in a case file. If you have it with you, you will be able to flick back and forward to refresh your memory according to the questions asked. There is one problem. When it comes to cross-examination, the opposing lawyer will ask to take a look at the notes. If the notes are contained in a file, you have to hand over the whole file. There will be a dramatic pause while the lawyer peruses the notes, and suddenly you may get a totally unexpected question: 'But it says here that. . .' How will you cope with the realistic need to refresh your memory without the problems caused by handing your whole file to the opposition? The simple answer would be to extract only those notes which are relevant, although under cross-examination about incidents you had thought irrelevant, the absence of your notes will now be painful. And the court may object to your selection only of parts of what, in essence, is one continuous document, and refuse to allow you to rely on the extract.

There are two safe options. One is to rely on memory only. This is advisable only if your memory is clear, for it will be fully tested under cross-examination.

The other (recommended) option is to use the whole file. You should, as a matter of course, have prepared every entry in the knowledge that it may be the subject-matter of skilled cross-examination. Every opinion must then be justifiable, every fact accurately recorded, with the name of the person making the note (and the time and place) also recorded.

In a children case, the decision whether to rely on your notes to refresh your memory should be discussed with your lawyer and your line manager.

Can I Give the Court my Opinion?

Courts have traditionally had an abhorrence of witnesses offering opinions: 'Give us the facts. We will form our own opinions.'

The rule excluding opinion is easy to state but hard to apply with certainty. What appears to be a simple fact, such as 'The car was going fast', or 'She was drunk' or even 'The person I saw was John' is, on reflection, nothing other than the observer's opinion as to drunkenness, speed or a person's features. But the court allows a witness to give their opinion of facts that could not easily be conveyed in any other way, so the examples above cause no problem. The opinion can be stated: whether it is believed is another matter. Coming closer to the borderline, statements such as 'She looked frightened' or 'He was trying to avoid me' — statements which are giving an opinion as to someone else's state of mind — will usually be admissible as the only way of saying what was observed. But from a lay person, a statement such as 'This injury was not an accident', or 'I think she was behaving negligently' will be refused.

Sometimes courts cannot make up their minds about the evidence without the help of an expert. In areas such as mental health and child care, opinion evidence is allowed and is usually crucial. The Civil Evidence Act 1972 expressly permits experts to give their opinion to the court on any relevant issue, if they are experts in that subject (*Re M and R* [1996] 2 FLR 195: see p. 87). The courts presume that as a qualified social worker you are an expert on issues of general child care (see *F v Suffolk County Council* [1981] 2 FLR 208).

Sometimes you will be an expert witness, and sometimes not. In conveying opinions about one sample of handwriting matching another, or interpretations of medical symptoms, you are not an expert, and not entitled to offer opinions to the court. But in areas such as child behaviour, or causes of stress in families, if it is relevant, the court will allow you to voice those opinions, because you are in a better position than a court to judge these matters. In fact, frequently, a large part of what you have to say will consist of your opinion; but you must confine your opinions to areas where you have expertise. (Courts do not consider that social workers generally have expertise in diagnosing sexual abuse: *Re N* [1996] 2 FLR 2. You will therefore need to tell the court what you have directly observed, not what you think it means. Nor are you expert in matters of credibility of child witnesses — see p. 87.)

You will of course be required to defend your opinion. You will have to state what experience, or research, or reading, you based that opinion on, and in what circumstances you might modify it. You must be prepared to hear it contradicted by another witness, and to have it dismissed in favour of another interpretation of the facts. It is therefore worth anticipating very hard questions on your opinions in cross-examination; and if you cannot justify them before you get to court, perhaps they are unjustifiable, or perhaps you are the wrong person to call as the witness on this point. (See comments in the next chapter on reports.)

What if my Opinion is Different from that of my Agency?

Imagine that your opinion was not accepted at a case conference, and it was decided to apply for a care order, even though you think that this is not in the child's best interests or that the relevant admissible evidence is weak.

As an employee of your agency, you must abide by directions given to you by your seniors. If you are told to instruct your lawyers to commence care proceedings, you do so. Of course, as a professional, you make plain that in your view this is not the best course. If at all possible, you should avoid going into the witness-box. It may be that your lawyer decides there is sufficient evidence from other witnesses to make out the grounds. But the other parties may notice and comment on your absence, and may even serve you with a witness order, in which case you will have to attend. Alternatively, your lawyer may decide that without your evidence of the facts of which you have firsthand knowledge, the case will not be made out.

So you find yourself in the witness-box and the cross-examination begins. You are asked directly whether you think these parents are incapable of caring for the child. What is the answer?

You are now a professional social worker under oath, sworn to tell the truth. Your duty is to the court first, to your employer second. You state as accurately as you can what your observations and opinions are. Any alternative would be perjury. There is nothing unprofessional about giving evidence which damages your agency's case. What would be unprofessional would be if you had not made the difference in viewpoint known to your agency before giving the evidence. If you fear that this situation may arise, you should inform your lawyer and your senior at the earliest opportunity.

One example of this dilemma is *Re C (Interim Care Order: Residential Assessment)* [1997] 1 FLR 1. A psychologist and the social workers gave evidence in care proceedings that they considered that a residential assessment of the child and parents would help to determine whether the parents should have the child returned to them. The Assistant Director of Social Services refused to pay the estimated costs of £24,000, and gave evidence contradicting that of her team, who had said that an assessment was needed. The House of Lords considered, on balance, that an assessment should be ordered. What matters for the present discussion is that there was no suggestion in the judgment that there was anything wrong with social workers disagreeing with their manager in the witness-box.

Am I Allowed into Court when I am not Giving Testimony?

This matter was considered in the case of *R* v *Willesden Justices ex parte London Borough of Brent* [1988] Fam Law 341. At the commencement of the care proceedings the mother objected to the presence of the social worker in court, as she was later to be called as a witness. The justices excluded her, and the local authority applied to the High Court for judicial review of that decision. The court decided that as a general rule the party to the case has a right to be present throughout. If an agency is the party, it is represented through the social worker who deals with the case and therefore he or she retains the right to be present. But this is subject to the court's overall discretion always to allow witnesses and non-parties to be present and also to exclude people, even the social worker who personifies the agency. But as a general rule, even in children and family cases where proceedings are not open to the public, the social worker who gives instructions to the lawyer, and the expert witness waiting to be called, not only may, but should, be present in court.

How does the Hearsay Rule Affect Me?

The rule is best understood in the light of what it sets out to achieve. The court wants to hear the best evidence available. Rather than hear witness A say what witness B told her, it would prefer to hear and test the evidence of witness B in person. Rather than hear what a person wrote about the facts in a letter, or a prepared statement of evidence, the court likes him or her to come to court to tell all orally. The great dread of the courts has been of fabricated evidence which cannot be tested.

Hearsay is defined as evidence of a fact given to the court in some way other than through the oral testimony of a witness who has firsthand knowledge of that fact, and as evidence of the truth of that fact. The second part of this definition is important, for not all reported speech is excluded. So the words 'You are a fascist' could be repeated in court by a person claiming to have been slandered; the very last reason for giving this evidence would be as evidence of the truth of its contents. It would be tendered as evidence merely of the fact that it was said. 'I've just seen a flying saucer' could be evidence of the arrival of flying saucers, in which case your repetition of my statement in court would be hearsay; or it could be evidence of my intoxication, or poor eyesight, or declining faculties, in which case the issue before the court would not be whether there really were flying saucers, but the mere fact that I uttered those words.

The 'hearsay rule' looks simple enough: hearsay evidence is not admissible. The trouble is, the rule excludes much potentially helpful evidence. Case law recognises some exceptions to the severity of the rule, and statute has made significant inroads. (We have already noted that the rule does not apply to representations in any event, and much of what you have to say to the court will therefore not be evidence at all (see above). The Children Act clarifies the position as to representations made in a report to the court; under s. 7, any matter referred to in the report, whether hearsay or opinion, is admissible so long as it is relevant.)

To provide a complete list of the exceptions would be unduly lengthy; if you become absorbed in this subject, take a look at, for example, Spencer and Flin, *The Evidence of Children*, 2nd edn (Blackstone Press, 1993). Here we consider the significant occasions when the courts will allow second-hand, i.e., hearsay, evidence.

Hearsay in Child Protection Proceedings

The most significant hearsay evidence, from your point of view, is probably the evidence of children. If a child tells you that he or she has been hit, or sexually abused, by their parent, that statement is of crucial importance to a care case or a criminal case. There is often no other convincing evidence of the relevant facts, particularly the identification of the perpetrator.

Under s. 96 of the Children Act, in cases involving the upbringing, maintenance or welfare of children, hearsay evidence is welcomed. Out of court disclosures by children can be evidence in any case in which matters concerning children are in issue. In fact anything written or said out of court, by any person, not just a child, can be evidence in this type of case.

But if an alleged abuser is prosecuted on the same allegations, out of court statements, by a child or anyone else, are (with many exceptions) not allowed to be part of the evidence.

On top of this general relaxation of the anti-hearsay rule, s. 45 creates an exception where an emergency protection order is sought (see further Chapter 6). In such an application, any relevant evidence can be heard, opinion and hearsay notwithstanding.

So you can perhaps now see the philosophy behind this part of the legislation: if a court is considering the future of children, it should do so with all the available information before it. It would rather receive the information, weigh it and reject it, than not hear it at all. Only in that way can all relevant issues be considered, and the child's best interests protected. This philosophy is catching on in all civil proceedings, although in criminal cases there is always likely to be a wariness of allowing juries and magistrates to have untrammelled access to hearsay evidence on which they may place undue reliance.

Hearsay in Criminal Cases

In criminal cases the court generally expects a witness to come to court, or what they have to say will not be used. So evidence of what other people said which is in your file notes, interviews with the child and reports from neighbours are all inadmissible, except in special circumstances such as the witness dying or going abroad. At present even videos of interviews with children are only admitted if the child is available for cross-examination at or before the trial (see p. 181 below). So you have to understand why the police may be reluctant to take action when you yourselves have an open and shut case showing child abuse.

There is an important exception to the hearsay rule in criminal proceedings, the relevance of which will be further understood when you read Chapter 12 on criminal procedures. It is known as confession evidence.

Words that go against the interest of the party speaking them, for example a suspect 'coughing' to the police, can be quoted back in court as evidence of the truth of what was said, so long as the confession was not extracted improperly (see Chapter 12 for more detail). A simple example in a careless driving prosecution would be a driver after a road accident who says: 'I'm sorry, I just wasn't paying attention'. These words can be quoted back in court as evidence of carelessness. Such 'I wish I'd never said that' statements are called confessions (or admissions in a civil case).

The judges have always allowed confessions because they believe they are a sensible exception to the rule preventing hearsay; the reason for this is the somewhat dubious belief that a person will not make such a statement unless it is true. For this reason, a statement out of court which damages a party's case in court is considered persuasive evidence, regardless of any question of hearsay and admissibility. Therefore, if a parent admits to a social worker 'I hit my child', the court will pay considerable attention to the social worker repeating that admission in care proceedings as well as in a criminal prosecution.

The parent may of course deny that he or she did say those words. You will have to be able to convince the court of the accuracy of your recollection, backed up by meticulously kept notes. You will also have to be careful to avoid receiving information in confidence from a parent, or anyone else, since you know that it may become key evidence in court proceedings involving children. There is nothing to stop you discussing your allegations with the parents out of court, and repeating to the court what they tell you, but we suggest that, just as the police caution suspects before they are questioned, you should inform people that what they say to you cannot be guaranteed complete confidence — such an assurance would be wrong, because your duty to protect a child through giving all relevant evidence to the court would override any personal preference for confidentiality.

You will now have the impression that a great deal of hearsay, i.e., secondhand evidence, can be admitted. But we do not wish to give the impression that this is desirable as an alternative to evidence from witnesses in court. Let us consider, for example, the welfare report. (See the next chapter for further discussion of reports.) It is based on discussion with various interested parties, and, to do a fair job, it must report the essence of the discussions. The welfare officer recommends to the court that, for example, the child should not live with the father. This is based on interviews with the mother, who makes allegations about the father's brutality. To act on the recommendation, the court inevitably places some weight on those hearsay statements. The opinion of the Court of Appeal (*Thompson v Thompson* [1986] 1 FLR 212, confirming what a judge had said in an earlier case) was:

> Some hearsay is unavoidable in such a document, and in respect of comparatively uncontroversial matters is likely to be unobjectionable; but I think it is important that a reporting officer should report his own observations and assessments, and that where he is constrained to pass on second-hand information or opinions he should endeavour to make this explicit and should indicate the source and his own reasons, if he has any, for agreeing with any such opinions. Where a judge has to arrive at a crucial finding of fact he should found them upon sworn evidence rather than on an unsworn report.

This opinion was supported by Butler-Sloss LJ in *Re W (Minors)* [1990] 1 FLR 203:

> I agree that the liberty to tender hearsay evidence could be abused. I cannot imagine that any judge would allow a grave allegation against a parent to be proved solely by hearsay, at any rate in a case in which direct evidence could be produced.

This means that hearsay will not be excluded, but a case where the relevant facts are entirely based on such evidence will not usually be easy to prove.

We would like to finish this section on hearsay with some words of common sense, which should be applied in the preparation of any evidence, not just material containing hearsay. They were written by Roger Maunday in the *Law Society's Gazette* (1986) 29 Oct 3221: '[E]vidence is appraised on its merits by a judicious application of common nous, a balance being struck between direct and indirect evidence, between reliable, confirmed or reasoned reports of facts on the one hand and fickle gossip on the other.' Our advice therefore is to go for the best evidence you can get, which means witnesses who can tell the court the facts from their own personal experience, but not to be afraid of bringing relevant, secondhand evidence, so long as you are prepared to be cross-examined on the sources and reliability of such evidence.

Can I Read from my File?

We have referred (p. 173) to how you can refresh your memory as a witness from your notes. But a problem for a social worker wishing to present evidence at court will be how to give the court all the relevant facts, when he or she has no personal experience of some of them but can only repeat and interpret what is recorded by others on the file. Clearly, to tell the court what happened in 1998, when the witness was not involved until 2001, is hearsay. Can the social worker state such information as evidence of the truth of the facts, and as the reason for reaching the opinion which he or she wishes to give to the court?

We already know that the hearsay is admissible (s. 96 of the Children Act). A pre-Children Act case tells us how to present this type of hearsay evidence. In *Re N (a minor)* [1987] 1 FLR 65, a social worker wished to refer in an affidavit to incidents going back 12 years before he was appointed, which meant repeating what he found on the files. The court held that the evidence was admissible, but it was necessary for the witness to state clearly in the affidavit — and the same is required in Children Act written statements — the fact that he did not himself have firsthand knowledge and to identify where he had got the information.

You, and your agency lawyer, must satisfy yourselves that the evidence from the file is the best evidence you can obtain on a particular point. If the incident recorded is of great importance to your case, and the person who originally made the note is available (which may mean issuing a witness summons if they have left your department), then oral evidence which can be tested under cross-examination is likely to be more persuasive to the court.

(As you saw in Chapter 4, a person called a children's guardian can inspect your file, take copies, and produce the contents in court whether you like it or not.)

EVIDENCE FROM CHILDREN

Children's evidence is a problem for two reasons: first, they are (often wrongly) considered less likely to give good evidence than adults; secondly, the experience of being a witness is unpleasant and potentially damaging for them. Nevertheless in many cases what has happened to them of is of integral importance, and what they have to say must somehow come before the court.

A third problem arises where the child is the alleged victim of criminal behaviour, such as sexual abuse. The needs of the courts for evidence and the needs of the victim for therapy come into conflict. Courts do not want evidence to be rehearsed or contaminated. Cases have been thrown out because social workers or therapists have talked to the child about his or her story. This does not protect the child. If a case is thrown out because of contaminated evidence, the child may then feel that he or she was not believed. Yet if no one can talk to the child until after the court proceedings, he or she will be denied the help and support that it is the social worker's duty to provide whenever '. . . his health or development is likely to be significantly impaired . . . without the provision for him of . . . services [from the local authority]': Children Act 1989, s. 17(10)(b). The Court of Appeal has advised social workers that an interview carried out for therapeutic purposes would very rarely be acceptable for use as evidence in a criminal court: *Re D (Minors) (Child Abuse: Interviews)* (1998) *The Times*, 11 March. You have to decide in advance what the purpose of the interview is. Childline has produced a report on this conflict between the needs of justice and therapeutic support — *Going to Court: Child Witnesses in Their Own Words* (available from Childline, tel. 0208 239 1000).

The case of *Re T (A Minor) (Procedure: Alleged Sexual Abuse) (No. 2)* [1997] FCR 55 provides a warning, as well as a depressing chronicle of bad practice which failed to protect a child who may indeed have been sexually abused. We quote from (or paraphrase) the judgment of Lord Justice Thorpe:

It is depressing to see how badly this case has been managed by all the professionals who have been involved in what is, after all, a classically simple case of possible child sexual abuse within a single family . . .

The social services department, quite rightly, referred the case immediately to a skilled physician. [His report was ignored.] It was followed by a joint investigative interview which was very badly handled. The one thing that all accept was that it was conducted so ineptly that it has no residual value but it seems to have convinced the social services that this was a family in which the only child had been sexually abused by the father . . . Thereafter, the social worker in the case seems to have impressed upon the mother the need to release the child from guilt feelings by repeatedly reassuring him that he was not bad and that all evil was attributable to his father. It seems to me that social services need to await the outcome of the family justice proceedings before initiating a management policy that creates a belief system in the child. The issue of whether or not a child has been sexually abused in our society is for decision by the court and it seems to be essential that other agencies await that decision before introducing management counselling or therapy that pre-judged the issue.

[The opportunity to obtain an opinion from a psychologist was then inexplicably ignored.]

The next mistake to bedevil the case came . . . when the court welfare officer embarked on a 90 minute play interview with the child . . . He started out with a complete misunderstanding as to what is the appropriate approach [having stated in his evidence that children cannot fabricate such evidence and that he was prepared to flout the recommendations of the Cleveland Report on interviewing children!].

The criticisms of accepting and reinforcing one view as to what happened continue for several more pages. As a social worker you may disagree with the idea that you are not entitled to decide on the truth of allegations of abuse. As a social worker within the legal system you are going to need to suspend such views if you want to bring credible evidence before the courts. Credible evidence will be enhanced if you follow the guidelines. Moreover, as pointed out by Thorpe LJ, if you are totally committed to one view of what happened and ally yourself closely with that view in your case management (in this case the view that the mother was right and the father had played with the son's penis), how will you work with the family if the court does not come to the same conclusion? And how will the mother feel about the court's decision? Is it appropriate for you then to tell the mother that the court got it wrong?

Evidence by Video and other Special Measures for Receiving Evidence

In civil trials (which includes care proceedings) hearsay evidence is admissible, and so there is rarely a need to hear directly from a child witness. In criminal proceedings there has been a possibility of protecting the child witness through using pre-recorded videos of the child's statement, or through cross-examining the child through a CCTV, since 1991. The Youth Justice and Criminal Evidence Act 1999 now contains and extends this legislation and provides for 'special measures' to apply to receive the evidence in criminal trials of 'vulnerable and intimidated witnesses'. Facilities must be available for the special measures in the relevant court.

Under s. 16 of the 1999 Act, a child aged under 17 (when the decision on special measures is taken) is automatically eligible for special measures. Any other witness is eligible if the court decides that the quality of her or his evidence is likely to be diminished by reason of mental disorder, intellectual or social impairment, or physical disability. In addition, any witness may become eligible for special measures if the court decides that the evidence will be diminished in quality as a result of fear or distress. This automatically applies if the witness is a complainant in a case involving a sexual offence.

The court will exercise its discretion to decide what special measures, singly or in combination, are appropriate. But where the witness is a child (under 17 for these purposes, which includes someone who becomes 17 after the video of the evidence is made), s. 21 provides that, where the relevant equipment is available:

(a)   evidence in chief must be by way of pre-recorded video;
(b)   any live evidence must be given by way of CCTV link.

A court cannot override these requirements if the child witness is a complainant in a sexual offence trial.

The special measures are as follows:

(a) *Screening (s. 23)*: This is to prevent the witness from seeing the accused (but strangely it does not provide reassurance that the accused cannot see the witness).

(b) *Evidence by live link (s. 24)*: A court is permitted to move to a different venue to avail itself of facilities for this.

(c) *Evidence in private (s. 25)*: The accused or his or her lawyers cannot be removed, and the press can be removed only if a sexual offence is alleged, or there are allegations of witness intimidation.

(d) *Removal of wigs and gowns (s. 26)*.

(e) *Video recorded evidence in chief (s. 27)*: Under this section the evidence in chief — that is the evidence the witness gives first, before cross examination — can be pre-recorded. The court has to be satisfied that this is in the interests of justice, weighing the prejudice to the accused against the desirability of seeing the evidence. The main issue with child witnesses is the risk, or allegation, that in preparing the video recording the child has been in some way coached. Details of the circumstances in which the video was made must be provided to the other side. See below for considerations arising with pre-recorded child evidence. The court will usually not admit the recording if the witness cannot be cross-examined on it.

(f) *Video recorded cross-examination and re-examination (s. 28)*: This is an entirely new departure and addresses the criticism of the old law which did not provide any safeguards for the child witness against the terrors of cross-examination. Cases collapsed because it could be too traumatic for a child to be cross-examined at trial by a barrister whose job it was to undermine his or her credibility. A special measures direction can now provide for the cross-examination of the witness (and re-examination) on pre-recorded video. It is a small step only, of course, because the cross examination is still carried out by a lawyer whose job it is to discredit parts of the evidence. The video must be made in the presence (which can be electronic presence) of the other party's lawyer and of the judge. The witness is usually then spared from participation in the trial, but exceptionally the judge can have the witness recalled.

(g) *Examination of witness through intermediary (s. 29)*: This permits a court to approve an intermediary who puts the questions to the witness. An interpreter has always been allowed to do this, but this could now include a social worker or other person who can assist the witness. This can be carried out with live video links and (probably exceptionally) in conjunction with pre-recorded video cross examination.

The social worker may have involvement in preparing a pre-recorded video. Although the Act came into force in 2000, in preparing you for the task, a number of cases and guidance documents relating to the earlier legislation remain relevant.

The pre-recorded interview can be with a social worker or other non-lawyer. It is attractive for two reasons. First, the interview is more relaxed for the child than an appearance in the witness-box; secondly, the evidence may be of higher quality, as the video can be made long before the trial, before detail is forgotten. There is, however, a serious problem in the procedure, if sparing the child an ordeal is an important factor. The person accused of the violence or abuse has the right to challenge the child's evidence by cross-examination, so the child still has to give live evidence, though as we have seen, this can be organised before the trial. But the task of the cross-examining defence lawyer is still to destroy the credibility of the child's evidence and to get an acquittal, not to protect the child from pain.

The Criminal Justice Act 1988, s. 23 allows evidence in the witness's absence (i.e., hearsay evidence) if the witness is too afraid to come, but the court has to be convinced that this would be fair to the accused. This is unlikely. Courts like to see prosecution evidence tested.

Under the Youth Justice and Criminal Evidence Act 1999, s. 27, the judge can require the pre-recorded material to be edited before it is shown to the jury to remove inadmissible or unfair evidence (such as a reference to a person's previous record, or irrelevant prejudicial material). And the court may require those who made the video to give evidence about how it was made (Court of Appeal *Practice Direction* [1992] 3 All ER 909).

It is not good practice to conduct an interview with a child without recording this. Butler-Sloss LJ in *Re W* [1993] Fam Law 313 quotes what Latey J said in an earlier case with approval:

[C]ases have shown . . . that the precise questions, the oral answers (if there are any), the gestures and body movements, the vocal inflection and intonation, may all play an important part in interpretation.

Also experts can watch the video, without further interviews with the child. So, unless you are reporting spontaneous statements by the child, courts will want to see the tape, not to hear your recollection of what happened in the interview.

Guidance on conducting evidential video interviews   The use of pre-recorded video material raises the whole question of 'disclosure' work with children. The first concern of a social worker or doctor will be to work with a child to try to overcome the damage caused by abuse. In this kind of therapeutic contact with the child, it may be necessary to encourage the child to bring up past events which the child is suppressing. But the evidential interview is not, and cannot be, conducted on the same lines, and is rendered worthless as evidence for a trial if there is a suggestion that the interviewer has put words in the child's mouth.

You must be specially trained for this kind of interview. You must be familiar with the Cleveland Guidelines and *Working Together* (see Chapter 5), and with the case law and guidance that have grown around the use of video material. We start by quoting Home Office guidance taken from the 'Memorandum of Good Practice on Video Recorded Interviews with Child Witnesses in Criminal Proceedings' (HMSO, 1992):

It is very important that those conducting interviews under this Memorandum have clear, agreed, objectives which are consistent with the main purpose, which is to listen with an open mind to what the child has to say, if anything.

This guidance is essential reading for any person undertaking evidential video interviews. The courts will expect that the person who interviews the child on behalf of the multi-disciplinary team investigating allegations of abuse will be a trained specialist. You must, if that person is going to be you, read the Memorandum in full, for if the guidance is ignored, the evidence may be thrown out. That does not help the child.

First, the Memorandum dictates, the word 'disclosure' is out. It implies prejudgment of what the child may tell you. Your opinion that the child is withholding what he or she knows is potentially relevant, because in court you are an expert witness interpreting for the court what the child's behaviour means. But if, because you 'know' what happened, you prompt the child in preparing or recording a video interview, you have destroyed the child's evidence. (In fact you do not 'know' unless you witnessed the abuse; you have an opinion about what happened, and the court does not want that opinion to influence what other witnesses say.)

You can see examples of the courts' attitude to bad questioning technique in civil cases in a series of reports in [1987] Fam Law 269 *ff*. The judges rejected suggestive questioning, particularly in combination with the use of the anatomically correct dolls, and they rejected the allegations of sexual abuse apparently made by children on tape. They did so notwithstanding expert evidence from psychologists interpreting the answers to the questions as being evidence of sexual abuse. If you are involved in 'disclosure' work, these cases (although old) must be read; they show clearly that the courts reject the idea of the interviewer going in with the preconceived idea that there is something there to disclose. The consistent theme of the judgments is that putting suggestive questions to a child leads to unreliable disclosure. So yes, the evidence is admissible, but no, it is probably not persuasive unless the questioning has been very open. Jenny McEwan put it well, writing in the *Journal of Child Law*, vol. 2, No. 1, p. 24:

Judicial dislike of cross-examination technique in disclosure interviews is well known. The courts frown upon hypothetical and leading questions, 'pressure', reminding the child of what she allegedly said elsewhere and disregard of the answers actually given.

Here are some key points from the Memorandum: the interviewer should start by building a rapport with the child, then move to questioning in a very open-ended style, only gradually moving towards closed questions, which the child should be able to answer in his or her own manner without interruption. It is safe to ask leading questions — that is, questions suggesting the answer you expect to get — only at the very end, if at all. You must be aware that the court will be balancing the interests of the child and society against the right of the accused to have the evidence fairly presented — which means hearing what the child has to say without any hint of influence. Remember that in a prosecution, whether you agree or not, the child's interests are not paramount. A fair trial is.

Guidance was also given on evidential interviewing in *R v H and others* [1992] 1 All ER 153. Hollings J insisted in particular that one person should coordinate the investigation on behalf of a multi-disciplinary team, and this includes preparation of video evidence.

If pre-recorded evidence is used in a criminal case, the prosecution have to supply details to the defence of when it was made, who was there and who conducted the interview. The recording will not be used if of poor quality, since the jury need to be able to assess the credibility of the witness, which means being able to see him or her and hear clearly. A side view from a distance led to valuable child evidence against a teacher accused of indecent assault being thrown out in *R v P* [1998] 1 CL 882.

A parent should not be present: *Re N* [1996] 2 FLR 2.

The availability of pre-recorded video evidence probably encourages guilty pleas, once the accused knows it is available and has seen it. Research at Leicester University has shown that this type of evidence is easier for lawyers, judges and juries to understand, and makes it more likely that children will testify ((1992) LS Gaz, 22 January, 10).

Everything said about good practice for interviewing in relation to criminal allegations is applicable where the court is deciding a civil law issue. In *Re M (Sexual Abuse Allegations: Interviewing Techniques)* [1999] 2 FLR 92, the father wanted contact, seven years after his children (then aged 2 and 5) had given an eight-hour taped interview containing allegations of abuse. Leading questions had been put and the mother had been present. The mother now wished to rely on this evidence to prevent resumption of contact. It was held that the evidence was badly flawed and breached the Cleveland Guidelines (but, given the children's hostility to seeing their father, contact was limited to post cards to the children, and photographs and school reports to the father).

Another Possible way to keep the Child Witness out of Court

The Children and Young Persons Act 1933 has always permitted hearsay evidence to be put into evidence in criminal cases, if attending as a witness would harm a child (including emotionally). A Government Circular (LAC 88(10) Annex C) encourages social workers and others to use this power. But the evidence has to be taken by questioning the child in front of a magistrate, and medical evidence is required of the likely harm. The child is spared some, but by no means the whole, of the ordeal and some delay is averted. The reason this procedure is hardly ever used is presumably that prosecutors do not believe that the child's evidence will be as strong as it would be if given at the trial.

Avoiding Delay where Children are Witnesses

Children should be spared the normal months of delay before a criminal case gets to trial. Under the Criminal Justice Act 1991, cases of violence or sexual abuse involving child witnesses should be given priority in the court's timetable.

Confidentiality of Video Tapes

This is a problem with several dimensions. A child may be prepared to talk only if assured, for example, 'Daddy will never be told'. This is a promise you cannot make, since the tape may be needed in evidence. The other significant problem is that the accused must have a fair chance to know exactly what evidence is going to be given against him (or occasionally her). Fairness, looked at from this angle, dictates that he sees the tape and has a chance to prepare his defence. But to have tapes of this sort circulating as currency in prison, as happens with some written statements, is recognised as unacceptable, and tapes will be passed to the lawyer only on strict undertakings not to release them to the accused or copy them.

How Credible is a Child's Evidence?

To appear as a witness, a child does not have to give sworn evidence. In fact, a child under 14 can only testify unsworn in criminal proceedings. In a civil case, a child who understands the 'solemnity of the occasion' can give evidence on oath. Criminal courts used to be cautious about receiving, let alone believing, the evidence of children. Now, it is presumed that a child can give evidence 'unless it appears to the court that the child is incapable of giving intelligible testimony' (Criminal Justice Act 1988, s. 33A). (There does not have to be a special hearing within a trial on this point, nor does the judge or magistrate need help on the child's capability from a psychologist or other expert. Assuming the child does give evidence, it is then for the jury or magistrates to decide what weight to give it (*Gibson* v *DPP* [1997] 3 CL 154).)

Children's evidence no longer requires independent supporting evidence (known as corroboration); this used to be required in criminal proceedings, but it was dropped in response to a growing recognition that even quite young children tend to be truthful, and because sometimes, particularly in child abuse cases, there is no evidence independent of the child's which points to the involvement of the accused. It was felt by the Government that the resulting inability to obtain convictions was unjust to the victims of abuse. So now a court can base its decision, if it wishes, entirely on what a child has told it. But common sense says that, child or adult, a single witness is not always persuasive without some other evidence to support the story told.

Nevertheless, in *R* v *B* [1990] 2 QB 355, the Court of Appeal upheld a conviction where the principal prosecution witness was the six-year-old victim giving evidence by video link. And in *R* v *Norbury* (1992) 95 Cr App R 256, the Court of Appeal upheld a conviction for rape and indecent assault based on the uncorroborated evidence of a six-year-old. The judge had stated that he was helped in deciding on her competence by seeing her video interview and hearing from the social workers and police officers who were present when the video was made.

There is nothing inherently wrong with using the video evidence of a child as young as four in a criminal case. The judge will first assess whether the child is capable of giving intelligible testimony, before the evidence goes to the jury (*DPP* v *M* [1997] 2 All ER 749).

There have been many cases where the courts have come up with different answers to an interesting question: can one witness (a psychologist) give evidence about whether another witness (a child) is telling the truth? Generally courts are unwilling to be told who is credible and who is not, and prefer to reserve such decisions to themselves (or to a jury in the Crown Court). We hope that the debate is now over, following the Court of Appeal case of *Re M and R* [1996] 2 FLR 195. The Court said that the Civil Evidence Act 1972 puts beyond doubt the admissibility of such expert evidence. But the opinion can be given only by someone qualified to give it: as a social worker you would not be seen as qualified to go beyond your observations of fact into opinions on credibility. (As we have seen in *Gibson* v *DPP* above, the fact that this evidence is admissible does not mean the court needs it, or even wants it, in order to decide whether to hear a child's evidence.)

Can a Child be Compelled to Testify?
The answer to this question is mixed. In principle, a child can be summonsed to attend, like any other witness. But under s. 44 of the Children and Young Persons Act 1933, a criminal court should have regard to the welfare of any child involved in proceedings, and may exceptionally decide that the child should be spared from giving evidence. The court may make this decision either after the child has been summonsed (*R* v *Highbury Magistrates' Court ex parte Deering* [1996] 11 CL 4), or even before issuing the summons (*Re P* (1997) *The Times*, 18 April). The welfare of the child is important but not paramount, as this is not a Children Act matter.

Further Support for the Child
Giving evidence, even with the benefit of a screen or by video link or pre-recorded interview, is bound to be distressing for a child. We quote some helpful advice from *Childright*, January/February 1990, No. 63, at p. 12:

> Not all child witnesses and their carers receive emotional support from an outside source, and even if they do it is not inevitable that a support worker will accompany them to court. After a not guilty verdict, family anger can be very intense. It is important for someone to be available to pick up the pieces and access to a private room is very helpful.
>
> The verdict must be explained to the child. He or she may need to talk, even if the parent/carer wishes to see the trial as a closed chapter. If the result seems unfair to the child, or even if it is what the child wanted, the court experience and its aftermath can churn up emotions of regret and guilt. In the event of an acquittal, children's feelings about not being believed can be devastating. Whatever the verdict, the explanation should relieve the child of responsibility for the outcome.

The Home Office (working with several other organisations) has prepared an information pack for children who may need to give evidence; it also contains information for parents. As it is written for young and lay readers, the language and style are clear, and you also may benefit from reading it. It has pictures as well! The police have been sent copies, but we suggest obtaining your own from Headley Library, NSPCC, 67 Saffron Hill, London EC1N 8RS (tel. 0207-242 1626).

NINE

Written Evidence: Statements and Reports

FILES

Before considering the use of statements and reports in court proceedings, a few comments about files. A social worker working in a local authority has the job of fulfilling the statutory responsibilities of that local authority. Records and files are kept for that purpose. At some stage it may be necessary to justify any particular course of action. Looking at this from the viewpoint of lawyers, a written record is the safest and most assured means of being able to justify actions taken. Files have many purposes, amongst which are the following:

(a)   a factual record of who is who — the persons involved, addresses, dates of birth, who is related to whom;
(b)   a factual record of what has happened — when and where;
(c)   a record of what was the assessment arising from what has happened;
(d)   a factual record of decisions made based on that assessment; and
(e)   a factual record to communicate this to others.

Within any local authority or agency there will be procedures and protocols about file keeping. Above all, a file should be a working tool for the field social worker not a form of penance! Files should be a means to an end, not an end in themselves. There is a danger that the more information contained in a file the less use it is. A file should put you in control. Therefore a good file should provide, in addition to the above:

(a)   a clear chronology of significant events;
(b)   a clear family tree or genogram;
(c)   a regularly updated summary; and
(d)   a complete record of all discussions during supervision.

Some social workers have difficulties preparing chronologies. If you remember that the purpose of a chronology is to provide a comprehensive, concise and objective overview of the case rather than a précis of every entry on the file, this should help. Try to provide an overview for anyone who has to read the file which will be useful to them before they do so.

One of the effects of having to go to court is to crystallise the mind. If you have to go to court, you will try to ensure that the file is in good order. It is good practice to do this on a day-to-day basis, not when forced to do so by pending proceedings.

'Someone Else's Children' stated:

The majority of [Social Services Departments] had policies on file formats and these were usually complied with. The actual filing within the modules was somewhat erratic. It was often difficult for us to find materials and key documents such as birth certificates, care orders and agreements to accommodate; these were frequently not on current files. (10.1)

. . . most files we saw were useful working tools. They contained copious, full and up-to-date recording. However, this was frequently poorly structured and often had little obvious focus. Except in court cases, most case records lacked social histories and chronologies, and regular summaries were also rare. We saw little evidence of files being properly audited by line managers. (1.43)

[Case notes] were usually up-to-date and for the most part readable. However, they rarely contained an outline of the purpose of the interview, such as the issues to be pursued or the social worker's evaluation of the interview. They appeared to reflect unstructured information gathering exercises rather than focused pieces of work. (10.3)

Social histories and chronologies were rare except where cases were involved with court proceedings and although transfer summaries were relatively common, regular three monthly case summaries were very rare even when it was clear policy and procedure to provide them. (10.5)

We saw no proper evidence of supervision discussions on any of the case files we examined. Although we were told that formal supervision records were kept, children's files did not show the detail. Very few authorities have systems to ensure that all children looked after were discussed during workers' supervision. (4.9)

In *Re E (Care Proceedings: Social Work Practice)* [2000] 2 FLR 254, FD, the judge gave guidance on the importance of maintaining good files in relation to families where there have been difficulties over a protracted period. He was particularly concerned about decisions to take no action. Such decisions should not be taken without full knowledge of the file and consultation with the professionals who knew the family. A file should not be closed because of lack of cooperation from parents, which on the contrary should provide a spur for further investigation. Where children are part of a sibling group, they need to be considered within the context of their family history. Working with families needs to be time limited and timetabled so that cases do not drift.

Once you have decided to take action, the production of good statements and reports, considered in the rest of the chapter, is dependent on the original file source. Not only is good file management good practice, it is also part of the accountability required when working in a statutory context. As such it is one of the social worker's legal responsibilities.

TYPES OF WRITTEN EVIDENCE

Writing statements and reports should not be a chore, neither must it become one. The written statement and report produced by the social worker is the key point of access to the legal system. For even if you understand all the law relating to social services, you will fail in your role in the legal system if you are unable to produce an effective statement and report.

Reports are the most common form of written communication that you will use. They are also the most powerful tool given to a social worker, but often social workers fail to appreciate their importance and, more significantly, fail to understand the effect the production of a report may have on the lives of their client in whatever forum it may be used.

There are three main types of report that you will have to produce:

Internal Agency Reports
These are used for management purposes, and decision-making in particular cases, for child abuse case conferences, for cases reviews etc.

Court Reports (Reports making Representations)
These may be referred to as 'welfare reports' or 'social enquiry reports' or 'probation reports' or pre-sentence reports. Often the report will be produced by the social worker after the relevant facts have been proved or agreed. The social worker is acting as an officer of the court and the report is primarily to assist the court in knowing what type of order then to make. An example of this would be a pre-sentence report required before sentence in youth court hearings.

Statements for your Agency Lawyer (or 'Evidential' Statements)
These are statements that form the basis of evidence that you are going to give in court. In all cases there will be a written document produced by your lawyer for use by you and your lawyer — this is referred to as the 'proof of evidence'. The actual evidence will be given to the court in a written statement and may be followed by oral evidence.

Let us try to clarify the difference between the different categories of report (while pointing out that there can be no rigid division). Let us assume your agency is seeking a care order. You will first have to produce for your lawyer an 'evidential' statement. This will form the basis of your proof of evidence. Its contents will have to be admissible under the rules of evidence when you go into the witness-box. (For questions of admissibility see Chapter 8.) From the proof of evidence it will be necessary to complete the application form to the court and also the written statement of evidence that has to be filed with the court under the court rules. If the court has decided on the evidence received that the grounds for making an order are proved, then the court may wish to see a welfare report making representations that will have been prepared. It may well give a wider picture of the child's family, situation, etc. The evidential statement will form the basis of that report.

Much of what is said about one report is applicable to another, although there are particular requirements for each that we will examine.

The Statements and Reports Machine

From the moment of first placement a social worker will become subject to the demands of a great monster that needs to be fed with a constant stream of reports and statements. Look around any team room and ask any member whether they have their reports and statements up-to-date and a haggard look will come over the social worker's face.

- 'I have to complete my monthly reports for the child abuse register'
- 'I have to complete a report for the next child case review'
- 'I have to complete my mileage report'
- 'I have to complete a statement for the lawyer for the magistrates' court hearing'
- 'I have to complete the report for the domestic hearing in the magistrates'/county court'

Just consider for a moment the variety of reports that a social worker produces — actually, as you will see, slightly more than a moment is required, such is the range of different reports and statements that you can be called on to produce.

TYPES OF PROCEEDINGS

To consider the different forms of report, we shall look at the type of proceedings that are common to the courts in which you will be asked to act: the magistrates' court, the county court, and the High Court. We shall then look at the contents of the report that you will have to make.

Care Proceedings

When a local authority or other authorised person applies to the court for an order under the Children Act 1989, s. 31, if the court is satisfied that there are grounds for making an order it will need to consider whether either a care order or a supervision order should be made. At this stage the court may consider a welfare report that it has asked for under the Children Act 1989, s. 7.

Additionally, under the Children Act 1989, s. 37, in any family proceedings in which a question relating to the welfare of any child is raised, the court may direct the appropriate local authority to undertake an investigation of the child's circumstances in order to ascertain whether or not an application for a care or supervision order should be made. These cover all the proceedings in which family matters are dealt with. So at any time during these proceedings there is the possibility of a court asking the local authority to consider making an application for a care or supervision order and additionally requiring a welfare report to assist the court in its decision-making process.

When the court is considering the question of the type of order to be made, as opposed to the evidence needed to show that the grounds for an order exist, you switch roles from being concerned with the proving of grounds to being concerned with assisting the court as to which is the best type of order to make. This is the second part of the two-stage process talked of in *Humberside County Council* v *B* [1993] 1 FLR 257 (discussed below).

Is there Still a Report Stage in Care Proceedings?
The requirement under rule 17 for all evidence that is to be used in care/supervision proceedings to be filed at the court in writing has blurred the distinction between what was known as the proof stage and the report stage that used to exist under the old legislation.

The decision in *Humberside County Council* v *B* [1993] 1 FLR 257 (also discussed in Chapter 7) points to the difficulties that can now occur. In this case the High Court found that the magistrates had confused findings about the threshold criteria (that is whether or not there was significant harm under s. 31) with that of the welfare principles contained in s. 1. The High Court said that there should be a two-stage decision process. The first part requires a finding of significant harm, and the second goes on to look at the wider issues of the welfare of the child and what sort of order, if any, should be made.

The local authority can ease the difficulties of the courts by means of careful use of witness statements.

Before the Children Act 1989 came into force the only written evidence the local authority would file with the court was the social inquiry report. (It was also known as the welfare report, or the court report.) It was considered by the court only after it had been satisfied that the grounds for making an order had been proved.

Now with written statements being filed, much of what would have been contained in the old style report will be found in the witness statements. However, the witness statement filed at the beginning of the proceedings will, inevitably, be largely concerned with proving the case: showing that the threshold criteria are met. With the leave of the court, additional statements can be filed. Immediately prior to the final hearing we would suggest that a further witness statement should be filed.

It is our view that if the court has not ordered a separate welfare report to be prepared under s. 7, the final witness statement filed with the court should always contain the following:

(a)   A summary of the local authority's case. The facts relating to the child and family; a chronology of events; a summary of the history of the case, and the reasons why the proceedings have been brought.

(b)   The results of any assessment that has taken place since the proceedings commenced. (This may refer to a witness statement of an expert who carried out the assessment or part of the assessment.)

(c)   Why the court should not apply the no order principle (s. 1(5): see Chapter 4).

(d)   The views of the local authority in relation to the welfare checklist and how it should be applied in this case (s. 1(3): see Chapter 4).

(e)   Why the court should make a care or supervision order (as is appropriate).

(f)   The local authority's care plan and its proposals for contact if a care order is made (s. 34(11)). (For further discussion of care plans see Chapter 10, Case Planning.)

All witness statements that are to be filed also need the same careful thought and preparation.

Family and Other Proceedings

Under the Children Act 1989, s. 8, there is a variety of orders that can be made: contact orders, prohibited steps orders, residence orders and specific issues orders. The court can consider making these in any family proceedings, whether or not they have been applied for. (For more on these s. 8 orders, see Chapter 16.)

The welfare report   Having heard evidence from the parents, and before actually making any of these orders, the court can ask either the local authority or the probation service to prepare a report to assist it in deciding what type of order should be made, even if there is no question of the children being made the subject of any care or supervision application (Children Act 1989, s. 7).

This type of report is often referred to as a welfare report. It is, not surprisingly, prepared by someone called a court welfare officer! Under s. 7 of the Children Act either a social worker or a probation officer can be asked by the court to produce a report. Rule 13 requires the welfare officer to prepare the report and serve it on the court at least five days before the hearing. It also requires the welfare officer to attend the court hearing unless excused by the court. Rule 14, covering the directions appointment, enables the court to give any specific directions about the preparation of the welfare report, so the decision to order one will be made very early on.

In family proceedings the court can, under s. 16, make a family assistance order. Before making such an order the court may ask for a welfare report. (For further discussion of this, see Chapter 4.)

Under the Children Act 1989, s. 37, if the local authority decides that an application for a care or supervision order should be made then it should make an application in the usual way. If the local authority does not consider that an application should be made it must report this fact to the court. It must give its reasons for not applying and set out any services or assistance it intends to give to the family.

Adoption/Freeing for Adoption Proceedings

There are two distinct types of reports that can be asked for in these cases. The first is the formal 'Schedule 2' report that needs to be filed with the court with, or soon after, the adoption application. This report takes its name from the Second Schedule to the Adoption Rules 1984 which sets out the details that are to be incorporated into the report. Fuller details are contained in Chapter 11; but, in essence, the report gives all the background details of the child, his or her parentage, health, and placement history. In fact it contains all the answers to every factual question that is likely to be asked. The report is either prepared by the agency that is commencing the proceedings or, in the case of an application by the adoptive parents, by the local authority in whose area the child is ordinarily resident.

At the time of the hearing the court will also want to have the benefit of yet another report as to whether or not an adoption order is the appropriate course of action. This will either be supplied by a reporting officer (RO), in the case where the adoption/freeing proceedings are not opposed, or a children's guardian, where the proceedings are opposed by the child's parents. An RO's role is to see the child's parents and to obtain the signature of the parents, if forthcoming, to the consent form for the adoption. In presenting this to the court the RO will be expected to supply a short report to the court indicating whether or not the RO considers that the proposed order is in the child's best interest. If the application is opposed, then the guardian's role is to represent the child and to tell the court what the guardian considers to be in the best interests of the child. This may mean making a recommendation that instead of a freeing order or adoption order, a residence or other order under the Children Act 1989, s. 8 should be made.

The function of ROs can be carried out by local authority social workers, but that of children's guardians can only be carried out either by guardians employed by CAFCASS or by probation officers, since those carrying out these functions must be independent of the adoption agency.

Lastly, if your agency is seeking to obtain a freeing order without the consent of the parents then there will be the need to file with the court a 'statement of facts' upon which the agency will rely when seeking to dispense with the parents' consent. This will set out the points which the agency thinks go to prove that the natural parents are unsuitable to retain parental responsibilities. The statement of facts will normally be prepared by your agency lawyer, but you will be required to provide a report upon which the statement can be based. If your agency has placed a child with prospective adoptive parents who are applying for an adoption order which is opposed, then you may well be asked by the parents' lawyers to provide a report upon which to base the parents' statement of facts.

Adoption proceedings are 'family proceedings' and under the Children Act 1989, s. 37, the court can require the local authority to investigate whether a care or supervision order should be applied for (as set out in Chapter 7).

The proceedings described above can take place in the magistrates' court, the county court or the High Court.

The Pre-Sentence Report

Under the Criminal Justice Act 1991, s. 3(1) (for further details of the Act see Chapter 12), there is a requirement for courts in all cases, except those triable only on indictment, to consider a pre-sentence report before it decides whether a custodial sentence is justified. There are particular statutory requirements as to what should be incorporated.

You will see in Chapter 12 that the basis on which the court considers sentencing is geared to what is defined as the seriousness of the offence. It is on this basis that a custodial sentence may be given. The report therefore must look at the seriousness of the offence. It must include any information that may be relevant to the length of sentence and look at the question of a sentence in the community where liberty would be restricted by means of supervision requirements etc.

You will see on p. 290 in Chapter 12 that there is a step-by-step approach to sentencing. This is the format that needs to be adopted for that part of the pre-sentence report looking at sentencing.

For juveniles the welfare question is relevant, although not paramount, when the court is considering sentencing.

There are national standards for the reports set out by the Secretary of State. Before writing a pre-sentence report you must read 'Pre-Sentence Reports — a handbook for Probation Officers and Social Workers' (NACRO 1992).

The Use of Reports and Statements

Before looking in further detail at the requirements of reports, especially court reports and statements, it is worth recalling that any social worker will also be asked to produce a great number of other reports that will not be directly concerned with court proceedings, for example internal agency reports. These need to be as carefully produced as any other report, since they too can have great repercussions.

REPORT AND STATEMENT WRITING

Why do we use reports and statements? Why this relentless urge to reduce everything to paper?

Most people would put forward some explanation to the effect that when you have the opportunity to see it in writing you have a better chance to consider the case that is the subject of the report.

There is also a demand within agencies for higher management to see reports, even though they may have no direct dealings with the individual case. One eminent director admitted at a conference: 'I wouldn't recognise a client if they walked through the door but I do read a lot of child protection conference reports.' Social workers, on the ground, may often not be able to appreciate the worry of senior members of the agencies. Any social worker who does not have some residual fear of a case 'blowing up in their face' does not understand the demands of their profession. Multiply that fear 20 times and you know why team leaders look worried and multiply that fear 'n' times again and you may have some sympathy with your director. As one assistant director said, after an all too infrequent chairing of a review conference, 'I'm glad I don't do that every day otherwise we wouldn't have any children at home — I'd take them all into care — just to be sure!'

The implications of your reports being read by higher staff have to be borne in mind. Their attitudes towards policy for the agency will be affected by the diet of reports that cross their desks. It is the one way in which they, possibly mistakenly, try and keep in touch with the street level. If a case has to be referred to higher management for a decision, then all that they will initially know about the case will be in that report. Before they take decisions that can have a profound effect on a person's life they will often only see what is there in black and white. Even before you open your mouth to say anything, if they have had the report in advance then they will have begun to form, or even will have formed, a view that you may or not may be able to change.

Facts and opinions are the very essence of evidence received by any court and those presiding will be endeavouring to distil the underlying issues from the mass of verbiage they hear. Therefore it is essential that preparations are made prior to going into court, to avoid disaster.

Whoever is sitting in the chair, be it a High Court judge or magistrate(s), they will be better able to grasp the written word than any amount of spoken evidence. This is true even if full notes of evidence have been written down, since the oral evidence will never approach the well ordered layout of a written statement or report.

Your initial evidential statement to your agency lawyer will have to be translated into a written form for the court. Rule 17 sets out the require-ments. It says that to be able to rely on any evidence, you must 'serve' it (i.e., deliver it to the court and other parties to the proceedings) in a written form that is signed, dated and contains a statement that the writer believes the statement to be true, and understands that it may be placed before a court. It will be the responsibility of your agency lawyer to draw up the statement, but you will have to check it and sign it. You need to be careful that the process of translation does not change the content and meaning.

Too often the practice has been for reports and statements to be collected from the typists as you are late leaving for the court, and delivered to the lawyer and the court a few minutes prior to filing them with the court.

In Children Act cases, rule 13 requires, in the absence of any specific direction, the report or statement to be filed with the court at least five days before the hearing. It is then served on all parties. The aim of the Children Act is that all concerned, including the judge or magistrates, should read all the relevant papers before the case begins.

If you prepare your reports and statements in time, then by the time you appear to give evidence in person, what you first set out in your report or statement will have been read by a considerable number of people. Your team leader will have seen it and approved it; it may have been read by your district leader. You will have discussed it with your agency lawyer. The report or statement will have been sent to the court and will have been read by the court. All of these people will have formed their views from reading the report or statement. They may be satisfied that they have understood it or they may wish to ask further questions. A final decision will be made, much of it dependent on what you have committed to paper.

How to Prepare Reports and Statements

You have to appreciate fully that those who are going to read your reports and statements are actually going to act on their contents. It is not a question of throwing down the first thing that comes into your mind in an effort to get the report, etc. finished, but of ensuring that you adopt a consistent approach to the preparation and production of reports and statements. This approach needs to become a habit.

You are required to do this because it must be part of your professional pride in your job; because by virtue of your contract of employment you are legally required to do so; and because you are required by the court to carry out your functions to the best of your ability. Other professionals, such as surveyors, can find themselves paying monetary damages to their clients if they are negligent in preparing reports. Social workers used to be protected from this type of claim, but in *Phelps* v *Hillingdon LBC* [2000] 4 All ER 504, the House of Lords recognised that a duty of care can arise where a person is employed by a local education authority to carry out professional services as part of the authority's statutory duty to children with special educational needs. As social workers are professionals, it is likely that they too may be sued for negligence and are no longer protected by the fact that they are acting in furtherance of a statutory duty. However, it must be shown that the damage suffered is foreseeable, closely related to the advice and serious. A shoddy report will not often produce such damage, but you should approach report preparation as a competent, skilled professional.

The following points and suggested format are written with the court statement containing representations principally in mind. Much of what is said is applicable to all reports, but internal evidential reports and statements, whilst perhaps containing the same full information, do not have to be laid out in such a formal way.

Several questions must first be asked:

1. What will be the conclusion of this statement or report?
2. To whom am I trying to express this conclusion?

Then there is a third question that needs to be asked, particularly in respect of the evidential type statement:

3. Can I defend the contents under cross-examination?

These may seem to be odd questions to start with, particularly the question about the conclusion. However, by adopting this approach you should avoid the habit of so many social work reports which often start merely by repeating the contents of a previous report and then changing the conclusion and possibly adding a new paragraph to 'bring the report up to date'. This trap can still apply to a 'new' initial report, if you look at the format of previous reports, possibly about members of the same family, adopt that format and then change the conclusion.

So you need to think about the conclusion that you are going to arrive at. This process is the same as recommended in 'Case Planning' in Chapter 10. This means that you are going to have to sit back and think about where you are going with the case. This may well be the first time that you have done this, since the pressures of social work practice inevitably mean that each day is a series of rushing from one crisis to another, responding on your feet to each as they gain in prominence. The more 'serious' a case is, the greater the pressures that prevent you thinking.

In all but the simplest case, if you are preparing a court statement presenting evidence or making representations, you should have had discussions with your lawyer prior to beginning the task. It is at this stage that your discussions with your agency lawyer can be most productive. (The actual discussion will be assisted, if you have given your lawyer, in advance, a report about the child's family background, the department's views etc., so that you both have something in writing to refer to.) At that discussion you will jointly examine the options that may be available in the court proceedings. The lawyer will be able to advise you as to the likely outcome of the proceedings. This may influence your approach to the case both in respect of the court hearing and in the day-to-day handling.

For example, if you felt in a particular case that to protect a child it was necessary to remove the child under a court order (and often you may be told by your team leader or recommended by a child protection conference to adopt that course of action) and the lawyer says that there is insufficient evidence to satisfy a court to enable it to grant the order, then you and your managers will need to reconsider the case. Such reconsideration may be either to collect such evidence or to change tack.

It would do nothing for your credibility with either your client, the court or the agency if you went to court seeking a form of order that was wholly inappropriate and for the granting of which there was not the required evidence. This is true whether you are seeking an order on behalf of your agency or merely writing a report at the court's request. Therefore to repeat — use your lawyer!

The process of deciding what your conclusion is to be should evolve from your discussions with your line managers and your legal advisers. Having arrived at this you then proceed to the next question: To whom am I trying to express this conclusion?

The answer to this will affect the form of your statement or report and its contents. The type of statement that is going to be effective in the magistrates' court is possibly going to be different to the type of statement that will be effective in the county court or High Court. This is true even though they all use written statements and reports, both for evidential purposes and as welfare reports. Consideration needs to be made of the type of language used. What is appropriate for this particular court?

(You need to remember that the talk of effectiveness reminds us that we are talking about the legal process, i.e., how do we get the court to order the result that we are seeking?)

Department of Health guidelines This chapter is not designed to be an exhaustive study of the writing of statements and reports. There are many fine books on the subject. In particular, no social worker should write any report without studying the guidelines issued by the Department of Health. The latest version of these was published in 1996. It is called: 'Reporting to Court under the Children Act: A Handbook for Social Services'. We are grateful to the Department for permission to reproduce at the end of this section extracts from this handbook.

A Framework for the Assessment of Children in Need and Their Families This publication (D of M, 2000) is of great help in compiling statements or reports. Use of the *Framework* should provide evidence to help, guide and inform judgments about children's welfare and safety from the first point of contact, through the processes of initial and more detailed case assessments. We have already referred to this in Chapter 4. The guidance and reference to research contained in it provide a wealth of resources. It should be in every social worker's top drawer — or even better, open on the desk!

Any statement or report you write for court during the course of family proceedings, as defined in the Children Act 1989, s. 8, will need to have regard to the welfare checklist that is contained in s. 1. This is reproduced in Chapter 4, p. 88.

As the court will need to take account of these matters it is essential that your statement or report deals with all these issues. The checklist will form a good framework of your statement or report since the court, in making a decision on the statement or report, must have regard to the checklist. This is especially true in the conclusion, where you will be directly addressing the type of order that the court should be making. More important is the need to remember that the court can always choose not to make any order, or the court can substitute a s. 8 order, even where such an order is not applied for. So, in your statement or report you need to explain why the court ought to follow your recommendation instead of making no order or making a s. 8 order.

REPORTS IN THE COURT: LAYOUT OF STATEMENTS AND REPORTS

In this section we look at the form of the witness statement in court or welfare report using the magistrates' court as an example. We use the term 'report' to cover either of these two documents.

The typical layout of a magistrates' court report should be as follows:

(a) Name of magistrates' court and date of court hearing.
(b) Name of person(s) about whom the report is prepared.
(c) Name of person preparing the report and the identity of their agency.

Only these details should appear on the front page of the report, which should otherwise be blank, apart from clearly indicating that the contents are confidential. This is because you owe a duty of confidentiality to the person(s) about whom the report has been prepared. If the front page sets out any other details then there is the danger that the information may be seen by people for whom it is not intended, merely by being left on a courtroom desk, whether by you or others to whom the report has been given. With this suggested layout, if that happens, then with the information that can be obtained from the front page the report can be returned to those in whose possession it should be without the finder being any the wiser as to the actual contents.

(d)   Sources of information from which the report is compiled.
(e)   Family members; names, dates of birth, marital status, address, education/qualifications/current occupation (if any) and financial details (if relevant).

This should be in diagrammatic form. You may understand that 'Billy' is in fact John Brown, who is Susan's second cousin's husband, but will anybody else? Diagrams make things clearer.

(f)   A narrative family history.
(g)   A narrative history of client.
(h)   A narrative history about the reason for the court appearance. In the evidential statement this will be the part that contains the evidence to satisfy the threshold criteria in s. 31 of the Children Act.

Which way round these appear can be a matter of personal choice. There may be some element of repetition in these sections.

(i)   The results of any assessment that has taken place since the proceedings commenced.
(j)   Why the court should not apply the no order principle.
(k)   The views of the local authority in relation to the welfare checklist and how it should be applied in this case.
(l)   Why the court should make a care or supervision order (as is appropriate).
(m)   The local authority's care plan and its proposals for contact if a care order is made (s. 34(11)).
(n)   A conclusion and final recommendation.

The actual recommendation should always be of a single order, never giving the court a choice, since your function is to advise the court what you, as a professional, think to be appropriate.

If the court does not accept your recommendation, then that it is a matter for the court. The function of the court is to arrive at its decision on the information before it and it is entitled to diverge from what you say. If the court does not follow your recommendation, then you should discuss the matter with your agency's legal adviser as soon as possible after the conclusion of the case.

You should understand the power that has been given to those who write reports. Where, in presenting a statement or report, you are acting for the court and not making representations to obtain an order on behalf of your agency, for example when acting as a guardian, or presenting a report that has been directly requested by the court, it is decided case law (*Devon County Council* v *C* [1985] FLR 1159) that if the court does not follow the recommendation contained in that report without giving cogent reasons then the parties to the proceedings will have good grounds for an appeal. A moment's reflection will show you what care, therefore, should go into the preparation of reports.

Pre-Sentence Reports

For these reports a similar framework should be adopted. We discuss here the particular requirements of such a report. It is suggested that the first page of the report has a statement to this effect:

> This is a pre-sentence report as defined in section 3(5) of the Criminal Justice Act 1991. It is prepared in accordance with the requirements of the Probation Service National Standard for pre-sentence reports.

It will also show the details of court, hearing date, name of person for whom the report is prepared and name of person and agency preparing the report. This should be all that is on the front page for the same reasons as for the general report.

Then inside the report will be:

(a)   Basic facts of name, address, age and date of birth and the offence charged.

(b)   Sources of Report.

(c)   Discussion of current offence(s). This should look at seriousness and questions of aggravation (if relevant).

(d)   Relevant information about the offender. This is where you would bring to the attention of the court any particular factors to be considered. Is this a first offence? If not, does it go against pattern? Are there special circumstances? Have previous sentences worked? etc.

(e)   Conclusion and Proposal. The report should make a clear recommendation about the type of sentence and the length of sentence. It should justify this by stating what effect the sentence should have.

What may I put into a Statement or Welfare Report?

To answer this we have to consider what a report's function is. (This section will repeat some of what has already been said in the chapter on evidence. We do not apologise for this, since you will need to apply these rules in the different contexts. If you have fully grasped all the evidential points in the preceding chapter then perhaps your true vocation is, in fact, to be a lawyer!)

A good example of what the court expects is to be found in the judgment of the Court of Appeal in *H* v *H*, *K* v *K* [1989] 3 All ER 740:

In the High Court and county court in child proceedings a welfare officer directed by court order to investigate and report has a duty to give to the court all the information which [the officer] considers to be relevant and is not restrained by the hearsay rule from including relevant but otherwise inadmissible information. [The officer] may consider it necessary to and often does provide the judge with a full picture of the family, investigate many sources and interview many people, including grandparents and other relatives, teachers, doctors and the children themselves. What the children have to say may be relevant not only to their state of mind but as to important facts derived from the child which the court should know. Unless [the officer] is entitled to present this information, it would be extremely difficult for [the officer] to comply with the task [the officer] is directed by order to perform. Equally, [the officer's] usefulness to the court would be substantially diminished. The reliance on the report and the weight to be attached to any information contained therein is, of course, a matter for the judge. I would just add for completeness that a social worker directed by an order of the court to provide a report in place of a welfare officer . . . would seem to me to be in the same position for that purpose as a court welfare officer.

Your report is presented to the court at the stage in the proceedings when the court has already, by listening to evidence, decided that there are grounds on which it ought to consider making *some* form of order. Again, it must be borne in mind that the Children Act 1989, s. 1(5), specifically lays a duty on the court not to make an order unless 'it considers that doing so would be better for the child than making no order at all'. Therefore your report should be designed to help the court decide, first whether making any order would be better for the child, and then what is the order that should be made in the best interests of your client.

If you are to be cross-examined on the contents of the report then you have the benefit of the Children Act 1989, s. 7(4), which we discussed in the previous chapter. This is the section that enables you to use evidence that would otherwise be hearsay evidence and therefore inadmissible.

Conclusion and Recommendations
The two most important parts of your statement or report are the final conclusion and the recommendation. In those you are drawing on the information contained in the rest of the report, applying your professional knowledge, experience and expertise to assist the court in reaching its decision about the correct order to make. The only person who can make that professional judgment is you. That part of the report cannot be changed by anyone, except yourself, it can only be attacked. It can be attacked for two reasons. Either it is a bad professional judgment based on incorrect principles or it is simply based on incorrect information.

If it is based on incorrect principles of social work then there is little that you can do apart from going away and studying the matter further, albeit that it would be too late in the particular case. This is a rather gross simplification, since within the body of learning upon which social work operates there will always be debate as to what is the best course of action within any given situation. There will be legitimate divergence of opinion, which may surface in the courtroom. For example, there may be the case in which a guardian makes a different recommendation to that of the agency social worker.

Differences of opinion   This presents great difficulties for the court, since, as set out above, if the court does not follow the recommendation of the guardian, there may well be grounds for a successful appeal. This situation should be avoided if at all possible by the recommendation and the case being discussed between all the parties prior to the court hearing. You must know before the date of the hearing what the guardian's report is going to say, as should your agency lawyer. Rule 13 requires that in the absence of a specific direction, a welfare report must be filed five days before the hearing. Any other written statement which is going to be relied on needs to be served before the hearing (rule 17).

Agreed orders   It should be for your lawyer to arrange for a meeting to see whether there can be agreement, if not between all parties then at least between the agency and the guardian. It should go without saying that all parties and their lawyers should be given the opportunity to attend such a meeting. This is not to usurp the function of the courts, or to compromise anybody's professional standing or their duties to their clients. If properly and professionally dealt with it should be in the very best interests of all, since it may avoid a contested hearing, which rarely assists anyone. All parties, including the parents, should be represented, and it will be their decision on legal advice as to whether or not to accept any compromise proposed.

This meeting may then produce an agreed draft order that can be put before the court. This course of action was approved in *Devon County Council v S* [1992] 2 FLR 244 (which we discuss in more detail at p. 155).

It is to be appreciated that none of the above can take place if the reports of both the guardian and the agency social worker are not available at an early stage prior to the hearing. If the parties do not have the reports early enough then the case will be adjourned to enable the reports to be properly considered. Therefore it is in everybody's interest to make the reports available as soon as possible, even before the dates set by any court directions.

Expert opinion and research findings   Aside from disagreements between children's guardians and social workers, the report may be attacked by, for instance, the parent's lawyer because the social work principles are wrong or weak. In difficult, complicated cases there may well be grounds for assisting the court by referring to particular 'learned' writings, either in the report or in oral evidence on a particular topic. (These comments are in relation to the 'representations' type report. For the considerations applicable to the situation where you are giving evidence to obtain an order and wish to use particular expertise to back up your opinion that a particular fact is true, please see the previous chapter on evidence.)

Let us take an unreal example to illustrate. You are dealing with a case of a 'battered' child. The local magistrates' court (for some unknown reason!) has never before dealt with such a case. To counter the obvious contention by the parents' lawyer that the series of injuries were all entirely accidental, you may well wish to draw the court's attention to the findings about the characteristics of families that are liable to batter their children. To do this you may may wish to refer to the conclusions contained in the work of Kempe and others, or refer to the findings of the various enquiries into the death of children at the hands of 'battering' parents. The findings of that work would show, for example, that such assaults are prevalent amongst families where the parents are under 21 years old, where neither works, where the child subject to the 'battering' is the father's step-child, and that such battering is likely to recur unless the family dynamics are altered. With that information the court may then be swayed both to accept the risk of significant harm and to agree with your recommendation as to the type of order that they make.

As an expert in social work, you are entitled to state your professional opinions and from where you derive these.

If you are going to refer to such published work then you have to be careful to ensure that it is within your competence so to do. This means that you have to have an expertise in the area, which may be because it is within the general body of social work knowledge (usually taught as part of general training) or you have a particular expertise. This may be because you have obtained a certain qualification or because you have had long experience in a given area. That being the case there is no reason why you should not include reference to such work in your report. You should discuss with your agency lawyer whether you will need to disclose in advance the opinion and the support for it to the other parties to the proceedings and, if appropriate, supply copies of the relevant passages to which you may refer.

The danger in including such references in your report is that the other side may have the opportunity to test you in cross-examination on your knowledge and if it is shown to be lacking then you may end up weakening, rather than strengthening, your case.

This danger is, of course, even greater where you seek to rely on a controversial or 'new' theory. If you are in any doubt discuss it with your agency lawyer. If there is any doubt then your lawyer may well advise that either a 'proper' (i.e., a more eminent) expert witness should be brought in or there should be no allusion to the point during the hearing.

Against that there is the other trap, that you ignore your expertise and your professional standing. The courts do accept that you, by virtue of being a social worker, are already an expert on questions of general child development (*F v Suffolk County Council* [1981] 2 FLR 208). Therefore do not be afraid to say, if it is true, 'In my professional opinion I think. . .'. This indeed is the essence of the service that you should render to the court, viewing the facts before the court through your professional eyes and giving the court the benefit of that expertise.

Disputed evidence in reports The other basis on which your report may be attacked is because the facts that are contained in it are incorrect. There may be two principal reasons for this. First you may have made a straightforward factual error. This can arise from bad investigation, bad reporting or plain misunderstanding. It is hoped that experience will help you to eliminate these faults. If not then you will be at risk when you go into the witness-box!

Secondly, there may be other controversial facts that will be the subject of dispute. Often this can be because you include in your report hearsay evidence. This is usually from two sources. Most reports, first of all, will include some information from your agency records. This information may not have been prepared by you, it may have been put on the file before the case was assigned to you. Can you use this information? The answer is yes, but you should be able to establish in the report whether the information consists of things that you have directly obtained yourself or that you have obtained from such sources.

Also, in the course of your investigation, it may well be that you obtain hearsay information from third parties. For example, you may need to find out background information from relatives or neighbours, who may not be able to give evidence in the court. This does not mean that you should not include such information. Again, you should identify where the information comes from.

When preparing your report you should discuss the contents with your clients and in children's cases with their parents. If at this stage there emerges a dispute over the matters of fact contained in your report then you should consider whether the offending parts should be removed. If you are unable to remove those parts then you should make it clear on the face of the report that there is dispute about the validity of the facts. This does not prevent you including your opinion on those facts but in such a fashion as 'If these are the facts then my professional opinion would be. . .'. It is then up to the other party's lawyers to challenge the facts in dispute and the agency's lawyer to 'prove' the facts if at all possible. Again, there will be the need to discuss the implications about this with your agency's lawyer.

Jargon in statements and reports   The greatest risk in producing reports and in giving evidence is that you fall into the trap of using jargon. Jargon is the common language that we use with our fellow professionals; largely as a form of shorthand or as a way of trying to classify a situation in an accepted manner within the profession. It assumes a level of knowledge and experience in the recipient.

Therefore it should never be used in the preparation of reports unless there is an adequate and understandable definition of what it means. By understandable we mean understandable to the lay person.

It has to be appreciated that in the magistrates' court the magistrates are only lay people who may have acquired an expertise in hearing cases and who may or may not possess some knowledge of the language that is used in such a setting. They do not usually possess any social work qualifications, and they do not usually associate with social workers outside court, and therefore have no particular need to use the shorthand of social work jargon. Remember that people such as your agency lawyer or even judges are lay persons in social work terms. If you use jargon then you will tend to lose the sympathy of the court either because they think you are being too clever or because they think that you are incomprehensible and therefore your opinion should not count. As lawyers spend a great deal of their time in the courtroom they more readily appreciate the dangers of slipping into jargon. Often the lawyer will be asked from the bench: 'What does your witness mean?'

For example: Which is better? Which is clearer to the lay person?

'Tommy in the educational setting has considerable difficulty in adequately relating to his peer group.'
'Tommy does not have many school friends.'

'Tommy finds difficulty with questions of autonomy within the family setting as the Smith family is a seriously disfunctioning unit.'
'Tommy is a handful at home as the Smith household is in domestic chaos.'

The more commonsense approach is going to find favour rather than the technical language approach. If you find that you cannot avoid jargon then include a definition of each jargon word. Having done this you should consider whether it would be possible just to use the definitions rather than the jargon!

To every piece of advice there is normally a counterpart. In respect of jargon it is to avoid treating the court as a collection of complete idiots and trying to simplify every statement you make. You should start by avoiding jargon and then use your experience to adapt your language to suit. The first time you hear from the bench the imperious tones saying 'Yes, thank you. I and my colleagues are quite aware what such and such is. . .', you will know that you have moved too far the other way.

Extracts from the Department of Health Guidelines 'Reporting to Court under the Children Act'

The local authority's evidence must demonstrate that the course of action it proposes is in the child's best interests. This must not be achieved by including in its statements only those facts and opinions which support the local authority's position. The courts have clearly established that where the welfare of children is the paramount consideration, there is a duty on all parties to make full and frank disclosure of all matters relevant to welfare whether these are favourable or adverse to their own particular case. This includes the disclosure of information by local authorities to parents which may assist in rebutting allegations against them.

In considering which facts are relevant and any opinion which you wish to add to your evidence, you should distinguish:

- matters to be described factually as a result of your direct observations;
- your opinion or interpretation of behaviour or events which you have observed;
- matters recorded on the file or told to you by others which are relevant to the case but which you cannot personally verify; and

- your opinion of the reasons for the order being sought and the care plan based on your overall professional experience.

Justifying your conclusion   The document should make it clear to the reader how you arrived at your conclusions. Have you demonstrated the factual basis for each part of your conclusion? In assessing the risk to the child, have you explained what would need to change for the child to be safe within the home?

Set out the options available to the court and assess each in turn. Your position on each option should be substantiated by the evidence in the body of the statement. Drawing these together is likely to assist the court in its own analysis and in drafting reasons for its decisions.

The conclusions of other parties should be taken into account and the reasons for differences of opinion should be clearly recorded.

Based on your analysis, present a recommendation where appropriate to do so. It may not be appropriate to put forward a 'hard and fast' position at an early stage. Giving a provisional opinion in an early statement allows for a later change of position, where justified, and is likely to be seen as more balanced and reasonable.

Always review what you have written. It is helpful if you can get a colleague to look at it as well. As you read, consider whether your statement:

- is well-focused;
- takes account of the guiding principles of the Children Act as appropriate;
- reflects the requirements of the relevant section of the Act;
- is balanced and fair overall, giving credit where it is due to family members;
- includes all relevant facts whether or not they support the local authority's conclusion;
- verifies significant facts and justifies opinions;
- avoids unnecessary repetition of material available in other court documents;
- presents information with sensitivity, in a way which does not make relations between parties worse;
- makes references to race, nationality, colour or country of origin which are relevant to the context;
- avoids applying your own cultural or moral values to other cultures (assumptions may be implicit in your choice of words); and
- takes account of changes that have occurred in the period leading up to the final hearing.

REPORTS OTHER THAN COURT REPORTS

Having finished all the reports that are required for court, you will still not have satisfied that ever-hungry monster!

You will still be required to write up your file and from the contents of that prepare reports for your team leader, your district manager, higher management, case discussions and child protection conferences or reviews. So we find in *Working Together:*

> 7.47   Good record keeping is an important part of the accountability of professionals to those who use their services. It helps to focus work, and it is essential to working effectively across agency and professional boundaries. Clear and accurate records ensure that there is a documented account of an agency's or professional's involvement with a child and/or family. They help with continuity when individual workers are unavailable or change, and they provide an essential tool for managers to monitor work or for peer review.

In doing these tasks you will still be required to have regard to the law. The information that you put into the case file, and hence the other reports, should, to the best of your knowledge, be truthful and as far as is possible within your direct knowledge. The comments on evidence above have already made it clear that when you are in court you may well be put in a position where the file has to be shown to the court and the other parties' lawyers. Or in the very worst of your nightmares you have to face a public inquiry when all of the files will be taken to pieces. Always bear that in mind when you are writing up your case file. Ask yourself 'If this entry were to be read out in court would I be able to justify it, explain it, clarify it etc?'.

A further point on the question of access to information is that presented by the Children Act 1989, s. 42, which states:

> (1)   Where a person has been appointed as a guardian *ad litem* under this Act he shall have the right . . . to examine and take copies of—
>   (a)   any records of, or held by, a local authority [and the NSPCC or other authorised person] which were compiled in connection with the making, or proposed making, by any person of any application under this Act with respect to the child concerned; or
>   (b)   any other records of, or held by, a local authority . . . [in its social services function relating] . . . to that child.

The section goes on to say that the guardian can use those records as evidence in the relevant proceedings. Bearing in mind that in most court hearings involving children there will be a children's guardian appointed, then your files are going to be open both to your clients and to the courts through the guardian.

It will be seen from these points that you should not slap into your file the first thoughts that come to mind, but that you should carefully consider the contents of any entry before committing it to paper. But do not despair. By judicious and careful use of your file, which should contain as much information as you have time to enter, entered as soon as possible after the events described, you will ensure that firstly you have the opportunity to reflect your actions (past and future) concerning the case and, secondly, that in the courtroom you will be able to rely on your file as a good friend. (As to whether or not you actually take it to court see the comments on this point in Chapter 8.) On the question of access to the file and confidentiality, see Chapter 2.

Final Thoughts

As a final comment on reports, remember that throughout the preparation of reports, and at the very least before you get the final form typed up, there is nothing better you can do than show it to a colleague. This gives the chance for another person to comment on the contents and the course of action proposed as well as possibly spotting the spelling mistakes, grammatical errors and typing errors. Imagine the social worker who could not understand why the court would not allow Susan to live with her stepfather. The same worker then noticed that in the report, the phrase 'Susan often said that her stepfather liked her' had become a simple typing error 'Susan often said that her stepfather licked her'! It is the opportunity for a colleague's comments on your work that is the most useful aspect. To quote from the evidence of the unfortunate, overworked team leader who received the most blame in the report into the death of Kimberley Carlile: 'It is a curious yet repeatedly observed phenomenon of social work that it is much easier to perceive the errors in other people's work than in one's own.'

TEN

Investigation, Assessment and Case Planning

We have now reached the end of the part of the book that looks at those areas of statutory responsibility that will involve the social worker going to court on behalf of the local authority. It is hoped you will have an understanding of how the courts work, what the law is and what the social worker's function is within the court setting. This chapter looks at how you put it all into practice: how all the bits of the jigsaw begin to come together when dealing with a case that ends up in court. We look at:

(a) safeguarding and promoting the welfare of the child;
(b) the process of investigation;
(c) the difficulties of investigating sexual abuse;
(d) case planning; and
(e) care plans.

Throughout the earlier chapters we have made numerous references to this chapter. In reading the chapter we assume that you have already digested the preceding chapters. If you are reading this chapter for an overview before turning your attention to the earlier material, do not forget that for the fuller picture you need to go back and look at that when you have finished.

SAFEGUARDING AND PROMOTING THE WELFARE OF THE CHILD

All we say in the chapter has to be set against the touchstone of statutory responsibility. This is the need to safeguard and promote the welfare of the child in all circumstances (s. 3, the general duty of any person having care of a child; s. 21, the duty of a local authority when looking after a child; and s. 47, Children Act, the general duty when investigating whether a child is suffering or likely to suffer significant harm, see p. 97). When asked why you are taking or not taking a particular action for a given child, your initial response must always be 'because I am safeguarding and promoting the child's welfare — that is what I am employed to do'.

You can then justify any decisions on this basis. This will require you to take court action on some occasions and not on others. You will need to bear in mind the principles in the Act. You will need to be aware of the difficulties of the legal process. You will need to realise that the court will have the final say and may not agree with you. You will remember that the court process can, particularly if there is no order made, in itself damage the child.

Having weighed all these points, you then look to see what will safeguard and promote the welfare of the child, and take the necessary action. Safeguarding and promoting are positive words. Inaction is rarely positive.

THE PROCESS OF INVESTIGATION

Now, it is important to say a little about the process of investigation. What is it for? As can be seen from what we have said earlier, the process of investigation is to ascertain what steps the local authority should take to safeguard and protect the welfare of the child concerned. This may include applying for court orders. That being the case, you will need to be aware of the difficulties that may be involved in the investigation process.

The process of investigation will always involve tensions between outcomes that sometimes may appear to be incompatible. In any situation the social worker will be involved in the following matters:

(a) *Therapeutic intervention*: This means that you are trying to help the child. The help offered can encompass the range of powers and duties and services we have discussed. But sometimes the situation of the child, and the law, will require that the social worker seeks statutory control.

(b) *Statutory control*: To do this you have to use the courts and produce evidence that the grounds for an order are satisfied. In doing that you are acting as a statutory agent, and people are not always comfortable turning to a statutory agent for help or therapy. Collecting evidence may not always be entirely compatible with giving therapy. But if it is necessary to have statutory control, then it will not be possible to continue to intervene therapeutically without it. In some extreme cases, in cases of abuse, there may be the need to invite/persuade the police to consider whether to prosecute the perpetrator.

(c) *Prosecuting the perpetrator*: Prosecutions are brought because society deems, for a variety of reasons, that they are necessary. If a man murders a child then it is accepted that the man should be prosecuted. The problem is that the prosecution does not restore the life of the child: crudely put — it does nothing for the child. This point was made by the judge at first instance in *Re EC (Disclosure of Material)* [1996] 2 FLR 123, when he said:

> I do not see that EC's welfare will be advanced by the prosecution of any members of her family. Equally, as I have already stated, I do not see that a decision about whether or not any member of her family should be prosecuted in relation to SC's injuries is necessary to planning for her

future. In this context, therefore I do not see EC herself as having any interest separate and apart from the general public interest in the proper investigation and prevention of crime. . . . Clearly, the public interest here relates to the appropriate institution of other legitimate proceedings: I am not concerned with the outcome of those proceedings.

We discussed this case on p. 42 — SC had been killed and the local authority sought a care order for her elder sister EC. The Court of Appeal felt that there was a benefit to the child EC, who was still alive. The fact that the Court of Appeal took a different view, believing that the public interest prevailed in assisting in the prosecution, shows the tensions in such cases.

Where the child is abused and not killed, the dilemma of those investigating, both social worker and police, will be in trying to balance the demands of society and the needs of the child. If the suspected perpetrator of the abuse is a parent or relative, then investigating the facts with the child and the child's family for this particular end, whilst still trying to give therepeutic support, becomes even harder.

The tensions between these aims will always be present. Trying to balance all three — therapy, statutory control and prosecution — may, at times, be almost impossible. The distinct aims of each have to be clear in the minds of those investigating. From the local authority social worker's point of view, the tension between the therapy and statutory control will be uppermost. Bearing in mind the statutory nature of local authority work, you have to ensure that it is always possible, if required, to obtain statutory control. This may limit the initial therapeutic interventions that you may wish to make. The question of prosecution is to be resolved with the police in the interdisciplinary setting. You do not have a statutory duty to prosecute abusers, or assist in the process. Your duty arises from a decision that this would safeguard or promote the welfare of the child.

Investigations should not form part of the therapeutic process. This point was clearly made by Butler-Sloss LJ in *Re M (Minors)* [1993] 1 FLR 822:

It is important to draw distinctions between interviews with young children for the purpose of:

- investigation,
- assessment and
- therapy.

It would be rare I would assume, that interviews for a specifically therapeutic purpose would be provided for use in court. Generally it is desirable that interviews with young children should be conducted as soon as possible after the allegations are first raised, should be few in number and should have investigation as their primary purpose. However, an expert interview of a child at a later stage, if conducted in such a way as to satisfy the court that the child has given information after acceptable questioning, may be a valuable part of the evidence for consideration as to whether abuse has occurred. No rigid rules can be laid down and it is for the court to decide whether such evidence is or is not of assistance.

When to undertake therapy during the process of investigation will always be a difficult decision fraught with potential difficulties. This applies when the investigation may lead to either criminal or civil proceedings or both.

A useful resource book that explores the issues involved here is *Rooted Sorrows: Psychoanalytic Perspectives on Child Protection, Assessment, Therapy and Treatment* (Family Law 1997). This is a book resulting from a joint conference involving the judiciary and leading experts in the field of child psychology. It gives an insight into the differing perspectives of those involved and how some of these problems may be overcome.

The starting point for any investigation has to be to establish the relevant factual circumstances and the possible sources of harm and danger. The aim of the investigation must be to establish what help, support and services may be offered, and also to consider whether there will be a need for court proceedings. At the earliest possible stage, as indicated in *Working Together* (DoH, 1999), you need to work with other professionals (including your agency lawyer, the police health authorities, etc.) on a collaborative basis. The collection of possible evidence, which can be in any form, needs to be undertaken by members of this team. By 'evidence' we mean both the information on which decisions will be made and that which may need to be used in court proceedings. Notice that *Working Together* ensures that assessment happens in parallel with investigation.

Working Together states:

5.14   The process of initial assessment should involve: seeing and speaking to the child (according to age and understanding) and family members as appropriate; drawing together and analysing available information from a range of sources (including existing records); and obtaining relevant information from professionals and others in contact with the child and family. All relevant information (including historical information) should be taken into account.

5.15   In the course of this assessment, the social services department should ask:

- is this a child in need? (s. 17 of the Children Act 1989)
- is there reasonable cause to suspect that this child is suffering or is likely to suffer significant harm? (s. 47 of the Children Act 1989)

5.16   The focus of the initial assessment should be the welfare of the child. It is important to remember that even if the reason for a referral was a concern about abuse or neglect which is not subsequently substantiated, a family may still benefit from support and practical help to promote a child's health and development.

5.17 Following an initial assessment, the social services department should decide on the next course of action, following discussion with the child and family, unless such a discussion may place a child at risk of significant harm. Where it is clear that there should be a police investigation in parallel with a s. 47 enquiry, the considerations at para. 5.36 should apply. Whatever decisions are taken they should be endorsed at a managerial level agreed within the social services department and recorded in writing with the reasons for them. The family, the original referrer, and other professionals and services involved in the assessment should as far as possible be told what action has been taken, consistent with respecting the confidentiality of the child and family concerned, and not jeopardising further action in respect of child protection concerns (which may include police investigations).

Paragraph 5.36 sets out some key concerns about interviewing children. (See also Chapter 8, above.)

5.36 Children are a key, and sometimes the only, source of information about what has happened to them, especially in child sexual abuse cases, but also in physical and other forms of abuse. Accurate and complete information is essential for taking action to promote the welfare of the child, as well as for any criminal proceedings which may be instigated concerning an alleged perpetrator of abuse. When children are first approached, the nature and extent of any harm suffered by them may not be clear, nor whether a criminal offence has been committed. It is important that even initial discussions with children are conducted in a way that minimises any distress caused to them, and maximises the likelihood that they will provide accurate and complex information. It is important, wherever possible, to have separate communications with a child. Leading or suggestive communication should always be avoided. Children may need time, and more than one opportunity, in order to develop sufficient trust to communicate any concerns they may have, especially if they have communication difficulties, learning difficulties, are very young, or are experiencing mental health problems.

Working Together gives guidance on the investigation process. It, in turn, refers to the *Framework for the Assessment of Children in Need and Their Families*. The *Framework* points out that assessment is based on full understanding of what is happening to the child in the context of the family and the wider community. The Department of Health has produced ten family assessment questionnaires, including the Strengths and Difficulties Questionnaire and the Parenting Daily Hassles Scale, but unfortunately this information is not included in the *Framework*. Nonetheless, it is essential that social workers carrying out any investigation should work within the framework supplied by these documents.

Additionally, the implications of the use of videotaped interviews as evidence in criminal trials of alleged perpetrators, as allowed under the

Criminal Justice Act 1991, will need to be borne in mind. There will be the need to work within the 'Memorandum of Good Practice' issued to deal with the running and recording of such interviews. (See Chapter 8.) The practical difficulties of the overlapping nature of the process of such investigations are fully explored in the Department of Health book, *The Challenge of Partnership in Child Protection: Practice Guide*. This should be added to your essential reading.

SEXUAL ABUSE

This area is one that continues to present great difficulty. It is an immensely complex sphere, both in questions of evidence and assessment. The interaction between social workers and the courts and legal system in this area has been less than positive in a whole series of cases. Cleveland, Nottingham, Rochdale and The Orkneys all come to mind.

The courts will expect that social workers investigating sexual abuse will be familiar with and follow the guidelines on investigation contained in 'Report of the Inquiry into Child Abuse in Cleveland' (Cm 412, HMSO, 1988) ('The Cleveland Report'). Chapter 12 of that Report is called 'Listening to the Child'. You should be familiar with the whole chapter, especially the recommendations on interviewing (para. 12.34) and the series of recommendations contained in Part 3, the conclusion to the Report. This is a minimum expectation.

Failure to be familiar with the Cleveland recommendations is almost guaranteed to mean that the local authority will fail in any attempt to obtain a court order. This is the lesson from cases such as *Re E* [1991] 1 FLR 420. In this case there were allegations made by a small child which involved a number of other children. The concerns of the social workers were allowed to override the process of investigation. Amongst other things, they took every detail of the child's story literally and they introduced sexually explicit dolls into the investigation process too early. They did not apply any of the 'checks' the law considers appropriate. As a result the child was dewarded.

In the Rochdale case, reported as *Re A (Minors) (Child Abuse Guide Lines)* [1992] 1 All ER 153, Hollings J gave the following suggestions. (We have summarised these.)

(a)   Children should not be taken into care without notice and for the purpose of a medical examination unless there is an emergency or there are grounds for believing that the parents would refuse medical examinations.

(b)   Save in emergencies, child protection conferences should be held before a child is sought to be removed.

(c)   Early morning removals of children should take place only if there are clear grounds for believing that significant harm would otherwise be caused to the child or vital evidence is obtainable only by such means.

(d)   Good quality video recordings of interviews should be the rule.

(e)   In child sexual abuse cases it is highly desirable when separate teams are working on interviews in connection with the same case, that the social services should appoint an overall coordinator:

(i)   to afford overall direction and advice; and

(ii)   to ensure that there is no unjustifiable contamination of the interview results from one team to another team.

The question whether or not the requirements imposed by the courts and the law when dealing with sexual abuse are correct or 'fair' is something we cannot discuss here. All that can be said is that any attempt to protect the child who may have been abused will be frustrated if these legal requirements are not followed. The courts may have to return the child to the situation from which he or she was removed. Those who sought the removal would have done it for the child's protection. The return of the child may mean that the child finds him or herself back in the situation of continuing abuse. A court will make its decision only on the balance of probabilities and may refuse an order even though it cannot say with certainty that there is no abuse. That is the reality of the situation. Therefore, to protect the child, steps must, as far is possible, be taken with the court proceedings in mind.

There is discussion of the topic of investigating sexual abuse and evidence in Chapter 8, at p. 164.

Throughout this process you should bear in mind who is your client. The clear answer is the child. This does not absolve you of your responsibility to be fair to any adults involved in the investigation. If you decide that court proceedings are needed, you owe it to those who care for the child to ensure that they have the best advice. Ensure they understand their legal rights and that they are put in touch with a good lawyer, preferably one on the Children Panel. You should inform them that legal aid is available without a means test.

We now move on to looking at the process of getting cases before the courts.

CASE PLANNING AND PREPARATION: CARE PLANS

Earlier, we talked about the idea of court work being a process, of getting the desired result. In this section we want to look at the need to prepare the case for court. It is not dissimilar to preparing a court report. For the preparation of a report we recommended that you first asked what conclusion you were going to arrive at. The same is true about case planning.

To ensure that you get the desired result you have to start with that result and then work back. If you go to see a lawyer wanting to take a case to court, the good lawyer should always ask 'what do you want out of the hearing?'. This is not to prejudge the court process, it is merely to make sensible preparation.

In day-to-day life, we often look at maps to find out how to get to a particular place. If someone asks us for directions to a particular town, we do not say 'It's 20 miles away, sort of north from here', we give precise details — the road names or numbers to follow, the distances down particular roads, where to turn left or right, etc. In preparing cases for court you need the same approach.

Example   Mary, the six-year-old child of Tom and Ann, was found at school with a series of dark bruises on her back. She was examined by a paediatrician who said that they were the result of being hit and that there were some additional fingertip bruises on her arm. Mary said her dad had hit her. When questioned Tom denies hitting Mary. Ann, whilst not saying what happened, talks about Tom's drinking and problems in the marriage. There are financial difficulties and the family want to be rehoused. There is a new baby, Peter, who is three months old. Ann appears to be finding coping a strain. Your initial conclusion (which may only be an instinctive feeling) is that the current pressures faced by the family are responsible for the situation in which Tom takes out his frustrations by hitting Mary.

You discuss the case with colleagues, there is a child protection case conference. It is decided to register Mary. The social services department decides that you need a court order to protect Mary. You do think that Mary and Peter should in the long term remain with Tom and Ann. This view is accepted. At some stage you hope that the department will have to have only minimal involvement.

It is no good saying that is what we hope and 'we get there by going sort of north'! Often the lawyer will be presented with a case by a social worker in which the social worker is saying 'We've started on this journey and we are not even certain of where we want to go or even how much fuel we have. ... Can you solve it?'. It is difficult for the lawyer, who is rarely there at the beginning of the journey, to then try and sort things out. This is why case planning and care plans are so important.

Case Plans

Aim   You need a map of how to get there. Wherever, that is, you have decided 'there' is: a care order, nursery care for the child, whatever. What is needed at the end is a care plan. The first question to ask is what do we want as a result, or what are we trying to achieve? Where are we hoping to go? What is our aim? Having done this, we then need to look at the issues that are raised.

Consider the guidance in Vol. 2 of *Regulations and Guidance* about the planning process for children's placements. In chapter 2 the guidance identifies four stages: inquiry, consultation, assessment and decision-making. This volume gives excellent suggestions and a checklist of whom to involve in the planning process and how to carry it out.

Chronology   The first thing is to assemble the different facts that make up the case. Then prepare a chronology of events. This is the backbone of the plan. It shows where you have been, the main road, the important landmarks. In assembling the facts and in preparing the chronology we are identifying two possible types of question. There are questions of fact and questions of law. These, in turn, break down into disputed and not disputed questions of fact and law. So the date of birth of the child may not be disputed — everyone accepts that Mary was born on 5 May 1995 — but it may not be accepted that, for instance, Tom is the father of Mary. This then would become both a question of fact and one of law because you will have to satisfy the legal requirements to prove or disprove paternity.

Evolving the chronology identifies what is in issue and what is conceded. This narrows down the case and begins to put it into manageable form. You then arrive at your statement of the case. This is the backbone, with sufficient flesh put on to enable the court to understand 'what it is all about.'

In our example there are issues of fact:

(a)   What is the nature of the bruises? Is the existence of the bruises disputed? Are there alternative explanations? (The paediatric evidence should deal with this.)

(b)   Who caused the bruises? Are there alternative explanations? (Will it be admitted, can we use Mary's evidence?)

These raise questions of law:

(a)   How do we use Mary's statement?

(b)   What are the legal requirements we have to satisfy to obtain a care order? (Significant harm, past or present or future harm, etc.)

(c)   Can we obtain an order for Peter? On what evidence?

(d)   If a care order is made, what powers does the local authority have to place the children?

These in turn lead on to other questions of fact:

(a)   Are there foster parents whom we could use?

(b)   What other resources can we utilise to assist Tom? Ann?

These may raise questions of law, such as 'Can we force Tom to get help for his drinking?'

You are then able to identify what questions of fact may be disputed or agreed, the legal issues raised, the resource issues.

Having arrived at the statement of the case, you then have to ask the important question, 'So what?'. This, like so many other important questions, is apparently so obvious that it may well be overlooked. This is the stage at which you stand back and ask 'What is all the fuss about?'. In some cases you may then say that there is no need for the concern that has been expressed. Or you will make inferences and/or deductions from the statement of the case that lead on to pursuing the case.

Now a number of different possible courses of action should appear. You will need to explore these. This is the point when you may wish to carry out an assessment. It may be necessary to obtain expert opinion about what may or what should happen in the future. From all this you will be able to distil a clear plan of action. It may contain a number of different options but from these you should be able to decide on the best course. (If an assessment is required, do you need court permission?)

Care Plans

Now you will be able to present to the court a map of the way forward; the care plan. It will say where you want to go and how you are going to get there, and what will be encountered along the way. You will also have dealt with the points that will enable the court to make the order, by addressing the legal difficulties of evidence. Not only is this of assistance to you in the preparation of the case, it is what is required by the law.

Local Authority Circular LAC (99) 29 (12 August 1999), 'Care Plans and Care Proceedings under the Children Act 1989', sets out guidelines for the preparation of plans for court cases. The guidance is important and can be obtained from the Department of Health (tel. 0541 555 455) and on the DoH website www.open.gov.uk/doh. The advised contents are set out in five sections:

- overall aim;
- child's needs, including contact;
- views of others;
- placement details and timetable; and
- management and support by local authority.

Local authorities are urged to bear in mind the principles underpinning Article 8 of the European Convention for the Protection of Human Rights, and consultation with parents is emphasised. The guidelines stress the need fully to consider contact (a requirement under s. 34(11) of the Children Act); and where adoption is confirmed as the preferred option, consideration should also be given to whether a freeing for adoption application is appropriate (see p. 240).

The care plan is to be distinguished from the statement, although it can be incorporated as part of a witness statement (see Chapter 9.)

Much of the case planning will need to be done in conjunction with your agency lawyer. If you can prepare your thoughts along the guidelines suggested, it will clarify and assist your planning with the lawyer.

Care Plans and Assessments are not just for Court Proceedings

Care plans should be prepared for all children looked after by the local authority. The guidelines set out in the Children Act 1989 Regulations and *Guidance*, Vol. 3, 'Family Placements', at paras 2.43–2.62, apply to children who are accommodated and to statutory reviews. Paragraph 2.62 sets out the key elements, as follows:

the child's identified needs (including needs arising from race, culture, religion or language, special educational or health needs);
how those needs might be met;
aim of plan and timescale;
proposed placement (type and details);
other services to be provided to the child and/or family either by the local authority or other agencies;

arrangements for contact and reunification;

support in the placement;

likely duration of the placement in accommodation;

contingency plan, if the placement breaks down;

arrangements for ending the placement (if made under voluntary arrangment);

who is to be responsible for implementing the plan (specific tasks and overall plan);

the extent to which the wishes and views of the child, his parents and anyone else with a sufficient interest in the child (including representatives of other agencies) have been obtained and acted upon and the reasons supporting this or explanations of why wishes/views have been discounted;

arrangements for notifying the responsible authority of disagreements or making representations;

arrangements for health care (including consent to examination and treatment);

arrangements for education; and

date of reviews.

Similarly, it is essential that in every case the process of assessment of the case is undertaken on a continuing basis. While we emphasise in this chapter the need to be able to produce evidence of the type and nature of the assessment to the court, do not forget that assessment is merely a normal part of good social work practice. It will be seen from the comments reproduced from 'Someone Else's Children' at the beginning of Chapter 9, that the Social Services Inspectorate often found that it was only in cases involving court proceedings that there was evidence of care plans being properly prepared. They further stated:

> As with previous child care inspection our consistent finding was that assessment practice was more structured and coherent where there had been child protection investigations or court proceedings. (7.4)

> Although most children looked after had care plans which they were aware of and felt involved in the production of, the quality of the plans were variable, frequently short term and often rather sketchy. (8.16)

> . . . We saw some evidence to suggest that social workers were beginning to see assessment as a separate task to be specially commissioned outside of the normal social worker's normal job. (7.3)

Working Together (DoH, 1999) places a great deal of emphasis on the child protection plan. The initial child protection conference is responsible for agreeing an outline child protection plan. The core group should then develop the details of the plan, with the key worker making every effort to ensure that the children and parents have a clear understanding of the objectives of the plan, that they accept it and are willing to work to it. As

Working Together says (para. 5.84): 'All members of the core group have equal ownership of and responsibility for the child protection plan, and should cooperate to achieve its aims.'

The Courts and Care Plans

The Children Act 1989 divided responsibility for children in the care system between the courts and local authorities. The courts had no role in controlling the method of looking after a child once a care order was made. Even the guardian's role ended with the end of proceedings. This meant that if, for instance, the care plan upon which a local authority had based its application for a care order was not delivered then there was no role for the courts to intervene.

This failure of the law was discussed in the context of the European Convention for the Protection of Human Rights and Fundamental Freedoms 1950 in a very important Court of Appeal case (*Re W and B; Re W (Care Plan)* [2001] EWCA Civ 757). The case involved two conjoined appeals. In the first, following the making of a full care order the local authority, mainly as a result of budgetary constraints, had failed to deliver the care plan. In the second, the judge had felt compelled to make a full care order, despite considerable doubts about the plans for the children.

The Court of Appeal held that there was no fundamental incompatibility between the Children Act 1989 and the Human Rights Act 1988. Difficulties had been caused not by the provisions of the Act but by what had been perceived to be its underlying philosophy.

Breaches or risks of breaches in care plans could be avoided by two major adjustments and innovations in the construction and applicantion of the Children Act 1989.

1. Where applicable the trial judge in care proceedings should have a wider discretion to make an interim care order or to defer making a care order.
2. Essential milestones should be collaboratively assessed and elevated to starred status. A failure to achieve a starred milestone in a reasonable time of the date set at trial should reactuate the interdisciplinary process. Either the guardian or the local authority should then have the right to apply to the court for further directions. The extended powers would arise only in cases of actual or prospective breaches of a right under Articles 6 or 8 of the Convention.

This case makes clear the critical importance of the care planning process and the necessity of producing and delivering good care plans to avoid the type of harm suffered by children in *Z and Others v United Kingdom* [2001] 2 FLR 612. It also demonstrates that the courts will devise flexible mechanisms to ensure compatibility with the European Convention. For you as a social worker it means there is a further layer of protection for children and increases the court's scrutiny of your work.

Planning for Directions Hearings

The Children Act gives a concurrent jurisdiction to all the courts. It also envisages transfer up from the magistrates' court to either the county court or High Court for more complex cases (we discussed this in Chapter 3). The decision to transfer is based on the complexity and gravity of the case, and the High Court has indicated that long cases (more than three days) should not be heard by the magistrates. The opportunity to have the case transferred presents itself at the directions hearings. These occur at the beginning of the case. To know which court to go to you will need to have completed your initial case planning before the directions hearing. Without this it may be difficult to argue that the complexity and gravity of the case require it to be transferred out of the magistrates' court.

The importance of this initial directions hearing is reinforced by the decision in *Newham London Borough Council* v *AG* [1993] 1 FLR 281. In this case the Court of Appeal said that the question of significant harm in s. 31 was one of fact and within the discretion of the lower court hearing the case. (We look at significant harm and this case in more detail in Chapter 7 at p. 138.) The implications are that in a case where to show that a particular action or course of actions is or are significant is complex, you only get the one attempt. If the court does not agree with you, then you may have great difficulty in appealing that decision. (You could appeal only if you were to show that the court got the decision entirely wrong because it misunderstood the facts.) Therefore you must get the choice of court right at the earliest stage. To do this you must case plan.

Conclusion   Often, when asked for directions, you may say, 'If I were going there I wouldn't start from here. But . . .' In case planning, whilst you rarely would want to start from here the process of constructing the map that leads to the care plan will ensure that you do not get lost on the way!

Planning is crucial. Time and space to do that planning is also crucial. You have a professional responsibility to ensure that you are given that time and space.

ELEVEN

The Child Looked After by the Local Authority

The title of this chapter has caused a great deal of head scratching. To arrive at a title that encompasses all the points covered has not been easy. The chapter covers a wide range of duties and powers.

In approaching it we have looked at the role of the social work field worker. Therefore we have not covered the finer details of the management structure of the social services department, except where it is necessary for an understanding of the function of the field worker. Neither have we looked at the details of control and registration duties such as for child minders and children's homes since this area is rarely the responsibility of field workers. It is worth pointing out, however, that Government concerns about the experience of children in care, and in particular the conclusions of 'Lost in Care — The Report of the Tribunal of Inquiry into the Abuse of Children in Care in the Former County Council Areas of Gwynnedd and Clwydd since 1974', have led to a major piece of legislation — the Care Standards Act 2000 — which, in addition to strengthening registration and regulation provisions for children's homes, will establish by 2003 a National Care Standards Commission for England. Provision is made for a similar body in Wales.

We shall look at the duties and responsibilities of a social worker when dealing with:

(a)   a child who is looked after by the local authority;
(b)   a child who is subject to a court order; and
(c)   the long-term placement of children.

The whole field of 'looking after' is dominated by regulations that have been issued under the Children Act 1989. The most important are:

(a)   Arrangements for Placement of Children (General) Regulations 1991;
(b)   Foster Placement (Children) Regulations 1991 (replacing the Charge and Control Regulations 1988 and the Boarding-Out Regulations 1988);

(c)   Placement of Children with Parents etc. Regulations 1991;
(d)   Contact with Children Regulations 1991;
(e)   Definition of Independent Visitors (Children) Regulations 1991;
(f)   Review of Children's Cases Regulations 1991; and
(g)   Representations Procedure (Children) Regulations 1991.

Copies of all these regulations are included in Vol. 3 of the Department of Health's *The Children Act 1989 Guidance and Regulations* — 'Family Placements'. This book is essential. The regulations set down procedures, specify dates, forms, the types and nature of review, and time limits. They govern who should be consulted about steps to be taken by a local authority concerning a child, and so on. In this chapter we only have the space to give outline coverage of this large area, and you must read this Department of Health guidance. Also the guidance from the Department of Health 'Looked After Children' project should be standard practice. *Volume 3: Family Placements* and *Volume 4: Residential Care* both contain identical chapters on some subjects. Table 11.1 below shows the overlap.

Table 11.1

Chapter Name	Family Placements Volume 3, Chapter Number	Residential Care Volume 4, Chapter Number
Arrangements for placements of children	2	2
Contact	6	4
Independent visitors	7	6
Review of children's cases	8	3
Aftercare	9	7
Representations procedure	10	5

A CHILD LOOKED AFTER BY A LOCAL AUTHORITY

This section of the chapter looks at *all* children who are looked after by a local authority, whether under a court order or not. The following section will look at the particular provisions applicable to a child who is subject to a court order, including those remanded into local authority accommodation in criminal proceedings.

To set this in context it is necessary to have a short historical discourse on the law that prevailed before the Children Act so that the philosophy behind the Act can be understood.

Prior to the Children Act there existed the concept of 'voluntary care'. This was where a parent of the child placed the child in the 'care' of the local authority. This could be done for any of a number of reasons, such as that the parents could not cope because of some family crisis. A major deterrent to the use of this process by parents was that there were powers for the local authority to take over their parental responsibilities by means of a mere administrative resolution being passed by its social services committee. This process was, rightly, viewed as being an unfair and unacceptable procedure by which to bring about such a major change in a child's life.

The consequence of the availability of this power was that those parents who had the slightest understanding of the law would feel reluctant to allow their child to go into voluntary care for fear of losing the child to the 'social'. This residual fear will remain for some time to come and must be appreciated by the social worker.

The aim of the new legislation was to remove this fear and to remove the stigma of a child going into 'voluntary care'. The Act aims at a partnership between parents and the local authority, both looking to the best interests of the child. If there is then a dispute between parents and local authority as to what is best for the child, that should be resolved only by a court applying the statutory tests, i.e., the likelihood of significant harm and the welfare principle.

Therefore the concept of 'voluntary' care no longer exists. Instead it has been replaced by the concept of being 'looked after'. Although it is an important concept it is, suprisingly, not fully defined in the Act.

The term first appears in s. 22(1):

(1)   In this Act, any reference to a child who is looked after by a local authority is a reference to a child who is—
    (a)   in their care; or
    (b)   provided with accommodation . . .

The term 'care' in this subsection means a child in the care of the local authority under a care order under s. 31. (We shall use care in this way in the rest of this chapter unless otherwise specified.)

So a child subject to a care order will automatically be looked after by an authority and provided with accommodation, and also is maintained by the authority (s. 23).

But it is not necessary for a child to be subject to a care order to be looked after by an authority. This is the voluntary aspect of 'looking after'. A child can also be 'looked after' merely by being supplied with accommodation. We have already discussed in outline the provision of accommodation in Chapter 5 but we look at it now in greater detail.

Accommodation

The supplying of accommodation by a local authority is, according to the philosophy of the Act, to be seen as a 'consumer led service'. It is supplied to support children in need and their families. It is not a means for the local authority to gain control over the child accommodated, but is a help and service to the child.

Section 20 places a duty on the local authority to provide accommodation for a child 'who appears to them to require accommodation' as a result of:

(a) there being no person who has parental responsibility for him;
(b) his being lost or having been abandoned; or
(c) the person who has been caring for him being prevented (whether or not permanently, and for whatever reason) from providing him with suitable accommodation or care.

Accommodation is defined in s. 22(2) as meaning accommodation which is provided for a continuous period of more than 24 hours.

There are provisions in s. 23 as to how the local authority may supply accommodation. These provisions are subject to the regulations. This accommodation can be 'supplied' by placing a child with his or her family or a relative or other suitable person, or by placing the child in a suitable home. But s. 23 makes the child's family the first choice when considering where to place the child. Other forms of accommodation can be local authority community homes, voluntary homes, registered children's homes or other homes provided by the Secretary of State. There is the opportunity to place children in refuges for children who run away, either those run by the local authority or by other voluntary organisations (s. 51 — see Chapter 5).

Before the authority proposes to 'look after' a child it must ascertain the wishes of the child in accordance with the respect for the child principle (s. 22(4)), discussed in Chapter 4.

Accommodation is a 'consumer led service'   Official guidance sets out the preferred approach:

> The accommodation of a child by a local authority is now to be viewed as a service providing positive support to the child and [the child's] family. In general, families have the capacity to cope with their own problems, or to identify and draw upon resources in the community for support. Some families however reach the stage where they are not able to resolve their own difficulties, and are therefore providing inadequate care for their child or are afraid of doing so. They may look to social services for support and assistance. If they do this they should receive a positive response which reduces any fears they may have of stigma or loss of parental responsibility. (*Children Act 1989 Guidance and Regulations*, Vol. 2, 'Family Support, Day Care and Educational Provision for Young Children'.)

Section 20 makes it quite clear that the provision of accommodation without a care order or criminal supervision order is only provided on a 'service' basis. This is spelled out in s. 20(7) and (8):

(7) A local authority **may not provide accommodation** under this section for any child if any person who—

(a)   has parental responsibility for him;
(b)   is willing and able to—
    (i)   provide accommodation for him; **or**
    (ii)   arrange for accommodation to be provided for him,
objects.

(8)   Any person who has parental responsibility for a child may **at any time** remove the child from accommodation provided by or on behalf of the local authority under this section.

Removal of a child from accommodation   The 'at any time' in s. 20(8) means that no notice need be given to the authority. This is in contrast to the previous law where, after a six-month period in local authority accommodation, notice of the removal of the child had to be given. If you are supplying accommodation to a particular child and you are notified of the possibility of the child's removal by the child's parents, and you consider this to be against the welfare of the child, then you should consider whether there are grounds for an EPO.

If a child is subject to a court order in favour of the local authority, a parent has no right to remove the child from the accommodation without the local authority's consent.

Disputes between parents over a child in accommodation   If one parent has a residence order in their favour, the other parent cannot remove the child without first successfully applying to the court for a residence order in their favour. If neither parent has a residence order and both parents have parental responsibility (see Chapter 16), then either parent could remove the child, as stated in s. 20(8). This could mean that one parent places the child into accommodation and the other parent removes the child from that accommodation. This would be a good example of where the parent who wants the child to stay in the accommodation should apply to the court for a prohibited steps order under s. 8 (see Chapter 16). Remember that s. 8 orders, other than a residence order, cannot be made where the child is subject to a care order.

Where there is no residence order in favour of a parent, then there can be management difficulties.

If during the breakdown of a marriage the mother were to place a child, under the age of 16, into local authority provided accommodation, what is to stop the father removing the child? The simple answer is nothing. The Act is quite clear that if a parent objects to the provision of accommodation, or seeks, at any time, to remove the child, then the local authority cannot prevent it.

The only guidance in this situation is to look to the Children Act 1989, s. 3(5), which states that a person without parental responsibility but who has care of the child may, subject to the Act, do what is reasonable in all the circumstances of the case for the purpose of safeguarding or promoting the welfare of the child. The local authority is covered by this section, not having parental responsibility, and it has to do all it can to safeguard and promote the welfare of the child. Unfortunately this does not give clear guidance as to what to do when the drunken father turns up at 2 a.m. It cannot be promoting the welfare of the child to allow the child to go with the father, and yet the statute says you should. What will be required here are negotiating skills. If these fail, then an application for an EPO would have to be made, or a request should be made to the police to take the child into police protection (see Chapter 6).

A young person in accommodation   A young person of 16 or over is in control of whether or not he or she receives or stays in accommodation. This is because of s. 20(11):

(11)   Subsections (7) and (8) [power of parents to refuse accommodation and to remove the child] do not apply where a child who has reached the age of sixteen agrees to being provided with accommodation under this section.

Accordingly, the parents may squabble about the young person but the choice is always that of the young person.

Maintenance of a Child Looked After
A child in care or being looked after on a voluntary basis can under s. 23 be provided with accommodation by being placed with foster parents. Foster parents are suitable people selected by the local authority to provide accommodation and maintenance for a child being looked after. The selection and registration of foster parents are subject to the detailed guidance of the Foster Placement (Children) Regulations 1991.

Section 23 allows the local authority to pay any person with whom it has placed a child, but the local authority can recover all or part of the costs from the parents unless the parents are on income support or family credit (s. 29).

Promoting Family Links for the Child being Looked After
One finding of research into children who have been looked after by local authorities in the past was the concept of the child being 'lost in care'. This arose when a child may have been provided with accommodation (placed in voluntary care under the old law) at some time of crisis within the family. The child being out of the family may have relieved that particular crisis, but the reception of the child took place without any forward planning and the child just went on to 'hold' in the accommodation. The parents, relieved of the pressures, were often not encouraged to keep up contact and time passed, so that links were lost. Further crises with other families meant that the original child was not given attention and eventually the child became 'lost' in care.

The Children Act addresses this problem in a number of ways.

It treats all children looked after by a local authority in the same way. We start with s. 23(6) and (7), which seek to promote this contact between child and parent:

(6)   Subject to any regulations made by the Secretary of State for the purposes of this subsection, any local authority looking after a child **shall** make arrangements to enable him to live with—

(a)   a person falling within subsection (4) [that is a parent]; or

(b)   a relative, friend or other person connected with him, unless that would not be reasonably practicable or consistent with his welfare.

(7)   Where a local authority provide accommodation for a child whom they are looking after, they shall, subject to the provisions of this Part and so far as is reasonably practicable and consistent with his welfare, secure that—

(a)   the accommodation is near his home; and

(b)   where the authority are also providing accommodation for a sibling of his, they are accommodated together.

The regulations set out the requirement for a written plan before any placement is made. All the people involved in the plan, including the child (so far as is consistent with age and understanding), should be consulted about it. The plan must include the proposals for contact. Volume 3 of *Guidance and Regulations* sets out at para. 2.62 the suggested contents of such a plan. This approach to producing the plan was endorsed in *Manchester City Council* v *F* [1993] 1 FLR 419. See case planning in Chapter 10.

It is important to note that the statutory duty to consider placing the child with the child's family applies even if the child is subject to a care order. See the comments of the Court of Appeal in *Re T (A Minor) (Care or Supervision Order)* [1994] 1 FLR 103. Put another way, the making of a care order *does not* require the local authority to remove the child from the child's home. This is often misunderstood, as in *Re A (Supervision Order: Extension)* [1995] 3 All ER 401, [1995] 1 FLR 335, [1995] 1 WLR 482, [1995] 2 FCR 114, 93 LGR 119:

> This was resisted by the mother and at that time by the local authority in the mistaken belief that they would not be able to leave the child with her mother if a care order was made.

If such a placement is made, it must be done in accordance with the Placement of Children with Parents etc. Regulations 1991.

There are also comprehensive powers contained in Sch. 2 to assist the maintaining of links with the child's family. By way of an example: one of the allegations that is levelled against local authorities is that having provided a child with accommodation, the child is placed with a foster parent remote from the child's parents. To visit the child, the parents may have to get two buses and a train, and find this difficult. As a consequence the visits to the child drop off, and this is then used as an argument for saying that the parents do not really care for the child. The parents would say: 'This, of course, was what the authority was trying to prove all along. Indeed this was the very reason why the child was placed with these particular foster parents.' Often the truth is closer to the fact that the harassed placement officer only had those foster parents available on the day the child had to be supplied with accommodation. Using the powers in Sch. 2, para. 16 should remove this argument. It provides that if the authority believes that visits could not be made without undue financial hardship, then the authority is permitted to make payments to any parent, or indeed any relative, friend or person connected with the child. These payments can cover not only the cost of travel but subsistence and other expenses that may be involved. The payments need not be subject to a requirement for repayment, and indeed cannot be subject to that condition if the parents are in receipt of income support or family credit.

Independent Visitor

A step that can be taken when links with the child's family have failed is the appointment of an independent visitor (Sch. 2, para. 17 and Definition of Independent Visitors (Children) Regulations 1991). The function of the visitor is not to encourage links but to act as a form of replacement for the family. If the child has had infrequent contact with his or her parents **or** has not been visited or lived with them during the preceding 12 months, the authority shall appoint such an independent visitor. Therefore, an independent visitor can be appointed at any stage if there is infrequent contact. An independent visitor must be appointed if there have been no visits to the child during the preceding year. The role of the visitor is to visit, befriend and advise the child. In doing this the authority must apply the 'respect for the child principle' and the child has the right of informed consent to object to the initial appointment and to the continuation of the appointment (Sch. 2, para. 17(6)).

The visitor is entitled to recover reasonable expenses incurred in the exercise of this function. The appointment of such visitors is subject to the reviews of children being looked after.

It is depressing to read the following:

> In our . . . inspection, we found that SSDs were not always aware of their duty to provide independent visitors for children who are not in regular contact with their own families
>
> - 9 out of 17 SSDs had no scheme at all.
> - 3 authorities were not meeting the need.
> - other authorities contracted with voluntary organisations to provide a service.
>
> We saw evidence from the files we looked at that social workers should have been aware of this duty and should have acted upon it. ('Someone Else's Children', 8.15)

It needs to be emphasised that this is a *statutory duty*.

Reviews of Children being Looked After

The consideration of the need to appoint an independent visitor is one of the matters that would arise in the course of the regular reviews that are required for every child who is looked after by an authority (s. 26(1) and (2)). The nature and format of these reviews is set down in the regulations. Reviews are to be held within four weeks of the initial placement, again not more than three months after that first review, and subsequently every six months. There are stipulations as to who should be consulted before a review, who should attend, and the matters for consideration. Again, the *Guidance and Regulations* needs to be consulted.

A CHILD WHO IS SUBJECT TO A COURT ORDER

All that we have said about the treatment of a child being looked after above will be applicable to a child under a care order. There are some additional provisions.

Contact
Under s. 34, where a child is under a care order there is a presumption that the child will have reasonable contact with his or her parents. Before the making of any care order the authority shall inform the court of the plans it intends to make for contact between individuals and the child (s. 34(11)). The court can then define the extent of the contact that should take place.

At the stage of making a care order the court does have power under s. 34 to make what is in effect an interim contact order, with specific provision for a further hearing with a view to making provision for contact at the subsequent hearing (*Re B (A Minor) (Care Order: Review)* [1993] 1 FLR 421).

At the same time, or following a later application by either the local authority or the child, or the child's parents or others who had a residence order, the court may vary the amount of contact (s. 34(2), (3)). The court may instead make an order authorising the local authority to refuse contact between the child and his or her parents (s. 34(4)). Section 34 — with the rest of the Children Act — was written to ensure compliance with the European Convention. This judicial scrutiny of contact is necessary to satisfy the Human Rights Act 1998, and means that decisions to terminate parental contact are very likely to comply with Articles 6 and 8 of the Convention.

The orders for contact under s. 34 are not contact orders made under s. 8. Section 8 orders are private law applications and cannot be made in relation to children in care.

Restriction of contact   There is also a general power given to the local authority in respect of contact under s. 34(6). If the authority believes that it would not promote the welfare of the child to allow contact, then it may refuse contact, but only as a matter of urgency and then only for a period of up to seven days. During that period it would have to make an application to the court for an order. The use of the word 'urgency' implies that the situation which has arisen must have occurred within the recent past, this power not being available to solve long-standing difficulties.

So, there is the presumption of contact between parent and child in care. This also applies whenever the local authority accommodates the child under an EPO or a CAO. The parent can apply to the court to vary or discharge the order under s. 34(9). The child concerned may also use both s. 34(4) to stop a parent seeing him or her, and s. 34(6) to vary such an order.

Contact with Children Regulations 1991 These Regulations cover contact between a child in care and the child's parents and others. The Regulations are applicable to all children looked after by the local authority.

Importantly, para. 3 of these Regulations allows the local authority and the parents to vary a court order under s. 34 by means of an agreement in writing.

What is contact? Under the old law there was much discussion as to what access amounted to — could it be less than a face-to-face meeting? The choice of the term 'contact' in the Children Act is clearly designed to reduce this confusion. 'Contact' can mean something far wider than a face-to-face meeting.

This is indicated in the wide definition of a contact order given in s. 8. This refers to allowing the child to visit or stay with the other person, or for that person 'otherwise to have contact with [the child]'.

Reviewing the local authority plans for a child subject to a care order by contact application We have previously mentioned the problem of a parent challenging the actions of the local authority once a care order has been made (see Chapter 7). Unless there has been an order to refuse contact under s. 34(4), or an order preventing a person from applying without leave of the court for contact under s. 91(14), then parents may apply to the court to consider the contact arrangements (s. 34(3)). If an application has been made and the application has been refused, then the parents must wait six months before applying again for contact unless they obtain the leave of the court (s. 91(17)).

Challenges to the local authority plans for the child in care can be made during the regular reviews. Importantly, the decision in *Re B (Minors) (Care: Local Authority's Plans)* [1993] 1 FLR 543 has indicated that the Court of Appeal views s. 34 as another possible way of challenge. In this case it was argued that the discretion of the local authority with a care order could not be challenged and the court could not look at the local authority's long-term plans. The court would not accept this and said:

> If, however, a court was not able to intervene, it would make a nonsense of the paramountcy of the welfare of the child, which is the bedrock of the Act, and would subordinate it to the administrative decision of the local authority in a situation where the court is seized of the contact issue. That cannot be right.

This means that whilst the local authority does have a wide discretion, this discretion as to how to arrange for the care of the child can be reviewed by the courts when looking at the contact issue.

Parental Responsibility during a Care Order

The making of a care order gives the local authority parental reponsibility for the child. But s. 33(3)–(5) makes it clear that a care order does not remove parental responsibility from the parents. However, the local authority has the power in s. 33(3)(b) to determine the extent to which the parents may meet their parental responsibility. That being the case, s. 33(4) may present the local authority with some management difficulties. It states that the local authority can only determine the extent of the parental responsibility in order to safeguard or promote the child's welfare.

This means that if the parent wants to do something with the child that the local authority does not approve of, they have no power to stop it unless the authority believes that it is contrary to the child's welfare.

For example, an authority may think that a parent having a contact visit and taking the child to see a particular relation or always taking the child to a fun-fair may not be very 'good' for the child. But this subsection means that if the authority wishes to stop such behaviour, it has to be convinced that the behaviour is contrary to the child's welfare and use its powers under s. 34(4) to apply to the court to stop the contact, or s. 34(6) temporarily to suspend that contact whilst applying for a court order. The authority cannot just say 'don't do that'.

If an authority believes, for example, that a child is being physically or otherwise abused during contact, it may stop that contact.

A Child Remanded into Accommodation of the Local Authority

Where, in the course of criminal proceedings, the court refuses the child bail and remands him or her into accommodation provided by the local authority, the authority does not acquire parental responsibility for the child. Instead, it has the power to detain the child for the period of the remand. The child will be looked after by the authority. It may be that the child will be one of the few who has to be kept in secure accommodation. This provision is discussed below.

Placement of the Child with his or her Parents whilst in Care

If it is intended to place a child in care with a parent of the child, s. 23(5) will permit this only if it is done in accordance with the Placement of Children with Parents etc. Regulations 1991.

The purpose of these Regulations is to ensure that when the decision is made to place at home a child who is the subject of a court order without the order being discharged, control and supervision is exercised over that procedure. The Regulations to some extent address the perceived fears that such a placement might go wrong and are designed to avoid such situations as happened with Maria Colwell (see Chapter 4).

Before deciding to return the child, the 'respect for the child' principle dictates that the child's wishes be ascertained. The local authority must also obtain the written comments of all those agencies involved in the welfare and protection of this child, including the health authority, the education authority and the police, and must notify the people it has consulted, in writing, of the decision taken.

The Regulations also provide a framework for the practical social work that will be needed to prepare the child and parent for the child's return. There has to be a written agreement with the parent recording the objective and plan of the placement, the arrangements for supervision, details of health, and educational arrangements. The agreement *must* record the fact that the child can be removed if the authority considers that the child's welfare is no longer being promoted. Whilst it need not be signed, guidance in Volumes 3 and 4 suggests that the signing of such an agreement may be good practice.

On the return home the register of such returned children which has to be kept must record the fact of the return and further record the regular visits of the social worker to the child that have to be undertaken. The first has to take place within one week and the visits then have to take place at maximum six-week intervals.

Having placed a child in care with the parents the authority must not allow the situation to drift. It must review the placement within the first three months and then at six-month intervals. The reviews are to see whether the purpose of the placement is being met. If the placement is successful, the authority should consider whether to seek to discharge the care order. These reviews must be recorded in writing, as must the regular visits. (There are more reports to be added to the social worker's list!)

A Child Ceasing to be Looked After by an Authority
If an authority considers that a child's welfare will be promoted by the child ceasing to be looked after, it should make arrangements for that to occur.

The authority has two duties to the child/young person in this situation:

(a) To prepare the child/young person for the time when he or she will not be looked after.

(b) To 'advise, assist and befriend' him or her as necessary between the ages of 16 and 21. This duty to help the young adult applies not only to someone who has just left local authority accommodation or other institutional accommodation, but also to a child/young person who has at any time been looked after by the local authority for at least three months.

The Children (Leaving Care) Act 2000 imposes new statutory duties in respect of children who are soon to leave or have left care. Social Services departments must keep in touch with care leavers, provide them with 'pathway plans' and a personal adviser, offer vacation accommodation where needed for those in higher or further education, and give assistance to care leavers (including in relation to training and employment). The commencement date of the Act is 1 October 2001.

A Child Leaving Care: Discharge of Care Orders
Unless a care order is discharged earlier, it will last until the child is 18 years old.

Discharge is dealt with in s. 39, which provides the powers for the variation and discharge of both care and supervision orders.

Applications for variation or discharge of either of these orders can be made by the authority, the child or the parent.

In the case of a supervision order the child may be living with a person who does not have parental responsibility, for example a relative. In that case that person may apply for the supervision order to be discharged.

A care or supervision order would have originally been granted if the court was satisfied that the child is or was suffering, or was likely to suffer, significant harm or was beyond parental control. This is the test in s. 31. You might expect the court to want to be satisfied that the risk has passed.

In fact, there are no particular requirements for a court faced with an application to have a care or supervision order discharged except to do what is best for the welfare of the child (the welfare principle). The court does have the power, when an application is made to discharge a care order, to substitute a supervision order. In those particular circumstances under s. 39(5) the court **does not** have to apply the significant harm test in s. 31 which would otherwise apply when considering a supervision order.

In attempting to rehabilitate a child the local authority does not have available any particular court order. The choice is either a care order or a supervision order, or no order at all. The court does not have the power to make an order requiring either the local authority or the parents to undertake a rehabilitation plan. This is a situation in which the absence of the availability of wardship for local authorities is a real loss. The problem is that the court cannot impose restrictions or conditions on a full care order. (See *Kent County Council* v *C* [1992] 3 WLR 808, discussed at p. 148.)

Discharge of Care Order by a Residence Order

There is an alternative way to have a care order discharged and that is by an application for a s. 8 residence order. Under s. 91(1), the making of a residence order discharges any care order. Applications for a residence order are made under s. 10(4) and (5). For the purposes of seeking to discharge a care order by this means the following people could apply:

(a)   The mother or father.

(b)   Any person with whom the child has lived for a period totalling at least three years out of the last five, ending at the latest three months ago.

(c)   Any person who has the consent of the local authority. A foster parent will come within this category unless the child has lived with the foster parent for a period of three years or the foster parent is a relative of the child. Then they can apply without consent. (A relative is defined in s. 105 as a grandparent, brother, sister, uncle, aunt or step-parent.)

This method can be used to seek to have the care order discharged against the wishes of the local authority, so it is unlikely that there will be many applications where consent is given.

In addition to these people, the court has power under s. 10(9) to grant leave to any person, except a foster parent, to apply for a s. 8 order. In considering whether to grant leave the court has to have regard to a number of points:

(a) what form of order is sought;

(b) the connection with the child;

(c) the risk that the application would disrupt the child so as to harm the child; and

(d) where the child is looked after by the local authority, what plans the authority has for the child and the wishes and feelings of the child's (actual) parents.

Whilst a hearing for leave ought to be shorter than the full hearing, experience does not always bear this theory out. In an extreme case an authority may be faced with a number of persons seeking leave to apply for a residence order with the consequent pressures on staff dealing with a series of legal proceedings. Of course, the granting of leave does not mean that the residence order itself will be granted. That is decided at a full hearing on the basis of what is in the child's best interest. The decision in *Re B (Minors) (Contact)* [1994] 2 FLR 1 said that a court could refuse leave without a full hearing, if it was clear that leave should be refused. Therefore, if an application had just been refused by the Court of Appeal and the same parent applied in the magistrates' court for leave for a contact order, the court could refuse.

Anybody entitled to apply for a residence order without leave may at any time seek to have such an order made in their favour. This may prove to be a popular way to seek to have a care order discharged.

There is little to prevent the beleaguered social worker being on a continual conveyor belt back to court where a child is the subject of a care or supervision order.

If an application to discharge a care or supervision order, or to have contact with a child in care, has been unsuccessful, then a further application may not be made for a period of six months (s. 91(15)). But there are provisions for the court to grant leave to make an application within the six-month period — which takes us back to the comments above!

From the point of view of the long-term planning of the local authority, the prospect of a never-ending series of applications for leave to make applications for discharge of care orders or residence orders, or the actual applications for these will seem somewhat daunting. It is hoped that the aim of the Act in trying to build cooperation between the authority and the child's parents will overcome this. But it does point to the need for the local authority to have clear plans as to both the short and long-term future of the child in their care.

Before looking at the law relating to long-term placement, the restriction of the liberty of a child being looked after will be considered.

The Restriction of the Liberty of a Child being Looked After

It is important for social workers to understand that the only basis on which the liberty of a child or young person accommodated by the local authority may be restricted is in accordance with the Children Act 1989, s. 25 (unless the child is remanded from a criminal court — see Chapter 12).

The restriction of liberty   The restriction of liberty does not only mean locking a door. Anything that goes beyond the bounds of ordinary domestic security will probably be a restriction of liberty. The failure to understand or accept this was the cause behind the 'pin-down' affair in Staffordshire. All social workers involved in caring for children and young persons should read the report on this experience (*The Pindown Experience and the Protection of Children*, by Allan Levy QC and Barbara Kahan: Staffordshire County Council, 1991).

In February 1997 new guidance, 'The Control of Children in Public Care: Interpretation of the Children Act 1989' was issued by the Department of Health. The Chief Inspector, commenting on the guidelines, said 'the proper use of physical restraint — which must be reasonable and justified — requires skill and judgment'. The guidelines make it clear that the use of physical restraint to prevent children putting themselves or others at serious risk or to prevent serious damage to property can be justified. Staff in these situations should act as a responsible parent would.

The attitude of authorities to the use of secure accommodation seems to be varied, and many social workers would regard the use of secure accommodation in any but the most extreme of cases as a failure. Others may be more sanguine about its use.

What is secure accommodation?   Secure accommodation is accommodation that restricts the liberty of a child (s. 25). Detailed regulations have been issued under this section (written in the light of 'pin-down') in respect of the type of accommodation and who may be placed in it. See *The Children Act 1989 Guidance and Regulations*, Vol. 4, 'Residential Care', and the Children (Secure Accommodation) Regulations 1991.

The section prescribes that the restriction of liberty and the use of secure accommodation is available only in these strictly limited circumstances. A child may not be placed in secure accommodation unless:

(a)   it appears that the child has a history of absconding; and
(b)   is likely to abscond from any other type of accommodation; and
(c)   if the child absconds, he or she is likely to suffer significant harm;
or
(d)   if the child is kept in any other type of accommodation, the child is likely to injure himself or other people.

Under this section a child or young person whom a local authority is looking after may be placed in secure accommodation by a local authority only for a limited period of time; up to 72 hours in any period of 21 days.

It is not necessary for the child to be the subject of a care order before he or she can be placed in secure accommodation. But if the parent objects and there is no care order, in that situation the child must not be placed in secure accommodation.

If the authority wishes to keep the child in secure accommodation for a longer period than that prescribed by the Regulations, then it must make an application for an authority from a court.

A court can grant such an authority only if it is satisfied that the criteria of a history of absconding etc., set out above, are fulfilled. In doing this the court does not apply the welfare principle (*Re M (A Minor) (Secure Accommodation Order)* [1995] 1 FLR 418). What is important, from the social worker's point of view, is the fact that the court cannot grant an authority unless the child is legally represented. Of course, obtaining legal representation for the child may mean that the lawyer successfully opposes the granting of the secure accommodation the authority sought! Section 99 states that where an application for a secure accommodation order is being made, the child/young person must be granted legal aid. Rule 25 requires notice of the proceedings to be served on all relevant parties. A children's guardian should be appointed. Secure accommodation orders involve a serious deprivation of liberty, and therefore procedural safeguards are extremely important. In the light of this, the decisions in *A Metropolitan Borough Council* v *DB* [1997] 1 FLR 767 and *Re C (A Minor) (Medical Treatment: Courts' Jurisdiction)* (1997) *The Times*, 21 March are worrying.

In the first case the court said that a maternity ward was secure accommodation and ordered that the 17-year-old be detained there. The young woman was a crack-cocaine addict, who lived in squalor and had received no antenatal care until very shortly before the birth of her child. Two days prior to the birth, she was admitted to hospital suffering from pre–eclamptic fits brought on by high blood pressure. She then discharged herself from hospital. The local authority obtained an EPO and sought permission to detain her in the maternity ward. The court granted permission, saying that it was the restriction of liberty that made a particular place into secure accommodation.

In the second case, the local authority was granted authority to detain an anorexic young woman without reference to s. 25 under the court's inherent powers contained in s. 100.

The question arises as to whether secure accommodation orders made under s. 25 comply with Article 5 of the European Convention on Human Rights. Article 5(1) lists a finite set of circumstances in which persons may be deprived of their liberty, one of which is educational supervision. Despite the fact that the Children Act criteria make no reference to such supervision, the Court of Appeal in *Re K (Secure Accommodation Order: Right to Liberty)* [2001] Fam Law 99, rejected the argument that s. 25 was incompatible, as the local authority has a duty to provide education for all those aged under 16. The Court did, however, leave open the question whether the words 'for the purposes of educational supervision' covered the facts of a particular case.

In *LM* v *Essex CC* [1999] 1 FLR 988, Holman J expressed the view that once the criteria justifying a secure accommodation order ceased to be made out, the local authority should no longer keep the child in such accommodation. He also held that the court had no power to discharge or set aside such an order. If a local authority declined to release a child once it appreciated that the basis for the order was no longer present, a writ of *habeas corpus* would be appropriate. If the local authority failed to conclude that the grounds for the order no longer existed, the appropriate procedure might be judicial review.

Seeking to place a child into secure accommodation will always cause the social worker the greatest of difficulties, both personally and professionally. It is difficult in such situations to see how to square your duty to the child with your wider duty to society.

THE LONG-TERM PLACEMENT OF CHILDREN: ADOPTION

There are some children for whom it becomes clear that they will never be in a position to return to their parents or any other family member. In those circumstances the authority, in order to safeguard and promote the child's welfare, must look for an alternative permanent substitute family, unless the child is one of those who would benefit from remaining on a semi-permanent basis in some form of group home. That decision is essentially a social work decision, requiring no further legal power, and as such it is not our intention to discuss it in this book. However, with the possibility of repeated applications by the parents to discharge care orders or orders regulating contact, the management of the long-term care of a child in a stable environment will not be easy.

Having come to the conclusion that a permanent substitute family is the appropriate course of action, what should the social worker do? The first thing is start to think about a different Act! Adoption is governed by the Adoption Act 1976 as modified by the Children Act. Therefore all statutory references in the rest of the chapter will be to the Adoption Act 1976 unless otherwise stated.

Modernising the Law

The law relating to adoption is (as it has been for some time) under review. A Bill was placed before Parliament in the 1996–97 session. The provisions included that the process of adoption should be opened up, and the contact between the child and the natural parents should not always cease on the making of an adoption order. The Bill was withdrawn. Following some controversy over the operation of the law on adoption, and evidence of personal commitment from the Prime Minister to a more flexible approach to adoption, a new White Paper, *Adoption — a New Approach*, was published in December 2000.

The key features of the White Paper were reproduced in the Adoption and Children Bill. This Bill was introduced to Parliament in March 2001 to provide the new legislative framework for a modernised law on adoption. Even at this stage its progress has been faltering as it fell with the general election in May 2001. It has now been re-introduced in the Queen's Speech of June 2001. The explanatory notes to the Bill published by the Department of Health summarise it as follows:

The Bill
- Aligns adoption law with the relevant provisions of the Children Act 1989 to ensure that the child's welfare is the paramount consideration in decisions relating to adoption;

- Places a duty on local authorities to maintain an adoption service, which must include arrangements for the adoption of children and for the provision of adoption support services (including financial support);
- Provides a new right for adopted children and adoptive parents to request an assessment of their needs for adoption support services;
- Enables the appropriate Minister to establish an independent review mechanism in relation to the assessment of prospective adopters;
- Makes provision for the process of adoption and the conditions for the making of adoption orders, including new measures for placement for adoption with consent and placement orders to replace the existing provision in the Adoption Act 1976 for freeing orders;
- Incorporates the relevant sections of the Adoption (Intercountry Aspects) Act 1999;
- Restates that it is an offence to 'make arrangements' for adoption or advertise children for adoption (through traditional media and electronically), and prohibits certain payments, other than through adoption agencies;
- Makes express provision enabling the Secretary of State to establish a National adoption Register to suggest matches between children waiting to be adopted and approved prospective adopters;
- Makes provision obliging courts to draw up timetables for resolving adoption cases without delay;
- Amends the Children Act 1989 to provide that an unmarried father acquires parental responsibility where he and the child's mother together register the birth of their child;
- Amends the Children Act 1989 to introduce a new special guardianship order, intended to provide permanence for children for whom adoption is not appropriate.

The provisions of the Bill will of course change during its parliamentary process. We hope that by the next edition of this book the new statute with the accompanying guidance and regulations will finally be in place. Updates on the progress of the legislation in the mean time will be available from the Department of Health website (www.doh.gov.uk/adoption). The Government's commitment to modernising adoption is evidenced by the publication of new standards.

The Current Law

A definition of adoption is found in s. 12 of the Adoption Act 1976. The effect of making an adoption order is to vest the parental responsibility for the child in the new parents and to extinguish the parental responsibilities of the child's natural parents. It is as if the natural parents had not existed. This is the aim of the procedure, which is complex. Although we give an outline of the procedure in this section, you should recognise that before you become too deeply involved with an intended adoption you will need to refer to two people within your agency: first, the specialised adoption and fostering unit; and, secondly, your agency lawyer. No successful adoption can take place without the involvement of these key people.

Any social worker involved in adoption needs to understand that there is a two-stage procedure. The first is the internal agency procedure and the second is the court application. Agency here means the technical term of an adoption agency under the Act. All local authorities with s. 15 functions are automatically adoption agencies under the Act, and any other agency that seeks to carry out placements for adoption needs to be registered with the Secretary of State. If you are working for an unregistered agency and are doing adoption work then you would be best advised to find a very good lawyer!

There are a number of different characters that have to be dealt with if there is to be a successful adoption. They are:

(a)   the child;
(b)   the natural parents;
(c)   the adoptive parents; and
(d)   the court.

It is the function of the adoption agency to link together, in an indirect way, all these people in order to bring about the adoption. Each has different requirements and will need different treatment.

Regulations set out in detail how the adoption agency is to go about its task. Once that is complete there are detailed rules that govern how the court is to handle the adoption application.

The work of the agency is governed by the Adoption Agency Regulations 1983. These require it to set up an adoption panel whose function is to make recommendations in relation to proposed adoptions. So the social worker will need to satisfy the requirements of the agency's adoption panel as a first step.

The panel's function is to make recommendations. (Reproduced at the end of this chapter is a copy of the diagram setting out the adoption agency's function taken from DHSS Circular LAC (84) 3.) These are the recommendations:

(a)   Whether adoption is in the best interests of the child. (Having considered that the child is suitable for adoption, the panel should consider whether or not the child should be freed for adoption. See below for an explanation of 'freeing'.)

(b)   Whether a prospective adopter is suitable to be an adoptive parent.

(c)   Whether a prospective adopter would be a suitable adoptive parent for a particular child.

To arrive at these recommendations the panel will require full details of both the child and any prospective adoptive parents. Therefore the social worker will be heavily engaged in collecting information to be used to complete forms for presentation to the panel. Most agencies use the forms supplied by the British Agencies for Adoption and Fostering (BAAF). As will be seen from these forms, details are required for the child, the child's parents and family; and of the prospective adoptive parents and their families.

The panel will need a current medical report from its medical adviser. Again it is common practice to use the appropriate BAAF form. The medical adviser must advise the panel from the medical point of view, i.e., difficulties on possible inherited diseases, on the suitability of the child for adoption, and of the prospective adoptive parents.

With all these details the panel must first consider the situation of the child and make its recommendation as to whether it is in the best interests of the child to be adopted and, if so, whether a freeing for adoption application should be made.

Having done this the panel should next consider any prospective parents. Any individual or set of parents should be considered in their own right as suitable adoptive parents. The panel then consider whether any of the prospective parents of whom they have details would make a suitable match for any particular child.

The regulations make clear that the approval and matching process need not take place at the same meeting of the panel. That means that the panel may have a 'stock' of prospective adoptive parents and then go through those to see whether any of those match the child whom they are considering.

Matching may cover a wide variety of the child's and parent's attributes, physical, mental etc. The aim is to try and ensure that when the adopted child grows up they will, as far as possible, be suited to the adoptive family and, crudely put, will not stick out like a 'sore thumb'. The actual process is very sophisticated. For greater details you will need to consult the BAAF forms and the guidance published by BAAF.

The adoptions panel, membership of which is specified in the regulations to include amongst others councillors, social workers, independent members, foster parents, can only make a recommendation to the agency. This is similar to the position of the child abuse case conference, which again can only make a recommendation. In both cases the agency could ignore the recommendation if it so chose but, in doing so, it would have to have very compelling reasons. It would be a very unusual case where a recommendation of the adoption panel was not followed.

Having been to the adoptions panel the social worker still cannot relax: there are more forms to be completed. Before you can know which forms, there has to be a decision as to whether or not a freeing application is to be made or a direct application for adoption.

Freeing Applications

The completion of an adoption involves the natural parents, if they have parental responsibility, and the adoptive parents. The freeing process has the effect of dealing with these two groups on a separate basis. A freeing application is solely concerned with the natural parents. This application can be made without there being any adoptive parents in mind. Its effect has been likened to a process of 'stamping' the child as 'free for adoption' and placing the child on a shelf to await suitable adoptive parents. Its actual effect is to transfer the parental responsibilities from the natural parents to the adoption agency, which will subsequently be able to transfer those responsibilities to the adoptive parents during an adoption hearing. So it is a halfway house towards a full adoption.

If freeing is to remove the natural parents' responsibilities, there are two ways in which this can be done. The first and easiest is where the parents agree and consent to the child being freed for adoption. The other is where the court dispenses with the parents' consent.

Where there is agreement, the process is relatively straightforward. Most cases concern the single mother who for any reason feels that it would be in the best interests of the child that the child be brought up by adoptive parents. In this case it will not be necessary for the father to consent since an unmarried father does not have parental responsibility. So when discussing an agreed freeing we will for convenience refer only to the mother. But the same considerations will apply to parents who jointly have parental responsibility. (That does not mean that details of the natural father's background do not have to be ascertained for the adoption panel since those details may affect the panel's recommendation.)

Court Procedure when Seeking Agreed Freeing Order

Freeing proceedings and adoption proceedings can be heard in the magistrates', county or High Court. The choice of court should be discussed with your lawyer.

Whilst the Adoption Agency Regulations 1983 cover the procedure relating to adoption panels, the Adoption Rules 1984 regulate the court procedures. To commence proceedings the agency will have to file:

(a)   An application form (which is called by different names depending on which court is used). This form gives brief details of the child, his or her parents, the agency seeking the freeing order, and will include the statement that the freeing order is consented to by the mother. (If she does not consent, there is a different procedure — see below.)

(b)   A 'Schedule 2' report. This is a comprehensive statement of the history of the child and the mother. It is called a Schedule 2 report because the required details are contained in the Second Schedule to the 1984 Adoption Rules. The Schedule is reproduced at the end of the chapter. The completion of this report is greatly eased if your report to the adoption panel was done on the BAAF form because you will have already obtained most of the relevant details.

(c)   A recent medical report covering certain prescribed points (Sch. 3). (This has to be not more than three months old — so even if you have obtained a report for the adoption panel it may well need to be updated.)

(d)   A copy of the child's birth certificate.

(e)   The appropriate court fee.

The court requires the consent of the mother to be adequately recorded. This is done by a reporting officer who will be appointed by the court as soon as the freeing application is filed with the court. As soon as the court receives an application indicating that a freeing is being consented to, then an officer of the court (as an administrative step) will appoint a reporting officer. Reporting officers are drawn from children's guardians (see Chapter 4). The reporting officer cannot be employed by the agency making the freeing application.

The task of the reporting officer is to see the mother and confirm that she is truly giving consent. This is done by the reporting officer completing the prescribed form and witnessing the mother's signature to the consent. The mother cannot give consent within six weeks of the birth of the child. It may happen that when the reporting officer sees the mother she indicates that she no longer consents. If that happens the reporting officer immediately switches hats and becomes a children's guardian for the child and the proceedings become contested. (See below — it is necessary for the reporting officer in this situation, to notify the other parties of this fact!)

At the time of obtaining the mother's consent the reporting officer can ask the mother if she wishes to be kept informed of the future of the child whilst freed. The procedure of being notified is available because, if following the freeing of the child a final adoption order is not made within 12 months, the mother has a right then to apply to the court to have the freeing order set aside. If the mother does wish to be kept informed, the agency must give reports at six-month intervals indicating whether or not the child has been placed for adoption and whether or not the adoption order has been made. (This procedure is normally more relevant where the freeing is opposed.)

Assuming that the reporting officer does obtain the signed consent, a report together with the consent form is filed with the court and the case proceeds to a hearing. It may be that in a freeing application the child has already been placed with prospective adoptive parents. In that case, although they take no part in the actual freeing proceedings, details of the prospective parents will need to be given to the court and at the same time a request for the prospective parents' identity to be kept confidential. This is always granted but needs to be watched as sometimes administration can fall down.

The hearing in a freeing application which is consented to is straightforward. The court needs to be satisfied that consent is freely given (s. 18), which is proved by the report of the reporting officer, and thereafter the freeing order can be made.

Having freed the child, the agency must place the child for adoption and ensure that an adoption order is made within 12 months or, as we have seen, there is the risk that the mother could come back to the court and seek to have the order set aside.

A freeing order is *not* an adoption order. When a child is freed for adoption the adoptive parents still have to apply to the court for an adoption order, though that will be straightforward. We discuss this after completing our study of freeing.

Dispensing with Parental Consent in Freeing Cases

Understandably, in some cases, the natural parents, which may include the father, if he has parental reponsibility, are not willing to give consent to the child being freed for adoption. In this case their consent must be dispensed with.

It is not possible for a contested freeing application to take place whilst the child is accommodated on a voluntary basis by the local authority (Sch. 10, para. 6(1)). This is because of the philosophy of the Children Act that accommodation should not be used by the local authority to obtain 'control' over the child.

This may mean that use of freeing for children not subject to a care order will diminish, since it cannot be guaranteed until the order is actually made that the mother will not object.

But if the child is subject to a care order, then it is possible to free the child even if it is contested. To do this it is necessary to have a hearing with evidence from all parties. We will again refer to 'mother' in this section, although there may be a father with parental responsibility who will also be a party to the proceedings.

The procedure in a contested freeing case   The application in these cases will be the same as for an agreed application with one additional document known as the 'statement of facts'. It gets this name as it is the statement of facts upon which the agency will rely in asking the court to dispense with the consent of the mother. This statement will set out the 'facts' that the applicant relies on to prove the grounds for the dispensation (see below).

The social worker will be responsible for obtaining the information that will be contained in the statement of facts. The actual preparation of the statement of facts should be the responsibility of the agency lawyer.

Grounds on which consent can be dispensed with   These are contained in s. 16(2) and are the same grounds on which a parent's consent to an adoption can be dispensed with.

(2) . . . the parent or guardian [meaning parent or guardian with parental responsibility]—
    (a)   cannot be found or is incapable of giving agreement;
    (b)   is withholding agreement unreasonably;
    (c)   has persistently failed without reasonable cause to discharge parental responsibilities in relation to the child;
    (d)   has abandoned or neglected the child;
    (e)   has persistently ill-treated the child;
    (f)   has seriously ill-treated the child.

The particular choice of a ground or grounds must be made in consultation with your lawyer.

Surprisingly the 'normal' choice of grounds is (b), that the parent is unreasonably withholding consent. This may seem a somewhat paradoxical ground. In finding it proved, the court will say that given the situation of this particular child a 'reasonable' parent would find that it would be in the best interest of the child that it be freed for adoption. (There is a 'Catch 22': only reasonable parents recognise their inadequacies.)

There is a considerable amount of case law surrounding adoption and freeing and it is not our intention to set this out in detail since it is an area about which the social worker must consult their lawyer or read more specialised texts.

In arriving at a decision to dispense with consent or make any order in any freeing or adoption proceedings the court needs 'to respect the child', and the court, by s. 6, 'shall have regard to all the circumstances, first consideration being given to the need to safeguard and promote the welfare of the child throughout his childhood'. This test is differently worded to the welfare principle in the Children Act (where the child's welfare is paramount, not just first), although in practice the result achieved will normally be the same.

A father without parental responsibility In *Re S (A Child) (Adoption Proceedings: Joinder of Father)* [2001] 1 FCR 158, the Court of Appeal upheld a judge's decision to make a father party to an adoption application. The father had never seen the child and had not pursued the issue of parental responsibility after the mother refused to consent to a parental responsibility agreement. The judge was concerned that the father might claim breach of his rights under Articles 6 and 8 of the European Convention on Human Rights and, wishing to avoid excessive litigation and adopting a precautionary approach to human rights law, had decided that it was appropriate to include the father at this stage.

Article 8 (the right to respect for family life) could have implications for involving the wider family in the adoption process. However, in *Re R (A Child) (Adoption: Disclosure)* [2001] 1 FCR 238, it was decided that where the mother was expressly opposed to this, and it was found that it was necessary and proportionate in the child's interests to refrain from contacting the family, the rights of the wider family did not displace those of the mother and child.

Adoption Proceedings

Time limits In a freeing application the only time restriction is that of the mother not being able to give consent within six weeks of the birth. Since adoptions are of a final nature, the court needs to be assured that the placement will be permanent, and therefore there are requirements for the child to have lived with the prospective adopters before an application can proceed. Section 13 states:

Where one of the applicants is a parent **or** step parent (in the case of remarriage) **or** a relative of the child **or** the child has been placed by an adoption agency then the adoption order cannot be made until the child is at least 19 weeks old **and** has lived with the applicants or one of the applicants for all of the preceding 13 weeks.

In all other cases the child must be at least 12 months old and must have lived with the applicants or one of the applicants for the preceding 12 months.

Adoption on a contested basis   If the adoption is opposed the procedure will mirror that of freeing, except that the adoptive parents will be a party to the proceedings and the agency will not be a party. It is for this reason that most agencies have a policy of using freeing whenever possible when seeking to place a child with a permanent substitute family. In freeing, the agency 'controls' the procedure leading to the hearing and can directly use its resources to ensure that it proceeds smoothly. With a direct opposed adoption, the adoptive parents have to start the proceedings relying on their own lawyer and have to cope with the undoubted strain involved in contested litigation.

If a direct opposed adoption takes place then the court must ensure that the natural parents do not know the identity of the adoptive parents by giving the case a serial number to be used on all court documents rather than the names of the parties which would disclose the identity of the adoptive parents. Similarly at the hearing, arrangements have to be made to ensure that the parties do not meet, which can prove problematic.

The court's grounds for dispensing with the consent of the natural parents are the same as those for a freeing application.

It is unusual for an agency to use a direct adoption except where a child had been placed with foster parents on a long-term basis and their identity was already known to the natural parents. But if the application would be contested, it may still be easier for the adoptive parents for the matter to proceed by way of a freeing application.

Uncontested adoption proceedings   It is possible for an adoption to proceed by consent as with freeing. In this case the court will proceed as in a freeing application with the same forms being filed and a reporting officer being appointed to confirm to the court that the mother and/or father (if appropriate) have freely given their consent.

Many adoptions involve the adoption of a stepchild where a second marriage has taken place. These are normally on an uncontested basis without the placement being carried out by an agency. A social worker's involvement in these will normally be to supply a Schedule 2 report to the court, which is required by the court under r. 22 of the Adoption Rules 1984. Three copies of the report must be supplied within six weeks of the court's request.

Beyond these situations the remaining adoptions will be in the situation where the child is already freed for adoption. The procedure for these applications is the same as for the initial freeing application except that there will be no need for a reporting officer, as the freeing order itself is sufficient for the court to deal with the question of the natural parents. The adoption order transfers the parental responsibilities from the agency to the new adoptive parents. The court, in such situations, is still required to consider whether or not the adoption is in the best interests of the child, although that step is normally straightforward.

Miscellaneous Matters relating to Adoption

Payments to adoptive parents   Where foster parents are supplying accommodation to a child placed with them by a local authority they will normally be paid for supplying the service. After a period of time the authority and/or the foster parents may feel that it is in the best interests of the child that the child be adopted by the foster parents to give the child a stable home background. As an encouragement to adoption, regulations made under the Children Act now allow these payments to continue after adoption. The Children Act also provides that regulations issued by the Secretary of State will regulate these schemes.

Adoption and freeing proceedings are family proceedings   Under the Children Act 1989, s. 8(4), any proceedings under the Adoption Act are deemed to be family proceedings. This means that the court, when faced with an adoption or freeing application, can exercise its powers under the Children Act, s. 10 to make any order under the Children Act, s. 8, i.e., contact orders, residence orders, specific issues orders or prohibited steps orders. This would mean that the court could make a contact or residence order in favour of persons other than the applicants. It can require an investigation by the local authority under s. 37 with a view to applying for a care or a supervision order. (See also Chapters 4, 7 and 16.)

The impact of the Human Rights Act 1998 on adoption law   As we have described, both Articles 6 and 8 of the European Convention are relevant to adoption law. Recent cases indicate that there is an increasing emphasis on the birth family in adoption cases. In particular, the need to notify natural fathers of the adoption proceedings and, where appropriate, the need to allow natural fathers to participate in the proceedings, are recognised.

Proportionality is also a key requirement. In *Re B (Adoption Order)* [2001] EWCA Civ 347 [2001] 2 FLR 26, a child who had been placed with a foster family when he was two years old retained an excellent relationship with his natural father. The local authority proposed that the adoption was in the child's best interests and that the father's agreement be dispensed with. The Court of Appeal allowed the father's appeal. The authority's decision that the child should be adopted was inappropriate given the strength of the relationship between the child and the father. The trial judge had not considered whether the interference which would result to the father's right to a family life under Article 8 was necessary and appropriate. Finally it was hard to label as unreasonable the father's refusal to consent when his opinion was shared by the children's guardian and the father is a well-respected forensic scientist.

The Adoption and Children's Bill will provide an excellent opportunity for a statutory statement of the appropriate balance between the child's, the birth family's and the prospective adoptors' rights. The proposed introduction of the new 'special guardianship' to provide an alternative to adoption will also give much-needed added flexibility.

Table 11.1   Schedule 2 Adoption Rules 1984
                        (SI 1984 No 265)

SCHEDULE 2   Rule 4(4)

MATTERS TO BE COVERED IN REPORTS SUPPLIED UNDER RULES 4(4), 22(1)
OR 22(2)

So far as is practicable, the report supplied by the adoption agency or, in the case of a report supplied under rule 22(2), the local authority shall include all the following particulars:—

1. *The Child*
    (a) Name, sex, date and place of birth and address;
    (b) whether legitimate or illegitimate at birth, and if illegitimate, whether subsequently legitimated;
    (c) nationality;
    (d) physical description;
    (e) personality and social development;
    (f) religion, including details of baptism, confirmation or equivalent ceremonies;
    (g) details of any wardship proceedings and of any court orders or local authority resolutions relating to the parental rights and duties in respect of the child or to his custody and maintenance;
    (h) details of any brothers and sisters, including dates of birth, arrangements in respect of care and custody and whether any brother or sister is the subject of a parallel application;
    (i) extent of access to members of the child's natural family and, if the child is illegitimate, his father, and in each case the nature of the relationship enjoyed;
    (j) if the child has been in the care of a local authority or voluntary organisation, details (including dates) of any placements with foster parents, or other arrangements in respect of the care of the child, including particulars of the persons with whom the child has had his home and observations on the care provided;
    (k) date and circumstances of placement with prospective adopter;
    (l) names, addresses and types of schools attended, with dates, and educational attainments;
    (m) any special needs in relation to the child's health (whether physical or mental) and his emotional and behavioural development and whether he is subject to a statement under the Education Act 1981;
    (n) what, if any, rights to or interests in property or any claim to damages, under the Fatal Accidents Act 1976 or otherwise, the child stands to retain or lose if adopted;
    (o) wishes and feelings in relation to adoption and the application, including any wishes in respect of religious and cultural upbringing; and
    (p) any other relevant information which might assist the court.

2. *Each Natural Parent, including where appropriate the father of an illegitimate child*

(a) Name, date and place of birth and address;

(b) marital status and date and place of marriage (if any);

(c) past and present relationship (if any) with the other natural parent, including comments on its stability;

(d) physical description;

(e) personality;

(f) religion;

(g) educational attainments;

(h) past and present occupations and interests;

(i) so far as available, names and brief details of the personal circumstances of the parents and any brothers and sisters of the natural parent, with their ages or ages at death;

(j) wishes and feelings in relation to adoption and the application, including any wishes in respect of the child's religious and cultural upbringing;

(k) reasons why any of the above information is unavailable; and

(l) any other relevant information which might assist the court.

3. *Guardian(s)*

Give the details required under paragraph 2(a), (f), (j) and (l).

4. *Prospective Adopter(s)*

(a) Name, date and place of birth and address;

(b) relationship (if any) to the child;

(c) marital status, date and place of marriage (if any) and comments on stability of relationship;

(d) details of any previous marriage;

(e) if a parent and step-parent are applying, the reasons why they prefer adoption or an order relating to the custody of the child;

(f) if a natural parent is applying alone, the reasons for the exclusion of the other parent;

(g) if a married person is applying alone, the reasons for this;

(h) physical description;

(i) personality;

(j) religion, and whether willing to follow any wishes of the child or his parents or guardian in respect of the child's religious and cultural upbringing;

(k) educational attainments;

(l) past and present occupations and interests;

(m) particulars of the home and living conditions (and particulars of any home where the prospective adopter proposes to live with the child, if different);

(n) details of income and comments on the living standards of the household;

(o) details of other members of the household (including any children of the prospective adopter even if not resident in the household);

(p)   details of the parents and any brothers or sisters of the prospective adopter, with their ages or ages at death;

(q)   attitudes to the proposed adoption of such other members of the prospective adopter's household and family as the adoption agency or, as the case may be, the local authority considers appropriate;

(r)   previous experience of caring for children as step-parent, foster parent, child-minder or prospective adopter and assessment of ability in this respect, together where appropriate with assessment of ability in bringing up the prospective adopter's own children;

(s)   reasons for wishing to adopt the child and extent of understanding of the nature and effect of adoption;

(t)   any hopes and expectations for the child's future;

(u)   assessment of ability to bring up the child throughout his childhood;

(v)   details of any adoption allowance payable;

(w)   confirmation that any referees have been interviewed, with a report of their views and opinion of the weight to be placed thereon; and

(x)   any other relevant information which might assist the court.

5.   *Actions of the adoption agency or local authority supplying the report*

(a)   Reports under rules 4(4) or 22(1):—

    (i)   brief account of the agency's actions in the case with particulars and dates of all written information and notices given to the child, his natural parents and the prospective adopter;

    (ii)   details of alternatives to adoption considered;

    (iii)   reasons for considering that adoption would be in the child's best interests (with date of relevant decision); and

    (iv)   reasons for considering that the prospective adopter would be suitable to be an adoptive parent and that he would be suitable for this child (with dates of relevant decisions) or, if the child has not yet been placed for adoption, reasons for considering that he is likely to be so placed.

    OR

(b)   Reports under rule 22(2):—

    (i)   confirmation that notice was given under section 18 of the 1975 Act, with the date of that notice;

    (ii)   brief account of the local authority's actions in the case; and

    (iii)   account of investigations whether child was placed in contravention of section 29 of the 1958 Act.

6.   *Generally*

(a)   Whether any respondent appears to be under the age of majority or under a mental disability; and

(b)   whether, in the opinion of the body supplying the report, any other person should be made a respondent (for example, a person claiming to be the father of an illegitimate child, a spouse or ex-spouse of a natural parent, a relative of a deceased parent, or a person with any of the parental rights and duties).

7. *Conclusions*

(This part of the report should contain more than a simple synopsis of the information above. As far as possible, the court should be given a fuller picture of the child, his natural parents and, where appropriate, the prospective adopter.)

(a)   Except where the applicant or one of them is a parent of the child, a summary by the medical adviser to the body supplying the report, of the health history and state of health of the child, his natural parents and, if appropriate, the prospective adopter, with comments on the implications for the order sought and on how any special health needs of the child might be met;

(b)   opinion on whether making the order sought would be in the child's best long-term interests, and on how any special emotional, behavioural and educational needs of the child might be met;

(c)   opinion on the effect on the child's natural parents of making the order sought;

(d)   if the child has been placed for adoption, opinion on the likelihood of full integration of the child into the household, family and community of the prospective adopter, and on whether the proposed adoption would be in the best long-term interests of the prospective adopter;

(e)   opinion, if appropriate, on the relative merits of adoption and custody; and

(f)   final conclusions and recommendations whether the order sought should be made (and, if not, alternative proposals).

DHSS Circular LAC (84) 3

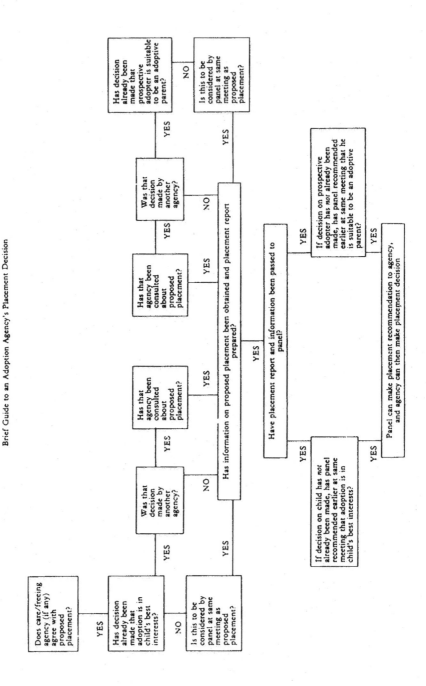

ANNEX B

Brief Guide to an Adoption Agency's Placement Decision

TWELVE

Your Clients and the Criminal Process

WHERE DO SOCIAL WORKERS HAVE RESPONSIBILITY WITHIN THE CRIMINAL JUSTICE SYSTEM?

Not every person in trouble with the police or before the courts is a social services client. Children are your main client group. In criminal matters they tend to be called juveniles, perhaps because it is easier to be tough on juveniles than on children. There are several areas of potential responsibility. In each your 'client' is the person to whom you have a statutory responsibility. (The extent of this statutory responsibility is indicated in italics.)

(a) Liaison with police before decisions are taken whether to charge, reprimand or warn (see below, p. 281). (*Children Act 1989, s. 17, Sch. 2; Children and Young Persons Act 1933 — keeping children out of court, liaising with police.*)

(b) During questioning of juveniles and members of other vulnerable groups by the police an 'appropriate adult' should normally be present (see below, p. 264). (*Children Act 1989 — protection of welfare of children. Note that the Police and Criminal Evidence Act 1984 creates no duties for social services authorities — see the table of statutory duties in Chapter 1, where it is not mentioned. National Assistance Act 1949 — protection of the vulnerable.*)

(c) If the police, or a court, remand a juvenile in local authority accommodation, social services must make the necessary arrangements (see below, pp. 278–80). (*Children and Young Persons Act 1969, s. 23; Children Act 1989, s. 20.*)

(d) If a juvenile is found guilty of an offence, a pre-sentence report will normally be required from you or the probation officer before the court makes an order. (*Children and Young Persons Act 1969, s. 9.*)

(e) If a community sentence is imposed social services will be involved in the supervision. (*Powers of Criminal Courts (Sentencing) Act 2000, ss. 63–67.*)

(f) Children in trouble, whether through their own behaviour or the way they are treated by others, trigger the social services duty to investigate and if necessary act to protect the child (see Chapter 5). (*Children Act 1989, s. 47.*)

(g)   Social workers may be involved when a court sentences a person with a mental disorder (see below, pp. 301–3). (*Mental Health Act 1983, s. 37.*)

Additionally, every social services department must produce an annual youth justice plan (Crime and Disorder Act 1998, s. 40) and every local authority must carry out all of its work in a way designed to reduce crime and disorder (s. 17).

In this chapter we concentrate on criminal procedure as it relates to these responsibilities.

To simplify the discussion, we have assumed that it is the police who instigate action in criminal proceedings; you should nevertheless be aware that an arrest may be carried out by a store detective, or a charge made by the transport police (e.g., where fare dodging is alleged). But by the time a social worker becomes involved the investigation will be in the hands of the police.

ANTI-SOCIAL BEHAVIOUR BY CHILDREN

Is this a crime? In earlier editions of this book the dividing line between crime and child protection or support was relatively easy to draw. If the police were involved and the child might appear in a criminal court, it belonged in this chapter. If the behaviour would not lead to a charge, the issue was one of providing for the needs of the child (dealt with in the earlier chapters). Now the Crime and Disorder Act 1998 has blurred the boundaries. It has introduced a range of quasi-criminal orders, aimed at tackling bad behaviour in order to benefit the community, but not actually taking the form of a criminal prosecution. One of these quasi-criminal orders, the child protection order, was discussed in Chapter 6. We put it there because, unlike the other orders, it is the responsibility of social services to apply for the order. The other quasi-criminal orders are not the responsibility of social services. It is for the district council to apply for these orders. However, the orders involve children, who are likely to be not only children in trouble but also children in need, so social services have to be closely involved under their Children Act s. 17 duties.

The 1998 Act is unusual in that it does not create new duties under the Local Authority Social Services Act 1971 (see Chapter 1). This means that although there is a new range of statutory responsibilities for the local authority on a corporate level, they are not specifically the function of the Social Services Committee.

A number of new court orders have been created, which we shall deal with in turn, together with the role that a local authority social worker is likely to play in obtaining or implementing these orders.

Anti-social Behaviour Orders (ASBO): Crime and Disorder Act 1998, s. 1

As you will have perhaps realised on reading Chapter 2, to obtain a criminal conviction the prosecution have to satisfy a court (or jury) beyond reasonable doubt that the allegations are proved. While anyone with experience of criminal courts realises that this formula is often ignored, it does not apply even in theory to this new court order. A person (child or adult) can be made subject to the ASBO if the court is satisfied on a balance of probabilities that the person has caused the harassment, alarm or distress as defined in the Act, or might have done so.

Making the application   The application for an ASBO can be made by the responsible authority, which is either:

(a)   the district council; or
(b)   the police.

There is a duty for the responsible authority to consult with the other responsible authority for the area. This is the district council (which in county areas is not the same as the social services authority), or the borough council (which is). There is no requirement for the social worker to be involved in an application. But the guidance states that the court hearing the application should satisfy itself that social services have been consulted, and that the person's needs have been assessed, before deciding whether an ASBO is appropriate. For a child, needs must be assessed under the Children Act; for adults, it will be under the NHS and Community Care Act 1990.

The grounds for the application are:

(a)   that the person has acted in an anti-social manner, that is to say, in a manner that caused or was likely to cause harassment, alarm or distress to one or more persons not of the same household as himself; and
(b)   that such an order is necessary to protect persons in the local government area in which the harassment, alarm or distress was caused or was likely to be caused from further anti-social acts by him; . . .

The evidence for proving these grounds may be presented anonymously, giving the person accused no chance to cross-examine the person making the allegations. The Court of Appeal has held that this is not a breach of the right to a fair trial under Article 6 of the Human Rights Convention (*Clingham* v *Kensington and Chelsea LBC* [2001] EWHC Admin 1 (2001) The Times, 20 February).

The order may be obtained against any individual over the age of ten. (Child safety orders (CSOs) are available for those aged under ten — see p. 117.)

The guidance states:

The process is not suitable for private disputes between neighbours (which are usually civil matters), but is intended to deal with criminal or sub-criminal activity which, for one reason or another, cannot be proven to the criminal standard, or where criminal proceedings are not appropriate.

However, although the ASBO is obtained in civil proceedings, breach of the order is a criminal offence. As it is a serious order, persons who may become liable to one should get legal representation.

What may be in the order? The simple answer is anything. The 1998 Act says:

> 1.—(6) The prohibitions that may be imposed by an anti-social behaviour order are those necessary for the purpose of protecting from further anti-social acts by the defendant—
>
> (a) persons in the local government area; and
>
> (b) persons in any adjoining local government area specified in the application for the order . . .

The problem with this section is that 'anti-social behaviour' is not fully defined. It relies on the concept of causing harassment, alarm or distress. What it amounts to will be a matter for the court finally to decide, as a matter of fact. The guidance makes the point:

> The orders should not be used against someone just because he or she is different, or is engaging in activities different from his or her neighbours for example because of difference in race or religion . . .

but it goes on to make clear the nature of the order:

> Some of those against whom an order is being considered may have other social or health problems, including drug and/or alcohol misuse, and/or mental health problems. These problems should be borne in mind — and in the case of mental health problems, may be addressed by referral to social care intervention. But these considerations should not override an application for an order where in the opinion of the relevant authority it is otherwise justified. It should always be remembered that the purpose of the order is to restrain serious anti-social behaviour caused to other individuals, who cannot be expected to tolerate the behaviour unchecked.

The responsible authority does not have to show that any other methods of controlling the behaviour have been used, or that it has exhausted all other methods.

Length of order Orders must last for *not less* than two years (s. 1(7)) and can last indefinitely. Although there are provisions to vary the order, the court cannot discharge an order that has not lasted for two years, unless all parties agree.

Breach of order Doing anything in breach of the order is a criminal offence. On summary conviction the court can exercise its maximum sentencing powers. The breach can be dealt with in the Crown Court with a maximum sentence of five years and an unlimited fine.

Parenting Orders: Crime and Disorder Act 1998, s. 8

The grounds under s. 8

8.—(1) This section applies where, in any court proceedings—

(a)   a child safety order is made in respect of a child; [*see p. 117*]

(b)   an anti-social behaviour order or sex offender order is made in respect of a child or young person; [*see pp. 256 and 303*]

(c)   a child or young person is convicted of an offence; or

(d)   a person is convicted of an offence under section 443 (failure to comply with school attendance order) or section 444 (failure to secure regular attendance at school of registered pupil) of the Education Act 1996.

If any of the above conditions is met the court can decide to make a parenting order. There is no need for anybody to make an application. The behaviour of the child or young person may either be criminal or merely anti-social.

The order can be made in:

(a)   a family proceedings court;

(b)   a magistrates' court acting under civil jurisdiction; or

(c)   all criminal courts, i.e. a youth court, an adult magistrates' court or the Crown Court.

What may be in the order?   An order under s. 8(4) has two elements:

(a)   compulsory attendance by the parent, once a week, at counselling or guidance sessions for a period not exceeding three months. (This need not be required if the unfortunate parent already has attended counselling or guidance sessions because of being previously subject to a parenting order (s. 8(5)). That fact appears to throw some doubt on the value of the sessions!)

(b)   to comply with such requirements as may be contained in the order. These requirements have to be designed to stop the repetition of the behaviour of the child that led to the parenting order being made. This requirement can last up to 12 months.

As the order must include the compulsory counselling and guidance, it follows that facilities have to exist. Therefore under s. 8(3) a court may make a parenting order only if it has been notified by the Secretary of State that those facilities exists in the area where the parent lives.

The guidance gives the following suggestions as to what might be included:

- the parent ensuring that the child attends school or any extra-curricular activities, such as sporting activities or homework clubs, that might be specified in any order directed at the child;
- the parent ensuring that the child avoids contact with disruptive and possibly older children;
- the parent ensuring that the child avoids visiting certain areas, such as shopping centres, unsupervised;
- the parent ensuring that the child is at home during certain hours, probably the evening, and is effectively supervised; or
- the parent attending or ensuring that the child attends a particular course or session to address specific problems.

The procedure for making a parenting order   Section 9 of the 1998 Act imposes specific requirements on the court before it can make an order. The court must:

(a)   obtain and consider information about the child's family circumstances and the likely effect of the order on those circumstances. This information can be either in oral or written form;

(b)   explain to the parent or guardian of the child in ordinary language—

(i)   the effect of the order and of the requirements proposed to be included in it,

(ii)   the consequences which may follow if the parent fails to comply with any of those requirements, and

(iii)   that the court has power to review the order on the application either of the parent or of the responsible officer.

This normally would be done at court, although the draft guidance does suggest that it could be done in the form of a letter sent by the court;

(c)   avoid, as far as practicable, imposing requirements which would either conflict with the parent's religious beliefs, or interfere with the times at which the parent normally works or attends an educational establishment.

It should be noted that the order will actually name the responsible officer. The guidance sets out what is expected of the responsible officer and how to implement the order.

Variation, discharge and breach of the parenting order   While the order is in force, the responsible officer or the parent may apply to discharge or vary it. Any provisions can be taken out or be added. The guidance states that it is not possible to extend the length of an existing order. It is not clear how the guidance comes to this conclusion.

A parent failing to comply with a parenting order commits a criminal offence and can be fined.

So we wish good luck to the social worker now trying to work with the family after making a criminal of the parent for the offence of deviant parenting!

Local Child Curfew Schemes: Crime and Disorder Act 1998, s. 14

These new powers of the district council should be noted, but (we are not unhappy to say) they have been ignored by those councils, despite Government exhortation. We would argue that blanket orders depriving individuals of liberty raise human rights issues under Article 5 and 6 of the European Convention.

These schemes should not be confused with curfew orders imposed on individual juveniles following their conviction for a criminal offence (see below, p. 298). This is not an order made in response to individual children but in response to the behaviour of children in general in the specified area. It is designed to keep all unsupervised children under the age of 16 off the streets in a particular area for a particular period of time, if the police and the local authority think that this is necessary. (Actually the order does not require anything to be proved, in an evidential sense; no evidence is needed of recent bad behaviour by children roaming the streets out of control. All that is required is that the Home Secretary agrees to the request and signs the order.)

Each order can last up to 90 days, but if the perceived troubles persist a new one can be made once the old one expires. The order empowers the police to take a child home (or elsewhere if they think the child would not be safe at home) if found out, without supervision from a parent or responsible person of at least 18, between the hours specified in the order (the order can be for any time between 9.00 p.m. and 6.00 a.m.). If a child is picked up in this way the social services authority must be notified, and they must start a s. 47 Children Act investigation into whether steps need to be taken to protect or assist the child (see Chapter 4).

If a child under the age of ten breaches a curfew order then this can trigger an application for a Child Safety Order (see Chapter 6, p. 117).

YOUNG PEOPLE/JUVENILES

Juveniles are under 18. Once people reach 18, the criminal courts treat them as adults, except for sentencing. Juveniles themselves are sometimes subdivided into children (aged 10 to 13) and young persons (14 to 17); but for most purposes, the word juvenile is sufficient, and we use the word to refer to people of 10 to 17 years inclusive. The age was raised from 16 to 17 by the Criminal Justice Act 1991. However, there has been no corresponding change in the age at which a person being questioned at a police station is treated as particularly vulnerable: that remains 16 and below. Similarly, where the police or the courts refuse bail, if the child is 17, he or she is treated as an adult and can be detained at the police station or remanded to a remand centre. As we explain shortly, for the child under 17 who is refused bail, the local authority must provide accommodation.

PHILOSOPHY OF THE YOUTH JUSTICE SYSTEM

Two statutory duties now contradict each other. The new, 'tough on crime' Labour Government made it clear under s. 37 of the Crime and Disorder Act 1998 that 'It shall be the principal aim of the youth justice system to prevent offending by children and young persons'. But s. 44 of the Children and Young Persons Act 1933 was not modified by the 1998 Act, and it continues to make the welfare of the juvenile the number one priority. This latter requirement is in accordance with the UN Convention on the Rights of the Child.

As an example of the approach of looking to the welfare of the child, s. 39 of the 1933 Act permits a court to restrict press reporting of the case, particularly to avoid any detail by which the child may be identified. The press can challenge such an order, in which case the higher courts which hear the application must balance the safeguarding of the child's welfare against the public interest in open justice. In *R v Manchester Crown Court, ex parte H* [2000] 1 WLR 760, the Divisional Court permitted identification of two 15-year-olds convicted of murder.

The Crime and Disorder Act 1998 is worded so as to impose the new responsibilities on the local authority as a corporate body. It does not impose those responsibilities on the Social Services Committee.

The effect of this confusion of duties will be worst in those areas where district councils exist within county council areas. Each of the different local authorities has different legal responsibilities.

For the social worker involved in youth justice, we suggest that you should be performing your duties with reference to the Children Act 1989, s. 17 and Sch. 2: promoting the welfare of children and keeping them out of the criminal courts (see further Chapter 4). This continues to be a duty of a Social Services Department under the Local Authority Social Services Act 1971. But you carry out this duty towards children in need in the new context of getting tough on crime, and the duty of every local authority under the 1998 Act to 'exercise its various functions with due regard to the likely effect of the exercise of those functions on, and the need to do all that it reasonably can to prevent, crime and disorder in its area'.

To provide direction to the drive to cut down youth crime, the Government has established a Youth Justice Board to set standards and give advice to the Government on policy. The Board can make grants to local authorities who have good ideas.

CAPACITY TO COMMIT CRIME

Under 10

A child who has not reached age 10 cannot, as a matter of English law, commit a crime, and so cannot be subjected to criminal proceedings (Children and Young Persons Act 1933, s. 50). Behaviour which in an older child could lead to arrest, charge and trial in the youth court will, if the alleged wrongdoer is under 10, either have to be dealt with informally by the police and/or social services (a telling off and a word with the parents), or formally, by application for a CSO (see p. 117), the institution of care/ supervision proceedings or, in an urgent case, by an application for an EPO (see p. 120). The deviant behaviour could be evidence of significant harm under the Children Act 1989, s. 31 (see further Chapters 6 and 7).

10 Upwards

A person aged 10 or older is presumed to have full capacity to commit a crime.

YOUTH OFFENDING TEAMS: LIAISON WITH POLICE AND OTHER AGENCIES

A Word About the Police

The reason you liaise with the police on questions of youth crime is your duty under the Children Act 1989. The police themselves must notify the local authority if they decide to prosecute a young person (Children and Young Persons Act 1969, ss. 5 and 34). Failure to do so, however, does not make the criminal proceedings invalid (*R* v *Marsh* [1997] 1 WLR 649).

The Youth Justice Plan
The framework for joint work with other agencies is set out in the Crime and Disorder Act 1998. Every local authority (at district, borough or county level) must now have a youth justice plan (ss. 6 and 40). The plan must contain a strategy for reducing crime and disorder, including setting performance targets.

The Youth Offending Team
Who is at the heart of this process? Not the police, not the probation services, but the local authority. Under s. 38, the local authority (in this case, those with social services functions) must secure all necessary youth justice services. They do this, under s. 39, by setting up for their area, or jointly with another social services department to cover more than one area, Youth Offending Teams (YOTs). The cooperation of police, probation, health and education authorities in establishing these teams is required by the statute.

Youth justice services must be secured — but what are these services? The YOT must ensure that the following are available in their area:

(a)   appropriate adults to be available when the police interview juveniles (below, p. 264);

(b)   rehabilitation following a police warning (below, p. 281);

(c)   support for children awaiting trial or sentence (below, p. 285);

(d)   accommodation for children who are denied bail (below, p. 278);

(e)   the making of reports to the court (below, p. 286 and Chapter 9);

(f)   persons to act as responsible officers where a court has made a parenting order (above, p. 260);

(g)   supervision of community sentences (for sentencing see below, starting at p. 285);

(h)   supervision of detention and training orders (below, p. 292) or supervision orders (p. 293);

(i)   supervision of children who are released from custody (below, p. 292); and

(j)   arranging for convicted juveniles to go into secure accommodation if sentenced to a detention and training order (below, p. 292).

All of these functions must be secured by the local authority, but need not necessarily be provided directly by them. Curiously, none of these functions appears in the Local Authority (Social Services) Act 1970 as statutory duties of Social Services Departments (see Chapter 1).

As stated already, your primary duties as a social worker, when carrying out the above functions, are still defined by the Children Act 1989, s. 17 and Sch. 2. Essentially social services departments have a duty under the Children Act 1989, Sch. 2 to stop children being the subject of criminal proceedings.

Two ways exist to achieve this ambitious goal: to cause children not to commit crimes and to persuade the police not to charge them. Neither is easy, but liaison with police at least does not require infinite resources. (Improving the lives of children — their self-esteem, their education, their housing, their financial security — would also make a difference, and is allowed under the Act, but resources are inadequate to eliminate crime in this way.)

THE SOCIAL WORKER IN THE POLICE STATION

What goes on when a suspect is held in the police station is governed by the Police and Criminal Evidence Act 1984, and the codes that are made by the Home Office. The particular code of interest here is the 1995 Code C on Detention Treatment and Questioning. The code is available for consultation in every police station, by detainees and members of the public; social services offices usually have a copy (and, if not, should acquire one).

Being at the police station for interview is stressful. Code C recognises that some groups of vulnerable people should not have to undergo the experience alone. An 'appropriate adult' should be called to assist the suspect, and no police questioning should normally take place until that person is available. A social worker will frequently be asked to be that appropriate adult.

The code recognises two groups as being vulnerable — juveniles (in the police station that means under 17) and the mentally disordered or handicapped (Code C, s. 11). How can the police be expected to know if a person falls into this category? Under s. 1, if they have any suspicion, or are told in good faith, that a person is a juvenile or mentally ill or handicapped, they must treat the person as such — i.e., if there is doubt, the detainee will be treated as being in a vulnerable category.

The Appropriate Adult

Code C contains several references to 'the appropriate adult'. Where it is or might be a social worker, we have highlighted this in italics.

Section 1.7 says that the appropriate adult means:

(a)   in the case of a juvenile:

(i)   his parent or guardian (or, if he is in care, *the care authority* or voluntary organisation). The term 'in care' is used in this code to cover all cases in which a juvenile is 'looked after' by a local authority under the terms of the Children Act 1989; so that includes accommodation without a care order.

(ii)   a *social worker*; or

(iii)   failing either of the above, *another responsible adult* aged 18 or over who is not a police officer or employed by the police.

(b)   in the case of a person who is mentally disordered or mentally handicapped:

(i)   a relative, *guardian* or other person responsible for his care or custody;

(ii)   *someone who has experience of dealing with mentally disordered or mentally handicapped people* but who is not a police officer or employed by the police (such as an *approved social worker* as defined by the Mental Health Act 1983 or a *specialist social worker*); or

(iii)   failing either of the above, *some other responsible adult* aged 18 or over who is not a police officer or employed by the police.

Do social services have to send someone to the police station on command in each of these situations? As we saw above, the department must ensure the availability of appropriate adults, but there is no duty to send someone to the police station under the Local Authority (Social Services) Act 1970 (see Chapter 1, p. 6).

Where a person at risk is detained, s. 3.9 of Code C requires the police to inform the appropriate adult as soon as practicable of the reason for detention, where the person is being detained, and to request the appropriate adult to come to the police station. They must not normally interview the detainee in the absence of the appropriate adult. This principle applies even if the mentally disordered person appears lucid at the time (see *R* v *Aspinall*, below).

But should you agree to be the appropriate adult simply because the police have requested a social worker, knowing that it is easier to contact your department than to get a parent along? Clearly where a juvenile is in your care, there is no doubt that a social worker from that authority is the appropriate adult. But in the other situations listed, someone else, a parent or carer, may be better. Where the detainee has a mental disorder or illness, Code C (Notes for Guidance 1E) recommends that someone with experience and training may often be better as appropriate adult than a relative. Home Office Study No. 174 of 1997 found that for juveniles the appropriate adult is a social worker in 23 per cent of cases. For mentally disordered detainees, the appropriate adult is a social worker in 60 per cent of cases.

The adult must be, to at least some extent, appropriate to the situation. Sometimes a social worker is more appropriate, and it is right to listen to the reason the police want you to attend rather than a parent. For example, in *DPP* v *Blake* [1989] 1 WLR 432, Norfolk social services, at the time, had a blanket policy of not sending a social worker to the police station as the appropriate adult if a parent was available. In this case the father of a 16-year-old had been contacted. The detained juvenile did not want him, as she had no real relationship with him. She wanted her social worker. During the police station interview the father played no part; in fact his daughter ignored him. She eventually confessed to the charge and was convicted. The Court of Appeal held that this confession should not have been put before the court as evidence, because of the circumstances in which it was obtained, notably the fact that the appropriate adult had not assisted the juvenile in any way. However, in *R* v *Jefferson* [1994] 1 All ER 270, the appropriate adult was the father, who intervened on the side of the police, often contradicting the boy's account. As we will see below, this is not what is expected of the appropriate adult — but the boy's eventual confession to riot and violent disorder was allowed to stand by the Court of Appeal. (See further p. 271 below for rules on excluding confession evidence.) The Home Office research confirms this impression that frequently the social worker does a far better job than parents, relatives or other adults. The social worker is calmer, more supportive and, of course, understands the task (having read this book).

There may be a temptation to use a family member as both appropriate adult and interpreter, where the detainee does not speak fluent English. The Queen's Bench Division, however, made clear that this flouts two important principles: first, that the appropriate adult must have only one task, that of assisting the detainee; secondly, that an interpreter must be wholly independent (*R v West London Youth Court, ex parte J* [2000] 1 All ER 823).

A social worker to whom the juvenile has previously admitted the offence is not the appropriate adult either — another social worker would be required (Code C, Notes for Guidance 1D). If you refuse to attend, do not, of course, give this as the reason to the police (see p. 33 on confidentiality).

In exceptional cases, Annex C to Code C, entitled 'Urgent Interviews', allows the police to interview a juvenile or mentally ill/handicapped person in the absence of an appropriate adult if an officer of at least superintendent rank believes that delay *will* lead to immediate risk of harm to anyone, or tip-offs to other suspects, or other interference with any evidence. If the police tell you on the telephone to be down within 10 minutes, otherwise they are going to interview anyway, with luck they are only bluffing. The police rarely carry out interviews of vulnerable groups without an appropriate adult present, since the courts will probably not allow any confession evidence they obtain to be used at trial. The Code states that such a course must be 'exceptional'. (The Home Office research found that in 9 per cent of juvenile interviews an appropriate adult was not present.)

A person who appears lucid and has been certified fit for interview by a police doctor, but who is known to suffer from schizophrenia, should not be interviewed in the absence of an appropriate adult (*R v Aspinall* [1999] 2 Cr App R 115). In that case, the interview should not have been used in evidence. Even with an appropriate adult to safeguard the detainee's interests, a confession obtained from a detainee who is suffering at the time of interview from a mental disorder is unlikely to be admissible at trial, and the appropriate adult is likely to be called to give evidence as to the circumstances surrounding the confession (*R v Heslop* [1996] Crim LR 730).

You should be aware that, entirely independently of the need to enlist an appropriate adult before interviewing, the police must attempt to inform the person responsible for the child's welfare (usually a parent or guardian) of the arrest and detention of any juvenile (Children and Young Persons Act 1933, s. 34(2)), and, if the juvenile is under supervision, the supervisor.

If you decide that you are the appropriate person to attend, it is important to go as soon as possible, to minimise the period of detention. Once you arrive, you should first talk to the custody officer to obtain basic details — suspected offence, time of arrest, what the police are intending to do. Beware of ever being asked at this stage to abandon your own professional judgment ('Between you and me, if you could persuade him to tell us what happened, he'll be out of here much quicker . . .'). Your role is described below; do not allow the police to define it for you.

You should then insist on talking to the suspect in private, for any overheard conversations could be repeated in evidence at trial (*R* v *Ali* (1991) *The Times*, 19 February). The police, some time ago, admitted that interview rooms routinely have eavesdropping facilities (*Law Society's Gazette*, 25 May 1991) and solicitors report that it takes place ('Anger at police station bugging', *Law Society's Gazette*, 23 October 1996). This is a breach of the suspect's human rights: *Brennan* v *UK* (2001) *The Times*, 22 October. Many solicitors refuse to talk to clients through partitions, which require microphones and are vulnerable to eavesdropping (*Law Society's Gazette*, 14 September 1994, p. 7). We advise you to insist on seeing your client in proper privacy. Your client is entitled to consult you privately at any time (Code C, s. 3.12).

If a solicitor is also to attend, he or she will probably wish to hold the first interview with the juvenile without you being present. This is based on Law Society guidance, because the solicitor's duty of confidentiality is almost always protected by courts, whereas something said in front of a social worker could, exceptionally, be ordered to be revealed in court. The Law Society guidance (*Law Society's Gazette*, 19 May 1993, at p. 41) sets out their view of your position as a professional social worker:

> [T]he appropriate adult may then disclose what was said during the consultation to the police as their Code of Conduct allows them to breach confidentiality in this way if they believe that the safety of the public may be at risk from the suspect.

This situation is exceptional, but because a breach of confidence by you is conceivable (see further p. 33), you can expect solicitors to insist on excluding you until they have taken instructions. Or you may be asked to help explain to the suspect why the lawyer needs a private talk, and then you should leave the discussions until the solicitor comes back to consider whether you should join in the consultation.

None of this affects the duty of the police to have the appropriate adult present during interview.

How effective are appropriate adults?   Research on what help juveniles and other vulnerable detainees get from the appropriate adult makes depressing reading. '[I]n the vast majority of cases, the adult in question (usually a parent or social worker) made no contribution at all to the proceedings, whilst the few who intervened were as likely to collude with the police as support the accused' (Morgan and Stephenson, *Suspicion and Silence*, Blackstone Press, 1994, at p. 11).

POLICE POWERS AND PROCEDURES

Now that you know how you might come to be in the police station, we shall explain some of the police powers and procedures, so that we can consider in context the role that the appropriate adult has to play.

The police have arrested a person and brought them to the police station. What they may then do or not do is governed by the Police and Criminal

Evidence Act 1984 (referred to as PACE) and Home Office codes of guidance – particularly Code C, which we have already touched on when considering the presence of the appropriate adult.

Powers of Detention

PACE empowers the police to hold an arrested suspect before charge for up to 24 hours from time of arrival at the police station (s. 41) for the purpose of obtaining evidence; the principal evidence will come from questioning the person who is detained. This period of detention can be extended to a maximum of 36 hours on the authority of an officer of at least superintendent rank (s. 42), and beyond that up to a maximum of 96 hours if a magistrates' court gives authorisation (s. 43). (The procedures are different under the Prevention of Terrorism Act 1989, but you are unlikely to be involved in such a case.)

Extensions of the period of detention before charge are only allowed if the offence is deemed to be a serious arrestable offence. It is up to the police to decide if a case falls into this category; s. 116 lists offences which are always serious arrestable offences, for example murder, rape, possession of firearms with intent to injure, and goes on to say that any arrestable offence can be serious if the consequences are serious, such as causing death or serious injury, or substantial financial gain or loss. This begs the further question of what an arrestable offence is, which would take too much space to describe. It is defined in s. 1, and it is normally safe (for the non-lawyer) to presume that the offence is arrestable if the person has been arrested!

The only purpose for which the police are allowed to detain someone before charge is to obtain enough evidence to make a decision whether to charge or not. In theory the police are not supposed to be looking for evidence to strengthen their case in court.

At the end of the maximum detention period, the police must either charge the detainee or release him or her. But they should take the decision to charge or release as soon as possible, which means as soon as they have obtained sufficient evidence on which to base such a decision (s. 37 and Code C, s. 16); they should not and do not usually rely on the maximum period as a matter of course.

All decisions concerning detention and charge are made by a police officer called the 'custody officer' (ss. 37 and 38), and he or she must be independent of the investigation into the offence. Complaints or problems should be addressed to the custody officer, so you should make sure you know who he or she is as soon as you become involved.

We have been talking here about detainees. People who have not been arrested are known, not always appropriately, as volunteers; they are free to leave the police station. One of the first things to ascertain therefore is whether the suspect is detained or not. Of course, once you inform a suspect that he or she is free to leave, and he or she chooses to do so, this may trigger an arrest; but at least at that point the time clock for maximum periods of detention before charge has started to run.

Right to Legal Advice

PACE, s. 58 gives all detainees the right to legal advice. Code C extends the right to 'volunteers'. Suspects in the police station are entitled to receive such advice, in person or on the telephone, and in private, before having to be questioned. They are entitled to have the legal adviser present during a police interview. This service is paid for out of legal aid and is not means tested; if the detainee cannot nominate a solicitor, a duty solicitor on a 24-hour rota must be contacted. The take-up of this right is surprisingly low; although a detainee must sign the custody record to signify that he or she does not want a solicitor, many appear to be unaware of the right. The Home Office research showed that 41 per cent of juveniles requested legal advice. This is higher than the adult rate and is attributed to the policy of social workers routinely insisting on a lawyer. Code C, s. 6 requires the suspect's reasons for refusing legal advice to be recorded in the custody record. A vital role of a social worker in the situation is to ensure that the detainee is aware of the right; and if the detainee has signed to say that he or she does not wish to see a solicitor, to explain that he or she is entitled to change his or her mind. An appropriate adult is in fact entitled to exercise the right to call a solicitor on behalf of the detainee. If a solicitor is called, the advice on law can usually be left to him or her, unless you have reason to fear he or she is not doing so adequately or at all (see below p. 272).

Right to have Someone Informed

A person held at a police station is entitled on request to have the police notify one person who is likely to have an interest in their welfare (s. 56 of the Act, s. 5 of the code). If the police cannot contact the person chosen, they must try at least two further people chosen by the suspect. The code requires the police in most cases to allow the detainee to speak to one person by telephone, and to have writing materials to send letters (Code C, s. 5).

Denial of Rights

Both the right to legal advice and the right to have someone notified depend on a request being made by the suspect; Code C provides in s. 3 that on arrival the suspect must be told of these rights, together with the right to consult the code. When the appropriate adult arrives, the suspect should be told this again, in the adult's presence.

Refusal of the right to legal advice and to have someone notified can be delayed only on the authority of an officer of at least superintendent rank, and only where the offence is a serious arrestable offence (discussed above). The delay cannot continue beyond 36 hours from the start of the detention in the designated police station. Grounds for a refusal are set out in PACE, s. 58 and Annex B to Code C; they state that the officer must be satisfied that the exercise of the right will (not might) lead to harm to others, interference with evidence or a tip-off of other suspects, or hinder the recovery of property. Refusal of the right to a solicitor requires the police to have actual grounds for suspecting the solicitor would be committing what amounts to a criminal offence.

Once a solicitor has been requested, there must be no further questioning until he or she arrives, unless an officer of at least superintendent rank believes that delay will lead to immediate risk of harm to persons or serious damage to property, or unreasonable delay to the investigation. Questioning before the solicitor arrives is permissible only if the suspect consents and signs the custody record accordingly. Even if that happens, the appropriate adult can override the juvenile's consent and exercise the detainee's right to insist on a consultation with a solicitor before questioning.

We have seen that the police can detain a person only for the purpose of deciding whether or not to charge. The decision is taken by the custody officer. This officer must also review the detention after six hours, and then every nine hours, to see if detention is still required in order to get the evidence to reach a decision on charging or not. If a person is charged, he or she should then be released on bail, unless the custody officer refuses it for the reasons set out below (p. 278). If a decision is made not to charge, the person must be released; but the release does not have to be unconditional, and can be subject to bail, with a requirement to report to the police station on a particular date and at a given time, by which time the police will have been able to decide whether to charge or not.

THE ROLE OF THE APPROPRIATE ADULT AT THE POLICE STATION

Section 11.16 of Code C is helpful, but brief:

> Where the appropriate adult is present at an interview, he shall be informed that he is not expected to act simply as an observer; and also that the purposes of his presence are, first, to advise the person being questioned and to observe whether or not the interview is being conducted properly and fairly, and secondly, to facilitate communication with the person being interviewed.

Let us take each aspect in turn.

Observer

You are an observer. Why is this important? First, your presence makes it more likely that correct procedures will be followed. Awareness of these procedures, and a willingness to object where they are not being followed, will usually ensure that the police act correctly in your presence. But what if there is impropriety, or even a refusal to allow you access to the suspect? Here we run into a problem of enforcement. The Act and Code C provide for good practice, but provide no immediate remedy for the victim for any breach. (Complaints against the police can be made to the police, which the Police Complaints Authority must investigate. It is wise to take legal advice before formally complaining; most solicitors believe that in cases of serious misconduct it is more effective to sue the police.) The most significant sanction is found in the rules of what evidence will be admitted at trial. So we must now take a digression to consider these rules; you may have expected to find this in the evidence chapter, but we felt it of most relevance to you in the context of police interviews.

The simple rule of evidence is that all relevant evidence is admissible, however it was obtained. If a person is searched illegally and incriminating evidence is found, it can be used at the trial (*Kuruma* v *R* [1955] AC 197). Tricks by the police, such as posing as a contract killer, do not normally result in the evidence being excluded (e.g., *R* v *Smurthwaite* [1994] 1 All ER 898).

However, that harsh rule is modified by ss. 76 and 78 of PACE. If the evidence obtained is a confession then that confession cannot be put into evidence against the defendant unless it is shown beyond reasonable doubt that it was not obtained improperly (which means under s. 76 by oppression, or in other circumstances which render it likely to be unreliable). As a social worker, you will not have to argue these points at trial. But as you may have been present at the police station and observed what actually happened, you can be sure that if there is a defence submission to the trial court that a confession is inadmissible, you will be an important witness.

Additionally, any unfair evidence can be ruled inadmissible in the discretion of the court; a factor taken into account can be the circumstances in which it was obtained (s. 78). An example would be where a confession has not been obtained by oppression, and is not inherently unreliable, but was nevertheless unfairly obtained. Examples have included telling the suspect that the solicitor was not available, when he was; or that they had obtained clear fingerprint evidence against the detainee, which they had not. Interviewing in a non-urgent case without the presence of an appropriate adult should lead to the exclusion of confession evidence (*R* v *Delaney* [1989] Crim LR 139).

The observer can become a witness when the circumstances in which the evidence was obtained are discussed in court. To anticipate being a witness yourself means to recall what happened. Therefore, bearing in mind the principle (see Chapter 8) that you can refresh your memory in the witness-box from notes made at or near the time of the facts you are talking about, you should always go to the police station with paper, pens and an accurate watch. You should record the time, to the minute, of every stage of the procedure — arrival, talking to the custody officer, waiting to see the detainee, length of interview etc. — and the names, rank and number of the persons you deal with. Ask them for this. If the police see you noting these details, they will respect your professional approach, and avoid the temptation to do anything in breach of the code. So keeping a careful note means you will probably not have to use it!

The police may talk to the suspect about the offence 'informally' before you or the lawyer are allowed to see him or her, and obtain damaging evidence. You obviously cannot prevent this, as you were not present. But if at the same time you have a record that you were waiting in the foyer, and available, it is possible that any evidence obtained will be ruled inadmissible (*R* v *Franklin* (1994) *The Times*, 16 June). If you are kept waiting unnecessarily, make a complaint to the custody officer, so that it is registered in the custody record and the defence solicitor will become aware of it.

More likely, the police will have conducted an informal interview in the police car on the way to the station. Code C (para. 11.1) expressly forbids this type of questioning, except where there is a risk to property or people, or the likelihood of evidence being tampered with, unless questions are asked. But you can have no influence over this.

Adviser

The formal interview, in the appropriate adult's presence, is the one that counts (for exclusion of the informal interview, see above). On arrival at the police station, you need to find out, in as much detail as possible, what has already been said, and what evidence the police have, so that you can discuss it with the detainee. You need then to find out from the detainee what he or she says has been happening. If there has already been an informal interview, it will help to advise the detainee to answer the questions in the formal interview afresh, or remain silent, and to avoid any reference back to earlier conversations and understandings reached with the police. For the contents of the earlier interview are less likely to be admissible at trial; what may have been happening is that the police have been preparing the detainee to give the 'correct' answers at the formal interview stage. If before the interview the suspect has made any statement that may be important, the police must put it to him or her at the start of the formal interview (Code C, 11.2A).

Are You Also a Legal Adviser?

Where a lawyer is available, legal advice is usually best left to the lawyer. However, some solicitors, or their representatives, fail in their duty. For example, in R v Miller, Paris and Abdullah (1993) 97 Cr App R 99, the Lord Chief Justice had this to say about the police: 'Short of physical violence, it is hard to conceive of a more hostile and intimidating approach by officers to a suspect.' Yet the solicitor had been present and done nothing to protect his client. Assuming you have confidence in the solicitor, you must help the suspect communicate with the lawyer, and ensure that he or she genuinely understands what the advice is. (At least the old practice of sending untrained staff to advise at the police station has been eliminated – to get legal aid for attending, the firm must send a solicitor or someone who has had special training.)

The appropriate adult, under the code, is entitled to exercise the right to call for legal advice on behalf of the detainee. But if no lawyer is called, because a delay in the exercise of the right is authorised (which is exceptional — see above), then you may have to give advice. If the legal adviser is giving poor, or no, advice, we advise you to speak to him or her first but, if necessary to protect your client, to give the advice yourself.

We cannot tell you what advice to give, because each situation will require a different approach; but any advice given must ensure that the detainee knows what is going on. Therefore, we shall explain what is going on.

As we saw earlier, the reason the police detain before charge is to obtain evidence, principally by questioning, to enable them to decide whether or not to charge. Gathering evidence for the trial is technically only a by-product, although the police will obviously see that as a high priority. They have a natural desire to get that evidence; the detainee has a desire to get out of this unpleasant environment. The detainee quickly realises — and may be encouraged to think — that there is a connection between confessing and getting out quicker. Confessing may indeed bring about an earlier release, because the police now have enough information to decide to charge. So the confession leads to charge, and court proceedings, and a likelihood of conviction.

The Right to Silence

This brings us to the right to silence. It is said that the right to silence was abolished during the passage of the Criminal Justice and Public Order Act 1994. The Act (ss. 31–38) does not, in fact, abolish the right so much as allow the court to draw adverse conclusions from a failure to answer questions. This makes it less tempting to remain silent. The European Court of Human Rights has ruled that to draw inferences from silence is not, of itself, a breach of Article 6 (right to a fair trial) (*Murray* v *UK* (1996) 22 EHRR 29).

A detainee must, nevertheless, still be cautioned before police questioning, in the following terms:

> You do not have to say anything. But it may harm your defence if you do not mention when questioned something which you later rely on in court. Anything you do say may be given in evidence. (Code C, s. 10)

The caution is unsatisfactory in that it suggests that there will be court proceedings — a decision the police should not yet have reached. It is also a long caution, containing information which is not easy to understand, particularly when under stress.

An adverse inference can be drawn only if at the trial the accused is basing his or her defence on facts that it would have been reasonable to mention at interview.

The fact that failure to answer questions can strengthen the prosecution case is not an automatic reason for answering questions. Police questioning is, even with the safeguards in Code C, a frightening affair. It takes great strength of mind to give simple, consistent answers, when put under pressure to explain this, account for that, comment on suggestions, and to do so despite being told that it is a pack of lies. A vulnerable person, who may have particular difficulties in dealing with others in positions of power, is tempted to confess, to please the questioner and escape the continuing questioning.

Silence, notwithstanding the risk of its strengthening the prosecution case, is better for the accused at trial than a confession. Solicitors are continuing to advise suspects to remain silent where appropriate, and are making sure that the reason for the silence ('My client will refuse to answer questions, in accordance with my advice') is recorded on tape and will be known to the court. But adverse inferences may be drawn against the accused even if he or she stayed silent on the advice of a solicitor (*R* v *Daniel* (1998) *The Times*, 10

April) and even if the detainee was of low intelligence (*R* v *Friend* [1997] 2 All ER 1012: 14-year-old with an IQ of 63). Silence on its own cannot prove guilt. This was established in *R* v *Condron* [1997] 1 WLR 827, where the appellants were advised by their solicitor to say nothing. The trial judge had said that the jury had the option of drawing an adverse inference from this silence. The Court of Appeal made it clear that the prosecution must still have good independent evidence of guilt. The judge had failed to explain this to the jury, who convicted the appellants. The Court of Appeal nevertheless upheld the conviction, on the ground that there was plenty of other evidence of dealing in drugs, and the conviction was safe. The European Court of Human Rights does not, however, like to see someone's conviction upheld if the trial was flawed, and it overturned the conviction as a breach of Article 6 of the Convention (*Condron* v *UK (No. 2)* (2000) 8 BHRC 290).

If the right is to be exercised, the whole of the formal interview should generally adopt the response 'no reply', for selective exercise of the right leads to the inevitable suspicion, which the prosecution will point out, that the accused was hiding something when the questions came too near to the target. But the case of *R* v *Welch* [1992] Crim LR 368, is encouraging: the Court of Appeal said that questions to which no reply was given should be removed from the evidence put to court. We still believe, however, that consistently answering no questions, or all questions, is the best advice. You will learn, too, that the police are very skilful at persuading a person who has said a little then to say more. The Home Office research indicates that only 6 per cent of interviewees make no comment. By contrast, 58 per cent confess.

Normally, the legal adviser will help the detainee come to the best decisions on how to approach the questioning, and your job will be to help the detainee to understand that advice and reach the best decision.

Advocating on Behalf of the Detainee

Decisions as to what happens are in the hands of the police. If, for example, a senior officer wishes to delay the right to see a solicitor, to continue to detain for questioning, or to refuse bail after charge, he or she does not require the consent of anyone else (subject to time limits being observed). However, police usually, in practice, listen to the views of the solicitor and the appropriate adult, and in relation to bail in particular, your views will be important.

Advocating on behalf of the detainee means noting when there is any breach of the proper procedures, ensuring it is noted on the custody record, and exercising, if appropriate, any rights the detainee has, for example to legal advice or to medical assistance (see below). It means interrupting during questioning if the questioning is oppressive (e.g., repetition of questions already dealt with) or incomprehensible. It means communicating the needs and wishes of the detainee, for example, for a break, for refreshment, or to have someone informed of the detention. (A disturbing article by Peter Lennon in the *Guardian* of 16 June 1993, indicated that there is a book used in police forces to assist interrogators in undermining the position of solicitors; for example placing them in a position where they cannot maintain eye contact with the client or the interrogator. The object of the exercise, according to the *Guardian* extract, is to ensure that the suspect is 'mildly stressed and a little apprehensive'. These tactics are not officially recognised by the police, whose training manuals recognise the importance of the solicitor–client–appropriate adult relationship. If you find police behaviour unacceptable, object and if necessary leave, having given your reasons. In the absence of an appropriate adult, the police should then stop questioning.)

The Right to know the Allegations

One important ground for a lawyer to advise a detainee not to answer questions is that the police have failed to outline the allegations which have to be answered. The normal right of disclosure of all relevant evidence in support of the allegations is only invoked later between charge and trial, but one of your functions at the police station is to ensure that the juvenile knows and understands the allegations themselves. In fact, failure to provide this information would be a breach of the European Convention on Human Rights, Article 6(1) (right to a fair trial), and the case of *Edwards* v *UK* (1992) 15 EHRR 417 establishes that this right to disclosure applies at all stages of a criminal case.

CONDITIONS FOR DETENTION AND QUESTIONING

We shall list the main aspects of Code C. It is necessary to understand these conditions, in order to be able to ensure that they are adhered to, or to complain and make a note if not.

The Custody Record

As soon as someone is detained (but not helping as a 'volunteer') at the police station, a custody record must be opened, to record all events, decisions and reviews, as well as listing the property of the detainee. Code C gives you a right to inspect the record at the time. You will particularly be looking to see reasons for any refusal of the right to legal advice, either by the detainee or by the police. If any complaints are made they must be noted in the record — this includes complaints by the appropriate adult. The detainee must sign the custody record if a solicitor is not wanted. If an interview proceeds after a request for legal advice, but before that advice has been obtained, the reasons must be recorded.

Conditions of Detention

The requirements cover, amongst other things, adequate heating and lighting, temperature, toilet facilities and sufficient meals, taking account of special dietary requirements. These could be summarised as an application of humane common sense.

A juvenile should not be kept in a cell unless the custody officer considers that no other suitable accommodation or supervision is available; the reason must be entered in the custody record. If you suspect treatment may be improper, check s. 8 of Code C (you must be allowed to see a copy) and if appropriate make your complaint, which has to be recorded.

Section 9 of Code C deals with medical treatment. A police surgeon must be called (or if unavailable another GP, or the detainee must be taken to hospital) if there is any indication of physical illness or mental disorder, injury, or other apparent need, or upon request by the detainee. It is therefore vital that if you are aware of any medical problem or needs of the detainee — for example, a supply of medication, such as insulin — the custody officer be told without delay.

Under s. 5 the police should allow the detainee to receive visits (but may refuse if short-staffed). A social worker can assist in this by contacting family or friends of a detainee. (Be careful of course not to pass on messages that may help to dispose of evidence or enable another suspect to avoid arrest.)

The Interview

We should distinguish between the formal interview, and its informal counterpart. It is only during a formal interview that the appropriate adult is required. Nevertheless, it may be that an informal interview, for example in the car on the way to the police station, is where the most damaging answers are given. So, after considering the formal interview, we will consider the status of the informal interview, and the admissibility at trial of any information obtained. A suspect must be cautioned before the formal interview starts (a caution is a reminder of the right not to answer questions — see p. 273 above).

For the formal interview, interviewing is almost always tape-recorded. If (exceptionally) the interview is not taped because of equipment failure, and no solicitor is present, you should try to record your own version of what is said. If, later, there is a dispute about what was or was not said, your notes may be requested by the defence solicitor. If the interview is taped, this need does not arise, as the recorders are tamper-proof, and the defence solicitor can obtain a copy of the tape on request.

If you are present during an interview, and are asked to sign a written record of what was said, read it and have it corrected, if necessary, before agreeing to sign. Otherwise refuse.

The interview should not proceed while the suspect is unfit through drink or drugs — if you think this applies, you need to insist on a delay. If necessary, ask for a doctor.

No interview should proceed for more than two hours without a break, and breaks should be taken at usual mealtimes. There must normally be a break of eight continuous hours every 24 hours, usually at night time.

Inducements to confess should not be offered, although if a suspect asks what course the police will take if he or she divulges certain information ('If I tell you, will I be out of here quicker?') the police are allowed to answer.

The informal interview lacks these safeguards. As a result, there is more likelihood of a confession. Generally, the courts take a robust attitude to such confessions, particularly where juveniles are concerned. For example, in R v Weekes (1993) 97 Cr App R 222, a 16-year-old seen in the area of a robbery was questioned in the police car. The safeguards of an appropriate adult, a tape recorder, etc., were unavailable. The confession was ruled inadmissible at trial.

Code C requires all questioning about suspicion of involvement in an offence to be conducted at the police station, recorded on tape or in notes, and subject to other safeguards already discussed. While it is doubtful if this will ever cause such interviews to disappear, they are less likely to be presented in court as evidence. And you should not get the impression from what we have said that questioning someone outside the police station is wrong. Police need to invoke the formal procedures only once they have formed a suspicion that the person has committed a crime. But evidence obtained from such earlier questioning will not normally be inadmissible in court (*R* v *Nelson* [1998] 2 Cr App R 399).

When talking to the detainee before the formal interview starts, therefore, it is wise to explain the difference between what has happened up to now, informally, and the evidential status of the formal interview. It is not necessary to tell the police something just because that is what the person told them earlier. It may be appropriate on the formal occasion to exercise the right to remain silent; or to tell the story as it should have been told. (A social worker, like a lawyer, must not in any way assist in fabricating a story.)

Identification, Taking of Intimate Samples, Fingerprinting

There are special rules governing these procedures, which we do not consider. The most important advice here is that the detainee, or you on his or her behalf, can and should exercise the right to legal advice before the juvenile agrees to any of them. The appropriate adult cannot as such give consent to fingerprints etc. on behalf of the juvenile; only a parent or guardian can. If the police insist on proceeding before the solicitor arrives, ensure that the reasons are given and recorded, and stay with the detainee, to observe what happens and also to reduce the risk of an informal interview taking place.

If an identification parade is offered, the opportunity should be given for a solicitor to be present if this is reasonable. The detainee has the right to refuse a parade. To hold a parade where a juvenile is the suspect, the police also require the consent of the parent or guardian. It is usually unwise to refuse, because the alternative methods of identification — direct confrontation or identification by photographs — are more likely to lead to a positive identification. But you should advise refusal at least until you, the solicitor and the detainee have had an opportunity to discuss the parade, and, if necessary, to read the *Code of Practice for the Identification of Persons by Police Officers*, Annex A. This, like the other codes, is available at the police station for consultation.

CHARGE

The custody officer must decide within the 24- or 36-hour time limits (or longer if extended by a court) whether the detainee is to be charged, released without charge, or released pending further investigation. The release may be on bail or unconditional. If released without charge, the detainee may be required to return at a later date once the police have made further enquiries or, in the case of a juvenile, had discussions with social services about whether they should charge, caution or do nothing. What follows assumes that the police have charged the detainee.

Refusal of Police Bail after Charge

The police can refuse bail to a juvenile only on grounds set out in PACE, s. 38. The first three also apply to adults:

(a)   the custody officer is not satisfied of the identity or address of the person charged;

(b)   the custody officer believes that the person will not answer to bail, will interfere with evidence or witnesses, cause injury to themselves or others or damage to property;

(c)   the custody officer believes that it is necessary for the person's own protection; or

(d)   granting bail would not be in the juvenile's own interests.

Section 38 does not, unfortunately, offer any guidance on what the interests of the juvenile are in this situation; but, as we shall see, on refusal of bail, the juvenile must be transferred to local authority accommodation, and it will be this that the police will probably see as being in the juvenile's interests.

The police (like the courts) have a power to make bail conditional — for example, to have the charged person live at a certain address, or keep away from the scene of the alleged crime or, a new power for courts, to make the defendant see his or her solicitor (Crime and Disorder Act 1998, s. 54). Someone can be asked to stand surety, which means becoming liable to pay a penalty if the person absconds.

A social worker present at the time these decisions are made will be able to offer relevant information and advice on some if not all of these points, and particularly on what is in the interests of the juvenile.

If a person is charged and bail is refused, he or she must be brought before a court at the earliest practicable time. Once the person is brought before the court, all decisions on whether to detain are now made by the court, and the word 'detention' is replaced by 'remand' (which is in custody or local authority accommodation, or on bail). (The grounds for refusing bail at court are similar to those outlined above: Bail Act 1976, s. 4.)

Detention after Refusal of Police Bail

We have seen above the circumstances in which the police can refuse bail. At this point, PACE, s. 38(6) requires the custody officer to make arrangements for the juvenile to be taken into accommodation provided by the local authority and detained by it. The subsection goes on to say that it shall be lawful for the local authority to detain the juvenile (but no mention is made of any obligation to do so). Therefore the local authority is entitled to keep the juvenile in secure accommodation until the court appearance. It will be up to the authority to transport the juvenile to court.

Under s. 38(6), following a refusal of bail, the custody officer can refuse to transfer the detained juvenile to local authority accommodation on either of two grounds:

(a) If the juvenile is 15 or older, the custody officer considers that the juvenile is a danger to the public *and* that the local authority lacks adequate secure accommodation.

(b) It is not practical to make the arrangements for a transfer. This should be exceptional, e.g., social services are on strike, or the roads are blocked by snow.

The custody officer must give a certificate to this effect and may then detain the juvenile in the same way as an adult until the first court appearance, i.e., in the police station (but not in a cell if this can be avoided — see above p. 275).

Detention after Remand by the Court

Remand is what happens every time a criminal court adjourns without unconditional release of the defendant. But if (see Chapter 3 for procedure) the magistrates send the accused for trial in the Crown Court, the word remand is replaced by the word committal. The effect is the same

There is no need to go into the circumstances in which the court is entitled to refuse bail, as a social worker plays no part in the decision, save perhaps by supplying information to the defence solicitor to use during a bail application.

All girls, and boys below the age of 16, cannot be sent to prison or to a remand home while awaiting trial. If the court decides to remand without bail, it must remand to local authority accommodation (Children and Young Persons Act 1969, s. 23). However, in order to protect the public from serious harm, a boy can be remanded to prison or a remand centre if he is 16 or 17 and either the alleged offence is a violent or sexual offence, or it is serious enough to warrant (for an adult) 14 years in prison or the boy has a history of absconding from local authority remands. We hope that this discrimination against boys will not survive a Human Rights Act challenge. If remanded to local authority accommodation, the remand is either with or without a 'security requirement'. The authority will be the one either where the defendant resides, or where the offence was committed.

Remand without a security requirement Once the juvenile has been remanded to local authority accommodation, the authority has a choice as to how to accommodate the juvenile, and the considerations are the same as for any child it is looking after (see Chapter 11) except that, under the Children and Young Persons Act 1969, s. 23, the authority can lawfully detain the child without a further court order. (Detention in secure accommodation would otherwise require a court order under s. 25 of the Children Act 1989 — see Chapter 11.) The court has no power to tell the authority where to accommodate the juvenile.

Remands with a security requirement The Children and Young Persons Act 1969, s. 23, allows the court to impose conditions when remanding a juvenile to local authority accommodation. These conditions are the same that a court can impose when granting conditional bail to an adult, and are designed to prevent the juvenile from absconding, offending while in local authority accommodation, or tampering with evidence. Typical conditions which a court may impose include: to report to a police station daily or, say, twice a week; not to approach a witness; to refrain from certain activities (perhaps not going to a particular part of a town where the offending has been taking place). The juvenile who breaches these conditions may be arrested and brought before the court, when further conditions may be imposed. As it will be for the local authority to enforce compliance with bail conditions, the court must consult the authority before imposing them.

In the absence of a security requirement, we saw that a court cannot tell the authority where to accommodate the juvenile. If a security requirement is imposed, the court can direct that the juvenile must not be accommodated with a named individual (perhaps an alleged accomplice or bad influence). In certain circumstances, the court can direct the authority to detain the juvenile in secure accommodation. These circumstances are:

(a) the juvenile is aged 12 or over; and *either*

(b) the alleged crime is a violent or sexual offence, or one which if committed by an adult could result in 14 years' imprisonment; *or*

(c) the juvenile has previously absconded while on remand.

THE SUMMONS

Police detention, followed by charge, is only one way in which proceedings can commence. In fact in most cases a different, less traumatic process takes place. An 'informant', usually a police officer, goes before a magistrates' court and 'lays an information' which describes the alleged offence and names the defendant. This information is then issued by the court in the form of a summons to attend court on the date given. It has to be served on the defendant, either by post or by the police.

The procedure is clearly appropriate in less urgent, less serious cases, and where there is no great doubt about the correct identity and address of the person concerned. If in doubt, the police will prefer to arrest and charge.

If a case is commenced by summons, no offence is committed by failing to turn up at court to answer it. It is, however, unwise not to attend; if the offence is arrestable — and the police are unlikely to be pursuing a case against a juvenile that is not arrestable — the court is entitled to issue a warrant to arrest the person who does not attend. Alternatively, the court is entitled to try the case in the defendant's absence. If a person is released on bail, failure to turn up without reasonable cause is an offence. A person who is summonsed can — at present — get free legal advice if eligible under the green form advice scheme. (The duty solicitor scheme applies only in the police station or at the first appearance at court.)

ALTERNATIVES TO CHARGE: REPRIMANDS, WARNINGS OR NO ACTION

The three alternatives open to the police with a juvenile suspect are to charge and prosecute, to reprimand/warn, or to take no further action. The decision must be taken before charge or summons, because after that stage proceedings can be discontinued only with leave of the court. If the police have arrested the juvenile, but have not decided what course to take, the juvenile will normally release on bail, as described above. Any decision will have to be made within the time limits to be laid down by the Home Secretary for delay between arrest and court appearance.

The case may be very serious; or it may be obviously trivial, taking into account what is known about the juvenile. In either of these situations, the police can make a decision without consultation, although they still have to notify social services when a charge is made. (This is independent of any requirement to obtain the presence of an appropriate adult for pre-charge procedures.)

In between these clear-cut cases, liaison with appropriate agencies is normal before a decision is made; but the decision is still that of the police. Home Office Circulars 59/1990 and 18/1994, *Cautioning of Offenders,* describe the old cautioning system, and encourage such liaison. The guiding principle in the 1990 circular was the desirability of keeping juveniles out of the criminal justice system, recognising that if their formal entry into the process can be delayed for long enough, it may never happen at all. The 1990 circular also emphasised the needs of victims of crime to feel that something has been done. This does not outweigh the public interest in keeping juveniles out of courts. However, since 1990 the political climate in relation to juvenile offending has moved, in the words of the then Prime Minister, away from understanding and towards condemning. The 1994 circular already discouraged repeat cautions and any use of cautions at all in serious offences. The new system of reprimands and warnings is guided by the belief that 'many young people can be successfully diverted from crime without recourse to court proceedings, provided the response is clear, firm and constructive' (Home Office Consultation Paper on Tackling Youth Crime, 1997).

As a social worker your involvement in all this focuses on the welfare of the juvenile and avoiding court proceedings.

Reprimands and Warnings

The system of reprimands and warnings is governed by the Crime and Disorder Act 1998, s. 65. Following pilots, it replaced cautioning altogether during 2001. The scheme is best viewed as a first step into the formal criminal justice system. It is not, therefore, available for anyone with previous convictions, who has reached the second step already.

Guidance has been published to help the police decide whether to prosecute, warn or reprimand. Essentially a reprimand is issued for a first offence if not too serious (however this is defined — the Act does not say what 'serious' means), and a warning for a subsequent or serious offence. The police cannot warn the offender again within two years, so a subsequent allegation of criminal behaviour would have to be dealt with (if at all) through the courts. This has meant more cases coming to court than previously. For example, a child who has been warned already will end up in court over the theft of a sandwich, unless the police take no action at all.

Warnings and reprimands for children under 17 have to be given in the presence of an appropriate adult. And a warning sets the YOT into action, who must try to get the offender involved in a rehabilitation programme (s. 66). There is no sanction for refusing to participate in these activities, except that failure to take part can itself be mentioned if the offender is ever before a court for sentencing.

The police can administer a reprimand or warning only if the juvenile admits the offence and his or her parent or guardian consents. That admission must not in any way be obtained by inducement or pressure (R v *Commissioner of Police of the Metropolis ex parte Thompson* [1997] 3 CL 167). A warning or reprimand does not count as a criminal conviction, for example for job applications; however, should a person later be found guilty of an offence, the earlier reprimand or warning can be mentioned when it comes to sentencing. A reprimand or warning, therefore, should not be treated as getting off lightly. The child also, in a sense, uses up a chance. This is because if convicted of an offence within the next two years, the court will not consider a discharge but will move to a more serious sentence (see p. 300 for discharge after conviction).

The guidance makes clear that a warning or reprimand should not be administered where the evidence against the juvenile is weak; unless a conviction is more likely than not to be the outcome, it is appropriate to drop the matter. The guidance has been reinforced by the case of *DPP* v *Ara* [2001] EWHC Admin 493 (2001) *The Times*, 16 July. The police, in this case, wanted to caution A, but his solicitor could not yet advise whether to accept the caution — nowadays, of course, a warning or reprimand — unless the police outlined what their evidence was. So the police went ahead and charged A instead. The magistrates dismissed the charge as an abuse of process, and the high court agreed. The police must reveal their evidence before a suspect has to decide whether to accept the reprimand or warning. Thus, if you are involved in a case where a reprimand or warning is a possibility, ask the police to outline their evidence and what they reckon the chances of a conviction would be; if there is no realistic prospect of a conviction, the police should take no further action.

Detailed guidance was published by the Home Office in 2000 — *The Final Warning Scheme: Guidance to Youth Offending Teams*. One aspect to be aware of is that child prostitutes should not be subject to warnings or reprimands. They are victims, not criminals.

WHICH COURT?

Whenever a defendant aged under 18 is before the court, a parent or guardian must be there unless the court dispenses with their attendance (Criminal Justice Act 1991, s. 56).

The defendant has now been charged or summonsed. Which court will deal with the case? There are three possibilities — the youth court, the adult magistrates' court and the Crown Court. (Refer to Chapter 3 for more on the courts themselves.)

But before considering how the cases are allocated, what happens if the juvenile turns 18 during the course of the proceedings? Before the Crime and Disorder Act 1998, a juvenile who turned 18 after the plea was taken stayed in the youth court. Now he or she can be sent to the adult court at any time before trial, or, after conviction in a youth court, before sentence (s. 47).

Powers of sentencing depend on the age of the offender at the date of conviction (*R* v *Danga* [1992] 2 WLR 277), so the youth court has the power to sentence as an adult the offender who has reached adulthood since conviction.

Use of Adult Courts for Juveniles

Most cases involving a juvenile will be dealt with, from start to finish, in the youth court. There are three exceptions to this:

1.   The juvenile's case is connected to that of an adult   Adults for this purpose start at 18. If the juvenile and the adult are jointly charged, or involved in cases which are factually connected, they will both be brought initially before the adult magistrates' court.

The adult can be tried only in the adult courts: if the offence is summary only, that is the magistrates' court; if it is either way, the magistrates or the adult can insist that it be tried in the Crown Court. If it is indictable only, the adult must be tried in the Crown Court.

So does the juvenile have to follow the adult? The general principle is for the courts to try to have connected matters dealt with together; the adult can never be tried in the youth court, so the juvenile normally follows the adult.

First, we consider cases where the adult is going to be tried in the magistrates' court. If the juvenile and the adult are accused of committing the same offence together (e.g., both are involved in an alleged theft), the juvenile will also be tried by the magistrates' court. But if the adult pleads guilty this leaves only the juvenile to be tried. In this case, the court may exercise its discretion to have the juvenile sent to the youth court. If, on the other hand, the juvenile and the adult are merely accused of committing connected offences — for example, the adult is charged with theft, the juvenile with handling — the court has a discretion: it can try the offences together, or send the juvenile to the youth court. It does not make any automatic difference how either of them pleads.

If the adult is to be tried in the Crown Court — i.e., the offence can only be tried there, or on an either way offence the court or the adult chooses for it to be tried there — the magistrates can separate the adult from the juvenile if they consider it to be in the interests of justice, regardless of the plea of the adult. This will be a matter of balancing the public interest of having the connected evidence dealt with together against the other public interest of keeping the juvenile out of the adult courts. Relative ages of the juvenile and the adult may be persuasive. If the offence is indictable only and the magistrates do not separate the juvenile from the adult, the case is sent for trial without committal proceedings (Crime and Disorder Act 1998, s. 51).

2.   *The charge is murder*   (Powers of Criminal Courts (Sentencing) Act 2000, s. 90.) This charge must be dealt with in the Crown Court.

3.   *Other very serious offences*   (Powers of Criminal Courts (Sentencing) Act 2000, s. 91.) Very serious means the following:

(a)   an adult could be sentenced to at least 14 years' imprisonment on conviction for this offence;
(b)   indecent assault on a woman or a man;
(c)   death by dangerous driving;
(d)   death by careless driving while under the influence of alcohol or drugs.

(For the driving offences, s. 91 applies only if the person was at least 14 at the time of the offence.)

In such a serious case, if the magistrates consider that the maximum powers of punishment of the youth court (two years' custody) would be insufficient, they must direct that the case (and any other indictable offence the juvenile is charged with) be dealt with in the Crown Court. (The decision must be made before conviction of the juvenile, which also means before a guilty plea.)

Although committal proceedings no longer take place where an adult is charged with an indictable only offence (see Chapter 3 and the Crime and Disorder Act 1998, s. 51), juveniles will be sent for trial in the Crown Court only if the magistrates are satisfied that there is enough evidence for a trial to take place. The only exception to the right to a committal is where the juvenile is sent directly to the Crown Court with a linked adult (see above).

LEGAL REPRESENTATION

Most juveniles will be eligible for a free defence lawyer on financial grounds, since it is their — not their parents' — means that are taken into account. Representation will be granted, however, only if the court thinks that it is in the interests of justice (see p. 371 — more likely in the case of a juvenile than in that of an adult). (See Chapter 15 for changes to criminal legal aid.)

THE TRIAL

Delay is not good for children. If a child has been arrested, a decision to charge and start court proceedings (or not) should be made swiftly.

The Prosecution of Offences Act 1985 allows the Secretary of State power to set time limits from arrest to first court appearance. These time limits have so far only been laid down where the accused is in custody.

The Prosecution of Offences (Youth Courts Time Limits) Regulations 1999 lay down limits where the accused is in custody while waiting for committal proceedings or trial. However, the time limits can be overriden if the prosecution can show good cause. The limits are as follows:

(a) between arrest and first appearance in court: 36 days;
(b) between first appearance and trial: 99 days; and
(c) between conviction and sentencing: 29 days.

(For the time limits in the Crown Court or adult magistrates' court, see the Prosecution of Offences (Custody Time Limits) Regulations 1987.)

If a juvenile under 16 is in care or in local authority accommodation, the Children and Young Persons Act 1933, s. 34(1) requires a social worker or foster parent to attend court with the juvenile. For any other juvenile the parent or guardian must attend. (The court can require attendance even if the juvenile is over 16.) The local authority must provide support for any child awaiting trial or sentence (Crime and Disorder Act 1998, s. 38).

SENTENCING OF JUVENILES

If the child was looked after by the local authority, you will have been in court during the trial. Otherwise, the social worker reappears in the proceedings at the sentencing stage. Nearly all the relevant legislation can now be found in one Act, the Powers of Criminal Courts (Sentencing) Act 2000 ('the PCCSA').

Which Courts have which Sentencing Powers?

You are likely to be involved in the sentencing process because you will be required to prepare a pre-sentence report for the court before a juvenile is sentenced. Your report must be prepared in the knowledge of which court is dealing with sentencing and what its powers are.

(When we talk about sentencing powers, there is a theoretical maximum sentence for each offence and a theoretical maximum for each court. The actual sentencing power in a given case is whichever of these is lower in the circumstances.)

Magistrates' court This court will be involved in sentencing only where it has dealt with a connected adult. It cannot impose custody on a juvenile: it can only fine, discharge, or order parents to enter a recognisance. If it wishes to impose any other type of order, it must remit the case to the youth court, which has greater powers (PCCSA, s. 8).

Youth court This court has the power to impose any of the orders discussed below. Its most severe sentence is custody under a detention and training order.

Crown Court A Crown Court dealing with a juvenile offender because of a linked adult should not normally sentence a juvenile but should remit the case to the youth court, unless the judge is satisfied that it would be undesirable to do so (PCCSA, s. 8). In practice, where the Crown Court is dealing with the matter because of a linked offence involving an adult, it will usually carry out the sentencing in order to avoid the undesirable delay that remission to the youth court would cause.

However, if the Crown Court has dealt with the case, not because of a linked adult, but because the case was sent by the youth court under the PCCSA, ss. 90–91 as a result of its gravity (see p. 284), then the case should not be remitted to the youth court since that court can only impose a detention and training order. Under ss. 90–92, the Crown Court has the power to order detention of the juvenile for a period up to the maximum that could have been imposed on an adult. So a juvenile can be detained 'during Her Majesty's pleasure' for crimes which carry a life sentence. (However, the court must set a target date for eligibility for release. Failure to do so, and leaving this decision in the hands of the Home Secretary, was a breach of the human rights of the juveniles who murdered James Bulger: see *T* v *UK* [2000] 2 All ER 1024; *Practice Statement (Juveniles: Murder Tariff)* [2000] 1 WLR 1655; *Re Thompson and Venables (Tariff Recommendation)* (2000) *The Times*, 27 October.)

Procedure

The court must order a pre-sentence report before dealing with a juvenile after conviction. Frequently, you will be asked by the court to prepare one before the finding of guilt, where it is known that the juvenile will admit the offence. The Children and Young Persons Act 1969, s. 9, requires you to start making the necessary investigations and preparing the information for the court as soon as the young person is charged, and not to wait until conviction. (Local authorities can leave this to probation officers where the child is 13 or over, if there is a local agreement.)

There is no reason why the juvenile should be required to cooperate with the preparation of the report if he or she intends to deny the charge. The preparation of the report is likely to make the juvenile think that his or her guilt has been pre-judged. So if you have not been able to prepare the report at the time of conviction, the case will be adjourned; as with all adjournments, the juvenile may be released on bail or remanded to the accommodation of the local authority.

How to approach writing the report was dealt with in Chapter 9.

Sometimes the court will dispense with a report. It should not do so in a serious case, unless there is only one sentence available (murder, in particular) or the matter is so trivial that a report would be a waste of effort (i.e., the court intends to discharge the case). However, the Magistrates' Courts (Children and Young Persons) Rules 1992 still require the court to have evidence on the child's circumstances before sentencing, so a report will be needed usually.

Your report will be in writing. You do not have to be in court to give it, but a representative of your department must be there. The court, or the defence, may wish you to be present, to explain and justify what has been put in the report. We suggest it is good practice to attend.

You are performing this reporting role as an officer of the court. The juvenile is not your client; it is not your job to move mountains to get a lenient outcome. Your role derives from your department's duties under the Children Act 1989, Sch. 2 — advancing the child's welfare. Your task is to advise on the individual needs and circumstances of the juvenile, something which cannot be done by the court without your help. As a result, the court is more likely to adopt an individualised, rather than a punitive, approach.

Sentencing Where Courts Have No Discretion
It is important to be aware that the courts may not have a choice of sentence. The penalty for murder is fixed, even for a juvenile (see above). The minimum penalty for a number of other offences can be fixed if the offender has a previous record of such offending. See the PCCSA, ss. 109–115, where, for example, domestic burglary committed for a third time attracts at least three years' imprisonment. These minimum sentences do not apply to offenders aged under 18. However, their juvenile offending record goes through with them into adulthood, and may trigger very harsh adult sentences where the offending is repeated.

For a social worker, the new referral order is the fixed outcome of perhaps the most relevance. Although currently only being piloted, it will probably become national during 2002.

Referral orders These orders are made under the PCCSA, ss. 16–32. The essence of the new system is that in suitable cases the court passes the decision to a special panel instead of deciding on a sentence in court. The panel's task is then to reach an agreement with the offender, failing which it gives the task back to the court to decide on a sentence. Here, in brief, is how it will work:

(a) *Compulsory referral.* A court must make a referral to the youth offender panel if the following conditions apply:
(i)   the offender is under 18;
(ii)   he or she pleads guilty;
(iii)   he or she has no previous convictions (a reprimand or caution is not a conviction);
(iv)   the court has decided that custody is not appropriate;
(v)   the court has decided that some punishment is appropriate (that is, no absolute discharge).
(b) *Discretionary referral.* This applies where the offender is charged with more than one offence and pleads guilty to at least one of them, but otherwise the conditions for compulsory referral apply.

Referral means that the young offender goes before a panel, and together with that panel works out a contract of behaviour which is to last between three and 12 months (the period is pre-determined by the court). The consequence of not agreeing (or of the panel deciding that this approach is not going to work) is that the offender will be sent back to court for sentencing.

The panel is nominated by the local YOT and must have a member of that team on it. A panel is constituted for each offender who is referred.

Reduction of court's discretion under Crime (Sentences) Act 1997 For repeat offenders in some categories of crime, the judges now have to impose minimum or fixed-term prison sentences unless they have particular reasons for departing from these:

(a) Life sentence (s. 2) Previously, the only offence which attracted a life sentence was murder. A life sentence is now mandatory for a person who commits a serious offence (as defined) after the age of 18, if he or she has previously been convicted of a serious offence in the UK (including before the age of 18). A serious offence consists of attempted murder, manslaughter, rape or attempted rape, intercourse with a girl under 13, certain firearms offences and robbery with a firearm (or imitation).

It is important to be aware of the effect of convictions for offences committed when a juvenile. Although the mandatory sentence is not imposed on a juvenile, the risk has been created if the juvenile commits a further serious offence after age 18. Possibly this will become an area where the judges exercise their exceptional discretion not to go for the mandatory sentence.

(b) Drug offences (s. 3) This involves the third conviction for class A drug trafficking ('A' is the most serious drug category). Again the third offence must be committed after age 18. The minimum sentence is then seven years.

(c) Domestic burglary (s. 4) For a third burglary committed after age 18 the minimum sentence is three years' imprisonment.

Sentencing Where Courts Exercise Their Discretion

Apart from circumstances in which courts are required to pass a particular sentence, they enjoy a wide discretion. Parliament lays down maximum penalties; the courts (guided by the Court of Appeal) then decide. In 1991, Parliament (in the Criminal Justice Act) brought in an element of control, in that courts were told to sentence only for the present offence or offences, and not to give an offender a greater sentence because of his or her previous bad record. The backlash against this humane approach was so enormous that in 1993 something close to the old *status quo* was restored. Courts can now look at the present offences and at any previous record before deciding how seriously the present offence is to be treated.

'Seriousness' is the key word. The court should first look at how serious the offence is, and the level of punishment appropriate to that seriousness. It is worth having access to the Magistrates' Association's own guidelines on offence seriousness, to see where the court will be starting from. (See, for example, in a good library, D. Thomas, *Current Sentencing Practice*, Sweet & Maxwell, looseleaf.) The Association sets an 'entry point' for each offence, then looks at aspects of the offence itself that are 'aggravating' or 'mitigating'.

For example, if taking a vehicle without the owner's consent (TWOC) is the present conviction (Theft Act 1968, s. 12), the guidelines suggest that a community penalty is a starting point. Unless it counts as aggravated vehicle-taking, the maximum penalty is six months' custody. Aggravating factors (if the conviction is for TWOC, not aggravated TWOC) could be, for example, driving while disqualified, offending on bail, driving badly, or that the taking was premeditated. Mitigating factors would be, for example, that no damage was caused, the owner left the keys in the car, or the driving was not itself bad.

Further guidance was given in the Court of Appeal case *R v Howells* [1998] Crim LR 836. The old 'what would right-thinking people regard as serious?' test was dismissed as useless — the judges simply have no evidence on this, only their own opinions. Instead the Lord Chief Justice, Lord Bingham, told the courts to look at the following issues: Was the offence spontaneous or premeditated? Was the victim physically or mentally injured? Was there an admission of guilt? Does the offender have a previous record?

The PCCSA gives further guidance on what makes an offence serious. Under s. 153, racial aggravation explicitly increases seriousness. Pleading guilty — the sooner the better — reduces seriousness under s. 152.

The courts will form an idea of seriousness in this way, and only then consider whether the seriousness is exacerbated by the offender's record. Section 151 of the PCCSA states:

In considering the seriousness of any offence, the court may take into account any previous convictions of the offender or any failure of his to respond to previous sentences.

Effectively, the court is entitled to say:

Because of your previous offences, this offence looks to us more serious, and our punishment is likely to be heavier.

However — in theory, perhaps less in practice — the court cannot increase a sentence merely because of an offender's record. The record must itself make the present offence look more serious. Probably this is just playing with words, and the offender is punished more severely because he or she is a 'bad person'.

Each penalty that a court is thinking of imposing — whether custody, a community penalty or a particular level of fine — should be imposed only if the court considers the offence to be so serious that only that level of sentencing is appropriate.

An example of the way a court should look at this requirement occurred in the highly publicised case of *Attorney-General's Reference (No. 3 of 1993)* (1993) 14 Cr App R(S) 739. (This kind of reference is an appeal by the prosecution against a lenient sentence.) A 15-year-old boy was convicted of raping a girl of the same age, and sentenced to a supervision order plus an order to pay compensation of £500 (for the girl to get herself a holiday). The Court of Appeal decided that the offence was so serious that *only* custody was appropriate.

Having decided on seriousness, with the offender's record taken into account, the court is then entitled to reduce the proposed punishment by taking into account the offender's personal circumstances, such as remorse or the effect that the punishment will have on the offender and/or other people. In particular, any sentence should be reduced for an early decision to plead guilty (PCCSA, s. 152).

There is, therefore, much for the probation officer or social worker to say in a pre-sentence report. A good record, or a bad record with redeeming features, can be used to mitigate the sentence — to reduce it below the sentence the court would think of imposing if seriousness alone were taken into account. Put another way, what is known about the offender can reduce the penalty but not increase it.

Here is a simplified step-by-step approach to deciding on sentence which courts should adopt:

(a)   Does the court have a choice, or is the sentence fixed by law? (See above.)

(b)   How serious is the offence? (Consider issues such as violence; effect on the victim; amount of gain or loss; planning; breach of trust; racial aggravation.)

(c)   Is it so serious that only custody is appropriate?

(d)   If not, is it so serious that a community sentence involving restrictions on liberty is appropriate? Is such a sentence appropriate for this offender?

(e)   If not, is another community sentence appropriate, or a fine?

(f)   If not, a discharge should be ordered, unless a warning or a reprimand was given within the last two years.

When sentencing juveniles, the courts should also be aware of s. 44 of the Children and Young Persons Act 1933:

> Every court in dealing with a child or young person who is brought before it, either as an offender or otherwise, shall have regard to the welfare of the child or young person, and shall in a proper case take steps for removing him from undesirable surroundings, and for securing that proper provision is made for his education and training.

This does not mean the child's welfare is paramount, for the court has a statutory duty — as do social workers as parts of the youth justice system — 'to prevent offending by children and young persons' (Crime and Disorder Act 1998, s. 37). But welfare must be a factor in deciding on the appropriateness of a sentence, and gives you some leverage if you wish to suggest outcomes which will benefit the child as well as punish. When we look at community sentences, you will see that the criteria tie in with s. 44, in that a community sentence must be appropriate to the seriousness of the offence, and also to reforming the offender.

SENTENCING OPTIONS

Age of Offender

In deciding on a penalty the age of the offender is relevant, as you will see throughout. The court will make its decision according to the age of the juvenile at the date of conviction. If the juvenile committed the offence before age 18, but is convicted on or after his or her 18th birthday, the court looks at the adult range of sentences which are outside the scope of this book.

Custody

We have to continually be reminded that the UK is signatory to the UN Convention on the Rights of the Child, and that custody has to be an absolutely last resort for the tiniest minority. What history does show us without a doubt is that the types of young people going [into custody] are going to be high- and multiple-risk. Everything has gone wrong for them, and they are among the most vulnerable people we will meet. We can change the name and culture of the intervention, but persistent young offenders are perennial. Whatever we do, they need very careful and — inevitably — very expensive interventions if we are actually going to reduce crime. (Ann Hazel, *Criminal Justice Matters* No. 41, Autumn 2000, p. 30).

There are two regimes for locking up children:

(a) *Custody for murder or grave crimes* (PCCSA, ss. 90–92, see above). The Crown Court sentences the juvenile to be detained for a defined term or 'during Her Majesty's Pleasure', and the place of detention is left to the Home Secretary to determine. It can include detention in local authority accommodation (Children and Young Persons Act 1969, s. 30).

(b) *A detention and training order.*

In either case, the statutory criteria must be met, which are:

(a) *the juvenile* must be represented (or has refused to apply for Legal Services Commission free representation, or it was withdrawn as a result of his or her behaviour); and

(b) *the offence* must meet one of the following three tests:

(i)   it was so serious, on its own or taking into account one or more associated offences, that *only* such a sentence can be justified; or

(ii) it is a violent or sexual offence and *only* custody will adequately protect the public from *serious* harm (injury or death); or

(iii) the juvenile refuses to accept the requirements of a supervision order.

The length of a sentence should be in proportion to the seriousness of the offence, or to the need to protect the public from violence. Seriousness is increased where the offender has committed and been convicted of 'associated' offences at the same time. 'Associated' means part of a pattern of offending. Seriousness, as we have seen above, may also increase in the light of the offender's record.

Even if the court decides that custody is justified, it is still entitled to consider whether what is known about the offender mitigates the sentence in favour of something non-custodial. Here a pre-sentence report can contain very important information about the likely effect of custody versus community or other sentences; the offender's past record and attitude, and prospects for avoiding further offending.

The minimum period for custody is four months and it cannot be suspended. (There is no corresponding minimum for an adult of 21 or over. Is this unfair on the juvenile? The idea is that courts are deterred from the idea of a short, sharp shock; custody is wrong unless the offence is serious enough to merit lots of it!)

Detention and training orders   These orders are now governed by the PCCSA, ss. 102–107. The provisions were implemented for 12- to 17-year-olds in 1999. The Act provides a power to make orders for 10- and 11-year-olds; according to the Government, these will be implemented only if it should prove necessary or desirable to include them. If these powers are brought into effect, the court must be satisfied that, in addition to the normal custody criteria, custody is the *only* way of protecting the public. (Until these powers are brought in, custody is a possibility for 10- and 11-year-olds only for the most serious of crimes, as described above, at p. 284.)

For all offenders, the custody criteria that we saw above apply: in particular, is this offence so serious that custody is the only answer?

For offenders below the age of 15, the courts additionally have to find that the child is a 'persistent' offender. The Home Office Circular 'Tackling Delays in the Youth Justice System' defines this as someone sentenced 'on three or more separate occasions' for a recordable offence. However, this is not a statutory definition, and courts will, it seems, define 'persistent' for themselves. See *R v C (A Juvenile) (Persistent Offender)* (2000) *The Times*, 11 October, where C was convicted of burglary and aggravated vehicle taking, committed while on bail for an earlier burglary. This was enough to make his offending persistent, even though he had no earlier convictions.

The maximum duration of the detention and training order is two years, or less if the maximum prison term for an adult would be less. The actual term imposed has to be one of the following: four months; six months; eight months; 10 months; 12 months; 18 months; or 24 months. Half of the term will actually be served in custody, undergoing training. For orders of eight, 10 or 12 months, an extra month can be taken off the custodial half of the sentence for good behaviour; for orders of 18 or 24 months, two months can be lopped off the custodial half for good behaviour.

The period of detention is to be served in an a secure training centre (at the time of writing only two exist), a young offender institution or in local authority secure accommodation.

After release the offender is supervised for the remaining period of the order by a social worker, probation officer or other member of the youth offending team. The offender must comply with the requirements of the supervisor. Unfortunately, as with the definition of 'persistent' offending, the nature of 'requirements' has not been specified in the legislation, but according to the Home Office guidance is similar to powers exercised where an offender is subject to probation or supervision: see below pp. 293–98.

Breach of any requirements can be reported to the court, which then has the power to fine or to order detention for up to three further months. Commission of an imprisonable offence during the period can put the offender back into custody for some or all of the remaining supervision period, with punishment for the new offence being added to the total term, so long as this does not exceed 24 months in total.

Community Sentences

Guidance for social workers on approaching community sentences is given in circular LAC (92)5, *Criminal Justice Act 1991: Young People and the Youth Courts.*

The Criminal Justice Act 1991 attempted to create a range of sentencing options which are not custodial but are nevertheless tough. These are called community sentences. The range and importance of community sentences for juvenile offenders were significantly increased in 2000, when action plan and reparation orders came into effect.

A principal feature of the community sentence is that it is a punishment, which supervision and probation were not, under the old regime, supposed to be. Therefore the offence must be serious enough to warrant the particular type of community order chosen. Seriousness was discussed above, and the same considerations apply: you cannot take previous offending into account, unless it throws light on the present offence. But seriousness can be increased by taking one or more 'associated' offences into account. What is known about the offender comes second, but is highly relevant in mitigating the punishment chosen and in matching the offender to an appropriate community sentence (PCCSA, s. 35). Where the result of the order is to impose restrictions on the offender's liberty, the court must match up those restrictions to the seriousness of the offence.

To pass a community sentence a court must take account of all the circumstances of the offence, including 'aggravating or mitigating factors' (s. 36(1)) and any information available about the offender (s. 36(2)). It will normally have a pre-sentence report before deciding, and must have one before imposing 'requirements' as part of supervision or probation, or before imposing a community punishment order.

An offender does not have to accept a community sentence. But refusal is not advisable, as this is itself a ground for triggering custody and enables the court to bypass the seriousness requirement.

What community sentence can be imposed also depends on the age of the offender, as we will see now as we look at each in turn.

Supervision Order   Age range: 10–17. You may recall that supervision is a possible outcome in civil proceedings about the child (see Chapter 7). Unless the juvenile is found guilty of murder, where an indefinite period of custody ('during Her Majesty's pleasure') is the only available outcome, supervision is also available after a finding of guilt in criminal proceedings. Although there are many similarities, particularly the supervisor's duty to advise, assist and befriend, the criminal supervision order is a different one from a civil supervision order, governed by different legislation: PCCSA, ss. 34, 63–67, and Schs 6 and 7. The court can designate as supervisor either the local authority, a probation officer, or a member of the youth offending team. An order can be made for up to three years, which means that it can continue after the supervisee reaches 18. (The supervisor would be a probation officer in such a case.)

The key difference between civil and criminal supervision orders is the restrictions that can be attached to the latter, which will give a bench a chance, if that is what they are looking for, to feel that they are imposing a punishment. The fact that conditions can be attached to an order is attractive to magistrates seeking to restrict the liberty, or correct the conduct, of a juvenile who they feel needs control. We list below the three types of condition that can (but need not) be imposed with a supervision order under s. 12.

1.   *Residence in local authority accommodation*   This is a surprising condition, given the abolition of care orders in criminal proceedings brought about under the Children Act 1989. It seems to bring about a similar result by the back door. Until the amendments brought in by the Crime and Disorder Act 1998, it was available only for serious offending. Now the criteria are no more than breach of a supervision order and a belief that such residence will sort out the bad behaviour.

The residence requirement can be imposed if the following conditions are *all* satisfied:

(a)   the relevant local authority has been consulted (but it has not necessarily agreed);

(b)   the juvenile is already subject to a supervision order with requirements for residence;

(c)   the juvenile has either breached a requirement or committed an offence;

(d)   the court is satisfied that the offending or the non-compliance results from the circumstances in which the juvenile is living and that a residence requirement will help towards rehabilitation;

(e)   the juvenile is represented at the time the order is made, or has refused the offer of legal aid or been turned down because of means; and

(f)   there is a pre-sentence report.

Your report must therefore address the issue of circumstances of the offence or breach of supervision and its seriousness, and of course give the view of the local authority as to whether a residence requirement is recommended, and why, and how it would be applied.

The maximum length of a residence requirement is six months, though the supervision itself continues after that. It is not a custodial sentence, and (in contrast to a remand after refusal of bail) does not give the authority a power to lock up the juvenile (though, as with all children looked after by local authorities, a court's permission can be sought to detain in secure accommodation — see Chapter 11). Where does the juvenile actually live while subject to this order? This is up to the local authority; he or she could live at home, with relatives, friends, in a foster home or a community home. But the court can order that he or she must not live with a particular individual while the order is in force.

2.   *Other requirements which the court may impose*   Subject to trying to avoid conflicts with the offender's religious beliefs or education, the court can impose any of the following requirements:

(a)   to live with a named individual;
(b)   to take part in certain supervised activities;
(c)   to present him or herself at stated times to the supervisor (e.g., Saturday afternoons if the offence is connected to soccer violence);
(d)   to make reparations to the victim or to the community at large (this is similar to the freestanding reparation order — see p. 296 below);
(e)   to observe a curfew in one or more designated places for up to 10 hours between 6.00 pm and 6.00 am (to a maximum of 30 nights, which do not have to be consecutive);
(f)   to comply with arrangements made for his or her education; or
(g)   to submit to medical treatment (before this condition is imposed there must be medical evidence in relation to the juvenile's mental condition).

The first four requirements can be imposed only for the 90 days following the making of the order (unless the juvenile is in breach of the requirements, in which case the clock stops running until the breach ends). After that the supervision order can continue, of course.

3.   *Requirements made by the supervisor*   If none of the above requirements are imposed the court can instead make an order requiring the supervised person to comply with the directions of the supervisor. These directions are then given at the discretion of the supervisor, but can only cover:

(a)   living at a specified address for a given period or periods;
(b)   presenting himself or herself to the supervisor at required times; and
(c)   participating in specified activities at stated times.

The court decides how long this power shall last, up to a maximum of 90 days.

You will see that it is this third option that gives a supervisor the real control over the offender; the others, by contrast, require the supervisor to operate within the pattern dictated by the court. If you wish to work with the offender, you should specify in your report what activities you — or you together with other agencies — have in mind for the initial up to 90-day period of the supervision order. (See further Chapter 9: Written Evidence: Statements and Reports.)

Supervision orders were previously an alternative to custody. That meant that an offence meriting custody because of its seriousness could be disposed of by supervision, if the defence solicitor was persuasive and the pre-sentencing report encouraging. As the current statute does not make super-vision a way of avoiding custody, the term 'intermediate treatment' (IT), used to describe the regime of a supervision order, is arguably no longer correct. But before making a supervision order, as before, the court will want to know, in the report prepared for sentencing, what regime is proposed for the supervisee, and to be satisfied that it is appropriate. Once the court makes the supervision order, it has no control on the form of the regime of activities and, strictly speaking, the supervisor can depart entirely from the proposals made. In the long term, that supervisor and that authority begin to lose credence with the court, however, if word gets around that the regime is not as 'tough' as the court was promised.

See p. 298 for what happens if the conditions of a supervision order are breached.

Reparation orders   Age range: 10–17. A juvenile convicted of an offence can, under the PCCSA, ss. 73–75, be ordered to make reparation either to specified persons (victims of crime or, at least, those affected by the crime) or to the community at large. A report will be needed from the social worker, probation officer or YOT member to indicate that appropriate work is available and, if the victims have been specified, that the victims are genuinely willing. The total work carried out must not exceed 24 hours, and the order should not be combined with a community service order or combination order (below, p. 297). The order must be completed within three months and is supervised by a social worker, probation officer or member of the YOT.

Action plan orders   Age range: 10–17. Any juvenile offender can, under the PCCSA, ss. 69–72, be placed under a three-month action plan order. The order will set out an immediate plan of action and whereabouts for the juvenile during this period. Activities can include doing good things, not doing bad things, education, and even reparation. Supervision is the same as for reparation orders. The court will, again, need a report setting out the proposed arrangements.

Probation   Age range: 16 plus. The court has to be satisfied that the offence is serious enough to warrant probation and that probation will either:

(a)   secure the rehabilitation of the offender; or
(b)   protect the public.

The offender is placed under the supervision of a probation officer for a period, fixed by the court, of between six months and three years. (For a shorter period, supervision is available.)

The probationer must keep in touch with the probation officer, and may have to comply with additional requirements under the PCCSA, ss. 41 and 42. These requirements are imposed by the court at the time of sentencing if the court thinks them necessary for securing rehabilitation or protecting the public (the same factors for imposing the order in the first place, but considered with the additional requirement in mind).

Possible requirements are:

(a)   residence at a particular address, such as a bail hostel;

(b)   participation in certain reforming activities, or keeping away from certain activities thought to be associated with offending. Participation or avoiding cannot exceed 60 days in total, unless the offence was sexual, in which case activities and — less importantly — prohibitions can continue throughout the probation. This enables longer-term therapeutic work to be undertaken;

(c)   treatment for mental disorder. The court requires medical evidence before making this a requirement; or

(d)   treatment for drug or alcohol problems, if such problems were connected with the offending. Treatment can be residential. (This power has hardly been used, and is effectively replaced with the new drug treatment and testing order — below, p. 298.)

Community punishment order   Age range: 16 plus. This order used to be called Community Service, and is governed by the PCCSA, ss. 46–50. It must be shown to be available in the pre-sentence report. The offence must be one for which an adult could have been sent to prison. The number of hours which must be carried out is between 40 and 240. Breach of the order, by committing a further offence or failure to comply with the requirements, can lead to the court revoking the order and sentencing the person afresh.

Combination orders   Age range: 16 plus (PCCSA, s. 51). Only probation and community punishment can be combined in this order. The seriousness and suitability criteria must again be met, and the court must believe the order is desirable to rehabilitate the offender or protect the public.

The court can attach requirements to the probation side of the order. The number of hours of the community punishment element is between 40 and 100.

Attendance centre   Age range: 10 plus. This is governed by the PCCSA, ss. 60–62. The offence must be one for which imprisonment could have been imposed on an adult.

The order will require the offender to attend between 12 and 36 hours in total, usually on a Saturday for perhaps two hours. (If the offender is under 14, less than 12 hours can be ordered. For an offender under 16, the maximum is 24 hours.) Attendance centres are usually run by police officers in places such as youth clubs and schools.

The court can only make an attendance centre order if it has been informed, through the pre-sentence report, that a suitable centre is available locally. Suitable, according to the Home Office, means within one-and-a-half hours' travel and not more than 15 miles; or one hour and 10 miles for an offender under 14.

The old rule that attendance sentence was not available if the offender had previously had a custodial sentence was abolished in 1992.

Curfew orders   Age range: 10 plus. This community sentence allows the court to impose a curfew from two to 12 hours a day for up to three months, or, for a juvenile of 16 or 17, up to six months (PCCSA, ss. 37–40), and the order must not interfere with the juvenile's education or religious practices. Powers to enforce the order by electronic tagging (s. 13) are available if the monitoring facilities exist in the juvenile's home area.

Drug treatment and testing order   Age range: 16 to adult. If the offender is a drug abuser, and agrees, this order provides for treatment over a period of between six months and three years (PCCSA, s. 52). The treatment may include residential treatment. It is supervised by an expert named in the order. The court must, of course, be informed that appropriate facilities are available. During the period of the order the offender must provide samples for testing and keep in touch with a 'responsible officer', normally a probation officer. The success, or otherwise, of this order is kept under review by the court which made the order — a unique provision which does not apply to other community orders unless there has been a breach.

Breach of Community Sentences
Whoever supervises a community sentence can report to the youth court a breach of any of the conditions in the order such as residence, activities, attendance, and the court (PCCSA, Schs 3, 5, 7–9) can then:

(a)   fine the juvenile up to £250 if he or she is under 14, £1,000 otherwise;
(b)   order up to 60 hours' community punishment (240 if the offender is already doing community punishment);
(c)   order attendance centre for a breach of probation;
(d)   order a curfew for a breach of supervision or reparation;
(e)   start again, i.e., sentence the offender afresh, and the court may then decide on custody on the ground that the offender's behaviour under the community sentence is effectively a refusal of a community sentence.

Fines
If the court decides to fine, whether for an offence or for breach of a previous order, it will fix the appropriate level according to the seriousness of the offence and the means of the person paying. The court cannot impose a fine greater than the maximum that an adult could be made to pay, and the youth court has a top limit of £250 for an offender under 14, and £1,000 for one of 14 to 17 (PCCSA, s. 135). There is no top limit in the Crown Court.

Who pays the fine?   If the offender is under 16, it is the parent or guardian who must pay, unless the court is satisfied that it would be unreasonable to make them pay in the circumstances (PCCSA, s. 137). It is unreasonable if the court thinks the offending is not in any way a result of parental influence or neglect.

For an offender of 16 or 17, the assumption is reversed: the offender pays, unless the court thinks the parent or guardian should pay in the circumstances.

The court must, before ordering the parent or guardian to pay, allow them to address the court and argue that they should not have to.

What if the juvenile is in local authority care? Then the local authority must normally pay the fine if it has acquired parental responsibility through a care order. The authority can, however, argue that it has done all that it reasonably could to keep a child in its care from offending, and avoid a fine if successful (*D v DPP* [1995] Crim LR 748). A remand (or provision of accommodation without a court order) is not the same as care, which arises only from a care order (see Chapter 7). In *North Yorkshire County Council v Selby Youth Court Justices* [1994] 1 All ER 991, the court had tried to make the council pay where the offenders had been remanded for an earlier offence to local authority accommodation. It was held on appeal that the authority should not have to pay the fine.

How is the amount of the fine calculated?   All courts must fine on the same broad principles — taking both the seriousness of the offence and ability to pay into account. The court must enquire into ability to pay (which means the parent's or guardian's ability — see above and PCCSA, s. 138). But the court is not told how to apply its discretion. The court fixes a fine that feels right, subject to any maximum levels set by statute for the offence.

Enforcement of fines   The court can order the fine to be paid by instalments. If it remains unpaid the court must hold a means enquiry. After such enquiry, the court can enforce the fine against the parents or guardian. It can make a money supervision order by appointing a suitable person to oversee the payments, make an attendance centre order (see above) or, where the juvenile is employed, an attachment of earnings order (i.e., deduction by the employer). It can also remit, that is cancel, all or part of the remaining balance.

Fines are deductible from income support, which could affect the parent or guardian ordered to pay the fine, or the young offender who, unusually, gets income support.

Binding Parents Over
When a court convicts a juvenile of under 16, it must normally also bind over the parents. If the juvenile is over 16 it can still choose to do this. This means the parent or guardian promises to take care of and exercise proper control over the child to prevent reoffending (PCCSA, s. 150).

A sum is fixed by the court, and the parent or guardian is liable on breach to forfeit some or all of this sum. Forfeiture is unlikely to be triggered unless a further offence is committed. The maximum sum is £1,000, and the period during which this sword of Damocles hangs over the parent must not exceed three years, or run beyond the offender's 18th birthday.

The court should take into account the relationship of the juvenile to the parents and whether the parents could have had any influence over the juvenile's behaviour, in deciding whether to use its power not to bind over. For more guidance see LAC (92) 5, para. 41.

A parent can refuse to be bound over but it is risky. If the court thinks a refusal is unreasonable, it can fine the parents up to £1,000. This is on top of any fine they may already have to pay for the juvenile's offence.

Some good news — the local authority cannot be bound over where the child is in their care.

Deferred Sentence
Under the PCCSA, s. 1, a court has the power to defer sentence. It should do so only if there is evidence before it that some change in the offender's life is imminent — for example leaving school and taking up employment — which the court ought to take into account. The offender must consent to deferment.

The maximum period of deferment is six months. On the appointed day the matter returns to court, with, usually, a fresh pre-sentence report, and the court will sentence in the light of the new circumstances. It will not normally be appropriate to order custody after deferment if the offender has carried out the improvements in his or her life which were originally suggested as grounds for the deferment.

The court can only order what the court could have ordered at the time of deferment — so the fact that the offender is now 18 does not entitle the court to treat him or her as an adult.

Discharge
This is an option where in all the circumstances for the offender and the offence no punishment is appropriate. It is governed by the PCCSA, ss. 12–15. With hindsight it might have been more appropriate to reprimand or warn the offender, if he or she had been prepared to admit the offence.

If the discharge is absolute then, apart from showing on the offender's record if ever he or she is sentenced again, it does not count as a conviction.

If the discharge is conditional, a period of up to three years is attached to the discharge. If the offender commits an offence within that period, the court dealing with the further offence can sentence for the original offence as well. The later court will only have the powers of the original sentencing court, save that if the offender has reached 18 he or she will be treated as an adult (unlike the deferred sentence described above). A conditional discharge is available only in exceptional circumstances if an offender has had a warning in the last two years from the police (Crime and Disorder Act 1998, s. 66).

Compensation Orders
Any person found guilty of an offence can be ordered to pay compensation to the victim. (This is one reason why a caution is sometimes inappropriate – there must be a conviction for a compensation order.) Indeed, a court should make such an order if appropriate, or give its reasons for not doing so (PCCSA, s. 130).

This order can stand alone, without the court making any other order against the offender, or it can accompany any other order made by the court.

As with a fine, the juvenile's means are taken into account; and the parents can be ordered to pay the compensation (but not where they were not in control of the juvenile at the time of the offence — for example, the child was in local authority accommodation — *A v DPP* [1996] 9 CL 61). Where the offender has limited means, a compensation order should be made before a fine.

SENTENCING THE MENTALLY DISORDERED

We look now at powers to make hospital and guardianship orders in relation to all ages of offenders (apart from those under 10, who by definition cannot offend — see above p. 262).

Home Office Circular 66/90 provides a useful background to work in this area. As with juveniles, police and Crown Prosecutors should first avoid prosecution altogether if this would not be in the public interest. Courts should if possible impose sentences which are therapeutic rather than punitive.

If a court is dealing with a person on whom it could have imposed a custodial sentence, it can also make a hospital order under the Mental Health Act 1983, s. 37. (Since a magistrates' court cannot impose custody on a juvenile, it would have to remit the case to the youth court if it felt this was an appropriate order.)

The court must be satisfied that the offender is suffering from mental illness, psychopathic disorder, mental impairment or severe mental impairment. These concepts are defined by the Mental Health Act (MHA) 1983, s. 1 and are discussed in Chapter 14. The court must be satisfied that detention in a hospital for treatment would be appropriate; and if the mental condition consists of mental impairment or psychopathic disorder, the court must also be satisfied that a hospital order would alleviate the condition, or prevent deterioration. There is no need for there to be any evidence of a connection between the mental disorder and the criminal offending. Medical evidence on these requirements will be required by the court from at least two doctors, and also evidence from the proposed hospital that a place is available. The court, in reaching a decision, must take into account the likely effect of any sentence on the offender's mental disorder (Criminal Justice Act 1991, s. 4).

The court can name the hospital that the offender is to be sent to (a power introduced by the Crime (Sentences) Act 1997) in order to achieve a particular level of security, rather than leaving it to the NHS to decide this.

The hospital order empowers the hospital to detain the offender for up to six months. Once the offender is in the hospital he or she is now a patient, and is treated the same as any other patient under a hospital order (see Chapter 14). The Crown Court can, however, add to a hospital order a restriction order designed to protect the public from serious harm (MHA, s. 41). A youth court or magistrates' court cannot do so, but may commit the offender, if he or she is over 14, to the Crown Court, notwithstanding that the offence is not triable in the Crown Court, if it considers that such an order would be appropriate. But the Crown Court is free to dispose of the case in any way which was open to the sentencing court in the absence of mental disorder. It is not obliged to make a hospital order or, if it does, to attach a restriction order.

The restriction period can be for the same period for which a court could have sentenced the offender to custody. The essence of a restriction order is that the detainee cannot be released, even for leave of absence, during the period of such order without an order of the Home Secretary or the Mental Health Review Tribunal. This is in contrast to other patients, who can be released by the hospital, if the doctors think this appropriate.

Transfers from Prison to Hospital and Back

Section 47 of the MHA allows the Home Secretary to make a transfer order to move any prisoner to hospital, on receiving reports from two doctors that certain conditions apply. Since these conditions are almost identical to the conditions which a court would look for before making a hospital order (see above), they are not repeated here. Once made the transfer order is identical to a hospital order with restrictions, which was described above. The patient remains in hospital until the mental condition which precipitated the transfer no longer requires treatment, or is not susceptible to treatment. He or she then reverts to being a prisoner for the remainder of the term or, if it has expired, until he or she is released.

Where the offender has been diagnosed as a psychopath, the Crown Court itself now has the power to direct in advance a transfer from hospital to prison (ss. 45A and 45B MHA (inserted by the Crime (Sentences) Act 1997). The Court will make this order, called a 'hospital and limitation' directive, when it first wishes to send the offender to hospital, but wants the offender also to serve a period of punishment through imprisonment if the condition improves and further treatment is not needed. So the sentence starts out with detention in hospital with restrictions (limitations is just another word for restrictions). The detained psychopath stays in hospital until the condition cannot be treated, or no longer requires treatment, and then he or she is taken back to prison for the rest of the sentence.

After-care of Prisoners Released from Hospital

You will discover in the next chapter that one of a Social Services Department's duties to the vulnerable is after-care of persons released from detention in mental hospitals (s. 117 MHA). This duty applies equally if the person was detained in hospital as a result of a criminal conviction, or was transferred to hospital from prison. It also applies to a person released after being transferred from hospital to prison.

If the person is either under 22, or was sentenced to at least 12 months in prison, the probation service must also supervise him or her on release (see above, p. 296), and this supervision requirement applies even though the person was released from detention in hospital, not from prison.

Guardianship Orders Following Conviction

As an alternative to the hospital order, s. 37 empowers the court to make a guardianship order on the offender. The guardian will be nominated by social services, who will have to provide the court with details of how the guardian will exercise his or her powers, and may well be an approved social worker. The guardianship order, once made, is identical in effect to such an order made outside criminal proceedings and is dealt with in Chapter 14.

Is Probation or Supervision an Alternative?

On pp. 295 and 297 we looked at probation and supervision orders, where one option before the court is to require the offender to receive treatment for mental disorder. But this is not an option if a hospital order under the Mental Health Act 1983 is appropriate (Powers of Criminal Courts Act 1973, Sch. 1A).

Unfitness to Plead

A person accused of a crime before the Crown Court may be declared unfit to plead. This is a matter for the jury, not for medical experts. If unfitness to plead is found, the Crown Court must still have a trial on the facts. If the facts of the crime are proven, the Court may order detention without time limit in a mental hospital (with or without a restriction order), a guardianship order, a supervision and treatment order or an absolute discharge. Details are set out in the Criminal Procedure (Insanity and Unfitness to Plead) Act 1991 and Circular 93/1991.

ADDITIONAL POWERS TO DEAL WITH SEX OFFENDERS

Sex Offender Orders: Crime and Disorder Act 1998, s. 2

These are civil orders obtained after conviction for a sexual offence. They keep sex offenders away from areas where they may commit offences. So a convicted sex offender may be ordered to stay away from school gates when he has been seen hanging about. As a social worker you may be involved either in asking the police to seek such an order, or in dealing with a client or member of a client's family who is subject to an order.

Who may apply for an order? The application for a sex offender order must be made by the police.

Grounds for an order (s. 2(1)) There are two elements that the police must satisfy when applying for an order:

(a)   That the person is a sex offender (as defined under the Sex Offenders Act 1997 — see p. 43). This means that there has to have been a conviction for a previous offence. An order cannot be sought if it is merely perceived that a person may be a danger to children. An order can be obtained against anyone over the age of ten.

(b)   That there is a risk of serious harm to the public. 'Public' in this context can mean one individual.

The application is made to the magistrates' court. As these are civil proceedings the court will apply the civil standard of the balance of probabilities. The Queen's Bench Division has confirmed that to require a civil standard of proof is not a breach of the Human Rights Act 1998, since an offender had already been convicted in a criminal court using a criminal standard of proof (*B v Chief Constable of Avon and Somerset* [2001] 1 WLR 340). What the police need to establish is that it is more probable than not that the person has acted in such a way as to give reasonable cause to believe that an order is necessary to protect the public from serious harm from him. Moreover, they do not need to prove this risk of harm in respect of any individual victim — only that the belief in such risk is reasonably held — or call for evidence from any potential victim. As such, it would only require the court to believe the officer who states that the police consider that there is a risk of serious harm. The magistrates do not need to be satisfied that the police have proved that an order is necessary to protect the public from serious harm from the defendant.

Length of order   The sex offender order lasts for a minimum of five years and can be imposed for as long as the court sees fit.

What may be in an order?   The only requirement that can be contained in an order is that the person does not do something. For example, the subject of the order must stay away from school gates or from a defined area.

It is in everybody's interest that the area involved is clearly defined. This means that the person knows where he may and may not go. It also enables the breach of such an order to be clear. The order can only be prohibitive: it cannot require the person to do anything, such as obtain treatment.

Breach of the order   Breach of the sex offender order is a criminal offence. On summary conviction it carries up to the maximum fine available to magistrates and/or six months' imprisonment. If dealt with in the Crown Court it carries an unlimited fine or up to five years' imprisonment.

THIRTEEN
Community Care and Residential Care

The Legislation
The principal Acts involved in this chapter will be referred to by their initials. These are:

- National Assistance Act 1948 (NAA)
- Disabled Persons (Employment) Act 1958 (DPEA)
- Mental Health Act 1959 (MHA 1959)
- Health Services and Public Health Act 1968 (HSPHA)
- Chronically Sick and Disabled Persons Act 1970 (CSDPA)
- Local Authority (Social Services) Act 1970 (LASSA)
- Supplementary Benefits Act 1976 (SBA)
- National Health Service Act 1977 (NHSA)
- Mental Health Act 1983 (MHA)
- Health and Social Services and Social Security Adjudications Act 1983 (HASSASSA)
- Registered Homes Act 1984 (RHA)
- Disabled Persons (Services, Consultation and Representation) Act 1986 (DP(SCR)A)
- National Health Service and Community Care Act 1990 (NHSCCA)
- Carers (Recognition and Services) Act 1995 (C(RS)A)
- Health Act 1999 (HA)
- Carers and Disabled Children Act 2000 (CDCA)
- Care Standards Act 2000 (CSA)

Guidance and Direction from Government
You may recall (Chapter 2) that under the LASSA 1970, s. 7A, social service functions must be exercised under the 'general guidance of the Secretary of State' (meaning the Health Secretary). This includes the exercise of discretionary powers, which play a prominent part in this chapter. Therefore, we shall make reference to the appropriate government circulars, since, as a

matter of law, you are obliged to pay attention to this guidance. (The guidance may, exceptionally, be wrong in law, in which case the statute — as interpreted by a court — prevails. See *R* v *Wandsworth BC, ex parte Beckwith* [1996] 1 All ER 129, below.)

There are many overlapping powers and duties. Some enactments deal with the old, some with the handicapped, some with people who are mentally or physically ill, and more, as we shall see. Your clients, of course, may refuse to fit neatly into one category only; but the authority's plan will normally promote integration of support services.

COMMUNITY CARE AND STATUTORY DUTIES

Warning: you are about to enter difficult territory. Why?

- There are many different types of vulnerable people needing support within the community or residential care.
- You may owe different types of duty depending on the client's needs.
- You will find descriptions of the types of clients, the range of needs and the powers and duties you must exercise in different pieces of legislation, regulations and circulars.
- Courts interpret your powers and duties in ways that may be hard to comprehend.

Let us take an example of the last problem. The House of Lords was faced with deciding whether a social services department could reduce care to a client on the grounds that it could not afford to maintain the previous level of care provided. Here is an extract from the judgment of Lord Nicholson in *R* v *Gloucestershire County Council ex parte Barry* [1997] 2 WLR 459:

> However neither the fact that the section imposes the duty towards the individual, with the corresponding right in the individual to the enforcement of the duty, nor the fact that consideration of resources is not relevant to the question of whether the duty is to be performed or not, means that a consideration of resources may not be relevant to the earlier stages of the implementation of the section which lead up to the stage when satisfaction is achieved.

What does it all mean? We think that Lord Nicholson is saying that:

(a)   statute requires the council to do certain things for Mr Barry;

(b)   Mr Barry is entitled to go to court to force the council to carry out its duty;

(c)   the council cannot plead poverty if it has this duty; and

(d)   there is nevertheless a case for looking at the council's resources in seeing how it should be carrying out that duty.

If this excerpt from a leading case is anything to go by, it is not going to be easy to find a pathway through the law in this field. A good starting point for a local authority social worker is to ask: 'What statutory duties and powers do I have?' Refer back to Chapter 1 for the full range, but according to NHSCCA 1990, s. 46(3), they can be summarised as providing or arranging:

(a) residential accommodation for the old, infirm, disabled or destitute;
(b) care services and employment facilities for the disabled;
(c) care services following discharge from mental hospital;
(d) welfare services for the old; and
(e) services for mothers of young children.

COMMUNITY CARE: THE CONCEPT

Community care means the provision of services in the community where possible for those who need them. What does 'in the community' mean? Essentially it means not as an in-patient in a hospital, and in practice it means care provided or coordinated by the social services department.

Community care was not invented by the NHSCCA. Before 1993, when the 1990 Act came into force, the social services department already had a wide range of powers and duties, and was able to make direct provision of services, or arrange with voluntary or commercial providers to meet the needs of the vulnerable.

The things shifted with the 1990 Act. The first was the emphasis towards managing services for the vulnerable, rather than providing these directly: 'It will be [social services'] responsibility to make maximum possible use of private and voluntary providers and to increase the available range of options and widen consumer choice' (DoH Circular *Community Care: Review of Residential Homes Provision and Transfers* (LAC (91) 12, para. 3)). The second was the requirement for social services to plan their services, and assess the need of individuals for those services, in partnership with health authorities and other agencies. (Other shifts, which we do not have space to develop in this chapter, included changes to the regime for inspection of care homes, transfer of staff between local authority and NHS, particularly as long-term hospitals close, and complaints procedures: see NHSCCA 1990, ss. 48 and 49.)

A third more recent shift is the government's determination to try to reduce the need for acute care services by getting all local authorities to try to improve welfare services. This is to be achieved through the creation of funding opportunities for welfare services under Part V of the Local Government Act 2000. All local authorities — not just those with social service functions — should take a lead and can obtain grants for developing welfare services for local people. Welfare, it is believed, should not be confined to the acute personal care services for which statute already provides, such as homelessness provision and the community care powers and duties we cover shortly. The Audit Commission identified the problem in its report 'Home Alone: The Role of Housing in Community Care', May 1998:

A picture emerges of significant resources invested by housing, social services and health authorities in crisis-based services — homelessness, high-intensity support in specialised schemes, hospitalisation in short-stay psychiatric beds, etc. — in large part because funding is available for these services, but is lacking for more basic, and often less costly, support . . . for all vulnerable groups . . .

All local authorities, whether they are at district, county or unitary level, with or without a social service function, will have a grant for supporting vulnerable people, using all relevant departments and co-operating with other agencies. However these new funds will not affect personal care by social services.

The actual wording of the legislation is vague. Under s. 93(1), which governs England:

> The Secretary of State may, with the consent of the Treasury, pay grants to local authorities in England towards expenditure incurred by them in providing, or contributing to, the provision of such welfare services as may be determined by the Secretary of State.

(Identical provisions in s. 93(2) apply in relation to the Welsh Assembly.)

The social worker's powers and duties in relation to community care provision are not changed by this legislation, even though the context in which you carry out your work is changed, with more agencies and authorities working on the same patch. The intention is laudable, as we said, but it remains to be seen if the funding might have been better targeted to improved social work resources.

The key elements of community care, since 1993, are:

(a)   Encouragement through financial incentives and government guidance to use the private and voluntary sector. All provisions described below may well be bought in rather than provided in-house.

(b)   Planning of community care services with all other service providers.

(c)   Social workers as assessors of need and coordinators of service provision, more than as care providers.

(d)   (Reading between the lines) careful scrutiny of budgets before assessing any vulnerable person as requiring services.

These elements will be mentioned where appropriate in what follows. We will take you through the legal framework by looking first at how community care services should be planned, and then at how they should be delivered. This will be followed by looking at services which do not require residential accommodation and at those which do.

Planning, Publicity and Research for Provision of Community Care

There are two levels at which a social services department must plan: for the whole community, and for the individual.

Planning at community level   NHSCCA, s. 46 requires every social services department to publish a plan for community care in its area, and to update the plan regularly (the Secretary of State has directed that this be at least every year). Your authority therefore already has a plan, and we advise you to obtain a copy if you are working in this field. The planning must be in consultation with the District Health Authority (i.e., hospital services), Family Health Services Authority, all relevant voluntary groups, housing departments (which usually means different local authorities from the social services departments), housing associations and any other appropriate organisations.

The intention behind the plan, revealed in government statements during the parliamentary debates on community care, is that authorities will devise services that meet the needs of the population, rather than plan the services first and then see who wants them second. Even if only a small number of people in the area have a particular need for a particular service it should be in the plan. Flexibility in meeting the various needs can then be obtained by using a range of service providers, with the department in the coordinating seat.

It is necessary for the department — with assistance from these other bodies — to assess the needs of all vulnerable people in the area. This does not require keeping registers, except in the case of the disabled (CSDPA, s. 1), but of course it is good practice to keep full records of assessments.

Planning for individuals   So much for the plans for the community's overall needs. What of the individual?

Before looking at your statutory duties, under the 1990 community care legislation, perhaps a perspective on what you will be trying to achieve for an individual will help you to see the overall picture. The Department of Health's *Policy Guidance*, at para. 3.24, states that 'service provision should, as far as possible, preserve or restore normal living'. The order of priorities in helping any individual will be:

(a)   support so that the client can live at home;
(b)   a move to more suitable accommodation;
(c)   a move to another household;
(d)   a move to residential care;
(e)   a move to a nursing home; and
(f)   long stay hospital care.

NHSCCA, s. 47 sets out the statutory duties governing assessments and plans for the individual. This is worth quoting in full:

(1)   Subject to subsections (5) and (6) below [which allow you to meet needs without an assessment in order to deal with an emergency], where it appears to a local authority that any person for whom they may provide or arrange for the provision of community care services may be in need of any such services, the authority—
(a)   **shall** carry out an assessment of his needs for those services; and
(b)   having regard to the results of that assessment, **shall** then **decide** whether his needs call for the provision by them of any such services.

According to Government guidance, the assessment should be carried out by specialist assessors and not by the department's service providers. The approach should be needs-driven, not defined by what is actually available. Where a person is disabled, there is special statutory provision for him or her to be listened to, or for his or her representative to make representations (DP (SCK)A ss. 2 and 3).

You are obliged to *assess* the needs and the court will order you to do so if you have not complied (*R* v *Sutton LBC ex parte Tucker* [1997] 2 CL 566). You must assess those needs even if your authority already knows that it cannot afford to meet them (*R* v *Bristol City Council ex parte Penfold* [1998] CCL Rep 315). An inadequate assessment can be struck down by a court on judicial review. In *R* v *Birmingham City Council ex parte Killigrew* (2000) 3 CCL Rep 109, the council had reassessed K as needing only six hours' daily care for her physical needs, where previously she required 12. There was, it was held, no basis at all for this reduction. The reassessment was carried out without even looking at medical reports or consulting K's GP.

Circular LAC (92) 12 requires the assessment to focus on the difficulties an individual is facing, and to take into account the following:

(a)   the capacity/incapacity;
(b)   the preferences and aspirations;
(c)   the living situation;
(d)   support from relatives and friends; and
(e)   other sources of help.

Whether to *meet* those needs is then a matter of discretion. Section 47 goes on to make special provision for persons who are 'disabled'.

(2)   If at any time during the assessment of the needs of any person under subsection (1)(a) above it appears to a local authority that he is a disabled person, the authority—

(a)   shall proceed to make such a decision as to the services he requires as is mentioned in section 4 of the Disabled Persons (Services, Consultation and Representation) Act 1986 without his requesting them to do so under that section; and

(b)   shall inform him that they will be doing so and of his rights under that section.

Section 47(3) requires you, when assessing, to notify the health authority or housing authority if you think that that agency may need to provide services. And s. 47(6) requires you, in urgent cases, to provide services first and to complete the assessment second — something which is common sense to any social worker.

So s. 47 does not require an individual to ask for help; it requires the local authority to carry out an assessment of anyone who might be eligible for community care services. The community care plan should already have identified, in broad terms, the numbers and needs of people who might need the services.

The reference in s. 47(2) to s. 4 of the DP(SCR)A is the beginning of a legislative paper chase; that section refers us on to CSDPA, s. 2, which refers us to NAA, s. 29. We will look at both of these sections later (pp. 315 and 320). These three sections of the three Acts mean, in outline, that certain individuals who are defined as disabled are *entitled* to have certain needs met, once the assessment shows those needs to exist. (The particular services a disabled person is entitled to receive, if he or she is assessed as needing these, are set out in CSDPA, s. 2(1) and LAC (93) 10 (see below, p. 319).) But only the disabled are entitled to be informed of this right before their needs are assessed. Is that clear? If not, rather than blame us, please blame the legislators who missed the opportunity to clarify the statutes.

Assessment of the carer's ability We have just examined the duty, under NHSCCA, of the authority to assess the needs for services of the vulnerable client. Under the C(RS)A, the authority must also assess the ability of any persons caring for that client. This assessment must be realistic and not turn a blind eye to the burden carers take on. A press release from Help the Aged dated 24 October 2001 states: 'more than a million older carers are having to look after the sick without adequate support from health, social services or homecare agencies'. They call for a complete overhaul of support services.

Despite the word 'services' in the title of the 1995 Act, the authority is not required to provide any actual services to the *carer*. The intention of the two Acts taken together is to ensure that the silent army of voluntary carers — including young children looking after sick parents — is monitored by the authority, and their efforts supplemented by social services provision to the *client* or payment to cover such provision. (The CDCA 2000 now provides that services can be provided directly to the carer, who therefore becomes a statutory client. See further p. 321 below.)

Assessment of means at this stage Government guidance makes clear that the individual client's needs are assessed, and decisions made on how to address those needs, before looking at whether that client can be called on to pay for or contribute towards any services. If the need is established it should be met. So far this is reasonably clear, but read in the context of LAC (92) 12, a Department of Health Circular, it is a little less clear: 'An authority may take into account the resources available when deciding how to respond to an individual's assessment.' This leaves the assessor being able to say that a need does not in fact exist because the client is in the position to buy that help.

Delivering the Service: An Overview of Community Care Provision

We will be looking at the detail of the legislation and Government guidance. Before you get bogged down in that detail, however, we offer an overview of the main client groups covered by community care. (The definition of what counts as community care is taken from NHSCCA, s. 46(3). The powers and duties in relation to each element of community care are then contained in further legislation.)

- Support services for those who have a physical or mental handicap (NAA).
- Support services for old people (HSPHA).

- Support services for expectant and nursing mothers (NHSA).
- Services for prevention of illness and after care of those who have been suffering from illness (particularly relevant for mental illness and drug or alcohol dependency) (NHSA and MHA).
- Home help and laundry services for those who need them (NHSA).
- Accommodation for people who need it because of age, illness, disability or other circumstances (NAA).
- Although not specified in s. 46, it may be convenient to add to the list any carer aged 16 or more (CDCA).

You can see that community care is mostly defined by the type of person who may need a service, not by the service itself. Taken together, the definitions of who needs community care seem wide. But not every vulnerable person is covered. In particular, the needs of children as a group — except the under-fives — are not to be met under community care legislation, but under the Children Act (see Chapters 4 and 11).

Community Care and the NHS
It is unlikely that social services can meet all the needs of a client for care services. The NHS is charged, under the NHSA, s. 1(1), with providing a 'comprehensive health service designed to secure improvement . . . in the physical and mental health of the people . . . and in the prevention, diagnosis, and treatment of illness'. Specific duties will include medical, dental, nursing and ambulance services, care for mothers and children, and preventative, care and after-care services for ill people and, of course, provision of hospitals. Inevitably, therefore, community care involves an overlap of functions (and financial responsibilities) between health authorities and social services authorities.

Health and local authorities are also under a statutory duty to cooperate to advance health and welfare (NHSA, s. 22) and to provide after-care for released mental patients (MHA, s. 117). As you will see below, NHSA, sch. 8 gives local authorities a wide range of powers in relation to mothers and young children, prevention of illness, care and after-care. These are services where the health service also has statutory duties. Circular 99 (30) is designed to ensure that the NHS does not abdicate responsibility for long-term health care need. No patient must be allowed to fall into the gap between social services and NHS services. There is not space here to set out the detailed provisions governing financial arrangements between health and social services authorities. Three circulars — LAC (95) 5 'NHS Responsibilities for Meeting Continuing Health Care Needs', HSG(95)45 'Arrangements between Health Authorities and NHS Trusts' and LAC 99 (30) (see below) — are useful, if for no other purpose than to ensure that there is no 'buck passing'.

The HA, ss. 28–31, require local authorities (not explicitly their social services departments) to cooperate with local health authorities to set up local Health Improvement Programmes. The Act permits — indeed encourages — a pooling of resources to achieve common aims, so the care services can be either jointly funded, or jointly provided or provided by one service and funded by the other. Statutory duties are not changed. For example, if the NHS pays for and provides after-care services for the patient discharged from a mental hospital, it still remains a social service duty under MHA, s. 117 to ensure that such services are provided. Further guidance on these partnership arrangements may be found in the LAC (2000) 9.

Support Services in the Community

Community care covers both services which can be provided to a person living at home and also the provision of non-hospital accommodation. In carrying out assessments of the needs of individuals, you have to be able to consider all possible outcomes together — if remaining in the community with support is not possible, is residential accommodation appropriate? However, the statutory criteria for offering a person accommodation are different from those that dictate who is eligible to receive services at home or in non-residential centres. For this reason we will take each in turn, starting with non-residential care services.

Financial grants instead of providing support services   The Community Care (Direct Payments) Act 1996 enables local authorities to pay all (or, subject to means, part) of the cost of buying care services direct to a disabled individual or his or her spouse, cohabitee or a relative living with the individual. The Act does not compel the local authority to provide care to any individual in this way, or compel an individual to accept money instead of services. Up to four weeks' respite care in any year can be purchased in this way.

NON-RESIDENTIAL CARE SERVICES

Our quick overview gives a flavour of the legal issues in community care. The next task is to define more carefully who is entitled to receive particular services. What kind of vulnerable people should you be taking into account? What should your department be doing for them? The answers to both questions are to be found in different legislation for different types of clients. All services can be bought in rather than provided by the authority. In the authority's community care plan there must be a statement of its plans to purchase from the independent sector.

Labelling Clients who may need Services

Most groups are easily identified — the elderly, children, or mothers of young children, for example (children are dealt with as a group in Chapter 5). But one group is defined in statute as 'disabled'.

Disabled Clients

The NAA, s. 29 refers to 'persons aged eighteen or over who are blind, the deaf or dumb, or who suffer from mental disorder of any description, and other persons aged eighteen or over who are substantially and permanently handicapped by illness, injury, or congenital deformity or such other disabilities as may be prescribed.'

Therefore, under this heading, we are looking at people who have some kind of mental or physical handicap; if they need help it is because of who they are, not because of the circumstances they find themselves in. Old age is not a criterion mentioned in s. 29: you do have special duties to the old (as we shall see in this chapter) just because of their age; but you have duties to any adult who falls within s. 29, whatever their age.

Circular DOH (93)10 gives guidance on what exactly is meant by words like 'handicapped' and 'deaf'. You will need a copy of this circular if you work with disabled clients.

Categories of Support Work

To make accessible the information about what support services you or your department can or must make available, we divide support work into two broad categories: the setting up of schemes (broadly a managerial decision), and the services offered to individual clients after an assessment (more an individual social worker's decision). Of course there is an overlap, and there are other ways of approaching the topic, such as to look at first the handicapped, then the elderly etc.

Schemes

The schemes that can be set up are not described in detail in the legislation or the circulars, so each authority can arrange them to the extent that their will matches their resources.

The schemes that all authorities must have in place are summarised in Table 13.1. The schemes that an authority has the power to make are summarised in Table 13.2.

Work with Individuals

Limitations on money, staff and expertise mean that not every possible welfare need of vulnerable groups can be met. As we shall see, even where you have not a discretion but a duty to provide the service to an individual, you only have to do so if the department first decides that the individual needs that service and (although there are conflicting court decisions on this point) that it is reasonable to meet it from within the department's available resources. In other words, the final say, the final discretion, remains.

If you are deciding what services to offer, you must take into account the ability of any person who is currently caring for the person to make the necessary provision (C(RS)A). This should mean more than saying 'Oh good, I see your daughter-in-law can look after you, so we don't need to bother'. It means assessing the meeting of needs in partnership, without exploitation. (See p. 321 below.)

Challenges to your decisions   Let's start, by way of a break, with a trip to the picture house. You may recall from Chapter 2 (p. 26) that there is a process called judicial review. This is how courts may be asked to rectify decisions of public authorities when such authorities are behaving irrationally. In the landmark case of *Associated Provincial Picture Houses* v *Wednesbury Corporation* [1948] 1 KB 223, Lord Greene stated:

Table 13.1   Schemes that a Department Must Make

Disabled persons under NAA, s. 29

a.   general social work support and advice, in the home or elsewhere (DHSS Circular LAC (93) 10)
b.   facilities for rehabilitation and adjustment (DHSS Circular LAC (93) 10)
c.   facilities for occupational, cultural and recreational activities (DOH Circular LAC (93) 10)
d.   keep a register of such clients (DOH Circular LAC (93) 10)

The elderly, the ill, expectant mothers, those handicapped by illness or congenital deformity, persons suffering from or at risk of suffering from mental disorder

e.   home help on an adequate scale (NHSA, Sch. 8)
f.   centres for training or occupation (DOH Circular LAC (93) 10)
g.   social work support (DOH Circular LAC (93) 10)
h.   appointment of approved social workers (DOH Circular LAC (93) 10)
i.   suitable staff to deal with assessment and mental health guardianship (DOH Circular LAC (93) 10)

Drug or alcohol abusers

j.   (if the Department receives a government grant) payments to voluntary organisations to provide both residential and non-residential facilities (Local Authority Social Services Act 1970, s. 7E(b) and Payments to Voluntary Organisations (Alcohol or Drug Misusers) Directions 1990)

The court is entitled to investigate the action of the local authority with a view to seeing whether they have taken into account matters which they ought not to take into account; or conversely, have refused to take into account matters which they ought to take into account . . . once that question is answered in favour of the local authority, it may still be possible to say that, although the local authority have kept within the four corners of the matters they ought to consider, they have nevertheless come to a conclusion so unreasonable that no reasonable authority could ever have come to it. In such a case . . . I think the court can interfere.

Unfortunately, but inevitably, the law is imprecise, and great discretion rests with the individual social worker or the department. It can only be challenged in a court if it can be shown that you acted so irrationally in making your

Table 13.2   Schemes that a Department May Make

Disabled clients

a. providing information about services available (NAA, s. 29)
b. giving instructions on overcoming problems (NAA, s. 29)
c. recreational facilities (NAA, s. 29)
d. holiday homes (DOH Circular LAC (93) 10)
e. travel subsidies (DOH Circular LAC (93) 10)
f. help with finding accommodation (DOH Circular (93) 10)
g. contributing to the cost of wardens in assisted housing schemes (DOH Circular (93) 10)

The handicapped or disabled

h. sheltered employment or training facilities and hostel accommodation for those whose handicap or disability makes them unlikely to obtain work (DPEA, s. 3(1) and NAA, s. 29)

The elderly

i. wardens (or part of the cost of wardens) (HSPHA, s. 45)
j. meals on wheels and recreational schemes (HSPHA, s. 45 DHSS Circular 19/71)
k. laundry facilities (NHSA, Sch. 8)

Parents and children

l. schemes for the care of expectant mothers and the under fives who are not at state school (NHSA, Sch. 8)

The physically ill or mentally disordered (including those at risk)

m. training, recreational and occupation facilities, including day centre, meals, social work support, respite care and night-sitting, for prevention, care and after care of the ill (NHSA, Sch. 8 and DOH Circular LAC (93) 10)

n. laundry facilities (NHSA, Sch. 8)
o. residential accommodation for expectant and nursing mothers (DOH Circular LAC (93) 10)

decision, for example by failing even to consider a request, that no reasonable person/department would have acted in that way. This is hard for the aggrieved individual to prove, although occasionally it is possible: for example, one service that must be provided, if needed, is to make holiday arrangements for a disabled client (see Table 13.3 below). In *R v Ealing London Borough Council ex parte Leaman* (1984) *The Times*, 10 February, the court ruled that a local authority had acted wrongly in refusing to consider help with a holiday. It was unreasonable to rule out help merely because the client had arranged it privately. Had it decided that she did not need a holiday at all, or could afford the arrangements herself, the result would probably have been different.

The normal principle, however, is that courts are reluctant to intervene. Lord Denning, for example, said that it was better to rely on the Secretary of State to use default powers to take over local authority services than for courts to order them what to do. So the woman who thought she should have more home help because of her incapacity was refused help by the court (*Wyatt v London Borough of Hillingdon* (1978) 76 LGR 727). The male client who was upset about having his carer withdrawn and replaced with a younger, female carer, had no success in a challenge in the courts (*R v Essex County Council ex parte Bucke* [1996] 11 CL 512. The court held that the local authority can decide how to provide the care the client needs. Similarly, the disabled client who had been promised a stairlift could not show that the council behaved unreasonably when it took the cheaper option of transferring the applicant to a ground-floor flat (*R v Kirklees MBC ex parte Daykin* [1997] CLY 4711).

What is the relationship between the needs of the individual and the resources of the authority? Mr Barry was 79 and severely disabled. He was assessed as requiring cleaning and laundry services. The authority decided, because of its own financial pressures, to reassess him as needing only reduced laundry services and no cleaning. Mr Barry's circumstances had not themselves changed, so could the authority say he no longer needed the same services? The Court of Appeal decided that under CPDSA, s. 2, he should have the services he was assessed as needing, and resource constraints could not change those needs. The House of Lords — in a majority decision in *R v Gloucestershire County Council ex parte Barry* [1997] 2 WLR 459 — ruled that the authority need provide only what it can reasonably afford, and can assess or reassess the individual client in the light of financial constraints. But — prepare for mental gymnastics here — if the need is found to exist, the authority must meet that need, even if it lacks resources. See *R v Sefton MBC ex parte Help the Aged* (1997) *The Times*, 23 August, where the authority was ordered to provide residential accommodation to an elderly client because she had been found to need that care and attention. How to make sense of these two decisions? It may come down to the language used in the assessment. 'We can't meet your needs because we can't afford it' won't work. 'We can meet your needs but only in this limited way because of our limited resources' may work. The *Barry* case will probably now go to the European Court of Human Rights. It clashes, in our opinion, with the later House of Lords decision on providing home education to a girl with ME. In *R v East Sussex County Council ex parte Tandy* [1998] 2 All ER 769, Lord Browne-Wilkinson stated:

Parliament has chosen to impose a statutory duty, as opposed to a power, requiring the local authority to do certain things. In my judgment the court should be slow to downgrade such duties into what are, in effect, mere discretions . . . If Parliament wishes to reduce public expenditure on meeting the needs of sick children then it is up to Parliament so to provide.

(The decision related to a different statutory duty and can technically be distinguished from *Barry*. In spirit, however, *Barry* is wrong if *Tandy* is correct.)

Following the *Barry* case, the Department of Health issued a Guidance Note (LASSL (97) 13) telling local authorities not to use the judgment as an excuse to take decisions on resource factors only. Decisions must always be based on a needs assessment.

Could a failure to provide a proper service also lead to a damages claim by the client. Although set in a different context, the case of *Phelps* v *Hillingdon LBC* [1997] 3 FCR 621 suggests that local authorities owe duties to their clients which can be pursued in a court. The plaintiff was dyslexic and had had a poor education. She succeeded in persuading the court that an education authority which failed to diagnose dyslexia and act on the findings was negligent. Could this principle work in the field of mental health? The *Clunis* case suggests that professionals may be protected from liability, although the case was decided on its particular facts. Mr Clunis had a mental disorder which needed treatment which the health authority should have provided. In his untreated state he attacked and killed an innocent man. In *Clunis* v *Camden and Islington Health Authority* (1997) *The Times*, 10 December, his case for compensation was eventually struck out by the Court of Appeal as being against public policy (Mr Clunis should not get compensation for committing a criminal act, even though he wanted to use the money to pay the victim's widow). But could the widow herself have sued? Although the Court did not have to decide this issue, it did state that s. 117 MHA (duty to provide after-care for patients released from mental hospitals) did not, in its view, create a right to sue for breach of statutory duty. The law is still developing in this area. In the most recent case a health authority was found liable to a patient whose suicide attempt left her disabled. The authority had not properly assessed and treated the patient for her suicidal tendency: *Drake* v *Pontefract Health Authority* [1998] Lloyd's Rep Med 425. In an important case relating to children, the European Court of Human Rights has made clear that children whose social services department failed to protect them from severe abuse must have a must have a right to sue (*Z* v *UK* [2001] 2 FLR 612).

Under NHSCCA, a local authority must have a well-publicised complaints procedure. Also, in theory, the Secretary of State can order the authority to carry out a particular duty, which might have solved the problem of Mrs Wyatt and her home help. However, since the *Barry* decision, in which the House of Lords pointed the finger of blame for inadequate services at central government cost-cutting, we are unlikely to see much use of this power in favour of increased, costly services. This power is relatively recent, and we do not yet know of any occasions when it has been exercised.

Services to individuals

Table 13.3 sets out the services that must be provided to individuals who normally live within your local authority's boundaries. (In cases of dispute as to where the person is ordinarily resident, the decision of the Secretary of State is final — NAA, s. 32(3). Guidance is available in Circular LAC (93) 7.)

Table 13.3 Services that Must be Made Available to Individuals who Need Them

Disabled clients (CSDPA, s. 2)

a. practical assistance in the home (no further guidance is given on this, so you are left with a wide discretion to weigh up what should be provided; it will cover home visits)
b. providing or helping to obtain radio, television, library or similar recreational facilities
c. providing, or assisting the person to take advantage of, lectures, games, outings, or other recreational facilities outside the home
d. providing travel or assisting with travel arrangements for the purpose of obtaining the services you provide
e. providing or helping with adaptations or special facilities in the home, for the purpose of greater comfort or safety. (DHSS Circular LASSL 20/73 gives guidance on such aids for the disabled, such as telephones, page turners, special locks, the costs of which can be recovered from the DSS)
f. providing or helping a person to obtain a holiday
g. providing meals, whether at home or elsewhere
h. providing a telephone, and if necessary any special equipment to enable person to use it (such as voice amplification for the deaf)

Disabled clients, the mentally disordered and physically ill

i. home help and laundry facilities if the person needs them because of the illness or handicap (NHSA, Sch. 8)

The elderly

j. home help and laundry if needed because of age (NHSA, Sch. 8)

Any person in hospital or local authority residential care

k. protection of property and possessions while away from home (NAA, ss. 43–45). (This requires liaison with the hospital and the managers of the residential homes)

Table 13.4   Services Offered to Individuals at the Department's Discretion

Clients who are registered disabled

a.   the person must be registered as disabled with the Department of Employment, and be unlikely to obtain employment for a considerable time because of the disability or handicap; you can then offer sheltered employment, training, and assistance in finding work (DPEA, s. 3(1))

The elderly

b.   meals and recreation, in the home or elsewhere (HSPHA, s. 45 and DHSS Circular 19/71). (District councils can also provide this service in county areas, HASSASSA, Sch. 9)
c.   practical assistance in the home to improve safety, comfort or convenience (HSPHA, s. 45 and DHSS Circular 19/71)
d.   helping an elderly person to find suitable accommodation (HSPHA, s. 45 and DHSS Circular 19/71)

Table 13.4 lists the services that may be offered to individuals, but which the department has no obligation to provide. To some extent this overlaps with the schemes described in Table 13.1. What we list in Table 13.4 is additional assistance to individuals.

Cooperation with other Bodies
Where, having assessed the needs of the individual, the local authority believes that the health or housing authorities could help, it should pass on the information (NHSCCA, s. 47). An important example of this cooperation arises with the housing of vulnerable people. The Housing Act 1996 introduced new powers to evict anti-social tenants. One of the measures allows local authorities and Housing Action Trusts to grant new tenants a year's trial tenancy (an introductory tenancy) before they gain proper security against repossession. The landlord has the legal power to evict them without any ground having to be proved during this period. Given the prevalence of prejudice against people with mental disorders, housing authorities may listen to neighbours' concerns (as they should, of course) and decide to repossess. Where the tenant is known to social services, your job is to assist him or her to retain the tenancy. This requires helping the tenant as necessary, and liaising with the landlord and, perhaps, the neighbours. For more detail see Chapter 17.

Charging for Welfare Services
Services provided by the NHS must be free of charge. However, a social services department may, with two exceptions, charge for any or all of the services which have been discussed above (HASSASSA, s. 17). The exceptions are:

(a)   after-care of mental patients under MHA, s. 117; and

(b)   advice on community care and assessment of need.

There are no national rates for charges. They must be reasonable, and it is good practice to inform the person concerned what the charges will be before providing the service and to publish full information on charging policy, including means testing. (It has been argued that it amounts to discrimination on grounds of disability to assess a client's means in light of their receipt of disability-related payments. In *R v Powys County Council ex parte Hambridge (No. 2)* [2000] 2 FCR 69, this argument failed in front of the Court of Appeal. The applicant had not suffered disability discrimination in the provision of the actual care services.)

Services should not be withdrawn on the ground of non-payment according to Government guidelines; instead the debt should be pursued in court as an entirely separate matter. (The charity 'Scope' has found that almost one in five people liable to charges for services turn down the help because they cannot afford it.) Where services are provided by voluntary or commercial agencies, the agency can receive payment from the individual and the local authority tops the payments up.

Further guidance on charging may be found in DOH Circular: Advice Note for Use by Social Services Inspectorate — Discretionary Charges for Adult Social Services, January 1994.

Working with the Family

How does the local authority assess what contribution to non-residential services a carer — friend or relative, it does not matter — can make? A carer is someone who 'provides or intends to provide a substantial amount of care on a regular basis' (C(RS)A, s. 1) and can be anyone aged 16 upwards (CDCA, s). 1. The C(RS)A clarifies the position.

When making an assessment of a client's needs under NHSCCA, s. 47, you must listen to the carer's views and consider the role that he or she can play. You must assess the carer's needs as well as those of the vulnerable person (CDCA, s. 1). You can then plan, for example, to supplement the carer's support, or to take over while he or she has a break. Your authority can make direct payments to the carer, or provide vouchers for a short-term break (CDCA, ss. 2 and 3).

RESIDENTIAL CARE FOR THE VULNERABLE

Providing or arranging for residential care is governed by another set of rules, which you will find target a narrower group of vulnerable people than the non-residential support services we have looked at. Apart from two limited situations, which we can deal with quickly, you will see that you are only able to arrange residential care for people if they cannot cope without going into residential accommodation.

Those two exceptions, where you can provide support by way of accommodation, even though the person is not necessarily incapable of coping on their own, are:

1. Disabled clients under NAA, s. 29   In addition to all the non-residential support work you can offer, social services can provide hostel accommodation to enable people to take up or train for employment; and residential holiday facilities (NAA, s. 29 and DPEA, s. 3(1)).

2. Mentally disordered or physically ill clients   The department can provide residential accommodation for the prevention of illness, the care and after care of the ill (NHSA, Sch. 8; DOH Circular LAC (93) 10). (This is particularly useful for those discharged from mental hospital; or admitted to guardianship.) The person does not have to have a 'mental illness' as defined in the MHA (see Chapter 14). Any person with any mental disorder, or recovering from one, or at risk of one, can be offered accommodation.

'Part III' Accommodation for Those who Cannot Cope

The NAA, s. 21 comes within Pt III of the NAA; it allows the social services department to arrange 'residential accommodation for persons aged 18 or over who by reason of age, illness, disability or any other circumstances are in need of care and attention which is not otherwise available to them'; NHSCCA has extended this provision to expectant and nursing mothers who need this care and attention. The government has indicated that s. 21 services must take into account drug and alcohol abusers, and must cover those with HIV or AIDS. Part III accommodation is particularly relevant for those discharged from hospital, who are not yet ready to live in the community.

Section 21 covers people who for some reason, normally because of age or some mental or physical incapacity, cannot cope at home. We are talking of people who cannot cope even with help; but if, from family, friends, social services or voluntary organisations, they are receiving sufficient help to manage, then the definition does not apply, for they do have care and attention available to them. As we saw above, residential care is to be used only where support in the home or in another household cannot be achieved. So Pt III accommodation cannot be provided where there are alternative ways of keeping the person within the community. (This does not mean that the family must support an impossible relative at all costs; the Act merely states that the person is not receiving care and attention. If the would-be carers refuse to provide it, they cannot be forced. But see 'Liability of the Family to Maintain', below.) A local authority cannot, now, expect a person to spend his or her own capital to obtain care and attention, unless the person has capital exceeding the means-tested limit (currently £16,000). This has been made explicit by the Community Care (Residential Accommodation) Act 1998. (See, for guidance, Circular (98) 19.)

The courts extended the scope of s. 21 in the case of *R v Hammersmith and Fulham LBC ex parte M* (1998) 30 HLR 10. The former Government had legislated to remove benefit entitlement from most asylum seekers (see page 410), so the Court of Appeal declared that financial destitution rendered them 'in need of care and attention' and therefore entitled to Pt III accommodation. (But Pt III assistance is only available for those whose destitution includes homelessness. It does not cover those who have a home but nothing to eat: *R* v *Newham BC ex parte Gorenkin* (1997) *The Times*, 9 June.)

DOH Circular LAC (93) 10 directs that social services must arrange the accommodation if the person in need lives in the authority's boundaries; and, if the need is urgent, they must do so even if the person normally lives elsewhere. (If the need is not urgent, your department still has a discretion to accommodate someone from another area.)

When accommodation is arranged under Pt III, the circular requires it to be backed up with necessary welfare services (i.e., social work support), proper supervision of hygiene, and medical attention, nursing attention during illnesses which would normally be nursed at home, and 'such other services, amenities and requisites' as the authority considers necessary: catering, cleaning, recreation, and so on — whatever is decided is needed must be provided.

There must be regular inspection by social services management of the level and quality of provision of Pt III accommodation (DOH Circular LAC (94/6). During 2002 the new Care Standards Commission will take over this function and will be required to inspect not only private homes but the authority's homes.

What Accommodation Must be Provided?

A local authority may provide the accommodation itself, or use commercial or voluntary organisations. Although Circular (93) 10 states that a local authority must retain some direct provision, the House of Lords was happy to declare this Circular to be wrong on this point (*R* v *Wandsworth BC ex parte Beckwith* [1996] 1 All ER 129). (This is a useful reminder that Government guidance is not law. Only statute, regulations and case law are law.)

How is Residential Care Paid For?

Provision of accommodation is mandatory if the need is accepted. A person's right to it is independent, therefore, of any decision by the local authority to enforce the payment of contributions. Non-payment is a debt-collection problem.

In principle, the system is simple. It is governed by NAA, s. 22 as amended. If a person is not assessed as needing residential care, any provision must be paid for privately.

If the social services department assesses the individual as needing residential care, the authority pays initially, either by directly providing the service, or by paying a private or voluntary registered home. Then it seeks to recover as much as it can. Subject to means testing, the authority must charge the resident the full cost of provision (NAA, s. 22(2)). All income of the resident (but not the spouse) is relevant. Whether the resident's income derives entirely from social security benefits or from private means, he or she must be left with a residual sum for personal expenditure (currently £14.75 — and not to be spent on basics such as food or essential clothing, which should be part of the care). This amount can be increased if the resident has dependants. A resident must pay for the accommodation out of capital if this exceeds £16,000. For this purpose capital given away to avoid liability to pay still counts. But the value of the resident's home is disregarded if it is on the market, if a return home is likely, or if a spouse/relative lives there (National Assistance (Assessment of Resources) Regulations 1992).

People approaching old age, and their families, naturally worry about the cost of (and the possible forced sale of the old person's home to pay for) care. Family pressure on the old person to give the property away to reduce the risk of a forced sale may be contrary to the interests of that person. The beneficiaries of such a gift (usually the children) cannot be guaranteed to keep it available for the former owner, whose state of dependency is increased to no advantage.

If the resident or family wish to obtain higher standard accommodation than the department provides as a standard, they must provide top-up payments to the local authority.

Special rates of income support were available to pay fees for private residential accommodation before April 1993. For existing residents, these arrangements continue until they leave residential accommodation.

Further guidance is given in DOH Circulars LAC (92) 19 and LAC (98) 19, and in a free pamphlet 'Charging for Residential Accommodation Guide' from the Department of Health, PO Box 410, Wetherby LS23 7LN.

Payment for residential care after Mental Health Act detention   Section 117 of the MHA requires after-care services to be provided to patients released from detention in a mental hospital. See Chapter 14 for detail. If the services include residential accommodation, it cannot be charged for (*R* v *Richmond LBC ex parte W* (1999) 2 CCL Rep 402). This is a quirk of the community care legislation and its piecemeal origins.

Choice of Residential Provision
DOH Circular LAC (92) 10 encourages choice for the resident. The local authority can restrict choice only on the grounds that the chosen accommodation is not suitable for the resident's needs, is more expensive than usually paid to meet those needs, is outside the UK, or does not meet the authority's standards, for example for access, monitoring anti-discriminatory practice or insurance. (It may still be registered without meeting the standards of the paying authority, as it could be in a different local authority area with different requirements.)

Guidance is also given in DOH Circular LAC (93) 18.

Does it have to be a care home?   Part III accommodation must meet the assessed needs of the client. If those needs are best met in a residential care home, a place must be found. If they are best met in other accommodation, such other accommodation must be found. This is the clear outcome of *R (on the application of Khana)* v *London Borough of Southwark* (unreported), 1 December 2000. The applicant was an elderly Kurd, whose family claimed they could provide extensive support if the applicant did not go into a home, and that their ability to support her would be seriously restricted if she did go into a home. What she needed, they argued, was moving from an upper-floor flat to a ground-floor flat, and that was what social services must provide. They also argued that the council had acted unlawfully in ignoring Government policy guidance (see p. 28) which says that normal living should be preserved for clients. As it happens, the court rejected the applicants' argument, preferring to accept on the facts that the council was correct in assessing Mrs Khana as needing 24-hour care and not just family support. But if the facts had been otherwise, accommodation in the community would have to have been found.

Liability of the Spouse to Maintain

What happens if a person has to be taken into Pt III accommodation because their family does not maintain them? Or if, having been taken into Pt III accommodation, their family does not contribute to their costs?

The relevant principle is set out in the NAA, s. 42. A person is liable to maintain his or her spouse and failure to do so is actually a criminal offence. If this failure to maintain results in reception into Pt III accommodation, this results in a further offence being committed under s. 51. Social Services are entitled to prosecute the alleged offender.

However, prosecution may achieve no useful result. If Pt III accommodation becomes necessary — perhaps despite your efforts with supportive social work — you can ask the spouse who would be liable to maintain the resident to *agree* a contribution towards the actual cost of accommodation. If agreement cannot be reached, the department may ask a magistrates' court under s. 43 to assess the amount that the spouse must pay and to order payment. If you take this course, do not forget that the spouse should be advised of their right to obtain independent advice.

Registration of Care Homes

Any establishment which provides residential care for illness, mental disorder, disability or dependency on alcohol or drugs must be registered. This applies to the local authority's care homes as much as it does to private homes.

Registration is with a new national body, the National Care Standards Commission (in Wales, with the National Assembly). Failure to register a care home is a criminal offence. Registration must be granted if the applicant meets the standards set out in CSA, s. 22 and regulations made under that section. The standards cover management, staffing, facilities, record-keeping, training, accounts, etc. The Commission can cancel registration where the manager has been convicted of an offence relating to registration, or if the home has failed to comply with the requirements. As the procedure allows the manager to be heard on whether registration should be withdrawn, the legislation permits the local magistrates' court to order immediate cancellation of registration in urgent cases (s. 20).

The registration authority has the power to inspect both premises and records (s. 31).

COMPULSORY POWERS

Every community care service discussed above is delivered on the basis that the client chooses to accept the service. Situations can arise, though, particularly with elderly people, where the client cannot make appropriate choices. If a person needs assessment or treatment for a mental disorder, compulsory powers are available under the MHA, and these are discussed in Chapter 14. Where a client does not have a mental disorder, powers of compulsory intervention are limited to the following two areas:

(a)   removal from home; and
(b)   managing the client's financial and property affairs.

No other compulsory intervention, however well motivated or desired by persuasive relatives, is acceptable or lawful.

Compulsory Removal from Home
Most people will enter hospital or Pt III accommodation voluntarily. What can be done if they refuse to go, but are a danger to themselves or others if they stay where they are living? We are in a difficult area, where the rights of the individual are set against what, in the opinion of someone representing state authority, is their own best interests, or the interests of society. For example, the person constantly leaves the gas on, or his or her living conditions attract rats. (We are not suggesting that these, on their own, are grounds for compulsory removal; there ought to be ways of overcoming such problems if there is some cooperation from the person concerned or his or her carers.)

The social worker is not the one who has powers to remove a person against his or her will, but you cannot wash your hands of responsibility in this area. First, you are in the front line of support work which would obviate any need for compulsory removal; secondly, in exercising your powers and duties to provide support to vulnerable people, you, sooner than anyone else, are the person likely to recognise when the need for residential accommodation has arisen. However, the person who actually exercises the power to apply for a compulsory removal is a person appointed by the district or borough council called the 'proper officer'. The person appointed will not be part of a social services team unless the authority is a unitary authority. Where a county council runs social services, the 'proper officer' will be an officer from the district or borough council, i.e. not a member of social services staff. Often the proper officer will be the medical officer of health.

The proper officer cannot remove a person without an order from the magistrates' court. The order can be obtained in an emergency without any notice being given even to the person concerned (see below), so you will appreciate that it is a Draconian power. It is essential to follow the correct procedure and be sure that the statutory criteria are met. Even if they are met, you should be aware that what is proposed is to remove basic liberties; could your goal — assisting the person to manage his or her life — be met without compulsory removal, by further support? Or could you justify allowing that person the dignity of living the way he or she wishes?

Criteria for compulsory removal   NAA, s. 47 applies to persons who:

(a)   are suffering from grave chronic disease or, being aged, infirm or physically incapacitated, are living in insanitary conditions; **and**

(b)   are unable to devote to themselves, and are not receiving from other persons, proper care and attention.

We have emphasised the 'and', because it is not enough merely to be infirm and living in squalor — it must be shown that the person is also unable to look after himself or herself, and is not just choosing to live in that way.

The proper officer must supply to the court a certificate that he or she has made thorough enquiries, and considers that it is necessary to remove the person from the premises where he or she is, either because:

(a)   it is in the interest of that person; or

(b)   removal will prevent injury to someone else's health, or prevent a serious nuisance being caused to someone else.

The proper officer must also give oral evidence of these facts at the hearing before the magistrates.

The person who is at the centre of these proceedings — or the person caring for him or her — must be given notice of the magistrates' court hearing at least seven days in advance. Also the manager of the proposed accommodation must be notified at least seven days before the hearing, unless the manager comes to court to give oral evidence that suitable accommodation is available. In the case of Pt III accommodation provided by the local authority, the manager means a person representing social services.

But in an emergency, the procedural safeguards drop away; an application can be made without informing the subject of the application in advance. Nevertheless, the proper officer plus another doctor must certify that it is in the person's interest to remove him or her without delay (National Assistance (Amendment) Act 1951, s. 1).

An order allowing removal in an emergency gives the applicant a power to detain the person for up to three weeks, during which period a further application can be made with the seven days' notice. A non-emergency order lasts for three months, which can be renewed by the magistrates as many times as necessary. If the compulsory detention lapses, the person can leave, or remain voluntarily.

The person can be detained against his or her will only in the place mentioned in the court order; any variation requires a magistrates' court order.

This is a sweeping power, made more so by the fact that there is often no legal help for representation before the magistrates for the 'victim'. The Access to Justice Act 1999, shamefully, explicitly excludes this from the scope of Community Legal Service funding (see Chapter 15). There is not even any requirement that the person be represented, or receive legal advice. The magistrates themselves can be asked to revoke the order, but such an application cannot be made until six weeks after the order was made — over halfway through the period of detention. There is no right of appeal, unless the magistrates have exceeded their powers or made an irrational decision. Judicial review in the High Court would then be possible.

Perhaps because of the Draconian nature of these proceedings, the delay before a challenge to an order, and the lack of any provision for representation, many district authorities and their community physicians are reluctant to invoke the s. 47 procedure at all. A challenge to an order as breaching the Human Rights Act could well succeed.

Managing the Affairs of the Mentally Disordered, Confused or Elderly Client

Community care legislation does not give any control over the client's property or affairs. The same issue can arise in relation to the property and financial affairs of a mental patient (see Chapter 14 for the law on mental health). You may find yourself advising a relative (not necessarily the nearest relative — a term used in the Mental Health Act and discussed in the next chapter) or friend of a client or patient about, for example, how to free some of the client's money to buy items for the client or their family, or to pay for residential care. You may exceptionally have to take steps on the client's behalf yourself.

Your involvement as a social worker is likely to come from your statutory duty to disabled clients under NAA, s. 29. 'Disabled' (see above pp. 316 and 319) includes mental confusion. The duty simultaneously arises from the fact that a social services authority must also have schemes for assisting the elderly (above p. 320).

The law will not uphold any transaction, or disposition of a person's property, where one of the parties was unable to understand the nature of the transaction. The only exemption from this is where the other party to the transaction had no reason to suspect any inability, or supplied to the confused person necessary goods or services — such as food or accommodation.

The result of this is that an obviously disordered person cannot make binding agreements; cannot run a bank account; go to court; sell property, or do any business except during lucid moments with strangers, or buy things like food. So no one will knowingly do much business with such a person, and special procedures are required.

If such a person has to take or defend a court case, a person has to act on their behalf as litigation friend. This person will normally be a close relative, but anyone with an interest in the person's affairs can take on the role. The litigation friend can give the lawyers all the necessary instructions to conduct the case. But the role of the friend is limited to that case only. It gives no powers to act in the person's affairs generally.

Who should take over the confused person's financial affairs? Is it a relative? The relatives may be squabbling. There is a risk of financial exploitation. Is it the local authority? This frequently happens, but is the finance department of a local authority likely to understand the issues? (See further Langan, 'In the best interests of elderly people' (1997) 19(4) CFLQ 494.) It may not be easy to find the selfless person who has the time and understanding necessary to take on the work. Advice given with the best of motives could lead to legal liability. Therefore your authority should be able to identify a specialist to undertake the giving of advice. If the person is in residential care, the staff of the home should not take on this role (see 'Home Life: a Code of Practice for Residential Care', Centre for Policy on Ageing, 1984, adopted by the Government and therefore equivalent to a circular). Here are some of the available mechanisms:

(a) Powers of attorney There are two other ways in which others can conduct the affairs of a mentally incapable person. The first is a device called a power of attorney, under which a person can, by executing a deed, confer powers on another person to carry out specified, or all, matters on their behalf. Until the Enduring Powers of Attorney Act 1985, such a power was legally useless (though widely used), for it lapsed when a person became incapable of handling their own affairs — the very moment when it was most needed. Now, if executed by a person who is in sufficient control of his or her faculties to understand broadly what powers he or she is giving away, and registered with the Court of Protection once it needs to be used, a power of attorney can continue to be valid, even though the person giving the power no longer has mental capacity to grant such a power. It is a useful mechanism for a person approaching old age, presently of reasonably sound mind, but fearing dementia. A person wishing to draw up such a power or have one created for a friend or relative should take legal advice from a solicitor.

(b) Court of Protection If the person cannot be caught in a lucid moment, the second way to intervene is a more cumbersome mechanism. This is an application to the Court of Protection, and its powers are set out in MHA, ss. 93–98. The Act uses the term 'patient', though such applications are not confined to mental patients. The application is supported by a medical opinion that the patient is unable to act, but there is no attempt to define what 'to act' means, and no scrutiny by the court's own medical experts of the opinion sent with the application. An application can be made by any interested person on behalf of the patient, and the Court can make decisions for the benefit of the patient in relation to his or her affairs. This can include drafting a will for the patient or giving away assets to family or charity. (The Court will assume that, but for the disability, the patient would have applied 'normal decent' standards in deciding how to dispose of his or her property (*Re C* [1991] 3 All ER 866).) The Court appoints a receiver who must — but often in fact does not — send in accounts to show how the money has been spent. Legal advice is generally desirable; but legal aid for representation before the court is not available; though preliminary advice under the green form is available to a relative or friend, subject to a means test.

(c) Miscellaneous ways of helping Where a person is in receipt of DSS benefits, arrangements can be made for payment to a person on behalf of a claimant unable to act. That person is appointed by the DSS. It can be anyone — a social worker, even a DSS employee. No medical evidence is

required. If the person is in residential care, the DSS will notify social services of any appointment. No other legal safeguards exist and no monitoring of the appointee's use of the money takes place, save for a requirement to keep a record of expenditure. If you take on this role you may become liable if the person then alleges that you mismanaged or appropriated the money. The procedure may even turn out to be a breach of the client's rights, under the Human Rights Act 1998, not to be deprived of his or her property without a proper legal process. However, this procedure is quick and easy, compared to the Court of Protection.

Apart from these specific powers to engage in the affairs of persons unable to understand for themselves what they are doing, there is no legal mechanism for running someone else's affairs without their genuine consent, and any such action could lead, for example, to the person who does so being sued after the recovery or death of the patient.

Age Concern have published an excellent guide to the area called *Managing Other People's Money* (Penny Letts, available from 1268 London Road, London SW16 (tel: 0208 765 7200). It gives guidance not just on helping people with mental disorder, but on simple issues like cashing someone's benefit giro when they are not able to walk to the post office.

People having difficulty managing their affairs are at risk of exploitation from friends and relatives. People may think they know better than the elderly person what is good for that person. Relatives may have become impatient at the perceived burden of care, and begin to look at the elderly person's money as their own to use. But social workers, and lawyers, must remind themselves that the client is the elderly person, whose wishes are to be respected unless the evidence is clear that intervention against their wishes is appropriate. Medical and legal advice will give some protection from exploitation and/or well-meaning but unnecessary interference. If you think you know best, check whether the action you propose to take is legal. Never allow yourself to be dictated to by the relatives as to what is best for the elderly person. The relatives are not your client.

FOURTEEN

Mental Disorder and Admissions to Hospital/Guardianship

MENTAL DISORDER

This area is of greatest concern to those social workers who choose to be specialists — approved social workers (ASWs). Perhaps the intricate details of the legislation can be left to them? But what are you going to do with a person who is showing clear signs of disturbance and threatening to jump off a window ledge, or to attack you? Or, even if there is no immediate threat to you or anyone, a person with whom you come into professional contact needs medical help because of what you see to be their mental disturbance? Or maybe you have a client who appears incapable of managing his or her affairs because of dementia?

You cannot avoid taking decisions in such a crisis; you cannot hide behind the fact that this is not your field. At the very least you need to contact the right person, sometimes urgently, and that involves knowing enough about the procedures to know who that person is. A social worker who is not an ASW may nevertheless be a patient's key worker and must be involved in decision-making. So we make no apology for covering this area in some detail.

Having said that, this is an area for specialists, and this is recognised under the MHA. Social work functions under the Act are almost entirely carried out by the ASW. It is the social worker's employing authority who gives this approval, after training (s. 114), and every social services department must have enough ASWs to deal with admissions of mental patients and their treatment (DOH Circular LAC (93) 10). Cover must be on a 24-hour basis (Mental Health Act 1983 Code of Practice, para. 2.37). We hope that this overview will provide a starting point in this area for those wishing to become ASWs.

The problem with mental disorder, from the legal point of view, is that the sufferer is sometimes not seen to be the best person to make decisions about his or her own welfare. Society expects judgments to be made by experts as to what is in the patient's best interests; but the power of the professionals to override the wishes of the patient, or sometimes the patient's family, is a power to deprive a person of his or her basic liberties. You should keep in mind the words of McCullough J, in the case of *R* v *Hallstrom* [1986] 2 All ER 314:

> Unless clear statutory authority to the contrary exists, no one is to be detained in hospital or to undergo medical treatment or even to submit himself to a medical examination without his consent. That is as true of a mentally disordered person as of anyone else.

This clear statement is underpinned by Article 5 of the European Convention on Human Rights, soon to be a part of UK Law, which provides a right to liberty. An example of the interpretation of this article can be seen in *Kay* v *United Kingdom* (1998) 40 BMLR 20. Mr Kay was subject to a hospital restriction order for a killing in 1971. He had been conditionally discharged in 1985 and committed two violent offences for which he went to prison. While in prison he obtained evidence that he was not suffering from mental disorder and tried to get the 1971 restriction order discharged. The Mental Health Review Tribunal agreed that he had no mental disorder but refused the discharge. The hospital then recalled him, so that on release from prison he was detained again under the 1971 order. A fair result for a dangerous man? Perhaps. But it was all done without considering up-to-date medical evidence. Mr Kay's right to liberty had been breached, because the evidence had not been presented which would justify the order, according to the European Court of Human Rights.

The MHA provides procedures to try to ensure that abuse of the powers of the professionals does not occur, while necessary treatment and containment can still be provided. It is not our task to comment on whether the balance achieved is the correct one.

The Mental Health Act 1983 Code of Practice (Department of Health and Welsh Office 1999) is essential reading for all professionals working in the mental health field. It replaces the 1990 Code.

The key features of the Code are set out in para. 1:

1. The detailed guidance provided in the Code needs to be read in the light of the following broad principles, that people to whom the Act applies (including those being assessed for possible admission) should:

- receive recognition of their basic human rights under the European Convention on Human Rights (ECHR);
- be given respect for their qualities, abilities and diverse backgrounds as individuals and be assured that account will be taken of their age, gender, sexual orientation, social, ethnic, cultural and religious background, but that general assumptions will not be made on the basis of any one of these characteristics;

- have their needs taken fully into account, though it is recognised that, within available resources, it may not always be practicable to meet them;
- be given any necessary treatment or care in the least controlled and segregated facilities compatible with ensuring their own health and safety or the safety of other people;
- be treated or cared for in such a way as to promote to the greatest practicable degree their self determination and personal responsibility, consistent with their own needs and wishes;
- be discharged from detention or other powers provided by the Act as soon as it is clear that their application is no longer justified.

Paragraphs 1.2 to 1.6 set out the steps that all mental health professionals must take to ensure effective communication with the individual, including suitable interpreters and intermediaries (not a role for friends or family), training of staff, and awareness that it may take several attempts to communicate with the individual about any particular issue.

The Code also stresses the need to bring into discussions not only the patient, but their family and friends and other relevant people, including victims of the patient's offending, if applicable. However, a patient's affairs are to be discussed with such people only with permission of the patient; a mentally disordered person is entitled to expect confidentiality, as is any other of your clients. (But, as with other clients, your statutory duties towards the patient sometimes require discussions with other professionals; confidentiality does not apply then — see Chapter 2.)

The following part of this chapter concentrates on the powers to admit, control and treat mental patients under the MHA 1983. Further detail on these procedures is contained in the Mental Health (Hospital, Guardianship and Consent to Treatment) Regulations 1983 (SI 1983 No. 893). But while looking at admission to hospital or to guardianship, and at control and treatment, it is important for the social worker to be aware that mental disorder is also an example of a vulnerability or handicap. Support facilities in the community can generally be offered to people with a mental disorder under the powers we have already considered in Chapter 13. Note also the obligation of social services to work together with the health authority in the after-care of patients discharged after hospital detention (MHA, s. 117).

Definitions — Patients and Relatives

The word 'patient' will occur frequently as a shorthand for a person suffering from mental disorder. It is not necessary to be a patient in hospital to be called a patient under the Act.

Definitions of mental disorder are given in Table 14.1.

The definitions contained in Table 14.1 require professional judgment as to whether a patient meets the criteria or not. This judgment should be formed by each professional independently of the others: the Code (para. 2.31) makes clear that there is nothing wrong with disagreement, so long as the needs of the patient are not ignored while the disagreement is resolved.

Table 14.1   Mental Disorders as Defined in MHA, s. 1

> *Mental disorder* is defined as 'Mental illness, arrested or incomplete development of mind, psychopathic disorder and any other disorder or disability of mind' (s. 1(2)). It is sufficient for a compulsory admission for assessment (see p. 339).
>
> *Mental illness* is not defined.
>
> *Severe mental impairment* is 'a state of arrested or incomplete development of mind which includes severe impairment of intelligence and social functioning and is associated with abnormally aggressive or seriously irresponsible conduct. Note that the aggressive or irresponsible behaviour of the person does not actually have to be caused by the impairment, so for example a patient whose violence is caused by emotional disturbance, and not mental handicap, could come within this definition.
>
> *Mental impairment* has the same definition as severe mental impairment, with the word 'severe' replaced by 'significant'.
>
> *Psychopathic disorder* is 'a persistent disorder or disability of mind (whether or not including significant impairment of intelligence) which results in abnormally aggressive or seriously irresponsible conduct'.

A social worker should not, therefore, automatically concur with medical opinion.

A diagnosis of mental disorder can *never* be founded *solely* on evidence of promiscuity, immoral conduct, sexual deviancy or drug abuse (MHA, s. 1(3)). Neither can it be founded on bizarre and irrational behaviour. A woman refusing to undergo a caesarian, despite advice that she was putting herself and her baby at grave risk by insisting on a natural birth, is not suffering from a mental disorder. This Court of Appeal ruling, in *St George's NHS Trust* v *S* [1998] 3 WLR 936, came too late to stop the caesarian being carried out against her will, but has made clear that the Act should be used to deal with mental health issues and not social control. Nevertheless, life-threatening anorexia nervosa can be a mental illness (*Re KB (Adult) (Mental Patient: Medical Treatment)* (1994) 19 BMLR 144).

The assessment, as stated above, is one for professional judgment. But it is reviewable by the courts, particularly where words like 'seriously irresponsible conduct' have to be interpreted. In *Re F (Mental Health Act: Guardianship)* [2000] 1 FLR 192, the Court of Appeal disagreed with the assessment of the doctors that the wishes of a 17-year-old boy to return to an unhappy, abusive home amounted to such conduct.

The final point to mention when defining the patient is that there is no age requirement. The MHA applies to children, except for admission to guardianship, where the child must be at least 16 years old.

The other definition required for an understanding of the workings of the Act is the 'nearest relative'. This is a person with whom the ASW often has to work. Only one person can fill this role for a particular patient. Section 26 defines who this is, and this is summarised in Table 14.2.

The list given in Table 14.2 presupposes that someone can be found from that list. But there may be no such person alive and in this country. Or the nearest relative may be unwilling or incapable of acting. Or there is a nearest relative willing to act but who wants to do the 'wrong' thing, such as discharging the patient against advice. In such a situation, any relative, any person with whom the patient normally resides, or an ASW, can apply to the county court to be appointed or to have someone else appointed — for example the ASW might apply to have a relative further down the list appointed (s. 29) or a suitable friend of the person. (Alternatively, the nearest

Table 14.2   The Nearest Relative

The order of priority is:

- Spouse (but excluding any spouse who has deserted the patient, or been separated by court order or formal agreement)
- If there is no spouse, a cohabitee of six months' standing
- Son or daughter
- Parent
- Brother or sister
- Grandparent
- Grandchild
- Uncle or aunt
- Niece or nephew
- Any other person who has lived with the patient for at least five years (but only if there is no spouse)

If a person on the list actually lives with and cares for the patient, he or she take precedence, even if lower down the list. Anyone who lives abroad is ignored altogether.

Illegitimacy is irrelevant; where there is more than one person competing for the position on the same level in the list (e.g., a brother and a sister; two parents) then the oldest takes precedence. Relationships of the whole blood take precedence over those of half blood (e.g., a sister comes before a half sister).

If a child is in care under Children Act 1989 the nearest relative is always the authority named in the care order, even if the child is accommodated at home (s. 27).

relative can give written authorisation to allow another person to discharge the role (reg. 14).)

The court can make this s. 29 order only if:

(a)   no nearest relative can be found; or

(b)   the present nearest relative is incapable of acting because of mental disorder or other illness; or

(c)   the nearest relative unreasonably refuses to consent to an application for admission to hospital or guardianship under the MHA; or

(d)   the nearest relative has unreasonably exercised his or her power to discharge the patient without taking into account the public interest or the welfare of the patient (s. 26(3)).

As soon as an application is submitted to the court under s. 29, right up to the court hearing, the existing nearest relative loses the power to discharge the patient. This s. 29 application, therefore, is one way in which an ASW can prevent the discharge of a patient. The hospital authorities also have ways of preventing discharge (below p. 344).

The nearest relative has the right, at any time, to appoint an independent doctor to visit the patient in hospital, and look at all relevant records. This is important, for the nearest relative has rights to apply to the Mental Health Review Tribunal, and to discharge a detained patient, and should be told of this right to obtain medical advice before taking that kind of decision.

ADMISSIONS TO MENTAL HOSPITAL

Informal Admissions

Before we talk about compulsory powers, it is useful to bear in mind that the majority of admissions to hospital are not compulsory. The MHA (s. 131) and the Code of Practice (para. 2.7) explicitly encourage non-compulsory admissions. These patients should not strictly be called voluntary, since it is the fact that they do not object to admission, or remaining in hospital, rather than their actual agreement that enables the hospital to admit or keep them there. The importance of admitting patients on this informal basis was reaffirmed by the House of Lords in *R* v *Bournewood Community and Mental Health NHS Trust ex parte L* [1998] 3 WLR 107. L had a 30-year history of in-patient treatment, but had recently been looked after in the community. His carers brought him in one day because he was getting agitated, only to find that they could not get him out again. L himself, being autistic, could not insist on leaving, but was not objecting to his stay. His carers, on L's behalf, claimed in judicial review that this amounted to compulsory detention and that the compulsory detention procedure, with all its safeguards and time limits, should have been used. They were successful in the Court of Appeal, but the *status quo* was restored in the Lords. The Code of Practice explicitly endorses this outcome: if a patient does not object, informal admission will be lawful (para. 2.8).

An informal patient is theoretically free to leave at will. Unfortunately, in the *Bournewood* case the patient could not begin to exercise this freedom himself. Two of the five Law Lords said that this in fact amounted to detention. If, on a Human Rights Act challenge, it was recognised that the patient had been detained without judicial process or right of challenge, this could amount to a breach of the right under Article 5 of the European Convention (discussed further at p. 341 below).

Even if the patient is capable of exercising his or her right to leave, no one is required to inform the patient of this right; and as we see later, as soon as he or she indicates his or her desire to leave, there are powers to detain the patient at the stroke of a doctor's or nurse's pen (see below p. 341). (Detained patients have greater rights: they must be informed that they can refuse treatment and apply for discharge (s. 132).)

Any person of 16 or over can become an informal patient regardless of the wishes of his or her parent or guardian. Below that age an informal admission is made by the patient's parent or guardian (s. 131(2)). (This gives a parent more control over the child in mental health than in other medical matters — see p. 71 for a discussion of informed consent to medical treatment.)

In *R* v *Kirklees MBC ex parte C (A Minor)* [1993] 2 FLR 187, the court, on a challenge by the parents, held that where a child is in care, the local authority, exercising parental responsibility, can admit the child to a hospital against his or her will, even if there are no grounds for a compulsory MHA admission, and even if the result is to deprive the child of his or her liberty without a court order. The Court of Appeal ruled that if the child had been 'Gillick competent' (see p. 71) she would have been entitled to refuse admission. This is still an 'informal admission' in that no powers under the MHA are exercised. The admission took place under the parental responsibility of the local authority. (In contrast, the local authority must have a court order to lock up children in care for more than 72 hours.)

As a result of the *Bournewood* decision (above), the Department of Health issued further guidance (HSC 1998/122), stating that the wishes of the patient and his or her carers must be taken into account before informal admission, and the fact that a patient does not object should not be taken as evidence of compliance with an informal admission.

Compulsory Admissions

'Compulsory admission should only be exercised in the last resort' (Code, para. 2.7).

There can be no compulsory admission without an application. Who is the applicant? An ASW is usually a better person to make the application than the nearest relative, 'bearing in mind professional training, knowledge of the legislation and of local resources, together with the potential adverse effects that an application by the nearest relative might have on the latter's relationship with the patient' (Code, para. 2.35). The ASW must consult the nearest relative, however (MHA, s. 11(4)). Consulting the wrong relative makes the ensuing admission and detention unlawful (*Re S-C (Mental Patient) (Habeas Corpus)* [1996] QB 599).

Compulsory admission does not require an order of any court or tribunal (apart from admission for treatment following a criminal conviction (see

Chapter 12, p. 301)). The liberty of the patient is removed on the completion of a purely administrative procedure: the ASW or the nearest relative makes an application, supported by two (or, in an emergency, one) doctors' statements.

The nearest relative's or ASW's application is addressed to the managers of the proposed hospital (s. 11); this means the health authority or, if it is a private mental nursing home, the person registered with the Department of Health (National Care Standards Commission from June 2002) to run it, or if the hospital is secure (e.g., Broadmoor) the Secretary of State for Health.

Although the Act calls the procedure an application, it is hardly that. Neither the managers nor the hospital doctors have to consider whether it has any merit. They only have to consider whether they have space. Indeed, once the application for admission has been completed, before the ink is dry, let alone read by the person to whom it is addressed, it gives rise to compulsory MHA powers: the applicant or his or her authorised agent is now empowered to take the patient to the named hospital. However, the detention ceases to be lawful if the hospital managers realise that the facts stated in the forms are untrue (*R* v *Central London County Court ex parte London* [1999] 3 All ER 991).

An ASW *must* make an application where in his or her professional opinion that is the appropriate course (s. 13(1)). This is a matter for the social worker as an individual; it is not a departmental decision. And he or she must reach the decision independently, even if it is a different decision to that of the doctors (*St George's Healthcare NHS Trust* v *S* [1998] 3 All ER 673, where the ASW might have realised that a woman refusing a caesarian was not necessarily suffering from a mental disorder). Before making the application, the ASW must interview the patient 'in a suitable manner', and be satisfied that compulsory admission is the most appropriate way of providing the care and medical treatment which the patient needs (s. 13(2)). A suitable manner means taking into account any language barriers, hearing difficulties, and other obstacles such as cultural differences which could interfere with communication with the patient. Guidance is given in the Code, para. 2.11. As soon as the ASW has made a decision — to apply or not to apply for compulsory admission — he or she must explain the decision to the patient, the doctors, the nearest relative (if possible), and the patient's key worker and GP (Code, para. 2.17).

The applicant must have seen the patient within the last 14 days. We would suggest in any event that a compulsory admission be based on more up-to-date observations by the applicant. The application must be supported by the signed medical recommendations of two doctors, one from a Department of Health approved mental health specialist, the other, if possible, from a doctor familiar with the patient. Both doctors must have examined the patient within five days of each other. They must sign the recommendations before the applicant signs the application, otherwise the application is invalid.

A completed application gives the applicant power to take the patient to hospital. This power lapses 14 days after the last of the two medical examinations (s. 6(1)), which means that the medical information must be reasonably up to date at the time of the admission.

The five-day and 14-day time periods are shortened in the case of an emergency admission: the applicant must have seen the patient not more than 24 hours before making the application, and the admission must be carried out within 24 hours of the medical examination (s. 6(2)(b)).

Once a patient is compulsorily detained, the managers must inform him or her of the grounds for detention, and of the patient's right to discharge and to apply to the Mental Health Review Tribunal. If the application was by an ASW, the nearest relative must be similarly informed unless the patient objects to this (s. 132).

Where the application was by a nearest relative, the managers of the hospital must notify the patient's local social services department; a social worker (who does not have to be an ASW) must then interview the patient and provide the hospital with a social circumstances report (s. 14). The report should set out not only the history of the patient and the disorder, but also state whether alternative methods of dealing with the patient are available and appropriate. Alternative methods means community care — can anything be organised under the powers described in Chapter 13?

We have not yet considered the medical grounds, what the doctors must be satisfied of before making their recommendations. This will vary according to whether the admission is to be for assessment under s. 2, treatment under s. 3, or emergency assessment under s. 4.

28-day admission for assessment   The doctors must certify on the application that they are satisfied that the patient:

> (a)   is suffering from mental disorder of a nature or degree which warrants the detention of the patient in a hospital for assessment (or for assessment followed by medical treatment) for at least a limited period; **and**
> (b)   he ought to be so detained in the interests of his own health or safety or with a view to the protection of other persons (s. 2(2)).

The words 'is suffering' still apply even if the patient's condition is currently controlled by medication (*Devon County Council* v *Hawkins* [1967] 2 QB 26).

The nearest relative cannot veto this application if it is made by an ASW. However, s. 11(3) and the Code, para. 2.15 require the ASW to take all practicable steps to inform the person (if any) who appears to be the nearest relative that an application for admission is about to be, or has been, made, and of the nearest relative's power to discharge the patient after admission (which we describe later).

We have seen that a correctly completed application gives the applicant immediate powers to convey the patient to hospital. The hospital may then detain the patient for up to 28 days (s. 2(4)). After that, the patient must be discharged unless he or she remains as an informal patient, or detention is renewed for treatment rather than assessment under the s. 3 powers discussed below.

72-hour admission for assessment in an emergency   The s. 2 procedure above requires two doctors' recommendations. But in an emergency an application can be founded on only one, if the applicant certifies that admission is of urgent necessity and that obtaining two recommendations would involve undesirable delay (s. 4(2)). The single medical recommendation should, if possible, come from a doctor who knows the patient; the grounds are the same as under a s. 2 admission for assessment. The doctor must also state that admission is a matter of urgent necessity.

The Code (para. 6.3) advises that urgency is more than a matter of administrative convenience. There must be evidence of:

— the existence of an immediate and significant risk of mental or physical harm to the patient or others, and/or
— the danger of serious harm to property, and/or
— the need for physical restraint of the patient.

The completion of the application gives the applicant a power to convey the patient to the hospital, where he or she can be detained for up to 72 hours. During these 72 hours, if the second doctor's recommendation is received by the managers, containing the required recommendation under s. 2, the detention is converted into a 28-day admission, starting from the day of the admission not the conversion (s. 4(4)). Otherwise, at the end of the 72-hour period the patient is free to leave, or remain voluntarily.

Admission for treatment   Admission for treatment is governed by s. 3.

One difference between admission for assessment, and for treatment, is that the ASW cannot usually proceed with admission for treatment against the wishes of the nearest relative. For the ASW must consult the person who appears to be the nearest relative before making an application for admission for treatment (s. 11(1)), unless it is 'not reasonably practicable or would involve unreasonable delay'; so consultation must be the rule, not the exception. The nearest relative can then prevent the application going ahead by simply informing the ASW or his or her department that he or she objects (s. 11(4)). If, therefore, an ASW wishes to make an application for treatment against the wishes of the nearest relative, an application to displace the nearest relative must first be made to the county court (see above, p. 335). The ASW will therefore find the admission procedure more difficult.

The medical grounds for admission for treatment are more rigorous than for assessment, which is not surprising given that the doctors are now, by definition, satisfied that treatment is appropriate. Suffering from a mental disorder on its own is now not enough. Both doctors making the recommendations must agree on which of the four defined categories of mental disorder the patient is suffering from — mental illness, severe mental impairment, mental impairment or psychopathic disorder (s. 1, see above, p. 334). (We saw in relation to s. 2 admissions that 'suffering from' applies even where the condition is currently controlled by medication.)

The doctors must also be satisfied that the patient's 'mental disorder is of a nature or degree which makes it appropriate for him to receive medical treatment *in a hospital*'. Just having one of the mental disorders is not ground enough, therefore, if it could be treated in the community. 'Treatment' itself is a broad concept. A patient refusing to eat was capable of treatment consisting of force-feeding (*B* v *Croydon Health Authority (No. 2)* [1996] 1 FLR 253).

If the patient is diagnosed as suffering from one of the 'minor' disorders only — mental impairment or pyschopathic disorder — the doctors must be satisfied that 'such treatment is likely to alleviate or prevent a deterioration of his condition' (the 'treatability test'). In other words, since the disorders are minor, no one should compulsorily be sent to hospital for treatment unless he or she will benefit from it. A psychopathic patient who is dangerous and yet untreatable cannot (until the legislation is reformed — see a summary of the proposals below) be detained under s. 3. (But where there was treatment available which the patient refused, she still counted as treatable (*R* v *Canons Park MHRT ex parte A* [1994] 2 All ER 659).) Note that the treatability test does not apply on admission for assessment, for assessment by definition has to precede a decision on treatment.

On top of the required diagnosis of a disorder, the doctors must be satisfied that treatment is necessary 'for the health or safety of the patient or for the protection of other persons' — that is, the patient is a risk to himself or others — and that 'it cannot be provided unless he is admitted *under this section*'. So if the patient could be treated in the community, or be admitted voluntarily, the s. 3 grounds would not apply.

There is no emergency admission for treatment. If the need is already known, it should be a s. 3 admission for treatment; if it has only just arisen, by definition, assessment is needed first, and if necessary an emergency admission for assessment could be sought.

Detention for treatment can last up to six months.

New grounds for admissions? *The Government has proposed legislation to create powers to detain 'dangerous people with severe personality disorder', even where the detainee does not meet the treatability test for detention under the MHA and has committed no offence. Any new legislation will have to comply with the Human Rights Act 1998 and Article 5 of the European Convention, which allows for detention of persons of unsound mind but, according to case law, only if the deprivation of liberty is outweighed by the public interest in protection.*

Conveying a patient to hospital The completion of the admission procedures gives the applicant (usually, as we have seen, the ASW) the power to convey the patient to hospital, or to delegate that power. The Code (Chapter 11) should be read before embarking on this, and you should be aware of any local agreements between social service departments, the ambulance service and the police. Taking a patient in your car without an escort is strongly discouraged. If the task is delegated to police or ambulance staff, the ASW is still in charge (Code, para. 11.4).

Admission for treatment from a criminal court We saw in Chapter 12 that a hospital order is a possible outcome following a criminal conviction. Once admitted, the patient is treated essentially the same as other patients, and the power of detention lasts an initial six months, renewable in the same way as admission for treatment under s. 3. There are slight differences in powers of discharge — see below p. 348. If a restriction order is attached, detention is lawful for however long that order lasts.

Admission for assessment or treatment from a police station There is no special procedure for admission from a police station. We saw in Chapter 12 that a doctor should be called to assess a detainee in the police station when mental disorder is suspected. From there, informal admission, or admission under the MHA, ss. 2–4, can take place. The decision whether to continue with any criminal proceedings will be taken by the police, who will probably need to defer that decision.

GUARDIANSHIP

We have seen when looking at admission for treatment that patients should not go to hospital if they can be treated in the community. But some power to direct the patient's life may be necessary, and this is where the concept of guardianship may fill the gap. The Code in para. 13.3 advises that 'ASWs and doctors should consider guardianship as a possible alternative to admission to, or continuing care in, hospital'. And in para. 13.4: 'An application for guardianship should be accompanied by a comprehensive care plan established on the basis of multi-disciplinary discussions'. A guardian can be either an individual or a social services department.

A person of any age can be admitted to a hospital either informally or compulsorily. However, age matters in guardianship. If the patient is under 16, guardianship is not available, and the parents (or other person with parental responsibility) are already the guardians. If the local authority wishes to intervene, mental disorder which the parents are unable to cope with could be grounds for care or supervision proceedings, as outlined in Chapter 7, or compulsory admission to hospital under ss. 2 and 3. Wardship may well be better suited to meeting the needs of a child of 16 or 17 (*Re F (Mental Health Act: Guardianship)* [2000] 1 FLR 192).

The application procedures for admission to guardianship are very similar to those for admission to hospital for treatment. In this case, however, the application is made not to a hospital but to a social services department (s. 11; 1983 Regulations, reg. 5). The application must be made by the ASW or nearest relative. But the mere completion of the application is not enough, unlike applications for admission to hospital (see above, p. 338). The application must then be accepted by the social services authority for the area where the proposed guardian lives, or the authority which it is proposed will be the guardian.

Procedures for an application for guardianship are otherwise the same as those for admission for treatment, which we looked at on pp. 337–39. The applicant must have seen the patient within the past 14 days, the nearest relative must be consulted and has the same power of veto, and there must be the two medical recommendations.

The grounds on which the doctors must be satisfied are slightly different from the grounds for admission to hospital (s. 7). The patient must still be suffering from one of the four mental disorders, to a degree that warrants reception into guardianship. This can be reviewed by a court, and if the grounds are not made out the guardianship order will be quashed. See *Re F* (above), which is discussed further at p. 355. The doctors must confirm that guardianship will benefit the welfare of the patient or, if not, will protect other persons. Welfare is not such a stringent requirement as the health or safety of the patient, which we have seen is the basis of admission for treatment; if the doctors think that guardianship would improve the quality of the patient's life, that is enough for reception into guardianship.

There is no requirement that the disorder be treatable, since guardianship is not, essentially, about treatment.

Alternatively, a criminal court can make a guardianship order instead of a hospital order (s. 37) (see Chapter 12). However it comes about, whether by order of a criminal court or by admission, the result of guardianship is the same.

Powers and Duties of the Guardian (s. 8 and 1983 Regulations reg. 12)
If the local authority accepts the application, the person named as guardian in the application assumes certain powers over the patient's life: to specify where the patient shall live, to require the patient to go for medical treatment, occupation, education or training, and to require whoever the patient lives with to give access to a doctor, ASW or other named person. The particular place the patient might be required to live could well be Pt III accommodation (see p. 322, above.)

There is no sanction against a patient who breaches these requirements, except the power to fetch back an absconding patient. If the patient cannot comply with the requirements then guardianship is not appropriate and the order should be discharged (Code, para. 13.8).

The 1983 Regulations, reg. 12, requires that the guardian visit the patient at least every three months, keep the social services authority informed of any changes of the patient's address, comply with any directions given by social services, and nominate a doctor to attend on the patient. Social services must arrange for the patient to be seen every three months, and by a doctor every 12 months (reg. 13).

Guardianship lasts initially for six months. The doctor in charge must review the guardianship during the last two months of any period of guardianship. If the doctor reports to the social services authority that he or she is satisfied that the conditions for continuation of guardianship are fulfilled, the guardianship is automatically renewed for six months on the first occasion, and after that for 12 months (s. 20).

Transfer from Guardianship to Hospital or Vice Versa
What happens if a patient presently under guardianship needs to be admitted to hospital, for assessment or treatment, and refuses? An application can be

made by the ASW or the nearest relative to the managers of the hospital. The procedure is similar to the original admission procedures, and in particular the same medical recommendations are required (s. 79).

The converse is a transfer from hospital detention into guardianship, either to an individual or to a social services authority. The full guardianship procedure is not necessary — if the proposed guardian and the relevant social services department agree, the hospital managers can simply authorise the transfer (s. 19; 1983 Regulations, reg. 7). Readmission to hospital after such a transfer would require consent or the usual application under the MHA, ss. 2, 3 or 4.

KEEPING THE PATIENT IN THE HOSPITAL

1. The Informal Patient

If there is time to do so before the informal patient leaves, the applicant can simply invoke the normal admission procedures. There will normally be no need for assessment, so admission is under the s. 3 treatment procedure.

But if time is short — the patient is packing his or her bags, the taxi is waiting — the informal patient can be temporarily detained under s. 5 powers.

First, the doctor in charge of treatment (or his or her delegate) can, without having to get any kind of second opinion, detain any hospital patient by writing a report to the managers of the hospital stating that detention is necessary. As soon as the report is delivered to the managers, a 72-hour power of detention commences. This then gives the authorities time to consider a compulsory admission for treatment.

Secondly, if the doctor in charge is unavailable, a six-hour detention can be made by a nurse (so long as she or he is registered for mental disorder work under the Nurses, Midwives and Health Visitors Act 1979.) In this case the power of detention begins as soon as the report is written, even before it is delivered to the managers. Again, there is no requirement for the nurse to consult anyone else.

The doctor can use this procedure to detain a patient who is in hospital for a totally unrelated matter, in which case the doctor is unlikely even to be a mental health specialist. The nurse, on the other hand, can only detain a patient admitted originally for mental disorder.

2. The Detained Patient

It is possible to convert one type of detention into another:

(a) The six-hour nurse's detention can become a 72-hour detention on receipt of the report of the doctor in charge.

(b) The 72-hour doctor's detention can become an admission for treatment or assessment by following the normal procedures.

(c) The 72-hour detention for assessment in an emergency can be converted to a 28-day detention by obtaining the second medical recommendation.

(d)   The 28-day detention for assessment can become a six-month detention for treatment under the normal procedure for admission for treatment.

(In all of these cases, any time already spent detained counts towards the new detention period.)

Review and extension of detention for treatment

Detention for treatment is the end of the road. It cannot be converted to anything more powerful. Instead there is a procedure for review and if appropriate renewal under s. 20. During the last two of the six months, the doctor in charge must do two things: first examine the patient, and, secondly, consult at least one other person who has been professionally concerned with the patient's medical treatment — such as a social worker in the hospital. The doctor must then report to the managers if he or she is satisfied that the conditions for continued detention apply. (However, if the patient came to hospital as a result of a criminal case, and a restriction order was imposed, there is no need for this review process to start until the end of the restriction period.)

The conditions for renewed detention mirror, with slight differences, the original conditions for admission for treatment:

(a)   one of the four disorders applies (it must be treatable if it is only a 'minor' disorder; if it is a major disorder, if discharged the patient would be at risk of exploitation, or unlikely to be able to care for himself or herself); *and*

(b)   detention is necessary for the health or safety of the patient or the protection of others; *and*

(c)   detention in the hospital is necessary for the treatment.

When the managers receive this report, they can detain the patient for treatment for a further six months on the first occasion, and on future occasions for a further 12 months. This review is then repeated during the last two months of each new period of detention.

Treatment while in hospital

Detention for the purposes of treatment under s. 3, or following a criminal conviction (s. 37), enables treatment to be given for the disorder that lead to the admission. 'Treatment' was held to imply a power to search patients and their property, to control and to discipline them, and even to override the objection of a doctor (*R v Broadmoor Special Hospital Authority ex parte S* (1998) *The Times*, 17 February).

A detained patient loses none of his or her human rights or civil rights, except those that are necessarily lost by the fact of the detention or by clear legal limitation (such as we see below regarding overrriding refusal of consent to specific treatments).

An example of a reduction in civil rights is the fact that the hospital can monitor the telephone calls of dangerous patients. This was ruled not to be a breach of the European Convention right (Article 8) to private life: *R (on the application of N)* v *Ashworth Special Hospital Authority* [2001] EWHC Admin 339; (2001) *The Times,* 2 June. The manner of the patient's detention may be reviewed under the European Convention on Human Rights and, since 2000, under the Human Rights Act 1998. An example of this is the case of *A* v *UK* (1980) 20 D & R 5, where a detainee in Broadmoor Hospital challenged the conditions imposed on him following his involvement in an arson incident. These included solitary confinement and deprivation of normal clothing and furniture. He alleged breach of Article 3, i.e. inhuman and degrading treatment. Although the matter was settled before final hearing, the preliminary opinion of the European Commission on Human Rights was that the complaint was admissible and the conditions of detention reviewable.

The Representation of the People Act 1983, as amended in 2000, allows all mental patients except those detained by a criminal court to vote in elections.

The basis upon which doctors normally treat patients is by consent. Where someone is too young to give consent (which is for the doctors to decide under the *Gillick* principle — see p. 71), it can be given by a parent or guardian, or by a High Court judge in wardship. But what is the situation where a mental patient withholds consent from treatment? Or the disorder is such that any consent is meaningless? Treatment in the absence of lawful authority would be an assault; so the Act clarifies the circumstances in which consent is needed or can be dispensed with. Further, it contains safeguards to try to ensure that any consent is real.

We only give a brief summary of the position; the likelihood of a local authority social worker becoming involved is small. But you need to know of these powers before admitting patients, to appreciate what the consequence of the admission may be, and to explain matters to the patient and others. The Code, para. 15.12, gives guidance on circumstances where capacity to consent may not exist.

Under the MHA, s. 57, certain drastic treatments cannot be given without the patient's informed consent; an independent specialist doctor, plus two mental health specialists who are not doctors, must vouch for the fact that the patient did understand the nature and consequences of treatment. This could involve the hospital social worker. Also, a second medical opinion is required, confirming that the treatment is appropriate. Only two treatments at present fall into this category: destruction of brain tissue or brain functioning (such as a lobotomy), and surgical implants to reduce male sex drive (1983 Regulations, reg. 16).

Lower down the scale of drastic treatments comes electro-convulsive therapy and long-term drug treatment (any regime of over three months). This can be administered only if the patient gives informed consent, or if an independent doctor agrees that it is necessary notwithstanding the lack of consent or the lack of capacity to give consent. There is no requirement for an independent specialist to confirm that any consent is informed. If treatment is to proceed without consent, the doctor providing the second opinion must have consulted two specialists who are not doctors, but can go ahead, whatever they say!

Regardless of these safeguards, the doctor in charge can administer any treatment where this is immediately necessary to save the patient's life. So long as the treatment is not irreversible, the doctor can also do anything to prevent serious deterioration or suffering by the patient, or to prevent the patient being violent or a danger to him or herself or others.

Treatments which do not relate to the mental disorder   No special rules apply to mental patients. If patients require treatment for physical ailments, their consent must be obtained. If it cannot be obtained, because of the lack of capacity of the patient, then there is a common law (i.e., judge-made, rather than statute) power to carry out any treatment necessary for the well-being of the patient. An example is the case of *F* v *West Berkshire Health Authority* [1989] 2 All ER 545. The authority sought a declaration that it would be lawful to sterilise a woman with a mental age of five who was deemed to be at risk of a pregnancy, which the doctors felt she could not cope with. The House of Lords agreed to declare this operation lawful. If the treatment is purely therapeutic, i.e., to treat a condition, the court's permission is not needed. So a mental patient suffering serious menorrhea could be given a hysterectomy even though she could not consent to it herself (*Re GF* [1992] 1 FLR 293). Not every mental patient automatically lacks the necessary understanding to give or withhold consent. In *Re C* [1994] 1 WLR 290 the patient refused to allow his gangrenous foot to be amputated. The court held that he knew what he was doing and the right to decide remained his. (His foot recovered too!)

Treatment can be to the benefit of the patient in an oblique rather than a direct manner. In *Re Y (Mental Incapacity: Bone Marrow Transplant)* [1996] 2 FLR 787, the High Court ruled that it was in the patient's best interest to donate bone marrow to her sister, whose death would distress the patient.

A person who understands what he or she is doing can give an 'advance directive', so that consent (or withholding of consent) applies even though at the time the need for treatment arises the person lacks capacity. (An advance directive would not limit the power to treat the mental illness itself, however.) See *Re C (Adult: Refusal of Medical Treatment)* [1994] 1 WLR 290; *Re AK (Adult Patient) (Medical Treatment: Consent)* [2001] 1 FLR 129.

If the patient is under 18, the proposed treatment can be authorised by the High Court (*Re M* [1988] 2 FLR 505). Any person sufficiently interested in the welfare of the young person could make the application, but normally this would be social services, after liaison with the medical staff.

No permission of the court is required, apparently, for an abortion for a mental patient, if doctors consider the criteria of the Abortion Act 1967 to be be met (risk to the mother) (*Re SG* [1991] 2 FLR 329).

DISCHARGE FROM HOSPITAL OR GUARDIANSHIP

Discharge of a Detained Patient

An informal patient can discharge himself or herself, unless this is prevented by admission or detention procedures described above. So we must consider how the detained patient can be discharged before the detention period has expired.

Where patients are detained for assessment or treatment the courts have declared that they should be discharged as soon as they are found not to be suffering from a mental disorder (*Kynaston* v *Secretary of State for Home Affairs* (1981) 73 Cr App R 281). So the 28-day, or six-month periods, are not to be seen as time to serve, but maximum periods.

Who can exercise this power of discharge? Section 23 gives the power to the managers, the doctor in charge, or the nearest relative. But the nearest relative has less power to discharge than the doctor or managers: first, he or she has no power of discharge during the period of a hospital order made by a criminal court (s. 23 and Sch. 1); second, the nearest relative must always give 72 hours' notice before exercising the power of discharge. During that period the discharge can be vetoed (see below). If the patient is still under a restriction order following a criminal conviction, even the doctors or the managers need the approval of the Secretary of State for Health before discharging a patient (s. 23 and Sch. 1).

The criteria for discharge are not stated in s. 23, but the case of *Kynaston* implies that those in charge should constantly be checking to ascertain whether the initial admission criteria are still met; they should not wait until the s. 20 review which takes place in the last two months of a detention for treatment.

Discharge Subject to Supervision

If the doctor in charge believes that the patient, on discharge, is a risk to himself or herself or to others, or open to serious exploitation, there are powers under the Mental Health (Patients in the Community) Act 1995 to obtain a supervision requirement, technically known as 'aftercare under supervision' (MHA, s. 25, as amended).

As the supervision of after-care gives a measure of control over the patient, there is an application and consultation procedure to attempt to ensure that powers to direct the patient's life are not obtained where it is unnecessary. Further details are set out below at p. 312.

Discharge from Guardianship

Guardianship can be terminated before the end of the six- or 12-month periods by the nearest relative, the social services authority, or the doctor in charge (s. 23) — but not by the individual guardian unless he or she is also the nearest relative.

But where the guardianship order was made by a criminal court, discharge under s. 23 can only be made by the social services department, and not by the doctor in charge or the nearest relative (Sch. 1, Pt I, paras 2 and 8).

Prevention of Discharge by the Nearest Relative

The doctors may not agree with the nearest relative that the patient should be discharged from hospital. They have 72 hours to decide their position. If the doctor in charge wishes to veto the discharge, he or she must submit a report to the managers of the hospital stating that the patient would, if discharged, be a danger to himself or herself or to others. If the managers agree with this view, this blocks the discharge (s. 25). In addition to risking having their decision overridden, nearest relatives have to think hard about even trying to discharge the patient; if the doctor reports against discharge, the nearest relative is barred from discharging the patient for the next six months. Neither the 72-hour notice period, nor the right of veto, applies in discharge of guardianship by the nearest relative, however.

Can an ASW block discharge, either from hospital or guardianship, by the nearest relative? The answer is yes, but unlike a doctor's immediate power to block discharge from hospital, the ASW must go through the more complex route of applying to the county court to displace the nearest relative (see above). Under s. 29, as soon as this application is filed with the court (which could be during the nearest relative's 72-hour notice period) the discharge by the nearest relative is blocked until the court has made a decision. It will probably be too late to use this power to block discharge from guardianship as there is no 72-hour notice requirement.

Discharge by the Mental Health Review Tribunal (MHRT)

The tribunal is empowered to order a discharge from hospital and also from guardianship (MHA, Pt V). Procedures are governed by the Mental Health Review Tribunal Rules 1983 (SI 1983 No. 942).

Tribunals, as we saw in Chapter 3, are in theory more simple, less orientated towards formal legal procedures, than courts. In the case of the MHRT this has long been a myth, and as a result of campaigns waged for the rights of patients, it is now recognised that applicants should have publicly funded specialist legal representation. A solicitor appearing before the MHRT has to be a member of an approved panel of specialists, for there will be a need to marshall evidence of fact and medical opinion, and cross-examine witnesses, including experts in mental health. The ASW will need to consult their own legal department.

Who can apply to the MHRT? It will be either the patient, or the nearest relative who has been barred from discharging the patient. The application is submitted to one of the four regional MHRTs and must be in writing; a letter will do (1983 Rules, r. 3), although forms are available.

It is important for any applicant to be aware of the time limits which apply to MHRT applications. These are set out in Table 14.3.

At any MHRT hearing there must be an up-to-date social circumstances report, which is usually submitted by the hospital social worker. Where the application relates to a discharge from guardianship, the social services department has three weeks to prepare a statement of information, including the factual background and social circumstances, together with the author's opinion on whether the patient should be discharged (1983 Rules, r. 6).

The task of the MHRT essentially is to consider whether the original criteria for detention or guardianship are still justified. It will take into account not just the evidence heard, but also a medical examination carried out by the medically qualified panel member (1983 Rules, r. 11). If it is satisfied that the criteria are no longer justified, it can order the discharge of

Table 14.3   Time Limits for Applications to the MHRT (MHA, ss. 66 and 68)

Application by the nearest relative

Discharge of patient blocked by the doctor in charge: within 28 days from the date of being informed.
Nearest relative displaced by county court order: within 12 months from that order, and thereafter once every 12 months.
Patient detained under a hospital order: not before six months; once during the second six-month period, thereafter once during every 12-month period.
Patient under a restriction order: as for hospital orders.

Application by the patient

Within 14 days of an admission for assessment.
Within six months of an admission for treatment/reception into guardianship.
Supervised after-care: no time limit.

the patient — either now, or at a specified date (s. 72). (Failure to order discharge where there is no further mental disorder has been declared wrong by the European Court of Human Rights: *Johnson* v *UK* [1997] 27 EHRR 296.) The Tribunal can also recommend leave of absence from the hospital (s. 73). Discharge can be subject to conditions, such as residence, so long as the conditions can be met reasonably soon.

But the grounds on which an MHRT can order release are broad, in that it can discharge a person even where there would be grounds for admission under s. 3. The MHRT must discharge if the mental disorder has ceased or if it would be otherwise appropriate. The criteria are set out in s. 72. It must discharge the patient if the treatability test is no longer met (see above, p. 341) (*Reid* v *Secretary of State for Scotland* [1999] 1 All ER 481).

Where a patient is discharged by the MHRT, compulsory readmission, even on the same day, under the s. 3 procedure appears to be lawful if the proper application procedure is used (*R* v *Managers of South Western Hospital ex parte M* [1994] 1 All ER 161). This decision may be rendered obsolete, however, by the Human Rights Act 1998, which is discussed below.

Where the patient is under a criminal court restriction order, discharge by the Tribunal can be made conditional. A conditional discharge then gives the Home Secretary a power of recall. Conditions commonly relate to residence, treatment and supervision. A patient who has been conditionally discharged may be sectioned under MHA, s. 3, and recalled by the Home Secretary (*R* v *N.W. London Mental Health Trust ex parte Stewart* (1996) *The Times*, 15 August). Even after such a further detention under s. 3, he or she may be recalled to the hospital chosen by the Home Secretary (*Dlodlo* v *MHRT for*

South Thames Region [1996] 8 CL 474). So the Home Secretary's powers remain undiminished.

(Guidance on recall of discharged patients is set out in Circular HSG(93)20: Recall of Mentally Disordered Patients. Any ASW who has not read this before taking part in a recall should do so.)

If the patient is detained for treatment beyond the first six months, and no one makes an application to the MHRT, the hospital managers must themselves refer the case to the Tribunal. There must be a further reference not more than three years later — so no patient should languish unnoticed for more than that time.

Human rights and the MHRT Article 5 of the European Convention on Human Rights requires there to be a mechanism for challenging the lawfulness of the detention of any person. The existence of the MHRT fulfils the form of such requirement, but does the practice of the Tribunal meet the substance of the right?

The case of *Winterwerp* v *Netherlands* [1979] 2 EHRR 387, laid down a number of tests, including a requirement for the state to prove the grounds for detention. Yet the MHRT has no duty to release unless it is satisfied that the person does not suffer from the mental condition. The negatives in the last sentence essentially mean that the Tribunal can, in theory, wait until it is proved that the condition no longer exists before ordering release, putting the burden of proving this on to the detained patient. This provision of the MHA has recently been successfully challenged in the case of *R (on the application of H)* v *Mental Health Review Tribunal for North East London* [2001] EWCA 415; (2001) *The Times*, 2 April. In fact the Court of Appeal declared it to be incompatible with Article 5, so there is a good prospect of amending legislation.

Another challenge may arise under the three-year automatic referral to the MHRT discussed above. This period may be too long, given that the patient may lack the capacity to make an application to the MHRT himself or herself. It could be argued that three years without being able to challenge the lawfulness of the detention is effectively a denial of the right itself.

Further, any recall of a restricted patient by the Secretary of State would be open to challenge if there has not been a proper examination of the grounds for renewed detention. Even with consideration of the evidence, recall by a politician on grounds not tested in a court or tribunal seems to amount to a denial of Article 5 rights.

ADDITIONAL POWERS TO DETAIN

Patients Absent from Hospital
A doctor in charge of a patient's treatment can give leave of absence under s. 17, and can recall a patient from leave. The power to renew the period of detention (see above, p. 345) can be used if the patient is still receiving some in-patient treatment. (*Barker* v *Barking Havering and Brentwood Community NHS Trust* (1998) *The Times*, 14 October, CA). But if the patient is on leave without treatment, renewed detention is impossible and, if grounds arise, a fresh application for admission would be needed.

However, powers to detain a patient who is absent from hospital without leave, or who fails to live at the place where their guardian requires, are more important. A detained hospital patient absent without leave can be detained and returned by an ASW, a member of the hospital staff, a police constable, or any person authorised by the managers of the hospital. A guardianship patient absent from the place where the guardian requires him or her to live can also be detained and returned by any of this list of people, except a delegate of the hospital managers (s. 18).

However, the power to return the patient lapses after whichever of the following happens last:

(a)   six months have elapsed since the 'escape'; or
(b)   the period of compulsory detention has expired anyway.

A patient can therefore be brought back to hospital even though the compulsory detention would have elapsed. There is then a one-week power of detention (MHA, s. 21, as amended in 1995) during which the hospital can consider extending detention under s. 20(3) (renewal of detention for treatment), or s. 20(6) (renewal of guardianship) or s. 3 (conversion of admission for assessment to admission for treatment by making fresh application).

Police Powers of Detention of Mentally Disordered Person
At the beginning of the section on mental disorder, we talked about someone threatening suicide or violence. Your natural instinct may be to call the police. That is probably correct. The police can arrest someone committing any kind of offence that is likely to be threatening, and in particular a person committing a breach of the peace. But the police also have powers to deal with the mentally disordered.

Section 136 enables a police officer to detain in a place of safety any person found in a public place who appears to be mentally disordered. Every police authority must have a policy on using this power, agreed between the police, social services and the health authority (Code, para. 10.1). A public place is defined in case law as somewhere to which the public have access (e.g., the landings in a block of flats — Knox v Anderton (1983) 76 Cr App R 156). The officer must consider that detention is necessary either in the interests of the mentally disordered person, or to protect any other person. The place of safety can be a police station, a hospital, Pt III accommodation provided by the local authority (see Chapter 13, p. 321), a mental nursing home or any other suitable place. 'The purpose of removing a person to a place of safety . . . is to enable him or her to be examined by a doctor and interviewed by an ASW and for any necessary arrangements for his care and treatment to be made' (Code, para. 10.2). The Code suggests that the best place of safety is the hospital (para. 10.5). Any person detained in a police station has the right to a lawyer under s. 58 of PACE 1984 (see p. 269). This power of detention lasts only 72 hours, and any longer detention requires an admission for assessment or treatment.

The power to detain in a place of safety is not given to an ASW. There is no alternative to using the police if you cannot yourself deal safely with the situation.

Searching Out and Protecting the Mentally Disordered

Section 135 enables a magistrates' court to issue a warrant for the police to enter premises, by force if necessary, and remove a mentally disordered person to a place of safety for up to 72 hours. Anyone, including a social worker, can apply. You will have to satisfy the magistrates that there is evidence that either:

(a)   a person suffering from a mental disorder has been or is being ill-treated, neglected or kept otherwise than under proper control, or is living alone and unable to look after himself or herself; or

(b)   you are being denied access to a patient who has absconded from hospital or the place the patient is required to live by the guardian; or in respect of whom the proper admission procedures have been completed.

AFTER-CARE OF THE MENTAL PATIENT

Where a patient is discharged from detention in hospital or from guardianship, s. 117 imposes a duty jointly on the health authority and social services to provide after-care services for as long as they are needed. The authorities should cooperate with suitable voluntary agencies. There is no statutory definition of what level of after-care is required. However, DoH Circular of 5 February 1995, 'After-care Form for the Discharge of Psychiatric Patients', sets out a good practice checklist for entering details such as the patient's nominated contact and details of the after-care plan. All discharged patients must have an individual care plan drawn up with an identified keyworker who will ensure that it is implemented.

We have seen in the last chapter that services can, or must, be provided to people who need them by reason of age, mental disorder or handicap. For example, a number of people in need of Pt III accommodation will be old, physically unable to manage, and mentally disordered. Support and accommodation is therefore available under the NAA, ss. 21 and 29 (see above).

After-care under supervision

Under the Mental Health (Patients in the Community) Act 1995, there is a new regime called 'after-care under supervision'. The hospital can now require a discharged patient to cooperate with a treatment plan under MHA, s. 117. Social services and the health authority will draw up this plan together. The patient who does not cooperate may be readmitted under the existing MHA powers (see above, p. 340), or be taken to hospital or submitted to other treatment compulsorily by a supervisor.

The power to supervise the patient's after-care — as contrasted with the existing power to work with the discharged patient voluntarily — is set out in the MHA, s. 25. It is obtained on the application of the hospital, made to the health authority responsible for the after-care services. The local authority must be consulted, and the application must be supported by both a doctor and an ASW. The application must include an after-care plan which names the doctor and the patient's supervisor after discharge. Social services will be closely involved in preparing this plan. The power lasts six months, renewable for six months and then a year at a time. (The health authority responsible for the patient's community care can bring it to an end earlier if the power is no longer needed.)

A patient who objects to receiving supervised after-care may apply to the MHRT under MHA, s. 66.

How does supervised after-care overlap with guardianship? The answer is that while the objectives of guardianship and supervised after-care overlap, the legal regimes do not. Indeed, if the patient in after-care is received into guardianship, supervised after-care terminates.

Guardianship is essentially a means of providing help independent of compulsory admission to hospital. Supervised after-care aims to keep the former detained patient out of hospital after release. Also the procedure for applying is different, particularly with regard to who is the applicant (ASW for guardianship, hospital for supervised after-care) and who the application is addressed to (local authority for guardianship, health authority for supervised after-care). The other key difference is that supervised after-care gives stronger enforcement powers than guardianship. The social services and health authority who are jointly responsible for the after-care under MHA, s. 117, can tell the patient where to live, to attend for treatment, occupation, education or training, and to let any person authorised by the supervisor see the patient. The supervisor can 'take and convey' (i.e., force) the patient to achieve these ends. If the patient still does not cooperate, there are no further powers, and compulsory re-detention may be necessary.

Lastly, whose job is it to supervise? The supervisor must be a named individual, under the amended MHA, s. 117 defined as 'a person professionally concerned with any of the after-care services'. This does not automatically mean a social worker; in theory the doctor in charge could double up as the supervisor (MHA, s. 34 as amended). The responsibility for ensuring that someone is appointed is actually that of the health authority, not the local authority (MHA, s. 117(2)).

POWERS TO CONTROL PEOPLE NOT COVERED BY THE MHA

You would be forgiven for thinking that the powers of compulsory intervention in the lives of vulnerable people would be clearly set out in the legislation. Two recent cases, taken together, cast doubt on this. They both concern the same mentally incapacitated young woman. She was 17 years old at the time of the first hearing — too old for a care order. The local authority tried guardianship as its preferred way of removing her from a sexually abusive home environment. There was no doubt that she suffered from a 'state of arrested or incomplete development of mind' under the MHA, s. 1, but her wish to return home, according to the Court of Appeal, could not amount to 'seriously irresponsible conduct'. So guardianship was not available, leaving an obvious gap in the law in terms of affording protection to such persons (*Re F (Mental Health Act: Guardianship)* [2000] 1 FLR 192).

The local authority tried another approach, using an old, previously thought defunct, common law doctrine of 'necessity'. The Court of Appeal in *Re F (Adult Patient)* [2000] 2 FLR 512, held that it had the power to make a declaration as to the living arrangements to be made for the mentally incapacitated person, allowing the local authority control. This would be in F's best interests.

See also powers of compulsory removal from home under community care legislation (at p. 325 above).

LIABILITY OF HEALTH AND SOCIAL WORK PROFESSIONALS

We mentioned in the previous chapter the case of *Clunis*, where a mental patient who had killed a stranger wanted to sue the health authority for not controlling his condition, but was refused leave (see p. 318). We mentioned that the whole area of law is developing, in that the rights of children whose needs were not met by social services departments, leaving them exposed to abuse, to sue those departments have been approved by the European Court of Human Rights. The same principles apply in the mental health field. The most recent case is *Palmer* v *Tees Health Authority* (unreported), 2 July 1999 (CA). The hospital trust had cared for a man for several years, but notwithstanding this the man had sexually assaulted and murdered the four-year-old daughter of Mrs Palmer. The Court of Appeal rejected her claim for damages on the basis that the hospital, in law, did not owe her a duty of care. Whether this judgment would withstand a Human Rights Act challenge is, in our view, very uncertain.

MENTAL HEALTH LAW REFORM

The present Mental Health Act is a consolidation of legislation designed in the 1950's, when residential treatment was the norm. Care and treatment in the community is now usual, and the 2000 White Paper, 'Reforming the Mental Health Act' envisages a complete rewriting of mental health laws. It also proposes new powers in relation to dangerous individuals. The key elements of new legislation are likely to include:

- *Entry into the mental health system to start with assessment, which covers risk and need.*
- *Drawing up a 28-day care plan which includes powers of compulsory treatment.*
- *Any further compulsory treatment to be authorised by a new tribunal.*
- *'Care and treatment' order to be based around a plan approved by the tribunal.*
- *Compulsory powers to last for up to six months on the first two occasions, then 12 months.*
- *Compulsory powers may be exercised in the community or a hospital.*
- *Compulsory powers available for dangerous individuals who are not treatable.*

A date for bringing forward this legislation or for implementation is not yet known.

CHANGES IN THE LAW RELATING TO MENTAL INCAPACITY

The Lord Chancellor has also issued a Green Paper on how best to protect the interests of those who cannot make decisions for themselves. His intention is to clarify the law to define incapacity, require all decisions to be in the person's best interests, to clarify the law on advance directives to terminate medical treatments (living wills — an area of law currently requiring some clear legislation), to tighten up the law on enduring powers of attorney, and to impose on social services a duty to investigate abuse of such people, together with powers to protect them. No legislation has yet been brought forward.

USEFUL WEBSITES

www.markwalton.net — Gives access to a wide range of materials, including the legislation and Code of Practice.

www.mind.org.uk — Access to a range of helpful materials to help those with mental health problems.

PART II THE LAW FOR SOCIAL WORKERS' CLIENTS

FIFTEEN
Introduction to Advice Work

This part of the book looks at areas of law where you do not have a statutory responsibility to take action. For example, if the mother of the child who is your client asks you how to get her welfare benefits sorted out, or what to do about the violence of her husband, you do not, as a social worker, normally have a statutory duty to play a part in the legal process that follows.

ADVISING CLIENTS AND NON-CLIENTS

But why are you giving advice in the first place? Many social workers assume that they have a role to give advice, to assist people in disadvantaged circumstances, but without knowing how this fits into their statutory duties. But clearly — at least we assume this is a clear starting point — social services are not in the business of giving advice to everyone who needs it. They do not have the resources and it is not their duty. The answer to this question takes us back to a question raised earlier — who is your client? Your client will be someone to whom you owe some kind of statutory duty, but you will inevitably form a relationship with someone looking after or involved with your client, such as a carer of the elderly, or a parent. And when you have a statutory role to play in the client's affairs, you will normally find a supportive role is required towards the client, the client's family, or the carer. We have seen this explicitly spelled out in relation to keeping children from being the subject of court proceedings (Chapter 4) which involves supporting the family, and in relation to providing services to vulnerable individuals (Chapter 13). By and large, when we use the term 'client' in this chapter it is the lawyer's client we are thinking of, and not your statutory client.

Support includes advice. And problems include legal problems. To give advice — even if the advice consists only of referring someone to another adviser — means knowing something about the legal process and the relevant problem area.

POINTING PEOPLE IN THE RIGHT DIRECTION

If a person has a legal problem, to whom does he or she turn? To say simply 'a specialist adviser' is wishful thinking. People turn to their friends, family, colleagues, and people they see as authoritative, like doctors and social workers. The problem is mulled over in their minds, and they will air it to a number of people while working out what to do about it. (If you doubt this, and have no experience of going to see a lawyer, ask yourself how many times you discuss an ailment with someone else before deciding to make an appointment with your doctor.) The first adviser they approach may well not be the solicitor or advice centre worker. They first seek informal advice, and if you have built up a relationship of trust with them, they may turn to you. They turn to you because they are not yet ready to take the step of seeing a legal adviser. Alternatively, you are the person who reveals to them that they have a legal problem and then they turn to you for help.

What happens at this stage is very important. For a long time lawyers, politicians, and pressure groups of all political persuasions, have identified something called 'unmet legal need'. Why this need is unmet is sometimes because there are not enough legal services available at a price people can afford. But this has never been the whole answer; it is also because people find it hard to go to a lawyer or an agency. They find it daunting, they have fears about the consequences, the costs, the formality; it is not, as they see it, their world. Having been practising solicitors and voluntary advisers, we have both frequently experienced the case of the client who makes an appointment, and is never seen again. We suspect that this is rarely because the problem has been resolved, but more frequently because the fear of the legal process has become too great.

Therefore a task of the social worker is to ensure that the legal problem is identified as such; that the fear of seeing an adviser is reduced; that, where possible, arrangements are made with the appropriate adviser for an appointment; and, as far as possible without getting out of your depth or making over-optimistic pronouncements about what a legal adviser can do, that some sort of explanation is given as to the advice and assistance the specialist is able to give. We do not think, unless you are trained in a particular field, that it is appropriate for you to give the advice itself. The law is complex, and certainly, in this section, we aim at best to give an overview of each area considered rather than to give you the tools a specialist adviser would have available.

Although we have divided the contents of this book into sections on statutory roles, and non-statutory roles, this is somewhat of an over-simplification. For example, in Chapter 12 on criminal procedure you saw the social worker playing many roles; in the police station, you have a role to play specified in the Police and Criminal Evidence Act codes, and in presenting your report to court before sentencing, your task is defined by statute. But at the same time, you have many opportunities, both in and out of the police station, to advise your clients about their relationship to the criminal law. In Chapter 19 on unlawful discrimination, you will see that it may, at times, be appropriate to advise a client of remedies available to him or her for an act of discrimination; but the chapter also tells you how the law defines your own professional behaviour, and your authority's duties to avoid discrimination and promote good practice. Your statutory duty to certain vulnerable groups is to provide support services, which by definition includes advice work.

Nevertheless, we hope that, having read Part I, you will usually be able to distinguish between an action that you carry out as part of your statutory duty, and a situation where your role is limited to advising and assisting.

Before we start to look at each area of law, chapter by chapter, there is one vital topic often relevant to all of them: the legal profession and the legal aid system. We frequently end up saying that specialist advice is necessary so you need to know something about the sources of such advice.

LAWYERS AND ADVISERS

Two Views

I don't think the English public appreciate just how lucky they are with the legal profession in this country. (Heather Hallett QC, 1998 Chair of the Bar Council, *Law Society Gazette*, 28 January 1998, at p. 24)

[Law is] a profession obsessively preoccupied with its own purity and solidarity at the expense of the common good which it exists to serve. (Ann Abrahams, Legal Services Ombudsman, (1998) August 1998, *Legal Action* 8)

Choosing a Lawyer

A word of warning. Just like social workers, there are good lawyers, experienced lawyers, hard-working lawyers, and their opposites. In highly motivated firms or advice agencies, you may still find the occasional person in whom you have little confidence. You are not assisting your client by making a referral to such a person — you are merely passing the buck. If you do not know who to refer to, ask around, among colleagues, or contact the local CAB or law centre, which tend to have a good idea of who is good in which field. Keep a contacts list.

All solicitors are obliged to advise clients whether they might be eligible for legal aid, which we are about to discuss. But some firms are far more familiar with legal aid work than others, and you should find out who these are by consulting colleagues or looking at the Community Legal Service (CLS) directory (see p. 367), or the CLS website (see p. 362). Your department should have directories, as should any library. The Legal Services Commission operates a system of contracts for legal advice and assistance work. Contracts are only given to those firms of solicitors which meet quality standards and which specialise in a particular area or areas of law. For example, a firm may be contracted to give specialist advice on crime, housing, family law, etc., or may be contracted for advice on one area only, such as immigration.

Solicitors and Barristers

These are the qualified lawyers, who are allowed to conduct cases and appear in court. Solicitors practise either alone or in partnership, and employ staff both for secretarial assistance and as advisers. So long as a solicitor supervises his or her staff, advisers do not have to be qualified as solicitors. Non-qualified staff, such as trainee solicitors or 'clerks' (who may have taken exams in law to become 'legal executives') may be excellent — but note that a client is entitled to know whether he or she is being dealt with by a solicitor or not. The names of the partners in a law firm are set out on the firm's notepaper. Legal executives can now qualify as advocates in the lower courts, but still need to work in solicitors' offices.

There are currently some 64,000 solicitors in private practice in England and Wales, operating from about 14,000 offices. Another 15,000 work in local government, industry or advice agencies.

Most solicitors cannot represent clients in the Crown Court or High Court, and have to 'brief' a barrister to do so. However, a small number of solicitors have obtained the right to appear in all courts.

There are some 10,000 barristers (also referred to as counsel). They are allowed to appear in all courts. They cannot at present be approached directly by the client, so they get most of their work from referrals from solicitors, who will choose from the available barristers which one they prefer for the case. (The preferred barrister may be replaced, to the anguish of client and solicitor, at the last minute because another case did not finish in time.) Barristers are seen, by and large, as the specialists — though many solicitors are in fact highly specialised too. Employment of a barrister inevitably increases the expense of a case, but if a client is legally aided, the barrister's costs are usually included.

Sometimes a person's legal problem consists of dissatisfaction with a solicitor. The client tells horrific stories of delay and incompetence. It may be that there is another side to the story, and the delays were inevitable and the incompetence an illusion. However, if this is how the client feels about it then the relationship with the solicitor is not working; at the very least, the solicitor has failed to explain fully what is happening. In any event, clients of solicitors are free to change to someone else, and should be told of this right. If they are receiving civil legal aid, the Legal Services Commission has to agree to the change. If a criminal client is legally aided, it will be at the court's discretion whether he or she can change solicitor. A reasonable request should not be refused. If the client is paying privately, the first solicitor has to be paid before the papers can be released to the new solicitor, which is a source of considerable anguish to someone who thinks he or she is paying for incompetence. (The bill can be challenged, but this takes time, which often cannot be afforded at the time of waiting for the papers.)

Complaints concerning solicitors can be made to the Office for the Supervision of Solicitors (OSS), Victoria Court, 8 Dormer Place, Leamington Spa, Warwickshire CV32 5AE (tel. 01926 820082), to whom written complaints can be sent. The OSS is funded by the Law Society, the solicitors' professional body. The client should first have attempted to resolve the complaint through the solicitor's firm's own internal complaints procedure. The OSS can refer the case to a disciplinary tribunal, and can also check the quality of a solicitor's work and order him or her to rectify mistakes, or to reduce the bill for shoddy work and to pay compensation of up to £5000. Solicitors' costs can also be challenged by a checking procedure called 'assessment', which is carried out by a judge or an officer of the court. A negligent solicitor can be sued to recover money lost as a result of that negligence — for example where the solicitor's negligent advice has meant abandoning a promising case. A person dissatisfied with his or her solicitor should seek advice from a law centre or CAB, or change to a new solicitor (but the new solicitor will have to be carefully selected to give the client confidence; anyone thinking of suing a solicitor will have the problem of finding a good solicitor to take on the job. The OSS has a list, and anyone on that list will advise without charge in a one-hour interview. After that, unfortunately, the work will have to be paid for or done on a 'no win, no fee' basis.)

Citizens Advice Bureaux
There are 2,000 CABs in England, Wales and Northern Ireland. Although there is a national federation, each CAB area operates independently, and will determine its own priorities. Some are able to provide not just advice but representation, which is of significance particularly in the areas which legal aid does not reach (see below p. 363). In the law relating to welfare benefits the CAB is often more specialised than solicitors.

CABs are dependent on large numbers of volunteers, in addition to their paid staff; but the volunteers are carefully selected and trained.

Law Centres
There is a much smaller network over 50 law centres, mainly in urban areas. Although there is a national Law Centres' Federation, the centres are each wholly independent, accountable to their own management committees, and each funded in whatever way it can raise money, many from local government, some from central government, and most topped up by income from Legal Services Commission contracts.

Law centres always employ at least one solicitor, and may also employ a barrister. They can represent a client in court, or instruct an external barrister. Law centres fight hard for their independence, and those that are funded by local government try to insist that the grant has no strings attached, so that they should be able to take action against the hand that feeds them. You should not be surprised to find a law centre occasionally taking on a case against your department.

Law centres try to meet the 'unmet legal need' we have referred to. But because they are limited in number and resources, they have to take difficult decisions about the types of case they will take on. Many prefer to adopt a campaigning and educational role, to make people aware of rights, to help communities to organise, and therefore have to limit severely the number of individual cases they can take on; most will be delighted to take on a test case if winning it would benefit others who they do not have the resources to help individually. Therefore you need to know what your local law centre can do, and what types of cases it takes on. Most publish leaflets about what they do, and when they are open to the public. Some offer training sessions to people like social workers and housing advisers. Some are more effective, of course, than others.

Other Agencies

Other than CABs and law centres, a large variety of individual agencies has grown to fill a particular need — the Federation of Independent Advice Centres has 2500 member organisations. Their website (www.fiac.org) gives useful information on how to find the relevant agency for a particular service. Some social services authorites operate specialised welfare benefit advice units, or provide grants to agencies offering such advice. There are particular local and national organisations to assist the homeless, the young, the unemployed, or people of different ethnic backgrounds. Usually these organisations operate in the knowledge of what each other is doing, and ensure that CABs and libraries have details of their work. You will need to build up your own list of appropriate referral agencies.

Agencies that employ solicitors can represent a client in courts as well as tribunals, so they are like law centres. Those that do not employ solicitors can still represent clients in tribunals, provided they have an adviser who specialises in the relevant area.

There are also national bodies involved in particular rights issues, such as the Child Poverty Action Group (94 White Lion Street, London N1 9PF, tel. 0207 837 7979) and the Children's Legal Centre (University of Essex, Wivenhoe Park, Colchester, tel. 01206 873820). The CLC gives legal advice to children and those concerned with children — see www.2.essex.ac.uk/clc.

Choosing the Right Agency

We have mentioned the fact that clients miss appointments. It is also very easy for a client to 'get lost' between one agency and another. There are three ways of reducing this risk: first, to make sure the client understands why help of a particular sort is needed; second, to send the client to the appropriate agency first time, so there are no further referrals; and third, to contact the agency yourself and discuss whether you have in fact identified the best place to refer your client to, and make an appointment for the client while the client is still with you. All advice agencies or solicitors receiving Legal Services Commission funding must be aware of the services provided by other agencies and make appropriate referrals. The idea is that for each local community there will be a 'seamless referral network'.

Self-help

The Government believes that part of the solution to the problem of unmet demand for legal services is better information about law. As well as putting more and more information on to the Internet (new Acts of Parliament, Consultation Papers, etc.), it has instructed the Legal Services Commission to put information about the law directly on to the Internet for public consultation. The Commission's website for getting information about who can give what advice and, in due course, about the law itself, is at www.justask.org. There are already several websites for those with access to the Internet, most linked to further sources. A useful starting point is www.venables.co.uk.

SOLICITORS' COSTS AND THE LEGAL AID SYSTEM

The Right to Assistance

The right to a fair trial, in both civil and criminal matters, is a fundamental human right, and with the enactment of the Human Rights Act 1998, is now part of English law (European Convention on Human Rights, Article 6). The Government intends to meet its obligations under this article in part (we say 'in part' because providing fair court procedures is another major element) through legal services to be provided by, or obtained by, the new Criminal Defence Service and the Community Legal Service. The right does not automatically lead to representation in every case. Existing human rights case law shows that the European Court of Human Rights balances cost, the means of parties, the importance of the case and its complexity. There are few instances of European states being found in breach of this right.

Solicitors' Costs

One of the greatest reasons for fearing lawyers is costs. This is not surprising since fees of well over £200 per hour are mentioned in the newspapers. The cost of non-commercial solicitors will be around half that, or less for non-partners, but still a daunting figure. The agencies we have looked at above do not charge, though they may collect a contribution if using the legal aid scheme.

But solicitors in private practice are commercial concerns, and seek to make a profit out of their work. How will the client fare on crossing the threshold of a solicitor's office?

Some solicitors offer a free initial half-hour interview. In this way the client can have a preliminary discussion about the problem, and the costs implications of taking it further, without worrying about open-ended costs. It is hard, even for an experienced solicitor, to predict what the eventual costs outcome may be. If a case is won, the usual way of dealing with the costs is for the loser to pay the winner, so long as the legal costs are reasonable. But of course there is never a certainty of winning, and even after a great victory, the loser may not have the funds to meet the costs ordered. And in some cases, matrimonial in particular, there is no 'winner' and usually no costs order. But at the very least, a solicitor should discuss with the client what it will cost to take particular initial steps, and how his or her costs are calculated (which is normally an hourly rate). The client is entitled to this information but must insist if it is not volunteered. The solicitor must confirm it in writing. The government has talked about legislating to restrict costs to the amount quoted — 'Modernising Justice' White Paper.

LEGAL AID

The Government spends over a billion pounds each year on legal aid. Civil legal aid is administered by the Legal Services Commission and is dealt with first. Criminal legal aid, as far as the applicant is concerned, is handled by the courts. The Government is keen to prioritise its expenditure on legal aid, and it does this in many ways. The means test is one important way, and the refusal of legal aid for some types of legal problem is another. A third is the likely refusal if there is any other way the person could find to pay for legal representation. If the person could fund the case through legal expenses insurance, trades union membership or 'no win, no fee' arrangements, legal aid is likely to be refused.

The term 'legal aid' has been since 1949 a well-understood 'brand name' for publicly-funded legal services for individual clients. As conceived in the idealism of the post-war welfare state, the aim was that clients should receive exactly the same service whether funded by the state or privately. So legal aid was grafted on to existing solicitors' firms and barristers' practices. A client with a potential or actual legal case would have to pass two tests before legal aid was granted: a means test and a merits test (known in criminal cases as an 'interests of justice' test). The means test was initially quite generous, so that even people in salaried employment could secure help (subject to a requirement to make contributions towards the cost when their disposable income or capital reached prescribed limits). The merits test for a civil case was intended to replicate the process whereby a person would decide whether to finance a case out of their own money — would a person paying privately pay for the legal costs?

Legal aid was restricted to court cases, and was not available for tribunal cases. But in 1949, tribunals, such as social security, mental health or employment tribunals, either did not exist or handled small numbers of cases, and the intention was to extend legal aid to these as resources became available. When the extension happened, it was quite radical. In 1970 a 'green form' scheme was introduced. Any person who wanted advice on any aspect of English law which affected them could approach any solicitor for an on-the-spot means assessment; if they passed the means test they could immediately get two hours of a solicitor's time, for advice or assistance but not representation. It also saw the establishment of duty solicitor schemes at court in criminal cases, where everyone on their first appearance in custody would be entitled to assistance, followed in the 1980s by a similar scheme for advice during questioning in police stations, again not means tested.

The effect was a massive expansion of the availability of solicitors and barristers, and an increase in Government expenditure. Following a period in the 1980s and early 1990s when the means criteria became increasingly restrictive, a series of reforms started, with the intention of changing the system from a reactive one, where every demand that fits the criteria must be met, to a planned one, where services are provided according to an assessment of the need for the service in the particular locality. That system is now falling into place, but the transformation is, from the client's perspective, still gradual. The basic elements we have outlined above are in place: an advice scheme, a representation scheme, and, by and large, the exclusion of tribunals. (The Scottish Executive has, by contrast, decided that to deny funded assistance for tribunal representation for unusually difficult cases where the applicant is particularly vulnerable could be challenged as a human rights breach under Article 6 of the Convention.)

The term 'legal aid', perhaps regrettably, will be gradually discarded for the harder to grasp concept of Legal Services Commission publicly-funded legal services. However, at the moment it is still widely used to describe the range of publicly-funded services to help people obtain legal assistance.

The Legal Services Commission

The Access to Justice Act 1999 replaced the Legal Aid Board with a Legal Services Commission. This organisation has two arms: a Community Legal Service (CLS), responsible for advice and assistance in civil matters, and a Criminal Defence Service. This new body is required by the 1999 Act to establish provision of legal services in civil and criminal matters. We will discuss each in turn below.

Civil Legal Aid

The word 'civil' in this context means any assistance out of public funds which is for a non-criminal legal problem. Civil legal aid, for our purposes, can be divided into two concepts. First, there is Legal Help, which means advice and assistance with a legal problem but not representation in a court or tribunal. Legal Help is the flagship of the CLS, which aims to bring all providers, whether voluntary agencies (e.g., Citizens Advice Bureaux), statutory bodies (e.g., social services) or solicitors, to offer targeted help in the parts of the local area where it is most needed. In each area the advice providers are expected to cooperate, to share information, and to refer clients to other agencies. In each area a priority is to compile a directory of services to which the person seeking advice, or advisers such as social workers or librarians, can refer in order to direct them towards appropriate provision. Secondly, there is legal representation, which means getting the Legal Services Commission to agree to pay for, or pay towards, the costs of representing the client in a court case.

Before considering Legal Help and legal representation in further detail, a word is needed about means testing. All provision of civil legal aid is subject to a stringent means test. Not everyone can get legal aid. Where representation is provided, the client of even modest means will have to pay a contribution out of income and/or capital during the lifetime of the case. So in advising any person about legal aid, bear in mind that, even if there is an advice agency next door with an appointment available, that person may not be eligible or, if eligible, may have to pay towards the costs. These costs may be recovered from the opponent if the case is won, but applicants must know that this is not guaranteed.

The Access to Justice Act 1999 provides that assistance to the individual with a civil legal problem can take many forms, the main ones being:

- signposting — pointing enquirers to those who can advise or represent;
- help with a legal problem short of representation, or mediation;
- help at the court or tribunal short of actual representation;
- investigative help — preparing a case for court or tribunal; and
- representation.

The old legal aid scheme essentially dealt with only two of these areas — advice and assistance (in the above list, help short of representation) and representation. These are the principal areas of provision at present and these are what we focus on below.

Advice and assistance — 'Legal Help'   It is the long-term intention behind the reforms culminating in the Access to Justice Act of 1999 to pay only those providers of legal services who meet the LSC 'quality mark' standards as specialists in a particular area of law. This aim has not been fully achieved in respect of representation in court, but it has been achieved in relation to advice and assistance work, which now goes under the name 'Legal Help'. If a provider does not have a quality mark and a contract to provide legal help, that agency cannot claim payment. The provider must pass a regular quality audit and have in place adequate supervision for all work. (Before these reforms any solicitor could operate what used to be called the legal aid 'green form' advice scheme merely by virtue of being a solicitor. There was no limit on the number of clients or queries she or he could deal with, so long as clients with problems and limited means could be brought through the front door. There was no audit of quality. And previously such advice could be provided in any area of English law save advising on conveyancing and wills.)

Legal Help is, since April 2000, provided under the umbrella of the CLS, which we discuss below. Areas of law in which a contract to give Legal Help is available include family law (in which there is no shortage of provision from private solicitors who built up their practices under the legal aid scheme), housing, debt, community care, employment, mental health, education and immigration. (Do not be deterred from referring if a problem cannot exactly be fitted into one of these categories, as providers are allowed to do a certain amount of additional advice and assistance work under what are called 'tolerances'.) In each local area contracts for different types of help will be awarded only in those areas of law where the need for the service has been identified as a priority.

The Community Legal Service — a partnership of providers of advice and assistance   The Community Legal Service (CLS) took over the provision of all forms of publicly-funded legal advice and assistance from the Legal Aid Board in April 2000. The CLS is not itself an organisation but comes under the umbrella of the Legal Services Commission. (The Commission, which replaced the Legal Aid Board, remains the Government body which controls funding, quality assurance, and contracts for legal service providers.)

Under s. 4 of the Access to Justice Act 1999, the Legal Services Commission:

> shall establish, maintain and develop a service known as the Community Legal Service for the purpose of promoting the availability to individuals of services . . . for securing that individuals have access to services that effectively meet their needs.

Under s. 4(2) of the 1999 Act, the services to be secured by the CLS are:

(a)   the provision of general information about the law and legal system and the availability of legal services,

(b)   the provision of help by the giving of advice as to how the law applies in particular circumstances,

(c)   the provision of help in preventing, or settling or otherwise resolving, disputes about legal rights,

(d)   the provision of help in enforcing decisions by which such disputes are resolved, and

(e)   the provision of help in relation to legal proceedings not relating to disputes.

Providers of CLS legal help are not necessarily solicitors, as non-solicitor voluntary organisations can apply on equal terms for funding. Social services departments are themselves frequently already active as advisers in categories of law such as welfare benefits, and are themselves obtaining contracts in many parts of the country to boost the provision of the service.

In each CLS partnership area (which typically covers a metropolitan or London borough, or all or part of a county) providers must share information on the services they can provide. Typically, advice providers are expected to refer clients to specialists if they are not contracted to assist in that area of law. However, if an agency is seeing a client within the specialist area, mechanisms called tolerances exist to permit a certain amount of advice to be given outside the specialist area, except for family and immigration advice which may be given only by the contracted specialist. In each area available services are listed in a local CLS directory (which will eventually be replicated on the CLS website, www.justask.com, and will be available in places like public libraries and should be available in social services offices).

The decision to award contracts for the provision of services is to be based on research into priority needs, so help in a particular area of law may be available in one ward of the borough and denied next door. (Though people with a problem should be told that they can travel outside the area to seek legal help from another provider.)

Referral   How does a person who needs advice or representation get it? You will need to have access to the local CLS directory. You will be required, if you are yourselves CLS accredited, to keep records of any referral you make for advice or assistance with a legal problem. Your local 'referral protocol' will probably require you to contact the agency you make a referral to, and require them to provide you with feedback on whether the referral was appropriate. The directory will provide details of who has expertise in which category of law. Services such as libraries which themselves do not provide advice are expected to become part of the referral network.

Means testing   To qualify for Legal Help, an applicant must normally have income and capital below set limits. But there is no means test if the case concerns care or emergency protection proceedings, mental health review tribunal proceedings or child abduction, or help from the duty solicitor in a criminal case. Eligibility on income grounds is automatic if the person receives income support or income-based job seekers allowance.

The figures for 2001–2002 are indicated below, but they change every year.

Representation in a civil case *Advice* about tribunal or court cases may be available under the Legal Help scheme (above). However, if the client needs *representation* different criteria and procedures apply. In a tribunal, there are only a few situations, particularly mental health and immigration cases, where a client can be represented using legal aid.

If the case is going to go to a court, as opposed to a tribunal, only solicitors (or barristers) can generally represent the client. This does not mean you must refer to a firm of solicitors, as many agencies, most notably law centres, employ solicitors or barristers.

The availability of legal aid for representation in court depends on the area of law to which the dispute relates. Some areas are excluded altogether under Sch. 2 to the Access to Justice Act 1999. The Government does not wish to use public money on these court cases. The main areas excluded are personal injury (though not if the claim is that it was caused by clinical i.e. medical, negligence) and business or property ownership problems. The reason for excluding personal injury is that the Government believes that any injury case worth bringing can be funded on what is, slightly misleadingly, called a 'no win, no fee' basis. (There is likely in fact to be a fee for insurance against paying the opponent's legal costs.) The 1999 Act permits the Lord Chancellor to add other types of legal problem to this list of excluded areas.

Representation in court through a legal aid certificate is not restricted to the advice categories outlined earlier when we discussed Legal Help, e.g., family, debt, housing. So long as the area of law is not excluded the application must be considered on its merits. Some factors the Legal Services Commission will take into account are listed in the Access to Justice Act 1999:

(a)   Is there going to be sufficient benefit for the applicant to justify the work?

(b)   Is it reasonable to grant funding, taking into account any other ways of funding the case that may be available, such as a conditional fee ('no win, no fee')?

(c)   Does the applicant actually need help at court?

(d)   Does the applicant have other ways of resolving the case, such as complaints to an ombudsman, or in (say) a family law case, access to mediation?

(e)   For representation or investigative help, is the case worth at least £5,000, or alternatively of significant public importance?

(f)   Is it reasonable in all the circumstances to fund the case, given the likely costs?

(g)   Are the prospects for success unclear or borderline?

Application of these criteria may mean that after the initial interview, or the provision of some help or perhaps investigation, no further help is available unless provided by an agency with other funding, or paid for privately.

In court cases apart from the excluded areas a client can be represented, but only if the Legal Services Commission decides to grant a certificate for representation having considered the merits of the case and the client's means. Applying for a certificate is itself a difficult legal problem and will require legal help (see below).

In some areas (clinical negligence cases, family cases and immigration) representation is only available from a specialist who has obtained a Legal Services Commission franchise. In other areas of law, such as housing, any agency employing a solicitor can provide representation in court if a certificate is granted to cover it, though the policy of the Government is to move towards specialist provision only.

Subject to finding an appropriate solicitor (which can include an agency employing a solicitor), a client with (say) a family problem or a housing problem, or even a consumer problem if it is a very big one, can apply to the Legal Services Commission for representation under a legal aid certificate based on a means test and a merits test. It is difficult even to make such an application without legal assistance, but this assistance may not be available if the problem does not fall into one of the Legal Help areas mentioned above in which the lawyer or agency has a contract to provide this assistance. Some solicitors provide free initial interviews as a way of attracting business and can help with the application form then.

Applicants will normally be means tested for both Legal Help and for representation. An exception to this is public law children cases (such as care proceedings), mental health tribunal representation, and child abduction cases, in all of which cases the parties are not means tested. Different thresholds apply in immigration cases. The figures given below are in force December 2001 but they will change annually. Therefore they are provided for indicative purposes only.

Where phrases like 'disposable income' or 'disposable capital' are used some allowances are permitted, for example to take into account travel to work costs or the value of work equipment. In some circumstances allowances are made for the cost of dependants, or for ignoring assets which are the subject matter of the dispute (e.g. ownership of matrimonial home); and the rules generally require aggregating the applicant's income and capital with that of the spouse or cohabitee if they are not on opposite sides of the case.

Four general principles are worth noting: Firstly no-one can get help if their monthly gross income exceeds £2000 — there are no exceptions and no allowances. Secondly any value of a home above £100,000 counts as capital (after taking off the outstanding mortgage up to £100,000). Thirdly there is no point giving away resources in order to come within the limits — they will still be calculated. Fourthly some legal help and representation is available without a means test — see p. 368.

Legal help (i.e. general advice, including help but not representation at court), plus advice and representation Capital limit £3000, disposable income £601 per month (no assessment of income for those receiving income support or income-based jobseekers allowance).

Family mediation, family case in magistrates courts, representation under a legal aid certificate in court Capital limit £8000, disposable income limit £683 per month. Below this income limit monthly contributions out of income must be paid towards the cost; anyone with capital over £3000 must pay the excess towards the cost.

Representation and Legal Help without legal aid Can representation be found for tribunals such as employment tribunals and benefit tribunals which are excluded from LSC legal representation? Can Legal Help be offered to those who do not qualify on means test grounds? Most CLS not-for-profit agencies (such as CABs, law centres, or indeed your own social services department) will have other sources of funding than just the CLS contract. It may also be possible to find a lawyer or paralegal to represent an applicant in an employment case on a conditional 'no win, no fee' basis, but such services, unless provided by a solicitor who is subject to codes of conduct and complaints procedures, are not subject to any regulation by a professional body or to quality assurance requirements, and so you would be wise to avoid a referral until you know the provider's reputation. Where solicitors operate conditional fees they are subject to strict guidelines.

The statutory charge Legal Help is not always free, even where there is no contribution payable. The Commission has first claim on any money or property recovered or preserved in the course of the proceedings, and will deduct any costs it has paid out before letting the client have the balance. Even if there is only a small deduction, or none at all, this requirement that all money recovered be paid to the Commission can cause a delay in the successful litigant actually getting hold of the fruits of victory. (Solicitors can reduce the delay by putting a ceiling on their costs, and only handing over to the Commission enough to cover that amount. The client can then be handed the balance.)

This clawback of costs from a client's winnings is known as the 'statutory charge', and it can come as a great shock to the client. It is perhaps worst in matrimonial cases, for in these cases there is usually no loser, and no costs order in favour of the winner, and therefore the Commission will be looking to 'property recovered or preserved' to recover its costs. It can take its costs out of lump sum payments or the value of the matrimonial home (if ownership or occupation was in dispute). It is frequently cheaper to settle for an unsatisfactory compromise of a matrimonial claim than to fight on to victory, for the extra legal costs may outweigh the advantage gained. If the property recovered in the case consists of a home for a party, or a lump sum for the purpose of buying a home, then the charge is not enforced immediately but is registered against the home in the same way as a mortgage, meaning that the home cannot be sold without the charge also being paid off; meanwhile, just like a mortgage, the legal costs owing to the Commission accrue interest.

Maintenance payments and the first £3,000 recovered in matrimonial cases are not subject to this charge.

Other ways of funding court action   A person interested in bringing a claim in a civil court for an award of damages (i.e., payment of money on winning the case) can enter a 'conditional fee' arrangement with a solicitor. No costs are payable if the claim fails. They are payable — with a fees increase of up to 100 per cent to cover the risk to the lawyer — only if the case is won. Insurance will be needed against paying the other side's costs on losing, but this is becoming costly. We saw above that the Access to Justice Act 1999 removes personal injury from the scope of legal aid. So personal injury claims will now be funded by conditional fee agreements in almost all cases. The costs of the insurance premium can be recovered from the other side if the case succeeds.

We would not enthuse about 'claims assessors'. Despite their attractive boast of 'no win, no fee', they are not qualified as lawyers, they are unable to make full use of the courts, and they are consequently likely to settle for too little. If the case requires court proceedings claims assessors therefore have to contract out work to solicitors on their panels.

A person may also have access to legal expenses insurance, as most household insurers and motor insurers try to tack on cover when selling a policy.

However, clients who can get CLS Legal Help have a significant advantage. If they lose the case the court may award costs against them only to the extent that it is reasonable to do so, and 'reasonable' includes consideration of affordability.

Criminal Legal Aid

It is encouraging to see that the Government White Paper which preceded the Access to Justice Act 1999 quoted the European Convention on Human Rights as the basis for its thinking: a defendant has a right 'to defend himself in person or through legal assistance of his own choosing or, if he has not sufficient means to pay for legal assistance, to be given it free when the interests of justice so require' (Article 6).

The Criminal Defence Service   As with Civil Legal Aid, equally radical changes are underway with criminal defence work. The Access to Justice Act 1999 required the Legal Services Commission to establish a Criminal Defence Service (CDS) for securing, under s. 12:

> . . . that individuals involved in criminal investigations or criminal proceedings have access to such advice, assistance and representation as the interests of justice require.

The CDS was launched in April 2001 and has contracts with about 3,000 firms of solicitors which are 'franchised' (i.e., have been found to meet specialist quality standards) for criminal work. The CDS is entitled to run such services itself, or to authorise others to provide the services. Such providers must meet quality assured standards set by the CDS. The Legal Services Commission has launched a salaried public defender service which is now running in four parts of the country. The private practice firms specialising in crime are very hostile to the public defender service. It remains to be seen how successful it is — the pilot will be subject to a research study. At the time of writing it is mainly solicitors in private practice who do criminal work, and any change is likely to be gradual. Therefore the lawyer's client will not see major amendments to the old scheme during the currency of the present seventh edition of this book.

Under s. 13 of the 1999 Act, the CDS is to ensure availability of advice and assistance services; and under s. 14, representation in court. Solicitors wishing to provide these services must have a contract with the Legal Services Commission. What matters, perhaps, from the client's perspective is whether she or he will be automatically eligible, or subject to a means and/or merits test.

Free advice, assistance and representation   Any person, regardless of means or the merits of the case, is entitled to free legal advice from a specialist solicitor or solicitor's representative at the police station. This was discussed above in Chapter 12. The solicitor can either be chosen by the client, or taken from the list of available solicitors kept by the police.

When a person appears in a criminal court for the first time after the charge (for a first hearing this will be in the magistrates' court), the duty solicitor can provide free non means-tested, non merits-tested advice and representation on matters such as bail and, if the plea is guilty, mitigation of sentence.

Alternatively, a person charged or expecting to be charged can ask a solicitor of their choice to provide initial assistance — called litigation assistance — in preparing the case and helping in the early hearings at court. If the solicitor thinks the case suitable, she or he will take it on without means testing.

If the client is on bail or not yet charged, free advice and assistance from a solicitor is available subject to the same means test as applies for CLS Legal Help.

Legal aid for representation   All representation must be either by solicitors who have a specialist contract with the CDS, or by solicitors employed by the CDS. (At present the latter applies only in the pilot scheme areas. Clients must have a free choice of eligible solicitors and cannot be forced to use a salaried defender.) The application is submitted to the court currently dealing with the case and will be considered on its merits (Is it in the interests of justice to pay for representation?) and according to the means of the applicant (Could she or he afford representation privately?)

Few criminal defendants fail the means test. But getting legal aid may still carry a cost: if the defendant is convicted the judge or magistrates can order him or her to pay a contribution once the case is over. The contribution can be 100 per cent of the costs of the case, but the defendant's means are taken into account before the amount is decided.

The interests of justice test involves factors such as the risk of imprisonment, the risk of loss of livelihood, age, or the complexity of the case. Refusal of legal aid where it is clear that the defendant's liberty is at stake can be a human rights abuse (*Maxwell* v *UK* (1995) 19 EHRR 97).

Legal Aid Public Law Cases Involving Children
The principle that legal aid for parties involved in care proceedings, supervision proceedings or emergency protection proceedings should be available without a means test and without a merits test has survived the reorganisation of legal aid. Only the local authority (or NSPCC) are excluded from this eligibility. The children's guardian is entitled to appoint a solicitor funded in this way. (If the case is to be dealt with in the High Court or the county court, legal aid will be civil and granted by the LSC. In the family proceedings court, which is a branch of the magistrates' court, criminal legal aid has to be granted by the court.)

SIXTEEN
Family Relationships

You have statutory responsibilities to children (see Chapter 2). These are your clients, not the families they live with. But of course, you cannot exercise those responsibilities without taking an interest in families. You will find yourself assisting and advising families in order to provide services for children in need, and to avoid the need for children to come before a court, civil or criminal.

This chapter is about private law proceedings, i.e., disputes initiated by members of families not the local authority. But remember (see Chapter 4) that any private family proceedings can lead to public law proceedings if the court directs a local authority investigation. Similarly, many private law orders — in particular Children Act, s. 8 orders — can be made in the course of public law proceedings. The labels 'public' and 'private' are not watertight.

The range of problems that might affect your clients' families is huge. We aim in this chapter to identify the legal aspects of the most pressing or common problems. Legal Help is available to consult a solicitor for most disputes involving family law, although the initial advice is restricted to those on subsistence incomes. While it is important to steer those who need it towards legal advice, the deterrent of costs is a real obstacle (see Chapter 15). Even if a person gets help for representation, say, in a family property dispute or a conflict over the children, the Legal Services Commission will want all its costs back if that person 'recovers or preserves' money or property. That means that the value of the family home can, in effect, pay the legal costs, not the Legal Services Commission. The use of family mediation may be far cheaper, even for the 'winner'.

The most urgent problems faced by people you are advising will probably relate to violence, and occupation of the home on relationship breakdown. We shall look at these areas as soon as we have clarified a few basic concepts. We shall then consider how relationships are dissolved, and finish by considering what happens to the children, and property and finances when a relationship ends.

For simplicity, we have called the person seeking protection from violence, or seeking financial help, 'she'; this reflects our experience that it is more often women who need these legal remedies than men.

SOME DEFINITIONS

If two people decide to have a relationship which involves living together with some degree of permanence, or they have or adopt children, or they are or have been married, there is a family relationship recognised in law. There is also a family relationship between parent and child, regardless of who or where the other parent is. But English law does not recognise a same sex relationship as creating family rights and duties, even following gender reassignment treatment. (The law is beginning to recognise same-sex relationships as equivalent to heterosexual family relationships in other areas, such as housing law and the right to take over a tenancy when a partner dies.)

Married or Not?

The law carefully defines the ritual necessary to create a valid marriage in this country; but it is rare that the validity of a marriage ceremony is in dispute. In such a case, for example where there is doubt about whether a person was actually divorced at the date of the marriage ceremony, specialist legal advice is required.

It makes no difference if the parties married abroad. English courts recognise foreign marriages, and, so long as one of the parties is now living with some degree of permanence in this country, courts here can make decisions about, and even dissolve, a marriage that took place abroad. Similarly, English courts recognise divorces obtained abroad, and other court orders concerning families.

A Human Rights Dimension

The Human Rights Act 1998 incorporates the European Convention on Human Rights into English law. The most significant Convention article in the family context is Article 8, which decrees that, in relation to family affairs:

> 1.   Everyone has the right to respect for his private and family life, his home and his correspondence.
> 2.   There shall be no interference by a public authority with the exercise of this right except such as is in accordance with the law and is necessary . . . for the protection of health or morals . . .

Article 12 establishes the right to marry and to found a family.

Case law is beginning to develop where there are allegations that existing law does not adequately protect these rights. For example, in *G v UK* [2001] 1 FLR 153, a case decided by the European Court of Human Rights, a father's complaint that the UK authorities had not done enough to facilitate contact with his children was rejected as not being a breach of his Article 8 rights. The authorities had taken all reasonable steps, but could not coerce the mother without breaching her rights. Another example is that of the prisoner denied the right to provide sperm to his wife to start a family. In *R* v *Secretary for the Home Department ex parte Mellor* [2000] 2 FLR 951, the Queen's Bench Division held that the denial of the Article 12 right was justified given the lawful imprisonment.

Marriage and Immigration Status

Being married to someone who has the right to stay or reside permanently in the United Kingdom does not give that spouse an automatic right to enter the UK. However, the rules made under the British Nationality Act 1981 state that a spouse in such circumstances will normally be allowed entry, so long as the marriage is genuine and not primarily designed to be a means of gaining entry to the UK. After three years married to a British citizen and living in the UK, a spouse can apply for naturalisation as a British citizen.

Be aware that divorce can occasionally affect immigration status. Where a person is not a British citizen, and his or her right of abode is derived from the fact of being a spouse, legal advice should be obtained before decree absolute. It should not be assumed that the solicitors dealing with the divorce will automatically advise a client on this point.

Cohabitation

Cohabitation is a relationship without a marriage ceremony. To what extent does cohabitition give rise to a legal relationship? The answer is that cohabitation is usually not, in itself, recognised in law as a type of legal status. (However, the state does not always turn a blind eye to the nature of a relationship when it comes to assessing cohabitees' means for state benefits, or entitlement to Legal Help, or the council tax — then cohabitation 'as man and wife' brings with it legal responsibilities for the partner.)

Because cohabitation does not change legal status in the same way that marriage does, most disputes between cohabitees are resolved not according to matrimonial law, but according to the law which governs relationships between any two members of society; if there is a dispute about the ownership of property, it is resolved according to the laws of property ownership, not according to the laws of marriage; and unlike a spouse, a cohabitee has no chance of maintenance in his or her own right, unless there is some binding contract for such provision.

The status of the unmarried father When we consider the relationships between people and their children, we find that the law makes less of a distinction between married and unmarried parents. The reason behind this convergence of the law is that the state has an interest in defining the status of children, and parents' duties towards them, so it cannot leave matters solely to the agreement and actions of individuals. One significant difference which still applies is the status of the unmarried father, who does not have 'parental responsiblities' at law without a court order. Parental responsibility for the unmarried father can be obtained on application to the magistrates', county or High Court, or by an agreement between himself and the mother and registered with the court (Children Act 1989, s. 4). The father's status as a parent is then equal to that of the married father or the mother, for example, in making decisions about the child's upbringing. There are very few circumstances in which a court will refuse to grant a parental responsibilities order to a father (even, for example, where the child is in local authority accommodation and the father cannot do much for the child: *Re G* [1996] 1 FLR 857). But it can happen, as where the father had seen an 11-year-old child only six times in her life and she viewed him as a stranger: *Re J (Parental Responsibility)* [1998] 12 CL 220). Again, the court refused an order where the father was likely to take a sexual interest in the child (*P (A Minor) (Parental Responsibility)* [1998] 2 FLR 96). The s. 4 order is considered again below.

PROTECTION FROM VIOLENCE

This topic is intimately connected with rights of occupation of the home, which is dealt with below.

A good place for a social worker to start to understand the implications of violence for his or her statutory duties is Circular (97) 15, *Family Law Act 1996 Part IV, Family Homes and Domestic Violence.* This shows the close link between child protection and dealing with violence, and explains who you will need to liaise with, particularly health professionals, children's guardians, any local domestic violence forum, child protection team and the police.

The law is a blunt instrument in protecting a person from domestic violence. It can make orders forbidding the person from being violent; it can send people to prison when they breach these orders (though this is in fact rare). It cannot deal with the causes of violence, or resolve the family tension that may be the underlying problem. And it is usually available too late — after the violence has occurred.

Alongside the legal process, or instead of it, other strategies for protecting a woman, and perhaps children, may be necessary. She may be advised to go to a secret address: you will need to be aware of the availability of women's refuges in your vicinity (Women's Aid National Helpline: tel. 08457 023 468; www.womensaid.org.uk). Refuges strive to protect women and children in their care, and are very reluctant to divulge details of who is staying there. They work hard to build trusting relationships with the police, so it is gratifying that a 1998 Court of Appeal decision upheld a refusal by the police to disclose to a father the whereabouts of his child and the child's mother since this would make the refuge less safe (*Chief Constable of West Yorkshire* v *S* (1998) *The Times*, 24 August). (The father would still be able to apply to the court for contact or residence — see below.) If the victim of violence sees the rift as permanent, and she does not want to apply to get the man out of the home, she can seek rehousing from the housing department as a homeless person. Since no one can be required to live under threat of violence, she should not be treated as intentionally homeless, which is a ground for refusing accommodation (see Chapter 17). Problems such as the sudden drop in income will loom large, and an immediate application for income support will be necessary for a woman who has no other source of income. An application to the court for maintenance for herself (if married) and to the Child Support Agency for the children should be urgently considered (see below).

Using the Police

The criminal courts — with the authority of the House of Lords — recognise the crime of rape within marriage (*R* v *R* [1992] 1 AC 599). (This is an unusually clear example of the evolution of the common law, i.e. the powers of judges to make new law rather than leave it to Parliament. Until 1992, the law did not recognise marital rape as a crime. The House of Lords decided that this should change. If this looks like convicting a person for something that was not a crime when committed, it might amount to a breach of Article 7 of the European Convention — no retrospective punishment. When this argument was put to the Court in Strasbourg in *SW and CR* v *UK* (1995) 21 EHRR 363, it was rejected on the ground that gradual clarification of the law by the courts is desirable. The rapist defendant should have known that attitudes and laws were changing.) The Court of Appeal has also ruled that the sentence should be no less than for rape of a stranger (*R* v *W* (1992) *The Times*, 21 September). Indeed, very heavy sentences are sometimes imposed, e.g., in *R* v *Montaine* [1998] 2 Cr App R 66, where the rapist had had a ten-year relationship with the victim and they had two children. He raped her repeatedly at knife point. The sentence was 12 years, upheld by the Court of Appeal.

All physical or sexual assault is a criminal offence. Behaviour which causes psychological injury can also be an assault (*R* v *Burstow* (1996) *The Times*, 30 July), and the Protection from Harassment Act 1997 creates the offence of putting a person in fear of violence. These types of offence can lead to lengthy custodial sentences. For example, the accused was sentenced to a total of six years' imprisonment following a concerted campaign of stalking (*R* v *Haywood* [1998] 1 Cr App R 358).

The police are more willing to get involved in 'domestic disputes' than they were a few years ago. Most forces train recruits to be aware of domestic violence as a serious crime, and have set up specialist units to assist victims. In deciding whether to prosecute, the police know they can compel the victim to give evidence, even though witnesses in other cases cannot be forced to testify against their spouses (Police and Criminal Evidence Act 1984, s. 80). This improves the chances of arrest and conviction, since they know from the beginning that they can call the principal witness, even if the victim changes her mind about wanting to prosecute or is put under pressure to do so.

The advantage of using the police over any other procedure is their day and night availability in serious cases. (If a solicitor can be contacted, injunctions can also be obtained round the clock (see below).) In addition, the police may decide to arrest a person suspected of violent crime, which provides immediate short-term relief for the victim while she considers what else to do.

Sometimes the victim of violence is reluctant to bring in the police; but this is the quickest, and cheapest, process. If the fear is that the husband will be all the more violent when he comes out on bail, there is not a great deal of hope that an order from the civil courts will have much more of a deterrent effect.

As we shall see below, the civil courts can themselves involve the police where an assault has caused actual injury.

Orders in Children Act Cases Where There is Family Violence

When a court makes an order for interim care or emergency protection (see generally Chapter 6), it can also, under powers inserted by the Family Law Act 1996, order a suspected abuser to be removed from the home. The court must be satisfied that removal of the person is likely to reduce the significant harm or risk of it. If the child is subsequently removed from home, this order lapses — remember to tell the adult victim of this.

Using the Civil Courts

The police may not wish to arrest or charge the violent partner; in any event, he may be released on bail or after conviction, or the victim may want action that the police cannot provide, particularly an order to remove a person from the victim's home. So she has to take her own case in the civil courts. It is possible to do this without legal representation, particularly in the magistrates' court, but we would recommend that you advise a victim of violence to see a solicitor in any event. There may be other issues which require legal advice, and the solicitor may advise using the county court, or commencing divorce proceedings; or may, after talking it all over, agree with his or her client that no action should be taken at the moment.

Initial advice on this type of problem is available instantly for the least well-off under the CLS help scheme (see Chapter 15); emergency legal aid, for the magistrates' court, the county court or the High Court, is available in the worst cases at short notice. (A firm with a CLS family law contract (see Chapter 15) can itself grant emergency legal aid to its client.)

Protection from domestic violence is intricately tied up with rights to live in the property. Both these areas of law are governed by the Family Law Act 1996. We look first at non-molestation orders, which are governed by s. 42. What does 'non-molestation' mean? Who can apply for this kind of order? What protection does it provide?

Non-molestation Orders

The 1996 Act does not actually define 'molestation'. Fortunately the old law (the Domestic Violence and Matrimonial Proceedings Act 1976) used the same term, and the old cases make it clear that the concept is wide, covering physical and sexual violence, or the threat of it; annoying phone calls and letters. In fact the word 'pestering', which is usually the word used in the order which is served on the respondant, sums it up.

Who can apply? The most common situation is where the person making the application claims to be the victim of molestation. So the applicant applies for an order against her alleged molester, who is called the respondent.

However, three new concepts were introduced by the Family Law Act 1996:

(a)   The court (s. 62), without an application necessarily being made by anyone, can decide to make an order on behalf of the victim against the molester. As with similar powers under the Children Act (see p. 74), to make orders that have not been asked for the court must be already dealing with 'family proceedings'. The order can only be made against a molester who is himself involved as a party in the proceedings. This power can overcome the situation where, under the old law, there was no power to protect a child victim by getting the abuser out of the home, leaving two equally unsuitable choices to the court — no action, or removal of the child into care.

When we say that no application need be made for this kind of order, it does not mean that you have to wait and see if the court will spot such an opportunity. It can be part of your strategy in child protection proceedings to seek such an outcome; but would it be an abuse of the procedures to bring care or supervision proceedings solely to obtain a non-molestation order? You may — which we do not recommend — be tempted to pretend that you really do want the care/supervision order! (But see point (c) below.)

Allied to this power to make an order in family proceedings is an amendment to the Children Act 1989 which enables the court to make an exclusion order in the course of making an interim care order or an emergency protection order — see p. 120.)

(b)   A child can apply (s. 43), although if under 16 the court's leave is required. The child will need a children's guardian for such an application. This is the child's application, and it is likely the courts will not be pleased with adults manipulating children to bring applications to achieve other purposes. You may wish to tell a child of this route to an order, and arrange for the child to receive independent legal advice.

(c)   If the necessary rules are brought in — Parliament has enacted a power but the Government is still not sure how (and, after five years, we assume is unwilling) to move forward — a third party (s. 60) such as the police or a social worker may apply directly on behalf of the victim. You might wish to do so, if and when the rules allow, in order to protect a child where, guided by the 'no order' principle in Children Act cases (see p. 86), you would not need to start child protection proceedings if the abuser could be removed. Be aware that intervention on behalf of a woman in this context, without a clear reason under the Children Act aimed at the welfare of a child, would be merely (in our view) to disempower a victim further. It is also not within your statutory powers. If matters are serious, is action by the police more appropriate, if they will take it?

The relationship between the victim and the molester   The court will not grant a non-molestation order under the Family Law Act 1996 unless the two people concerned are 'associated'. Powers to obtain orders against strangers (e.g., stalkers) do not exist under the Family Law Act 1996. (However, there is no need for the victim and harasser to be connected under the Protection from Harassment Act 1997. This Act gives similar powers to courts to order, on pain of committal to prison, the harassment to cease. Breach of this order is also a criminal offence in itself.)

An associated person is:

- a spouse or a 'cohabitant' (this means a heterosexual cohabitant; 'cohabitant' is the new term under the Act for the old term 'cohabitee');
- a former spouse or former cohabitant;
- a relative;
- a man and a woman linked by being parents of the same child; or
- a person who shares a household (but not as a lodger or tenant). Persons sharing a household clearly covers same-sex couples (as well as platonic companions): this is an implicit recognition of a homosexual relationship within the concept of family law.

From now on we will call the applicant and respondent, for the sake of understanding, the victim and the molester. But strictly speaking, the victim might be a child on whose behalf the applicant is applying; or someone might be applying on the adult victim's behalf; and of course the term 'molester' assumes that the allegations will be proved.

How is an application for a non-molestation order made?   The Family Law Act 1996 provides that an application can be made to the magistrates' court, to the county court, or to the High Court. If Legal Aid is available, solicitors will probably continue to prefer the county court. If it is not available the victim is best advised to make her application to the local family proceedings court. The court staff should help the victim with the paperwork, and the evidence will be given from the witness-box. In the other two courts the evidence will be prepared initially in affidavit form, on which the victim can expect to be cross-examined.

What protection does a non-molestation order provide?   Section 42 of the Family Law Act 1996 states:

(6)   A non-molestation order may be expressed so as to refer to molestation in general, to particular acts of molestation, or both.
(7)   A non-molestation order may be made for a specified period or until further notice.

The actual wording of an order will reflect the particular circumstances. The molester may be ordered not to molest, not to approach, and not to pester the victim. Together with a property occupation order (see below), it may require the molester to stay out of the home and not come within, say, 100 metres of it. The courts do not generally like open-ended orders; three months is the normal duration. However this is not a rule, and orders can be indefinite: *Re BJ (A Child) (Non-molestation Order)* [2000] All ER 874.

How is a non-molestation order enforced?

(a)   A power of arrest   If the court, when making an order, concluded that the molester had used or threatened violence against the applicant or a child,

the order *must* have a power of arrest attached. (No power of arrest is available under the Protection from Harassment Act 1997, so where victim and molester are 'associated' we advise use of the Family Law Act 1996.) A power of arrest means that a police officer can arrest without warrant anyone suspected of breaching the terms of the order, and bring him before the court for punishment for contempt of court. Without this power of arrest the police would need a warrant, or would have to wait for a further offence to be committed. The power of arrest must be registered at the nearest police station, and the victim should keep the police telephone number handy if she fears attack.

(b)   The court's powers   If, with or without a warrant, the molester is brought back to the court and the court accepts the evidence of breach of the order, it has power to commit to prison for contempt of court, or to remand the molester in custody or on bail so that a medical report can first be obtained. It can send a molester to hospital under the MHA 1983, s. 37, or make a guardianship order under s. 38 (see Chapter 14). However, there is no reason to assume that the courts will abandon the general preference for giving a molester in breach of an order a telling off and 'one last chance' before sending him to prison. Even after 18 separate breaches of a non-molestation order, 13 months in prison was considered manisfestly excessive in *C* v *G* (1996) *The Times*, 14 October. Compare the six weeks' prison sentence for the mother who defied a court and obstructed a violent father's contact with his child. But perhaps the courts are beginning to get tougher here. In *N* v *R* (1998) *The Times*, 1 September, the Court of Appeal agreed that an immediate custodial order could be necessary to make a violent man obey court orders. (As contempt of court is treated as a criminal matter under the European Convention, it is possible that a committal to prison will be challenged as a human rights abuse under Article 6 (right to fair trial), since the procedure does not at present involve setting out precise allegations in the form of a charge.)

Applying for a non-molestation order in an emergency   Imagine a situation where there has been a serious and violent incident. The victim is scared that if the molester hears she is going to court, he will become even more violent. In such a case Legal Aid can be sought as an emergency and a judge made available very quickly in court, elsewhere if out of hours, or even over the telephone. The court can make an order without the paperwork being ready, and without the molester having any notice of the case. You may have heard lawyers calling this type of application *ex parte*. However, the Civil Procedure Rules changed this term to 'without notice' in the county court (but not the family proceedings court). A person who has an order made against him without notice can apply to have it set aside, and a full hearing with notice and paperwork will generally be held within seven days.

Courts do not like the inherent unfairness of deciding, even for a few days, to grant an order having heard only one side of a case. A court will make an order without notice only if it believes that the applicant or a child will otherwise suffer significant harm, that delay would deter the victim from making an application at all, or that the molester is trying to avoid being served with the papers for a hearing with notice. Having said that, many judges faced with a desperate and distressed applicant will use humanity and common sense and grant an order without notice even where these requirements are not strictly met. A good lawyer who knows the individual judges is essential.

Molestation and Property Occupation

Often the most important matter in cases of family violence is getting the molester out of the home. The kind of order necessary to achieve this used to be called an 'ouster order', and sometimes the old language survives alongside the current term 'occupation order'.

Although the power of the court to adjust rights to occupy property is based on different grounds from a non-molestation order, the things you need to be aware of in deciding whether an application can be made are almost the same. The law is set out in ss. 30–41 of the 1996 Act.

Everything we have already said about powers of arrest, applications without notice, punishment by committal to prison, and the need for the victim and the molester to be associated in some way applies when the court is considering an order to do with occupation rights. A child can again make an application, as can the court in the course of family proceedings. It is worth bearing in mind, in care proceedings in particular, this power for a court to exclude an abuser, rather than removing a child victim into care.

The type of order that can be made, and its duration, depends on the marital or cohabitation status of the parties, and their existing property rights in the home. Please note that the order does not adjust property *ownership* rights. It cannot make the victim a tenant instead of the molester, and cannot put her name on to the title deeds of freehold property (see below, by contrast, for property adjustment powers where the parties are divorcing).

Rights of occupation Before looking at the power of the court to adjust occupation rights, we think it helpful to set out in a simplified way the rights of occupation that exist before the court intervenes.

For married parties, regardless of who owns the property, a spouse has a right of occupation of the principal matrimonial home; but if that spouse does not also own the property (solely or jointly), the right must be registered to protect the spouse against the home being sold or mortgaged to someone who does not know of the spouse's interest. A solicitor can register this right quickly and cheaply, and in an ideal world the time to do so is before there is a problem. It is no longer possible to register this right of occupation without the person's spouse finding out. This, the Land Registry has decided, would breach that spouse's human rights. Legally, this is a correct decision, but the result may be that women are deterred from registering their right of occupation.

For a non-spouse the right to occupy a property depends on whether they own it or whether the owner has granted them a licence or tenancy. A non-married person without ownership or tenancy rights, or a licence to occupy granted by the owner or tenant, has no right of occupation unless the court grants it. On the other hand, the owner or tenant cannot have his or her rights interfered with unless the court so orders.

What can the court actually order? Sections 33–38 describe the circumstances in which a court will adjust occupation rights and the matters it will have to take into account. A court should make an order if to do so would prevent the victim or a child suffering significant harm. If the court is being asked to interfere with someone's occupation rights to protect a victim who has no rights as an owner or spouse, the court is required to consider the conduct of the parties before making an order. (An Englishman's home is his castle — until he behaves badly.)

The things a court must consider in every case are the financial and other needs of the parties and the children, including issues such as health.

The court can order a person to leave all or part of the home; to keep away (say, not come within 100 metres); and to allow the victim back in (including, for example, ordering the means to achieve this, such as giving her a key). But remember, it cannot change ownership rights, so it is important to know how long this occupation order can last. Where the victim has no property ownership rights, and is not now married to the molester, the order can last only for six months. What happens, then, after the six months? If the parties are or were previously married, the victim can go back to court for renewals, if the circumstances justify it, for six months at a time. In any other situation, one six-month renewal is possible, but then the order must lapse. This means that the occupational rights of the molester cannot be interrupted indefinitely and the victim will have to find some other solution to her accommodation needs. (If there are children, some property ownership adjustment can be applied for; and on divorce, even without children, the court can order property adjustment. See below.)

Will the court be willing to make a person leave? Occupation orders are to be seen as exceptional orders, and in particular they are hard to obtain without giving notice to the alleged violent person and holding a full hearing of all the evidence. Although the legislation has changed, the leading case is still *Richards* v *Richards* [1984] AC 174. Here the House of Lords said that the court has to look not only at the conduct of the parties, which is what the applicant is most concerned with, and the needs of any children, but also at the needs of the parties and their financial resources (so it may be easier for the wealthy to get an order, since the ousted person can find somewhere else to live). But the court has a discretion on the evidence before it, and some judges are more inclined to grant an order than others. Solicitors know this and may time their applications accordingly. You might think that violence is necessary to justify an order — not so. For example, in *Scott* v *Scott* [1992] 1 FLR 529, an order was made where the husband would not stop pestering his wife for a reconciliation, despite his undertakings to the court. However, an occupation order cannot be granted just because the parties do not get on (*Grant* v *James* [1993] 1 FLR 1008).

The balance of harm test Domestic violence tends to evoke images of innocent victim and guilty perpetrator. Sometimes the law is asked to intervene in less clear-cut circumstances. In *Banks* v *Banks (Occupation Order: Mental Health)* [1999] 1 FLR 726, the wife suffered from dementia, on top of previous mental illness, but was currently living at home. She was very aggressive towards her husband. He was under great strain, though no physical attack had been made on him (only threatened). The court had to apply (as it does in every case) the 'balance of harm' test. It decided that to evict the wife would be more harmful to her than her staying would be to the husband. Any non-molestation order would be wasted on the wife, given her mental state.

Another case showing the balancing act was *B* v *B* [1999] 1 FLR 715. The Court of Appeal allowed the violent man to remain because of the needs of his dependent child from a former relationship. His violence, if evicted, made him 'intentionally homeless' (see next chapter), whereas his wife would be 'unintentionally homeless' and could look to the housing department for housing for herself and their younger child. On balance he could stay and she ended up going, notwithstanding his violence.

RELATIONSHIP BREAKDOWN

If a person is not married, no formal steps need be taken to end the relationship itself, though there may be a need for formal agreement or a court order to decide children's future arrangements and division of any property. It may be that the parties have to live together until property matters are sorted out.

If parties are married, they have a theoretical legal duty to live together. However, it is unenforceable, and if a spouse wants to leave (and of course has somewhere to go — see Chapter 17 for a discussion of homelessness) he or she can do so. He or she is free at law to form new relationships; the only restriction is on marrying again before obtaining a decree absolute in divorce. That would be the crime of bigamy. The new marriage would be void.

So there is no immediate practical difference between terminating a married or an unmarried relationship. There is nothing to compel a person to seek a divorce just because he or she has abandoned the marriage. However, if divorce proceedings are undertaken, all the 'ancillary' matters — children's arrangements, property, maintenance, where to live — will be dealt with (if at all) through the divorce court, and that court can make a wider range of orders than a court dealing with the problems of the cohabiting or non-divorcing couple.

Divorce
Divorce is not the only way in which a marriage comes to an end. It ends on death; a court can presume death after a spouse has not been heard of for seven years. Sometimes it can even be declared void — for example, where it has never been consummated by sexual intercourse. But if a party to a marriage wishes to have it dissolved, he or she must issue a petition for

divorce. A fee is payable, although those on means-tested benefits are exempted.

The ground for divorce is that the marriage has broken down irretrievably. Such breakdown can be shown only by evidence of one (or more) of the five grounds which are set out in the Matrimonial Causes Act 1973, s. 1(2):

(a)   The respondent (that is the other spouse) has committed adultery and the petitioner finds it intolerable to live with him or her.

(b)   The respondent has behaved in such a way that the petitioner cannot reasonably be expected to live with him or her.

(c)   The respondent has deserted the petitioner for a period of at least two years. To be in desertion, the respondent must have left against the petitioner's will.

(d)   The parties have lived apart continuously for two years and the respondent consents to the divorce. (It is possible to live 'apart' under the same roof, if the spouses' lives are conducted separately.)

(e)   The parties have lived apart for at least five continuous years.

A divorce can still be based on desertion, or a period of separation, even where the period of living apart was interrupted by a period of living together, as long as that period did not exceed six months. If reconciliation fails, the period of desertion or separation can start running again.

The bulk of petitions are based on behaviour, adultery or agreement after two years' separation; adultery and behaviour offer the quickest route to divorce, because there is no waiting period. But no petition can be brought until the marriage is a year old; the hope is that parties will at least give it a try, although they may have separated after the wedding reception!

A no fault divorce procedure was due to come into effect in 2000 but has been scrapped. For the forseeable future, divorcing couples will have to continue to hurl unpleasant allegations at each other to get a divorce in less than two years, or find a way of living apart for at least two years.

Most divorces, after the bluff and bluster encountered when the respondent spouse first receives the petition, are undefended. Most respondents can be persuaded that there is nothing to gain from defending the divorce, since this leads to complicated High Court proceedings and the need to give oral evidence about the breakdown of the marriage. There is rarely anything to be gained by trying to keep a marriage alive that is really dead.

If the petition is not defended, the divorce is dealt with in a county court. Legal Help is available, subject to the means test (see Chapter 15), to enable a solicitor to draw up the petition, and to assist with the response by the other party. Later on the solicitor can assist by drawing up the simple affidavit which is the petitioner's evidence that the grounds given in the petition are true. A statement has to be submitted to the court to say what the arrangements are for the children. Both parents must sign this unless arrangements are disputed.

Apart from unresolved disputes over property, money and children, there is no need to attend court for the divorce itself unless the court is in some way worried about the welfare of the children; it can then hold up the divorce until there is a chance for a judge to interview the parties about the children's arrangements.

If everything goes smoothly, as most petitions do, the decree nisi should be made about eight to 12 weeks after the petition; but that is not a divorce. A petitioner can apply for decree absolute six weeks after decree nisi, and the respondent three months after those six weeks.

Judicial Separation

There is also a procedure called 'judicial separation', which mirrors the divorce petition right up to decree nisi but there is no termination of the marriage. Instead of decree nisi, a decree of judicial separation is made which terminates the obligation to live together and, like divorce proceedings, provides a vehicle for the court to make orders in respect of children, property and maintenance. Judicial separation does not prevent a person later applying for divorce. It is favoured by those who have moral objections to divorce, or who do not want to let their spouses 'off the hook' — although after five years of living apart the respondent spouse has a ground for divorce anyway.

CHILDREN, PROPERTY AND MAINTENANCE FOLLOWING RELATIONSHIP BREAKDOWN

The unmarried partner simply got up and went; the married person got a divorce in three to four months. In both instances, that was probably the easiest bit. The hard bit is untangling the consequences of a defunct relationship. The Family Law Act 1996 was supposed to usher in a new era of non-confrontational divorce procedures. Most of it has been scrapped. However, s. 29 — one of the few parts to survive — promotes the use of mediation to resolve these types of dispute. Mediation can be funded through the Legal Services Commission. But the idea to make mediation compulsory before getting public funding for help from lawyers has been dropped.

So what is mediation? The fundamental principle is that the mediator does not advise and the parties have to arrive at their own solution. Such face-to-face discussions can be very demanding for separating couples, and out of the question where violence has entered the relationship. But mediation has the very clear advantage that couples 'own' the solution and are encouraged to think through how to make it work.

All negotiation and mediation takes place in the shadow of the law. What follows is a description of how a court can sort out the issues of children, property or finance if the parties cannot reach their own agreement.

What Happens to the Children?

The types of decisions a court can make about where children live, who they have contact with, etc. can be made at any time. This sort of dispute is not limited to the situation where a couple breaks up.

This type of child law is private law; public law involves the state protecting children (see Chapters 5 and 6).

Most of the legal principles have now been brought together under one Act, the Children Act 1989. Before considering these, and the types of orders that a court can make, we need to look at the different ways in which the future arrangements for a child can come before a court.

In divorce proceedings, a petitioner or respondent can apply to the court in the course of the divorce proceedings, or, as we have seen, the court can itself require a hearing if it wants to consider the arrangements for the children. And in any 'family proceedings' (defined in Chapter 4, p. 89) the court can make orders about the children whether or not any person has asked it to; it can also order the local authority to carry out an investigation into whether care proceedings should be brought (see further Chapter 5, p. 102). So even where the parties themselves are only concerned about, for example, maintenance or protection from violence, the court can look at whether orders ought to be made in respect of the children. Any order can now include orders relating to occupation of the home (above, p. 383). In most cases, however, the parties can agree about the arrangements for the children and do not need to make any application for the court to decide.

Who can apply for an order in relation to children? A parent can apply for an order. A guardian can apply, as can a step-parent who treated the child as a member of the family during the marriage, or indeed any person with whom the child has lived until no more than three months ago for at least three years. Anyone else can also apply to the court, with leave — which will be refused if the application will be disruptive to the child — and even the child can apply if he or she has sufficient understanding.

How the court decides If you have already read Chapter 4, you will know the factors the court takes into account in making any order in respect of the upbringing of the child or the administration of the child's property; under the Children Act 1989, s. 1, 'the child's welfare shall be the court's paramount consideration'. This means the needs and desires of the parents, society at large and others come second — but are not ignored altogether.

The court will take into account all the circumstances in deciding what order, if any, to make in relation to a child: the child's own wishes, needs, the likely effect of any change in circumstances (i.e., the status quo is likely to be favoured); age, sex and background; whether the child has suffered harm or is at risk; and the capability of the parents and other relevant persons to meet his or her needs. Above all the court will consider whether it is worth the effort of making an order at all, in that if it would be better to make no order, it should do just that (s. 1(5)). The court must also hear evidence of any relevant facts. If allegations of abuse or inadequate parenting are made, they must be substantiated by credible evidence. Therefore, where a mother resisted contact and relied on a video tape containing allegations of sexual abuse, the video would not persuade the court if it was made in breach of the safeguards outlined in Chapter 8 (*Re M (Sexual Abuse Allegations: Interviewing Techniques)* [1999] 2 FLR 92; see p. 185).

In making its decision, the court will not only hear the parties and the argument by their lawyers, it can also call for a report (oral or in writing) from a probation officer or social services department and take into account the contents. (See Chapter 9 for more on reports.)

Orders which a court can make   The type of order that a court can make about the future of children is dictated by the Children Act 1989, ss. 5 and 8, and Sch. 1.

Section 5 deals with the child who has no parent or guardian. The court can appoint a guardian to take up parental responsibilities for the child. (This section also enables a parent to make a written declaration appointing a guardian for the child after the parent's death, which may avoid the need for someone to apply to the court for a guardian to be appointed where both parents are dead.)

Section 8 enables a court to make — of course — a 's. 8 order'. Section 8 does not cover orders about money (dealt with below), the appointment of guardians under s. 5, and care or supervision (see Chapter 7); but s. 8 covers almost any other dispute about the future of a child.

The orders we are about to describe can be made in favour of any person the court thinks appropriate, after hearing all the evidence, not just the applicant and not just a parent; for example, a grandparent, step-parent, an unmarried father, or even a sibling (e.g., *Re W* [1996] 3 FCR 337, where an older brother applied for contact with his younger brother).

1. Contact orders   David McKee, writing in [1997] Fam Law 386, cited research showing that 40 per cent of fathers lose contact with their children after divorce: 'It emerged that the major difficulty facing fathers was in . . . renegotiation of their role. Research on complete families shows that the father role is negotiated by the mothers, with the children. On the breakup of the marital relationship a father needs the goodwill of the mother . . .' Contact negotiations take place in the shadow of the law, which enables a court to order contact. However, the law cannot renegotiate roles. Perhaps a social worker, providing support on behalf of a child in need, can help in this respect.

The s. 8 *contact* order itself provides that a person with whom the child is not living shall have specified contact with the child. An application can be made by anyone, not just a parent — for example, a grandparent. The court can lay down the exact nature and extent of the contact, for example, overnight stays, supervised visits, telephone contact. The right to contact is that of the child. The contact must be in the child's welfare interest. Starting from those two fundamental principles, each case must be decided on its own facts, and the judge or magistrates, after hearing the evidence, have a wide discretion. Certain predictions can be made about how the courts make contact decisions. For example, a court will be likely to want a child to have some form of contact with his or her natural father, even if there has been no previous contact, even, in fact, where the child had no knowledge that the applicant, a man serving a long prison sentence, was their father (*A v L (Contact)* [1998] 1 FLR 361). In fact the Court of Appeal has recently stated that the presumption is in favour of contact with a parent — so the burden of proof rests with the person who claims he should not have contact: *F (A Child) (Contact Order)* [2001] 1 FCR 422. For example, contact beyond cards and letters would not be in a child's interest whether the father was serving a life sentence for murder and the mother wanted to protect the child from this violent past (*P (Minors) (Contact)* (1998) *The Times*, 30 July).

Once a contact order has been made, the courts may take a hard line with parents who obstruct contact. In *Re O* [1995] 2 FLR 124, the Court of Appeal said that non-cooperation was not an option, and ordered the mother not only to allow reasonable contact with the father but also to send progress reports, photographs, etc. to him in between contact visits. In *A v N (Refusal of Contact)* [1997] 1 FLR 533, the Court of Appeal would not allow an appeal by a mother who was jailed for six weeks for obstructing contact which a court had ordered, even though the father was violent and even though sending her to jail was not in the children's best interests. Again, in *F v F (Contact: Committal)* [1998] 2 FLR 237, the President of the Family Division said that the mother must not sabotage contact by indoctrinating the children against it. However, the pendulum is now swinging back. In *Re M (Minors) (Contact: Violent Parent)* (1998) *The Times*, 24 November, the Family Division refused contact to a man whose violence to the mother made contact with the children a disturbing experience. The court said it was time to start expecting violent men to change their behaviour. And in *Re M (Contact: Family Assistance: McKenzie Friend)* [1999] 1 FLR 75, the mother's genuine fear was held to be a good enough reason to prevent face-to-face contact, in the interests of the children who were upset by their mother's distress when they returned from seeing their father. Similarly, in *Re K (Contact: Mother's Anxiety)* [1999] 2 FLR 703, where the father had previously kidnapped the child, the mother's anxiety made it in the child's best interest to reduce contact, even though the child was enjoying the contact.

Supported contact may be facilitated by the National Association of Child Contact Centres (www.naccc.org.uk; tel. 0115 941 4557), which has 277 centres nationally.

2. Residence orders   A s. 8 *residence* order settles the arrangements to be made as to whom the child is to live with. A residence order in favour of any person gives that person parental responsibility for the child. This can, in itself, be sufficient reason to make an order, in spite of the 'no order unless necessary' principle. In *B v B* [1992] 2 FLR 327, a grandmother needed a residence order so that she could give consent for school trips, etc. If an unmarried father obtains a residence order, he also gets the parental responsibilities under s. 4, which then continue even if the residence order is cancelled. A residence order can be granted in an emergency without hearing evidence from anyone other than the applicant (*M v C* [1993] 2 FLR 584). Generally, advance notice is required.

The courts are reluctant to presume that one parent is 'better' than another, except in the case of a newborn baby, where it will be hard for the father to obtain a residence order at the expense of the mother (*Re W* [1992] 2 FLR 332). In *Re A (A Minor)* [1997] CLY 447, the Court of Appeal confirmed its reluctance to make presumptions in favour of the mother. What makes this case particularly interesting is that the court considered the relevance of the UN Declaration of Human Rights, which states that a child of tender years should only exceptionally be separated from his or her mother. Thorpe LJ dismissed the argument on the ground that the presumption contained in the Declaration was now out of date.

The courts will always presume that residence with the natural parent is best, unless the evidence against this is strong (*Re D (A Child) (Residence: Natural Parent)* [1999] 2 FLR 1023). This automatic preference was summed up by Lord Templeman in *Re KD (A Minor) (Access: Principles)* [1968] 2 FLR 139: 'The best person to bring up a child is the natural parent. It matters not whether the parent is wise or foolish, rich or poor, educated or illiterate, provided the child's moral and physical health are not endangered.' This is arguably more in keeping with the right to family life approach of the European Convention on Human Rights than the welfare principle of the Children Act 1989.

A residence order can be made in favour of more than one person, even specifying how the child's time will be split, if this serves the child's interests. For example, in *G v G* [1993] Fam Law 615, the father looked after the children when he was not on shift work; the mother covered during the shift work. The court approved a joint residence order because it was working well for the children. The principle was reaffirmed in *Re D (Children) (Shared Residence)* [2001] 1 FCR 147. In *G v F* [1998] 3 FLR 1, a lesbian couple both wanted a residence order in relation to the child, born to one of them by artificial insemination. The biological mother opposed her former partner's application. The judge recognised that both parties loved the child, and the nature of their lesbian relationship should not prevent the court doing what was best for the child: a shared residence order. Nevertheless, split residence orders are rare.

Once a residence order has been made, the child's surname cannot be changed unless all those with parental responsibility agree, or the court orders a change (which it will generally be reluctant to do: *Re F* [1994] 1 FCR 110).

3. Specific issue orders   A s. 8 *specific issue* order takes away the responsibility of a parent to make a specified type of decision, and requires the decision to be made instead by the court. This order ensures that, where there is disagreement, major decisions, such as where the child is to be educated, or whether he or she should have certain treatment, are brought before the court. So it is essentially a negative type of order, reducing parental power. It can be used in cases such as *Re B* [1991] FCR 889, where the court overruled a mother and permitted her 12-year-old daughter to have an abortion. (In fact, the courts seem to prefer to use wardship for dealing with this type of problem, rather than s. 8. See Chapter 4 for more about wardship.) Another example of a specific issue order is to change a child's surname, where a parent objects. The courts, applying s. 1 of the Children Act, generally consider that the interests of the child require there to be no change. They may be more sympathetic where a child has already become used to using a new name before the application comes to court. *Dawson* v *Wearmouth* [1999] 2 AC 308 is the House of Lords' confirmation that each case must be decided based upon an assessment of the child's welfare.

In *Re K (Specific Issue Order)* [1999] 2 FLR 280, a mother had told her son that his father was dead. In fact the father was an alcoholic whom the mother hated intensely. The father wanted his son to be told of his paternity and applied under s. 8 for a specific issue order. The court held that while in principle it would be in the son's interest to know who his father was, in this instance it would be damaging because of the mother's attitude.

4.Prohibited steps orders A corollary of the specific issue order is the s. 8 *prohibited steps* order. This could, for example, prevent a child being taken abroad or living with a certain individual. In *Re J (A Minor) (Prohibited Steps Order: Circumcision)* [1999] 2 FLR 678, the court granted a prohibited steps order where the father wanted to have the child circumcised in accordance with his religious beliefs and the mother, not herself a Muslim, resisted.

What else can the Court Order?

If an application comes before a court, the court looks at all the circumstances and will make any order under s. 8 that it thinks appropriate on the evidence. So the result may be different from that for which the applicant was hoping. What is more, the family may find the probation service or social services involved, since the court can make a family assistance order under s. 16. This requires the probation officer or social services department to advise, assist and befriend the person named in the order; this may be the child, or any parent or person who lives with or has contact with the child and who consents. This order lasts for up to six months, but can be revoked earlier on the application of the probation officer or social worker, or any party to the s. 8 proceedings.

The family assistance order can in fact be made in the course of any 'family proceedings', which are defined in Chapter 4.

Another possible outcome of any hearing is that the court may consider that local authority care or supervision may be appropriate. The court may, under s. 37, require a social services department to investigate, and specifically to consider whether they should themselves apply for a care or supervision order, or provide assistance to the family or take any other action with respect to the child. They must inform the court within eight weeks of the results of the investigation and any decision made.

Any order made in respect of a child's upbringing, or agreement made between the parties without a court order, can be altered by the court on further application.

What happens if the court makes no s. 8 order? Or, which is the case with most children, what if no one has ever thought of bringing the arrangements for the children before a court? What is the status quo before a s. 8 order? The answer depends initially on whether the parents are married or not. If the parents are unmarried, only the mother has any 'parental responsibility' and there is no ambiguity about who is legally responsible for making the decisions. In fact, the father will frequently be fully involved in taking responsibility for the child — but the law allows the mother to pull the rug from under his feet, and in cases of dispute, he will have to apply to the court for a s. 8 order or a parental responsibility order.

Parental responsibility orders   If an unmarried father is unhappy about not having the power to take decisions which goes with parental responsibility, he can apply to a court under s. 4 for a declaration that he has parental rights and duties jointly with the mother. It does not require a relationship breakdown or a court order for this step to be taken; many stable couples regard this as a sensible move to formalise the father's position. Orders can be made where the father is abroad or in prison, or the child is abroad. But there are limits. A father who managed on home leave from prison both to conceive a child and commit a robbery for which he got 15 more years, was denied a parental responsibility order (*Re P* [1997] 2 FLR 5). He should have thought about the consequences of his actions. But if he had married the mother, his irresponsibility would have been of no consequence. A father married to the mother, at conception, birth or any time subsequently, automatically has parental responsibilities, and the termination of the marriage makes no difference.

Where parental responsibilities are shared, either parent can exercise them independently of each other; where the parents are, or were, married, the law has made an underlying assumption of trust between them, and assumes agreement as to the arrangments for the children. The same assumption applies where a s. 4 parental responsibility order has been made. If that trust is not justified, either party can apply to the court for one or more of the s. 8 orders.

Maintenance and Property Disputes on Relationship Breakdown

The law's philosophy   The Matrimonial Causes Act 1973 does not make it easy to predict how property and finance issues will be sorted. The system is not like that in Scotland, where there is an initial presumption of a 50:50 split of property and savings acquired during the marriage (although see below). It is not like Germany or Sweden, where maintenance for the spouse is extremely rare and the welfare state picks up the additional costs. It is not even like other areas of English law, where previous cases decided on similar facts enable lawyers to make sensible predictions. If you are asked — indeed if an experienced matrimonial lawyer is asked — by a client to advise on money and property matters, remember the following extraordinarily unhelpful remarks of Ormrod LJ in *Sharp* v *Sharp* (1981) 11 Fam Law 121:

> It was often said that the Court of Appeal was inconsistent when considering family finances. Each family was unique and often decisions decided on different facts or even similar facts were not helpful. Sometimes a *Mesher* type order [postponing sale of the matrimonial home until the children leave] was appropriate, but again on very similar facts such an order might

not be appropriate. The judge has to go through the exercise of s. 25 [discussed below] of the Matrimonial Causes Act 1973. There was no need to look at the reported cases.

In other words, in trying to settle a marriage breakdown without litigation, a divorcing person is navigating blind. In addition, parties should constantly be aware of the costs of litigation, and the devastating cost of appeals. By the time the case of *Piglowska v Piglowska* [1999] 1 WLR 1360 had reached the House of Lords, legal costs were £128,000, whereas the total combined assets were worth £127,000. Their Lordships gave lawyers a lecture on costs, stating that a wrong settlement for something may be better than a successful appeal gaining nothing.

For most couples there simply are not enough assets to allow for easy decision-making. The needs of the children are the first (but not paramount) consideration. Once these needs are catered for, is there any presumption in favour of equality? We would not have even raised this question in earlier editions, because there was no such presumption. Rich men generally took more out of the ruins of the marriage than their spouses. Now, however, there is (belatedly) a presumption of equality; but it is only a presumption, and there has to be something available to be equal about (*White* v *White* [2000] 2 FLR 981 (HL)).

The home   A person starting a property dispute with the benefit of funded Legal Aid should be reminded of the right of the Legal Services Commission to deduct legal costs from the value of any assets recovered or preserved in the forthcoming proceedings. The home may end up subject to a massive extra charge. The same applies to those paying their own costs. In *White* v *White*, above, legal costs have exceeded £1 million, in relation to joint assets of £4 million (Law Society Gazette (2001) 24 October, p. 5).

Both parties may want to continue to live in the home, or to have the sale proceeds; how does the law apportion the rights in the property?

The first possibility is that the parties agree on who will live where, and how the ownership will be adjusted. This is the simplest option, but not necessarily the best; for example, the wife may think she is entitled only to a half share, but a court may be likely to award more. So legal advice is recommended before agreeing any property division. Legal advice is not a panacea. A settlement based on bad legal advice can occur, and the courts will not overturn it (*Harris* v *Manahan* [1996] 4 All ER 454). The only choice then is to sue the bad legal adviser. (Because of legal costs, disputes are not recommended, however.)

If the parties cannot negotiate an agreed settlement of property questions, the court has to resolve the dispute.

If there are no children, unmarried parties have to apply to the Chancery Division of the High Court for an order that the property be sold and divided up. The court is empowered to do this, because the 'trust' which is implied when parties jointly own property subsists only while the purpose for which it was conceived also subsists. If a property is bought for a relationship, the trust ends with the end of the relationship. However, if there are children, the trust normally continues until the need to house the children in the trust property has also ended. So an order for sale may be obtained, but postponed.

To avoid going through the expense, delay and frustration of Chancery proceedings, the party who wishes to live in the property may be able to buy the other party out. To determine what price to offer, legal advice should be obtained. If the matter comes to court, in determining shares of ownership, the court will only look at the financial aspects of the input to the property in the light of any evidence of what the parties intended when the property was acquired. Unless she can prove that an explicit promise was made to give her a share of the property, a woman who has stayed at home to bring up the children gains no credit for this in the final balance sheet; but if she built an extension, or paid money into the common kitty for household and mortgage expenses, then she may build up a financial interest in the property accordingly. This area is legally very complicated and constantly changing. Your best advice is to put your client in touch with an appropriate lawyer.

Divorcing couples have a much simpler, but often less predictable, task. At the same time as dealing with a divorce petition, the court can adjust all the interests in ownership of the property to suit the current position of the parties and the children (Matrimonial Causes Act 1973, s. 24). The starting point will be who owns what, as with the unmarried parties, but the idea of adjustment is that everything can be varied, taking all factors into account. (But there is no presumption that the overall goal is equality. Needs must be met, particularly the needs of children; but after meeting needs, including the 'need' to continue living in luxury, any surplus wealth should in principle be divided equally, according to the House of Lords in *White* v *White* (above).) For this purpose, the home is just one asset amongst all the others, and the principles operating when the court makes property adjustment and financial provision orders are dealt with in the next section. Note that the tenancy of the matrimonial home is also subject to adjustment in divorce proceedings: it can be transferred from one spouse to the other, or from joint names to one only. The landlord cannot veto such a court order.

If parties are unmarried, or married but not going through divorce, and there is a child of the relationship, the court can order amongst other things a transfer of property between the parents for the benefit of that child. However, an order cannot be made against a non-parent, whatever the circumstances, except in divorce proceedings (*Re D* [1993] 2 FLR 1). An order of this type is only designed to benefit the children, and the transfer may be only for the duration of their dependence, leaving the parent who looked after them with nothing once they leave home (*T* v *S* [1994] 2 FLR 883).

Who will live where?   How will the court approach the division of the income and assets? It cannot usually make any order until it is known where the children are to live, as this affects the earning capacity of the parents and their housing needs.

Once the arrangements for the children are known — if necessary the court has to make a s. 8 residence order if the parties cannot agree — other parts of the jigsaw begin to fall into place. The parent with whom the children will live will, if at all possible, have to keep the matrimonial home or be assured of a suitable substitute. If the matrimonial home is owned, the other parent will hope to realise enough of his or her share in order to buy somewhere else. The party moving out, albeit that he may have been the breadwinner paying the mortgage and the bills, may be entitled to well under half the value of the home, in recognition of his greater earning capacity now, the wife's needs and the children's needs for a home (if they are staying); the wife can often increase her share by forgoing maintenance for herself in the future.

If the wife can raise the cash to buy out his share then the problem is relatively simple (except for the huge mortgage repayments). If, on the other hand, there are not enough resources for one to buy the other party out, it will be necessary either to order the property sold, or to make a deferred order, whereby the parent looking after the children can continue to live there until the children grow up. (Usually both parties remain liable for the mortgage, as the lender will refuse consent to a transfer of ownership to a low earner.) This is all very well while the children are there, but it leaves a divorced wife in middle age facing homelessness when, finally, the husband's share is realised. An alternative order may be for her to have the home until she remarries or cohabits. This is also unjust: the husband may never get his share; the wife feels that she is prevented from starting a new life with someone else. But the real problem is the enormous cost of housing, which overstretches one family's resources on breakdown.

Who has what resources and what needs? The other factors the court will consider, after looking at the needs of the children, are the needs and resources of the parties, and their relative capacities to earn (including potential, where, e.g., a wife could return to work). The length of the marriage will be relevant; the shorter the marriage, the less the obligation between the parties is likely to be. The court also considers the ages of the parties, what contributions each has made over the years to the welfare of the family, and lastly, the behaviour of any party if it has been extreme. For example, in *Kyte* v *Kyte* [1987] 3 WLR 86, the wife had not only had an adulterous and clandestine relationship with another man, but had encouraged the husband to attempt suicide. Her lump sum award was reduced in the light of this conduct. In *L* v *L* [1994] 1 FCR 134, the husband had squandered most of his assets through his compulsive gambling. His share of what the wife had managed to keep out of his hands was ordered to be much less than half because of his behaviour. Note that behaviour is not allowed to take precedence over the needs of the children, which is the court's first consideration (but unlike proceedings *about* children, their needs are not paramount).

In passing, we note a remarkable case, *J* v *S-T* (1996) *The Times*, 25 November. It is not a divorce case but a case on nullity, but where property and finance are involved the law is identical. The 'husband' in this case was actually a woman. When the wife eventually discovered this she petitioned for a declaration that the marriage was void. The 'husband' claimed a share of the wife's property. Under the Matrimonial Causes Act 1973, s. 25 the court said that the 'husband's' behaviour was so extreme that she should get no financial adjustment.

It has already been noted that the court can adjust shares in the ownership of the home, and order it to be sold, or transferred from one spouse to the other, or order the transfer of a tenancy. The court also has power to adjust ownership of other property (for example, furniture or a car), to order payment of a lump sum from one to the other, and to order maintenance, either for a period or indefinitely.

Maintenance payments and divorce If parties are going through divorce, the court can adjust their rights to ownership of the matrimonial assets; and it can order payment of maintenance between spouses. Maintenance of children is now normally governed by the Child Support Act 1991 (see below and p. 397).

An interim maintenance order — known as maintenance pending suit — can be made before the divorce itself is granted. An application may be necessary as soon as the petition for divorce has been commenced.

The courts are encouraged, under the Matrimonial Causes Act 1973, ss. 25(1) and 25A, to try to obtain a clean break between the parties, by adjusting property once and for all, and, if a maintenance order is made between spouses, limiting its duration. There is, however, no such thing as a clean break in responsibilities to the children, since the duty to maintain continues until 17, or beyond if they remain in full-time education. (While the Matrimonial Causes Act encourages clean breaks, the Child Support Act 1991 promotes the opposite. And if a person obtains income support for a child, the ex-spouse can be ordered to pay maintenance to the DSS not only to cover the cost of the child, but also as an allowance to the parent who looks after the child. So a person effectively pays some maintenance towards a spouse even after a clean break.)

If a maintenance order is made in favour of a spouse, it is possible to go back to the court which made it and to apply for a variation based on new circumstances. For this reason a wife is best advised to agree nominal maintenance — say 5p a year — which can be varied if her needs change, rather than to agree to no maintenance order at all. She should have legal advice in any event.

A question which a party (let us here presume it is the wife) might ask is whether an application for maintenance for herself is worth the bother, given the limited resources available to the husband. It frequently happens that, however much maintenance he pays, she will still have to rely on income support (IS), and (see Chapter 18) the maintenance received will simply reduce the amount of benefit. There are two reasons why an application for maintenance should still be considered: first, if the wife later becomes employed, the maintenance will be a real addition to her resources; secondly, (ex) spouses are obliged to maintain each other. If they are able to do so, but fail, throwing their dependants on to the state, the DSS can itself take proceedings against them for the maintenance. If the wife fears that her ex-partner's maintenance payments will not be reliable, she can sign the maintenance over to the DSS while she receives IS. The DSS then pays the full amount of IS, however much maintenance they actually receive from the husband.

Pensions The court has power to order pension fund trustees to make pension payments directly to a former spouse. Therefore a divorce court can treat present or future pension expectations as part of the matrimonial assets.

However, unless the court exercises its new pension splitting power, the payments will cease on the death of the person whose pension it was or on remarriage of the recipient. This means that a lump sum now may well be preferable as a trade-off against a possible pension benefit in later years.

In 2000 the court also gained power to order pension payments to a divorced person to continue beyond the death of the spouse, or on remarriage of the beneficiary. This is called pension splitting. This will reduce the amount of pension benefits available, because the pension fund is now required to pay out on two lives, not one.

Property and maintenance orders for married parties who are not divorcing Married parties not going through a divorce can apply for a maintenance order (and a modest lump sum order of £1,000) against their spouse (Domestic Proceedings and Magistrates' Courts Act 1978, ss. 2, 6 or 7). At the same time, if there are children, an order can be sought for them. Maintenance orders made by the magistrates are often lower than those made by the county court; if the marriage is over, then it is usually better to deal with financial matters as part of the divorce proceedings.

Married parties can also apply to the county court for a determination of their rights in property under the Married Women's Property Act 1882, s. 17. This was the Act that first enabled women to own property independently from their husbands. But unlike divorce proceedings, the Act provides no mechanism for the adjustment of shares of ownership. So if divorce proceedings are contemplated, all property issues are probably best resolved there.

Interim orders Where a court has a divorce case before it, it can make the final, considered maintenance and property adjustment orders only when a divorce order has been made. However, the court may make an interim maintenance order as soon as divorce proceedings start.

Enforcement and Variation of Orders
Unlike child support (below), court maintenance orders for a spouse have no automatic enforcement mechanisms. If a maintenance order falls into arrears, the unfortunate payee has to go back to court to get it enforced. There are various possibilities. Commonly, a court will order the payer's employer to make regular deductions from wages and pay them direct to the court. Or a court can order the non-payer to be committed to prison — usually a threat of last resort.

But on any application for enforcement, the court may also remit, i.e. cancel some or all of the arrears, or may vary any maintenance order. It can also do this on the application of a person — payer or recipient — whether or not there are arrears. Many men, in our experience, are quick to assume new financial burdens after a relationship breakdown, and then to ask the court to reduce their payments and remit the arrears. Since their ability to pay has to be taken into account, it may be better for the recipient of maintenance to try to obtain the best possible property and lump sum order initially, and trade that off against uncertain maintenance in the future. (As we see below, the maintenance of the children cannot be traded in this way.)

Maintenance for Children

Non-resident parents are expected in law to pay towards the maintenance of their children. This principle applies regardless of whether the children need the payments (for example, the parent with care may be very rich). And it applies regardless of whether the payments will actually benefit the children, for in cases where the parent with care receives means-tested benefits, the maintenance simply reduces the benefit entitlement.

Child maintenance can be paid by agreement. Otherwise an absent parent can be made to pay maintenance in one of two ways: exceptionally, by a court order; or, usually, by the Child Support Agency.

The Child Support Agency   The arrival of the Child Support Agency in 1993 was greeted with mixed feelings. Many, ourselves included, see the courts as very blunt instruments for dealing with delicate issues of family finances. The adversarial tradition, whereby the parent with care has to apply and prove her right to payments, favoured the absent parent who chose to be obstructive. Without legal aid the expense was prohibitive; and even with legal help, if there was any property settlement the then Legal Aid Board clawed back its costs.

Additionally, the courts had such a wide discretion in deciding what should be paid that advisers could never predict the outcome with confidence, making sensible negotiations harder.

The Child Support Agency, which was set up by the Child Support Act 1991, approaches maintenance from a more mechanical point of view. How much the absent parent pays is calculated according to formulae available to advisers. These formulae initially had a reputation for extraordinary complexity. In 1998 the Government sought to simplify them. Now, the starting point is that the non-resident parent pays 15 per cent of net income for the first child, 20 per cent for two children, and 25 per cent for three or more. (Those on low incomes or with second families pay less.)

That seems like good news. The bad news takes three forms, which we examine below.

Parents with care who receive state benefit   The first problem is the Agency's brief to save money for the Treasury. If it can obtain maintenance for children of single parents who are living on means-tested benefits (income support, means-tested jobseeker's allowance, family credit or disability working allowance) then the DSS can reduce the benefits paid out. (Though in relaxation of the rules, the parent with care may now keep the first £10 before seeing benefits reduced pound for pound.) The Agency can force the parent receiving these state benefits who is looking after the children to make an application. It cannot force any other lone parent to make an application. The philosophy is therefore clear. In benefit cases, the Agency has the right to enquire into the identity and whereabouts of the non-resident parent, usually the father, whom the mother may have every reason not to want to bring back into her life. In the past such parents would have chosen not to make a maintenance application; now they can have their benefits reduced for not cooperating with the Child Support Agency. The only way out for a parent with care receiving means-tested benefits is to convince the Agency that there is a good reason for not divulging the information. Privacy is not considered a good reason, but fear of harm or 'undue' distress is a good reason under s. 6 of the Act. The word 'undue' is broad enough to leave a huge discretion to the Child Support Agency. Agency guidelines suggest that only physical violence counts, or fear of it. But the guidelines are not legally binding. On the positive side, the Agency guidelines say the claimant should be believed, and is not required to prove the violence.

Failure to cooperate with the Agency leads to reduced benefits for 18 months. This reduction does not start straightaway: the parent with care has an agonising six weeks either to change her mind and supply details of the father before the cuts bite, or to prepare for existence below subsistence level.

The Child Support Agency as a cause of disputes The second way in which the Agency can be bad news is that it can influence the arrangements for caring for children. A non-resident parent gets to pay less in maintenance if the child stays with him for 104 nights or more a year. This is an incentive to fight contact battles for the wrong reasons. (From 2002 there will be a discount for overnight stays of at least 53 nights a year.)

The Child Support Agency and inefficiency This is the third bit of bad news about the Agency. It has been 'the greatest failure in public administration in the present century' according to Stephen Cretney, a leading family law expert ((1998) 95/28 LS Gaz 33). The delay in processing cases and then enforcing payments has been monumental, throughout the Agency's life. Parents with care have suffered. Errors in calculations, leading to hardship for the paying parent, are regular. The National Audit Office recently found that the Agency made large numbers of miscalculations (NAO, *Child Support Agency: Client Funds Account 1999–2001*, HC 658). Formulae have been rigid, in some cases harsh, even leading to suicides by distraught fathers trying to meet the demands of the old and the new family.

How the Child Support Agency calculates payments from the non-resident parent The calculation of how much is payable by an a non-resident parent is set out in complex tables. (Some advisers have computer programs to carry out a calculation.) The sum is arrived at by first looking at the basic (that is income support levels) needs of the child; then the ability of the non-resident parent to pay; and lastly the means of the parent with care.

The scheme has been amended, following protest from non-resident fathers, to give the Agency some discretion to leave more money to the paying parent and take account of the particular financial circumstances of either payer or recipient. Allowance is made for the cost of second families, and a parent cannot be made to pay more than 30 per cent of net income. Where, before the Agency scheme started in 1993, a 'clean break' order had been made whereby, in effect, property was traded for liability to maintain the children, the paying parent now receives some credit for this 'wasted sacrifice'. Another recent relaxation of the calculation rules allows the Agency to make an award of maintenance based on apparent wealth, even though the paying parent's actual (or revealed) income is low.

Who is a non-resident parent?   This is normally not a problem for the Agency, but if a man denies paternity the Agency has to apply to a court under s. 26 for a declaration. The court will rely on scientific evidence. However, no further proof is necessary if the man has previously adopted the child, or if in other proceedings (such as Children Act 1989 contact proceedings) he was already found to be the father.

Enforcing an Agency order   Once a payment has been calculated, the Agency is responsible for enforcement. Payments can be made by standing order or direct debit. Enforcement can be via deductions from earnings (s. 31), or direct from benefits (s. 43). Property of a non-payer can be seized by order of the magistrates' court (ss. 33 and 35), and ultimately he can be committed to prison.

Agency inspectors carrying out an assessment of the non-resident parent's means have powers to interview him, to search property, and to inspect documents. They can obtain information from the tax office, housing benefit department, and the Benefits Agency or Department of Employment (ss. 14 and 15). From April 2002, they will have the power to apply to a magistrates' court to get the non-paying parent disqualified from driving. There is every chance that such a parent will claim breach of his right under the European Convention First Protocol not to be deprived of property, or of his Article 8 right to a fair trial.

More details of the Agency can be obtained free from www.dss.gov.uk.csa. There is a free advice phone line on 08457 133 133. A CAB, Law Centre or solicitor can also help. An application to obtain an assessment is made on a form available from any Benefits Agency office. (A child cannot apply, only the absent parent or the person caring for the child.)

Appeals against Agency decisions   Agency decisions, including reductions of benefit for non-cooperation, but also relating to assessments of maintenance payments, can be appealed to the Child Support Appeals Tribunal. The right to appeal must usually be exercised within 28 days of the decision. There is also a right to a review of the decision, which is carried out by the Agency itself.

The role of the courts in provision for children   The court, not the Child Support Agency, continues to decide questions of maintenance from an absent parent in the following circumstances:

(a)   where the child is disabled;
(b)   where the application relates to school fees;
(c)   where the application is for a top-up over and above the Agency assessment (relevant to the rich only);
(d)   where there is already a pre-1993 maintenance order or agreement in effect (but if the parent with care gets means-tested benefits, the Agency takes over).

Where paternity is disputed, the courts must settle that issue before the Agency can decide on the correct level of maintenance. (But a court will not necessarily order a blood or DNA test, because doing so may exceptionally not be in the child's interests.)

The diminished role of the courts is a cause for some celebration, as we mentioned. It is also a cause for concern, because courts no longer have the ability to look at the whole of a divorcing family's financial affairs and decide on a complete package. It has been policy for some time to aim to reduce continuing dependence between spouses, to achieve a 'clean break' on divorce in particular, and, where appropriate, to order smaller or nil mainten-ance for the children in return for a larger share in property. Such clean break orders are more difficult now because of automatic continuing liability under the Agency to maintain the children. Any agreement not to approach the Agency is unenforceable, and anyway, if the parent with care needs to apply for benefits, the Agency will want to pursue the non-resident parent regard-less of an agreement.

Other financial and property matters   In deciding the other issues — lump sum payments to spouse and children, property division, spouse maintenance — the court will have to take the assessment of the Child Support Agency as given, and adjust everything else with that in mind.

Courts continue to have powers to make lump sum orders in favour of children, whether or not the parents were married. We look briefly at how they make this kind of decision; these considerations also apply where the court is (exceptionally) making a decision in relation to maintenance for children.

The considerations taken into account are set out in Sch. 1 to the Children Act 1989. (If there is a divorce petition, similar considerations are set out in the Matrimonial Causes Act 1973.)

If a child normally lives with a particular person then that person can apply to the court for a lump sum order for the benefit of the child. Lump sum payments can cover expenses incurred before the application, for example in connection with or anticipation of the birth.

It is not just the other parent who can be ordered to make a payment: it could also be a step-parent who accepted the child as a child of the marriage. (In contrast, the Agency has no powers to make a step-parent pay.)

Orders for children are rarely made in isolation. If the parents are splitting up, their needs and resources have to be taken into account too. Indeed, the court may at the same time be hearing applications for property adjustment and maintenance between spouses. When considering financial orders in favour of a child, the court does not have to make the welfare of the child its paramount consideration, as it does when considering where the child shall live and who he or she shall have contact with. What the court must consider are the needs of the child, the child's resources, physical and mental attributes, and educational expectations, and also the needs and resources of both the paying party and the party who the child is living with. It may decide, in the end, to balance these requirements instead of putting this child's needs above all other needs (such as those of other children to whom a parent may have acquired a responsibility).

Any financial order that relates to children, or agreement between the parties — even an agreement expressed to be unalterable and final — can be varied by the court on application, and a child of 16 or over can him or herself apply to vary an order.

Court orders for child maintenance generally last until the child is 17, or ceases full-time training or education.

Child Abduction

A parent may decide to take questions of residence and contact with a child into his or her own hands. If the child is removed within England and Wales, the court can make a residence, contact or specific issue order (see above p. 389) to ensure the child's return. The bigger problem arises if there is a risk of the child being taken abroad. If that risk is foreseen, urgent action is necessary, and it is wise to instruct a specialist lawyer. Assuming, for the sake of simplicity, the child is living with the mother, and it is feared that the father may remove the child abroad, steps can include:

(a)   an agreement, or court order, for the father to surrender his passport (not always effective if the father has a foreign passport, as a replacement may be provided by an embassy);

(b)   a ports warning, carried out by the police. Again this is not guaranteed to succeed, especially with the reduction of passport controls in the European Union.

Where the child has already been removed, legal action becomes necessary in the country to which the child was taken. This is horrifically distressing and difficult. In some countries, laws give custody to fathers automatically, so a court order will be impossible. However, any country which has signed the Hague Convention on Civil Aspects of Child Abduction is bound to assist with returning a child to the country where he or she is 'habitually resident', unless this is quite clearly contrary to the best interests of the child (for example where the children are violently opposed to returning and evidence suggests this will cause psychological harm: *Re M (Abduction: Psychological Harm)* [1997] 2 FLR 690 — an application to return abducted children to

Greece). The Lord Chancellor's Department in the United Kingdom contacts the authorities in the country concerned, and those authorities must take steps to obtain the child's return.

Child abduction (removal of a child from the United Kingdom without the consent of the other parent) is a criminal offence. (For this purpose, consent of a father without parental responsibility is not required.)

An organisation providing support to parents whose children have been abducted is: International Child Abduction Centre, PO Box 4, London WC1X 3DX; tel 0207 357 3440; www.reunite.org.

SEVENTEEN
Housing Problems

The social services department itself has certain duties to provide accommo-dation, especially to vulnerable people (see Chapter 13) and to children (see Chapters 4–7 and 11). But that is not what this chapter is concerned with. Your involvement arises because you are dealing with people — children, the elderly, the handicapped, etc. — to whom you have statutory duties. And these clients may suffer housing problems; if you can assist them in sorting these out, you may have avoided the need for more social work intervention.

The law is complex. It is often ignored, both by tenants, who do not know that they have rights, and landlords, who may rely on or share this ignorance. It is an area which tenants frequently do not recognise as having a legal dimension; we hope that where a client has a legal problem, the social worker will be able to diagnose it as such and point the person towards more specialist advice.

For example, there are arrears with the rent, the landlord is threatening to throw the tenant out, and the flat is damp. The tenant may see this as an insoluble problem — the social worker, on the other hand, should be recognising rights and obligations; the landlord may have a legal duty to repair; the tenant cannot be thrown out without a court order; the rent may be too high — and, once you have told the tenant that there may be something he or she can do, specialist advice should be sought.

We have omitted the housing problems of owner occupiers. They are spared most of the problems which beset the tenant, except the threat of repossession for failing to pay the mortgage, or, for many flats, the ground rent. The most important advice to those with mortgage difficulties is to contact their building society or bank immediately to discuss ways of meeting or rescheduling the payments. (We looked at rights of ownership and occupation of property on relationship breakdown in Chapter 16.)

The key issues for the non-property owning client are the following:

(a) obtaining a property;

(b)   homelessness;
(c)   rent control;
(d)   keeping the property; and
(e)   keeping it in repair.

These issues are considered further below, once we have discussed the social worker's roles in housing advice.

THE SOCIAL WORKER'S ROLES

Signposting

Your main role is signposting. By this we mean spotting legal problems and telling people where to go for advice. Many people find it hard to go for advice, and need encouraging that they have rights, or at least that they may have. You must take a positive, though not necessarily optimistic, role.

A problem of conflicting loyalties could arise here. In metropolitan or London boroughs you are employed by a local authority which may also be the landlord of your client. How will your employer react if you appear to be advising clients against them? If you suffer doubts, you must discuss these with a senior person in your department. But we have no doubts. You are advising people to whom you often have a statutory duty; and you are advising tenants about rights which they themselves have under statute. Whoever the landlord may be, if there is a failure to carry out, say, certain repair obligations, by pointing this out to the tenant and pointing to sources of specialist advice, you are doing what you are employed to do — to be a professional social worker.

Looking at this issue the other way round, remember that the housing department owes different duties to its clients. Under the Children Act 1989, s. 27 it must cooperate with social services, but does not have to *provide* housing to your clients. The case of *R v Northavon District Council ex parte Smith* [1994] 3 WLR 403 illustrates the different duties. The family was 'intentionally homeless' which meant that the housing authority had no obligation to house them (see below p. 416). The social services authority (as it happened, a different authority) did have a duty to accommodate the children, who were 'in need' (Children Act, s. 17(6)). It could not force Northavon to provide this accommodation, and therefore should have addressed the children's needs through other means (e.g., helping find the rent for private rented accommodation).

Advocating/liaising

Some of your clients, particularly those for whom you are providing community care services, may be homeless, or have problems with the landlord or neighbours. We will see below that you have a direct responsibility to assist the client towards obtaining or keeping accommodation.

Picking up the Pieces

Whether or not the client's housing problems are dealt with, a client of social services who meets the relevant definition — a child in need under the

Children Act, a disabled person under the National Assistance Act, etc. — remains a client. *R v Newham LBC ex parte P* (2000) 9 Nov QBD Admin Ct, reported in Legal Actions (2001) January 28, reminds us of the continuing statutory duty. When the council evicted P from her temporary accommodation (which it was lawfully entitled to do because she was 'intentionally homeless'; below, p. 416), she began to sleep rough. She had mental health problems. P was offered a hostel bed; she turned it down. The council argued that it had discharged its statutory duty to her as a homeless person. The Queen's Bench Division held that, at best, it might have done, but the council had overlooked its community care obligations. This person had to be assessed under s. 47 of the National Health Service and Community Care Act 1990 (Chapter 13, above) and accommodated under Pt III of the National Assistance Act 1948 'forthwith'.

Asylum Seekers

We warned in Chapter 1 that the powers and duties of social services departments under LASSA 1970 do not apply to asylum seekers. The Immigration and Asylum Act 1999 does the same to housing departments, who owe no duties to asylum seekers. Such rights as asylum seekers have to housing are covered briefly in Chapter 18 (briefly, because they are pathetically few).

OBTAINING A TENANCY

You may be asked to help someone who is looking for accommodation. The choices open to people are taking up a private sector tenancy, a Housing Association tenancy or a local authority tenancy.

Private Sector Tenancies

Some people may prefer to rent property in the private sector, or have no choice because they are not in priority need or have been found to be intentionally homeless. Renting in the private sector may reduce their legal rights (see later) but it can offer greater choice, particularly as to the type of accommodation available and its location. Private accommodation is advertised in local papers and the Housing Office may have a list of landlords. Accommodation agencies may offer a service to people looking for private sector accommodation, but their services are often expensive and may not be relevant to people on benefits. Their operation is covered by the Accommodation Agencies Act 1953. Note that private sector landlords can select their tenants in any way they choose, and have no obligations over and above anti-discrimination legislation.

The most important advice for those seeking accommodation in the private rented sector is to check that it is affordable. Most private sector landlords require deposits and rent in advance which are not automatically covered by income support payments. More importantly, housing benefit, which covers rent payments, is not only means-tested but also has limitations with regard to the level of payments which can be made on any particular property.

Several local housing departments run schemes to help people rent in the private rented sector which aim to speed up housing benefit decisions and support tenants in their dealings with their landlord. You should check to see what services are offered in your local area.

Private sector landlords are most likely to offer assured shorthold tenancies under the Housing Act 1988.

Housing Association Tenancies

Housing Association tenancies are generally obtained either through a waiting list run by the individual housing association, or via nominations from the local housing department. Again, you should get to know which Housing Associations offer accommodation in your area and what their criteria are. Housing Association landlords are most likely to offer tenancies which are assured tenancies under the Housing Act 1988.

Local Authority Tenancies

The Housing Act 1996 provides that local authorities are permitted to allocate housing only to qualified people appearing on the register. Thus the first and most important advice to give someone looking for local authority accommodation is to get on the housing register. Local authorities are obliged to allocate housing in accordance with the law.

The Housing Act 1996 and a code of guidance lay down principles for allocation of local authority housing. 'Reasonable preference' must be given to helping people to move out of bad or insecure housing, to those with dependent children, to expectant mothers, and to people with medical or other problems (s. 167). Additional preference may be given to people who have a particular need for settled accommodation on medical or welfare grounds. The authority must publish its criteria, including how it will apply these statutory priorities.

The 1996 Act and the local authority's criteria do not create rights: no one can take the authority to court for not granting a tenancy unless the authority has plainly behaved irrationally. For example, a rigid refusal to allow a transfer because the applicant is in rent arrears (*R* v *Southwark LBC ex parte Melak* (1997) 29 HLR 223) is unreasonable. Refusing to consider transfers on grounds other than being the victim of violence is equally unreasonable (*R* v *Islington LBC ex parte Nelson* [1997] CLY 2697, where the applicant needed to move because the premises she occupied were unfit for habitation and making her seriously ill). Complaints can be made to the ombudsman or to a councillor, or legal action may be taken via judicial review proceedings.

The 1996 Act limits the powers of the authority to choose who to grant public housing to. A person subject to immigration control is not qualified to come on to the register unless he or she is:

(a) a person who already has a public sector tenancy;
(b) a person accepted by the Home Office as a refugee;
(c) an asylum seeker whose claim was lodged before 4 February 1996; or
(d) a person with unconditional leave to be in the UK.

A person who is not eligible for public housing cannot be granted assistance under the homelessness provisions of the Housing Act either (with very limited exceptions for asylum seekers whose status is not determined — see below, p. 412).

Does Homelessness Create a Right to Local Authority Accommodation?

As we see below, in certain circumstances a local authority must provide, or help find, accommodation for a homeless person. If the accommodation provided is a council house/flat, this used to be permanent. From the commencement of the Housing Act 1996 the duty on housing authorities has been limited to two years unless the authority decides to extend it. The Homelessness Bill currently going through Parliament (at the time of writing) will restore the permanent duty (see p. 421).

Introductory Tenancies

A local authority or a housing action trust is entitled to grant new tenants a tenancy for a trial period of up to a year as 'introductory tenants' (Housing Act 1996, Pt V). The stated purpose of the tenancy is to enable public housing authorities to get rid of tenants who behave anti-socially, and it is part of a series of measures designed to improve life for the majority of residents on local authority estates. The provisions also allow tenants with introductory tenancies to be evicted for rent arrears.

The landlord can obtain possession at the end of the year by applying to the court, and the court must order it if the correct procedure has been followed. There is no need to prove any grounds such as bad behaviour or non-payment of rent; all the tenant can do is to ask (within 14 days of the notice that the landlord intends to evict the tenant) for the landlord to review the decision. This power of summary eviction with no consideration of grounds or evidence has been challenged under the Human Rights Act 1998, since the tenant can lose his or her property without any trial, in breach of Article 6 and the First Protocol of the European Convention. The Court of Appeal in *McLellan* v *Bracknell Forest DC* [2001] EWCA 1510 (unreported) decided that introductory tenancies are Human Rights complaints on the basis that judicial review combined with the internal review procedure provided sufficient safeguards for tenants. Moreover the procedure was necessary for the protection of the rights and freedoms of others. Guidance provided by the Department of the Environment, now the Department of Transport, Local Government and the Regions, emphasised that the provisions should not be used against vulnerable tenants when providing support via social services would be more appropriate.

Following the introductory year the tenancy becomes secure, and grounds are needed before a court can order eviction.

HOMELESSNESS

It is not easy for people with limited resources to obtain and keep accommodation. The law does not provide a welfare safety-net for everyone via homelessness legislation.

This area of law is governed by the Housing Act 1996 (references to sections are to this Act unless otherwise stated). Many cases decided under the old legislation remain valid, as the basic principles were retained in the 1996 Act. District and borough councils must also take into account the Code of Guidance on Pts VI and VII of the Housing Act 1996 published by the Department of the Environment (now the Department of Transport, Local Government and the Regions) in October 1996; this sometimes takes a fairly generous view of the council's obligations, and is worth having and quoting on behalf of a homeless applicant. It contains extensive references to the duties of social workers where their clients are vulnerable and at risk of homelessness. It is available free of charge.

Social Workers' Duties

The Code clarifies the respective duties of housing departments and social service departments. There is a duty to liaise with the homelessness unit of the housing department on questions of vulnerability and need. There is an overlap between your duties: under s. 20 of the Children Act 1989, social services must accommodate children in need where appropriate, out of social service resources (see p. 227). But the housing department (which will be a different authority except in London or metropolitan districts) must respond to a request from the social services for accommodation (Children Act 1989, s. 27(2)) — but not if, the Code admits, this is going to be too much of a burden on the housing department (para. 14.13). So it is not an entirely clear-cut duty, and there is a real risk of buck-passing. The case of *R v Northavon District Council ex parte Smith* [1994] 3 WLR 403 (see above, p. 406) makes clear that the buck stops with social services, which cannot make a housing department provide accommodation where the need arises under the Children Act. The social services department had a continuing obligation to help find accommodation for a homeless family where there was a child in need under s. 17 of the Children Act, even though the housing department had fulfilled its minimum obligations, in *R v Barnet LBC ex parte Foran* (1999) 31 HLR 708. On the other hand (Code, para. 14.13) 'Children should not be provided with accommodation by the social services authority as a result purely of family homelessness'. If you think the law is unclear, we agree. We think you have a duty to children in need, however that need arose. Nothing in the 1996 Act contradicts that part of the Children Act. Indeed, you are at risk of judicial review if you do not assess the needs of a child to be housed under s. 17 of the Children Act 1989 (*R v Tower Hamlets LBC ex parte Bradford* [1997] CLY 2639).

There is a risk of people being shuttled to and fro between departments. This is unacceptable, and liaison between authorities must take place and policies be established. If such liaison is not effective, and an individual client falls between two departments, this could lead to a complaint to the local Government ombudsman (see p. 30), or under the Children Act complaints procedure (see p. 82). The field social worker, on behalf of a vulnerable client, will have to test his or her assertiveness skills both with his or her own line manager (or whoever controls the purse strings) and the housing department. Good luck!

The Extent of the Local Housing Authority Duties to the Homeless

The basic objective of Pt VII of the Housing Act 1996 is to place a duty upon local authorities to provide advice and assistance and, in certain limited circumstances, accommodation for the homeless. You will realise from this that local authorities do not have to house everyone who is homeless. In many parts of the country there is a shortage of decent affordable housing and the law serves to ration that accommodation to those who are both in need and, according to the criteria set out in the Act, deserve it. The statutory obligation placed upon local authorities is to make available suitable accommodation for a person who is eligible for assistance, homeless, in priority need of accommodation and who did not become homeless intentionally. The duty is also subject to the local connection provisions of the Act. Your clients may seek your advice and support directly about their homelessness, but may also need advice in the context of relationship breakdown, mortgage possession proceedings, eviction, immigration or dissatisfaction with their housing conditions.

The key definitions of 'eligibility for assistance', 'homelessness', 'priority need' and 'intentionality' need to be understood before advising on anyone's rights under the legislation. It is also important to be aware of the relevant local authority's policies and practice and the local authority's allocation scheme and to understand what accommodation can be described as suitable. We will examine these questions shortly. First of all, it is important to understand who can apply as homeless and the system of inquiries that follows an application. The key word that triggers the process is that a person must *apply*. There is no reference to an age limit in the Act, so in theory a minor can apply, but courts have excluded applications from dependent children (see p. 416). An authority only owes a duty to someone who has the mental capacity to understand and respond to an offer of accommodation and, if accepted, to understand the responsibilities involved. Whether a person has sufficient mental capacity to make an application is to be decided by the authority and its decision can be challenged only on the basis that no reasonable authority could make such a decision. Although joint applications can he made, for instance by husband and wife, each individual is entitled to separate consideration of his or her case.

The duty then on the authority is to take reasonable steps to hear and adjudicate upon applications and to make reasonable provision for receiving applications. Applications need not be in writing, or in any particular form. An application can be made by any member of a household. On completing its inquiries, the authority must notify the applicant of its decision and, so far as any issue is decided against his or her interest, inform him or her of the reasons for the decision. Any notice of any decision by the authority must inform the applicant of his or her right to request a review of the decision and of the time limit for doing so (s. 184).

There is an interim duty to accommodate in the case of apparent priority need while inquiries are on-going (s. 188). The duty ceases when the authority's decision is notified to the applicant, even if the applicant requests a review of the decision, although the authority may continue to secure that the accommodation remains available.

Inquiries by the housing department should be made in a caring and sympathetic way directed towards the relevant issues. They should not be carried out in the manner of a CID inquiry but can be, and indeed should be, rigorously and fairly pursued. The applicant must be given an opportunity to explain matters which the authority is minded to regard as weighing substantially against him or her. If inquiries lead to doubt or uncertainty, the issue should be resolved in the applicant's favour. A 10-minute conversation was not sufficient exploration of the reasons why the applicant was homeless in *R v Dacorum Borough Council ex parte Brown* (1989) 21 HLR 405. If medical evidence is relevant, where the council's decision was based on the report of a doctor who had not even seen the applicant, the investigation was ruled inadequate by the court: *R v Lambeth London Borough Council ex parte Carroll* (1988) 20 HLR 142. The greater the applicant's problem, the more thorough the assessment required. In *R v Ealing LBC ex parte C (A Minor)* (2000) 3 CCL Rep 122, C was a nine-year-old suffering from dyspraxia, asthma, incontinence, dyslexia and partial blindness. He was having to share a bed with his mother in a small flat. The council's failure to assess his practical difficulties before turning down his application as homeless was unlawful because it was unreasonable. If the person is homeless because he or she failed to pay rent, the department must find out if it was deliberate or accidental (*R v Westminster City Council ex parte Ali and Bibi* (1992) 25 HLR 109).

Social workers must, of course, help the housing department where it is in their clients' interests. The Code (Part 11) requires the homelessness unit to liaise with *other bodies*. These include, of course, social services and health authorities 'where applicants appear to have care, health or support needs'.

The authority is under a duty to inquire into:

(a)   whether the applicant is eligible for assistance;
(b)   homelessness or threatened homelessness;
(c)   priority need; and
(d)   intentionality.

There is a power, not a duty, to make inquiries into local connection.

The first key inquiry — eligibility for assistance   No duty is owed by the housing department to anyone, however dire their situation, if the legislation and the regulations taken together make them ineligible for assistance (s. 185). The philosophy behind this is to remove the right to emergency housing assistance for anyone whose immigration status is restricted. The same people are defined as ineligible as are barred from going on to the public housing register in the first place (see p. 409). (There is one exception: a duty is owed to a person seeking asylum but whose status as asylum seeker has not yet been accepted by the Home Office. However, no duty will by owed if that person has any accommodation of any sort, including hostel accommodation but excluding totally unsuitable accommodation.)

The second key inquiry — homelessness   If the person is eligible then the authority moves on to investigate his or her homelessness. It is not necessary to have, literally, no roof over a person's head. A person is homeless if he or she, together with any person he or she can reasonably be expected to live with, has no accommodation which they are entitled to occupy and which it would be reasonable for them to continue to occupy (s. 175). In *R v Newham LBC ex parte Sacupima and others* (2000) *The Times*, 1 December (CA), it was made clear that tenants did not become homeless until actual execution of a bailiff's order, despite the fact that there was no defence to the proceedings and the tenants had to bear the cost of the court proceedings. Accommodation includes accommodation overseas. A person does not have to be actually homeless to qualify under the Act, if he or she is likely to become homeless within the next 28 days.

This definition of homelessness raises several questions. *First, what is meant by accommodation which the applicant is entitled to occupy?* A person is entitled to occupy a place he or she owns, or has a tenancy or licence of, or has a right to occupy by marriage (under the Family Law Act 1996, see Chapter 16). An informal licence, which a person has by virtue of living with relatives, could be terminated at any moment; it nevertheless constitutes a right to occupy, so a person is homeless 'intentionally', with all the disastrous consequences that follow from this label, if he or she gives this up for no valid reason. But if the hosts genuinely want that person to leave, and are not colluding to get him or her a home with the local authority, that person is threatened with unintentional homelessness. A cohabitee living in his or her partner's premises has an entitlement to occupy as a licensee, unless that right is withdrawn on relationship breakdown.

We cite two further examples of a right which the applicant cannot exercise. The landlord has changed the locks — the tenant has the theoretical right to occupy, and may eventually be able to enforce it. Or the applicant has a caravan, but nowhere where he or she is entitled to place it. People in these circumstances are usually treated as homeless.

Secondly, when is it reasonable to continue to occupy accommodation? The Act gives some indication of when it would *not* be reasonable. For example, under s. 177(1), it will not be reasonable:

> . . . if it probable that this will lead to domestic violence against [the applicant] or against—
> (a)   a person who normally resides with him as a member of his family, or
> (b)   any other person who might reasonably be expected to reside with him.

Domestic violence is defined as violence from an 'associated person' with whom the applicant was living, such as a relative, a cohabitee or a member of the same household or threats of violence from such a person which are likely to be carried out.

Victims of domestic violence can go to court to obtain an injunction to enable them to return to a property. Quite often a victim does not want to do this as he or she is frightened to do so. Will your client be obliged by the local authority to obtain an injunction to allow him or her to return to the property? The Code of Guidance says: 'Injunctions ordering persons not to molest, or enter the home of, the applicant will not necessarily deter people and the applicant should not necessarily be asked to return to his or her home in this instance. Authorities may inform applicants of the option to take out an injunction, but should make it clear that there is not an obligation to do so, if she or he feels it would be ineffective.' Some local authorities try to insist that an applicant obtains an injunction. You should support your client by referring to the Code.

What of the person who commits the violence? Such a person is not homeless within the Act; he is able to exercise his rights of occupation. (If an injunction is obtained requiring him to leave the property, or if his local authority or housing association landlord evicts him under a ground specifically designed to remove the perpetrators of domestic violence from family homes, he is then homeless; but as we shall see below, it is treated as intentional homelessness, because he is the cause of his own misfortune.) However, while it is not necessarily your job to worry about such a person, you should bear in mind the provisions of the Children Act 1989, para. 5 of Sch. 2 (see Chapter 5); a suspected abuser of children can be assisted by social services in finding accommodation, including cash assistance such as paying a deposit or even an advance of rent. (No statutory obligation is placed on the local authority housing department by this provision, but the social worker should liaise with them when helping the abuser find somewhere to live.) Note that the Homelessness Bill (see p. 421) proposes extending s. 177 of the Housing Act to other violence and amends the local connection provisions (see p. 417) in a similar way. This means that being the victim of violent or intimidating anti-social behaviour from outside the home may well justify a decision to cease his or her occupation of a property.

Matters other than domestic violence can make it unreasonable to continue to occupy accommodation. These could include affordability, physical conditions in the property, overcrowding, type of accommodation (so that, for instance, crisis accommodation such as women's refuges or direct access hostels should not be regarded as suitable for occupation in the longer term) and violence or threats of violence from persons not associated with the applicant. It is important to note, however, that in deciding whether it is reasonable for a person to continue to occupy accommodation, a local authority may have regard to the general circumstances prevailing in relation to housing within its area. So if the prevailing housing conditions are overcrowded or in serious disrepair then the local authority is unlikely to find that it is unreasonable to continue to occupy the accommodation. If your client is not accepted as homeless on these grounds, you should advise him or her to use the review proceedings (see p. 421).

Thirdly, who may live with the applicant? The right to family life is a fundamental human right and suggests that families should be able to live together. The 1996 Act recognises this. The definition of homelessness covers not only the applicant, but people he or she could reasonably be expected to live with (s. 176) — a spouse, a cohabitee, dependent children or relatives. A pregnant woman should be considered as herself plus the baby (the baby being a person she could reasonably expect to live with – *R* v *Newham London Borough Council ex parte Dada* [1995] 1 FLR 842). In *R* v *London Borough of Ealing ex parte Sidhu* (1983) 2 HLR 41, the court said the Borough housing department was wrong to require that the applicant, a single parent, have a custody order (now known as a residence order) before it would be reasonable for the children to live with them.

The third key inquiry — priority need The authority has to decide if the applicant, or someone who can be expected to live with the applicant, is in *priority need* (s. 189), which means:

    (a)   a pregnant woman;
    (b)   dependent children (including a child who could reasonably be expected to if the applicant had a home);
    (c)   a person who is old, mentally disordered, or handicapped, or who has some other special reason for being vulnerable; or
    (d)   a person whose homelessness, or threatened homelessness, results from flood, fire, or similar emergency.

The Code (para. 14.10) advises the homelessness unit — in consultation particularly with social services — to be sensitive to the vulnerability of young people, to the risk of violence, sexual abuse, drug or alcohol abuse or prostitution. Those leaving institutional care, including a young offender institution, are likely to be vulnerable — and therefore in priority need. The Homeless Persons (Priority Need) (Wales) Order 2001 (Welsh Statutory Instrument 2001 No. 607) has extended the descriptions of those who have priority need partly in response to the Children (Leaving Care) Act 2000, which came into force on 1 October 2001. In particular, the following persons are to be considered as having priority need: those persons who are care leavers or persons at particular risk of sexual or financial exploitation; persons who are over 18 but under 21, or 16 or 17 years old; persons fleeing domestic violence or threatened domestic violence; persons homeless after leaving the armed forces; and former prisoners homeless after being released from custody. At the time of writing (October 2001), it is anticipated that a similar statutory instrument will extend priority need for England very soon.

Vulnerability was somewhat restrictively defined in the case of *R* v *Camden LBC ex parte Pereira* [1998] 4 CL 369. A drug addict was vulnerable only if his condition made him less able to obtain and keep a home than other homeless people. The fact that, like an applicant with children, being housed is a good thing for a drug addict, does not seem to have convinced the Divisional Court. On the other hand, an alleged paedophile who had been driven from his home and who received death threats in temporary accommodation was vulnerable and entitled to accommodation (*R* v *Tower Hamlets LBC ex parte G* (2000), November 2000, Legal Action 23).

Problems can arise where a child shares his or her time with two parents living apart. It is not a requirement in law, but is nevertheless helpful to the homeless applicant, to have a s. 8 residence order. If the child normally lives with the applicant, or would do so but for the lack of a home, the applicant is in priority need (*R* v *Lewisham Borough Council ex parte C* [1992] Fam Law 329). Social workers, in liaising with the housing department, should bear in mind that their duty under the Children Act includes keeping families together, if this is in the child's interests. The housing department does not have this duty (see p. 418).

Dependent children can never be vulnerable, even if they suffer from one of the specified conditions, as Parliament has provided for them by giving a priority right to accommodation to their parents or carers (*R* v *MBC of Oldham ex parte G*; *R* v *LB Bexley ex parte B* (1993) 25 HLR 319).

Impecuniosity is not sufficient to amount to 'other special reasons', but total resourcelessness caused, for instance, by excluding asylum seekers from benefits is (*R* v *Kensington and Chelsea ex parte Kihara* (1997) 29 HLR 147 (CA)). Asylum seekers excluded from benefit are now excluded from the provisions of the legislation by means of s. 185, but extending vulnerability to those who are totally without resources may be useful for a wide range of single people.

The fourth key inquiry — intentionality   The authority has to decide if the homelessness is *intentional* (s. 184), which means that the applicant has accommodation which it would be reasonable to continue to occupy, and by some deliberate act loses it (s. 191). The same criteria apply to threatened homelessness (s. 196).

The key to this is 'deliberate'. A person who suffers domestic violence leaves in consequence of an act of someone else — this is not deliberate. (The code of guidance suggests that if a person has not yet suffered violence, but has been threatened, and leaves, that is not deliberate either.) This interpretation is upheld in several cases. For example, in *R* v *Northampton Borough Council ex parte Clarkson* (1992) 24 HLR 384, a woman suffering sexual advances from her half-brother applied to another authority as a homeless person. Without investigating her allegations of harassment, they said she could have carried on living near the half-brother. The court said that the council must investigate the circumstances. Exactly the same happened to a wife who left the area because of her husband's violence: *R* v *Tynedale District Council ex parte McCabe* (1992) 24 HLR 384.

According to the Code, a person in rent or mortgage arrears through careless financial management whose property is repossessed is homeless intentionally, whereas the person whose arrears arose from genuine difficulties will be unintentionally homeless (para. 15.6). But who makes the decision? It is the housing department, subject to review and appeal procedures. The applicant can try to blame his or her partner for the failure to pay the mortgage (and therefore prove that he or she had no intention of default). This argument failed in *R* v *Barnet LBC ex parte O'Connor* (1990) 22 HLR 486, but in this case the applicant was partly to blame for remortgaging the house beyond the family's means. It should succeed if she was genuinely blameless — see para. 15.2 of the Code. In *R* v *Exeter City Council ex parte Trankle* (1993) 26 HLR 244, the applicants had lost their home by securing a loan to run a hopeless pub. They had acted unwisely, but in good faith, so their homelessness was not intentional.

A vulnerable person who does not know how to manage his or her affairs, thereby becoming homeless, cannot be said to have acted intentionally (Code, para. 15.6); but with proper support from social services (see Chapter 13 and Code, para. 15.8) that person would not have been allowed to drift into that position in the first place.

There is much litigation on intentional homelessness. For example, the court upheld the local authority who considered a person intentionally homeless who left a home because of poltergeists (*R* v *Nottingham County Council ex parte Costello* [1989] HLR 301); tenants who had a reasonable counterclaim for disrepair but consented to the landlord's possession application were held to be deliberately homeless (*R* v *London Borough of Wandsworth ex parte Henderson and Hayes* (1986) 18 HLR 522); where the tenant's children caused the nuisance which led to the possession claim the tenant herself was held to be deliberately homeless (*R* v *East Herts District Council ex parte Bannon* (1986) 18 HLR 515). The tenant who lost his home through being sent to prison for child abuse was intentionally homeless (*R* v *Hounslow LBC* (1997) *The Times*, 25 February). But when children damaged property in *R* v *Rochester City Council ex parte Williams* [1994] EGCS 35, and the landlord locked the applicant out, she was held to be unintentionally homeless.

The 1996 Act introduced two traps that can make a person intentionally homeless. One is — if applied fairly — a reasonable measure. Under s. 191(3), collusion between the landlord and the applicant ('You kick me out so that I can get a local authority tenancy') is intentional conduct. The second is more worrying. As we see below, unintentional homelessness triggers a duty for the housing department to provide advice and assistance. A person who is offered advice and assistance and rejects it becomes labelled intentionally homeless, and the housing department owes him or her no further duty. (A child or a vulnerable person may still need help from social services in this situation.)

The authority must review each individual applicant's circumstances carefully. Challenges against the authority's decision on intentionality may well be successful; decisions can be reversed without necessarily taking the case to court, especially if someone will speak up on behalf of the applicant. You, the social worker, can contact the district or borough housing department, and if you are unsuccessful, refer the applicant to a lawyer.

Passing the buck — the local connection provision   Once an applicant has been accepted as in priority need and not intentionally homeless, there can occasionally be a problem over which local authority housing department has the duty of providing accommodation.

Under s. 198, local connection means being normally resident in the area, or employed there, or having family ties. It should not be misunderstood: the applicant is *not* required to have a local connection to obtain housing under these provisions. It is more subtle; if neither the applicant nor a person who would reasonably be expected to live with them has a local connection, but does have a local connection with another local authority's area, the buck can be passed by notifying that other authority. It is therefore unlawful for a housing authority to refer all cases elsewhere just because the applicant has a connection elsewhere (*R v Harrow London Borough Council ex parte Carter* (1992) *The Times,* 3 November). It is also unlawful to pass the buck where the applicant has a good reason to leave the area where she had a connection (*R v East Devon DC ex parte Robb* (1998) 30 HLR 922, where Aberdeen was too cold for the applicant's skin condition). While the buck is in the process of being passed, the first authority approached must provide temporary accommodation until accommodation is available in the area where the local connection applies.

The local connection proviso does not apply to an applicant who has a local connection, if to return there would be to return to domestic violence.

The Housing Department's Duties to Homeless Persons
The duties in respect of homeless people are the duties of housing departments. Do not confuse these duties with those of social services. The remainder of this paragraph is concerned with the duties of social services departments to people who are ineligible for housing department help. Your duties to the vulnerable and to children are not affected in any way by immigration status, and a child in need of protection or services under the Children Act, or an adult under the National Assistance Act, must be catered for whatever their background. The Court of Appeal ruled in the case of *R v Hammersmith and Fulham LBC, ex parte M* (1998) 30 HLR 10, in a landmark judgment, that social services must accommodate a person who is financially destitute (in this case an asylum seeker whose entitlement to benefit the Government had just abolished) because that person meets the criteria of being 'by reason of age, illness, disability or any other circumstance . . . in need of care and attention which is not otherwise available to them' (National Assistance Act 1948, s. 21). The duty may even be owed to a person who has entered, or remained in, the country illegally. In *R v Brent LBC ex parte D* (1998) 1 CCL Rep 234, the applicant was too ill to leave the country, and the court had to decide between two competing principles: compassion, and not benefiting from his own wrongdoing. Compassion won in this case, and social services were ordered to accommodate the applicant, but only until he was fit to return home. This duty, incidentally, cannot be discharged by giving the homeless destitute person cash instead of accommodation. (*R v Secretary of State for Health ex parte Hammersmith and Fulham LBC* (1998) *The Times,* 9 September).

Now we return to the duties of the housing department. The 1996 Act reduced the obligations of the housing department, reflecting (then) Government attitudes towards those who failed to thrive in the so-called enterprise culture. The two significant changes from the old entitlement are:

(a)   If there is accommodation available for rent in the local area, the department can advise and assist the applicant to get that rather than provide or secure housing for the applicant itself.

(b)   If the department does provide or secure housing, this does not create a secure tenancy, it simply provides a two-year breathing space for the applicant who meanwhile works his or her way up the register of housing applicants. At the end of the two years he or she has to apply again as homeless, or find something else in the meantime. Even if homeless at the end of two years, the housing department only has a power, not a duty, to provide accommodation (s. 194). However, the Homelessness Bill currently (October 2001) going through parliament proposes the abolition of these changes (see the note at p. 421).

Here, then, is a summary of what the housing department must do in the different circumstances after its investigations are complete. It is based on the Code (paras 17–21) which sets the duties out clearly:

Notification and review   Under s. 184, the department must tell the applicant, in writing and with reasons, the result of its enquiries and what help, if any, it will give. It must give the applicant details of the right to seek, within 21 days of notification, a review of the decision (s. 202). One of the following then applies:

No duty is owed   This may be because the applicant is ineligible (wrong immigration status), or not deemed homeless/threatened with homelessness. Actually a duty is still owed, in the sense that under s. 179 the department must give free advice on homelessness to anyone in its district. The department has a power, not a duty, to assist such a person to obtain housing.

The applicant is homeless/threatened with homelessness but not in priority need   The duty is confined to giving advice and assistance to help the applicant to get or keep housing (s. 192). (A social worker is unlikely to be involved, since your statutory clients are likely to be in priority need.)

The applicant is homeless, is in priority need, but the situation is intentional   The duty is to provide interim accommodation, or to secure it from elsewhere for the applicant, but only for such a period as will enable the applicant to find accommodation with the department's assistance (s. 190) .

Case law under similar legislation before the Housing Act indicates that an interim period is short, even a few days, and that use of bed and breakfast accommodation is frequent. The Code (para. 20.3) suggests a period of 28 days, although a department that did not consider each case individually would be acting unreasonably. The interim accommodation does not, under the legislation, have to be 'suitable', unlike the accommodation provided under the next heading but one. It must be capable of being called accommodation, of course. And it is not good enough if it splits up the family unit (*R* v *Ealing LBC ex parte Surdonja* (1998) *The Times*, 29 October, where the local authority split the family between hostels in Ealing and Southall).

The applicant is threatened with homelessness, is in priority need, but the situation is intentional   The duty is to give such advice and assistance as will avert the homelessness (s. 195), failing which the need for interim accommodation (see above) arises.

The applicant is homeless, in priority need and it is unintentional   This used to be the passport to a local authority secure tenancy. Now the duties are limited to giving advice and assistance in securing accommodation (s. 197), or providing/securing accommodation for two years (s. 193). A refusal by the applicant to act on the advice offered or to accept the assistance turns the homelessness from unintentional to intentional, with the disastrous consequence that the department can wash its hands of the problem after a period of interim accommodation is secured. (Leaving the problem, almost inevitably, with social services, since priority need plus homelessness probably means a child in need or a vulnerable adult.)

The applicant is unintentionally threatened with homelessness, and in priority need   The department must help prevent the homelessness occurring (s. 195). If it fails, the situation is dealt with under the previous heading. In trying to avert the homelessness it may be that social services can help; for example, a vulnerable person is at risk of eviction from an introductory local authority tenancy because of behaviour that upsets neighbours. Talking to all parties, and support to the vulnerable person, could make a difference.

Don't Forget the Children
As a social services department, not a housing department, you can ignore intentionality in the interests of children. Under the Children Act 1989, s. 17, for example, the department can provide rent money to keep a family together.

Securing Accommodation
The Act does not specify within what time limit accommodation must be secured for those in priority need who are unintentionally homeless, and it is well known that many people have to wait indefinitely in unsuitable temporary accommodation. The Code (para. 20.16) suggests temporary arrangements should be as short as possible. An applicant in priority need (or a member of their household) who is homeless intentionally can expect no more than temporary accommodation in any event (see above, p. 419).

Suitable accommodation for families and vulnerable people   One matter of particular relevance to social workers involved in liaising with the housing authorities is to note the particular needs of children. We have referred to the need to avoid them having no home because of their parents' intentional homelessness. Another factor you should be aware of is the exhortation (spelled out in the former Code but a human right in any event) that splitting families is to be avoided wherever possible, unless there is a compelling reason such as abuse or domestic violence. Quite oddly, the exhortation to housing departments to keep families together is dropped from the 1996 Code. The housing department is expected to liaise with social services in such a case.

To put a homeless Bangladeshi man into housing where there were intolerable levels of racial harassment was not considered an offer of suitable accommodation in *R v Tower Hamlets London Borough ex parte Subhan* (1992) 24 HLR 541. Likewise, to place a woman on the 27th floor of a tower block when she produced psychiatric evidence that she and her daughter suffered from vertigo, was unacceptable (*R* v *Kensington and Chelsea RLBC ex parte Campbell* (1996) 28 HLR 16). Sending a family to accommodation a long way from the children's school also was unacceptable (*R* v *Newham LBC ex parte Ojuri* (1998) *The Times*, 29 August) but, in the absence of special needs, a mere change of school was acceptable (*R* v *South Holland DC ex parte Baxter* (1998) 30 HLR 1069). Sending a homeless family to live in seaside accommodation, applying a policy that took no account of children's schooling needs, was, however, declared unlawful (*R* v *Newham LBC ex parte Sacupima* (2000) *The Times*, 1 December). Expecting a Nigerian family to live in a house daubed with racist slogans was hard for the housing department to justify (*R* v *Islington LBC ex parte Okocha* [1997] CLY 2672).

An applicant thinking of refusing an offer of accommodation should take legal advice first. The council is entitled to refuse to make any further offers, unless the applicant satisfies the council (or court) that what was offered was unsuitable.

Challenging the Local Authority's Decision

Section 202 of the Housing Act creates a right to a review by the housing department of a decision on homelessness, followed by a right to appeal to the county court. The review must be requested within 21 days of the authority's decision. Advice should be obtained urgently if the decision is unfavourable. The time limit both for applying for internal review and to the County Court is strict and may be subject to a Human Rights Act challenge. In *R* v *Newham LBC ex parte P* (unreported), 9 November 2000 (QBD Admin CT), solicitors for the applicant requested the council to accept an appliation for a review out of time. They submitted evidence that the applicant was mentally ill. The council refused. On an application for judicial review, the judge indicated that had he not granted other relief, he would have made a mandatory order requiring the council to carry out a review of the original decision out of time.

Proposals to Change Homelessness Law

The Homes Bill, which contained provisions to extend and amend the allocation and homelessness provisions of the Housing Act 1996, fell with the general election in May 2001. However, those provisions have been republished by the new government as the Homelessness Bill. This Bill will, if it becomes law, make the system of allocating local authority tenancies more flexible and extend the choices available to prospective tenants. It will abolish the housing register. It will impose a duty on local authorities to produce a strategy to reduce and prevent homelessness. In addition, it will abolish the two-year limit on the provision of accommodation following accepting someone as homeless, in priority need and not intentionally homeless and the current duty on housing authorities to consider whether other suitable accommodation is available before they can secure the accommodation themselves. It also contains a power for authorities to secure accommodation for homeless applicants who are not in priority need. At the time of writing, it is anticipated that the Bill will become law in 2002 when it will provide welcome evidence of the commitment of the government to tackling homelessness.

THE LEGAL RIGHTS OF TENANTS

The main practical problems which affect occupiers during the course of their occupation are to do with the rent level, the state of repair of the property and the right to stay in the property. We shall consider each of these in turn, but since the legal rights of tenants and licensees are dependent upon their legal status we must spend some time describing the different legal arrangements that exist within the rented sector.

Legal status depends on a number of things. First, it has to be established whether someone has a tenancy or a licence and then, if a tenancy exists, what kind of tenancy it is. The answer largely depends on the date of commencement of the tenancy and who the landlord is.

Tenancy or Licence?

People who pay money to live in someone else's property are normally called tenants. However, in law, the word tenant describes a particular type of arrangement. To be a tenant, the person or persons renting must be entitled to three things: (i) to exclusive possession (ii) of identifiable premises (iii) for a known period (such as a weekly period) (*Street* v *Mountford* [1985] AC 809). So they must be able to say that under the contract (that is the verbal or written tenancy agreement), while the tenancy continues, they are entitled to live there and to exclude anyone else from being there. A guest, or a cohabitee, or a live-in granny, or grown-up child would all fail these tests. Such occupiers are in the premises by permission of the occupier, their right to continue there can be withdrawn, and they are called not tenants but licensees.

Why does it matter if a person is a tenant or licensee? The advantage of being a tenant is that it is harder for the landlord to recover possession of the premises, because the protection provided by the Rent Act 1977 and the Housing Act 1988 extends to tenants only. We shall examine this protection below. But most licensees, like most tenants, cannot be evicted without a court order, because of the Protection from Eviction Act 1977, which we discuss below at p. 435. Also the landlord must repair premises let on a tenancy (see below, p. 437) — this obligation does not apply with a licence, unless the landlord has actually agreed to repair.

A landlord may try to describe a letting as a licence, when in fact it is a tenancy. The House of Lords in *Street* v *Mountford* said it does not matter what the letting is called; what matters is what the person actually gets from the landlord under that agreement.

Difficulties have arisen for the courts in deciding whether an arrangement is a lease or a licence in two particular areas. First, where occupiers share accommodation. These multiple occupancy agreements were discussed by the House of Lords in *Atoniades* v *Villiers* [1990] AC 417; and *AG Securities* v *Vaughan* [1988] 3 WLR 1205. In the *Atoniades* case, a young couple were looking for accommodation together. They each signed a separate agreement, described as a licence agreement to share a one-bedroom flat. Each agreement provided that the 'licensor' also had the right to occupy the premises and that he might license others to share occupation with the licensees. The House of Lords held that the arrangement was clearly a lease and that the young couple were joint tenants of the flat even though they had signed separate agreements. The terms allowing occupation by the landlord or others were clearly shams not intended to be used in reality. This contrasts with the case that the House of Lords heard at the same time, *AG Securities*. Here the premises comprised a flat which had four bedrooms, plus bathroom and kitchen. The flat was occupied by four people who were selected by the owner and who did not previously know one another. Each had arrived at a different time and each paid a different amount for the use of the flat. No exclusive possession of any part of the flat was given. It was a typical student-type house-sharing agreement. The House of Lords was clear that these were genuine licences.

There have been a number of cases since 1988. What we can learn from them is that agreements for flat-sharing should be understood in the light of all the circumstances — the relationship between the sharers, the negotiations which led up to the agreement, the nature and the extent of the accommodation, and the intended and actual way in which the accommodation was used. Do not be swayed by what the landlord or the occupiers think the arrangements are. What matters is the objective reality of the situation.

The second difficulty has arisen around the nature of exclusive possession in the context of hostel accommodation provided by social landlords. Following the decision in *Westminster City Council* v *Clarke* [1992] 2 AC 288, it was generally understood that where social landlords provided bedsitters for the vulnerable homeless in hostels and maintained strict controls over the management of the residents and the hostels, licences as opposed to leases were created. This allows a social landlord to optimise short-term provision of accommodation without granting security of tenure. However, in the decision of the House of Lords in *Bruton (AP)* v *London and Quadrant Housing Trust* (1999) 31 HLR 902, the judges returned to a very straightforward interpretation of *Street* v *Mountford*. As Mr Bruton had exclusive possession for an identifiable period (here, for a weekly term) at a rent of a room in the Housing Trust's hostel, he was found to have a tenancy. This was despite the fact that the trust itself only had the premises on licence and that Mr Bruton had understood that he only had a licence. What this means is that in most circumstances, residents who are paying rent for the exclusive use of accommodation will have tenancies, even if this causes difficulties for social landlords attempting to accommodate some very vulnerable people in short-term accommodation.

Unfortunately, even when you have solved the initial problem of tenancy or licence, the law governing tenancies is complex, and rights vary dependent upon the statutory regime that the tenant falls under. Before we start to unravel those matters, however, we should consider some basic principles which apply to all tenancies.

Written or Oral Agreement?

Many people renting homes do so without a written tenancy agreement. They may therefore wrongly assume that there is no enforceable contract. This is untrue; only an agreement for a fixed term of over three years has to be in writing. Sometimes the absence of a written agreement is to the tenant's advantage, since most of what is put in tenancy agreements is worked out by lawyers for landlords, not tenants. A binding agreement comes into effect when its terms are agreed; the best evidence of what has been agreed is what is written. Failing that, the evidence of what has been agreed is what actually happens. If the landlord says you can live here for £30 a week, and the tenant pays rent on that basis, a weekly periodic tenancy has been formed. Those terms which are not expressly agreed, such as who does what repairs, or what notice has to be given before leaving, are implied by law.

If the rent is payable weekly, the landlord must supply the tenant with a rent book (Landlord and Tenant Act 1985, ss. 4–7).

Young Tenants
Technically you have to be 18 or over to acquire an 'interest in land', which is what a tenancy is. Notwithstanding this legal hurdle, there is a willingness amongst some local authorities and housing associations, acting as landlords, to grant tenancies to 16- and 17-year-olds (reported in *Legal Action*, December 1996, p. 12). This may assist you if you are trying to help a young person to become established on leaving home or residential care. The landlord may want a guarantor for the rent. Any proposed guarantor should not sign anything before getting independent legal advice.

The Legal Significance of a Lease
Because tenancies are contractual agreements they are subject to the same legal regime as all contracts. So they are subject to human rights legislation, anti-discrimination legislation and to the Unfair Terms in Consumer Contracts Regulations 1999. These Regulations mean that the courts will strike out terms which breach the Regulations, and may provide a useful remedy where, for instance, the tenant has had to agree to rent increase provisions which are considerably in excess of the annual inflation rate. In *Camden LBC v McBride* [1999] 1 CL 284, a county court judge ruled that Camden Council's anti-nuisance clause could not be enforced against one of its tenants because of the 1999 Regulations.

In addition, tenancies have other characteristics. First, what is called the covenant of quiet enjoyment is implied by law into every tenancy. What this means is that the landlord makes a legally binding promise that the tenant's lawful possession of land will not be substantially interfered with by the landlord. In practical terms, therefore, the landlord cannot go into the tenant's home without permission, he cannot send the tenant threatening letters, neither should he stop the tenant using the premises as he wishes. The covenant is particularly useful in the context of harassment and illegal eviction. The second characteristic of which it is useful to know is the tenant's obligation to behave in a 'tenant-like' manner. This means that the tenant should look after the property, carry out minor repairs and not let damage occur through carelessness.

Recognising the Relevant Statutory Framework
In order to recognise the relevant statutory regime you need the answers to two key questions:

(a) Who is the landlord?
(b) When did the tenancy commence?

The potential landlords are local authorities, housing associations and private landlords, who can be individuals or companies. The most significant date is 15 January 1989, the date of the commencement of the Housing Act 1988. However, the commencement date of the relevant sections of the Housing Act 1996 — 28 February 1997 — is also important.

In simple terms, all private tenancies created on or after 15 January 1989 are governed by the Housing Act 1988 and must be either assured tenancies or assured shorthold tenancies. All private tenancies created before that time are governed by the Rent Act 1977 and are regulated tenancies. Where the local authority is the landlord then the Housing Act 1985 is the relevant piece of legislation, and local authority tenants have secure tenancies regardless of the commencement date. Do not forget that some local authorities use introductory tenancies for the first year of the tenancy (see p. 409). Housing Association tenancies are slightly more complex, in that the legislation has treated them in different ways depending on whether the Government of the day saw them as part of the private or public sector. Pre-January 1989, the Housing Association tenant was seen as part of the public sector, with the rent governed by the Rent Act 1977 and the other terms determined by the Housing Act 1985. New tenancies created on or after that date by Housing Association landlords are governed by the Housing Act 1988 and are generally assured tenancies, although some Housing Associations are using assured shortholds for probationary periods. The Housing Act 1996 added a final twist from its commencement on 28 February 1997. Prior to that date a private sector landlord had to comply with rigorous technical procedures to create an assured shorthold tenancy. From that date all new tenancies created are assured shorthold tenancies unless the landlord informs the tenant that the agreement is for an assured tenancy. These complex provisions have real significance, particularly in relation to the tenants right to remain in the property.

Statutory Rights
You should now be able to work out which statute covers the tenancy agreement. If so, you can identify the rights which are relevant to the tenant and give an indication of the answers to the problems which we discussed at the beginning of the chapter, i.e. what legal protection does the tenant have from rent increases and from eviction from the property. Note, however, that not all tenancies are covered by statutory regimes, either because the tenancy is one which is specifically excluded from protection by the statute, or because the tenancy agreement itself does not comply with the statute. So, for instance, a tenant of a private landlord started living in the property in

Table 17.1   Main Statutory Framework — a Summary

Legislation	Type of tenancy and its characteristics	Applicable to
Rent Act 1977	*Protected tenancies* • strong security of tenure • 'fair' rent regime (including Housing Association tenancies created prior to commencement of Housing Act 1988) • strong succession rights	Private residential tenancies created prior to 15 January 1989
Housing Act 1985	*Secure tenancies* • Tenants' Charter rights • strong exit rights • some succession rights	Local authority and Housing Action Trust tenancies whenever created which comply with landlord and tenant conditions set out in ss. 79–81 Includes Housing Association tenancies created prior to 15 January 1989
Housing Act 1988	*Assured tenancies* • market rents • strong security of tenure — but with mandatory ground for eviction where there is 2 months' rent arrears • limited succession rights *Assured shorthold tenancies* • must comply with statutory criteria including notice • very limited security of tenure • market rents	Private residential tenancies and Housing Association tenancies created on or after 15 January 1989
Housing Act 1996	*Assured shorthold tenancies* • created automatically *norm is now security limited to 6 months* *Assured tenancies* • notice must be given	Private residential tenancies and Housing Association tenancies created on or after 28 February 1997

July 1990. On the face of it that means that the relevant statute is the Housing Act 1988. However, the tenant also owns a property where she lives five days a week. The Housing Act 1988 requires that for the tenant to receive protection, she must occupy the property as her only or principal home. Clearly this tenant does not, so she will not be protected by the Act. What protection would such a tenant have? She would be a common law tenant whose tenancy can be ended by a notice to quit. Her only (and limited) protection would be via the Protection from Eviction Act 1977, which we will discuss later (see p. 435).

Our second example relates to those tenancies which are excluded from protection. The same basic facts apply — a tenant who moved into the property in July 1990. This time, however, it turns out that she has a resident landlord. Such an agreement is excluded from the Housing Act 1988 on the basis that a landlord should not be obliged by statute to allow a tenant to continue to live in his own house when that relationship has broken down. Again, what the tenant has is a common law tenancy with only the Protection from Eviction Act 1977 for protection — and in this case that protection is even more limited.

You may begin to agree with us that the law is complicated and that you are happy to have your role limited to signposting! However, a large number of tenants are covered by the statutory regimes, so we will now consider the rights which these create.

The Rent Act 1977   This Act created regulated tenancies. Such a tenancy will be either a protected or a statutory tenancy. No new tenancies can be created under the statute and so they are a dying breed. We will limit our discussion here to statutory tenancies because those represent the vast majority of tenancies under the 1977 Act.

The rights the 1977 Act created are much greater than those in subsequent statutes, so anyone who has the benefit of a statutory tenancy has something of great value and should not give it up without legal advice. The key features of the statutory tenancy are that the tenancy was created before 15 January 1989 and that the tenant resides in the property. The key exclusions from protection are tenancies with payments for board and attendance, holiday tenancies and student lettings provided by an educational establishment, along with the most important exclusion, that of tenancies with a resident landlord. Once it is established that an occupier has the benefit of a statutory tenancy, however, then he or she becomes entitled to leave the tenancy to a spouse or a member of the family, to the fair rent regime and to strong security of tenure. In *Fitzpatrick Sterling Housing Association* [1999] AER 705, a same-sex partner was allowed to succeed to the tenancy as a member of the original tenant's family. What is required from a potential success or for someone other than a blood-relation is something akin to the characteristics of a family such as a mutual degree of interdependence and the sharing of lives in a single-family unit.

By creating these strong rights the Rent Act created a regime which gave benefits very similar to those enjoyed by owner occupiers. However, the

Housing Act 1988 had two impacts upon these rights. First, it amended the succession provisions so that in general a member of the family, while they may inherit the tenancy, will do so only under the assured tenancy regime. Secondly, the increase in the availability of private sector tenancies led to landlords successfully arguing in the courts that rents of Rent Act tenants should rise to the level of market rents. This led to a great deal of hardship. Tenants who had anticipated that their rents would remain relatively stable found that they were doubled and tripled over a period of a few years. The Government intervened to provide additional protection for these tenants. The Rent Acts (Maximum Fair Rent) Order 1999 (SI 1999 No. 6) sets a maximum fair rent limit for regulated tenancies where applications for a fair rent are made after 1 February 1999. An arithmetical formula provides a maximum rent of the existing registered rent plus the difference in the retail price index since the last registration, plus 7.5 per cent for first applications or 5 per cent for subsequent applications. The limit does not apply if there is no existing registered rent, or if the increase requested is more than 15 per cent because of improvements carried out by the landlord.

The Housing Act 1988   This Act, as amended by the Housing Act 1996, governs private sector and Housing Association tenancy agreements commencing from 15 January 1989 to date. It creates two forms of tenancy: the assured tenancy and the assured shorthold tenancy.

The key feature of the assured tenancy is that the tenant must occupy the property as his or her only or principal home. The key exclusions are the same as under the Rent Act 1977. Succession provisions in the 1988 Act are limited. There can only be one succession, and only the spouse or partner of the tenant can succeed. The rent regime is a market system. The tenant is taken to have freely agreed the original rent with the landlord and therefore cannot legally challenge it. If he or she has agreed rent review clauses then, she is similarly bound. If there are no provisions for rent increases, the landlord may increase the rent annually via a notice procedure. The tenant can challenge the increase, but the Rent Assessment Committee will intervene only if the rent has been raised above the market rent level; and as the Committee can raise the rent as well as lower it, the tenant has to be very sure before challenging any increase.

Assured shorthold tenancies (ASTs) are tenancies which are similar to assured tenancies but with very limited security of tenure. Essentially, tenants can be evicted from the tenancy with two months' notice once the first six months has expired. When the Housing Act 1988 was originally passed there were some procedural requirements which needed to be conformed with before an AST could be validly created. So the tenant had to be given notice that the tenancy was an AST and there had to be a fixed term of a minimum of six months. However, landlords seemed to have difficulty complying with the requirements of the Act, so in the Housing Act 1996 the requirements were abolished. All tenancy agreements created on or after 28 February 1997 are automatically ASTs unless the landlord serves notice otherwise. The rent control provisions for ASTs are more rigorous than for assured tenancies.

The tenant is allowed to challenge the initial rent during the first six months, but only if the rent is significantly higher than the market rent. It is also extremely unlikely that any tenant with such limited security is going to risk his or her future in the property by commencing such a challenge.

The Housing Act 1985 The Housing Act 1985 creates secure tenancies. It covers all local authority tenancy agreements whenever they were commenced, and Housing Association tenancies created before 15 January 1989. (Do not forget that for such tenancies, their rent regime is that of the Rent Act 1977). The key feature of the secure tenancy is that the tenant occupies the property as his or her only or principal home. Therefore if the tenant moves out and lets out the property, he or she loses security of tenure and can be evicted easily. The way the statute is worded, however, means that the tenant can regain his or her secure tenancy status if he or she manages to move back into the property before the landlord commences proceedings against him — a saving provision that does not exist in the private rented sector and means that local authority landlords have to be on their toes if they want to evict someone for illegal subletting. The principal exclusions to the 1985 Act are set out in Table 17.2 below.

There can only be one succession under the Housing Act 1985, which can be either by a spouse or a member of the family. Because there is a statutory list of family members who can succeed and that list does not include same sex partners, unfortunately same sex cohabitees cannot succeed to the tenancy. There are no rent control provisions in the statute other than the right of the landlord to charge reasonable rents for their properties. Tenants must be given notice of rent increases.

Security of Tenure

While we have given you an outline of the rent control and succession provisions under the various statutes, the most important statutory rights are those which govern security of tenure. Security of tenure is the extent to which the tenant has the right to remain in the property after the landlord has decided he or she no longer wants to let to the tenant. It will not surprise you

Table 17.2   Principal Categories of Public Sector Tenancies Excluded from Security (Housing Act 1985, Sch. 1)

— Introductory tenancies
— Property let to employees to carry out their job (e.g., a warden's flat)
— A letting to a homeless person (see above, p. 418)
— Temporary lettings to people moving into the area for work (the first year only)
— Lettings to students
— Lettings to squatters

that Rent Act 1977 statutory tenants have much stronger rights to remain in the property than Housing Act 1988 assured tenants, and that assured shorthold tenants (particularly since the commencement of the Housing Act 1996) have very little security of tenure.

In each of the statutory regimes the landlord must serve a notice. This will be either a notice to quit under the Rent Act 1977, or a notice of seeking possession under the Housing Act 1985 and the Housing Act 1988. The notice must specify the grounds for possession. The grounds for possession in each of the statutory regimes are set out in Tables 17.3 to 17.5 below.

Grounds on which a court can order possession: private landlords   Table 17.3 summarises the grounds that have to be proved for a post-January 1989 tenancy (a Housing Act 1988 assured tenancy), and Table 17.4 shows the grounds that the landlord must prove for the earlier kind of tenancy (the Rent Act 1977 statutory tenancy).

Grounds for possession: public sector   The grounds on which a court will grant possession are divided into three categories. These are found in Housing Act 1985, Sch. 2 (see Table 17.5). Except for an introductory tenancy, possession is never automatic for a public sector landlord. There is always a discretion; in each case the court must be satisfied that a possession order is reasonable, or that there is suitable alternative accommodation for the tenant. Where the property is of a particular type — for example, adapted for a disabled person, or adjacent to special facilities for the elderly — the court has to be satisfied both that there is suitable alternative accommodation and that possession is reasonable.

Terminating the assured shorthold tenancy   During the initial six months of an AST the landlord can recover possession only by obtaining a possession order from the court based upon a limited range of grounds (which, however, includes all of the rent grounds). After that six months is up a specific procedure for recovering possession is open to the landlord, who can give notice of not less than two months stating that he or she requires possession. The notice may be given before the expiry of the six months, although no order for possession can be applied for before the six months is complete. The court must make an order for possession and has no discretion at all, as long as it is satisfied that the correct notice has been served. No matter how long a tenant has been in the property, the two-month notice period is sufficient.

The accelerated possession procedure   Not all possession cases have to go to a full court hearing. If a landlord wishes to evict an assured shorthold tenant, he or she can use a paper only procedure. The landlord has to have given the tenant a written agreement and written notice to benefit from this much cheaper court procedure. If he or she is able to apply to use the accelerated possession procedure, the tenant has only 14 days within which to respond. If the tenant has any doubt about his or her status then it is critical to get

Table 17.3   Housing Act 1988 Assured Tenancies: Principal Grounds for Possession for Tenancies Created on or after 15 January 1989

---

1.   The main mandatory grounds — court must grant possession

(a)   Landlord must have given notice on creation of tenancy for these grounds to apply:

— The landlord shares the accommodation with the tenant.
— The tenancy is 'shorthold'.
— The landlord lived in the property before the tenancy.
— The landlord now needs it as a home for him- or herself or spouse (but only if there has been no change of landlord since the tenancy was granted).
— The landlord has defaulted on the mortgage, and the bank or building society wants to sell the property without a tenant.
— The property is a holiday home let out of season.

(b)   No requirement of notice before tenancy created

— The landlord intends to carry out major reconstruction or demolition.
— The tenant inherited the tenancy under the will of the old tenant in the last 12 months.
— At least 8 weeks' rent arrears have accrued (both at the date of the notice and not below 8 weeks by the date of starting court proceedings).

2.   Discretionary grounds

— Suitable alternative accommodation (not necessarily equally good).
— Rent arrears (of any amount), both at the time of the notice of seeking possession and again at the start of proceedings.
— Persistent delay in paying the rent.
— Allowing the property or furniture to deteriorate.
— Causing a nuisance.
— Tenant no longer employed by the landlord.
— The tenant's violence has caused his/her spouse/partner to leave permanently (this ground is available only to social landlords and charitable trusts).

---

legal advice as soon as possible. If no defence is made then the judge may simply make an order for possession. This procedure can only be used to grant possession. If the landlord wishes to claim arrears of rent then he or she must issue small claims proceedings in the county court.

Table 17.4   Rent Act 1977 Statutory Tenancies: Principal Grounds for Possession for Tenancies Created Before 15 January 1989

---

1.   Mandatory grounds (* notice required before letting)

— An owner occupier or a member of his or her family wants to move back in (or sell in order to buy another home).*
— The owner bought the property as a retirement home, and now wants to live there.*
— The property is normally a holiday home.*
— The letting is a 'shorthold' tenancy.*
— The letting was by a member of the armed forces.*
— The landlord shares the accommodation with the tenant.

2.   Discretionary grounds

(a)   Breach of the tenancy agreement

— Arrears of rent.
— Subletting without permission.
— Allowing the property or furniture to deteriorate.
— Annoying neighbours.

(b)   Balance of inconvenience

— The tenant is no longer an employee of the landlord; the landlord needs the property for a current employee.
— The landlord, or a member of his or her family, wants to live there.
— Suitable equivalent alternative accommodation is available.

PROCEDURES AND TACTICS IN POSSESSION CASES

Having served the required notice — called a notice to quit or a notice of seeking possession — the landlord will issue a summons. The time between notice and summons can be as little as two weeks (and where anti-social behaviour is alleged by a local authority landlord, the notice and the summons may be served together), so the tenant cannot delay seeking advice. The summons sets out what it is that the landlord claims — possession, and sometimes rent arrears or compensation for damage as well. It will state when the court will hear the claim for possession. The court sends this to the tenant, together with a document setting out what the landlord's grounds for the claim are. The landlord's grounds must be precise and must be recognised under the relevant Act (one of the grounds in our tables, probably, though we have not included each and every ground). The tenant is entitled to know exactly what is alleged. 'Noise and disruptive behaviour', without details of the alleged incidents, was held not to be enough, and the landlord's claim for possession

Table 17.5   Principal Grounds of Possession for Public Sector Tenancies

1.   Grounds where the court need only be satisfied of reasonableness

— The tenant has failed to pay rent.
— The tenant (or tenant's visitor) has caused a nuisance in the property or locality (including commission of any arrestable offence by the tenant).
— The tenant has allowed the property to deteriorate.
— The tenant's violence has caused the spouse/partner to leave permanently.

2.   Grounds where the court must be satisfied that there is suitable alternative accommodation for the tenant

— The property is overcrowded.
— The landlord wishes to demolish or renovate the building.

3.   Grounds where the court must be satisfied both that it is reasonable and also that there is suitable alternative accommodation for the tenant

— The property is let to a former employee (e.g., a cemetery keeper or school caretaker).
— The property is specially adapted for a disabled person who is not living there any more (e.g., the tenant had a disabled parent living with him or her, and the parent has died).
— The property is located close to special facilities, for example for old people, and there is no one living with the tenant who now needs those facilities.
— The tenant has succeeded to the tenancy on the death of the tenant and it is too big for his or her needs. (The widow or widower of the tenant cannot be evicted under this ground, only other successors.)

was thrown out (*Slough BC* v *Robbins* (1996) December 1996 Legal Action 13). There must be a court hearing, unless the tenant fails to reply to the summons. In that case, the order will simply be made evicting the tenant.

Does the tenant need a lawyer at this stage? Yes, the tenant needs advice on his or her position, for example what the landlord is going to have to prove and what the tenant can do to disprove the grounds; the lawyer can obtain evidence in relation to the reasonableness of a possession order, if reasonableness has to be proved. The lawyer can negotiate with the landlord, for example agreeing a rate of payment of the arrears. The lawyer can advise if there is any ground for counterclaiming against the landlord if the property is in disrepair. The lawyer can ensure that a reply is sent to the court, which prevents an order being made without a hearing taking place.

If a tenant receives a notice to quit or a notice of seeking possession as a prelude to possession proceedings, it may not automatically mean that the landlord wants possession. It may be the best way the landlord sees to apply pressure on the tenant, in particular to bring rent arrears up to date.

If the ground that the landlord relies on is discretionary, the court can at any time adjourn the proceedings; it can suspend any order made, or delay the date on which it is to come into effect; a suspended order for possession is common in Rent Act arrears cases, and means that the order for possession will not be 'executed' while the current rent plus an agreed figure towards arrears is being paid (Rent Act 1977, s. 100; Housing Act 1985, s. 85; Housing Act 1988, s. 9(6)). To give heart to Rent Act tenants, we cite a case quoted in (1989) December 1989 Legal Action 14, in Newport County Court, where the court suspended a possession order while arrears were paid at a penny a week. (They will be paid off in 865 years. The current rent, of course, will still have to paid as well as the instalment of arrears, otherwise the possession order becomes active again.)

If you ever have the chance to be in court on possession day, you could be forgiven for thinking that the court is there to rubber-stamp the wishes of the landlord, particularly the local housing department, whose officer will know the procedures and court personnel so well that he or she will appear to be part of the same apparatus. Once you have seen this process — and once is enough — you will know for evermore how important it is to get representation and negotiation at an early stage. We can think of no possession application where the tenant would not be better off having obtained legal advice.

Rent Arrears Tactics

If the ground for possession is rent arrears, and the court has no discretion to grant or not grant the possession order (Housing Act assured tenancies), see if the arrears can be brought down to eight weeks or less by the time of the hearing (see Table 17.3). The court has no discretion and must grant an order to the landlord if the arrears exceed eight weeks, and cannot grant an order on this ground if they do not — at the date of the hearing, not at the date of the notice. Unlike Rent Act cases, the court has no interest in the cause of the arrears. It may be entirely the fault of the housing benefit department, which would be persuasive in a Rent Act case where the court has to exercise discretion, but irrelevant in a Housing Act case where the court has no discretion once the arrears are proved.

If your interest in the family's plight arises from your duty to children in need, you have powers to assist, including putting in money (Children Act 1989, s. 17), and this may deal with the rent arrears.

Rent arrears and disrepair   A traditional weapon for a tenant whose property the landlord has failed to repair is to withhold rent. If the landlord then seeks repossession on grounds of arrears, the tenant can say 'Taking into account the money you owe me as compensation for the disrepair, I am not in arrears.' Lawyers have become cautious about this tactic, particularly since the Housing Act regime takes away the court's discretion in arrears cases. What if the evidence of disrepair is not accepted by the court? What if the compensation is calculated on a less generous basis than was hoped for? It could mean that the arrears, and the possession ground, are proved. It could lead to a decision, on a homelessness application, that the loss of the home was intentional (see above, p. 416; *R v Harrow LBC ex parte Fahia* (1997) 29 HLR 974). No one is recommended to withhold rent if they can possibly afford to pay it, at least until they have received expert advice.

Execution of a Possession Order
If possession is granted, the landlord still does not have the property until the order is 'executed' by the court bailiff. The landlord must apply for a warrant of possession, which gives the bailiff the authority to take possession at a given time and day. All of this takes time, and at any time before execution has taken place, the tenant can apply for suspension or setting aside of a warrant. Whenever the ground is discretionary, and possession has not yet actually been lost, it is not too late to seek legal advice. Even if the ground for possession is mandatory, the tenant may find upon legal advice that there has been a defect in the procedure, and an application could be made to set an order aside.

No tenant should ever be advised to accept the landlord's wish to repossess as unchallengeable. Even if it appears that the grounds for an order are satisfied, the procedural requirements are detailed and must be correctly followed. Unless the tenant in any event wants to leave the premises, they should seek immediate legal advice.

Furthermore, even if the tenant is advised that the landlord is entitled to possession, to leave voluntarily is to risk being treated as intentionally homeless for the purposes of the local authority's duty to rehouse those who are unintentionally homeless (see above, p. 413).

Termination of a Private Sector Tenancy by the Tenant
Although a *landlord* cannot remove a tenant without a court order, the *tenant* is free to end any tenancy, apart from a fixed-term tenancy, by giving four weeks' notice, or longer if the tenancy agreement requires. With a fixed-term tenancy there is no means to end the tenancy before it expires, except where the landlord has breached the agreement (for example, failing to make repairs) and it would as a result be reasonable for the tenant to leave. If the tenant does leave early, the landlord can recover the rent owing for the remainder of the period, but must try to reduce his or her loss by seeking new tenants.

PROTECTION FROM EVICTION

What happens if the landlord does not follow the procedures set out in the statutory regimes, that is illegally evicts the tenants, or if the tenancy is only protected by the common law, or if the occupier only has a licence? The Protection from Eviction Act 1977 provides remedies for illegal eviction and harassment and sets out procedures which provide a minimum of protection for all residential occupiers. Section 1(2) of the Protection from Eviction Act 1977 states:

> If any person unlawfully deprives a residential occupier of any premises of his occupation of the premises or any part thereof, or attempts to do so, he shall be guilty of an offence unless he proves that he believed, and had reasonable cause to believe, that the residential occupier had ceased to reside in the premises.

The key word is 'unlawfully': the landlord cannot change the locks, or throw out the tenant's possessions; he or she must obtain possession, if at all, by way of court order and the court bailiff, as we have already described.

Section 1(3) also makes it an offence to harass the occupier knowing that this is likely to make him or her leave, or to prevent him or her from exercising a right connected with the occupancy. Cutting off services is a prime example of such harassment, and is a specific offence under s. 3A. If a landlord's actions appear to be harassment, a tenant should seek urgent legal advice.

But the Act no longer protects all occupiers. Where a letting made on or after 15 January 1989 is a holiday let, or a temporary letting to squatters, or the landlord shares living accommodation with the tenant, the Housing Act 1988, s. 30 excludes the letting from the Protection from Eviction Act 1977. Therefore the landlord can recover possession without court proceedings, so long as reasonable notice is given, which will usually be at least four weeks.

A landlord who unlawfully evicts or harasses the tenant in breach of the Act can be prosecuted by the local authority (districts and London boroughs (s. 6)). This applies even if the landlord has cast-iron grounds in law for possession, and even if the tenancy was granted for a fixed period which has now expired. You should report cases to the appropriate person from the housing department, who is probably called a tenancy relations officer. If the landlord is found guilty, the court can make a compensation order in favour of the tenant. Also, tenants may themselves bring a case for damages for harassment or unlawful eviction, and should be advised if they wish to regain possession or prevent further harassment to apply to the county court for an injunction. Such proceedings can be taken whether or not the local authority has decided to prosecute; or even if the landlord was acquitted. Subject to satisfying the means test, the tenant can usually obtain legal assistance, and in an emergency this can be granted very quickly (see further, Chapter 15).

Harassment can lead to very large awards of compensation in the civil courts. In *Tagro* v *Cafane* [1991] 2 All ER 235, the Court of Appeal upheld an award of £46,538 against a landlord who ransacked the tenant's bedsit. Some £30,000 of this represented the increase in value of the property to the landlord once the tenant had left. Lord Donaldson described the case as 'a cautionary tale for landlords'!

The other important provision of the Protection from Eviction Act is that, so long as the property is rented as a home, both landlord and tenant have to give at least four weeks' notice before ending the tenancy, whatever the agreement may say to the contrary (s. 5(1)). But this four-week period does not apply to licences, which may be terminated at shorter notice. (Expiry of the four weeks does not in itself allow eviction — a court order is required.)

REPAIR PROBLEMS

The owner-occupier cannot look to anyone else if the wallpaper is peeling or the roof leaking, but the tenant is entitled to a certain level of repair from the landlord.

Sections 11 and 13 of the Landlord and Tenant Act 1985 set out the obligations of the landlord, who must keep in repair the structure and exterior of the residential premises. This includes drains, gutters and pipes. The landlord is also responsible for keeping in working order the supply of gas, electricity and water, and any appliances for heating and water heating. Additionally, the landlord must ensure the sanitation facilities are in working order — lavatories, sinks, baths and showers. This leaves the tenant responsible for internal decoration. But if the need to redecorate is the result of the landlord's repairs, the landlord, not the tenant, must carry this out.

The landlord cannot escape these obligations; for they are statutory, and cannot be written out of a tenancy agreement for residential premises (unless it is for a fixed term of at least seven years). However, the landlord is not obliged to repair damage caused by the tenant, unless the damage amounts to no more than normal wear and tear.

Sections 11 and 13 do not write any obligations into a licence. A licensee, as opposed to a tenant, can only insist on such repairs as are included in the agreed licence.

A landlord's duty to repair does not arise until he or she knows of the defects, and the tenant should be encouraged to report disrepair in writing as soon as it arises. The landlord must be allowed reasonable access to the property from time to time, both to inspect and to repair.

Suing the Landlord

These repairing obligations are implied into the contractual relationship between landlord and tenant. Therefore, a failure to carry out the repair is a breach of contract, on which the tenant can sue. Damages may include not only the cost of putting the premises right, if the tenant has had to do this, but may also include resulting losses, such as damage to clothing and furniture, additional heating costs, and compensation for health effects and inconvenience. If it is suspected that disrepair has caused medical symptoms, the sufferer should see a doctor at a very early stage, so that if the matter ever comes to court, the evidence is documented in health records from the start. If it can be shown that the disrepair has caused problems for other persons living with the tenant — particularly spouse and children — the effect on them, and damages for such effect, can be included in the claim, for example children suffering from respiratory disease caused by damp.

The obligation of the landlord to carry out repairs does not always ensure that homes are in good condition. Properties may be in appalling condition, not because of disrepair so much as poor design. The Housing Act does not require the landlord to *improve* property. Frequently, a landlord can defend a repairs case by showing, for example, that serious damp is a design fault and not a disrepair matter.

However, there is another approach, where the state of the property leads to injury (not just to the tenant, but to anyone) or to damage to the tenant's possessions. In this case, it does not matter if the damage was caused by disrepair or bad design — the property should be safe (Defective Premises Act 1972, s. 4). The landlord must make the premises safe if he or she knew or ought to have known of the defect. Again, it is wise to notify a landlord in writing of any potential problem; cases can be lost because there is no evidence that the landlord knew of the defect, although the tenant had been aware of it for years.

The tenant can therefore claim damages from a landlord in breach of the repair obligations. The tenant can also apply to the court for an injunction against the landlord, ordering him or her to carry out the repairs or improvement. Legal aid may well be available for such an application. Of course, the first step is for the tenant to inform the landlord of the defects.

Other Action to Bring About Repairs

Is there anything a tenant can do without actually commencing proceedings? Withholding rent should never be considered without legal advice, for reasons discussed on p. 434. But if there are arrears and the landlord sues for the rent, the claim by the tenant for damages for disrepair can be either offset against the amount owed, or claimed by a process called a counterclaim. If the court agrees that the tenant is entitled to compensation, the amount goes to reduce or cancel altogether any rent arrears — so the landlord may find that the ground for possession disappears.

There are other ways of making a landlord repair. A local authority or a tenant can prosecute a landlord under the Environmental Protection Act 1990, s. 82 where residential premises are a danger to the health of the occupants. If a landlord is convicted, the court has a power and, unless there is a good reason to the contrary, an obligation to make a compensation order to the tenant. Cases involving unhealthy premises should therefore be referred to the environmental health department, who may be able to obtain improvements by threatening prosecution. A local authority (district or borough) may also serve a notice on the landlord requiring work to make property fit for habitation, and in default the authority can carry out the work and recover the cost from the landlord (Housing Act 1985, ss. 189 and 193).

Where the tenant is a secure (i.e., public sector) tenant, he or she can notify the landlord of a disrepair; if the landlord then fails to repair, the tenant can, with the landlord's agreement, carry out the work and deduct the cost from the rent (Housing Act 1985, s. 96). The procedure looks simple, but the tenant has to be aware that they become liable to pay the contractors in the first place; and, remote possiblity though it is, if the repairs were badly carried out the tenant, and not the landlord, would be liable if anyone were injured.

PROBLEMS WITH NEIGHBOURS

There has been a great deal of media concern about 'neighbours from hell' and a corresponding amount of political and legislative activity. As a social worker, you may be working with a family who are suffering from anti-social neighbours, or who are accused of behaving in an anti-social manner. The range of legal powers now open to landlords, in particular local authority landlords, is extensive. We referred earlier to introductory tenancies as a device to enable local authority landlords to evict trouble makers quickly. In addition, landlords can seek an injunction at common law to restrain breaches of tenancy agreements.

Since the commencement of the Housing Act 1996 local authorities have been able to apply for an injunction against anyone — not just a tenant — causing annoyance to their tenants. There must be evidence of violence, or at least threats of violence. The Housing Act 1996 also strengthens the grounds for possession open to landlords where the tenant, or anyone residing with the tenant or visiting the tenant, causes nuisance or annoyance to people residing, visiting or working in the locality. The courts are also working to make it easier to evict tenants who are responsible for anti-social behaviour as they have been taking a robust approach to the 'reasonableness' requirement in evictions under the Housing Act 1985. Essentially it has become very difficult for tenants to demonstrate that it is unreasonable to evict them for serious allegations of anti-social behaviour. Even at the stage of application to suspend warrants of possession issues of anti-social behaviour may be of importance. In *St Brice* v *Southwark LBC* (*The Times*, 6 August 2001) the Court of Appeal allowed the local authority's appeal against a decision of the lower courts that matters occurring after the order for possession was granted could not be taken into account in decisions about staying or suspending orders. There the council applied to the court to bring evidence that the tenant was guilty of nuisance. Lord Woolf held that the court was not limited to the grounds for possession originally relied upon. As long as the additional material was relevant and complied with the European Convention in terms of proportionality and notice to the tenant it could at the discretion of the trial judge be relied upon. Lord Woolf mentioned in particular that courts should bear in mind the responsibilities of public landlords to other tenants.

Some limits on the courts' interpretation of reasonableness were set out in *Castle Vale HAT* v *Gallagher* [2001] Legal Action (2001) 20 April, in the light of the Human Rights Act 1998. The Court of Appeal substituted a suspended possession order for the outright order made in the county court. The Court held that Article 8 of the European Convention served to reinforce the importance of making an order ousting a tenant from his or her home only where that was shown to be both necessary and proportionate. In this case the daughter, who had been the perpetrator of the anti-social behaviour, had moved out of the property, which was a significant change of circumstances justifying suspension of the order.

In addition, the local authority has the power to apply for anti-social behaviour orders under the Crime and Disorder Act 1998. These are available in respect of anyone aged ten or over. The grounds for the grant of the orders are (i) that the person has acted in an anti-social manner, that is to say, in a manner that caused or was likely to cause 'harassment, alarm or distress to two or more persons not of the same household as himself', and (ii) that the order is necessary for the protection of persons in the area. The order will last a minimum of two years and will prohibit the defendant from doing anything described in the order. Breach of the order will amount to a criminal offence punishable by imprisonment. While few landlords have obtained anti-social behaviour orders to date, their existence is a powerful response to the problem of anti-social behaviour.

The Government remain concerned about the impact of anti-social behaviour on law-abiding neighbours. Recent ministerial speeches (October 2001) have indicated that procedural reforms will be introduced to speed up evictions where appropriate. The Homelessness Bill (see p. 421) includes a provision which will allow a local authority to decide that an applicant for local authority housing is ineligible on the basis of unacceptable behaviour. On the other hand, if your client is the victim of anti-social behaviour the law provides no means whereby tenants of local authorities can force their landlord to take action against the perpetrators — see *Hussain* v *Lancoder* (1999) 31 HCR 164 and *Mowan* v *Wandsworth LBC* (2001) 33 HLR (forthcoming). This gap in the law is likely to be the focus of a European Court of Human Rights Challenge.

EIGHTEEN

Income Maintenance and Money Problems

This chapter is mainly about welfare benefits. This area is a potential minefield. But unless you specialise as a welfare benefits adviser you are not expected to be an expert; indeed we would rather you took a straightforward approach and did not try to provide answers to your clients' benefit problems, saying instead 'I'm not sure, but I *think* you *may* be entitled to X or Y benefit, but you should get specialist advice from Z agency'.

Wrong advice can actually be harmful. If you tell someone that he or she is not entitled to a particular benefit, when he or she is, it is easy to see that you have caused harm. You may in fact be right in what you tell the client, and able to correctly identify the benefit to which he or she is entitled, but not aware of all the ramifications: for example, you may advise someone to apply for a social fund loan, when it would be better to apply for a non-repayable community care grant; or it may not be a good time to apply for working families' tax credit, because the applicant has just had unusually high earnings, which will be used for the calculation of what is payable for the next six months. You have to be aware of the effect of one type of benefit on another — for example, reduced earnings allowance may simply be lost because it reduces the amount of income support or housing benefit payable. And you have to remember that anything that causes a loss of income support may leave the person worse off, because of the loss of advantages such as mortgage interest payments, free school meals or social fund payments.

Unless you become a specialist it is not your job to be an expert on income maximisation or debt management. You do, however, have statutory duties towards children, the elderly, and others needing community care, which you cannot always discharge without taking an interest in their financial situation. For example, you must take action where possible to prevent the need for care proceedings (see Chapter 5) — preliminary advice to the parent about benefits may lead to more money coming into the household, and reducing some of the stress that poverty causes to parents and children. And if you assess someone as needing residential care, the local authority is going to have to pay for it if the client has insufficient resources. So your finance department will want you to maximise your client's benefit income.

Also, a social worker cannot help sometimes getting directly involved. You may be approached by the Benefits Agency (BA) for information about an application for a discretionary loan; you may be asked by your client or a carer to get in touch with the local authority to find out why the housing benefit is not arriving. What role should you play? We start by emphasising what we consider the most important consideration. We saw in Chapter 2 that the social worker generally has a duty of confidentiality towards his or her client, and in what circumstances it can be overridden. Liaison with the BA is not one of those circumstances; therefore, any divulging of information must normally be with the consent of the person concerned. This applies even though BA guidance tells benefit officers to consult social services in certain circumstances, particularly after a request for a social fund loan. Do not be forced into saying anything until you have your client's authority or you know why you need to divulge the information relating to your client, and do not go beyond that by saying things you have not been authorised to disclose.

Where do you turn to for help in this area? If you are fortunate, there will be a welfare rights unit in your local authority you can consult, or to which you can refer clients. There may be a local law centre, or a CAB. It will help to find out which of the possible agencies specialises in what sort of work. Under the Community Legal Service Partnership, discussed in Chapter 15, advice agencies who obtain CLS money must be specialists in a particular area of client need. Debt and welfare benefits are areas in which the CLS is trying to increase the provision of advice. If you want to find out more for yourself, the Child Poverty Action Group, 94 White Lion Street, London N1 9PF (tel. 0207 837 7979), produces guides to welfare benefits, which are updated annually. You can obtain further information direct from the BA, of course, but be aware that they themselves are fallible, for each officer has not been trained in all the areas you might be asking questions about, and it is not unknown for BA officers to be too busy to check the accuracy of their advice.

A BRIEF GUIDE TO THE BENEFIT SYSTEM

A little history may help you to place the present scheme in context. In the early twentieth century the Government introduced compulsory insurance schemes for workers: at times of need, such as ill health, injury or unemployment, or old age, working people could claim against the national insurance fund, much as a person would against private insurance.

National insurance payments are still compulsory for those in work or who are self-employed, and there are a number of benefits which can be obtained only if you or a spouse have made payments of the required type and over the required period.

But what if you have not paid sufficient, or indeed any, contributions? Should you starve, or receive no assistance in meeting your housing, health or mobility needs? As the twentieth century progressed, and particularly after the Second World War, the answer to this question was agreed to be 'No': some needs must be satisfied, whether a member of society has paid or not. Indeed, under the UN International Covenant on Economic, Social and Cultural Rights of 1976, the state has a duty to ensure that such needs are met. Health and education to age 16 come into this category, but are not discussed further. What we are concerned with is the kind of welfare provision that means cash for the person in need; the safety net which keeps people above absolute poverty. The idea was that those few who had not been able to provide for themselves should be entitled to claim a basic level of material provision.

In order to assess whether a person needed such safety net provision, the state had to assess that person's resources. The means-tested benefit had arrived. We look at means testing below.

Table 18.1 (see pp. 449–60) summarises the principal benefits available. You will see that some benefits are contributory, and some not. For example, you can receive a retirement pension, or contributory jobseekers' allowance (JSA), only if you have made sufficient contributions; but other benefits, such as child benefit, income support (IS) and income-based JSA, or disability living allowance, are payable if your circumstances meet the set criteria, without anyone asking any questions about your contribution record.

The advantage of a contributory benefit, for those whose contribution record is in order, is that once the claimant can meet the other eligibility criteria — which may be extremely strict — no one can say: 'Oh, but you don't need this money'. For the concept of insurance dictates that you are entitled to the benefits whenever the situation that you are insured against actually arises. But some benefits are not means tested, even if they are non-contributory, as you will see from Table 18.1; child benefit or disability living allowance or attendance allowance, for example, are benefits that are not based on means or contributions but solely on the criteria of being, say, responsible for a child, or having particular care needs.

A contributory benefit may not be enough to live on. The claimant may also be entitled to a means-tested benefit. For example, a person with a family may get both contributory jobseeker's allowance *and* income-based jobseeker's allowance.

Those who claim means-tested benefits have to show that their financial circumstances satisfy whatever criteria have been set for that type of benefit. And a point that can upset many claimants is that no distinction is made, when looking at their assets, between those which are hard earned, such as an occupational pension or life savings, and windfalls such as inheritances or gambling wins. Other state benefits are often counted as means, so what the state 'gives' with one hand, it may claw back in reduced entitlement to other benefits with the other. Thus, for example, what a person gets by way of child benefit or retirement pension comes off their payment of IS, but disability living allowance does not.

These rules are said to penalise the thrifty and benefit the profligate. You might like to know, however, that deliberately depriving yourself of resources for the purpose of obtaining benefit is of no help — if found out, you are still treated as possessing those resources. Even worse is not divulging income or assets, as social security fraud is increasingly a target for Government passion.

MEANS TESTING IN INCOME SUPPORT

The concept of means testing deserves a little more exploration. You can see from Table 18.1 on pp. 449–60 which benefits are means tested. What means are taken into account when eligibility is means tested? And whose means? Unfortunately, the exact criteria will differ between benefits, and you need the exact criteria, and current figures, to be able to make any assessment. To give a flavour of the criteria, we take a look at IS, and the way that is means tested — but even though we look at only one benefit, there is not space to cover all the criteria in sufficient detail for you to use this as a safe source of reference. It will give you an idea of the sort of questions that an expert adviser, and the BA, will be asking.

Income
This ought to be straightforward, but is not. Income means both earned and unearned income, and even includes notional income — that is, income that the claimant is assumed to have, but in fact does not. Let us consider a few common items.

Earnings from employment — these are counted, but a small amount is 'disregarded', which gives a small incentive to take up part-time work while receiving IS or income-based JSA. Only one-third of a childminder's earnings (after tax and insurance), however, is treated as income. If the earnings come in a lump sum, for instance accrued holiday pay, or compensation from an employment tribunal for unfair dismissal from work, these are normally treated as income spread over the relevant period.

Then there is income that does not come from work — for example, you let a room and receive rent. There is no single rule for treating this money; it depends on whether you provide board, when a larger sum can be ignored than if you do not.

If you receive maintenance for yourself, or children, this is taken into account. But what if a parent is owed maintenance, but, as frequently happens, the money fails to arrive? It is technically part of your income, but the BA will not include it in the calculation for that week of assessment, if satisfied that it did not arrive. But if the arrears do get paid, they will deduct that amount from later benefit.

Then there is the question of other state benefits. For example, if you receive a pension, that is part of your income when IS is assessed. So are child benefit, statutory sick pay, industrial injuries payments and several others. But there are some benefits which the state does not claw back from the IS recipient: for example, attendance allowance and disability living allowance are ignored as income, and are therefore benefits that should be seen as very worthwhile.

Lastly there is notional income. You do not see this money, but the BA treats you as receiving it. It comes from having capital of over a certain amount (currently £3,000). For each £250 over this figure, you are deemed to earn £1 per week, a staggering rate of return on any investment! Especially when interest actually earned is also treated as income! Alternatively, you can be deemed to be earning money if you do work for someone without pay when that work would normally command a wage — for example, helping a friend out in a shop.

Capital

This means more than just money in the bank. It includes property (apart from the value of the home you live in), shares, and lump sum payments received on divorce. But it does not cover personal possessions, such as a car or jewellery. Savings out of income become capital — even if they have been put aside to pay next month's gas bill. So if a claimant's capital is getting near one of the thresholds it is wise to pay bills regularly, such as monthly rather than quarterly.

Whose Means?

Obviously, for a means tested benefit the means of the claimant are taken into account. If she or he lives alone without dependants, that is simple. But if living with a spouse or cohabitee (of the opposite sex) then the partner's means have to be taken into account as well. If the claimant or his or her partner has a dependent child who has income from earnings such as a newspaper round, or maintenance from another parent, what then? The rules are quite complex: the child's earnings while at school are normally ignored, but any other money received by the child, including maintenance, is added on to the claimant's income for the means test.

The child's capital normally is ignored, and not added to that of the claimant. But if it exceeds a certain level, no IS can be paid to the claimant for that child as a dependant.

The Need to Refer to Specialists

What we have done is to look at a sample of the rules for assessing income and capital for a single benefit. We hope, first, that you will see the range of means that the BA takes into account, and secondly, the reason why we urge you to treat this area as one calling for specialist advice.

DISCRETION IN AWARDING BENEFIT

To receive a benefit, a claimant must satisfy the criteria laid down in the relevant Act, regulations and, sometimes, guidance given by the Secretary of State. The question is whether, if you satisfy the BA that you fall within the criteria, you now have a right to that benefit, or whether you have to rely on the BA to use its discretion in your favour. Most benefits, at present, are available as a right. This does not mean they are easy to get, because the officer at the BA may think that you do not satisfy the criteria; he or she may, for example, place more weight on a medical opinion that you are fit for work than another opinion that you are not. So evidence has to be weighed up by the benefit officer before a conclusion is reached. Unless it is a discretionary benefit, you can appeal if you think the decision is wrong.

However, there is also a system called the Social Fund. Although Social Fund payments include some non-discretionary claims — funeral, maternity and cold weather payments — most Social Fund payments, whether loans or grants, are discretionary. The area office of the BA is given detailed guidance by the Department of Social Security, in the form of a Social Fund manual, but this does not give the claimant any right to the benefit. An adviser can only look at the factors that the Social Fund officer is required to take into account in reaching a decision, for example, what kind of people get priority, in predicting how the discretion will be exercised. If the officer refuses your application, there is no right of appeal to an independent tribunal which will look again at the facts, hear your evidence and argument, and reach its own conclusion. (The BA can, however, be asked to review the decision, but the Social Fund inspector still has to exercise a discretion at the end of the process. Since all that is needed is a letter requesting a review, if possible giving reasons, it is worth trying.)

The use of this kind of discretion puts the claimant into a weak position. It is made worse by the fact that the grants/loans are limited by budget; when a particular area runs out of money for the month or year, then no payment can be made, however sympathetic the officer is to the applicant's needs. It is a harsh regime. However, payments by social services to families under the Children Act 1989 are also cash limited, discretionary, and vary from one area to another.

CHALLENGING DECISIONS ABOUT BENEFITS

The criteria for reaching a decision about whether a person is entitled to a particular benefit are numerous; there may be a means test, there may be medical criteria, the claimant may have to satisfy the BA that he or she is available for work (or exempt) and actively seeking it, the local authority has to consider whether premises are too large for a person's needs, and so on. Whenever a decision has to be made as to whether a person meets the necessary criteria, there is room for the officer concerned to get it wrong, and for the claimant to disagree with the decision. A difficult area is backdated payments, when a person was entitled, but had not claimed. The BA, or local authority housing department for housing benefit, may disagree with the claimant as to whether it can be backdated.

Errors can be in the claimant's favour, resulting in an overpayment. Or the BA may seek to recover what it thinks to be an overpayment, when in fact the amount paid was correct or is not recoverable.

The first thing to do is to ask for written reasons for any unfavourable decision; no advice can be much use if these reasons are not known. You do not have to be an expert to advise the client to ask for reasons if these have not been given. But how do you take a challenge any further? Appeals can be carried out without advice or representation; but research has shown that the chance of success is greatly reduced. (But the single biggest reason for appeals failing is not turning up, according to research by Dr Eileen Fry of North-umbria University.) Community Legal Service Legal Help is not available for representation in social security appeals, but advice can be obtained from an advice agency or a solicitor (see Chapter 15).

Getting a Decision Reviewed

There is an appeal process. But even before embarking on it, the claimant may be able to persuade the BA or, where applicable, housing benefit office to change its mind: the normal reason for asking for a review is either that the claimant's circumstances have changed since the original decision, or that the claimant believes the officer misunderstood the original circumstances or the relevant law.

With some benefits there is no right to appeal to a tribunal — notably most social fund loans and grants. There is no way of challenging an adverse decision through appeal — unless there has been a breach of natural justice, when judicial review of the decision is a possibility. Apart from that instance, a review is the only challenge, and should not be overlooked when people (including BA officers) suggest that nothing can be done.

The request for a review does not have to be in writing, but written reasons for thinking the decision should be altered are likely to be more persuasive than simply a verbal request for review.

Appealing a Decision

The claimant does not, as we have seen, always have a right of appeal to a tribunal. But if he or she does, perhaps the most important single fact you should be aware of is the need to send in a written notice of appeal to the office that made the decision within one month — although if a client has missed the deadline, he or she should get advice.

Appeals are heard by the Appeals Service Tribunal, which consists of a lawyer in the chair and two lay members. Tribunals hear evidence and argument. Often the principal source of the evidence for the appeal will be the claimant himself or herself. But in a medical appeal, it is the opinion of an expert that is wanted; the problem is paying for that expert. Welfare benefits advisers funded by the Legal Services Commission may be able to use funding to pay for a medical report. But other agencies, and unrep-resented clients, are at a disadvantage against the BA's own doctor, who usually is the doctor who made the decision in the first place. The only hope is to persuade a sympathetic GP to write an opinion for the tribunal (or attend, but that is unlikely to be agreed).

The decision of the tribunal is open to further appeal, if necessary all the way up to the House of Lords, or beyond to the European Court of Human Rights (see Chapter 3).

Appeals against housing benefit and council tax benefit decisions do not fit into the tribunal system. They are made, after the review process has failed to satisfy the claimant, to a review board made up of members of the local authority.

AN OVERVIEW OF THE MOST SIGNIFICANT BENEFITS

You now have a bare outline of some of the concepts involved in the benefit system. The overview of important benefits on pp. 449–60 is designed to enable you to refer quickly to the essential features of each type of benefit; the aim is for you to realise that there is a wide range of potential benefits, and a person may not be getting the appropriate benefit; if you spot a potential gap for a client, refer him or her for expert advice as soon as possible. Table 18.1 does not aim to cover all possible benefits. Use the Child Poverty Action Group welfare benefits handbook (above at p. 442) for a complete list.

Table 18.1

Features of Principal Benefits

BENEFIT (and main legislation)	WHO CAN CLAIM?	WHO CANNOT?	IS IT MEANS TESTED?	IS IT CONTRIBUTORY?	IS IT DISCRETIONARY?	COMMENTS
1. Income Support (IS) Social Security Contributions and Benefits Act 1992, s. 124; Income Support (General) Regulations 1987	Only available to claimants who do not have to sign on, e.g., because sick, single parent, disabled, over 60 or a carer. Can work part time (under 16 hours p.w., or more if child minder or voluntary worker).	Full-time students and under 18s (some exceptions). Many persons from abroad.	Yes – means of claimant and spouse/cohabitee, capital limit currently £8,000 (£16,000 if in residential care); income measured against amount fixed by DSS for claimant and dependants, payments reduced by amount of income taken into account.	No	No	Mortgage interest payments (unless excessive) can be claimed on top (but not during first 39 weeks for loans after 1 October 1995; for old loans not for first 8 weeks, then 50% for 18); does not cover rent (claim housing benefit); some payments (mortgage interest, fuel, water, child maintenance) may be paid direct; entitlement affected if involved in trade dispute.
2. Jobseekers' Allowance (JSA) Jobseekers Act 1995; Jobseekers Allowance Regulations 1996	Person available for employment (full- or part-time) immediately (or on 48 hours' notice for carers) and actively seeking work.	Person who gave up job, or who was fired or fails to seek work (up to 26 weeks withdrawal of benefit).	See below.	See below.	No	Claim at a Job Centre; claimant signs on fortnightly and signs a jobseeker's agreement. Claimant must take part in initial, 13-week and 6-monthly Restart interview; must comply with directions for seeking work or obtaining training. Deductions can be made from payments for, e.g., child support, water charges.

BENEFIT (and main legislation)	WHO CAN CLAIM?	WHO CANNOT?	IS IT MEANS TESTED?	IS IT CONTRIB-UTORY?	IS IT DISCRET-IONARY?	COMMENTS
A. Income-based JSA	See above.	See above.	Yes	No	No	Means test applies to partner as well as claimant. Amount of payment calculated on personal allowance plus amounts for dependants. Can cover some housing costs (restrictions apply as with IS).
B. Contributory JSA	See above.	See above.	No	Yes	No	Payable for 6 months; then claim income-related JSA or IS. If means insufficient and claimant has partner or family, can claim income-related JSA.
3. Working Families Tax Credit (WFTC) Tax Credits (Decisions and Appeals) (Amendment) Regulations 1999; Family Credit (General) Regulations 1987	Claimant (or partner) working full-time (at least 16 hours p.w.), and supporting a dependent child.	Foster parent (unless other dependent child also in household). Many persons from abroad.	Yes – claimant and spouse/cohabitee; capital limit currently £8,000.	No	No	Payable for 6 months at a time even if means change, or lose job, so long as dependent child in household. Does not include housing costs – HB and council tax benefit may be available.

BENEFIT (and main legislation)	WHO CAN CLAIM?	WHO CANNOT?	IS IT MEANS TESTED?	IS IT CONTRIB-UTORY?	IS IT DISCRET-IONARY?	COMMENTS
4. Disabled Persons Tax Credit Tax Credits (Decisions and Appeals) (Amendment) Regulations 1999 Disability Working Allowance (General) Regulations 1991	Age 16 working full-time (at least 16 hours p.w.), with physical or mental disability which causes disadvantage in getting a job.	Person receiving WFTC. Some persons from abroad.	Yes. Capital limit £16,000.	No	No	Must also receive or have recently received DLA, AA, ICB, SDA, or IS with disability premium.
5. Housing Benefit (HB) Social Security Contributions and Benefits Act 1992, s. 130; Housing Benefit (General) Regulations 1987	Person, or partner of person, liable to pay rent or board and lodging.	Person in residential care; students (some exceptions). Many persons from abroad.	Yes – claimant and spouse/ cohabitee; capital limit currently £16,000; amount of HB payable tapered according to income.	No	No	Administered by district councils, or London/Metropolitan boroughs. Does not cover mortgage payments. Rent can be paid direct to landlord by local authority. If a private tenancy is entered into on or after 2 January 1996, new formulae will apply to push the level of benefit towards the bottom end of local rent levels. Benefit may be payable where person not living in home because of violence.

BENEFIT (and main legislation)	WHO CAN CLAIM?	WHO CANNOT?	IS IT MEANS TESTED?	IS IT CONTRIB-UTORY?	IS IT DISCRET-IONARY?	COMMENTS
6. Council Tax Benefit (CTB) Local Government Finance Act 1992; Council Tax Benefit (General) Regulations 1992	Occupant of property who is liable to council tax.	Full-time students (some exceptions). Many persons from abroad.	Yes – similar test to HB.	No	No	Administered by local authority (as HB). 'Second adult rebate' available if the taxpayer shares with another adult on low income. (Liability for council tax reduced if only 1 occupant, or disabled person lives in property, or students. This 'status reduction' is not part of CTB scheme.)
7. Social Fund A. Budgeting and crisis loans Social Security Act 1986, s. 167; Social Security Contributions and Benefits Act 1992, s. 140; Social Fund (Applications) Regulations 1988; guidance and directions given in Social Fund Guide (HMSO)	Budgeting loan – applicant has received IS for 26 weeks (2-week break permitted). Crisis loan – any person of at least 16 who does not have the resources to meet crisis.		Yes – must either be in receipt of IS, income-related JSA, or have no resources to deal with crisis; and capital over £500 reduces the loan £ for £. For crisis loans ability to raise loans by other means considered.	No	Yes	Refusal of loan means no further application for that purpose for 6 months without change in circumstances. SF officers have fixed budgets. Repayment deducted from IS, or recoverable through the courts. No right to apply to a tribunal, but right to have refusal reviewed. Criteria set out in Social Fund Manual. Loans usually not made to person involved in trade dispute.

BENEFIT (and main legislation)	WHO CAN CLAIM?	WHO CANNOT?	IS IT MEANS TESTED?	IS IT CONTRIB-UTORY?	IS IT DISCRET-IONARY?	COMMENTS
B. Community Care Grants Legislation as above	Person leaving residential institution; person at risk of admission to residential institution; families under exceptional stress. Applicant must be in receipt of IB, JSA or IS, or likely to receive it on leaving institutional care.		Yes – in receipt of IS or income-related JSA, or likely to get it; as above. Capital over £500 as above for loans.	No	Yes	May be available for person of 16 when leaving local authority care. Liaison with social services normal before decision. Fixed budgets apply. As above, no right of appeal against refusal, but right to a review. Grants usually refused if involved in trade dispute.
C. Social Fund Funeral Grant Legislation as above (plus Social Fund Maternity and Funeral Expenses (General) Regulations 1988)	Applicant responsible for funeral arrangements, in receipt of IS, WFTC, HB, income-related JSA, DPTC, or council tax benefit.		Yes – savings above £500 count and are deducted from grant paid.	No	No	Claim within 3 months of funeral; repayable out of estate of deceased. Claim refused if close relative of deceased has over £500 or is not eligible for benefits (see 'Who Can Claim?').
D. Sure Start Maternity Grant Legislation as above	Woman who receives (or whose partner receives) IS, WFTC, DPTC or income-related JSA.		Yes, as for funeral grant.	No	No	Claim can be made from 11 weeks before expected birth, up to 3 months after birth or adoption. Single lump sum payable.

BENEFIT (and main legislation)	WHO CAN CLAIM?	WHO CANNOT?	IS IT MEANS TESTED?	IS IT CONTRIBUTORY?	IS IT DISCRETIONARY?	COMMENTS
8. Statutory Sick Pay (SSP) Social Security Contributions and Benefits Act 1992, ss. 152–155; Statutory Sick Pay (General) Regulations 1982	Employee absent through sickness for over four days.	Employee who has used up the 28-week entitlement; employee whose average pay for previous 8 weeks is too low, or aged 65 or over. Employee on a contract for less than 3 months.	Yes – but in reverse, not eligible if earnings too low.	No – but employment necessary.	No	Payable for 28 weeks. Employer may have to pay above minimum level under contract of employment. Medical certificate required after 1 week. Administered by employer. Small employers can reclaim from DSS. Disputes between employer and employee about entitlement can be decided by the Benefits Agency. Income support may also be claimed.
9. Incapacity Benefit (ICB) Social Security Contributions and Benefits Act 1992, ss. 30A–30B; Social Security (Incapacity Benefit) (General) Regulations 1995	Person incapable of work.	Age 65 or over (men), 60 or over (women). Person receiving SSP. Claimant with insufficient contributions.	No, but payments increased for dependants.	Yes	No (but most claimants will at some point be subject to All Work Test).	Payable at higher rate after a year of incapacity. Also at higher rates where incapacity started below 35 or 45. Not payable if claimant refuses suitable treatment. Counts as income for IS. Taxable after first 6 months. Incapable of work means doing own job for 28 weeks, then any job claimant could reasonably do.

BENEFIT (and main legislation)	WHO CAN CLAIM?	WHO CANNOT?	IS IT MEANS TESTED?	IS IT CONTRIB-UTORY?	IS IT DISCRET-IONARY?	COMMENTS
10. Disability Living Allowance						
A. Mobility Component Social Security Contributions and Benefits Act 1992, s. 73; Social Security (Disability Living Allowance) Regulations 1991	Unless terminally ill, must have satisfied following criteria for 3 months and be likely to for 6 months. Higher rate: Person unable or virtually unable to walk due to physical cause. People who are deaf and/or blind. Lower rate: People who cannot walk along unfamiliar routes without assistance.	People under 5 or over 66. Person whose immigration status is subject to any limitation or condition.	No	No	No	Claimed on complex self-assessment form DLA1. DSS can visit for help with form. Medical evidence not usually required in initial assessment. Not counted as income for IS or other benefits.

BENEFIT (and main legislation)	WHO CAN CLAIM?	WHO CANNOT?	IS IT MEANS TESTED?	IS IT CONTRIB-UTORY?	IS IT DISCRET-IONARY?	COMMENTS
B. Care component Legislation as above	Person who needs attention or supervision because of a physical or mental disability. Unless terminally ill must have satisfied criteria for three months and be likely to do so for further 6 months.	Persons whose care needs start after age 65. *No lower age limit, except lower rate not available to under 16s.*	No	No	No	Covers blind/partially sighted and deaf claimants – but seek advice. Claimed on same form as mobility component. Very complex self-assessment form – help needed. May elect to complete a short claim for and be examined by a doctor instead. Payment ceases after 28 days in hospital/res. care. Not counted as income for IS or other benefits. It is paid at three rates.
11. Attendance Allowance (AA) Social Security Contributions and Benefits Act 1992, s. 64; Social Security (Attendance Allowance) Regulations 1991	Claimant needs help with bodily functions; need for attendance must have existed for at least 6 months (unless terminally ill)	Age under 65. Person whose immigration status is subject to any limitation or condition.	No	No	No	Covers blind/partially sighted and deaf claimants – but seek advice. Can only be claimed for people whose care needs start after age 65 (otherwise see DLA). Payable at two rates: lower for day *or* night time care; higher for day *and* night time care or terminally ill. A person does not have to be receiving care to get AA, just be in need of care. Payment stops after 28 days in hospital – resumes automatically on discharge.

BENEFIT (and main legislation)	WHO CAN CLAIM?	WHO CANNOT?	IS IT MEANS TESTED?	IS IT CONTRIBUTORY?	IS IT DISCRETIONARY?	COMMENTS
12. Invalid Care Allowance (ICA) Social Security Contributions and Benefits Act 1992, s. 70; Social Security (Invalid Care Allowance) Regulations 1976	Carer of person receiving AA or DLA care component (middle and higher rates).	Carer is aged under 16 or is in full-time education; carer is over 65 unless would have been entitled before that age. Person whose immigration status is subject to any limitation or condition.	No	No	No	Carer must regularly spend at least 35 hours p.w. caring for the person who gets AA and must not earn, if working, more than a certain amount.
13. Statutory Maternity Pay (SMP) Social Security Contributions and Benefits Act 1992, s. 164; Statutory Maternity Pay (General) Regulations 1986	Pregnant employed woman with 26 weeks' continuous service at 15 weeks before expected date of birth.	Woman whose earnings are too low, or who is self-employed.	No	No	No	Payments start from 11 weeks before expected birth and last for 18 weeks; first 6 weeks paid at higher rate (90% of average earnings for last 8 weeks). Contract of employment may give better entitlement. Administered by employer who recovers money from DSS.

BENEFIT (and main legislation)	WHO CAN CLAIM?	WHO CANNOT?	IS IT MEANS TESTED?	IS IT CONTRIBUTORY?	IS IT DISCRETIONARY?	COMMENTS
14. Maternity Allowance (MA) Social Security Contributions and Benefits Act 1992, s. 35; Social Security (Maternity Allowance) Regulations 1987	Woman expecting child in next 11 weeks (or child already born prematurely). Must have been employed for half of the past year.	Working woman; woman receiving SMP.	No	Yes	No	Payable for 18 weeks. Additional amount payable for adult dependant.
15. Bereavement Payment Social Security Contributions and Benefits Act 1992, s. 36	Men and women under retirement age at spouse's death.	Spouse cohabiting with other partner at time of spouse's death.	No	Yes, unless spouse died in industrial accident.	No	Lump sum payment for surviving spouse and dependants. Entitlement depends on deceased spouse's contributions.
16. Bereavement Allowance As for Bereavement Payment	Men and women of 45 to 65 at spouse's death.	Men and women of 65 or over.	No	Yes	No	Entitlement depends on spouse's contribution.

BENEFIT (and main legislation)	WHO CAN CLAIM?	WHO CANNOT?	IS IT MEANS TESTED?	IS IT CONTRIB-UTORY?	IS IT DISCRET-IONARY?	COMMENTS
17. Retirement Pension (RP) Social Security Contributions and Benefits Act 1992, s. 44	Man of 65 or over; Woman of 60 or over.		No	Yes – but can be based on ex-spouse's contribution.	No	Receipt of RP can be deferred for up to 5 years, which increases weekly payments. Amount increases if claimant has dependant(s). Taxable.
18. Child Benefit (CB) Social Security Contributions and Benefits Act 1992, ss. 141–146; Child Benefit (General) Regulations 1976; Child Benefit and Social Security (Fixing and Adjustment of Rates) Regulations 1976	Person responsible for child under 16 (or 19 in full-time secondary education).	The child is married, works over 16 hours a week, receives IS or SDA or an allowance under training scheme. Person whose immigration status is subject to any limitation or condition.	No	No	No	Only one claim per child – person who child lives with has priority; not available if person looking after child receives boarding out allowance; not available once child in local authority accommodation for 8 weeks, unless actually living with claimant. In some circumstances additional benefit can still be claimed for single parent where claimant does not live with spouse, cohabitee, or child's parent, 18-year-old for whom CB received exempt from council tax. Counts as income for means tested benefits.

BENEFIT (and main legislation)	WHO CAN CLAIM?	WHO CANNOT?	IS IT MEANS TESTED?	IS IT CONTRIBUTORY?	IS IT DISCRETIONARY?	COMMENTS
19. Guardian's Allowance Social Security Contributions and Benefits Act 1992, s. 77; Social Security (Guardian's Allowance) Regulations 1975	Person looking after child who has no known parents, in receipt of CB.		No	No	No	Can be claimed by step-parent.
20. Benefits for Industrial Diseases and Injuries Social Security Contributions and Benefits Act 1992, ss. 94–103; Social Security (Industrial Injuries) (Prescribed Diseases) Regulations 1985	Employed person who suffered work-related accident or prescribed industrial disease.	Certain relatives of employer; person less than 1% disabled	No	No	No	Detailed regulations specify prescribed diseases and ways of assessing percentage disablement. For *disablement benefit* (a weekly benefit) disability must normally be at least 14% disablement, and claimant injured before October 1990, may; if less than 14% disablement, be entitled to *reduced earnings allowance*.

SUPPORT FOR ASYLUM SEEKERS

The right of an asylum seeker to use the welfare state alongside other members of society has been progressively eroded over the past ten years. Such support for asylum seekers as exists is now set out in the Immigration and Asylum Act 1999. (Not every immigrant is an asylum seeker of course. An asylum seeker is defined as a person of at least 18 claiming that his or her removal from the UK would be a breach of the UK's international obligations under the UN Refugee Convention, which obliges states to accept those fleeing from genuine fear of persecution. Once their status is determined by the Home Office they cease to be asylum seekers, unless appealing against refusal.)

The essence of the regime established under the 1999 Act for 'support' for asylum seekers waiting to have their status determined is threefold:

(a)   compulsory dispersal;
(b)   maintenance without cash; and
(c)   removal of asylum seekers from protection of significant areas of social services legislation (summarised in Chapter 1, p. 5).

We will look briefly at the second of these issues. Part IV of the Act establishes a support regime entirely separate from the benefit system. Asylum seekers are entitled to support if they — taken together with any dependants — are likely to be destitute. Destitution means they do not have any right to occupy accommodation, including shared and temporary accommodation, and/or they are not able to meet essential living needs (as defined by the Government).

The support which the Home Office provides, under s. 96, amounts to accommodation and other needs to a level which the Secretary of State considers adequate. Payment by way of money is not allowed and the Secretary of State is forbidden to take into account the preference of the asylum seeker in determining where the person will live. Support will be capped at around 70 per cent of the IS equivalent level. Section 99 allows the Secretary of State to pay local authorities to provide the support to the asylum seekers. Support includes accommodation, and the local authority must provide information on request so that the Home Office can decide on dispersals. Although the regime assumes cooperation between Home Office and local authorities, the Act allows the Government to direct a local authority to receive and accommodate asylum seekers.

If any support is provided for a destitute asylum seeker it can be made subject to conditions, though there is no requirement to set these out in a language which the asylum seeker can understand.

OTHER FINANCIAL ISSUES

The final part of this chapter looks at a collection of financial issues which may be relevant to your client's circumstances. There is not scope to go into detail, and all we can do is to flag a few ideas. If your client may have a claim for accidental injury, he or she will need to seek legal advice — preferably from someone who does not charge for the first interview — as soon as possible.

Compensation for Dismissal from Work

Until a person has been employed for one year at more than eight hours per week, the only protection from arbitrary dismissal is the notice period. Unless the contract stipulates longer, notice, or pay in lieu, must be one week for each year worked — so this gives little protection from dismissal in the early stages of employment. The amounts which can be claimed in such a wrongful dismissal case are low — usually up to one week's wages, plus holiday pay if that is owing. The claim can be heard in the county court or industrial tribunal. Help may be available from an agency specialising in employment advice or, for a member, a trades union.

Neither wrongful dismissal — the claim for pay in lieu of notice — nor unfair dismissal, which we look at next, are claims that will succeed if the employee brought on their own dismissal by behaving in a way totally inconsistent with the requirements of being an employee, i.e., by being guilty of some type of gross misconduct which entitles the employer to say 'go'.

Once the full year of employment with this employer has been notched up, greater security is available under the Employment Rights Act 1996. Someone sacked before one year's employment may still qualify if their notice period would take them over the one-year period, or if the dismissal is connected to grounds of race or sex, or trade union activities. If the firm has been taken over in the past year, that does not usually mean the time has to be served again.

A person employed for at least 12 months has a right not to be unfairly dismissed. What does this mean? A dismissal is 'fair' if the employer has behaved reasonably in deciding to sack someone; it is up to the employer to prove fairness, rather than the other way round. A fair dismissal usually requires misconduct on the part of the employee, and unless it is gross misconduct, there must be a reasonable disciplinary system allowing the employee to put his or her side of the case, and to receive warnings before being sacked. Dismissal because of a genuine redundancy is fair, but the employee is still entitled to compensation from the employer by way of a redundancy payment, which is partly financed by the state.

A person dismissed in circumstances which appear unfair should immediately take legal advice; it is available, subject to means, from a solicitor or an advice agency under the CLS scheme (see Chapter 15); law centres and CABs are usually able to advise. It is vital to act swiftly; if a case is to be brought to an employment tribunal, the correct form must normally be lodged within three months of the dismissal. CLS funding does not, unfortunately, extend to representation in the tribunal. This will have to be paid for, obtained from an agency which has other sources of funding, obtained from a trades union or on a 'no win, no fee' basis, or done without. It is arguable that the lack of funded representation is a denial of the right to a fair hearing under Article 6 of the European Convention. The Scottish Executive believes this, and has extended the right to representation to employment tribunals ((2000) December 2000 Legal Action 4)).

A problem can be that the employee resigned. But a person who leaves because his or her work situation has been made intolerable by the employer, or who is told to resign, may be treated as 'constructively dismissed', and therefore should not be deterred from seeking advice.

A tribunal cannot force an employer to take back an unfairly dismissed employee, although it can penalise an employer who refuses to do so by making a bigger award to the sacked employee. An award will be based on the number of years the employee has worked for this employer, plus compensation for any actual losses incurred by the sacked employee. If there was an element of racial or sex discrimination in the dismissal, the compensation will be increased.

Criminal Injuries Compensation

This scheme is governed by the Criminal Injuries Compensation Act 1995, which set up a Criminal Injuries Compensation Authority (CICA) (formerly the Criminal Injuries Compensation Board). Compensation may be available to a person injured or killed by a criminal act. The amount awarded is based on a tariff. Temporary partial deafness, at one end of the scale, is worth £1,000; serious brain damage, at the other end, merits £25,000. On top of the tariff amount the CICA awards compensation for loss of earnings, except for the first 28 weeks.

The scheme does not cover road traffic accidents but, as we have seen, a claim for personal injury can be made through the courts or the MIB.

It does not matter that the criminal cannot be prosecuted, because, for example, he or she cannot be traced, or is not prosecuted because it is not in the public interest — for example, a mentally disordered person. It does not even matter if the person who committed the act was acquitted. The CICA merely has to be satisfied that the injury was caused by a criminal act.

It costs nothing to make a claim, and the forms can be obtained from the CICA at Morley House, 26–30 Holborn Viaduct, London EC1A JJQ (tel. 0207 436 0804; www.cica.gov.uk). Once the form has been filled in, the claim is assessed without a hearing, and it may take more than a year for a decision to be made. A claim must be made within two years of the criminal act, except where the victim is a child. It is possible to appeal against a decision of the Authority to an internal panel.

Social workers should be aware of the possibility of making a claim on behalf of a child in care, or advising a parent or guardian where the child is not in care. Child abuse, whether or not a prosecution ever takes place, is a criminal offence. It is a crime even if the child 'consents' to the assault (*R* v *Criminal Injuries Appeals Panel ex parte B* (2000) *The Times*, 1 August). Psychiatric, as well as physical, injuries are covered. But the CICA is unwilling to make an award if this is not in the interests of the child, and the old CICB published a short guide on how it viewed such cases (*Child Abuse and the Criminal Injuries Compensation Scheme*). Also no award will be made if there is a possibility of the abuser benefiting from the money.

The child may be eligible separately for free legal advice, and we suggest advising the person helping the child to obtain legal help. The more quality information supplied to the CICA, detailing the extent and effects of the abuse in particular, the better the likely outcome. Medical evidence is, of course, vital.

The Court of Appeal considered when it is appropriate to apply on behalf of a child in the case of *Re G* [1990] 1 WLR 1120. The key feature in that case pointing towards making a claim (the court had to decide as the child was a ward of court) was that there was no further contact with the abuser, so a CICB claim would not damage an important relationship.

Note also that if the person who caused the injury is successfully prosecuted, the criminal court can award compensation — the court must give reasons for not making such an order where it is appropriate (see Chapter 12). The payment of such compensation may be less than the amount which could be awarded in a civil court, or by the CICB, because the offender's means and the victim's own conduct will be taken into account. There is, somewhat surprisingly, no procedure giving the victim the opportunity to appear in court or write to the court to ask for compensation in a criminal court.

Rewriting a Will

A cause of financial problems can be the death of a person who fails to provide for a dependant in a will. Despite the general principle that people can leave their property without interference, a dependant can make a claim against the estate under the Inheritance (Provision for Family and Dependants) Act 1976. This is expensive, may be contested by other beneficiaries, and is not guaranteed to succeed. Prevention is better than cure, and if possible a dependant should try to ensure that he or she is named in the will.

Managing Debt

Debt is a specialist area for legal advice. In the CLS Directory for your region you should be able to find details of who to refer to for such specialist help.

There are no panaceas, since debt usually results from not having enough money. An adviser cannot often solve that problem — though Children Act money, or good advice on benefits, may do just this. If a person falls into debt and cannot repay, what advice can you give him or her? Again, we consider this to be an area where expert advice is better than partially informed advice. So we have only indicated certain priorities, as you need a separate book to give detailed advice on debt management.

Useful volumes are the CPAG's annual *Debt Advice Handbook*, and *Fuel Rights Handbook*.

A social worker need not be passive; you can sit down with the client and work out a schedule of income against outgoings, assets against liabilities, to help the client understand his or her position and the choices that are open (if any). You can help the client face up to the fact that there is a real problem, so that advice is sought.

Nearly all creditors are open to negotiation; whether or not they are humane, they have an interest in talking to the debtor as a way of obtaining satisfaction of the debt. An agreed arrangement to pay less than the whole amount of a debt, or, for example, to freeze interest, may in the end yield better rewards to the creditor than holding out for payment of the whole sum, when payment in full is unrealistic. Against a person of no resources, a court judgment may not be worth the paper it is printed on — the knowledge of this helps encourage a creditor to talk to the debtor or his or her adviser. But to get anywhere in negotiations, the creditor needs to know about the debtor's current financial position, because only the knowledge of the debtor's difficulties and proposals to allocate the limited money available will force on the creditor the realisation that compromise is better than nothing.

In the case of each type of debt, you have to ask: how will it be enforced? This answers some of the questions about priorities. All debts can be enforced through court action. But sometimes the outcome of one court action is worse than others: in particular, if the debt consists of rent or mortgage arrears, the court can order repossession of the home. The local authority does not have to rehouse such a person if the debt arose through his or her own wilful mismanagement of his or her finances — that is intentional homelessness (for more on homelessness, see Chapter 17).

In these circumstances, the payment of the arrears (or renegotiation of the arrears with the creditor) should assume a high priority.

Debts carrying a high rate of interest are also high priorities; often the accrued interest exceeds the original loan.

Debts to gas and electricity boards are high priorities, since these creditors have a course of action open to them which is immediate and drastic — cutting off the service. There is a code of conduct delaying the supply being cut off in cases of hardship; this applies only if the debtor contacts the board and informs them of the reason for not paying. Having a child under 11 in the premises, or being in receipt of IS, means the boards will automatically delay any action for a further two weeks, to give the BA or social services time to try to arrange some scheme for sorting out the debt. The result may be payment direct (see below); a meter, calibrated so that some of the payments go towards the arrears; or an agreement to pay off the arrears at a set rate. So the code does not prevent the boards cutting off the supply; it means that it will not be carried out without a chance to make a satisfactory arrangement. But the code does prevent a household being cut off during the winter months where all the occupants are pensioners.

(Telephones can also be cut off because of non-payment; it depends on individual circumstances whether this is a priority.)

Fuel, water, mortgage interest, arrears of these, and rent and council tax arrears can be paid direct by the BA out of IS (but not out of any other benefit — so claiming a benefit which reduces entitlement to income support may destroy this option). The amounts paid will not automatically be the exact amounts for any period, because consumption of fuel cannot be exactly estimated. Only a certain proportion of IS can go on direct payments, so if there is not enough, rent arrears take priority, followed by fuel and water. The landlord or fuel/water company will usually take no further action, once current payments and arrears are being made directly.

A typical client will have a number of small debts, rather than one very large one. If a court judgment is obtained against the debtor, he or she can apply to the court for an administration order. This requires the court to administer all the debts, including those where there is no judgment, so long as they do not together exceed a set figure (currently £5,000). The court decides on a monthly figure that the debtor can pay towards all the debts, and then parcels out the available money to the creditors. The creditors can refuse to agree to join such a scheme, but at least if they do join they know they will be getting something.

Even on a single debt, the court can, and usually will if the debtor asks, order payment of the outstanding sum by instalments based on the debtor's ability to pay. Knowing that this is the likely outcome, a creditor who is told of the debtor's financial circumstances may be willing to accept instalments without a court order.

Possibly the strongest temptation to someone running into debt problems is to turn a blind eye, to hope the problems will go away. The specialist debt counsellor can advise only if approached, whereas a competent social worker may spot signs of debt problems before the client seeks advice. It does not help the client to ignore the problem — interest accumulates, arrears of rent may exceed the threshold for an automatic possession order (see Chapter 17), and the creditor ends up taking court proceedings, without any hope of negotiations. Even court summonses get ignored by anxious debtors, who then find judgment is granted by the court and the bailiff is knocking at the door to take away possessions for sale. Even at this stage, it is not too late to take advice and action. Courts can grant orders suspending the action of the bailiff in return for proposals to pay the debt by instalments.

But if you are aware that a client has debt problems, helping the client to face up to them sooner not later is the best (but not necessarily the most welcome) help you can offer.

NINETEEN
Unlawful Discrimination

HUMAN RIGHTS AND DISCRIMINATION

Human rights are on the agenda in England and Wales, and the right not to be unfairly discriminated against is one of the most important ones. The rights have existed, on paper, since the United Nations adopted the Universal Declaration of Human Rights shortly after the Second World War. Take a look at the rights contained in Articles 2 and 23:

Article 2
Everyone is entitled to all the rights and freedoms set forth in this Declaration, without distinction of any kind, such as race, colour sex, language, religion, political or other opinion, national or social origin, property, birth or other status. . . .

Article 23
  1. Everyone has the right to work, to free choice of employment, to just and favourable conditions of work and to protection against unemployment.
  2. Everyone, without any discrimination, has the right to equal pay for equal work.

These rights are supplemented in further treaties to which the UK is a signatory. The contents of four key conventions are summarised in Table 19.1 below. You can get the flavour of the way these are worded by looking at the Convention relating to women where we include more of the actual wording.

Table 19.1 Human Rights Treaties on Discrimination to which the UK is a Signatory

Convention on the Elimination of All Forms of Discrimination against Women 1981

Article 1

For the purposes of the present Convention, the term "discrimination against women" shall mean any distinction, exclusion or restriction made on the basis of sex which has the effect or purpose of impairing or nullifying the recognition, enjoyment or exercise by women, irrespective of their marital status, on a basis of equality of men and women, of human rights and fundamental freedoms in the political, economic, social, cultural, civil or any other field.

Article 2

States Parties condemn discrimination against women in all its forms, agree to pursue by all appropriate means and without delay a policy of eliminating discrimination against women.

Article 3

States Parties shall take in all fields, in particular in the political, social, economic and cultural fields, all appropriate measures, including legislation, to ensure the full development and advancement of women, for the purpose of guaranteeing them the exercise and enjoyment of human rights and fundamental freedoms on a basis of equality with men.

Article 4

1.   Adoption by States Parties of temporary special measures aimed at accelerating de facto equality between men and women shall not be considered discrimination as defined in the present Convention, but shall in no way entail as a consequence the maintenance of unequal or separate standards; these measures shall be discontinued when the objectives of equality of opportunity and treatment have been achieved.

Article 5

States Parties shall take all appropriate measures:

(a)   To modify the social and cultural patterns of conduct of men and women, with a view to achieving the elimination of prejudices and customary and all other practices which are based on the idea of the inferiority or the superiority of either of the sexes or on stereotyped roles for men and women;

(b)   To ensure that family education includes a proper understanding of maternity as a social function and the recognition of the common responsibility of men and women in the upbringing and development of their children, it being understood that the interest of the children is the primary consideration in all cases.

Article 11

1.   States Parties shall take all appropriate measures to eliminate discrimination against women in the field of employment in order to ensure, on a basis of equality of men and women, the same rights, in particular:

(a)   The right to work as an inalienable right of all human beings;

(b)   The right to the same employment opportunities, including the application of the same criteria for selection in matters of employment;

(c)   The right to free choice of profession and employment, the right to promotion, job security and all benefits and conditions of service and the right to receive vocational training and retraining, including apprenticeships, advanced vocational training and recurrent training;

(d)   The right to equal remuneration, including benefits, and to equal treatment in respect of work of equal value, as well as equality of treatment in the evaluation of the quality of work;

(e)   The right to social security, particularly in cases of retirement, unemployment, sickness, invalidity and old age and other incapacity to work, as well as the right to paid leave;

(f)   The right to protection of health and to safety in working conditions, including the safeguarding of the function of reproduction.

UN Declaration on the Elimination of All Forms of Racial Discrimination 1963

1.—Discrimination between human beings on the ground of race, colour or ethnic origin is an offence to human dignity and shall be condemned as a denial of the principles of the Charter of the United Nations, as a violation of the human rights and fundamental freedoms proclaimed in the Universal Declaration of Human Rights, as an obstacle to friendly and peaceful relations among nations and as a fact capable of disturbing peace and security among peoples.

2.—1.   No State, institution, group or individual shall make any discrimination whatsoever in matters of human rights and fundamental freedoms in the treatment of persons, groups of persons or institutions on the ground of race, colour or ethnic origin.

2.   No State shall encourage, advocate or lend its support, through police action or otherwise, to any discrimination based on race, colour or ethnic origin by any group, institution or individual.

3.—Special concrete measures shall be taken in appropriate circumstances in order to secure adequate development or protection of individuals belonging to certain racial groups with the object of ensuring the full enjoyment by such individuals of human rights and fundamental freedoms. These measures shall in no circumstances have as a consequence the maintenance of unequal or separate rights for different racial groups.

4.—1.   Particular efforts shall be made to prevent discrimination based on race, colour or ethnic origin, especially in the fields of civil rights, access to citizenship, education, religion, employment, occupation and housing.

2.   Everyone shall have equal access to any place or facility intended for use by the general public, without distinction as to race, colour or ethnic origin.

The remaining articles include the following (summarised) obligations on the signatories to combat discrimination or prejudice founded on race, colour or ethnic origin:

- to address laws that encourage or permit discrimination and, take steps to combat prejudice;
- to legislate against discrimination in employment, political or citizenship rights and public service;
- to secure equal access to justice, security and state protection;
- to secure remedies in law through independent tribunals for discrimination suffered;
- to undertake positive steps in education and public information; and
- to condemn persons claiming superiority of one group against another and to criminalise incitements to violence and organisations which promote violence.

UN Declaration on the Rights of Disabled Persons 1974

1.   The term 'disabled person' means any person unable to ensure by himself or herself, wholly or partly, the necessities of a normal individual and/or social life, as a result of a deficiency, either congenital or not, in his physical or mental capacities.

2.   Disabled persons shall enjoy all the rights set forth in this declaration. These rights shall be granted to all disabled persons without any exception whatever.

These rights may be summarised as rights to:

- dignity;
- a decent and normal full life;
- social and political rights;
- all possible measures to be taken to facilitate self-reliance;
- treatment and retraining towards rehabilitation; economic and social security;
- proper employment opportunities;
- family life as near to normal as possible;
- legal aid for the protection of rights;
- protection from exploitation; and
- the right to be informed of these rights.

Convention on the Rights of Mentally Retarded Persons 1971

These rights may be summarised as the rights to:

- proper care;

- education;
- rehabilitation;
- guidance;
- economic security;
- work to the fullest extent possible;
- family life as far as possible, with support if necessary;
- guardianship;
- protection from exploitation and abuse; and
- proper procedures to be adopted before any deprivation of normal rights.

These Articles are, unfortunately, merely statements intended to bind the UK Government to good practice. Unlike in some countries, treaty obligations in the UK do not create enforceable rights. However, under the Human Rights Act 1998, the United Kingdom has taken on board the European Convention on Human Rights. The following Article of the Convention is now to be taken into account by courts in England and Wales:

Article 14
The enjoyment of the rights and freedoms set forth in this Convention shall be secured without discrimination on any ground such as sex, race, colour, language, religion, political or other opinion, national or social origin, association with a national minority, property, birth or other status.

These protections against unreasonable discrimination seem to extend way beyond the rights currently enshrined in our legislation, and which this chapter now discusses. All we have at present are rights not to be discriminated against on grounds of race, sex or disability. However, we must restrain an overjubilant anticipation of Convention rights significantly extending English law. The right not to be discriminated against is in respect of the enjoyment of the treaty rights — things like a right to privacy and a right to a fair trial. The European Convention, which now has legal effect, offers no rights not to be discriminated against in relation to work or social security, unlike the UN Declaration which is not legally enforceable.

Meanwhile, the law of the European Union has been enforceable in the UK since accession to the Treaty of Rome in 1973. So Article 141 (ex 119) of that treaty, which outlaws discrimination on grounds of sex, has been our law for a long time. However, the treaty, being in origin an economic one interested in improving economic productivity and labour mobility, did not start from a rights perspective and does not yet look at issues of race or disability. So European Union legislation may well move from centre stage as the European Convention on Human Rights begins to influence the decisions of tribunals and courts. It has already had an impact on discrimination against homosexuals.

An example of sex discrimination in the enjoyment of a European Convention right can be seen in the case of *Abdulaziz, Cabales and Balkandali* v *UK*

(1982) 7 EHRR 471. The new Conservative Government wished to restrict immigration, particularly at a time of mass unemployment. New rules were introduced which prevented a man joining his wife in this country unless he could show that his wife was a UK citizen born, or descended from parents born, in the UK. The allegation against the UK was a breach of the right to family life (Article 8) and of the right to found a family (Article 14). This allegation was strengthened by demonstrating that the rule discriminated against women, since men could be joined by their wives, the latter being presumed to be not so likely to seek employment. The final decision of the Court on Article 8 was disappointing: the European Court of Human Rights found no breach of the right to family life, since the couple were not prevented from living together in the wife's country of origin. But taking account of Article 14, the Court held that the applicant (a woman) was discriminated against. The UK could not protect its labour market against immigrant men but not immigrant women. (Despite the immigration rule clearly favouring whites over other racial groups, the Court held that there had been no racial discrimination.)

THE LIMITATIONS OF THE LAW

The law will never outlaw all discrimination. Some discrimination is unobjectionable: for example, the targeting of welfare services towards certain sectors of the population; medical services for the elderly; obstetric facilities for women, etc. The law can, and should, move in the direction of preventing those with access to goods and services — jobs, housing, recreational facilities, pay — offering these to some segments of the population in preference to others. The law can occasionally accept, or require, discrimination in favour of certain sectors: for example, facilities to enable workers with disabilities to carry out employment tasks, or training for groups who have had less access to certain jobs.

DISCRIMINATION AND LAWYERS

Another reason for not expecting all discrimination to become outlawed — even all discrimination that we would like to see disappear — is the fact that the legal profession and the judges have made so little progress in removing the kind of discrimination that comes from prejudice.

The legal profession is not yet in a good position to preach anti-discrimination practice to social workers. Here are a few recent examples:

- There are 423 women judges of all ranks, compared to 3,112 men (Lord Chancellor's Department website, November 2000 — up from 10 per cent to almost 14 per cent since the last edition of this book). So don't be surprised to read below that English judges (subsequently overruled) thought that dismissing a woman for pregnancy had nothing to do with her sex (*Webb* v *Emo Air Cargo* [1993] IRLR 27).
- No judge in the High Court or above comes from an ethnic minority background (LCD website, May 2001).

- The youngest judge in the High Court and above in December 2000 was 46 years old. In the House of Lords, the youngest Law Lord was 62.
- 'About 11% of women trainee solicitors and 9% of ethnic minority trainees reported discrimination or harassment . . . The equivalent figures for trainee barristers were 40% and 33% respectively. . . .' Minorities and women may find it hard to progress: 'Professional sponsorship is most likely to go to those who . . . need it least. Around 74% of Oxbridge graduate Legal Practice Course students received funding, compared with 3% of new university graduate students; and 27% of white students, compared with 8% of ethnic minority students.' ([1997] *Law Society's Gazette*, 24 September, p. 30)
- Even the Lord Chancellor has been found liable by an employment tribunal for appointing a male former colleague to a top job. He didn't advertise or interview. No women had a chance to apply. This was sex discrimination. (The Lord Chancellor appealed successfully in *Lord Chancellor* v *Coker* (2000) *The Times*, 23 January 2001. It was held that for a political appointment he was entitled to choose whoever he liked. In other words, he would be allowed to follow worst practice. A further appeal is likely.)

THE LEGAL FRAMEWORK

You need to know the legal framework, but do not rely on all lawyers to set good examples! Awareness of the prevalence of discrimination is important, and anti-discriminatory practice is a required part of social work training. But good practice is way ahead of the minimum that the law requires.

There are also two simple reasons why this area of law is important to you. You are obliged, as an individual and a department, to act within the law. And you will deal with people who may need advice on discrimination they have suffered. A third reason is that the Children Act 1989 requires you to be aware of racial origin when placing children with foster parents or providing day care. Guidance is set out in a letter Cl 90(2) from the Social Services Inspectorate.

A local authority should have a written policy on sexual, racial and disability discrimination (an equal opportunities policy). This policy, it is hoped, will go beyond the bare minimum of what the legislation requires, and will attempt to promote genuine equality of opportunity and sensitivity to relevant difference for all people affected by the work of the authority. From April 2001, all public bodies — for example, police, immigration authorities and, of course, local authorities — have a general duty to work towards the elimination of unlawful discrimination and to promote equality of opportunity and good relations between different racial groups (Race Relations Act 2000, s. 1).

We first focus the discussion on sex and race discrimination, where each of the Acts was drafted in the 1970s on very similar lines. At the end of the chapter we look at more recent legislation in relation to disability.

Sex Discrimination Act 1975 (SDA) and Race Relations Act 1976 (RRA)

Definitions can be difficult. For sex discrimination, English law recognises only two sexes, men and women, which means the sex which went on to your birth certificate. A challenge before the European Court of Human Rights failed to overturn this rule: *Sheffield* v *UK* [1998] 3 FCR 141. This meant that the UK was not in violation of the Human Rights Convention for failing to register as father of a child a man who had been female at birth. However, the European Court of the EU has ruled that dismissal of a person on the ground that she changed sex from male to female amounted to sex discrimination against her as a woman in breach of (then) Article 119 (now 141) of the Treaty of Rome (see below): *P* v *S and Cornwall CC* [1996] IRLR 347. As a result of this decision, the SDA has been amended to include discrimination on grounds of gender reassignment.

Sex discrimination seems to be defined in the SDA only in terms of sex, not sexual orientation. It was not unlawful to discriminate against a man because he was gay, or against a woman because she was a lesbian. Therefore, when Lisa Grant could not get her employer to issue a free travel pass to her lesbian partner, and complained to the industrial tribunal that a man living with a woman would have received one, the European Court, who finally decided this question, said that this was discrimination on grounds of sexual orientation and lawful (*Grant* v *SW Trains* [1998] IRLR 206). However, if male homosexuals are treated differently to female homosexuals, this is straightforward sex discrimination and unlawful (*Smith* v *Gardner Merchant* [1998] 3 All ER 852).

But overlaid on this fairly clear reading of the meaning of 'sex' is the new Human Rights Act 1998. This, as we pointed out in Chapter 1, does not override all UK statutes, but it does require a court to bend over backwards to find a meaning within any legislation in a way which is consistent with the rights set out in the European Convention. In a Scottish case, *MacDonald* v *Ministry of Defence* [2000] IRLR 748, the Employment Appeal Tribunal decided that 'sex' could be read as including 'sexual orientation', and therefore the dismissal of an RAF officer because of his sexual orientation was unlawful sex discrimination. This decision is not binding outside Scotland, but will be highly persuasive in relation to a discrimination case based on sexual orientation in England and Wales.

For race discrimination, the RRA, s. 1, defines race in terms of colour, nationality or ethnic or national origins. It does not yet cover religion, although a group of people that has established its own racial identity around its religion, such as Sikhs, has been treated under the Act as a distinct ethnic group — *Mandla* v *Dowell Lee* [1983] 2 AC 548. Jews are an ethnic group (*Seide* v *Gillette Industries Ltd* [1980] IRLR 427). By contrast, Rastafarians are not treated as a racial group because the movement is too recent in origin — so it was lawful to refuse a man a job unless he cut his hair (*Dawkins* v *Crown Suppliers* [1993] IRLR 284). Gypsies have been accorded the status of a racial group (*Commission for Racial Equality* v *Dutton* [1989] 2 WLR 1989), although the same case decided that discrimination against travellers was not illegal, since they represent a mode of life rather than a racial grouping. Scots are not a separate ethnic or national group (*Boyce* v *British Airways* (1997) 581 IRLB 7).

There is currently nothing to stop discrimination on grounds of religion. In 1997, the Government pledged to introduce legislation to fill this gap. In the meantime, the British National Party can attempt to stir up hatred against muslims, without contravening the Public Order Act 1985, because of the technicality that muslims are not a racial group (*Guardian*, 28 October 1998).

Neither is discrimination on grounds of age unlawful (though if such discrimination also affects more women than men, because of time taken out to raise a family, that will be sex discrimination). The Government has introduced a Consultation Paper on age discrimination and intends to issue a Code of Practice.

What is Discrimination?

The simple principle of the legislation is that it is unlawful to discriminate against a person on grounds of his or her sex or race unless a statutory exception applies. So first we have to define discrimination, and then look at the exceptional circumstances in which sex or race discrimination is allowed.

Discrimination can be direct — treating a person less favourably on grounds of sex or race. This covers the now illegal job or property advertisements which used to state, for example, 'no coloureds or Irish need apply'. Sexual or racial harassment is considered to be direct discrimination. Employers cannot plead ignorance if harassment occurs — they must stop their employees harassing others. See, e.g., *Burton* v *De Vere Hotels* (below).

It can be indirect — imposing requirements that a person of that sex or race would have greater difficulty in complying with than others: for example, a height requirement would exclude more women; a requirement to wear a particular piece of headgear may be difficult to comply with for a particular racial group. However, indirect discrimination is not unlawful if the requirement can be justified on its merits on non-sex or non-racial grounds — for example, to seek workers with experience of senior management may well discriminate against women, or members of some racial groups, who for a variety of reasons are less likely to have such experience, but it will not be unlawful if that experience is genuinely necessary. But, by contrast, an unnecessary upper age limit, which indirectly discriminates against women who have spent time bringing up a family, is unlawful (*Price* v *Civil Service Commission* [1977] IRLR 295).

Discrimination also arose in the case of *Weathersfield* v *Sargent* [1999] ICR 425. An employee was instructed not to rent vehicles to black or Asian customers, and left the employment in disgust. His claim to have been discriminated against on racial grounds was upheld — a decision showing the Court of Appeal working to achieve justice rather than following legal tramlines.

Sex discrimination is unlawful not just against women, but also men. Furthermore, it is illegal to discriminate on grounds of marital status, if a person of one sex is treated less favourably because he or she is married or single. There have been very few cases where this — as opposed to sex — has been the real issue. For example, refusing to train a woman social worker on the ground that she was going to follow her husband to another part of the country was unlawful not because she was married, but because the employer should not have been making prejudicial assumptions about married *women* (*Horsey* v *Dyfed County Council* [1982] IRLR 395).

The Importance of European Community Law for Sex Discrimination Cases

Back in 1975, English legislation on sex discrimination was required under the Treaty of Rome which required member states to remove discrimination on pay and treatment (Article 119 (now 141) and subsequent directives). But even where the UK Parliament has not brought in legislation to implement European Community law, the latter is still applicable in our courts. Using European Community, as opposed to English, law, it has been possible to get pension and retirement ages equalised, and clearer recognition of pregnancy-related discrimination as being unlawful. It is worth asking in any case of sex discrimination that English law seems to turn a blind eye to: can this be challenged as unlawful under European law? An example of a case being sorted out by the European Court is this Danish one: *Tele Danmark AS* v *Handels-og Kontorfunktionaerernes Forbund i Danmark HG* (4 October 2001, not yet reported). The employee had not told her new employers that she was pregnant. It was only a six month contract, and the employers dismissed her as soon as they found out, since she would be absent for a large part of the contract. It was held that she did not have to reveal her pregnancy, even where the contract was very short. The dismissal was unlawful, as are all pregnancy-related dismissals.

EXAMPLES OF UNLAWFUL RACIAL AND SEXUAL DISCRIMINATION

Employment

Discrimination on grounds of race or sex in the field of employment is unlawful. This means not just refusal of employment in the first place on sex or race grounds, but discrimination in all aspects of work, including the provision of facilities, promotion prospects, training or deciding who to dismiss. Moreover, the employer carries a responsibility for what goes on in the work situation; he or she has to take positive steps to stop employees behaving in a discriminatory way towards each other. Therefore, if a person is discriminated against by fellow employees, the employer is liable unless he or she can show that he or she was not only unaware of the acts of the employee, but also had taken reasonable steps to prevent such discrimination from occurring (such as training or supervising the workforce). An example of how this works is *Enterprise Glass Co. Ltd* v *Miles* [1990] ICR 787. A female employee was subjected to suggestive remarks by a colleague. The employers not only ignored her complaint, but promoted the perpetrator. The Employment Appeal Tribunal made the employer pay the victim compensation. The same principle applies with race discrimination. In *Burton* v *De Vere Hotels*

[1996] IRLR 596 a speaker at a dinner made extremely offensive racist comments to two black waitresses. He then encouraged guests to make offensive remarks to them. The hotel, knowing the propensities of the speaker, should have protected these black employees in particular from such an attack.

How far must an employer go? In *Stewart* v *Cleveland Guest (Engineering) Ltd* [1994] IRLR 440 the Employment Appeal Tribunal upheld a tribunal's finding that it was not sex discrimination for the employer to allow male workers to put up offensive pin-ups. The employer did not have to act on the female employee's complaints. (The EAT rather confusingly added that allowing pin-ups can sometimes amount to sex discrimination, so it is still worth complaining to an employer.)

Employers must not discriminate in rates of pay. There is a separate process for dealing with equal pay claims for women, under the Equal Pay Act 1970, which involves complex rules for making comparisons between the value of different kinds of work. Is canteen work, for example (typically work done by women), worth as much as shipyard work (more often done by men)? The answer was 'Yes' in *Hayward* v *Cammell Laird* [1988] ICR 464. To bring this kind of case an expert in job evaluation is necessary. The Equal Opportunities Commission may be able to help (address below).

Exceptions where discrimination is allowed in employment Not all discrimination in employment is outlawed; we shall look at only the most significant exceptions, and anyone needing more comprehensive advice should either read the Acts in full (maybe your legal department has them, or otherwise a public library), or take legal advice or contact the Commission for Racial Equality (10/12 Allington Street, London SW1E 5EH, tel. 0207 828 7022) or the Equal Opportunities Commission (Arndale House, Arndale Centre, Manchester M4 3EQ, tel. 0161–833 9244). North Lambeth Law Centre has set up a do-it-yourself guide to the race discrimination law: www.rdu.org.uk.

Occupational requirements If a person of a particular sex or racial group is required for a job for genuine occupational reasons, it is lawful to choose only that kind of person. It is therefore permissible to employ an actor of a particular sex or racial group to play that part; it is lawful to choose to employ a person of Bengali origin to do welfare work within a Bengali community; a woman can be sought to work in a women's refuge; to provide authenticity an Indian can be sought as a waiter for an Indian restaurant (but probably not as a cook, since appearance is in itself irrelevant to cooking). But each exception, if challenged, has to be justified as genuine. Do you have to be a Bengali to work with Bengalis?

Small employers As an exception it is lawful to discriminate in choosing to employ someone in a person's own home for domestic service; firms with fewer than five employees may discriminate on sex grounds, but never on race grounds.

Positive discrimination In certain situations, there is an exception which allows for positive discrimination. Thus where a particular racial group, or one sex, is under-represented in a field of employment (throughout the UK), training organisations may offer members of the disadvantaged group special training and facilities to attempt to equalise the position. Employers can also offer special training if during the past 12 months a racial group or a sex has been under-represented in that establishment.

Positive discrimination is also permitted to allow training to be offered to people who have had family or domestic responsibilities. This can help women come back into the workforce, and apart from this exception it would constitute unlawful discrimination against men.

The European Court — whose decisions bind English courts — has ruled that positive discrimination must remain within boundaries. Giving preference to women just because they were women was not acceptable (*Kalanke* v *Freie Hansestadt Bremen* (1995) C-450/93).

Statutory exceptions It is lawful to discriminate, in employment as well as other fields, if statute makes that lawful: for example, the fact that women cannot work underground in the few remaining coal mines (but we suspect that this legislation would be hard to justify before the European Court, given that mining techniques have changed). Race discrimination is also lawful if a government minister authorises the act. Otherwise many decisions and rules in relation to immigration and residence requirements for state benefits would be unlawful indirect discrimination.

The statutory exception allowing men's and women's retirement ages to be different — always a rather bizarre exception on grounds of logic — was declared illegal by the European Court (*Marshall* v *South West Area Health Authority* [1986] ICR 335). But discrimination based on age is still permitted in relation to social security benefits (see pp. 448–60). Cheap bus fares at age 60 for women and age 65 for men remain — despite all commonsense — legal discrimination (*Atkins* v *Wrekin DC* [1996] 9 CL 622).

Other Examples from the Acts

Discrimination in membership of trades unions and in provision of goods and services is unlawful, or in partnership agreements where there are at least six partners. A private club with fewer than 25 members is exempt from the RRA, so long as it does not discriminate on grounds of colour. So a small Irish-only club would be lawful, but not the exclusion of a black Irish person.

Discrimination in the provision of rented property is unlawful, with the regrettable exception that a resident landlord can discriminate on race or sex grounds in his or her choice of tenants. And where premises are used as a hospital or prison, or for caring for certain groups, such as children or people with special needs, single sex establishments are permitted.

Race or sex discrimination in schooling is not permitted, except that single-sex educational establishments are allowed. For example, Birmingham City Council was found to have breached the SDA by giving fewer grant aided places to girls (*Birmingham City Council* v *EOC* [1988] 3 WLR 837).

Dismissal from work on grounds of pregnancy is an example of sex discrimination. So to select a woman for redundancy because she was about to go on maternity leave was unlawful (*Brown* v *Stockton on Tees Borough Council* [1988] 2 WLR 935).

A spate of sex discrimination cases involving the Ministry of Defence hit the headlines in the late 1990s. Courts now accept that the armed forces are subject to the operation of anti-discrimination rules, and that dismissal for pregnancy is unlawful. Several large awards of damages for lost careers and hurt feelings have been made.

Amazingly a recent doctrine arose, almost as far-fetched as the pregnant man. In *Webb* v *Emo Air Cargo* [1993] IRLR 27, the House of Lords allowed an employer to dismiss a woman on grounds of pregnancy, if the employer would have dismissed a man with a similar condition. An example given was a man taking time off for a hip replacement. The European Court of Justice has fortunately overruled this approach and re-established the principle that discrimination on the grounds of pregnancy is sex discrimination (*Webb* v *Emo Air Cargo (UK) (No. 2) Ltd* [1995] IRLR 645). In fact, under Articles 2 and 5 of the Equal Treatment Directive any dismissal for illness related to pregnancy is automatically unlawful (*Brown* v *Rentokil* [1998] IRLR 445).

Undeterred, the Employment Appeal Tribunal sometimes turns a blind eye to the real differences involved in child care. In *British Telecommunications plc* v *Roberts* [1996] ICR 625, it held that a woman returning from maternity leave and seeking a job share was no different to a man suddenly deciding that he wants to change his hours of work. A better decision was *London Underground* v *Edwards* [1995] IRLR 355, where a woman train driver had to resign when the shift rotas were changed with the result that she could not look after her son. It was held that this shift pattern discriminated against women (who were more likely to be single parents than men).

How would you decide this one fairly? Mr Smith had long hair. His supermarket employers told him to smarten up by having his hair cut to what would be a more normal length for men. He refused and was dismissed. Mr Smith claimed sex discrimination. The employers argued that there was no discrimination since all employees were expected to look smart, regardless of sex, and that meant accepting conventions on hair length. The Court of Appeal held that Mr Smith had not been discriminated against (*Smith* v *Safeway plc* [1996] IRLR 69).

Sexual harassment is a clear example of discrimination which tribunals have a good record of combatting. For example, a woman who rejected her employer's advances and who was, in retaliation, subject to unjustified criticism, was awarded £12,000 for injury to feelings (*Hay* v *Bellhaven Brewery Co. Ltd* (1996) 28 EOR DCLD 8). Allegations of harassment require the employer to investigate. Failure to do so can amount to discrimination since it is a detriment (*Reed* v *Steadman* [1999] IRLR 299).

ENFORCEMENT

In both areas, there are publicly-funded bodies whose task it is to review the operation of the Acts and to take steps in individual cases. The Equal Opportunities Commission (EOC) and the Commission for Racial Equality

(CRE) both have powers to hold investigations, and to require persons or bodies to answer questions about their practices, and if necessary to appear before the Commission. They can issue non-discrimination notices requiring a person or organisation to desist from specified discriminatory practices, which can be enforced by injunction in the High Court. The Commissions can also assist individuals in bringing cases against a person or body that has discriminated against them.

The victim of discrimination has two forums, apart from enlisting the help of the CRE or EOC. If the discrimination occurred at work, he or she can bring a case in an employment tribunal — but he or she must not delay, as the time limit for starting the case is normally three months from the date of the last discriminatory act. For example, where a black nurse claimed she had been regraded at a lower level than equivalent white nurses, her application to the tribunal failed because it was started more than three months after the regrading, even though she could clearly show the discrimination continued after then in her relatively lower pay packet (*Sougrin* v *Haringey Health Authority* [1992] ICR 650). (The European Court of Justice has since been asked to rule on the legality of these time limits since they make it excessively difficult for claimants to exercise their rights. In *Preston* v *Wolverhampton NHS Trust* [2001] UKHL 5; [2001] 2 WLR 448.) The House of Lords applied the ruling obtained from the ECJ. Workers barred from joining occupational pension schemes over the past 30 years because, the rules stated, they worked too few hours each week to join, had already successfully challenged their exclusions. But in this case they had to challenge the Government again when it laid down rules that to join the pension scheme the women had to make their claim within two years of the employers' refusal to let them join. Guided by the ECJ the House of Lords held that such rules effectively barred them from enjoying the equality that European law dictated.

A tribunal can declare the rights of the individual, can order compensation to be paid (which can include a sum for distress to feelings, even if there is no other financial loss), and can order the employer to take specified steps to prevent further discrimination against this employee, failure to do so leading to a possible further award of compensation.

Legal aid is not available in tribunal cases, but as we saw in Chapter 15, preliminary advice can be obtained from some solicitors or advice centres.

If the discrimination takes place outside the employment field, for example, refusal to serve someone in a restaurant or to consider them for a partnership, the case is brought in the county court. Proceedings have to be started within six months of the last act complained of, or eight months in the case of discrimination in education. Legal aid may be available, subject to the means and merits tests (see Chapter 15). The court can order damages to be paid, including for distress to feelings, and an injunction requiring the discriminator to do or stop doing certain acts (e.g., ordering a landlord to cease harassing a tenant).

RACE AND CRIME

A racial element can be part of the definition of a crime. An important example is incitement to racial hatred under the Public Order Act 1986,

s. 23, or racially aggravated assault under the Crime and Disorder Act 1998, s. 29. A racial element can also increase the seriousness of an offence when the court decides on sentence (Crime and Disorder Act 1998, s. 63).

RACE AND SEX DISCRIMINATION
AND THE SOCIAL WORKER

We take for granted that a social worker should not discriminate unlawfully in carrying out his or her duties. Your duty, however, as a local government employee, goes further than that. Under the RRA, s. 71, all local authorities must have due regard to the need:

(a)   to eliminate unlawful racial discrimination; and
(b)   to promote equality of opportunity and good relations between persons of different racial groups.

How do you go about this? The following ideas came from Duncan Forbes, *Action on Racial Harassment* (Legal Action Group, 1988). He suggests careful vetting to ensure that registration is refused of any homes under what is now the Care Standards Act 2000 where there is no system for preventing discrimination; and provision of facilities, by way of counselling, rehousing, play groups or day care, for victims of racial abuse. Racially abusive behaviour will be a breach of the terms of a council letting, and you can ask a housing department to take steps to stop it, if necessary by instituting possession proceedings against the perpetrator. You may also need to refer cases of racial abuse to the police, as this is likely to involve an offence under the Public Order Act 1986. An employer should take available steps to protect an employee against discrimination or abuse by others, e.g., to protect a teacher from racist abuse by pupils (*Bennett* v *Essex CC* (2000) 666 IDS Brief 8). This would apply equally where a council takes no interest in protecting its social workers from racial or sexual abuse.

Positive discrimination is permitted in the provision of education, training, or welfare to meet the special needs of persons of a particular racial group — for example, language assistance for Asian women. A circular from the DHSS (11/77) states that this exemption 'will, for example, enable consideration to be given to special housing or social service arrangements where for example particular Asian or West Indian groups have special needs. These may include residential home provision for children and the elderly'.

You are exempted from the RRA in choosing foster parents or making boarding out arrangements for children, elderly persons or persons requiring special care. Indeed in making arrangements for day care for children, and selecting foster parents for children, your duty goes the other way: the local authority is obliged by the Children Act 1989, Sch. 2, para. 11 to 'have regard' to racial groups. But in making each individual placement decision you still have to choose — depending on whether this is considered best for the child — to place them with someone from their own racial or national background, or not. A blanket policy based on race would be open to challenge.

THE DISABILITY DISCRIMINATION ACT 1995

Disabled persons are the largest minority in the world encompassing more than 500 million persons, of which ⅔ live in developing countries. For a very long time disabled persons have been confronted with different kinds of disregard and mistreatment. Together with women and children, legal systems have excluded disabled persons as non-persons. Eugenic population policies were carried out with the aim of eliminating those deemed disabled through sterilization and killing programmes . . . Modern disability policies [are] much more benign but [are] also based on the assumption of disabled persons not being real citizens. (Theresia Degener, 'Disabled Persons and Human Rights: The Legal Framework', in Degener, T. and Koster-Dreese, Y., *Human Rights and Disabled Persons* (Martinus Nijhoff Publishers, Dordrecht, 1995)).

Using this quotation as a yardstick, how well do the long overdue arrival of disability discrimination laws and enforcement mechanisms work to promote equality of opportunity and rights of full participation for those with disability?

Anyone invoking the 1995 Act must have a disability, which is defined as 'a physical or mental impairment which has a substantial and long-term adverse effect on ability to carry out normal day-to-day activities.' Long-term means 12 months (or less if an illness is terminal). Disability can include severe disfigurement and mental impairment. It can also include learning disorders. Paranoid schizophrenia was ruled to be a clear instance of a disability in *Goodwin* v *Patent Office* (1998) *The Times*, 11 November, since it impaired the applicant's ability to carry out normal day-to-day activities. Reactive depression can amount to a disability (*Kapadia* v *Lambeth LBC* (2000) *The Times*, 4 July). However, the Employment Appeal Tribunal was not prepared to view the side effects of gender reassignment treatment as constituting a disability, so a trainee police constable's dismissal because of the effect the treatment was having on her work was lawful. (*Ashton* v *Chief Constable of Mercia* (2000) *The Times*, 14 November). (Unfortunately that disability does not cover people who have a condition (such as HIV) which causes other people to stop them from doing day-to-day activities which they are otherwise perfectly capable of doing.)

It is now unlawful to discriminate on grounds of disability in employment (but education, the police, the forces, prisons and firms employing fewer than 15 staff are excepted), in services (such as shops and restaurants, but public transport has yet to be included) and in selling/letting property. A victim can bring a case before an employment tribunal or a county court.

There are many exceptions to the right not to suffer discrimination, including:

(a) unsuitability for the job;
(b) a candidate without disability is genuinely more suitable;
(c) the buildings which cause the discrimination complied with building regulations relating to disabled access;

(d) provisions for disabled service-users (e.g., shops, cinemas) would cause real and unavoidable safety problems, or would be too expensive;

(e) all publicly-funded or voluntary education (but not employment in those fields); and

(f) lettings where the landlord lives in the premises.

Case law in the employment field has begun to show how the Act is working. We predict that the 'too expensive' let out will be widely cited — but it applies only to services, not employment. There is an automatic assumption that discrimination is not justified. Anyone claiming that discrimination is justified therefore has to prove it.

Disability and Employment

There are two important differences between this legislation and that relating to sex and race discrimination. First, there is the defence of justification, which is not arguable in sex and race cases. Secondly, there is no distinction here between direct and indirect discrimination.

An employer must not discriminate against a disabled person in terms of selection procedures or in terms of employment (s. 4), unless such discrimination is justified (s. 5). Discrimination cannot be justified, however, unless the reason is 'material to the circumstances of the particular case and substantial'. This requirement would rule out the defence of 'well, we'd be happy to take you on, but the rest of the workforce wouldn't like it'. Discrimination is not justified if the employer could have made reasonable adjustments to accommodate the needs or abilities of the employee or applicant. Adjustments (s. 6) can include physical changes to premises, changes to work arrangements, training, supervision, or the provision of a helper to the disabled person (for example, a signer for a deaf person). (The Code of Practice issued by the Department for Education and Employment in 1996 provides extensive guidance and examples. The conclusion we draw from this is that an employer or tribunal will have to show real attempts to meet the needs of an otherwise suitable employee.)

Case law in the employment field is mainly encouraging. Let's start with the good news. In *British Sugar plc* v *Kirke* [1998] IRLR 624, compensation of over £100,000 was paid to a 40-year-old worker selected for redundancy on grounds of his disability (partial blindness). In a case settled before tribunal proceedings were finished, a supermarket employee who was sacked when he was found to be HIV positive obtained £300,000 in compensation. (As there is no official case report, only a newspaper report (see *Guardian*, 11 April 2000, p. 9), we do not know how the HIV status was defined as a disability. See above, where we note that prejudice against a sufferer is not itself within the Act.) In *Kenny* v *Hampshire Constabulary* (1998) *The Times*, 22 October, the applicant had cerebral palsy. He was offered a job, but his needs included help getting to the lavatory. The employers could not find any volunteers, made an application to the Access to Work scheme for help, but gave up waiting and withdrew the offer. The EAT held that the employer's duty to make reasonable adjustments for disabled employees had not been discharged. It was wrong to give up before learning if the grant had been awarded.

Now the bad news. In one case it was decided that an employer would not have to make reasonable adjustments, or avoid discriminating, if he or she could not have been expected to know the person was disabled. In *O'Neill* v *Symm* [1998] IRLR 233, the applicant had been dismissed because of recurrent sickness absences. She had chronic fatigue syndrome, which the appeal tribunal accepted as a disability. The employer had not been told the reason for the absences, and had not enquired if there might be a disability. It was therefore held that the discrimination was lawful, an encouragement to turn a blind eye. Fortunately, a conflicting decision in 2000 will help to force employers to take more care to find out. In *Hammersmith and Fulham LBC* v *Farnsworth* [2000] IRLR 691, the applicant was dismissed when her history of mental illness was discovered. She had not disclosed this at interview, but the mental illness was not affecting this employment (and had not affected her previous employment). The Employment Appeal Tribunal held that the council could not use its own lack of knowledge of the applicant's illness as a defence, especially as, once the council discovered it, it discriminated against her by sacking her.

The legislation does not prevent justified discrimination. For example, when a person with chronic fatigue syndrome is incapable of returning to work after a prolonged absence, any dismissal is not automatically unfair. But it will be if the employer fails to consider adjustments such as lighter duties (*H.J. Heinz Co. Ltd* v *Kenrick* [2000] IRLR 144).

Goods and Services

Few cases have yet reached the court. In *Blankley* v *Lyden*, reported in an article in *Legal Action*, December 1998, p. 19, a group of ten people were refused admission to a pub because of their learning difficulties. They were each awarded £800 in the county court.

The law is gradually being brought into force, between now and 2004, by a series of Parliamentary Orders extending the Act to different services. A Code of Practice, *Rights of Access, Goods, Facilities, Services and Premises*, may be obtained free from the Disability Rights Commission (below).

Enforcement

The Act may have started to alter the culture, but it is not going to abolish discrimination against disabled persons. One expert has described it as 'riddled with vague, slippery and elusive exceptions making it so full of holes that it is more like a colander than a binding code' (*Hansard*, 22 May 1995, cited in C. Gooding, *Blackstone's Guide to the Disability Discrimination Act 1995*).

The 1995 Act did not originally create the equivalent of the CRE or EOC. However, a Disability Rights Commission was created under the Disability Rights Commission Act 1999, with a statutory duty to promote 'equalisation of opportunities for disabled persons' and to 'work towards the elimination of discrimination against disabled persons'. It has £14 million to spend each year, which is an excellent commitment, together with powers to investigate, to assist individuals, to issue non-discrimination notices, and to negotiate with employers to ensure compliance with best practice. The Commission has already won its first case before the Employment Appeal Tribunal (see (2000) 27 (24) LS Gaz 5). It may be contacted at DRC Helpline, Freepost MID 02164, Stratford-upon-Avon CV37 9BR (tel. 0845 7622633; www.drc-gb.org/).

OTHER FORMS OF DISCRIMINATION

Two forms of discrimination are still lawful, even when based on prejudice alone. Homosexuals and transsexuals can be lawfully discriminated against, unless they can show that sex discrimination was also involved. People can be discriminated against on grounds of age (whether too young or too old), unless this can be proved to lead to indirect race or sex discrimination.

These vestiges of lawful prejudice are under gradual but steady attack. In 1999, the Department for Education and Employment published a voluntary code, *Age Diversity in Employment*, and promises a code relating to sexual orientation.

THE FUTURE

We noted earlier that the Human Rights Act 1998, by incorporating Article 14 of the European Convention, prohibits discrimination only where this prevents enjoyment of Convention rights. The Twelfth Protocol to the Convention is not yet in force, but when ratified by the UK it will bind the UK not to permit discrimination by any public authority on grounds such as 'sex, race, colour, language, religion, political or other opinion, national or social origin, association with a national minority, property, birth or other status'. But even when in force as a treaty, it will not change the law in England and Wales without an amendment to the Human Rights Act 1998. The EU, meanwhile, has set the following requirements relating to discrimination in employment:

- End 2002: Legislation to outlaw discrimination on grounds of sexual orientation.
- End 2003: Legislation to outlaw discrimination on grounds of religion.
- End 2006: End discrimination on grounds of age.

INDEX